OUTSIDE READINGS
IN
ECONOMICS

The Editors

ARLEIGH P. HESS, JR.

Associate Professor of Economics
Wharton School of Finance and Commerce
University of Pennsylvania

ROBERT E. GALLMAN

Instructor in Economics
The Ohio State University

JOHN P. RICE

Formerly, Wharton School of Finance and Commerce
University of Pennsylvania

CARL STERN

Associate Professor of Economics
Randolph-Macon Woman's College

OUTSIDE READINGS IN *Economics*

SECOND EDITION

Hess

THOMAS Y. CROWELL COMPANY

New York-1957

Library of Congress Catalog Card Number 56-7456

(c. 9. 57)

MANUFACTURED IN THE UNITED STATES OF AMERICA

Preface to the Second Edition

In order to provide in accessible, inexpensive form a wealth of collateral reading material for the introductory course in economics we compiled the first edition of this book. The wide acceptance of the volume during the past five years indicates that it has achieved its purpose.

The passage of time, however, has brought new developments that should receive attention and has lessened the significance of some of the original articles. We have, therefore, thoroughly revised the book, omitting some selections and adding new ones. In this revision process the suggestions of teachers who used the first edition have proved very helpful. Also, because so many of the users reported lack of time for assignment of a considerable proportion of the selections, the volume has been shortened and the price further lowered. In its present form and at the new price no student need forego this opportunity for acquaintance with some of the foremost literature of the subject. The new edition should thus prove still more useful in meeting the need created by the inability of libraries to cope with assignments because of increasing enrollments.

In this new edition, as in the first, we have at all times tried to keep clearly before us the following basic objectives:

1. The volume should be aimed primarily to meet the needs of students for materials that complement the standard introductory texts in economics.
2. The volume should be well balanced.
3. The selections shoud be readable, stimulating, and provocative.
4. The reading should be significant.

To augment the effectiveness of the readings themselves as a tool, we have continued the following four features: (1) a headnote for each selection to outline its significance and to orient the student; (2) a brief biographical sketch of each contributor; (3) a table correlating the readings for use with leading standard texts; and (4) an index in which the topics, as far as practicable, parallel those found in economics texts.

In the final analysis such value as may inhere in this volume is due primarily to the work of the original writers whose materials have been included. Individual acknowledgments to them and to the publishers who have cooperated so graciously are made throughout the volume at the beginning of each selection. We should like, however, to take this opportunity to express to them collectively our deep appreciation for their courtesy, generosity, and understanding in making their work available to a new and important group of readers.

A. P. H., Jr.
R. E. G.
J. P. R.
C. S.

Contents

I

RESOURCES, PRODUCTION, AND ECONOMIC GROWTH

II

PRICES AND COSTS

III

THE CONSUMER

IV

NATIONAL INCOME, BUSINESS CYCLES, AND STABILIZATION POLICY

V

BIG BUSINESS

VI

LABOR AND ENTERPRISE

VII

MONEY, BANKING, AND PRICE LEVELS

VIII

INTERNATIONAL ECONOMICS

IX

COLLECTIVISM AND PLANNING

I

Resources, Production, and Economic Growth

1. THE PIN FACTORY *

SPECIALIZATION of function and division of labor are fundamental to the processes of economic society. The following excerpt from Adam Smith's *Wealth of Nations,* which was published in 1776, is still the classic discussion of the division of labor.

THE GREATEST improvement in the productive powers of labour, and the greater part of the skill, dexterity, and judgment with which it is anywhere directed, or applied, seem to have been the effects of the division of labour.

The effects of the division of labour, in the general business of society, will be more easily understood, by considering in what manner it operates in some particular manufactures. It is commonly supposed to be carried furthest in some very trifling ones; not perhaps that it really is carried further in them than in others of more importance; but in those trifling manufactures which are destined to supply the small wants of but a small number of people, the whole number of workmen must necessarily be small; and those employed in every different branch of the work can often be collected into the same workhouse, and placed at once under the view of the spectator. In those great manufactures, on the contrary, which are destined to supply the great wants of the

* Adam Smith, *An Inquiry into the Nature and Causes of the Wealth of Nations* (New York, G. P. Putnam's Sons, 1904, and London, Methuen and Co., Ltd., 1892). Reprinted by permission of the publishers.

The author (1723-1790), a Scottish economist, was Professor of Logic and Moral Philosophy at the University of Glasgow. Many trace the history of economics as a science from the date of publication of his book, *The Wealth of Nations.*

great body of the people, every different branch of the work employs so great a number of workmen, that it is impossible to collect them all in the same workhouse. We can seldom see more, at one time, than those employed in one single branch. Though in such manufactures, therefore, the work may really be divided into a much greater number of parts, than in those of a more trifling nature, the division is not near so obvious, and has accordingly been much less observed.

To take an example, therefore, from a very trifling manufacture; but one in which the division of labour has been very often taken notice of, the trade of the pinmaker; a workman not educated to this business (which the division of labour has rendered a distinct trade), nor acquainted with the use of the machinery employed in it (to the invention of which the same division of labour has probably given occasion), could scarce, perhaps, with his utmost industry, make one pin in a day, and certainly could not make twenty. But in the way in which this business is now carried on, not only the whole work is a peculiar trade, but it is divided into a number of branches, of which the greater part are likewise peculiar trades. One man draws out the wire, another straights it, a third cuts it, a fourth points it, a fifth grinds it at the top for receiving the head; to make the head requires two or three distinct operations; to put it on, is a peculiar business, to whiten the pins is another; it is even a trade by itself to put them into the paper; and the important business of making a pin is, in this manner, divided into about eighteen distinct operations, which in some manufactories, are all performed by distinct hands, though in others the same man will sometimes perform two or three of them. I have seen a small manufactory of this kind where ten men only were employed, and where some of them consequently performed two or three distinct operations. But though they were the very poor, and therefore but indifferently accommodated with the necessary machinery, they could, when they exerted themselves, make among them about twelve pounds of pins in a day. There are in a pound upwards of four thousand pins of a middling size. Those ten persons, therefore, could make among them upwards of forty-eight thousand pins in a day. Each person, therefore, making a tenth part of forty-eight thousand pins, might be considered as making four thousand eight hundred pins in a day. But if they had all wrought separately and independently, and without any of them having been educated to this peculiar business, they certainly could not each of them have made twenty, perhaps not one pin in a day; that is, certainly, not the two hundred and fortieth, perhaps not the four thousand eight hundredth part of what they are at present capable of performing, in consequence of a proper division and combination of their different operations.

In every other art and manufacture, the effects of the division of labour are similar to what they are in this very trifling one; though, in many of them, the labour can neither be so much subdivided, nor reduced to so great a simplicity of operation. The division of labour, however, so far as it can be introduced, occasions, in every art, a proportionable increase of the productive powers of labour.

---

2. DIRECT AND INDIRECT PRODUCTION *

Of the alternative methods of production the most direct way offers the fastest manner of satisfying a need or a want. However, as the noted Austrian economist, Eugen von Böhm-Bawerk, shows in three simple illustrations in this selection, roundabout or indirect production often obtains superior results or results impossible to achieve by direct methods.

A peasant requires drinking water. The spring is some distance from his house. There are various ways in which he may supply his daily wants. First, he may go to the spring each time he is thirsty, and drink out of his hollowed hand. This is the most direct way; satisfaction follows immediately on exertion. But it is an inconvenient way, for our peasant has to take his way to the well as often as he is thirsty. And it is an insufficient way, for he can never collect and store any great quantity such as he requires for various other purposes. Second, he may take a log of wood, hollow it out into a kind of pail, and carry his day's supply from the spring to his cottage. The advantage is obvious, but it necessitates a roundabout way of considerable length. The man must spend, perhaps, a day in cutting out the pail; before doing so he must have felled a tree in the forest; to do this, again, he must have made an axe, and so on. But there is still a third way; instead of felling one tree he fells a number of trees, splits and hollows them, lays them end for end, and so constructs a runnel or rhone which brings a full head of water to his cottage. Here, obviously, between the expenditure of the labour and the obtaining of the water we have a very roundabout

* Eugen von Böhm-Bawerk, *The Positive Theory of Capital* (London, Macmillan, 1891), Book I, Chapter II.

The author (1851-1914) was Professor of Economics at the University of Innsbruck and the University of Vienna. He was for many years a member of the ministry of finance of the empire of Austria-Hungary. Known for his development of the ideas of marginalism, opportunity costs, and roundabout production. *Capital and Interest* and *The Positive Theory of Capital* are his chief works.

way, but, then, the result is ever so much greater. Our peasant needs no longer take his weary way from house to well with the heavy pail on his shoulder, and yet he has a constant and full supply of the freshest water at his very door.

Another example. I require stone for building a house. There is a rich vein of excellent sandstone in a neighbouring hill. How is it to be got out? First, I may work the loose stones back and forward with my bare fingers, and break off what can be broken off. This is the most direct, but also the least productive way. Second, I may take a piece of iron, make a hammer and chisel out of it, and use them on the hard stone—a roundabout way, which, of course, leads to a very much better result than the former. Third method—Having a hammer and chisel I use them to drill a hole in the rock; next I turn my attention to procuring charcoal, sulphur, and nitre, and mixing them in a powder, then I pour the powder into the hole, and the explosion that follows splits the stone into convenient pieces—still more of a roundabout way, but one which, as experience shows, is as much superior to the second way in result as the second was to the first.

Yet another example. I am short-sighted, and wish to have a pair of spectacles. For this I require ground and polished glasses, and a steel framework. But all that nature offers towards that end is silicious earth and iron ore. How am I to transform these into spectacles? Work as I may, it is as impossible for me to make spectacles directly out of silicious earth as it would be to make the steel frames out of iron ore. Here there is no immediate or direct method of production. There is nothing for it but to take the roundabout way, and, indeed, a very roundabout way. I must take silicious earth and fuel, and build furnaces for smelting the glass from the silicious earth; the glass thus obtained has to be carefully purified, worked, and cooled by a series of processes; finally, the glass thus prepared—again by means of ingenious instruments carefully constructed beforehand—is ground and polished into the lens fit for short-sighted eyes. Similarly, I must smelt the ore in the blast furnace, change the raw iron into steel, and make the frame therefrom—processes which cannot be carried through without a long series of tools and buildings that, on their part again, require great amounts of previous labour. Thus, by an exceedingly roundabout way, the end is attained.

The lesson to be drawn from all these examples alike is obvious. It is—that a greater result is obtained by producing goods in roundabout ways than by producing them directly. Where a good can be produced in either way, we have the fact that, by the indirect way, a greater product can be got with equal labour, or the same product with less labour. But, beyond this, the superiority of the indirect way manifests itself in being the only way in which certain goods can be obtained; if I might say so, it is so much the better that it is often the only way!

---

3. THE BIG CHANGE *

The Coming and Disciplining of Industrialism, 1850-1950

IN ONE hundred years this country has been transformed from an economy based largely on agricultural production to the vast and complex industrial society we know today. Mr. Allen, a veteran chronicler of Americana, describes vividly the changes which rapid and large-scale industrialization has wrought in our way of life and in our national economic personality. Although he recognizes dangers that threaten our future progress, his reaction to the developments since 1850 is one of optimism.

IN AN upper hallway of the New York Public Library there have been hanging, this year, a series of prints of American cities dating from about 1850. To the eye of today these pictures show what look like overgrown villages and small towns—clusters of red brick and white wooden houses, here and there crowded closely along narrow streets, elsewhere set comfortably apart from one another, with clumps of trees about them and green gardens sloping down to the inevitable river. In a few of these towns one will see a factory chimney or two rising above the roof-tops; but the striking thing, to the eye of 1950, is that in most of the pictures—whether they are of Davenport, Iowa, or Hartford, Connecticut, or even New York City—the skyline is broken only by church spires. Hence the village effect; for today it is only a village which is dominated by its steeples.

If we should wish to see where we have come from in a hundred years—how the everyday life of American men and women and children has changed since 1850, what people lacked then that we take for granted now, what people possessed then that is only a memory now, and whether the gap between rich and poor has narrowed or widened

* Frederick Lewis Allen, *Harper's Magazine,* August, 1950, pp. 245-60. Copyright 1950 by Harper & Brothers. Reprinted by special permission on behalf of *Harper's Magazine* and the author. Mr. Allen expanded these materials into a book with the same title.

The author (1890-1954) was Editor in Chief of *Harper's Magazine* and Vice Chairman of the Board of Directors of the Foreign Policy Association. Author of *Only Yesterday, Since Yesterday,* and *The Big Change.*

since industrialism began to transform American life—I suggest that we begin by trying to look through those pictures to the reality that lay behind them, a full century ago.

To begin with, are those engravings fair portraits of the America of 1850? Well, we must remember that American life was vastly more varied geographically then than now. At that moment in the mid-nineteenth century when the United States had only just reached out to its present continental boundaries (as a result of the Mexican War), and when California had only just become, abruptly, a land of bright American opportunity (as a result of the discovery of gold at Sutter's Mill), America was still a land of violent contrasts. A silk-waistcoated merchant prince of Boston or New York or Philadelphia lived in a wholly different world from a family of homespun pioneers setting out by covered wagon from the bleak and muddy streets of Independence to cross the "Great American Desert." The high-thinking Transcendentalists of Concord, strolling about Walden Pond to note the blooming of the arbutus and to discuss natural aristocracy, were continents apart, in their way of life, from Brigham Young's Mormons building their new city beside the Great Salt Lake, or from the black slaves of a Georgia plantation, or from the gold-hungry prospectors in the town of tents and shacks that was San Francisco, or from the farmer trying out a new McCormick reaper on a quarter-section of scraggly Illinois prairie.

If America was so varied geographically, this was largely because it took so much time and effort for either people or goods to get about. When young Joseph Jefferson, the actor, traveled from New Orleans to New York in 1846, what he had to do was to take a Mississippi River steamboat to Wheeling, in what is now West Virginia (being delayed for days by ice, for it was winter); then bump for twenty-four hours in a chilly stagecoach over rutted roads to Cumberland, Maryland, stopping every few hours for a meal while the horses were changed; then proceed by primitive train to his destination. Early in the eighteen-fifties Ralph Waldo Emerson, taking a lecture trip in Michigan, had to make a forty-eight-mile journey through the woods from town to town by horse and buggy. And the fastest time anybody could make from New York to San Francisco was eighty-nine days by swift clipper ship around the Horn.

We must remember, too, when we look at those engravings of American cities in 1850, that the men who made them did not show us the grimier streets, or the citizens eating with their knives or blowing their noses with their fingers. They could not show us the smell of household privies. Yet those pictures of red and white and green towns clinging to the banks of sailboat-studded rivers do reflect the central fact of the United States of 1850; that as a whole it was still a land of farmers, shopkeepers, merchants, and artisans—above all, farmers. Today, among "gainfully employed" Americans, only about one in five works on a farm; at that time, over half of them did. And the cities were small. New York, then as now the biggest of them, had about one-tenth of its present population.

To be sure, industrialism had long since begun its smoky invasion of the land. Along the banks of the Merrimac and other New England rivers, big textile mills were turning out cotton and woolen cloth, and there were a few scattered factories even west of the Alleghenies. But the basic units of American life were still the village and the farm; and the great majority of the American people—the lively, sociable, irritable, dyspeptic, boastful, uncouth, energetic, disorderly, wasteful, and hospitable American people—were villagers at heart.

How well did they live? It is easy today to forgt that many comforts and conveniences which we now take for granted were then available to nobody, or almost nobody. For one thing, cities were just beginning to install water-supply and drainage systems. Philadelphia had been an early innovator with its Fairmount Water Works, which long had been pumping water from the Schuylkill River, but New York did not have Croton water till 1842, and Boston did not introduce Cochituate water till 1848. Before public water supplies became general, you either subscribed for water provided by a private company such as the Jamaica Pond Corporation in Boston, or, if you were not within reach of its piping system or could not pay the price, you relied on a well of your own. In Boston, for instance, a census taken in 1845 showed that the 10,370 houses in the city got their water from no less than 5,287 separate wells, and supplemented this supply with rain water collected (for washing purposes) in 4,445 cisterns. (As the city gradually became smokier, cistern water naturally became sootier.)

Even after public reservoirs and aqueducts had been built, it took a long time to lay the water mains to take this new blessing to people's houses. All through the late eighteen forties, for example, New York was busily constructing mains along the streets of the city, and the authorities were discovering to their dismay how much water people used when all they needed to do to get it was to turn a tap. In 1853 the head of the Croton Aqueduct Department, in his annual report, remarking that a modern hotel on Broadway had installed "more than four hundred openings through which water is delivered, and discharged into public sewers," said in tones of despair, "With such arrangements for the consumption of water, under the control of a little army of careless servants, and irresponsible guests, how is any reasonable economy in its use to be expected?"

The sewers that this official mentioned were brand new; for as late as 1845 even the biggest city in the country had had no public sewerage system at all. And although the modern hotel which he described had had a number of suites equipped with bath and water closet, and had installed in the basement six water closets for domestics, and had provided, adjacent to the barroom, nine public water closets and three wash basins with hot and cold water, these were innovations connoting extreme luxury. In all or almost all private houses there was still no such thing as a water closet; people relied upon chamber pots or upon a drafty expedition to the privy; or—in the case of the prosperous—upon commodes which the servants would periodically empty. And except along the chief streets of the chief cities, they relied too upon cesspits and culverts and the gutters of the streets to dispose of their sewage.

No wonder their well water was widely contaminated; and no wonder the term of life was so short, particularly in the cities. Today the average expectation of life in the United States is over 67, and rising; in 1850 it was under 40. A health report published in Boston in 1850 disclosed that the average age of all who died in the city was 21.43 years, and that among the Catholic population—who were, of course, mostly poor immigrants from Ireland—it was less than 14 years. Those grim figures reflect not only a general ignorance of antisepsis and sanitation, but also the result of living, in fast-growing cities, under conditions which were still those of primitive village life.

Nor were private houses centrally heated. Even the wealthy depended on kitchen stoves, Franklin stoves, and open fireplaces for warmth in winter. Mark Twain describing in *Life on the Mississippi* the typical big house of any town along the river in about 1850—"a big, square, two-story frame house painted white and porticoed like a Grecian temple behind a white paling fence," noted that there was no bathroom and added that there might be, but wouldn't certainly be, a pitcher and washbowl in each of the square bedrooms upstairs. The first duty of the average American householder, in the morning, was to light the fires and empty the slops; until the fires really took hold, the chill of the house made any but the most cursory washing an ordeal. And the German writer, Ole Munch Raeder, describing a trip which he took in 1847 through what we now call the Middle West, remarked on the lamentable but general custom of spitting at the stove, not always accurately, adding with evident relief that there were cuspidors in some of the better homes in Madison, Elkhorn, and Janesville. All in all, it is likely that if we of 1950 were to visit the United States of 1850, we should find it a dirty place inhabited by dirty people.

Ready-made clothing was limited in amount and kind, ill-fiitting, and hand-sewn. Accordingly, shirts and underwear were generally stitched at home by the housewife, from materials spun by the textile mills and bought by the yard at the store; shoes were made by shoemakers, suits by tailors (or sometimes by the housewife), dresses by the housewife or by steamstresses and dressmakers. The well-to-do imported their suits from London, their dresses from Paris, or else employed tailors and dressmakers versed in the foreign modes to fashion them out of fine imported materials. Naturally a new article of clothing represented a considerable expense, in either money or toil; the people in any gathering were far more varied in costume than today; and the women of the family were perpetually sewing.

Against these and other lacks and inconveniences must be set certain advantages. First of all, space and air. The shopkeeper or blacksmith in an Ohio town was likely to have a house with more room in it than can be found today in the New York or Chicago apartment of a $30,000-a-year executive. In Philadelphia, my grandfather as a young man could take his wife skating in winter, or sailing in summer, on a Schuylkill River as yet undarkened by commerce or industry. Not yet was there any need for week-end escape from the cities, or for summer places, or for elaborately organized sports; the vast majority of the people found chances to walk, ride, drive, skate, swim, fish, or shoot, within ready reach on almost any day when the weather suited—if their long labors left them time enough. Although the American public school system was only partly established, although great numbers of chidren could not get even elementary schooling, and few went on to high school, and far fewer yet to college, at least the average American boy and girl had a countryside close at hand to run wild in when the chores that were their share in the work of family life were done. And one final advantage was possessed by nine families out of ten; when the crops failed, when the family store went broke, when their jobs folded up, they could tighten their belts and go on working—if not in their home communities, then at least in the beckoning West. In a land still dominated by small-scale and individual enterprise, a self-reliant man could be far more independent than could his son or grandson in later years.

The gulf between rich and poor was great, both in income and in the nature of their clothing, equipment, and pattern of life. At a time when the dollar was so big that $5,000 a year was an inviting salary to offer to the head of an insurance company, there were merchants in the seaboard cities who were making hundreds of thousands a year; one

Boston merchant is said to have cleared $100,000 from one voyage of one of his ships. Not only was such a man rich—with of course no income tax to pay—and not only did he have fine carriages, and a splendid house with satin-covered furniture and a paneled library and a cellar full of Madeira and other imported wines, and a staff of dutiful servants, but his wealth was instantly apparent to anybody who saw him and his lady on the street. You could tell at a distance of fifty paces that their clothes were quite different in material and cut from those of ordinary folk.

By contrast, not only the slaves of the South (who were looked after well or ill according to the whim of their slaveholders) but also the poorer people of the Northern cities and towns, were in miserable plight. For the floor of wages had been dropping. Years of famine in Ireland had brought into the country a horde of newcomers willing to work for next to nothing. In earlier years the rising textile mills of Lawrence and Lowell and Fall River had largely employed farmers' daughters; but as Irish labor became available a change was taking place. Wages fell—even when profits were booming—until whole families labored at the machines for three or four dollars a week per worker; a twelve-hour day was average, and a fourteen-hour day was not unusual. Stop for a moment and reflect upon what it would be like to work a fourteen-hour day—say from five o'clock in the morning till eight at night, with half an hour off for breakfast and half an hour for dinner—six days a week, in an ill-lighted, ill-ventilated factory; and ask yourself how much recreation, how much sunshine, how much education for children of fourteen or less, such an appalling routine permitted.

Meanwhile the wages of seamen, which in the early years of the century had been as high as $18 a month, had fallen to $8 or $10 or $12 a month, and the adventurous farmer boys who had formerly yearned for two years before the mast had been supplanted by foreign deckhands, until the slim and beautiful clipper ships of the eighteen-fifties were manned by the drifting scum of many continents. When, for example, the *Reindeer* sailed from Canton to Boston in 1851 she had as her crew 2 French, 1 Portuguese, 1 Cape Verde Islander, 1 Azores man, 1 Italian, 1 Dutchman, 1 Mulatto, 2 Kanakas, 1 Welshman, 1 Swede, 2 Chinese, and 2 Americans.

One catches a glimpse of the labor market in the mid-century in an article in *Harper's* for October, 1866, outlining a reasonable budget for a young couple living in the outskirts of New York on $2,000 a year—roughly equivalent to perhaps $6,000 or $7,000 now—with one servant. At a time when roast beef cost 35 cents a pound, corned beef 23½ cents a pound, fish 12 cents a pound, bread 10 cents a loaf, milk 10 cents a quart, and sugar 15 cents a pound—prices which were mostly, though not all, a fraction of what they are today—this family was allowed $114.75 a year for coal (for the kitchen range and a "portable furnace" in the cellar), and a mere $96 a year for the servant's wages—*at the rate of $8 a month!*

What did people think of these contrasts? Most people apparently regarded them as part of the order of nature. That men and women of the favored class approved of them is of course not surprising; the striking fact is that the tailor, the farmer, and the mill-hand on the whole agreed. For the reigning idea in America was that every individual should have a fair chance in the contest of life, and that he should be on his own, beholden to no man; to work for somebody else was spineless unless one were a young apprentice, or a girl waiting for marriage, or an immigrant who didn't know any better; and if such people chose to work for very little, this was their own affair. Couldn't they break away and get better jobs if they had the ability and the will? Meanwhile employers had a virtually unquestioned right to make all the money they could lay their hands on. For America was a young country with a future, in which it was considered every man's duty to play a constructive part; and if he made money—a lot of it—this was a good sign that he was contributing to the common weal. If he made a million while paying his workers a pittance, that was mighty smart. If he outwitted his neighbor in a slick trade, that was mighty smart. Disapprove of him? People admired him, and hoped to be as fortunate themselves one day.

For the tide of industrialism was only beginning to run strong, and opportunity still seemed to be within reach of all. Americans felt this in their bones, and held their heads high. Said Oliver Wendell Holmes to Edward Dicey, an English visitor, "We should find it hard to match five thousand American gentlemen with five thousand English, but we could match five million ordinary Americans against the same number of your countrymen, without fear of the result." If there were almost 25,000 paupers in Massachusetts, were not 91 per cent of them foreigners, and were they not therefore simply people who had not yet got off to a start in the free-for-all race? Even the ill-clad immigrants felt the breezes of hope in the air. Said a poor Irishwoman to Dicey, "This is a blessed country, sir; I think God made it for the poor."

As the second half of the nineteenth century began, industrialism took a new lease on life. Samuel Colt, making revolvers at Hartford, had pushed to a new perfection Eli Whitney's principle of the use of interchangeable parts; Colt had completely mechanized his factory, so that presently, with the aid of some 400 machines, his men were turning out over 24,000 revolvers a year. Such a performance was an eye-opener to inventors, manufacturers, investors; couldn't you make almost anything cheaply and swiftly, provided you had the right machines to do it with? And now the most essential tools for the making of such machines were ready; for the stocking lathe, the universal miller, and the turret lathe had all been invented. Elias Howe, Jr., had conceived the sewing machine, and now Isaac Singer was producing this new contrivance in quantity. Telegraph lines were being extended from town to town. In 1858 the first cable was laid across the Atlantic Ocean. The next year oil was discovered in Pennsylvania—an event destined to end the era of the whale-oil lamp. Meanwhile thousands of miles of railroad track were being laid; and as the fat-funneled locomotives wound their way through the wooded Alleghenies and chugged across the vast flatlands of the central basin, they brought town after town into new and exciting contact with the news and ideas of the outside world.

Each new miracle of invention seized the public imagination. When Joseph Jefferson received the first telegram of his life in Cumberland, Maryland, he could hardly believe that he was actually hearing from the partner in Baltimore to whom he had written only the day before. "I called at the office to inquire if it were really so; yes, there could be no doubt of it. A small group of people had collected about the operator . . . all wearing a look of surprise and incredulity. We began showing one another our dispatches. . . . People were rushing to and fro with little messages in their hands, and stopping one another in the street to talk and wonder over the new event." Just so, in scores of American towns, the new instruments and gadgets set boys and men to dreaming fantastic dreams—of getting a scientific training, devising some new wonder which would simplify the long labor of manufacturing, setting up a company to produce it, selling it by the thousands, and making a fabulous fortune. The future seemed full of wild promise.

The Civil War, though it left the South prostrate, did not halt the march of industrialism in the North, but rather accelerated it, bringing as it did outsize demands for weapons and equipment and quicker communication, and especially for uniforms in quantity. By the war's end industrialism was in full flood, irrestible and tremendous.

It brought with it both wonders and abominations. The wonders have become so familiar to us that it is hard for us to imagine a world in which they did not exist. Yet even a short list of the changes that came between 1850 and 1900 is staggering. Here are some of them:

A vast growth of steel production, resulting from the Bessemer process, the multiplication of steel mills, and the coming of the open-hearth furnace. (This meant more and better steel for rails, wires, bridges, ships, steel-skeleton buildings, and a host of other uses; steel became the basic material out of which the new industrial era was built.)

An equally vast boom in railroad-building, till the rails not only crossed the Rockies to unite East with West, but made a network tying the whole country together into one economic unit.

The installation of improved water and sewerage systems for cities and towns, making possible—for those who could afford it—the immense convenience of modern plumbing.

The lighting of homes, as well as city streets, by gas light and then by the magic of electric light.

Electrical transportation: the coming of the cable car, the trolley car, the elevated railroad (powered at first by steam, then by electricity), and the subway.

The development of electric motors and dynamos to do more and more of the work of the country; the introduction of the electric-power plant and of modern hydro-electric systems, so that the virtue of electricity could be on tap miles—or hundreds of miles—away from its source.

That incredible annihilator of distance, both between friends and between business offices, the telephone.

The revolutionizing of business life by the invention of the typewriter—which incidentally began to bring women into business life—and by the electric elevator, which, along with the development of steel-skeleton construction, made possible the skyscraper.

And, finally, the beginnings of that prime revolutionizer, the automobile, which had been introduced abroad as early as 1884 but did not begin to take its American forms until the early nineties.

To these wonders one might add the introduction of seaworthy ocean-going steamships; the opening of the Great Plains to settlement with the aid of the invention of barbed wire; the simplification and improvement of photography, and the coming of the half-tone process which accommodated it to publication; the invention of the linotype, to the great benefit of printing; and the contriving of all the machines which supplemented Elias Howe's sewing machine to facilitate the growth of the clothing and shoe industries. Yet even if we extended this list of new marvels indefinitely, we could hardly begin to convey a sense of the magnitude of the change which was wrought between

1850 and 1900. A land of formerly separate communities had been linked together. A land mostly of farmers and villagers had become a land mostly of cities and roaring industrial towns. Comforts, conveniences, and wealth had so piled up as to make possible a great extension of education on every level and a general widening of horizons. It was almost as if a whole new world had been invented for people to work and play in.

But industrialism in those days of its raw growth brought abominations too. To begin with, wherever it advanced, ugliness came with it —smoke, soot, grime, the darkening of skies once clear, the withering of foilage once green, the pollution of rivers once clean. Indeed, so completely did men assume that money-making and beauty lived in separate compartments—beauty being something which you could buy after you made the money, or must run away to, from the city or the factory where the money was produced—that even the profitable building of houses, except for the rich, was undertaken as if by blind men. It should come as no surprise that the grimmest sections of most of our cities today date from between 1850 and 1900.

Not only did industrialism uglify the land wherever it moved; it also, while subduing it, despoiled it. Forests were hacked to pieces, farm land misused and overused, natural resources plundered right and left as if the bounties of America would be forever inexhaustible.

Morally, too, industrialism proved at first to be a destroyer of standards. So thoroughly had the idea sunk into men's minds that it was smart to make money in any way, straight or crooked, that the third quarter of the nineteenth century brought a contagion of fraudulence. It brought, too, a trend toward monopoly that if unchecked would have drawn all the economic power of the country into the hands of a few men. But the most disturbing thing about industrialism, in those days of its spring blooming, was the way in which is disturbed the wealth it produced.

In the early days of the factory system in England, David Ricardo had enunciated the grim principle which he called the Iron Law of Wages: the principle that all wages tend to fall to the level which the most unskillful or most desperate man will accept. In pre-industrial times this Iron Law had not often operated unchecked. The prince, or the baron, or the squire, or the neighbors had tended to look after those who by reason of incompetence or illness or adversity were in want. And in the pre-industrial United States, as we have seen, men and women who were in want could at least go on working, for whatever pittance they could command, or could move on elsewhere to try again. But the new industrial community brought a change. For when a man built a mill or factory surrounded by a mill village or factory town, those who came to work for him were in great degree imprisoned by their choice. They did not own the tools with which they worked, and therefore were dependent on what employment the mill offered; and anyhow there was not enough other work in such a community for all who would be looking for it if the mill shut down. And if their wages were low they could not afford to look elsewhere for jobs. So they ceased to be free agents. They were at their employer's mercy. And the Iron Law really went into action.

One great advantage the American workingman had—if he could raise the cash. He could still go West. But as the discards of industrialism, along with the men of most adventurous ambition, became Western pioneers, their places were taken by an important proletariat—the incoming immigrants. First it was the Irish, who in the eighteen-fifties were the diggers of ditches, the builders of levees, the new class of mill-workers; then, as the Irish bettered themselves, it was the Italians, and then the Slavs of Eastern Europe. Each group tended to form a proletarian layer under the previous one. (At the bottom, in the most menial and ill-paid jobs of all, remained our own Negro population, slaves no longer, but remaining largely in a servitude of ignorance and exclusion from opportunity.) Thus the very hope that was smybolized by the Goddess of Liberty brought immigrants in such vast numbers as to glut the labor markets and delay the modification of the Iron Law.

As time went on there were to be other mitigating factors. One was the slow and uneven growth of labor unions. Another was the belated recognition, by a gradually aroused public conscience, of the horrors of American poverty; little by little the law began to prescribe more decent conditions of work. And another, of course, was the fact that the abounding flow of wealth from hugely increased productivity *did* tend to percolate down through the ranks of society and lift the living standard for the great majority. By 1891 wages in twenty-two industries had increased since 1860 on the average over 68 per cent, while wholesale prices had declined over 5 per cent. Yes, the *average* well-being, even in industry, was rising fast.

But there were sub-average areas where the terms of life were miserable. As late as 1887 a writer for *Harper's* found a coal-yard laborer in an Eastern mill town who earned seven dollars a week, while his wife earned five dollars, their elder daughter four dollars, and their fourteen-year-old daughter three dollars and a quarter, working from 6:30 in the morning till 6:30 at night in the mill. Total per year for *four* money-earners—$924. Not much improvement there over the conditions of the mid-century. The status of the anthracite workers in the Pennsylvania coal fields was sharply worse: there the workers who slaved grimly and dangerously underground were kept in a state of perpetual debt to the company on which they were dependent for their meager housing, their food, everything. And worse still were the conditions on New York's Lower East Side, where 290,000 people were packed into one square mile of tenements; where, in the filth and stench of Mulberry Bend, Jacob Riis found twelve men and women sleeping for "five cents a spot" in one room not thirteen feet square; where the wife of an incapacitated invalid earned an income of $1.20 a week making shirts, while her oldest daughter cut out Hamburg edging for the noble wage of 2½ cents per hour for ten hours of steady labor. Here, at the very bottom of the pit of poverty, the Iron Law was iron indeed.

Meanwhile at the other end of the scale there was magnificence unstinted. Consider, for example, the mansion which Samuel Colt had built near Hartford out of the profits of his industrial pioneering. In 1876, reported a rapt chronicler in the *Art Journal,* the Colt lawn was daily rolled, cut, and trimmed to perfection by thirty men; while the greenhouses, 2,634 feet in length, produced yearly at least a ton of grapes, to say nothing of 8,000 figs, peaches, and other fruits, and 400 quarts of strawberries. By the early eighteen-eighties American millionaires, led by the Vanderbilts, had become possessed with the idea that a successful man should build himself a mansion suitable for a European prince. They hired accomplished architects to produce for them Renaissance palaces, monumental Italian villas, or turreted French châteaux, with authentically princely bronze doors, grilled iron gates, ancient fireplaces, tapestries, and paintings imported from abroad; and in these feudal edifices, staffed in many cases by thirty or more servants, they lived in marble grandeur. Nor was the luxury of the rich limited to their palaces. Pierpont Morgan, whose house in New York was comparatively unassuming, as were his house in London, his country estate outside London, his American country estate on the Hudson, his Adirondack estate, his fishing box at Newport, and his suite at Jekyll Island, satisfied his desire for big things by building in 1898 a steam yacht 302 feet long, and by amassing an art collection worth at least fifty million dollars. Those were the days when private yachts, private art galleries, and racing stables were multiplying; when dinner parties included up to twenty courses; and when one young blood would be heard remarking to another, "Never ask the old man for less than fifty thousand."

It was on contrasts like these, at an early stage of European industrialism, that Karl Marx had predicted his theory of revolution. But one did not have to have a radical bias to be dismayed at the gulf one saw widening between rich and poor. In the year 1882—just a few months before the Vanderbilt fancy-dress ball on which was spent an estimated quarter of a million dollars (equivalent to much more than half a million today)—Junius Henry Browne wrote in *Harper's:* "Year after year New York seems to justifiy the painful, dispiriting averment that it is a city of paupers and millionaires. Are not the rich growing richer and the poor poorer as time moves on? Will there ever be a period when the distance between them will be less? Hope answers, 'Yes'; Reason answers, 'No.' "

The answer was still "No" at the turn of the century. At about that time—a period of relative prosperity—the mass of unskilled workers were receiving less than $460 a year in wages in the North, less than $300 in the South; while Andrew Carnegie's *personal* share of the profits of his steel company was a little over six and a half million dollars for the year 1898, a little over twelve million dollars for 1899, and more than twenty-three million dollars for 1900. With no income taxes whatever to pay.

It could not go on without making a mockery of democracy. It did not go on. The story of American progress during the first half of the twentieth century has been the story of repeal of the Iron Law and of the slow disciplining of an industrialism still expandingly and excitingly productive.

A vehement rebellion against the way things were going had begun during the latter decades of the nineteenth century, chiefly among the farmers and small business men of the Midwest and the Great Plains, where the old Jeffersonian idea of a nation of self-reliant free men had been reinforced, within living memory, by frontier experience. It was the indignation of these people against the greedy and arbitrary power of the big railroad and manufacturing companies that was chiefly responsible for the passage of the Interstate Commerce Act of 1887 and the Sherman Anti-Trust Act of 1890, and for the fervor of the Populist movement of the early nineties. This grass-roots rebellion was reinforced by the anger of industrial workers, who were making grim and often bloody attempts to unionize. And as time went on it was still further reinforced by what might be called the revolt of the American conscience: a widespread and rising disapproval, among citizens by the millions, of what looked to them like the coming of a new feudalism. When they read the eye-opening reports of men like Jacob Riis on slum life, when the muckraking journalists uncovered for them the sordid business deals and political corruption of the day, their dismay had a moral basis: the way things had been going was not right.

And so the center of gravity of American opinion began to shift. In all walks of life, during the first fifteen years or so of the twentieth century, people began to think of society at large as an entity for which they were partly responsible. This feeling lent strength to politcial progressives and liberals like Theodore Roosevelt, the elder LaFollette, and Woodrow Wilson. In the churches there was a new emphasis on the "social gospel"; social service began to be recognized as a profession; economists for the first time produced the concept of the "national income"; the two richest Americans, Carnegie and Rockefeller, converted great parts of their fortunes into foundations for the public weal; and Henry Ford, by voluntarily raising wages and cutting prices, dramatized a concept of industrialism as different from that of the nineteenth-century mill-owners as his assembly line was different from their crude mechanization. The Iron Law was on its way out.

Meanwhile invention continued at a breathless pace. We are all familiar with what it has brought us in the half century since 1900: such marvels as the airplane, the movies, the radio, television, a bewildering array of plastics and synthetics, and electronics. If we broaden the term "invention" to include a wider range of research, it has brought us a greatly increased knowledge of nutrition, a new battery of useful drugs, and—along with innumerable other wonders—the certainty of the future boon of atomic power, a certainty which only the misuse of atomic knowledge for purposes of mutual human destruction can long forestall. Likewise our increase in technological efficiency has been steady and formidable; during World War II our rate of production astonished the world. But along with this furious advance of industrialism has gone the disciplining of industrialism: its transformation from a force which made the rich richer and the poor poorer into a force which has narrowed the gulf between rich and poor.

For this great change there has been a surprising variety of causes. We need not detail here the long series of events through which they have manifested themselves—World War I, with its demand for high production at high wages; the confident competition of the nineteen-twenties; the crisis of the Great Depression, which dramatized the helplessness of the unemployed; the resulting spate of New Deal laws; World War II, with its unprecedented need for goods in quantity and its unprecedented government controls; and the post-1945 boom. Let us forget chronology and look at the tamers of industrialism group by group, in all their wild variety. We can lump them into five general classes:

(1) *Legislation*—including not only all manner of laws to protect

the health and safety of the worker, to grant him a minimum wage, to permit him to organize, and to protect him as tenant and consumer, but also laws for the regulation of business practices, and—immensely important—the graduated income tax, first adopted in 1913, which has increasingly redistributed the national prosperity.

(2) *Public Services*—including the vast expansion of public school systems, state universities, highway systems, park systems, and government aids and benefits of innumerable kinds. Municipal, state, and federal governments have all grown colossally; for instance, the federal government now spends *eighty* times as much money annually as in 1900. Most of the expansion of the public services has been attributable, not to any conscious trend toward socialism, but to recognition of the simple fact that in a complex urbanized society, people cannot live decently unless the organized community provides them with services and opportunities which in earlier days the self-reliant man could get for himself.

(3) *Union action*—which, especially during the past fifteen years, has helped to lift wage-rates and standards of employment far above the level they would have remained at under the Iron Law.

(4) *A change in the attitude of business managements*—a growing realization that good working conditions, handsome factories, acceptable housing for workers, and an intelligent concern with worker relations, and also with public relations, can be business assets. This change has been gradual and in some degree forced by public hostility, as well as by government regulations which have placed big business in the bright glare of publicity: a goldfish has got to be good. But the change has been pervasive and salutary.

And (5) *the logic of mass production*—which is that the more goods you can produce, the less it costs to produce them; and that the more people are well off, the more they can buy, thus making this lavish and economical production possible. The continuing discovery and demonstration of this logic has been, in some ways, the most powerful force for change of the lot. For it has had its corollaries: that a nation of men and women secure against exploitation and acute poverty is a nation of delighted buyers of goods, to everybody's profit; that it pays better to produce the same sort of food, clothing, and equipment for everybody, of all income levels, than to produce luxury goods for a few, and second- and third-rate goods for the rest; and that therefore one can make money by lowering class barriers. Thus is Marxism confounded—not by dogma, but by the logic of advanced industrialism itself; or, to put it another way, by capitalism turned to democratic ends.

So much for generalization. Now let us glance at a few of the specific things that this modernized and disciplined industrial order has brought us during the past half century.

In fifty years, the amount of goods consumed per person in America has gone up 2½ times, while the average work week has dropped from about 58 hours to about 40.

The telephone dates from 1876, but in 1900 there were only a little over a million and a third telephones in America. At the end of 1949 there were over forty and a half million—just about thirty times as many.

The automobile, too, dates from the late nineteenth century, but in 1900 there were still only a few thousand of them in the country. They were a rich man's luxury (and a mechanic's despair). Now there are over forty million—with paved roads everywhere to drive on.

And not only has the radio, which as a distributor of entertainment dates only from 1920, become a possession of almost every family in the country, but its new-come rival, television, has not even begun its career in the old-time way, as a plaything of the rich: from the beginning of the television boom in 1947, sales of sets have been distributed fairly evenly among all income groups. The logic of mass production has dictated for them a falling price and a mass appeal; and the purchase of a set has been, accordingly, an index less of wealth than of gadget-mindedness.

Or, to move into another field, take a look at education. In 1900 less than one American boy or girl out of ten of high school age was actually at high school; now over four out of five are. Meanwhile the number of students in American universities, colleges, and teacher-training institutions has increased eightfold. If we have a crisis in education today, this is because our training and paying of teachers has not yet caught up with the spread of American opportunity.

What has been taking place has been both a narrowing of the gap *in income* between rich and poor—though there are still islands of deep poverty in America, and there are also families and individuals by the millions who, through illness or adversity, live on the ragged edge of want—and, even more impressively, *a narrowing of the difference between rich and poor in their ways of living.*

For instance, consider the matter of personal appearance, remembering that in 1850 the merchant prince and his wife, or in 1900 the frock-coated, silk-hatted banker and his Paris-gowned wife were recognizable at a distance, if they ventured among the common herd, as beings apart. Forty or fifty years ago the countryman in a metropolis was visibly a "hayseed"; the purchaser of inexpensive men's clothing was betrayed by his tight-waisted jackets and bulbous-toed shoes. Today the difference in appearance between a steel-worker (or a clerk) and a high executive is noticeable only to the attentive eye. And as for women, the difference in appearance between the one who spends $5,000 a year on clothes and the one who spends $250 is by no means as conspicious as the difference between the woman who has good taste and the woman who lacks it. The fact that the wealthy woman has thirty dresses to the poor woman's three is not visible on the street, and the fact that her dresses are made of better materials and are better cut is observable only by the expert eye at close range. Fashion used to be decreed by Paris, imported by the most expensive dress shops, then modified by the more expensive American dress manufacturers, and finally—after an interval of six months to a year—modified still further, almost beyond recognition, by the manufacturers of cheap dresses. The process is now quicker and the differences much less sharp. Women of every income group wear nylon stockings (which offer the perfect illustration of the democratic logic of mass production). Unless the poor woman is exceptionally poor—or indifferent—she like the rich woman has had her hair recently shampooed and set. It could almost be said that the only easily visible mark of wealth which a woman can put on is a mink coat. A generation ago the great mail-order houses produced different clothes for the Western farmer's wife and for the city woman in the East; today there is no such distinction, and a friend of mine whose train stopped recently at a small Oklahoma town remarked that the girls on the railroad platform there were virtually indistinguishable in appearance from girls on Madison Avenue or Michigan Boulevard.

Let us proceed from clothes to the equipment of daily living. As Professor H. Gordon Hayes pointed out in *Harper's* in 1947, the rich man smokes the same sort of cigarettes as the poor man, shaves with the same sort of razor, uses the same sort of telephone, vacuum cleaner, and radio, has the same sort of lighting and heating equipment in his house, and so on indefinitely. The differences between his automobile and the poor man's are minor. Essentially they have similar engines, similar fittings. In the early years of the century there was a hierarchy of automobiles. At the top, as marks of dashing wealth, were such imported cars as the Rolls-Royce, Mercedes-Benz, and Isotta Fraschini. There was also an American aristocracy of the Pierce Arrow, Peerless, and Packard. Then came group after group, in descending scale, till you reached the homely Model-T Ford. Today, except for a few survivals such as the obstinately rectangular Rolls-Royce of the old school, and a few oddities such as the new British sports cars, there is a comparative uniformity; and although the owner of a big, brand-new car probably has a large income, he may merely, like the purchaser of a television set, be someone who adjusts a slender budget to cover the machines that entrance him.

In the matter of running water and plumbing, uniformity has approached much more slowly but nevertheless steadily. Throughout the latter part of the nineteenth century the rich and the middle-income group in the cities and towns were progressively installing running water, bathrooms, and water closets in their houses; but at the turn of the century not only did factory workers and farmers (except for a few owners of big farms) hardly dream of enjoying such luxuries, but even in the houses of well-to-do people beyond the reach of city water and sewerage lines, there was likely to be no bathroom. Not until 1908 did Ellsworth M. Statler build in Buffalo the first hotel which offered every guest a room and private bath at a moderate price. Not until 1916 did the double-shell enameled bathtub go into mass production, replacing the painted cast-iron tub with roll-rim and claw feet. Today only the older and poorer tenements and dwellings in American cities and towns lack bathtubs or showers and water closets, and these conveniences are fast being installed in farmhouses.

Meanwhile the electrification of American farms has reached a point which would have been unimaginable in 1900, when even the prosperous city-dweller had only just begun to install electricty in his new house without adding gas, too, lest the current fail suddenly. The coming of the electric refrigerator and also, increasingly, the deep-freeze unit have not only made for domestic convenience but also—along with our expanding knowledge of nutrition—have improved the year-round diet of millions. (Where, today, is the once-famous American dyspepsia?) Meanwhile the servant class has almost vanished, although servants' wages have a purchasing power today from five to ten times bigger than in 1900; its virtual disappearance—which has imposed upon all but a tiny percentage of American families the chores of cooking and cleaning and washing (with, increasingly, the aid of a dishwasher and a washing machine)—marks the virtual absorption of the immigrant proletariat of yore into general American society, in which domestic service has always been regarded as humiliating.

One of the most striking effects of the logic of mass production has been the way in which the mass circulation magazines, the movies, and the radio have tended to impose upon Americans of all income levels the same patterns of emulation: in other words, to make them all want to be the same sort of people. This has been a purely twentieth-century phenomenon, for the big magazines were just beginning to push their circulations over the million mark in 1900, while the first nickelodeon theaters did not begin to show movies till about 1905, and radio broadcasting dates only from 1920.

In the movies, popular stars like Clark Gable, Cary Grant, Gary Cooper, Humphrey Bogart, and Gregory Peck may play the parts of people who are supposed to be rich and stylish, or of people who are at the end of their economic rope; but whatever role any one of them assumes, his popularity depends upon his representing a kind of charm that any young American male can appreciate and at least approach; in other words, upon his conforming to what old-fashioned people would call middle-class standards of speech and behavior—standards which might more properly be called classless or all-American. Whether he is cast as a millionaire's son or as a truck driver, he remains essentially the same. In radio Jack Benny, for all his big income, plays the part of a Jack Benny who lives in a modest house, owns a wheezy old car, watches the pennies, and has for his sole servant a jack-of-all-trades helper with whom he is on the breeziest of terms. Thus the logic of mass production pushes the idols of Hollywood into roles which represent general American behavior.

And what is the result? Both the rich man's fourteen-year-old son, who dismays his conservative parents by trying to talk like Humphrey Bogart, and the truck-driver's son, who longs to be as funny as Bob Hope, will grow up to behave more like their idols—and thus, more like one another—than they would have otherwise. And something else happens too. Half a century ago a coal-miner who found himself at a fashionable restaurant would not have had the faintest notion of how to behave; nowadays he has only to ask himself, "How would Gregory Peck do it?" In short, the social distance between the extremes of American society is shrinking.

Whenever I think of this change, I think of something I saw the other day in New York City. A street was being torn up for repairs, and while the workmen were standing waiting for the arrival of new equipment, one of them, who had in his hands an iron rod presumably used for prying off manhole covers, was enjoying a little relaxation. I looked twice to see what he was doing with that rod. He was practicing a graceful golf stroke.

So much for the change since 1850. And where are we headed now—during the next half century, or century, if you will?

I believe that we have hardly started; that the expansion of industrialism is still in its early stages, and its civilizing is in a still earlier stage. Professor Sumner H. Slichter says that by such an early date as 1980 the annual output of goods and services in the United States should rise from about $4,065 per worker to at least $5,744 per worker (at present prices), and probably more, while the labor week is being reduced from an average of 40 hours to an average of 30 hours. That seems to me a modest estimate—if we can surmount certain dangers which threaten us.

The first danger is, of course, that total war may smash the whole system. But in this particular context, even this danger can be exaggerated. It is quite true that the existence of atom bombs, and the possibility of hydrogen bombs, threaten millions of us with annihilation. But it is useful to recall that in the twenties and thirties many people predicted that another world war would "end civilization"; but that when the war came, on a lethal scale, it was accompanied and followed by an unexpected *increase* in population, not only in the United States but in other warring nations; and that although international trade has since then been hobbled, production has more or less recovered in Europe and has been given a new boost in the United States. The danger of extinction for whole communities is real; the danger to the progress of industrialism is not necessarily final.

The second danger is that we may defeat our great experiment in the negating of the Iron Law by applying the lessons of that defeat on too rapid a scale. We may get the fatal notion that benefits to various sections of the population can be brought about by government handouts and guarantees larger than the increase in our national productivity can support. This is not primarily a danger of socialism, which in its doctrinaire form is almost as outdated a concept as communism; among the guarantees and handouts that could most endanger our national solvency are the kind that even the most conservative citizens (such as potato-growers) delight in—when they are the beneficiaries. The balance between economic liberty and political intervention offers a delicate problem in adjustment.

There is a third danger: that the trend toward American uniformity may reach the point where we are standardized into universal acceptance of the second-rate—or even worse, incomplete susceptibility to mass emotion, which in turn could be manipulated to turn the United States into a police state. Well, possibly. Every wave of hysteria which crosses the country—like that which today fills many people with a preposterous terror of American communism—reminds us once more than eternal vigilance is the price of liberty. But if American flexibility, horse sense, and humor carried us through the dark days of 1933, they ought to be able to do it again.

If these dangers can be surmounted, the prospects are exciting. The remaining islands of real poverty in America are a challenge; so are our congested and debt-laden cities, which become more expensive to run, and offer their inhabitants a more unnatural and nerve-racking life, as they lure more and more people to enjoy their glitter; so is the failure, thus far, of most Americans to get any chance to savor the joy of work done under agreeable conditions for a satisfying purpose. The best of our factories, today, are things of a new and lively beauty; the worst—which include most of the older ones—are still in essence "dark, Satanic mills." More satisfaction and enjoyment on the job might prove even more desirable for the general well-being than more pay for less work. But in all these directions progress can be made, with luck, if we can keep wide open the roads along which scientific research and technology are taking us—and can steer around those other dangers that I have mentioned. The technicians were never more active than today; science, like industrialism, is still in its youth; a single new discovery, like that of atomic power, if harnessed for peaceable use, could by the year 2000 help to make 1950 seem as primitive a time as 1900, to say nothing of 1850, seems to us today.

Those villages of 1850 were mighty pretty, with their lawns reaching to the river. I see no reason why—if we keep our wits about us—American communities of 2000 and 2050 should not be just as satisfying to the eye; far cleaner, more convenient, more comfortable; far prouder as residences for even the least fortunate man, woman, and child who live in them; and more favorable as seed-beds of the human spirit.

---

4. THE COMING LABOR SHORTAGE *

THE INCREASE in population that has marked the war and post-war years has served as a stimulus to demand for many capital and consumer goods. Professor Drucker is here concerned with the fact that this increase in numbers has shown up in the older and young groups but has not been felt to any extent in the middle group, those between the ages of 25 and 65, and it is this middle group that constitutes the lion's share of our labor force. For at least the next decade, it appears that the size of our working force will remain fairly constant. Does this necessarily mean inflation? Professor Drucker thinks not, though he admits the possibility; he

* Peter F. Drucker, "America's Next Twenty Years," *Harper's Magazine,* March, 1955, pp. 27-32. Reprinted by permission of the author.

The author (1909——) is a frequent contributor to *Fortune, Harper's Magazine,* and *The Harvard Business Review.* Author of *The End of Economic Man, Concept of the Corporation, The Practice of Management* and many other works in the field of economics.

does, however, feel that this coming labor shortage may have profound effects on our manufacturing system.

THE MOST important economic event of 1954 went almost unreported in the newspapers. It was the announcement that four million sixty thousand babies had been born in this country during the past year—the largest baby crop ever. Yet 1954 should have brought a record low in births rather than a record high. For the young women who reached marriageable age, married, and had their first child during 1954 were born, for the most part, in the dark Depression years of 1933 and 1934, when the birth rate ran 30 or 40 per cent below the present figures. The number of marriages last year was smaller than usual, but the total married population had more than the usual number of children.

Between now and 1975, that is, the number of young people reaching marriageable age will tend to increase. Since romance is reliably constant, this means an appreciable increase in the rate of family-formation and in the number of births to be expected each year. Eight or ten years from now the birth figure should take another mighty leap upward as the children born in the years of the "baby boom" since 1942 begin to reach maturity and form families of their own.

What now appears to be true, therefore, is that the low birth rate of the Depression decade was a freak. The higher birth rate which reasserted itself in the early forties now appears to be the "normal" rate at which the American people reproduce themselves. Only ten years ago the Census Bureau, misled by the Depression birth date, predicted that the American population would become static within a few years and start to decline soon thereafter. It was this interpretation which underlay most of the talk about a "mature economy" that played such an important role in American public policy during the thirties and early forties. But now we can say with some certainty that nothing short of a tremendous catastrophe—that is, an atomic war—could possibly stop or even slow down the growth of the American population for the next twenty years.

The reason we can be so certain, of course, is that in reckoning the adult population for the next two decades we do not have to predict; we know. *The major events that determine the future have already happened—irrevocably.* Everybody who will reach marriageable age during the next eighteen or twenty years has by now been born. Everyone who will join the work force within the next eighteen or twenty years has by now been born. And so, obviously, has everyone who will retire. The economic population of the next twenty years—its numbers, its age and sex distribution—is not just predictable today; *it is already in being.*

This article will examine some of the implications arising from the single stupendous fact of 1954's birth rate. As in any prophecy, there will presumably be some boners—but with a difference. In order to keep them to as few as possible, we will severely limit our forecasting to those future happenings that are already under way. There will be no need for crystal-gazing. We will find plenty to occupy us in what we *know* about America's next twenty years from events that have already occurred.

MORE JOBS THAN WORKERS

We start with a paradox: there are going to be more people, and hence more jobs, but not more people to fill the jobs. It is more than possible, in fact, that a continuing feature of the next two decades will be a labor shortage—and that the basic problem of the period will not be unemployment but inflation. Let's look at some of the figures which show why this is true.

The total population of the United States, now at 162,000,000, can be expected to top 190,000,000 by 1965 and 220,000,000 by 1975. These are conservative assumptions. They make full allowance for a continuing drop in the birth rate in the one major sector of the populace where it is still high, and still dropping: the Negro. They allow for several years of birth rates as low as those of the thirties. They hardly take into account at all the fact that ten years hence the number of young people old enough to start their own families will be very much larger than it is at present. And they do not make allowances for any growth in the size of families. If the three-child family again becomes the norm, of course, as against the present average of two-and-a-half, the growth of population will be much faster.

The *rate* of population growth which the figures anticipate is no larger than our rate of growth for the past fifty years, including the thirties. It is the rate of population growth which has prevailed in this country virtually since colonial days, and which has brought about the steady doubling of the American people every half century. But the *total* number of new Americans this rate will add to our population is now exceptionally large. It took forty years—from 1910 to 1950—for America to grow by forty million people. Now it should take only twenty years.

At the same time that the total population will grow very rapidly, however, the *working population* will grow very slowly, if at all. With total population increasing by thirty million, the number between twenty and sixty-five years of age (the bulk of our working population) will go up at the most by seven million. In the group from twenty-five to forty-five—the one from which every employment manager in the country prefers to choose—there will actually be a shrinkage of two million. On the other hand, there will be six million more people over sixty-five, and at least sixteen million more under twenty, than there are today.

From 1965 on, in the second decade ahead, total population and working population should be in better balance. Beginning in the early sixties, the large baby crops of the forties will reach maturity. Population of working age will thus increase by twelve million or so during the second decade. And assuming that there is a slight drop rather than an increase in the birth rate of the families these grown-up children form, the subsequent increase in total population and in working population will stand in the same ratio (five to two) in which they stand today.

EXPLOSION IN THE COLLEGES

But the size of the working population is not entirely determined by the number of people of working age. An important factor is the number who are not available for work because they are in school.

If the 1954 birth rate was the year's most important economic event, the second most important was the announcement that the number of full-time and part-time college students had increased by 10 per cent, to an all-time high of two-and-a-half million. The increase in the birth rate was contrary to all expectations; the increase in the number of college students was nothing short of miraculous. Not only did an abnormally low number of young people reach college age during the past year (the delayed result of the lean thirties) but the veterans studying under the GI bill have all but disappeared. Five or six years ago, three-quarters of the male students in many undergraduate colleges were GIs; today the figure is down to 10 or 15 per cent, most of them in the older classes. Yet the 1954 jump was in the *freshman* class, which contains almost no GIs and was drawn from the smallest college manpower reservoir of the recent past or the foreseeable future.

It had long been clear that the early fifties would show whether there had been any real change in the educational habits of the country, or whether the GI Bill (and the attempt of many young veterans to make up for lost time) had just created a temporary "bulge" in college enrollment. A drop of one-third during these years would have been mild; indeed, it would still have supported the conclusion that going to college was rapidly becoming the normal thing to do. That there has been an *increase* rather than drop is thus overwhelming proof that —far from being a freak—the jump in college enrollment is another new "normal." The college enrollment figures now show exactly the same trend that high-school enrollment showed after World War I, when a high-school education first became "normal" throughout the country.

Twenty years from now, at least nine and perhaps as many as twelve million young people can be expected to attend colleges and universities. Therefore, even though they are of working age, they will not be available for full-time work. Such a projection is again a conservative one; twelve million college students will still be less than half the young Americans of college or university age. Yet within a similar period—from the early twenties to the early forties—the number of young people in high school increased from a little under 20 to close to 90 per cent.

Such a substantial gain in college enrollment would come none too soon. For our problem is not the breeding of an "intellectual proletariat" for whom there will be no jobs, but a greater need for trained and educated man- and woman-power than the country can possibly supply. Indeed, the technological revolution of "Automation," already under way, primarily requires a tremendous increase in the number of trained and educated people. And it is already true today that the short supply of such people is *the major limiting factor* on the rapid growth of our economy and of our principal industries. We need not worry, therefore, about our ability to absorb these millions of college-trained people; we have to worry principally about increasing their number and quality fast enough.

The explosive growth of college enrollment will create problems which lie well beyond the scope of these articles. It certainy raises the most serious questions of educational policy, curriculum, and educational standards. It makes me wonder whether the colleges, especially the independent liberal-arts colleges, really know what they are doing in their fund-raising and other campaigns. If I were a college president I would not—as so many seem to be doing—lower educational standards in the belief that this is the way to draw more students. I would try instead to raise standards, so as to make my college known for the quality of its education and the toughness of its academic requirements. There will be students aplenty.

What concerns us here, however, is merely the impact of this development on the size of the working population. We can expect that there will be only four million more men and women available for work

Here, in summary, is the basic population structure within which the American economy will function during the next twenty years:

There will be a population increase of one-fifth *in the next ten years.*

But total population of working age will increase only by one-tenth.

Population actually available for work will increase only by 6 per cent.

And total hours worked by the whole economy in the course of one year *may not increase at all.*

And in the next twenty years, total population will increase by at least two-fifths.

Population of working age, however, will increase by less than one-third.

Labor force will go up by one-fifth, and total hours worked by 10 per cent.

And even more intensive employment, on a larger scale, of older people who are willing and able to work—however desirable in itself—would not materially affect these conclusions.

in 1965 than there are today—that is, an increase of seven million of working age minus an increase of three million in college attendance. And, of the twelve million who will be reaching working age between 1965 and 1975, five may go to college rather than straight to work, leaving a net increase for the second decade of only seven million.

Finally, the size of the working population must also be adjusted for time at work. There can be little doubt that total hours worked will continue to decline as a result of longer vacations, more holidays, and a shorter work-week. The American people have made it thoroughly clear that they have decided to take, in the form of greater leisure, a big slice of any increase in productivity.

The statements in the box at the top of this page define a trend exactly opposite to that which dominated the twenties and thirties. Then, partly as a result of the drop in the birth rate and partly because of the cutting off of immigration, the population of working age tended to grow faster than the total population. It is the exact opposite, in other words, of the basic assumptions that underlay Keynesian economics; and the basic problem of economic policy in the two decades ahead should therefore not be unemployment but inflation.

A DIFFERENT KIND OF DEPRESSION

The supply of people to do the work, and of hours to do it in, will in fact be so short as to make any prolonged period of large-scale national unemployment highly improbable. This does not mean that we shall have no depression, or even that a depression is unlikely (though the constant new demands created by a rapidly growing population can be expected to act as a substantial cushion). It also does not mean that there may be no serious and chronic unemployment in any one industry, or in one area dependent on a decaying industry—as there is today in the Pennsylvania anthracite fields. But though depressions—even serious ones—may well happen, depression unemployment of the kind that characterized the thirties is unlikely.

Lest this be considered incongruous, if not silly—for we have come to consider the two words "depression" and "unemployment" as interchangeable—let me refer only to Soviet Russia, where for the past thirty years there have been violent and extreme economic fluctuations without unemployment; and where, though for entirely different reasons, there has been a labor shortage much like the one we are about to experience. What form such a depression-without-unemployment might take may be suggested by our experience from 1946 to 1949, when the three-quarters of the working population who were not unionized (and were therefore not protected against inflationary price increases) suffered a cut in their real purchasing power fully comparable to the impact of a severe and prolonged depression. Even with high employment, inflation could have the same kind of destructive effect over the next twenty years.

Now, there is only one effective way to control long-range inflationary pressures, and that is increased productivity. Certainly it is the only way to convert inflation from a serious threat of economic and social disruption into an opportunity for economic and social advance. As one of several consequences of the population revolution, therefore, *increased productivity* will be the paramount need of the American economy in the decades ahead.

Mr. Ralph J. Cordiner, the president of General Electric, announced last December that by 1965 his company will have to produce and sell twice the volume of goods it turned out in 1954 with only 11 per cent more people on its payroll. Adjusted for the expected decrease in working hours, this means that ten years hence General Electric must be able to produce twice as much for every hour its employees work.

This is a sharper increase in both production and productivity than the over-all economy will have to show, for the electrical industry is growing a good deal faster than the national average. But even for an industry that grows only as fast as the nation at large, the increase ahead will have to be tremendous. A company that intends to maintain its competitive position in its own industry will have to be able, ten years from now, to produce two-fifths more than it does today without much, if any, increase in its hours worked. Twenty years hence it will have to be able to turn out twice as much with only one-tenth more hours of work.

Put it in another way. Today every American at work supports himself (or herself) and one-and-a-half other people besides. Twenty years from now every American at work should produce enough to support, at today's standard of living, himself and three-and-a-half other people. And he will have to do this in fewer working hours.

This assumes, moreover, that the standard of living will only go up at the same rate it has been advancing for the past twenty-five years, half of which were years of depression and war. To achieve this—hardly an ambitious goal—productivity will, however, have to increase 40 per cent in the next ten years; it will have to be almost doubled in the next twenty years.

Despite all the emphasis we have given to productivity in recent years, we really know very little about it—and we certainly do not know how to measure it. But even if we take the most optimistic of the various guesses about the rise in productivity in the past few years—a guess that puts the net annual increase above 3 per cent—we are going to have to step up the rate considerably to make possible increased growth.

PAYING FOR PRODUCTIVITY

The first requirement is capital. We may not know much, but we do know that an increase in capital investment and an increase in productivity are tied together, and that the higher the capital per worker the higher the productivity—and, incidentally, the wages and salaries paid.

We are at present spending forty billion dollars a year on capital investment. A good many economists consider even this tremendous sum to be too low; they feel that we have not yet made adequate allowance for the inflation of the forties, and they point to the fact that a good many businesses (especially the small ones) still base their provision for future new equipment on the deflated prices that prevailed in the thirties. These economists feel that in three major areas of the national economy we have an over-age plant which needs more capital investment than it gets: in housing, in transportation, and above all in education. They feel, too, that in many industries the machinery is rapidly wearing out and that American equipment, far from being modern, might well—in important respects—be on the verge of obsolescence.

But let us assume that forty billion dollars in capital investment are adequate for the needs of the 1955 economy. We would then need sixty-five billion dollars a year in 1965 and at least one hundred billion dollars twenty years from now. To obtain such gigantic sums would not be easy under the best of circumstances. To make matters worse the large investment trusts and pension funds are currently emerging as the country's only real "capitalists"; and this development by no means encourages the supply of that kind of capital.

But there is another and more important question: can the nation afford investment at such a rate? Today eleven cents out of every dollar produced in this country is put back into capital for the future. To obtain an adequate amount in 1975, however, we would have to put back fifteen cents out of every dollar. Eleven cents is already high—higher than we have ever ploughed back except in wartime. Fifteen cents may be wholly impossible, except under such stringent government control of interest rates or installment buying as would be considered unbearable—and rightly so.

We must, if this is the case, find ways to obtain more productivity for our investment dollar than we do today. If capital investment is to be kept at or below 10 per cent of national product, we must learn by 1965 to get as much additional productivity out of fifty-five billion dollars per year as we now would get out of sixty-five—as much, in 1975, out of seventy billions as we now would get out of a hundred. We must, in other words, increase the productivity of capital itself by one-sixth during the next decade and by one-third during the next twenty years.

This is not a new problem, to be sure. Economic progress might even be defined as the process of continually obtaining more productivity for less money. The means to achieve this is *innovation*. Without constant innovation, that is, all the capital invested in this country since 1750 might have been barely enough to permit the present population to live at a 1750 scale of living; the entire improvement in living standards since then is the result of innovation. Innovation has been the real "frontier" of the Western world these past two centuries. And what now distinguishes an "underdeveloped country"—and *keeps* it "underdeveloped"—is not so much a shortage of capital as it is shortage of innovation.

THE CHALLENGE TO INNOVATE

To the layman—and the typical businessman—"innovation" means "research" or "engineering," new products or new productive processes.

These are indeed important aspects of innovation; and the fourfold increase (from one billion dollars in 1950 to four billion dollars in 1954) in the sums spent by American business on research and engineering for new products and new processes is therefore a highly encouraging sign. We already know that the next twenty years will bring about major changes in manufacturing, amounting to a technological revolution. And we also know that in a major industry like housing we badly need both radically new products and much more efficient production. But it is a serious mistake to think of innovation exclusively as technological innovation. The most important area of innovation—and the most productive one—may well be the opposite of technological.

During the past ten or fifteen years, the innovations that have had a major impact on the American economy were nearly all non-technological, were nearly all innovations in something else than product or process. First among them certainly stands the tremendous changes in distribution methods. Hardly less important, especially in its impact on productivity, has been the development of new concepts of business organization. There have been tremendous innovations in plant, store, and office architecture; similarly in respect to the management of worker and work, whether industrial engineering, human relations, or personnel management. Finally there is the emergence of new basic management tools, especially measurements and controls like budgets, cost accounting, production scheduling, and inventory controls.

Among the major innovations of the past ten or fifteen years, only one can even remotely be called an innovation in product or productive process. That is the development of systematic and organized methods of materials handling. Otherwise, in their aggregate, the basically non-technological innovations have had a greater impact on the American economy, and have contributed more to the increase in productivity in this country, than all technological innovations of the past ten or fifteen years. In the long view of history, it is for social inventions—and not technical ones—that Americans may be best remembered.

During the period ahead, in any event, the greatest need for innovation seems more likely to lie in the social than in the technological area. Indeed, the technological revolution itself will be totally unproductive unless it is accompanied by major innovations in the non-technological field. Among them, above all, is again innovation in marketing. Equally badly needed are innovations in methods, tools, and measurements for doing the managerial job in the modern enterprise, large or small; for the development of competence, skill, and imagination among managers (still considered a luxury by many companies) is probably the greatest necessity any business, let alone economy, faces. Finally, the need is for effective innovation in the management of workers and in the organization of work; despite the progress in this area, it may well be the most backward sphere, and the one with the greatest potential for increased productivity.

Compared to electronics, rocket engines, or synthetic chemistry, these are unglamorous subjects.They are rarely discussed except by professional managers, and not as often as they should be, even so. Yet our success at innovating in these four areas may very well decide whether the population revolution, which has already taken place, will be an opportunity for further growth and strength, or whether it will prove a strain, a burden, and perhaps even a threat to social and economic stability.

---

5. THE MODERN FARM PROBLEM *

"THE ANCIENT farm problem was how to find enough to eat. The modern problem is that of finding enough eaters able to pay the cost of producing." After he makes this statement, Professor Zimmermann proceeds to analyse the modern farm problem and to consider certain remedies. The ultimate solution to the farm problem he finds in the expansion of non-agricultural activities. The reasons underlying his conclusions and his evaluation of the importance of agriculture in the world economy are found in the following seceltion from his book on *World Resources and Industries.*

AS ONE review the progress of the mechanization and rationalization of agriculture, he can hardly fail to feel proud of the material achievements of our age. Is it not glorious to reduce backbreaking toil and, at the same time, increase the productivity of the laborer, to make more land arable, to widen the choice of crops, to improve the genetic qualities of both plants and animals, to fight their enemies more effectively, to open new and larger markets for farm products, and, in addition to all this, to reduce the isolation and boredom of farm life, bringing farmers better educational opportunities, better health, and in

* Reprinted with permission from *World Resources and Industries* by Erich W. Zimmermann, pp. 163-174. Harper and Bros. Copyright 1951.

The author (1888——) is Graduate Professor of Resources and Economics at the University of Texas. He was Director of the National Bureau of Economic Research, 1941-42. Author of numerous publications.

general more of the blessings of our industrial civilization? To ask the question is to answer it.

And yet, despite all this progress, agriculture throughout the western world for most of the twenty years between the two World Wars was in dire distress, being kept alive by artificial respiration as it were. And what is worse, the outlook for the future is by no means rosy. At least this is the view taken by thoughtful observers who look beyond the prosperity which agriculture in many lands enjoyed during World War II and its aftermath.

HISTORICAL SETTING

This agricultural distress, born of man's desire to solve the age-old problem of hunger, paradoxically brought on by the very success he attained in solving that problem, made itself felt on a large scale after World War I. For decades, in fact for a century and more, inventors had been at work trying to mechanize farming and scientific discoveries had contributed their share to agricultural progress. And everything seemed well. Europe produced more per acre and gave her crowded millions more and more wholesome food. She bought readily from the overseas countries whose agriculture, thriving on both export trade and on increasing domestic demand, expanded by leaps and bounds. How could such success lead to failure?

One could almost say that this failure was the result of the improperly correlated effects of the commercialization of agriculture and its mechanization and rationalization. Commercialization means dependence on a market and this dependence is safe only so long as equilibrating forces are at work to keep supply and demand in balance. The secret of the farm problem may be found in the crossing of two curves suggesting vital secular trends; one curve shows the growth of agricultural production in the countries of the West, especially in those exporting overseas. That curve goes up and up. The other curve shows the rate of increase in the number of people who consume purchased agricultural products and in their purchasing power. After rising sharply during the nineteenth century, this curve began to flatten in the twentieth century, until in some countries population stood still or actually declined and purchasing power ceased to grow. This crossing of the curves occurred somewhere around the time of World War I. It signalized a major dislocation of the world market for farm products. In part, perhaps in large part, this major dislocation was caused by the simultaneous opening up of the grasslands as the major granaries, made possible mainly by mechanization, and the remarkable renascence of European agriculture based chiefly on science.

For decades the United States, Canada, Argentina, and Australia had expanded their agriculture without apparent ill effect. On the contrary, for a long time it appeared as if at last man had succeeded in achieving an economic development which favored both buyer and seller, both consumer and producer. Costs were low because land values were low, soils were fertile, and little attention was paid to depletion. Rising land values paid deferred rebates or veiled subsidies to the cropper. Exports expanded. Domestic industry and cities grew apace. The future looked rosy indeed.

The era 1895-1914 in particular is often referred to as the golden age of United States agriculture. Farm output rose 50 percent. At the same time, however, industrial output rose 150 percent (as against 50 percent during 1920-1939). Exports were holding up well; land values increased. The success story of American agriculture was told to all the world. Old Europe was derided for her conservative soil protection policies, for not selling long-run assets for quick market gains, for not commercializing her peasant agriculture with the same speed and abandon displayed in the New World, for not following the example of England where agriculture was sacrificed to other interests.

World War I came as a great shock to the agriculture interests of overseas countries. But this did not last long. Soon the war boom was on. Acreage expanded as perhaps never before. Large sections of the Great Plains felt the sharp edge of the plow for the first time. The United States and Canada especially, being nearest to the theater of war, were called upon to make up for the deficits of war-torn Europe and to still the voracious appetites of large armies in the field.

And then came the collapse, followed by violent convulsions, then by lingering sickness—pernicious surplusitis. The richest farm lands of the earth lay blighted as if under a curse. In Canada whole provinces faced bankruptcy, as did wide areas of the agricultural sections of the United States.

While it is true that World War I with its sudden insistence on expansion did much to hasten the catastrophe and to aggravate the trouble, it would be a grave error to look upon that war as the primary cause of the trouble. The evil lies more deeply embedded in the casual background of history. The roots reach much deeper—down to the very nature of agriculture itself and its incompatibility with the nature of industry. The roots can be traced to basic institutional developments. These underlying forces had been at work decades before their effects became visible on the surface. They were long hidden by compensatory or neutralizing forces—expanding exports, rapid industrialization, rising land values, and finally the war boom. "The mills of the Gods grind solwly, but they grind exceeding fine."

While the taproots of the modern farm problem are found in the surplus-producing overseas countries, other roots are spread far and wide, reaching far beyond the boundaries of the export countries. The simultaneous increase in European productivity has been mentioned. Its effects were aggravated by a rising nationalism, the fear of war and the consequent desire to be more self-sufficient than World War I had found the countries of Europe, the inability of statesmen to get world trade moving after the war, increasing interference with trade, currency disorders, and many other factors. As will be shown later, commercial agriculture can expand with impunity only if the industrial, i.e., the nonfarm, market expands at a far greater rate than does agriculture itself. And that market seemed to be suffering from a malignant disease. The rate of expansion of industry in the United States in 1920-1939 was only one-third of what it had been in 1895-1915.

In a *sense* there can be no surplus of farm products so long as millions are "in want," undernourished, or starving. But until mankind develops a great deal more compassion and foresight than it seems to possess now, that *sense* is highly theoretical. For what counts in this workaday world is hard cash on the barrel head or a cashier's check. The pieman's query to Simple Simon is still heard around the world. One could say, therefore, that the modern farm problem has a religious tinge—"Am I my brother's keeper?"

SYMPTOMS

The ancient farm problem was how to find enough to eat. The modern problem is that of finding enough eaters *able to pay* the cost of producing.[1] The problem is that agriculture, stimulated by outside forces, produces beyond the capacity of the market to absorb. It is a problem of imbalance, of disequilibrium. Surely, there is imbalance when farmers let their crops rot in the fields and on the trees while people are hungry, undernourished, or inadequately supplied with clothing and shelter. Surely there is disequilibrium when farmers are asked to pay grossly inflated prices for what they wish to buy while receiving deflated prices for what they sell.

The most telling symptom of farm distress in surplus-producing countries is the low return farmers earn as compared with those engaged in industry, secondary or tertiary. The difference in earnings is

[1] What is said here of food, the chief product of agriculture, applies with almost equal force to agricultural products in general.

TABLE 1

Net Income of Persons on Farms from Farming (Including Government Payments), Compared with Income of Persons not on Farms, United States, 1929-1945*

Year	*Income per Person*		*Index Numbers of Income per Person*[b]	
	On Farms from Farming	Not on Farms[a]	On Farms from Farming	Not on Farms
1929	$223	$ 871	166	179
1930	170	761	126	156
1931	114	605	85	124
1932	74	442	55	91
1933	93	419	69	86
1934	111	488	83	100
1935	159	540	118	111
1936	171	626	127	128
1937	197	671	147	138
1938	165	622	123	128
1939	173	663	129	136
1940	181	721	133	148
1941	253	850	186	174
1942	389	1046	287	215
1943	522	1250	384	257
1944	550	1320	405	271
1945	585	1294	431	266

[a] The income of the nonfarm population as shown here is national income minus the net income of persons on farms from farming. Income of persons on farms from nonagricultural sources has not been deducted.

[b] 1910-14 = 100.

clearly shown in Table 1. The difference ranges from over 100 percent in 1945 when wartime earning and protection policies had given farm income an unheard-of boost, to almost 500 percent in 1932 when, under the hammer blows of the Great Depression, farm prices fell faster than other income-determining factors.

The table also illustrates the instability of farm income. It will be noted that the index numbers of per capita farm income range from 55 to 431, a range of almost 1:8, while those for nonfarm income range from 86 to 271, a range of little more than 1:3. Another way of showing this instability is through the fluctuation in the "terms of trade." This is the ratio of the index number of prices of goods sold by farmers to the index number of prices of goods bought by farmers.

The meaning of these figures comes home with a shock when it is

* U. S. Department of Agriculture, *Agricultural Statistics 1946,* Washington, 1946, p. 566.

realized that in 1937 there were about the same number of people working on the nation's 6,000,000 (plus) farms as in the nation's 200,000 (minus) manufacturing establishments—about 10,000,000 workers in each. The farmers earned 9 percent of the national income, the factory workers 23 percent!

The relationship between supply, demand, and price is typically quite different in competitive agriculture and not-so-competitive industry. In agriculture vast numbers of producers, scattered over wide areas and more or less unknown to one another, sow their crops and then wait for the results, i.e., both physical results in terms of size and quality of crop and the economic result in terms of market price. Many industries, on the other hand, produce *not* in anticipation of a future demand which may or may not materialize, but only as that demand manifests itself in increasing prices and in orders. Thus in agriculture the crop is "made" first; it determines the supply and this in turn determines the price in the light of the demand. In industry rising demand raises price and only then is a greater output stimulated.

In importing countries the main symptoms of distress caused by the general dislocation of trade and finance are excessively high food prices, due mainly to the uneconomical production of foodstuffs behind tariff walls and other restrictive barriers but also due to rising taxes and to diversion of resources from agriculture to war industries.

NATURE OF THE PROBLEM

The modern farm problem is just one more illustration of the fundamental difficulty facing western civilization which was previously referred to as "social lag", i.e., the lagging of the societal arts behind the technological arts. To be truly successful, every new invention, every new machine, should have a counterpart invention, a counterpart device, in the realm of social institutions and social relationships. Not only must the potency of the social adjustment be comparable to the power of the impact, but also its tempo, its speed. A society that blindly promotes technological advance and one-sidedly pushes the progress of natural and applied science, relying on fate to provide the necessary corollaries in the field of societal adjustments, is bound to come to grief.

It is an old story that the introduction of every machine was accompanied by misery and resentment, and often by strife and bloodshed, on the part of workers displaced by it. There is hardly an industry which has not gone through that bitter experience. But again and again industry, benefiting from lowered costs and larger output resulting from the faster and cheaper machine processes, soon managed to employ more people than the machine displaced. So a strong faith in automatic adjustment developed and the terrors of "technological unemployment"[2] were soon forgotten or pooh-poohed as needless fears of faint-hearted souls.

It was only natural that the same reasoning should be applied to agriculture. But, as will be shown later, this was a fatal error. For not only is agriculture far less able to adjust itself smoothly to innovation, but that which proved the saving grace in the case of industry—elasticity of demand—is largely absent in the case of agriculture. What made possible the expansion of output of machine-made products was the ease and, one may say, the enthusiasm with which the cheaper machine-made products were snapped up by eager buyers—in other words, elasticity of demand. Agriculture, by and large, is deprived of the safety valve without which uncontrolled mechanization and rationalization appear as dangerous as raising the temperature in a steam boiler without providing for the escape of the excess steam.

There is another aspect to be considered. It is always dangerous to transfer the arts and devices created spontaneously in one environment to another, wholly different environment. Industry and agriculture are essentially different. This difference, which rests ultimately on the basic dualism of nature, fully developed elsewhere in this volume, renders the application to agriculture of machines and science sired by industry a precarious undertaking that should by no means be stopped but that needs to be watched with the utmost care as to its effects, including its repercussions.

The problem of the economic order, meaning the problem of preserving the proper balance between a diversity of producing and consuming interests, is difficult even under relatively static conditions marked by a modicum of homogeneity of factors and forces. It becomes complex and even more difficult in this age of accelerated technological and scientific progress. It is greatly aggravated by the clash of such heterogeneous elements as agriculture and industry within the same market economy.

CAUSES

Incompatibility of Agriculture and Industry

This incompatibility of agriculture and industry is one of the chief causes of the farm problem. The congenital weakness of agriculture

[2] But see the analysis of the problem by Emil Lederer, *Technical Progress and Unemployment,* League of Nations, International Labour Office, Geneva, 1938.

which derives mainly from its dependence on nature, the living forces of the plant and animal world, and its implications have already been discussed. Here the question is how this congenital weakness manifests itself when agriculture, no longer left to itself as in ancient vegetable civilizations, is harnessed to the same yoke, as it were, with a far faster, stronger, and more high-strung animal—when, in other words, agriculture is tied with industry into the exchange economy. In this exchange economy, industry—secondary and tertiary industry—sets the pace, is the active force, and agriculture must follow passively.

In this new setting, the congenital weakness of agriculture, always manifest in some way or other, takes on new meanings. Left to its own devices, agriculture is inefficient, its *per-man* productivity is low, the standard of living it assures is modest at best. It leaves largely unsolved the problems of crop failure and famine. When linked up with industry through mechanization and rationalization, it becomes highly efficient, its *per-man* productivity rising to amazing heights.

Over the amount of output, the farmer has not as full control as has the manufacturer or the miner or, for that matter, most people engaged in secondary or tertiary activities. Weather still plays a dominant role in the determination of output, i.e., weather acting directly on growth or indirectly through insect pests, diseases, length of growing season, etc. Nor does the farmer possess full control over quality. Nor can he definitely determine the exact time of the harvest. Typically the farmer sows in the spring, takes as good care of the growing crop as he knows how and as his means permit, and lets nature take her course. To a large extent he is helpless before the uncontrolled forces of nature.

He is equally helpless before the mysterious forces of the market. The typical farm is small—a one-family enterprise. Vast numbers of farms are needed to supply the main staples such as wheat, corn, cotton, etc. Market supply has to be built up out of very small parcels varying in size, quality, time of delivery, etc.

So the middleman steps in between the farmer and the ultimate buyer to assort crops by grades, collect homogeneous parcels, and deliver them where needed. Frequently the crop goes through a processing industry—milling, baking, canning, packing, etc.—before reaching the final consumer. Vast numbers of farmers therefore do not face vast numbers of consumers, but face a far more limited number of buyers, middlemen, and processors. The farmer's market position as a seller is generally weak.

It is equally weak as a buyer of industrial products such as tractors; service materials such as gasoline; or consumers' goods for his own use.

In general, both as a seller and as a buyer the farmer is in a weak position in the market. He may be "the last stronghold of competitive enterprise in America," but his is one of the few forms of business enterprise left that is afflicted with the old-fashioned variety of competition and not blessed with some newfangled monopolistic sort.[3]

How competitive agriculture fares in an industrial world became exceptionally clear during the Great Depression of 1929-1933. Figure 1 deserves careful study. The figure contrasts agricultural implements and agricultural commodities. Such a contrast is effective but not quite scientific. One should not contrast a single branch of manufacturing industry with the aggregate of agriculture. However, a sufficient number of industrial examples are cited to indicate the general character of the industrial aggregate corresponding to "agricultural commodities.". . .

FIGURE 1

Price and Production Trends of Agriculture and Industry During Depression (1929-32)

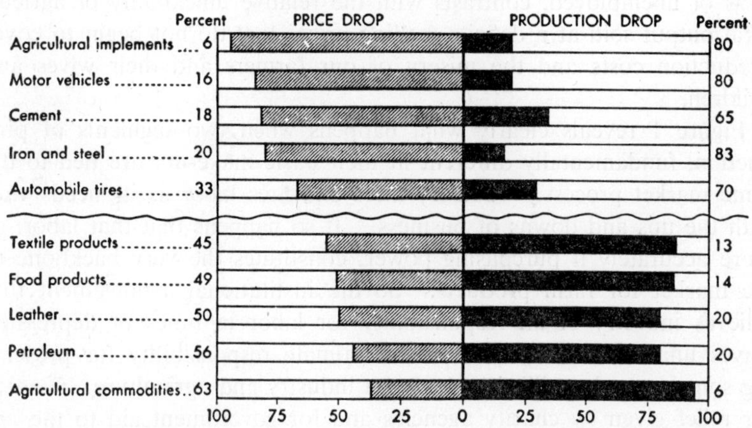

Note that above the wavy line the output drop is greater than the price drop; below this line the price drop is greater than the output drop. (From Gardiner C. Means, *The Relative Inflexibility of Industrial Prices,* Senate Document No. 13, 74th Congress, p. 8.)

Further comments on Means' significant diagram seem called for. The industries listed can be divided into two groups: those whose output dropped more than price and those showing the reverse behavior. The

[3] In this connection, one should bear in mind that the strong market position of industry is reinforced by such institutional developments as patents, the corporate form of enterprise entailing limited liability, holding companies, cartels, etc. Few farmers are in a position to take advantage of these devices.

division is clear-cut. In the first group are found mineral-using industries relying on inanimate energy and on science more than on hand labor; in the other are agriculture and agricultural industries (textile, food, and leather products). Evidently auto tires, though containing agricultural products, follow the lead of automobiles and therefore fall into the first group. Petroleum is in the second group by a mere accident of history—the discovery of the east Texas oil field (at that time, 1929-1933, a large share of the crude oil output of the United States was still produced by independents and thus resembled agriculture structurally).

The contrast is striking: agricultural implements, 6 and 80; agricultural commodities, 63 and 6! The price of the former holds up, come what may, while output drops to a mere 20 percent of peak production. The price of the latter drops 63 percent while output is virtually constant through the biggest boom and the worst depression in history. The relative inflexibility of industrial prices, bought at a fearful cost in idle resources and paid for largely by the misery of millions of unemployed, contrasts with the relative inflexibility of agricultural output sold at a deficit, spelling prices that do not begin to cover production costs and the misery of our farmers and their wives and children.

Figure 1 reveals clearly what happens when two segments of production, fundamentally different in their basic make-up, are tied to the same market process. Industry hires and fires labor as its needs vary with the ups and downs of business. It so happens that that labor, or more accurately it purchasing power, constitutes the very backbone of the market for farm products. So the institutional arrangement that relieves industry of all responsibility for labor in times of depression leaves unanswered the question of ultimate responsibility for preserving some sort of equilibrium between industry and agriculture. Except for relief given by charity agencies and for government aid to the unemployed, the bulk of the burden falls on those who constitute the weakest link in the economic chain—the farm population.

When domestic agriculture, by giving up its self-sufficiency, lost its independence and became commercialized, looking to the market for both the disposal of its products and the fulfillment of its needs, two mathematical ratios assumed fateful importance for the farmer's weal or woe. One is the ratio of the *price* which the farmer receives for his products, to the *cost* of producing them (this cost is affected by the prices he must pay for what he buys as a producer); the other is the ratio of the *price he receives* for what he sells, to the *price he pays* as a consumer. With the price he receives he is expected to cover:

1. Cost and maintenance of his farm, including interest on money borrowed for its purchase and improvement.
2. Cost and maintenance of equipment, barns, machines, etc.
3. Cost and maintenance of livestock, if any.
4. Services and supplies (seed, fertilizer, fuel, electricity, etc.).
5. Consumers' goods and personal services for himself and his family.

The proceeds of a sale depend on both the amount sold and the price. Ordinarily there is a negative correlation between these two: the more farmers sell in the aggregate, the lower the price.[4] Thus amount and price tend to offset each other to a certain extent, not necessarily in all individual transactions, but in the typical case and in the overall effect.

Unfortunately, too often and on too general a scale the prices received by farmers do not cover farm costs, if the latter are reckoned in any manner acceptable to cost accountants. The late Lord Stamp once characterized the failure of nonfarm consumers in industrial countries to pay adequately for farm products, as a blotch on the escutcheon of the West. Another Englishman once berated his countrymen for being willing to live well at the expense of the women and children of the Ukraine. (That was at a time when Britian was importing much if not most of her wheat from Russia.)

In the ideal economic world, governed by perfect competition, in which all resources are mobile enough to respond to every turn in the market, there should be no terror in these ratios. Automatic adjustments should keep them continually equilibrated. But unfortunately, the real world in which we live does not know perfect competition, and mobility is reduced to a snail's pace. The result—constant maladjustments and violent fluctuations.

By nature, agriculture is not nimble. It is sluggish, slow to respond to stimuli, especially to stimuli calling for contraction rather than expansion. Fixed charges constitute a high percentage of total farm costs. In fact, practically all costs are fixed. The direct exceptions are purchased seed, fertilizer, and hired labor (not much hired labor is employed on the "one-family farm," the mainstay of American agriculture). The biggest portion of the cost is the investment in the farm itself, including interest on any loans incurred in its acquisition or improvement. Another big item nowadays is equipment; a third one, taxes. Even

[4] This negative correlation need not be taken for granted in the case of industry. Industry generally produces the largest volume when prices are highest, whereas in agriculture a bumper crop spells low prices. The income of industry expands under the simultaneous dual stimulus of volume and price. The farmer must multiply his large crop by a low unit price; only a short crop can be multiplied by a high unit price. Thus what is cumulative in industry is neutralized in agriculture in the offsetting action of opposing forces.

labor (except hired labor) is a fixed cost, for there is no hiring and firing on family farms as in industrial and commercial establishments. One does not hire or fire his own family, and the family must live. If prices go down, the family is apt to work harder to make up in units of output for the low return per unit. Thus there is an element of *inverse* price elasticity in the expenditure of farm labor and the resultant supply of farm products, a tendency for output to increase rather than decrease in the face of falling prices.

The difference between farm and factory in this respect is striking. When times are bad, factory labor is dismissed and less raw and service materials are purchased. Under such conditions, it may pay to cut output to the bone. The savings in reduced variable costs outweigh the loss from fixed charges. In agriculture variable costs are of such little importance in determining total cost that their reduction in times of depression is frequently offset by fuller use of fixed capital—farm, equipment, family labor.

It was pointed out that the proper functioning of an exchange economy requires mobility of the factors of production, including labor. A word must therefore be added concerning the mobility of farm labor. One might expect that as farm prices drop and farming becomes progressively less remunerative, labor would leave the farms, i.e., that farms would go out of production, that farmers would sell out and their sons would move away, etc. Actually it does not work out that way. For one thing, farm foreclosure and bankruptcy seldom mean farm abandonment; they generally mean that one farmer tries where another has failed. One should expect that man power would leave the farms when times are bad. The exact opposite is true—additional man power streams in.

Paradoxical? Yes, but only in the eyes of the superficial observer. As soon as one probes deeper, the paradox dissolves into thin air. When times are good, industry jumps ahead by leaps and bounds while agriculture walks a little faster perhaps, but not much. Under these conditions the pull of rapidly advancing and expanding industry on labor is far stronger than that of slowly advancing agriculture. Agricultural labor prospects may look good, but industrial opportunities look better; and that is what counts. Therefore, in good times, labor shifts from farm to factory. Vice versa, when times are bad and the industrial labor market collapses, things in factory towns look desperate. They are bad on the farm too, but at least one can eat, and sleep in the hay. So the farm appears the lesser of two evils. But the farmer who receives perhaps half of what it costs him to "make" a crop is caught between inadequate cash income and an unwelcome plethora of labor.

The problem of adjusting farm personnel to the figure set by *per-man* productivity as affected or determined by the interaction of pertinent forces of nature (weather, fertility, etc.) and of culture (implements, mechanical horsepower, science, etc.) on the one hand, and by demand as reflected in price on the other hand, is seriously aggravated by the fact that people living in rural farm areas characteristically 'multiply" faster than do people in nonfarm areas. Thus in 1940 in the United States "the number of children ever born per 1000 mothers" was 3984 for rural farm classes, 3201 for rural nonfarm classes, and 2846 for urban classes. This differential fertility is in sharp contrast to the reverse differential in per capita income. Thus it was found that in 1937 farm people earning 9 percent of the national income had nearly one-third of the nation's children. The tempo of the transfer of people from farm to nonfarm areas, therefore, has to exceed that set by economic forces. Even if there were no mechanization or rationalization, there would still be a transfer problem. Without its solution, farm labor cannot be expected to earn wages comparable to those earned by nonfarm labor.

Under these conditions, business fluctuations, business cycles, booms and depressions affect the farmer in a way altogether different from that in which business—i.e., industry and trade—is affected. Being able to hire and fire labor in accordance with his needs and the employment opportunities, the entrepreneur finds rapid adjustment possible, not to say almost painless. Depending on inanimate energy for heat, light, and power, industry is free to turn the current on or off more or less at will, whereas agriculture is tied to the biological rhythm of nature.[5]

Effects of the Mechanization and Rationalization of Agriculture

The mechanization and rationalization of agriculture meet difficulties not altogether different from those found in some other economic activities. The procedure is typically as follows. The new machine or the new scientific discovery is adopted by an individual farmer who feels or knows that he is going to profit from the innovation. If his expectations are fulfilled, his example is soon followed by others who wish, like him, to enlarge their profits. As the application of the innovation keeps spreading, there comes a time when, in response to the greater profits, the production of the crop or commodity in ques-

[5] It goes without saying that industrial plants working at capacity are far more satisfactory all around than idle factories. The point made here refers merely to the difference in the degree of shock and pain suffered by agriculture and by industry.

tion increases, because of high yields or expanded acreage, or both, over and above previous production records. Unless, for some strange reason, the demand for the product happens to have increased at the same time and at a similar pace, the price must come down. To be more exact, if the innovation has reduced costs, the farmers whose costs have been reduced sufficiently to break even at the lower market price can stay in. Others still working on the old high-cost basis are forced out—or at least according to theory they are supposed to be forced out. If they are forced out, they constitute an employment problem unless they can grow something else, the demand for which is not yet fully met by existing facilities. If they are not forced out, chronic oversupply will tend to depress the market price below a remunerative level. The consumer or somebody else will gain unduly at the expense of producers in general and of high-cost producers in particular.

Frequently submarginal farmers are not forced out. Farmers whose costs are not covered by the proceeds of their sales are apt to defer maintenance of their land and equipment. Thus capital losses are incurred and the soil, the nation's number-one basic asset, suffers.

The problem, then, may be viewed as a conflict between immediate market gain (derived from the adoption of new mechanical and scientific discoveries) of individuals on the one hand, and long-run agriculture-wide interests with regard for general social assets on the other. This is one of the crucial problems of our time.

It seems hardly reasonable to expect that these difficulties are bound or even likely to resolve themselves through automatic market-wise adjustments. Such adjustments assume a minimum of self-determination and largely ignore the fundamental differences between agriculture and industry in the national economy. As has been shown, this minimum of self-determination is frequently absent in the case of farmers. It is different with a small group of giant manufacturers who constitute a modern industry and are their own inventors, research workers, machine suppliers, etc. In other words, they themselves provide the stimuli to increase production—if they want to. If obsolescence is too costly, they may decide to wait a while before adopting the new machine or process.

Demand for Farm Products

Up to this point the emphasis has been on supply factors. It is time that our attention is turned to the demand aspects of the problem. They materially add to the difficulties.

The demand for farm products suffers from several serious afflictions: (1) low price and income elasticity for farm products, (2) secular trends that unfavorably affect demand per person, (3) the instability of consumer purchasing power caused by the instability of business (cyclical disturbances), and (4) the absorption of some consumer demand by competitive products of industry. These will now be discussed.

1. The ease with which adjustment to market changes can be made depends largely on the elasticity of supply and demand. By elasticity is meant the responsiveness of one factor to changes in some other factor. Thus when economists speak of price elasticity of *supply* they mean that increases in the price received for a specific product readily elicit an increase in market offerings and perhaps also in the output of the product, and that price decreases have an opposite effect. It was shown that agriculture possesses relatively little supply elasticity. While it manifests little response to price increases, it is even less responsive to price decreases. Economists also speak of price elasticity of *demand;* this refers to the readiness with which demand responds by expansion to falling prices and by contraction to rising prices.

There is also income elasticity of demand, which means the readiness with which the demand for certain goods expands or contracts as the individual's or family's income increases or decreases. Since the bulk of farm products are foodstuffs (or feedstuffs that eventually become foodstuffs when finished) and since food is a basic necessity, the demand for farm products is in general rather inelastic as to both price and income. With exceptions, lower prices for foodstuffs do not greatly stimulate demand nor do high prices readily cause contractions. However, demand for *specific* farm products does show considerable elasticity in response both to price and to income changes. Thus changes in milk prices result in considerable variation in milk consumption. By and large, however, the income elasticity of the demand for farm products is very low. The result is that as the incomes of families rise, a progressively smaller percentage of the family budget is devoted to food purchases. This progressive decline would appear even sharper if food purchases at the retail level, which cover a great many materials or services not of farm origin, could be reduced to actual farm products. Fancier foods tend to come in fancier packages and to include costlier service items.

The fundamental significance of this declining importance of food purchases is that the demand for farm products behaves quite differently from the demand for nonfarm products. Wealth does not increase the appetite for food but it creates innumerable and insatiable desires for nonfarm products. Not only are progressively fewer farmers needed to produce a given amount of farm products (because of the ever-increasing per capita productivity of commercialized agriculture) but agriculture plays an ever-smaller (relative) role in the national economy as the national income rises. To maintain the equilibrium between supply and demand, a cumulative (relative and/or absolute) contraction of agriculture is called for.

2. Nor is this all. The occupational shifts associated with industrialization and urbanization—involving change-over from physical labor outdoors to indoor labor and exacting nervous rather than physical strain—justify a considerable curtailment of average per capita food consumption. This trend is accentuated by the decline in the rate of increase of total population which is observed in all industrial countries. The effect of this decline is aggravated by changes in the age composition which further contribute to low per capita food requirements. New knowledge of nutrition as well as new popular ideas about diets brings about shifts in consumer preferences for various foods; again there is expected from agriculture an adjustive capacity which is alien to its nature. (Not all these nutritional innovations have negative effects on agriculture. In fact, entire new branches of agriculture are brought into being by newly developed consumer tastes, desires, and demands, e.g., the citrus fruit industry.)

3. The demand for farm products is adversely affected by the instability of industrial employment. However, this aspect has been discussed (see pp.000 ff.) and nothing further will be said here.

4. Finally, the demand for agricultural products may at times be affected unfavorably by competition between them and products made by industry. History is full of such examples. The case of vegetable and animal dyes such as indigo, madder root, and cochineal being replaced by coal-tar dyes comes to mind. The substitution of mineral soda for vegetable soda is another example. Steel rope has replaced rope made from hemp; candles made from petroleum derivatives have replaced those made from tallow. Rayon and nylon compete with cotton and silk. More recently, synthetic rubber has made serious inroads into the market for "natural" rubber. Numerous other examples could be cited. There is no intention of implying that such substitutions are harmful to the common good or even to agriculture in the long run. Their effect may be favorable, unfavorable, or indifferent. All that is claimed here is that they constitute another factor in the equation that needs watching.

Under these conditions—low supply elasticity, especially on the downbeat; the unrelenting push from the outside in the form of technological advance and scientific progress; the release of millions of acres for food products resulting from the displacement of work animals by tractors; low price and income elasticity of the demand for farm products; the declining per capita demand for food in general; shifts in demand for specific products; and the declining rate of increase of the populations of industrialized countries—the only salvation for agriculture is an expansion of nonfarm activities, secondary and tertiary, so powerful and so sustained that all the negative forces at play will be at least compensated if not overcompensated. Such powerful and sustained expansion, by the irresistible force of tempting nonfarm employment opportunities, would bring about the withdrawal of man power from agriculture at a speed sufficient to keep *per-man* productivity on the farm on an even keel with *per-man* productivity elsewhere.

Society cannot afford to let the food getter down. Its great opportunity lies in the unlimited expansibility of the demand for nonfarm products and services. The whole ingenuity of the institutional inventor should be pointed in that direction. If the farm problem is to be solved, national income must go up at a rate infinitely greater than the rate at which technological advances and scientific progress accelerate the productive achievements of farmers. If this cannot be accomplished, calling a holiday for such technological and scientific advance may make more sense than modern man is generally disposed to admit. Industrial man hates to throttle technological and scientific progress as much as the farmer hates to throttle the God-given forces of nature. Yet situations may arise when such throttling will prove the lesser of two evils.

The farm problem as it has developed since about 1920 is, then, made up really of two problems: (1) the instability of farm income which results from the impact of an erratic industrialism on a way of life and a way of producing that are constitutionally incapable of adjusting smoothly and promptly to the constant ups and downs, shifts and changes; and (2) the relatively low average income of those engaged in agriculture, which suggests that, by and large, agriculture is overstaffed and overextended. This second problem is due partly to the relentless stimulation to which agriculture is constantly submitted both by industry-furnished machines and by government-furnished science and to which it does not respond with sufficiently prompt and effective expulsion of man power from its ranks. This second problem, in other words, is at least partly one of overemployment and resulting underproductivity.

REMEDIES

In considering the solution of the problem one thing seems clear enough, i.e., that agriculture cannot be expected to solve its own problems. In the first place, the roots of most of its troubles stem from outside the realm of agriculture. In the second place, agriculture retains little self-determination or autonomy. Economically the farmer is dependent on a market over which he has little or no control (which is supposed to be automatic but its automaticity has been a little one-sided of late). Financially he is dependent on banks, on corporations, on wealthy landowners, or on the government. Technologically he is dependent on the outside, mainly on industry. His research is done for him by the government, and for information he must rely mainly on the government. In industrial countries agriculture constitutes a political minority group.

That this dependent minority group of the national economy should be hailed by some as the most vital sector of our economy seems strange. Yet one can understand such "agricultural fundamentalism." Is not food vital to life? Is not the soil the basis of human existence? The answer is clearly yes. But to deduce therefrom that agricultural production should be maintained at a high level, or that the farm population should be held constant, or that farm prices should be firmly riveted to a certain ratio regardless of changes in cost, would seem to draw wrong conclusions from the vital significance of the products of agriculture. As Davis well states,

> In this field, as in many others, we may wisely seek to temper the cruelty of these forces; but far-sighted statesmanship will undertake, not the Canutian task of sweeping back the tides, but appropriate methods of making adaptations to them. . . . Agriculture has, and probably always will have, an important place in the life of every nation. Measures to protect agricultural resources from needless depletion, to facilitate physical and economic processes of agricultural production and marketing, to mitigate the severity of fluctuations in farm income, and to raise the plane of living among farmers are in the general interest; but they are justified on grounds independent of an allegedly peculiar importance of agriculture or farmers. Efforts to raise the level of attractiveness of farming, financially and otherwise, are desirable as part of a general policy; but most attempts to raise it in relation to the level of attractiveness of other occupations tend to be self-defeating. Efforts to make farming profitable for all who may choose to farm are foredoomed to failure.
>
> The wealth and welfare of nations depend upon many complex conditions. Today, agriculture is not uniquely basic and the prosperity of a nation depends largely on other factors than the work of those who till the soil.

Solutions are of two kinds: quick, short-run remedies designed to meet an immediate emergency; and slow, long-run permanent solutions. Subsidies, stamp plans, credit moratoriums, price support, acreage curtailment, etc., may be justified for limited emergency needs. Permanent solutions must go to the roots of the problem. There are congenital weaknesses of agriculture to be overcome. Science may find more and better ways of doing this. There are business cycles which are at the root of the instability of farm income. Their frequency and violence must be reduced. There are monopolistic practices in our economic make-up which interfere with the proper allocation of resources and challenge those suffering from the result to retaliate with generally unsound practices. If such monopolistic evils—for reasons of technology or politics or what have you—cannot be removed, agriculture must be protected by countervailing measures. But ultimately the solution lies in nonfarm expansion, both domestic and world-wide.

The reader may wonder why in a treatment of agricultural resources so much space is given to the discussion of history and the analysis of economic forces, to the farm problem, to industrial economics, etc., and relatively so little to actual bona-fide down-to-earth facts such as acres of this, yields of that, prices of the other. The answer is simple. If, as is maintained throughout this volume, "resources *are* not but *become,* resources evolve out of the dynamic triune interaction of natural, cultural, and human forces," it is this interaction that is the crux of the situation, the key to resource availability Unless man learns to solve problems such as the farm problem the fruits of both nature and culture will rot on the ground, and a detailed description of both the ground and the rotting fruit would be little more than mockery.

---

6. THE CRISIS IN RAW MATERIALS *

Condensed from a Report by the President's Materials Policy Commission

THE UNITED STATES has been fortunate in that it has enjoyed a generous supply of certain strategic natural resources, but our country has never had an adequate supply of all vital raw materials. The report below points to the rising real costs of raw materials as a threat to our continued economic development. In presenting the following article to their readers the Editors of *Fortune* wrote:

* Reprinted from the August 1952 issue of *Fortune* Magazine by Special Permission of the Editors; Copyright Time Inc.

"It has taken a massive, five-volume report by a special commission to show that the U.S. has reached a major crossroads in resources. From here on out, the U.S. will be running into increasing deficits and rising costs in materials to sustain its growth—unless it takes thought and uses all the weapons of economics and technology in coordinated attack on the problem. The report is one of the greatest, most readable government documents of the century.

Below is an eloquent statement of the problem, condensed by *Fortune* from the opening to the Summary of Volume I. Its eloquence derives in part from the sweep of data, in part from the caliber of the commission. Known informally as the Paley Commission, after its chairman, William S. Paley, chairman of Columbia Broadcasting System, Inc., its members are George R. Brown, chairman of Texas Eastern Transmission Corp., Arthur H. Bunker, president of Climax Molybdenum Co., Edward S. Mason, dean of the Graduate School of Public Administration, Harvard University, and Eric Hodgins, long associated with *Fortune*. The lucid Hodgins style is perceptible throughout this statement. *Fortune* prints it in the hope that it will lead readers to the five supporting volumes, which should be a 'must' for corporate management's libraries."

The question, "Has the United States of America the material means to sustain its civilization?" would never have occurred to the men who brought this nation into greatness as the twentieth century dawned. But with the twentieth century now half gone by, the question presses and the honest answers are not glib.

The full report of the President's Materials Policy Commission, "Resources for Freedom," has as its central task an examination of the adequacy of materials to meet the needs of the free world in the years ahead. In area after area we encounter soaring demands, shrinking resources, the consequent pressure toward rising real costs, the risk of wartime shortages, the strong possibility of an arrest or decline in the standard of living we cherish and hope to share. As a nation, we are threatened, but not alert. The materials problem now demands that we give new and deep consideration to the fundamental upon which all employment, all daily activities, eventually rests: the contents of the earth and its physical environment.

None of us in the U.S., whether in civilian or military life, is easily accustomed to the idea that raw materials can be a problem. Indeed, all our tradition has accustomed us. A hundred years ago resources America's problem today is precisely the reverse of the problem to which seemed limitless and the struggle upward from meager conditions of life was the struggle to create the means and methods of getting these materials into use. In this struggle we have by now succeeded all too well: so efficiently have we built our high-output factories and opened the lines of distribution to our remotest consumers that our sources are faltering under the constantly increasing strain of demand. We have always been more interested in sawmills than seedlings. We think about raw materials last, not first.

The Materials Problem

Today, throughout the industrial world, but centering inevitably in the heavily industrialized U.S., the resulting materials problem bears down with considerable severity. The nature of the problem can perhaps be successfully oversimplified by saying that the consumption of almost all materials is expanding at compound rates and is thus pressing harder and harder againt resources which, whatever else they may be doing, are not similarly expanding. This materials problem is thus not the sort of "shortage" problem, local and transient, that in the past has found its solution in price changes. The terms of the materials problem we face today are larger and more pervasive.

Powerful historical streams have converged to make the problem uniquely intense today. First, there has been a profound shift in the basic *materials position* of the U.S.—a worsening relationship between our requirements and our means of satisfying them. Second, other high-consuming nations, primarily in Western Europe, are in difficulties which stem from the serious depletion of their own domestic resources coupled with the weakening or severing of their former colonial ties. Third, many resource-rich but less-developed nations, especially of former colonial status, now focus on industrialization rather than materials export. Fourth, there lingers from the great depression a worldwide fear of the possible collapse of markets, which dampens the willingness of private investors and resource rich countries to develop new free-world resources. Finally, a great schism divides the world between the totalitarian and democratic nations, disrupting normal trade patterns and making necessary costly measures of armed preparedness.

The nation's economic life calls for a vast and delicate balancing of multitudinous resources against continually changing needs and demands. The American pioneers had to destroy trees so that they could plant corn. In a more complex world, minerals, fuels, forest and agricultural products, the land on which these grow and the water that nourishes them must be variously dug, burned, felled, cropped, and constrained in interactions that reach further than we are aware of when we induce them. We grow and we destroy. We concentrate and we disperse. We nurture and we abandon. A chemist makes a crucial discovery, and the resource base for the production of women's stockings shifts from mulberry leaves in Japan to bituminous coal underlying West Virginia. A war occurs, and the materials for tires and teething rings no longer comes from *hevea brasiliensis* in Malaya but from Texas petroleum, natural gas, or ethyl alcohol made from molasses.

But these colossal interplays between resources more often take place in less dramatic ways; more often entirely within our own domestic economy and so slowly that we may be unaware of their significance for a decade. Energy for farming operations, once supplied almost entirely by draft animals, now comes chiefly from tractors, stationary gasoline engines, and electric motors. This considerable fact carries with it another, even wider ranging: in this process of change, the petroleum industry releases for other use no less than 60 million acres that would be necessary to feed draft horses. (The nitrogen cycle is upset in the same process, and the loss of manure fertilizer must be compensated.) . . . As prices rise and fall, the resultant of thousands of forces, steel replaces wood in housing construction, or vice versa, or concrete replaces both. Glass increases while brass diminishes; plastics from coke ovens supersede porcelain enamels; paint pigments begin to come from sands in Florida instead of from galena deposits in Missouri. The rise and fall of materials streams constitutes the great fugue of our industrial times.

To anticipate such moves in detail is beyond the capacity of even the most electronic intelligence; to attempt to plan them in detail would be like planning the finger prints of one's great-grandchildren, and would fail for the same reason: too many accidents and unforeseeable forces. But because we cannot plan fingerprints we do not disregard the laws of genetics; and our inability to plan in detail does not mean that we can withdraw our intelligence from contemplating the future.

The Continuing Task

Clearly, the task of examining such matters cannot be completed in one attempt. Nor can it ever be safely regarded as complete. A major important conclusion presented by the President's Materials Policy Commission is thus that the job of materials-problem study must be carried on, cooperatively by government and private citizens, not periodically at wide-spaced intervals, but hereafter day by day and year by year. [A major recommendation is that this continuing task be centered in the existing National Security Resources Board, which has the authority, needs only funds and staff to perform it.]

In contemplating the future, a prudent man can base his actions only on the best estimates he can make; commissions weighing policies can do no better. This report attempts no prophecies. But if our current generation is responsible for passing on to the next as best it can the prospects for continued well-being, then the first requisite is that we plan to meet successfully those requirements and challenges that now can be foreseen. Therefore, the commission has chosen, as the period to review, the quarter century stretching from the present to the year 1975—a date which seems sufficiently distant not to be strongly affected by our current (1952) defense-production problems, yet not so far off as to be dominated by technological and other developments now wholly unforeseeable.

The eruption of war would alter the pattern of materials demand and the adequacy of supplies in swift and drastic ways. Yet if complete peace, confidence, and prosperity were to descend upon the world tomorrow, the materials problem would not vanish. Nor might it become less severe. If all the nations of the world should achieve the same standard of living as our own, the resulting world need for materials would increase to six times present consumption. Today's rearmament emergency may best serve us as a set of binoculars that brings apparently closer to us circumstances which would in any event confront us were we to take no action to avert them; in this sense it can be of great usefulness to us in emphasizing the problem we shall face and the actions we must pursue, *war or no war.*

The Fundamental Concepts

This report can have significance only as the convictions held by members of the President's Materials Policy Commission are clearly stated:

First, we share the belief of the American people in the principle of growth. Granting that we cannot find any absolute reason for this belief, we admit that to our Western minds it seems preferable to any opposite, which to us implies stagnation and decay. Whether there may be any unbreakable upper limits to the continuing growth of our economy we do not pretend to know, but it must be part of our task to examine such apparent limits.

Second, we believe in private enterprise as the most efficacious way of performing industrial tasks in the U.S. With this belief, a belief in the spur of the profit motive and what is called "the price system" obviously go hand in hand. This method, motive, and system have served uniquely well in America. We believe in a minimum of interference with these patterns of private enterprise. But to believe this is not to believe that this minimum must be set at zero. Private enterprise itself has from time to time asked for helps, or restraints, or counterpoises from government to keep the system working at its best. The commission sees no reason either to blink this fact or to decry it; as we see the future, the coexistence of great private and public strength is not only desirable but is essential to our preservation.

Third, we believe that the destinies of the U.S. and the rest of the free non-Communist world are inextricably bound together. This belief we hope will color everything we have to say about the materials problem. It implies, for example, that if the U.S. is to increase its imports of raw materials—as we believe it must—it must return in other forms strength for strength to match what it receives. It is this commission's belief that if we fail to work for a rise in the standard of living of the rest of the free world, we thereby hamper and impede the further rise of our own, and equally lessen the chances of democracy to prosper and peace to reign the world over.

It is by these avenues of thought that the commission arrives at the formulation of the major premise upon which all the rest of its report is based: the over-all objective of a Materials Policy for the U.S. should be to ensure an adequate and dependable flow of materials at the lowest cost consistent with national security and with the welfare of friendly nations.

The Basic Appetite

The U.S. appetite for materials is gargantuan—and so far, insatiable. At mid-century, the nation uses up over 2.5 billion tons of materials each year to keep itself going and support its standard of living. With a population of 151 million, each person consumes, on an average, 18 tons a year. He uses about 14,000 pounds of fuel for heat and energy. He uses 10,000 pounds of building materials, 800 pounds of metals (winnowed from 5,000 pounds of ores). He eats nearly 1,600 pounds of food; this, together with cotton and other fibers for clothing, and with pulpwood for paper, and other miscellaneous products, mounts up to 5,700 pounds of agricultural materials. In addition he uses 800 pounds of non-metallics, such as lime, fertilizer, and chemical raw materials.

Such levels of consumption, climaxing fifty years of phenomenal economic progress, levy a severe drain on every kind of resource we have: minerals, forests, soil, and water. In the first fifty years of the twentieth century, as population doubled and our total national output reached five times the 1900 level, the stream of raw materials increased in volume and value until, in 1950, it was worth two and one-half times as much (in constant dollars) as it was in 1900. In the mixture that made up this stream there were some significant differences, of which the most startling was that whereas our use of forest products actually declined 1 per cent in 1950 compared to 1900, our consumption of minerals, including fuels, was six times 1900 totals. In 1950 we were taking from the earth two and one-half times more bituminous coal, three times more copper, three and one-half times more iron ore, four times more zinc, twenty-six times more natural gas, thirty times more crude oil than in the year 1900. *The quantity of most metals and mineral fuels used in the U.S. since the first world war exceeds the total used throughout the entire world in all of history preceding 1914.*

This vast drain, greater today than yesterday, and inescapably greater tomorrow than today, upon resources that cannot be renewed has become the most challenging aspect of our present-day economy. A ton of ore removed from the earth is a ton gone forever; each barrel of oil used means one less remaining. Neither the next fifty years nor even the next twenty-five can see a growth in minerals consumption at the same increasing rate unless profound changes in trade and technology occur.

Even though they have been less urgently demanded, "renewable" resources have also felt the strain. Ninety per cent of our virgin timber stand in the commercial forest area has been cut, and thus far we have done a poor job in growing replacement crops. At present we are using up our inventory of saw timber at a rate 40 per cent faster than its annual growth. Millions of acres are no longer in forest; other millions have gone to brush and inferior trees. Upon our agricultural land we have imposed a heavy burden of depletion; we have opened it, exploited it heavily, abandoned much of it after its fertility had been drained, and moved on to repeat the process elsewhere. Partly because of soil erosion, even water, once regarded as a "free commodity" of virtually unlimited supply, has become a problem.

The time has clearly passed when we can afford the luxury of viewing our resources as unlimited and hence taking them for granted. In the U.S. the supplies of the evident, the cheap, the accessible, are running out. The plain fact is that we have skimmed the cream of our resources *as we now understand them;* the pause must not be too long before our understanding catches up with our needs.

With less than 10 per cent of the free world's population and 8 per cent of its land area, the U.S. has come to consume almost half of the free world's volume of materials. It is such growth of demand that is at the core of our materials problem; it is mainly our unwillingness to accept the status of a "mature economy" that challenges the adequacy of our resources to meet our needs. All the copper ever discovered in the U.S. would last only twenty-five years at the rate of consumption projected for 1975; all the lead would last only eighteen years, all the zinc only thirty years. In short, handing over the U.S. mineral deposits, intact and pristine as they were in Columbus' day, to our children in 1975 would scarcely help them solve their materials problems at all.

As a nation we have yet to face squarely such growing inconsistencies between our ambitions and the domestic bases upon which they rest. How did we get this way? And what are we going to do about it?

The Basic Shift in Position

The U.S. has never been completely self-sufficient in raw materials: had we insisted on being so, our economic output and living standards today would be considerably lower than they are. We began as an "underdeveloped" nation, with rich resources but a shortage of manpower and capital, and little industry. Our own manufacturing grew: our foreign trade burgeoned and its composition underwent drastic change. U.S. exports of crude materials slowly fell in proportion as exports of manufactured products slowly rose. Opposite changes occurred in our pattern of imports. Finally, the decade of the 1940's marked a turning point in the long-range material position of the U.S.; historical trends long in the making came to a climax when the national economy moved just prior to the war from a long period of depression into a period, still continuing, of high employment and production. By the mid-point of the twentieth century we had fully entered an era of new relationships between our needs and resources; our national economy had at last not merely grown up to our resource base but in many respects had outgrown it. We had completed our slow transition from a raw-materials *surplus* nation to a raw-materials *deficit* nation.

The symptoms of this changed materials position are today numerous: We have become the world's largest importer of copper, lead, and zinc, whereas once we were huge exporters. We have begun to meet from foreign sources a sizable and growing portion of our needs for petroleum and iron ore, long the hallmarks of U.S. self-sufficiency. We have shifted from net exporter to net importer of lumber. There are today only two metals (magnesium and molybdenum) for which we are not wholly or partially dependent on foreign supplies. At the start of the century we produced some 15 per cent more raw materials than we consumed (excluding food); by mid-century we were consuming 10 per cent more materials than we produced.

The Projected Demands

The size of future materials demands, and the adequacy of supplies, will depend upon the rate at which the U.S. economy and that of the whole free world expands. If we assume for the moment a favorable set of materials-supply conditions, the size of our national output by 1975 will depend mainly upon the size of total population and working force, the number of hours worked per week, the accumulation of capital that has occurred by then, and the rise of man-hour productivity.

Estimates of U.S. population for the future range between 180 million and 220 million; the commission has assumed, after consultation with the Bureau of the Census, a population of 193 million by 1975 and a working force of 82 million, in contrast with the 1950 figures of 151 million and 62 million. It has assumed a work week perhaps 15 per cent shorter than in 1950. It has further assumed an annual rise of about 2.5 per cent in production *per man-hour* against a somewhat smaller past rate of 2.1 per cent, because the commission thinks it reasonable to expect steadier levels of employment and economic activity in the future, in line with the avowed national objective of making major depressions a relic of the past. This does not preclude the possibility of milder fluctuations.

The fundamental assumption, drawn from this, may be wrong but seems unquestionably conservative: it is that the rate of growth of the economy in the next twenty-five years will be neither more nor less than what it has averaged over the last century, or about 3 per cent per year. Three per cent compounded results in a doubling every twenty-five years; thus by 1975 our total output of goods and services (the gross national product or G.N.P.) is assumed to be twice what it actually was in 1950. . . . Although it is assumed that our G.N.P. will double, past experience indicates that less than a doubling of total materials input can achieve this owing to the fact that G.N.P. will reflect more value added to materials by higher fabrication and a greater proportion of services. It thus seems that an increase in the total materials stream of between 50 and 60 per cent will suffice to achieve a doubling of the G.N.P. by the 1970's.

Based upon the foregoing, the commission has projected the general magnitude of demand in the decade 1970–80 for various major materials. These projections do *not* predict how much of each material will actually be available and consumed. Instead, they are estimates of what might be demanded *if relative prices of various materials remained the same as in early 1950,* which they are most unlikely to do. Moreover, the projections can make no allowance for unforeseeable new uses, sharp substitutions, or dramatic technological improvements.

In the difficult matter of projecting future demands, one point of overriding importance stands out: despite wide differences of judgment as to whether demand for some material will rise 50 per cent, or 100 per cent, or 200 per cent, the central point is that demand for everything *can be expected to rise substantially.* This may not be a popular dictim, particularly among some businessmen who may be more fearful of creating too much future capacity than of having too little. But the economic history of our times records more estimates of the future that were too small than those that erred on the other side. Many unexpected turns of fate will occur in the next quarter-century; one or more of them may have some deplorable effect upon business. But this commission sees no reason to assume that a world that has been growing economically by leaps and bounds for many generations will suddenly become static in this one.

The Essence Is Costs

The threat of the materials problem is not that we will suddenly wake up to find the last barrel of oil exhausted or the last ton of lead gone, and that economic activity has collapsed. The real and deeply serious threat is that we shall have to devote constantly increasing efforts to acquiring each pound of materials from natural resources which are dwindling both in quality and quantity—thus finding ourselves running faster and faster in order to stay standing still.

In short, the essence of the materials problem is *costs.*

The real costs of materials are not measured primarily in money; they lie *in the hours of human work and the amounts of capital required to bring a pound of industrial material or a unit of energy into useful form.* These real costs have for some years been declining, and this decline has helped our living standard to rise. In this commission's view, there is a serious possibility that this downward trend in real costs may be stopped or reversed tomorrow—if, indeed, this has not already occurred.

There is no completely satisfactory way to measure the real costs of materials over the long sweep of our history. But clearly the man-hours required per unit of output declined heavily from 1900 to 1940, thanks especially to improvements in production technology and the heavier use of energy and capital equipment per worker. This long-term decline in real costs is reflected in the downward drift of prices of various groups of materials in relation to the general level of prices in the economy. Since 1940, however, this downward trend has in some cases been reversed. Whereas wholesale prices of commodities in general advanced an average of 105 per cent from 1940 to 1950, in that decade petroleum rose 149 per cent, zinc 119 per cent, farm products 152 per cent, lead 157 per cent, lumber 218 per cent. Others, including aluminum, iron ore, nickel, sulfur, and even copper, moved up less than the general level of wholesale prices, although some might have moved further in the absence of price ceilings.

This upward thrust of materials prices since 1940 is accounted for in part by failure of supply to adjust rapidly enough to sharp increases in demand. To this extent prices can be expected to settle back as supply catches up. But in many cases there is cause to suspect that present high prices show that pressure against limited resources is boosting real costs.

The Costs Solution

If costs are the problem, what is the solution? The answer of this commission is that there is no *one* solution. There are, however, many flexibilities in our materials position, and we can succeed in averting the threat in the materials problem if we undertake a series of simultaneous actions which utilize these flexibilities to the full.

We can get more materials and more energy from domestic resources by pushing back the technological, physical, and economic boundaries that limit presently the *supply.*

We can alter our patterns of materials *use* by more efficient designs and processes—and by shifting the burden of use away from scarcer materials toward more abundant ones.

We can get more materials from abroad, on terms beneficial to ourselves and other free nations.

These opportunities are real and promising, but their full benefits will never be realized except by earnest and unremitting effort.

More from the U. S.

The U.S. even today makes practical use of only a small fraction of its total resource base. Past depletions notwithstanding, we still possess a broader and stronger usable fraction of our resource base than ever before—mainly because, over the years, we have discovered resources and uses unsuspected by our ancestors. The bayberries of Cape Cod and the sperm whales off Nantucket were vital resources to the early inhabitants of Massachusetts; so was the buffalo to the plainsmen. It was irrelevant to them that nature had created huge pools of petroleum under the soil of Texas, great bodies of iron ore in Minnesota, waterfalls in Washington, and phosphates in Florida. It is equally irrelevant to us today that the candles, the whale, and the buffalo have all but vanished; it is of high importance that the resources of the West have been opened up, that the invention of the internal-combustion engine has made petroleum a valuable resource, that technology has taught us how to make aluminum from bauxite, and plastics from such abundant resources as coal, water, and air. By discovery, development, and technology, the materials stream which flows from our resources has been enlarged and its composition vastly altered.

To improve our balance, we need to work increasingly in six areas of supply and three of use.

SUPPLY

Exploration and discovery: Most major metal discoveries have been made by following surface ore exposures in mountain regions. By now few of these exposures remain undiscovered, but perhaps half the surface of the U.S. is covered by a mantle of "young" rocks, and geologists infer that ore deposits exist hidden below them as large and as rich as have ever been found in the exposed areas. We must improve geophysical and geochemical prospecting methods swiftly in the hope of discovering such ore bodies.

Fuller use of known resources: In coal mining we leave about 50 per cent of commercial grades of coal behind in the ground; we leave more than 50 per cent of petroleum in an average pool. Enough natural gas was wasted in 1950 to supply the gas needs of 11 million of the nation's homes. A considerable fraction of harvested resources also goes unused: only 65 per cent of the average tree that is cut ends up as useful material. These physical wastes are not necessarily economic wastes, but many extraction practices need intensive improvement.

Using lower-quality resources: The richest-grade resources are usually the cheapest; hence we skim the cream. Yet we have frequently found that today's use of the second best has advantages over yesterday's best. The newsprint industry, once confined to using northern spruce, can today use a faster growing southern pine, once useless to it. As the rich iron ores of the Mesabi approach exhaustion, we are learning to use lower-grade taconite ores.

Renewing renewables: The U.S. for generations has been mining out its renewable resources—forests, soil, and water. Restoration of severely depleted resources is slow and costly, if possible at all. We must learn more speedily that it pays to use such resources on a "sustained-yield" basis.

Finding work for presently unemployable resources: Perhaps the greatest increases in our usable-resource base could be achieved by learning to tap certain abundant components of our total resource base which hitherto we have not known how to use. The mix of materials we use today has little to do with the way in which these materials occur in nature. Among the ninety-odd known chemical elements only a third enter strongly into modern industry. Another third enter weakly if at all; the final third is just now beginning to step out of the textbook pages. There is much more aluminum in the earth's crust than there is iron—yet we use sixty times as much iron as aluminum. The most abundant metal in the earth, silicon, finds as a metal almost no use at all.

Synthesizing new materials: The most notable supplements to our materials stream in recent years have been the array of various highly versatile plastics, artificial fibers, synthetic rubbers, and the like. These synthetic materials may, in many cases, be superior to the article replaced, and cheaper as well. Science and technology, which have created many materials shortages by expanding demand, are challenged now to help solve the materials problem in a host of ways, not least of which is by synthesizing additional important materials from abundant or renewable resources.

USE

Shifting from scarce to abundant: The way we can shift our materials mix toward more abundant materials is seen in the case of copper and lead. As copper became scarcer relative to aluminum, aluminum moved in to perform certain of copper's functions. As lead became scarcer, plastics began to supplant it for such uses as cable covering. These examples make it clear that our attention should be focused just as much on expanding the output and use of *abundant* materials as upon enlarging the supply of *scarce* materials; for some purposes an extra pound of aluminum or plastics may ease the situation as much as another pound of copper or lead.

Making materials work harder and longer: The U.S. has been lavish in its use of materials, because of their comparative abundance in the past. Vast quantities of material have been wasted by overdesigning and overspecification. We have frequently designed products with little concern for getting maximum service from their materials and labor. We drive heavier automobiles than is necessary for mere transportation, and we adorn them with chromium because we like it that way. We blow thousands of tons of unrecoverable lead into the atmosphere each year from high-octane gasoline because we like a quick pickup. We must become more aware that many of our production and consumption habits are extremely expensive of scarce materials and that a trivial change of taste or slight reduction in personal satisfaction can often bring about tremendous savings. If we fail to act from such awareness, rising costs and shortages will eventually force us to it.

Giving materials a second life: The more materials we put into goods and structures, the larger becomes our stockpile of potential scrap. Frequently the man-hour cost of reclaiming this material is so great that recovery does not pay, but better techniques and better organization for handling scrap can add great tonnages to total supply.

Our strongest weapons for accomplishing improvements in supply and use, and fighting the threat of rising real costs wherever encountered, are in the application of larger quantities of energy to *work* and larger quantities of technology to *working methods.* How well supplied are we with energy and technology, *as resources,* to give us the flexibility we must have to support the burdens of the future? As of today the simple answer is: not well enough.

The previous contributions of technology to materials supply have been great, but the future contributions must be greater still. Most Americans have been nurtured on the romantic notion that technology will always come to the rescue with a new miracle whenever the need arises; after all, it gave us synthetic rubber and the atomic bomb in a hurry when the need was urgent. But isolated solutions of problems relating to individual materials are no substitute for the broad frontal attack technology needs to make on the problem as a whole. The criticism is not of our technologists but of our lack of national concern for the materials problem.

More from Abroad

Even if no threat of war overhung today's world, the U.S. would still have to face the fact that our high-consumption economy no longer makes our domestic resource base adequate even to our civilian needs. The U.S. will find it increasingly worth while to turn abroad for more supplies of basic materials.

Some alterations in political thought may be necessary before such a policy becomes accepted as an everyday matter. Actually, there is little to be lost and enormous advantages to be gained by importing a much greater volume of raw materials in the future than we have in the past. We are in a good position to make bargains advantageous to buyer and seller alike.

The fact that nature distributed resources very unevenly over the face of the earth in relation to human population and consumption alone argues in favor of increasing integration of the various national economies of the free world. But the hard political facts of the mid-twentieth century add further great weight to the proposition that it will be to the mutual advantage of all freedom-loving peoples of the earth to achieve a greater measure of cooperation than ever before, founded on the principles of mutual help and respect. Such cooperation can succeed only if it is based on a clear understanding of the varying needs and resources of all the nations concerned, and the opportunities which lie in mobilizing the strength of all to meet the particular weaknesses of each.

It would be folly for policy makers in this or any other nation to assume that the present turmoil of the world will work itself out in ideal fashion. The violent political upheavals of this century clearly have not yet spent their force. What happens internally in the less developed nations, and to their economic and political relations with the industrially advanced nations of the free world, will largely determine whether materials development can be used to help world progress.

At the Least Cost

The task of overcoming the materials problem is far greater than one of merely locating enough physical resources. The task is to overcome the social, economic, and political obstacles in the way of foreign trade; to develop and apply more energy and technology to the materials field; to ensure a sufficient flow of capital into it; to guard our security, and concern ourselves at every point with insurance against rising cost. Such accomplishments can only be achieved by a consistent policy—that is, by intelligently directed action toward determined goals—as distinct from aimless drift and blind faith. A materials policy, broadly conceived, must provide a framework for public programs and for private actions such that all will move with reasonable harmony toward the same national objectives. It will not do to wait, and solve the problem "eventually"; while we are waiting we can encounter such a succession of shortages as to disrupt our cost pattern and defeat an "eventual" solution altogether.

The tests to be applied in government policy making are even more complex than those in private business. There is no magic formula to yield the right answers to the myriad questions that arise; each one must be judged on its merits and in its context. Yet there is one basic economic principle which, if applied to the limit of available facts and injected consciously into each judgment, can provide a basic thread of consistency throughout the whole field of materials policy. *With our economy facing stronger and stronger pressures toward rising real costs of materials, this commission believes that national materials policy should be squarely founded on the principle of buying at the least cost possible for equivalent values.*

This cardinal principle of least cost has application to all major sectors of materials policy: to development of resources, to energy and technology, to the difficult problem of weighing the claims of the present against those of the future, to imports of foreign materials, and to security. Its application is most often challenged, however, with respect to imports and security.

The Protection Argument

That our economy can best develop by obtaining its materials at the lowest possible cost is most often attacked by those whose costs are higher than those of foreign competitors. It is they who ask for restriction of imports on the grounds of "protecting the American standard of living from the competition of lower-paid foreign labor." This argument is often buttressed with the assertion that we should strive to be as self-sufficient as possible in view of the security risks we face.

The commission feels strongly that this line of argument is fallacious and dangerous. The idea that the American standard of living must be protected from low-cost foreign supplies based upon "cheap labor" is an idea based on unemployment psychology. In a full-employment situation the supply of any material from abroad at a price below that of our domestic costs (provided it does not represent a temporary dumping) does not lower the standard of living but actually helps push it higher. In the U.S. it enables us to use manpower and equipment to better advantage in making something worth more than the cheaper material obtained from abroad. Abroad, our purchases will contribute to a strengthening of economic life and improvement of working conditions in the nations from which we import.

It is true that where our industries face a considerable reduction in output, with employees and capital unable to transfer quickly to more remunerative activities, the government has the responsibility of easing the transition to the new situation. This, however, is hardly likely to be an important problem in the materials field, where even the declining industries are more likely to be faced with a shortage of manpower than with a surplus.

The Security Problem

As, in one material after another, we reach the stage at which we must turn abroad for additional supplies, the point may be raised that we are endangering our security by dependence on foreign sources; on "fair-weather friends" whose supplies in time of war will not be available to us.

This point is substantial enough for serious consideration. The issue must be defined. *It is to gain the greatest security at the lowest cost.* Sometimes the least-cost route to security is to give special aid to domestic industry; sometimes it is not. When aid is indicated it is always best to tailor it to the specific situation. Self-sufficiency for many materials is impossible; for many others it is economic nonsense. It is certainly not true that for all materials an unqualified dependence on domestic supplies is the best in the end, even when physically possible. With some materials, peacetime dependence on domestic supplies may mean such depletion that, if war comes, a reserve which might otherwise have existed will have been destroyed. With some materials it is much more economical to depend upon expanded output in safe areas abroad and on stockpiles built in whole or in part on foreign supplies than to maintain a domestic industry behind elaborate and expensive protection. With some materials it may be advisable to maintain a domestic industry which normally supplies only part of our requirements but is capable of a rapid expansion.

The fallacy of self-sufficiency as a basic guide to a sound materials policy is that it costs too much. A 50-cent increase per barrel of petroleum or a 2-cent increase in the average price per pound of basic metals would add to our annual bill for these materials about $1 billion and $2.5 billion respectively. Yet it is not in dollars alone that the increased costs of self-sufficiency would be paid. Other countries in the free world find markets for their exports in the U.S., and we, to our profit, are a principal source of industrial products for them. Interferences with these normal channels of trade in the name of self-sufficiency would inevitably check economic growth both at home and abroad. The *political* consequences of self-sufficiency, with its accompanying damage to carefully established security arrangements, would prove even more serious.

In time of war the overriding problem of materials is to have enough safely available, and the question of costs becomes subordinate. In the period of preparation against the threat of war, however, costs remain a major concern.

Every war consumes more and more massive amounts of materials. The U.S. is becoming increasingly vulnerable through the growing military importance of metals and mineral fuels and our shrinking resources for supplying them. Of more than 100 mineral materials we use, about one-third—for example, sulfur, coal, phosphates, magnesium, molybdenum—are at present fully supplied from our domestic resources. Another third we get almost entirely from other lands; this fraction has assumed greater importance as advances in the technology of high-temperature alloys and electronics have brought into greater prominence such minerals as columbium, cobalt, high-grade quartz crystals, and others we do not possess. The final third we obtain partly from abroad and partly from domestic output—materials like iron ore, petroleum, copper, and lead.

To meet or anticipate our needs from the supply side, we stockpile, and we seek reserve capacity in safe areas, domestic and foreign. On the supply side, civilian authority remains more or less in control. But on the demand side, the military, particularly in wartime, is in a commanding position. With each successive war, and now with preparation against the contingency of another, the military has become a greater and greater claimant against the materials of the whole economy. It would be impossible to fix a maximum percentage of military claims to the total economy and say "beyond this point you may not go." But even though the point cannot be fixed, it is known to exist. The military thus carries a heavy responsibility to hold its drain against the materials supply to the lowest levels consistent with adequate military strength; although progress has been made here, there is room and pressing need for much more.

Toward Policy and the Future

Closely linked with the least-cost principle is the notion of conservation of resources and materials. It is also linked with the question of this generation's responsibility to help provide for the next. Most thoughtful persons agree to some variation of this conservation idea, but there are wide differences as to how best—and how much—to protect the future claimants against the nation's resources.

The nation faces a very real and growing conservation problem, but many of our difficulties of agreement arise from a failure to recognize the economic dimensions of the problem and give proper weight to its dynamics. It is a popular fallacy to regard our resource base as a fixed inventory which, when used up, will leave society with no means of survival. A related fallacy is that physical waste equals economic waste; that it is improper to use materials in ways that make them disappear. This attitude can lead to devoting a dollar's worth of work to "saving" a few cents worth of waste paper and old string.

These fallacies together lead to a hair-shirt concept of conservation which makes it synonymous with hoarding. A sound concept of conservation, in the commission's view, is one which equates it with efficient use of resources, manpower, and materials: a positive concept compatible with growth and high consumption in place of abstinence and retrenchment. In developing America our forebears consumed resources extravagantly, but we are certainly better off in materials supply than they. It would be unreasonable for us to suggest that they should have consumed less so that we might consume more. If, then, through developing the opportunities inherent in the flexibility of our resource base, we can provide posterity with a better return of goods and services for its labor than we get for our own, we need not feel compelled to restrain specific consumptions of materials to make theirs even larger—any more than our New England forebears needed to conserve bayberries for candles to light a generation that lives by kilowatts.

Uncertainty over the future is the source of greatest difficulty in formulating national materials policy, yet it is basically because of this uncertainty that public policy has such an important role to play. In a sense, policy making and administration for materials is a huge national insurance business which seeks to protect the nation against tragic contingencies such as the collapse of living standards or defeat in war. More positively, it seeks to provide the best continuing chance for achieving the maximum growth and prosperity consistent with its means. Predictions have a useful role to play, but the nation cannot risk its future welfare by placing heavy bets on extremely optimistic assumptions. Neither can public policy be guided by the extreme of pessimism, let we pay so much for insurance that we have little left for anything else.

An adequate materials policy for the U.S. must balance considerations of cost and security. It must take account not only of our own requirements and resources, but of those elsewhere in the free world. It must be concerned not only with our own economic growth but with the growth possibilities of the whole complex of nations of which we are inevitably the center.

The U.S., once criticized as the creator of a crassly materialistic order of things, is today throwing its might into the task of keeping alive the spirit of Man, and helping beat back from the frontiers of the free world everywhere the threats of force and of a new Dark Age which rise from the Communist nations. In defeating this barbarian violence, moral values will count most, but an ample materials base must support them. Indeed, the interdependence of moral and material values has never been so completely demonstrated as today, when all the world has seen the narrowness of its escape from the now dead Nazi tyranny, and has yet to know the breadth by which it will escape the live Communist one—both materialistic threats aimed to destroy moral and spiritual man. The use of materials to destroy *or to preserve* is the very choice over which the world struggle today rages.

II

Prices and Costs

---

7. PRICING POLICIES FOR NEW PRODUCTS *

PRICE THEORY deals with hypothetical conditions and is not intended to explain why, for instance, a bottle of Macbeth Spot Remover sells for 39¢ at the corner drug store. Therefore, it is sometimes useful to supplement theory with material relating to some of the procedures actually followed by business firms in pricing their products, as is done in the following article. After reading this selection, the reader may find it interesting to attempt reconciling theoretical principles with the practices described by the author. As a start, he might first ascertain how many of the assumptions underlying the theory are also descriptive of the circumstances under which these prices were set. Anyone making such a study should remember that, while the sellers may initially "set" the price of a good, the buyers determine the quantity sold.

HOW TO price a new product is a top-management puzzle that is too often solved by cost-theology and hunch. This article suggests a pricing policy geared to the dynamic nature of a new product's competitive status. Today's high rate of innovation makes the economic evolution of a new product a strategic guide to practical pricing.

MARKET BEHAVIOR

New products have a protected distinctiveness which is doomed to progressive degeneration from competitive inroads. The invention of

* Joel Dean, *Harvard Business Review,* November, 1950, pp. 45-52. Reprinted by permission of the author and the publisher.

The author (1906——) is Professor of Economics at Columbia University. He is a management consultant. Author of *Statistical Cost Functions of a Hosiery Mill* and *Long-Run Behavior of Costs.*

a new marketable specialty is usually followed by a period of patent protection when markets are still hesitant and unexplored and when product design is fluid. Then comes a period of rapid expansion of sales as market acceptance is gained. Next the product becomes a target for competitive encroachment. New competitors enter the field, and innovations narrow the gap of distinctiveness between the product and its substitutes. The seller's zone of pricing discretion narrows as his distinctive "specialty" fades into a pedestrian "commodity" which is so little differentiated from other products that the seller has limited independence in pricing, even if rivals are few.

Throughout the cycle, continual changes occur in promotional and price elasticity and in costs of production and distribution. These changes call for adjustments in price policy.

Elements of cycle. Appropriate pricing over the cycle depends on the development of three different aspects of maturity, which usually move in approximately parallel time paths: (1) technical maturity, indicated by declining rate of product development, increasing standardization among brands, and increasing stability of manufacturing processes and knowledge about them: (2) market maturity, indicated by consumer acceptance of the basic service idea, by widespread belief that the products of most manufacturers will perform satisfactorily, and by enough familiarity and sophistication to permit consumers to compare brands competently; and (3) competitive maturity, indicated by increasing stability of market shares and price structures.

Of course, interaction among these components tends to make them move together. That is, intrusion by new competitors helps to develop the market, but entrance is most tempting when the new product appears to be establishing market acceptance.

Speed of degeneration. The rate at which the cycle of degeneration progresses varies widely among products. What are the factors that set its pace? An overriding determinant is technical—the extent to which the economic environment must be reorganized to use the innovation effectively. The scale of plant investment and technical research called forth by the telephone, electric power, the automobile, or air transport makes for a long gestation period, as compared with even such major innovations as cellophane or frozen foods. Development comes fastest when the new gadget fills a new vacuum made to order for it. Electric stoves, as one example, have risen to 50% market saturation in the fast-growing Pacific Northwest, where electric power has become the lowest cost energy. Products still in early developmental stages also provide rich opportunities for product differentiation, which with heavy research costs hold off competitive degeneration.

But aside from technical factors, the rate of degeneration is controlled by economic forces that can be subsumed under (1) rate of market acceptance and (2) ease of competitive entry.

By market acceptance is meant the extent to which buyers consider the product a serious alternative to other ways of performing the same service. Market acceptance is a frictional factor. The effect of cultural lags may endure for some time after quality and costs make products technically useful. The slow catch-on of the "electric pig" (garbage-disposal unit) is an example. On the other hand, the attitude of acceptance may exist long before any workable model can be developed; then the final appearance of the product will produce an explosive growth curve in sales. The anti-histamine cold tablet, a spectacular example, reflects the national faith in chemistry's ability to vanquish the common cold. And, of course, low unit price may speed market acceptance of an innovation; ball-point pens and all-steel houses started at about the same time, but look at the difference in their sales curves.

Ease of competitive entry is a major determinant of the speed of degeneration of a specialty. An illustration is found in the washing machine business before the war, where with little basic patent protection the Maytag position was quickly eroded by small manufacturers who performed essentially an assembly operation. The ball-point pen cascaded from a $12 novelty to a 49-cent "price football," partly because entry barriers of patents and techniques were ineffective. Frozen orange juice, which started as a protected specialty of Minute Maid, is speeding through its competitive cycle, with competing brands now crowding into the market.

At the outset the innovator can control the rate of competitive deterioration to an important degree by nonprice as well as by price strategies. Through successful research in product improvement he can protect his specialty position both by extending the life of his basic patent and by the keeping ahead of competitors in product development. The record of the International Business Machines punch-card equipment illustrates this potentiality. Ease of entry is also affected by a policy of stay-out pricing (so low as to make the prospects look uninviting), which under some circumstances may slow down the process of competitive encroachment.

STEPS IN PIONEER PRICING

Pricing problems start when a company finds a product that is a radical departure from existing ways of performing a service and that is temporarily protected from competition by patents, secrets of production, control at the point of a scarce resource, or by other barriers. The seller here has a wide range of pricing discretion resulting from extreme product differentiation.

A good example of pricing latitude conferred by protected superiority of product is provided by the McGraw Electric Company's "Toastmaster," which, both initially and over a period of years, was able to command a very substantial price premium over competitive toasters. Apparently this advantage resulted from (1) a good product that was distinctive and superior, and (2) substantial and skillful sales promotion. Similarly, Sunbeam priced its electric iron $2 above comparable models of major firms with considerable success. And Sunbeam courageously priced its new metal coffee-maker at $32, much above competitive makes of glass coffee-makers, but it was highly successful.

To get a picture of how a manufacturer should go about setting his price in the pioneer stage, let me describe the main steps of the process (of course the classification is arbitrary and the steps are interrelated): (1) estimate of demand, (2) decision on market targets, (3) design of promotional strategy, and (4) choice of channels of distribution.

Estimate of demand. The problem at the pioneer stage differs from that in a relatively stable monopoly because the product is beyond the experience of buyers and because the perishability of its distinctiveness must be reckoned with. How can demand for new products be explored? How can we find out how much people will pay for a product that has never before been seen or used? There are several levels of refinement to this analysis.

The initial problem of estimating demand for a new product can be broken into a series of subproblems: (a) whether the product will go at all (assuming price is in a competitive range); (b) what range of price will make the product economically attractive to buyers; (c) what sales volumes can be expected at various points in this price range; and (d) what reaction will price produce in manufacturers and sellers of displaced substitutes.

The first step in an exploration of the *preferences and educability of consumers,* always of course in the light of the technical feasibility of the new product. How many potential buyers are there? Is the product a practical device for meeting their needs? How can it be improved to meet their needs better? What proportion of the potential buyers would prefer, or could be induced to prefer, this product to already existing products (prices being equal)?

Sometimes it is feasible to start with the assumption that all vulnerable substitutes will be fully displaced. For example, to get some idea of the maximum limits of demand for a new type of reflecting-sign material, a company started with estimates of the aggregate number and area of auto license plates, highway markers, railroad operational signs, and name signs for streets and homes. Next, the proportion of each category needing night-light reflection was guessed. For example, it was assumed that only rural and suburban homes could benefit by this kind of name sign, and the estimate of need in this category was made accordingly.

It is not uncommon and possibly not unrealistic for a manufacturer to make the blithe assumption at this stage that the product price will be "within competitive range" without having much idea of what that range is. For example, in developing a new type of camera equipment, one of the electrical companies judged its acceptability to professional photographers by technical performance without making any inquiry into its economic value. When the equipment was later placed in an economic setting, the indications were that sales would be negligible.

The second step is marking out this *competitive range of price*. Vicarious pricing experience can be secured by interviewing selected distributors who have enough comparative knowledge of customers' alternatives and preferences to judge what price range would make the new product "a good value." Direct discussions with representative experienced industrial users have produced reliable estimates of the "practical" range of prices. Manufacturers of electrical equipment often explore the economic as well as the technical feasibility of a new product by sending engineers with blueprints and models to see customers, such as technical and operating executives.

In guessing the price range of a radically new consumers' product of small unit value, the concept of barter equivalent can be a useful research guide. For example, a manufacturer of paper specialties tested a dramatic new product in the following fashion: A wide variety of consumer products totally unlike the new product were purchased and spread out on a big table. Consumers selected the products they would swap for the new product. By finding out whether the product would trade even for a dish pan, a towel, or a hairpin, the executives got a rough idea of what range of prices might strike the typical consumer as reasonable in the light of the values she could get for her money in totally different kinds of expenditures.

But asking prospective consumers how much they think they would be willing to pay for a new product, even by such indirect or disguised methods, may often fail to give a reliable indication of the demand schedule. Most times people just do not know what they would pay.

It depends partly on their income and on future alternatives. Early in the postwar period a manufacturer of television sets tried this method and got highly erratic and obviously unreliable results because the distortion of war shortages kept prospects from fully visualizing the multiple alternative ways of spending their money. Another deficiency, which may, however, be less serious than it appears, is that responses are biased by the consumer's confused notion that he is bargaining for a good price. Not until techniques of depth interviewing are more refined than they are now can this crude and direct method of exploring a new product's demand schedule hold much promise of being accurate.

One appliance manufacturer tried out new products on a sample of employees by selling to them at deep discounts, with the stipulation that they could if they wished return the products at the end of the experiment period and get a refund of their low purchase price. Demand for frozen orange juice was tested by placing it in several markets at three different prices, ranging around the price of fresh fruit; the result showed rather low price elasticity.

While inquiries of this sort are often much too short-run to give any real indication of consumer tastes, the relevant point here is that even such rough probing often yields broad impressions of price elasticity, particularly in relation to product variations such as styling, placing of controls, and use of automatic features. It may show, for example, that $5 of cost put into streamlining or chromium stripping can add $50 to the price.

The third step, a more definite inquiry into the *probable sales from several possible prices,* starts with an investigation of the prices of substitutes. Usually the buyer has a choice of existing ways of having the same service performed; an analysis of the costs of these alternatives serves as a guide in setting the price for a new way.

Comparisons are easy and significant for industrial customers who have a costing system to tell them the exact value, say, of a fork-lift truck in terms of warehouse labor saved. Indeed, chemical companies setting up a research project to displace an existing material often know from the start the top price that can be charged for the new substitute in terms of cost of the present material.

But in most cases the comparison is obfuscated by the presence of quality differences that may be important bases for price premiums. This is most true of household appliances, where the alternative is an unknown amount of labor of a mysterious value. In pricing a cargo parachute the alternatives are: (1) free fall in a padded box from a plane flown close to the ground, (2) landing the plane, (3) back shipment by land from the next air terminal, or (4) land shipment all the way. These alternatives differ widely in their service value and are not very useful pricing guides.

Thus, it is particularly hard to know how much good will be done by making the new product cheaper than the old by various amounts, or how much the market will be restricted by making the new product more expensive. The answers usually come from experiment or research.

The fourth step in estimating demand is to consider the *possibility of retaliation by manufacturers of displaced substitutes* in the form of price cutting. This development may not occur at all if the new product displaces only a small market segment. If old industries do fight it out, however, their incremental costs provide a floor to the resulting price competition and should be brought into price plans. For example, a manufacturer of black-and-white sensitized paper studied the possibility that lowering his price would displace blueprint paper substantially. Not only did he investigate the prices of blueprint paper, but he also felt it necessary to estimate the out-of-pocket cost of making blueprint paper because of the probability that manufacturers already in the market would fight back by reducing prices toward the level of their incremental costs.

Decision on market targets. When the company has developed some idea of the range of demand and the range of prices that are feasible for the new product, it is in a position to make some basic strategic decisions on market targets and promotional plans. To decide on market objectives requires answers to several questions: What ultimate market share is wanted for the new product? How does it fit into the present product line? What about production methods? What are the possible distribution channels? These are questions of joint costs in production and distribution, of plant expansion outlays, and of potential competition. If entry is easy, the company may not be eager to disrupt its present production and selling operations to capture and hold a large slice of the new market. But if the prospective profits shape up to a substantial new income source, it will be worth while to make the capital expenditures on plant needed to reap the full harvest.

A basic factor in answering all these questions is the expected behavior of production and distribution costs. The relevant data here are all the production outlays that will be made after the decision day—the capital expenditures as well as the variable costs. A go-ahead decision will hardly be made without some assurance that these costs can be recovered before the product becomes a football in the market.

Many different projections of costs will be made, depending on the alternative scales of output, rate of market expansion, threats of potential competition, and measures to meet that competition that are under consideration. But these factors and the decision that is made on promotional strategy are interdependent. The fact is that this is a circular problem that in theory can only be solved by simultaneous equations.

Fortunately, it is possible to make some approximations than can break the circle: Scale economies become significantly different only with broad changes in the size of plant and the type of production methods. This narrows the range of cost projections to workable proportions. The effects of using different distribution channels can be guessed fairly well without meshing the alternatives in with all the production and selling possibilities. The most vulnerable point of the circle is probably the decision on promotional strategy. The alternatives here are broad and produce a variety of results. The next step in the pricing process is therefore a plan for promotion.

Design of promotional strategy. Initial promotion outlays are an investment in the product that cannot be recovered until some kind of market has been established. The innovator shoulders the burden of creating a market—educating consumers to the existence and uses of the product. Later imitators will never have to do this job; so, if the innovator does not want to be simply a benefactor to his future competitors, he must make pricing plans to recover his initial outlays before his pricing discretion evaporates.

His basic strategic problem is to find the right mixture of price and promotion to maximize his long-run profits. He can choose a relatively high price in pioneering stages, together with extravagant advertising and dealer discounts, and plan to get his promotion costs back early; or he can use low prices and lean margins from the very outset, in order to discourage potential competition when the barriers of patents, distribution channels, or production techniques become inadequate. This question is discussed further below.

Choice of channels of distribution. Estimation of the costs of moving the new product through the channels of distribution to the final consumer must enter into the pricing procedure, since these costs govern the factory price that will result in a specified consumer price, and since it is the consumer price that matters for volume. Distributive margins are partly pure promotional costs and partly physical distribution costs. Margins must at least cover the distributors' costs of warehousing, handling, and order taking. These costs are similar to factory production costs in being related to physical capacity and its utilization, i.e., fluctuations in production or sales volume. Hence these set a floor to trade-channel discounts. But distributors usually also contribute promotional effort—in point-of-sale pushing, local advertising, and display—when it is made worth their while.

These pure promotional costs are more optional. Unlike physical handling costs they have no necessary functional relation to sales volume. An added layer of margin in trade discounts to produce this localized sales effort (with retail price fixed) is an optional way for the manufacturer to spend his prospecting money in putting over a new product.

In establishing promotional costs, the manufacturer must decide on the extent to which the selling effort will be delegated to members of the distribution chain. Indeed, some distribution channels, such as house-to-house selling and retail store selling supplemented by home demonstrators, represent a substantial delegation of the manufacturer's promotional job, and these usually involve much higher distribution-channel costs than do conventional methods. Rich distributor margins are an appropriate use of promotion funds only when the producer thinks a high price plus promotion is a better expansion policy on the specialty than low price by itself. Thus there is an intimate interaction between the pricing of a new product and the costs and the problems of floating it down the distribution channels to the final consumer.

POLICIES FOR PIONEER PRICING

The strategic decision in pricing a new product is the choice between (1) a policy of high initial prices that skim the cream of demand and (2) a policy of low prices from the outset serving as an active agent for market penetration. Although the actual range of choice is much wider than this, a sharp dichotomy clarifies the issues for consideration.

Skimming price. For products that represent a drastic departure from accepted ways of performing a service, a policy of relatively high prices coupled with heavy promotional expenditures in the early stages of market development (and lower prices at later stages) has proved successful for many products. There are several reasons for the success of this policy:

(1) Demand is likely to be more inelastic with respect to price in the early stages than it is when the product is full grown. This is particularly true for consumers' goods. A novel product, such as the electric blanket or the electric pig, is not yet accepted as a part of the expenditure pattern. Consumers are still ignorant about its value as compared with the value of conventional alternatives. Moreover, at least

in the early stages, the product has so few close rivals that cross-elasticity of demand is low. Promotional elasticity is, on the other hand, quite high, particularly for products with high unit prices such as television sets. Since it is difficult for the customer to value the service of the product in a way to price it intelligently, he is by default principally interested in how well it will work.

(2) Launching a new product with a high price is an efficient device for breaking the market up into segments that differ in price elasticity of demand. The initial high price serves to skim the cream of the market that is relatively insensitive to price. Subsequent price reductions tap successively more elastic sectors of the market. This pricing strategy is exemplified by the systematic succession of editions of a book, sometimes starting with a $50 limited personal edition and ending up with a 25-cent pocket book.

(3) This policy is safer, or at least appears so. Facing an unknown elasticity of demand, a high initial price serves as a "refusal" price during the stage of exploration. How much costs can be reduced as the market expands and as the design of the product is improved by increasing production efficiency with new techniques is difficult to predict. One of the electrical companies recently introduced a new lamp bulb at a comparatively high initial price, but with the announcement that the price would be reduced as the company found ways of cutting its costs.

(4) Many companies are not in a position to finance the product flotation out of distant future revenues. High cash outlays in the early stages result from heavy costs of production and distributor organizing, in addition to the promotional investment in the pioneer product. High prices are a reasonable financing technique for shouldering these burdens in the light of the many uncertainties about the future.

Penetration price. The alternative policy is to use low prices as the principal instrument for penetrating mass markets early. This policy is the reverse of the skimming policy in which the price is lowered only as short-run competition forces it. The passive skimming policy has the virtue of safeguarding some profits at every stage of market penetration. But it prevents quick sales to the many buyers who are at the lower end of the income scale or the lower end of the preference scale and who therefore are unwilling to pay any substantial premium for product or reputation superiority. The active approach in probing possibilities for market expansion by early penetration pricing requires research, forecasting, and courage.

A decision to price for market expansion can be reached at various stages in a product's life cycle: before birth, at birth, in childhood, in adulthood, or in senescence. The chances for large-volume sales should at least be explored in the early stages of product development research, even before the pilot stage, perhaps with a more definitive exploration when the product goes into production and the price and distribution plans are decided upon. And the question of pricing to expand the market, if not answered earlier, will probably arise once more after the product has established an elite market.

Quite a few products have been rescued from premature senescence by pricing them low enough to tap new markets. The reissues of important books in the 25-cent pocket-book category illustrate this point particularly well. These have produced not only commercial but intellectual renascence as well to many authors. The pattern of sales growth of a product that had reached stability in a high-price market has been known to undergo sharp changes when it was suddenly priced low enough to tap new markets. A contrasting illustration of passive policy is the recent pricing experience of the airlines. Although safety considerations and differences in equipment and service cloud the picture, it is pretty clear that the bargain-rate coach fares of scheduled airlines were adopted in reaction to the cut rates of nonscheduled airlines. This competitive response has apparently established a new pattern of traffic growth for the scheduled airlines.

An example of penetration pricing at the initial stage of the product's market life, again from the book field, is Simon & Schuster's recently adopted policy of bring out new titles in a $1, paper-bound edition simultaneously with the conventional higher priced, cloth-bound edition.

What conditions warrant aggressive pricing for market penetration? This question cannot be answered categorically, but it may be helpful to generalize that the following conditions indicate the desirability of an early low-price policy: (1) a high price-elasticity of demand in the short run, i.e., a high degree of responsiveness of sales to reductions in price; (2) substantial savings in production costs as the result of greater volume—not a necessary condition, however, since if elasticity of demand is high enough, pricing for market expansion may be profitable without realizing production economies; (3) product characteristics such that it will not seem bizarre when it is first fitted into the consumer's expenditure pattern; (4) a strong threat of potential competition.

This threat of potential competition is a highly persuasive reason for penetration pricing. One of the major objectives of most low-pricing policies in the pioneering stages of market development is to raise entry barriers to prospective competitors. This is appropriate when entrants must make large-scale investments to reach minimum costs and they cannot slip into an established market by selling at substantial discounts.

In many industries, however, the important potential competitor is a large, multiple-product firm operating as well in other fields than that represented by the product in question. For such a firm, the most important consideration for entry is not existing margins but the prospect of large and growing volume of sales. Present margins over costs are not the dominant consideration because such firms are normally confident that they can get their costs down as low as competitors' costs if the volume of production is large.. Therefore, when total industry sales are not expected to amount to much, a high-margin policy can be followed because entry is improbable in view of the expectation of low volume and because it does not matter too much to potential competitors if the new product is introduced.

The fact remains that for products whose market potential appears big, a policy of stay-out pricing from the outset makes much more sense. When a leading soap manufacturer developed an additive that whitened clothes and enchanced the brilliance of colors, the company chose to take its gains in a larger share of the market rather than in a temporary price premium. Such a decision was sound, since the company's competitors could be expected to match or better the product improvement fairly promptly. Under these circumstances, the price premium would have been short-lived, whereas the gains in market share were more likely to be retained.

Of course, any decision to start out with lower prices must take into account the fact that if the new product calls for capital recovery over a long period, the risk may be great that later entrants will be able to exploit new production techniques which can undercut the pioneer's original cost structure. In such cases, the low-price pattern should be adopted with a view to long-run rather than to short-run profits, with the recognition that it usually takes time to attain the volume potentialities of the market.

It is sound to calculate profits in dollar terms rather than in percentage margins and to think in terms of percentage return on the investment required to produce and sell the expanded volume rather than in terms of percentage markup. Profit calculation should also recognize the contributions that market-development pricing can make to the sale of other products and to the long-run future of the company. Often a decision to use development pricing will turn on these considerations of long-term impacts upon the firm's total operation strategy rather than on the profits directly attributable to the individual product.

An example of market-expansion pricing is found in the experience of a producer of asbestos shingles, which have a limited sale in the high-price house market. The company wanted to broaden the market in order to compete effectively with other roofing products for the inexpensive home. It tried to find the price of asphalt shingles that would make the annual cost per unit of roof over a period of years as low as the cheaper roofing that currently commanded the mass market. Indications were that the price would have to be at least this low before volume sales would come. Next, the company explored the relationship between production costs and volume, far beyond the range of its own volume experience. Variable costs and overhead costs were estimated separately, and the possibilities of a different organization of production were explored. Calculating in terms of anticipated dollars of profit rather than in terms of percentage margin, the company reduced the price of asbestos shingles and brought the annual cost down close to the cost of the cheapest asphalt roof. This reduction produced a greatly expanded volume and secured a substantial share of the mass market.

PRICING IN MATURITY

To determine what pricing policies are appropriate for later stages in the cycle of market and competitive maturity, the manufacturer must be able to tell when a product is approaching maturity. Some of the symptoms of degeneration of competitive status toward the commodity level are:

(1) *Weakening in brand preference*—this may be evidenced by a higher cross-elasticity of demand among leading products, the leading brand not being able to continue demanding as much price premium as initially without losing position;

(2) *Narrowing physical variation among products as the best designs are developed and standardized*—this has been dramatically demonstrated in automobiles and is still in process in television receivers;

(3) *The entry in force of private-label competitors*—this is exemplified by the mail-order houses' sale of own-label refrigerators and paint sprayers;

(4) *Market saturation*—the ratio of replacement sales to new equipment sales serves as an indicator of the competitive degeneration of durable goods, but in general it must be kept in mind that both market size and degree of saturation are hard to define (e.g., saturation of the radio market, which was initially thought to be one radio per home and later had to be expanded to one radio per room);

(5) *The stabilization of production methods*—a dramatic innovation that slashes costs (e.g., pre-fabricated houses) may disrupt what appears to be a well-stabilized oligopoly market.

The first step for the manufacturer whose specialty is about to slip into the commodity category is to reduce real prices promptly as soon as symptoms of deterioration appear. This step is essential if he is to forestall the entry of private-label competitors. Examples of failure to make such a reduction are abundant. By and large, private-label competition has speeded up the inevitable evolution of high specialties into commodities and has tended to force margins down by making price reductions more open and more universal than they would otherwise be. From one standpoint, the rapid growth of the private-label share in the market is a symptom of unwise pricing on the part of the national-brand sector of the industry.

This does not mean that the manufacturer should declare open price war in the industry. When he moves into mature competitive stages, he enters oligopoly relationships where price slashing is peculiarly dangerous and unpopular. But, with active competition in prices precluded, competitive efforts may move in other directions, particularly toward product improvement and market segmentation. Product improvement at this stage, where most of the important developments have been put into all brands, practically amounts to market segmentation. For it means adding refinements and quality extras that put the brand in the elite category, with an appeal only to the top-income brackets. This is a common tactic in food marketing, and in the tire industry it was the response of the General Tire Company to the competitive conditions of the 1930's.

As the product matures and as its distinctiveness narrows, a choice must sometimes be made by the company concerning the rung of the competitive price ladder it should occupy—roughly, the choice between a low and a not-so-low relative price.

A price at the low end of the array of the industry's real prices is usually associated with a product mixture showing a lean element of services and reputation (the product being physically similar to competitive brands, however) and a company having a lower gross margin than the other industry members (although not necessarily a lower net margin). The choice of such a low-price policy may be dictated by technical or market inferiorities of the product, or it may be adopted because the company has faith in the long-run price elasticity of demand and the ability of low prices to penetrate an important segment of the market not tapped by higher prices. The classic example is Henry Ford's pricing decision in the 1920's.

8. RCA AND THE RECORD DEALERS *

THE EFFECT of a price cut by a large manufacturer, both on other large manufacturers and on the retail dealers, is illustrated by the following press releases about RCA and the record dealers. The student may ask himself whether the market for records is characterized by oligopoly or by a reasonable amount of competition. As a buyer of records he may also inquire who the seller is—the large firm such as RCA or the numerous retail record dealers?

NEW YORK — Radio Corp. of America rocked the phonograph record industry yesterday with the announcement disc prices would be slashed as much as 40%, effective next Monday.

Under the new set-up, 12-inch classical platters will be cut 33% to \$3.98 from the present \$5.95 price tag. All ten-inch long-playing records will be reduced from a top of \$4.95 to \$2.98, a 40% slash. Classical 45-r.p.m. extended play discs will be reduced from \$1.58 to \$1.49. At the same time, the standard 78-r.p.m. platter will be raised from 89 cents to 98 cents.

The move caught the industry flat-footed. Indeed, Columbia Records—RCA's major competitor—notified its distributors over the weekend that it would guarantee prices through June, 1955, on its 12-inch classical records. These now sell for \$5.95.

Exclaimed one puzzled platter-maker:

"It's beyond me. I just don't get it."

Lamented another: "It's going to cut profits all around."

Frank Walker, president of M.G.M. Records, called it "very drastic action," but indicated his company probably will take similar action.

Milton R. Rackmil, president of Decca Records, Inc., stated: "We will have no comment until we've had a chance to study the announcement."

Similar statements came from Mercury Records and Capital Records. At Columbia there was understandable silence.

At Goody's, which has a policy of selling all records below list price, Sam Goody said he plans "to continue selling records of all labels below list price." Today, he's starting a general sale of all 12-inch labels

* Joseph M. Guilfoyle, "RCA Slashes Phonograph Records. . . ," and "Columbia Cancels Guarantee. . . ," a *Wall Street Journal* News Roundup. Reprinted with permission from the December 28 and December 29, 1954, editions of *The Wall Street Journal.*

Mr. Guilfoyle (1911——) is a feature writer on *The Wall Street Journal.* Some of his articles have appeared in *Saturday Evening Post, Coronet,* and *Better Homes and Gardens.*

at $3.50. After the first of the year, Mr. Goody said, he will announce "a definite policy" on the price of his records.

Frank M. Folsom, RCA president, said the new price plan was developed because of the firm belief that the record industry is on the threshold of its greatest expansion.

"The low prices will be made possible partly because of the decreased production costs that will result from the increase in volume. We are anticipating these savings and passing them on to the consumer immediately."

Backing up its optimism, RCA is embarking on the most extensive advertising campaign it has ever undertaken on records. During the next two months, it will place 300 pages of advertisements in newspapers across the land, in addition to magazine, radio and television plugs.

Despite RCA's fervor, competitors generally took a pretty dim view of the entire thing yesterday. Most of them felt there was a lot more to the move than was apparent on the surface. One exasperated platter-maker who declined to be quoted by name offered this explanation:

"I've got a hunch," he said, "this is RCA's way of striking a blow at its competitors, especially in the classical field. In the past few years many firms have dug a niche for themselves in the long-hair field and you can bet RCA isn't too happy about it."

Another competitor took the view that the lower prices will be a knockout blow to many marginal producers. "They're resorting to all sorts of short-cuts now to keep their heads above water. One reason many of them existed is because of the lower prices they charged for their platters. They could do this because usually they use 'no-name' talent. But now when the public can get records by big-name stars for the same price or nearly the same price they're not going to buy records made by unknown artists. That will be a serious blow to many a small record-maker."

Artists and dealers will feel the pinch of the lower prices, too. For the artist who receives a percentage of the record's selling price—usually around 2% to 4%, depending upon their popularity—it means they'll have to sell a lot more discs to keep up with past earnings.

Dealers and distributors, especially those with large inventories, will suffer because RCA is not giving them any rebate nor will it reimburse them for any losses they may suffer on records now in stock.

"We think dealers and distributors will do so much business in January and February and through the rest of the year they'll more than make up for any mark-downs they may have to take now," explained

L. W. Kanaga, general sales and merchandizing manager of RCA-Victor's record division.

RCA is making some changes in its dealer discount structure, too. Discounts on all single and extended-play records will be increased from 38% to 42%, starting next Monday. At the same time it is eliminating the 5% return privilege which it has extended to dealers on L-P platters.

. . . . .

"It's a pretty dirty trick."

"They've been miserable since they've been in business."

"RCA doesn't care any more about dealers than you care about a rattlesnake."

These outbursts by phonograph record dealers in St. Louis, Houston and Pittsburgh sum up some of the extreme reactions of retailers to Monday's announcement that RCA Victor is slashing disc prices as much as 40%, effective next Monday.

Late yesterday Columbia Records notified its distributors by telegram that effective immediately the price guarantee for six months on L-P records, announced over the week end, "is cancelled and withdrawn." It advised distributors that "a new statement of policy will follow."

Meantime, other disc makers remained on the sidelines. At London Records, for example, Harry Kruse, executive vice president, stated: "We haven't made up our minds yet."

At Westminster Recording Co., a spokesman said: "There is no basis for a price reduction on quality items."

"No comment" was the only thing representatives of Angel Records and Remington Records would say.

Many dealers were especially annoyed by the fact they had to read about the price cut in the press.

For example, V. H. Anderson, who runs the "Record Center" on Chicago's West Side, says his biggest complaint is that RCA "made its announcement to the public before it said anything to dealers." He adds: "It's a breach of faith any way you look at it."

In New York, a spokesman for the Record Hunter, a retail outlet, exploded: "We're hurt morally and annoyed by the fact they did not give us any notice. We consider ourselves being used. We only learned about it through the newspapers."

A Philadelphia dealer said he thought RCA was unfair in not giving advance notice of the change to retailers "so dealers could clean out their stocks."

Some dealers—they're definitely a minority—thought RCA's action would have a beneficial effect upon the industry. Typical was the comment of a spokesman for Liberty Music Shops, a four-store chain operating in New York and Westchester counties. He said:

"We feel the lower prices will increase the sale of records and be a healthy thing for business."

C. G . Inman, record buyer for Music City, at Sunset and Vine in Hollywood, said: "We think this cut will help boost sales. When RCA had a sale last February at $3.98 list, our volume shot up tremendously."

In Detroit, the buyer for one of the Motor City's leading department stores took the position that "as soon as other makers follow RCA's action, which they'll have to do, it will help our record sales."

Dan Danzinger, owner of The Disc Shop in Washington, describes himself as "very happy, thrilled" by RCA's action. Mr. Danzinger, who claims his shop is Washington's largest in the classical record field, figures the price cut puts "regular dealers" like himself back into competition with "the New York discount houses."

"I have notified RCA how happy I am, and have also urged Columbia to follow suit," Mr. Danzinger said. "The action has given us a hopeful outlook."

The Washington dealer said he stands to take a book loss of about $25,000 on his inventory if the other record companies also cut prices, as he expects. "That I don't like," he admitted.

But for the most part dealers were unhappy yesterday. They're especially bitter because RCA will not reimburse them for losses they may take on inventories.

FIRMS FACE INVENTORY LOSS

A spokesman for Grinnel Bros. Music House, a chain of record and musical instrument stores in Detroit, said his firm will suffer an inventory loss. His profit on a 12-inch record under the old pricing plan, he said, was $2.26 while under the new plan, it will be $1.67, a 26% drop, he explained.

Val Sherman, owner of Houston's Record Center who made the remark about RCA and rattlesnakes, figures he'll take a $3,000 inventory loss as a result of the price change. Cooling off somewhat, he added that the cut may stimulate sales "but not nearly enough to offset the price slashes."

Fred W. Mosher, head of Boston's Mosher Music Co., said the reduction would cause his firm a big inventory loss—over $1 a record. Another Boston firm—Charles W. Homeyer & Co., Inc.—anticipates "a big loss" as it will have to mark down about $5,000 RCA L-P discs from the former cost of $3.72 to the new replacement value of $2.40.

"If I still do my present volume in dollars I'll consider myself lucky," stated Frank Homeyer.

Herman L. Forst, an official of Hudson-Ross, Inc., Chicago's largest record seller, says the firm will "suffer a fair loss in inventory, but not a tremendous amount because our volume is big enough that inventory isn't a big percentage of sales." They'll most likely cut RCA records immediately," Mr. Morst said, adding, "would you pay $5.95 today if you knew you could get the same thing at a third off next week?"

Mr. Forst feels that if RCA makes its price stick, other major record makers will have to drop their prices.

Although groggy from the blow dealt their pocketbooks, some dealers felt the picture wasn't all black if it made life more miserable for their arch enemy—the discount house.

For instance, a spokesman for one of Cleveland's largest record stores said that although they don't like the loss they'll have to take, they were almost pleased about it because they thought it might drive the discount house out of business.

THE DISCOUNTERS

"But if they (the discount houses) continue to cut below the new price the situation will be worse than ever," according to this dealer. "If Sam Goody (New York discount firm) cuts the price again, the whole country will have to follow, because too many people are listening to records here, and then ordering them by mail from New York."

The owner of a San Francisco discount house offered this opinion: "With Victor down to their level, the small record makers are going to have a hard time competing, and that may take some of the best money makers away from us. We'll cut the price of Victor discs below the new list price immediately—probably to about $3.75 for a 12-inch L-P."

A large Boston dealer who'd been giving 20% off on purchases of long-playing records selling for more than $3 said he couldn't give a discount on the new list price "or I won't even get my money back. I don't think the cut was justified."

"We will be working on a 40 cent profit on an album selling at $3.99 and it won't even pay us to open our doors," he added. "However, if the cut kills price cutting I'll be satisfied."

RCA, informed of the reaction among dealers stated it felt it had taken a step in the right direction.

"We are convinced our efforts to bring more music to more people at lower prices is in the best interests of the consumer, the dealer, the distributor and the industry," stated L. W. Kanaga, general sales and merchandising manager of RCA-Victor's record division.

Mr. Kanaga added that the public reaction to the price cuts "is terrific" while they had received more "favorable statements than critical ones" from dealers.

---

9. FAIR TRADE: THE PROBLEM AND THE ISSUES *

FAIR trade is a method of price control by which the owner of a branded or trade-marked article establishes a minimum price below which a commodity may not be subsequently resold. In practice the producer who owns the brand name is able by means of a fair trade agreement to control the retail price of a good. This procedure is legal in most states and a Federal law permits state fair trade laws to cover interstate trade in those states. Many retailers strongly oppose this system of price maintenance; others firmly support it, and a controversy has been raging with renewed vigor during the past few years. In 1952 a Congressional committee studied the fair trade problem. In this excerpt from the com mittee's report, both sides of the issue are considered.

The Case for Fair Trade

The Objective of Fair Trade: Prevention of Unrestrained Price Cutting. The basis of all justification of control over resale prices is the alleged evils that result from price cutting at the retail level. It is contended that in the absence of control there is an inevitable tendency for prices on identified merchandise to fall to undesirably low levels. This leads to serious injury to manufacturers, non-price cutting dealers and consumers alike. "Predatory" or unrestrained price cutting is not deemed to be a legitimate expression of true competition and should, in fact, be included in the category of unfair practices.

In the debate on the Miller-Tydings bill a representative of the Nation Association of Retail Druggists described the evil which fair trade is designed to eliminate in the following words:

Serious-minded students of the social and economic problems in the field of distribution have been greatly disturbed by the destructive trade practices which have demoralized and undermined the retail system. These practices

* Report of the Select Committee on Small Business, House of Representatives, Eighty-Second Congress (Government Printing Office, 1952), pp. 37-56.

have been particularly hurtful to the small business man, who has clung to the traditional American principle that he had a right to engage in business on his own account, if he desired to do so.

These unfair trade practices have, on the other hand, been peculiarly helpful to those large distributors who have been willing to lend themselves to this type of commercial piracy and deception. Thus large concerns have become larger, and smaller concerns have either given up the unequal struggle or else been reduced to competitive impotence.

The claim is made that predatory price cutting is not based upon *bona fide* economies of operation and can rarely be justified in terms of profit-making possibilities. The real motive behind this type of price cutting is to obtain the advertising appeal that goes with the reputation for being a low-priced store. It is advertising which aims only to lure people into the store. The dealer knows that a large percentage of the customers who enter his store to purchase the leader will make other purchases upon which large profits may be realized. The point of view has been well expressed by the National Association of Retail Druggists in a booklet, "What About Fair Trade?" Under the system of free pricing, the statement runs, "merchants cut a few advertised items, sometimes below cost, in order to get customers into their stores; and then make up the loss by raising the prices on other merchandise."

Recently the attack on price cutting has taken a new direction. It is not the price cutter that is the main enemy of fair trade but the "price juggler." The "new approach" according to the Director of the Bureau of Education on Fair Trade, is "to stop talking about predatory price cutting" and "to start talking all over the place about *price juggling*." The reason is as follows:

> Nobody likes to be treated as a sucker. And nobody likes a businessman who juggles his figures, his books or his prices. In loss-leader selling, the familiar prices of a few well-known brands go down to bankruptcy levels to fool the customers—and a host of unfamiliar prices go up. This is the juggling act, the essence of the unfair competition that Fair Trade prevents.

The Tragedy of Price Cutting to the Producer of Branded Merchandise. Fair trade is confined to merchandise which carries the trademark or brand name of the producer or wholesaler. As we have seen, the original impetus for resale price maintenance came from manufacturers who felt that control over resale prices was necessary to protect their goodwill. Their views in substance are as follows: When a manufacturer develops a product which at the outset is unknown, he gives it a brand name and spends large sums of money in advertising. The product is accepted and sales mount. The factory may be expanded to take care of the increased demand. The producer has a large investment not only in a specialized plant but in goodwill. Soon, however, the outlook changes because dealers begin to slash the retail price of this product. At first, the lower prices may stimulate sales, but it is not long before the cut-rate stores begin to substitute rival products on which the margin of profit remains high. Reputable retailers find that price comparisons on the item are to their disadvantage; so they stop featuring the product. Dealers, both price cutters and others, refuse to push the sale of the item and actually may reach the point of taking it out of stock altogether. Sales drop and the manufacturer finds he is operating at a loss. It is said that the annals of American manufacturing are replete with examples of products which have been price-slashed out of existence.

The price cutter is thus a parasite, living off the good name of the manufacturer. He deprives the latter of his property and converts it to his own advantage. Price cutting is as unfair as physical misrepresentation. It is a theft of valuable goodwill.

The Disastrous Effects of Price Cutting on the Independent Retailer. As we have seen, the strongest support of fair trade in recent years has come from organized groups of retailers. Their case rests on the assumption that unrestrained price cutting presents a serious threat to their very existence. Their dilemma is illustrated by the following example: Suppose that a cut-price store reduces the price on a well-known and widely distributed brand of aspirin. It advertises its prices heavily and attracts many customers away from its competitors. It soon obtains the bulk of the trade in this brand of aspirin and by implication establishes a reputation for cheap selling on all merchandise. Competing druggists are compelled either to lower their prices or to discontinue selling the item. If they do the former, the price cutter slashes his prices still further until the product is handled at a loss by all dealers. If they discontinue the item, the price cutter merely shifts to products they do handle.

Extending this operation to the entire list of items carried by a store, one sees the real evil of price cutting. While one store is cutting on toothpaste, another is cutting on hair tonics and a third on soaps. The total results are a multiplication of what happened in the aspirin case. Each store is striving to convince the public of its low prices. Their efforts largely cancel one another. All will eventually suffer loss. Some will be forced out of business.

A representative of the National Association of Retail Druggists assured the House Judiciary Committee in 1937 that "Prolonged selling at cut prices results in freezing out small dealer competition." And the Director of the Bureau of Education on Fair Trade has recently declared that "the very existence of our small business economy is at stake."

Dangers of Price Cutting to the Consumer. The advocates of fair trade vigorously contend that price maintenance is beneficial even to the consumer. Price cutting means a lack of standardization and its elimination is merely an additional step to protect the purchaser. A standard price, it is argued, like a distinguishing brand name gives the consumer a yardstick of value. The standard price and the standard brand together enable the customer to determine for himself whether he is getting the proper quality at the right price. If he likes the price and quality of a given standard brand, he can buy it again and again in the sure satisfaction that he is getting adequate value for his money. Indiscriminate price cutting in effect drives the consumer back to the position he had years ago where haggling between customer and storekeeper was the accepted method of retailing. Consumers who were the best bargainers got the best prices. Consequently, nobody could be sure that the price he paid represented honest value.

We are also told that the consumer shares in the financial losses created by unrestrained price cutting. The argument runs something like this: Merchants consider loss-leader selling a form of advertising and charge up its cost as such. The more loss-leaders a store offers, the higher its operating costs go. Generally, therefore, the types of stores which depend on price cutting to attract patronage are the ones which exact the highest average margins. Moreover, in the last analysis all operating costs are paid by the public. A loss on one item must be balanced by a high profit on another. The public cannot get something for nothing.

The above point of view has been vigorously stated by the Director of the Bureau of Education on Fair Trade as follows:

> Why does the price juggler juggle his prices? This is one of the major points to get across to consumers and to Congressmen. The answer is a simple one. It's the motive behind all cheating. It's the motive of making a profit at somebody else's expense. The embezzler juggles his figures to cheat his employer. The price juggler does a sleight of hand trick with prices to trick his customers and destroy his competitors. He does it, purely and simply, to make a profit. What would be the point of selling a famous brand at a loss, a ruinous loss, if the price juggler didn't have a profit angle? He likes to pretend to the customers that he's a wonderful Santa Claus, giving them something for nothing. This is how he gets them to buy his overpriced phony bargains. But he's using deliberate trickery to turn his advertised losses, his bankruptcy prices, into a fat profit margin.

So tell your customers about price juggling when they ask you why you charge more for a well known brand of drugs than the price cutter down the street. Tell them the loss-leader bait sure is a bargain if they can walk in that store and just buy that bargain—and nothing else. But warn them that they'll find this mighty hard to do. For price jugglers have a way of making the real bargains, the price-slashed trademarked products, do a disappearing act. It's a case of "you see it advertised on the outside, but you don't see it inside." For inside that price juggler's store, the customer will be urged and pressured to buy everything else under the sun—everything but the bargain she came for. Maybe she's got enough will power to resist this Mickey Finn for shoppers. Maybe she can insist on getting the bargain she came for—even wait an hour as she may well have to—without succumbing to the impulse to buy the other things that are depicted as bargains too. *Maybe* she can. But 99 out of 100 shoppers can't. And that's what the price juggler gambles on. That's how he makes his money and kills off his competitors.

The Case Against Fair Trade

The Concept of Price Cutting Offered by Fair Traders Is False and Misleading. Although there is little disposition among opponents of fair trade to question the broad generalization that predatory price cutting is an evil, it is charged that the picture drawn by fair trade enthusiasts is one-sided and misleading in that it assumes that all price reducing tactics are basically alike and all equally bad. They object to the tarring of all forms of price cutting with the same brush. Price cutting in the broad sense, they contend, is a normal characteristic of any competitive market and is the only way a seller has of adjusting his supply to the demand. In fact a competitive market cannot function without continual price adjustment, of which price cutting is one manifestation. Some price cutting is not only good but necessary. Yet fair traders condemn all forms.

Most opponents of fair trade are inclined to agree that true loss-leader tactics are not desirable. They hold, however, that this type of price cutting is not common. It is contrary to the policy of most chain organizations which require each store to observe stipulated margins. Only a few large department stores in metropolitan centers make a practice of using loss-leaders. Consumers generally are too sophisticated to be fooled by loss-leaders for long.

In any event, although the advocates of fair trade claim to be shooting at loss-leaders, this is not their real target. What fair traders really want, according to the critics, is to eliminate the low prices that are made possible by improved merchandising methods, curtailed services, and other legitimate cost-reducing devices. This type of price reduction is much more prevalent than the loss-leader type and in most instances should not be viewed as price cutting at all. But the fair trade advocate does not discriminate and in fact would prohibit all price competition. Clear evidence that the real goal of fair trade is not the predatory type of price cutting is afforded by the fact that enthusiasts for fair trade are not satisfied with the simple prohibition of loss-leader selling.

The same is true of local price cutting of the discriminatory type. This clearly is undesirable, the critics agree. But there is other legislation on the books specifically aimed at discriminatory pricing, namely the Robinson-Patman Act, which is far more effective than the fair trade laws in attacking the evil of price discrimination. Again the advocates of fair trade are not content merely to eliminate the practice they publicly condemn but insist on extending their prohibitions to include all price reducing practices.

The Ill Effects of Price Cutting on Producers Have Been Grossly Exaggerated. That owners of trade-marked goods have suffered some losses through price cutting is freely admitted by opponents of fair trade. They contend, however, that the seriousness of these losses has been greatly exaggerated and that such as they are they result from the predatory type of price cutting, not legitimate price reductions arising out of low-cost merchandising. It is further denied that rights in good-will or brand names should extend to the control of resale prices.

From 1931 to 1937 when the fair trade issue was being hotly debated in Congress, the opponents of fair trade referred to the statement of the Federal Trade Commission in 1931 that "No instance, however, has yet been brought to the commission's attention in which there was conclusive evidence that an article of real merit has been driven off the market by price cutting alone" and repeatedly asked for specific instances of the disastrous effects of price cutting on manufacturers. They believe it highly significant that none was offered. Further evidence offered by the opponents that manufacturers do not consider price cutting to be a serious problem is the fact that in recent years manufacturers have taken little part in the controversy. Except for drug manufacturers, few have appeared at the many hearings held by Congressional committees on the various price maintenance bills.

Professor E. T. Grether, an authority frequently quoted by fair traders themselves, has observed that thoroughly entrenched brands, backed by powerful sales efforts and with large consumer preference, frequently have gained greatly from price cutting. It may even happen that the less well-known manufacturers whose brands are *not* used as leaders will be the ones to suffer. On the whole Grether believes, "The adjustments of dealers to their own local market demand factors are the essence of the play of competitive forces, and on the whole should serve the majority of manufacturers better than any alternative procedures because they allow a flexible, variable adjustment to the demand forces on the various consumer strata."

It is contended that it is not price cutting itself that injures the manufacturer, but the ill-will of retailers occasioned by the refusal of the manufacturer to fair trade his products. It is a form of pressure tactics on the part of retailers to force the manufacturer to keep his products out of the hands of retailers who are content with low margins. At times this pressure has amounted to outright boycotting. But this cannot be attributed to the intrinsic evil of price cutting. In this connection Grether states:

> In the United States the decisive aspect of the problem in relation to manufacturers' interests is the effect of price control in the short run upon the relative amount of support received from classes of dealers under conditions of price control by contrast with price cutting. . . .
>
> This state of affairs makes resale price control very hazardous for some manufacturers unless all of their near competitors adopt similar policies. Some manufacturers have learned from bitter experience that if one of them attempted to stabilize prices alone, he would be holding the umbrella for competitors whose brands were price free.

Finally it is denied that fair trade laws do or can protect the goodwill of the owner of a trade-mark in the proper sense of the word. This was a strong point made to the House Judiciary Committee in 1937. In substance the argument runs as follows: Goodwill is not entitled to protection against the economic effects of honest competition among retailers. It is entitled to protection against "passing off" and counterfeiting, but nothing more. Present laws fully grant this protection. In reality what fair trade laws do is to destroy the goodwill of retailers who have built up a reputation for low prices. When a retailer buys a branded article, he pays for whatever goodwill is in the brand name. He then has the right to sell that merchandise at any price he sees fit. What producers are trying to protect is not goodwill but a semi-monopolistic position.

Retailers as a Class Are Rarely Seriously Injured by Price Cutting. The opponents of fair trade refuse to accept the view that the existence of independent retailers depends on the suppression of all price cutting. They point out that there is no statistical evidence that any appreciable number of retail stores has ever been put out of business by price cutting alone. Prior to fair trade the incidence of business failure in the drug trade where price cutting was claimed to be rampant was no greater than in other lines. Attention is also called to certain studies of the Department of Commerce which were completed in 1933 and which showed only one instance in which failure seemed to be the result of excessive competition. The growth of small stores in non-fair trade areas has been as rapid as the growth in states with fair trade laws.

It is also contended that it is false to assume that the interests of all retailers in price control are alike. In fact there are large numbers of retailers who find a definite disadvantage in fair trade. If this were not true, it is suggested, there would be no need for coercive legislation. Such establishments as the following are particularly handicapped by price maintenance: (1) high-price stores which find that the standardizing effect of price control removes their differential advantage; (2) poorly equipped and located stores which attract customers by price concessions; (3) stores handling lines which change rapidly in respect to style, perishability, prices and other factors and are injured because of the inflexibility of prices; (4) limited service stores such as self-service and cash-and-carry markets which lose their chief attraction through price maintenance; and (5) department stores, mail-order houses and similar large-scale distributors who because of low costs can frequently sell consistently at lower prices. It is significant that the official organization of department stores, the National Retail Dry Goods Association, has long been an ardent foe of price maintenance.

Even the "typical" small neighborhood merchant will find that price maintenance presents serious problems. "From a long-run standpoint," Grether says, "the results should not be so beneficial to the majority of small dealers as anticipated." He points out the following reasons for this conclusion: (1) the large stores will adapt themselves to price control and by private brands and other expedients counteract the effects of price control on standard brands; (2) fixed prices and guaranteed margins will stimulate new stores; (3) absence of price competition in controlled items will make for increased competition in uncontrolled items with no increase in over-all profits; and (4) it will be necessary to expand advertising, merchandising services and other promotional activities with consequent increase in costs.

The contention is also made that the *efficient* retailer has nothing to fear from the price cutting activities of rival merchants. Attention is called to the studies of the Harvard Graduate School of Business Administration which, it is claimed, show that the efficient small retailer can compete successfully with large-scale merchandisers. Although large stores have some advantage in buying, this advantage is more than offset by higher operating expense.

The opponents of price maintenance thus conclude that the effects of price cutting on retail stores vary greatly with the type of price competition to which they are subjected. If the price cutting is merely of the loss-leader type, a moderately strong case for control can be made. But if the competition takes the form of legitimate price reductions based on efficient methods of distribution, then the long-run injury to well run and efficient stores cannot be demonstrated. Unfortunately, they claim, price maintenance today is primarily a device to release conventional retailers from the pressure of legitimate competition. Sound public policy is not to be measured by the effects of fair trade on its immediate beneficiaries.

Benefits of Free Pricing to the Consumer. The chief impact of fair trade on the consumer, according to the critics, is felt through the tendency of price maintenance to raise prices. This criticism is reviewed below (pp. 00-00). In answer to the specific contention of the advocates of fair trade that price cutting is detrimental to the interests of the consumer, the opponents usually enter a general denial. They reject the claim that the consumer knows any more about the actual worth of an article with fixed prices than without. In fact they believe the tendency with price maintenance is to over-price and by heavy advertising to convince the consumer that the high price is justified. As the Chairman of Legislation of the American Association of University Women testified on the District of Columbia Fair Trade Bill in 1939:

> Manufacturers realize that the fixing of resale prices tends to give their products prestige by establishing a definite so-called worth. Establishing this so-called worth of branded articles has not necessarily been based on content or ingredient value or even on personal value to the consumer when compared with other products but has been established by pressure-selling methods.

Nor is it a fact that housewives are as easily fooled as the advocates of fair trade would have us believe. Women are not usually deceived by bogus bargains and are highly resistant to attempts at substitution. As a representative of the American Home Economics Association once said:

> The reaction of consumer buyers to loss leaders has been sadly misinterpreted by those favoring resale price maintenance. Consumers are not inevitably taken in by loss leaders. They rightly interpret the use of loss leaders as advertising on the part of retailers. . . .
>
> And consumers do not always come out of a store featuring loss leaders laden with high-priced goods on which they have been gypped. Women buyers are not quite that gullible. They may buy other goods in the store

but they do not pay over the prevailing prices for them and they do not buy inferior goods.

Finally the contention of the advocates of fair trade that price cutting on some goods leads to high prices on other goods is dismissed on the grounds that it overlooks two important facts. First, some stores can cut prices on certain goods without raising prices on other merchandise. Stores do not have the same costs and some stores can consistently and for long periods of time undersell their rivals. Secondly, the argument fails to consider the price-raising propensities of fair trade itself. Even if price cutting were injurious to the consumer, price maintenance would be worse.

FAIR TRADE AND THE COMPETITIVE SYSTEM

A fundamental issue presented by the fair-trade program has to do with the effects that this type of price maintenance may have on the competitive system. Is vertical price control itself monopolistic? Does it indirectly lead to the suppression of competition? Which is the "unfair" practice, price cutting or price maintenance? Opinions on these matters vary widely. The opponents of fair trade challenge the whole program as being suppressive of competition, and a serious weakening of our antitrust policy. The advocates of fair trade deny this charge and point to a number of ways in which they claim that competition is strengthened rather than weakened.

Reconciliation of Fair Trade and Principles of Free Competition

Fair Trade Does Not Mean the Elimination of Price Competition. In presenting the case for fair trade, the advocates maintain that resale price maintenance does not mean the abandonment of price competition. They emphasize first the fact that control under price maintenance operates on a vertical basis rather than horizontal. They recognize that direct price competition between retailers is eliminated but believe this to be unimportant in view of the fact that competition between manufacturers continues to exist. A fair trade law merely permits the making of contracts by which an individual producer establishes minimum resale prices on his own products. These prices vary with each producer and respond fully to consumer preferences and the laws of supply and demand. "National brands compete with each other, and they all compete with the private brands. The result is that the consumer is always protected," to quote the National Association of Retail Druggists.

Secondly, attention is called to the fact that to be on the fair trade list, an article must be in free and open competition with similar articles produced by others. This is cited as a guarantee of free competition. To quote the National Association of Retail Druggists again:

The moment a branded product ceases to be in free and open competition with other products of the same use and general character, its manufacturer, under the Fair Trade laws, ceases to have the privilege of establishing minimum resale prices. A Fair Trade product therefore must always remain a competitive product.

Collusion between manufacturers of different brands to establish the same price and thereby to eliminate price competition with each other, is ruled out by the Fair Trade laws. It is also ruled out by the fact that when resale prices of national brands rise, private brands gain a competitive advantage.

In the third place, much also is made of the fact that state laws are entirely permissive. They permit a manufacturer to put his trademarked article on the fair trade list but do not compel him to do so. Price maintenance is purely voluntary. There is no basis to the accusation that a group of rival producers or dealers can force a manufacturer to maintain prices if for any reason he prefers not to do so.

For these reasons, advocates of fair trade insist that a fair trade act is not a price-fixing measure. They point to Justice Brandeis' famous comment that "You cannot fix prices where competition is present with every other producer of the same article you produce, or where 10,000 retailers are selling the same articles you are selling, so long as they are prohibited by law from agreeing on prices with one another." They also claim to have the support of the United States Supreme Court, which in upholding the constitutionality of the Illinois Fair Trade Act, declared that the Act "does not attempt to fix prices nor does it delegate such power to private persons."

Price Maintenance as a Positive Deterrent to Monopolistic Practices. Advocates of fair trade are convinced that not only is their variety of price maintenance in harmony with competitive principles, but also that in the long run it will be a strong deterrent to monopoly. This is based largely on the assumption that price cutting is discriminatory in effect and a powerful tool for the suppression of competition. By preventing price cutting, fair trade is a strong barrier to price discrimination and hence monopoly as well. The argument has been stated by the Bureau of Education on Fair Trade as follows:

The public has never hesitated to put curbs on competition which it regards as unfair and monopolistic. The anti-trust laws, the Robinson-Patman Act and many other statutes curb unfair competition in order to promote fair competition. So do the Fair Trade laws. They are intended to curb bold, relentless, predatory commercial behavior. They restrain the unfair competition of retailers who engage in pricing practices that bedazzle the consumer without benefit to her pocketbook and lead, inevitably, to the concentration of retailing in few hands—to monopoly.

Under Fair Trade, American consumers can shop with confidence in getting fair value in big and little stores, in villages as well as in great cities, in neighborhoods as well as on Main Street. Without Fair Trade, they lose their freedom to shop where they please, for most retailers in America cannot exist for long in a jungle of unrestrained price wars. Few people would care to argue that retail monopoly would be good for the buying public or for the country.

Once again Brandeis is quoted on the monopolistic effect of price cutting. He declared:

> Americans should be under no illusions as to the value or effect of price-cutting. It has been the most potent weapon of monopoly—a means of killing the small rival to which the great trusts have resorted most frequently. It is so simple, so effective. Far-seeing organized capital secures by this means the cooperation of the short-sighted unorganized consumer to his own undoing. Thoughtless or weak, he yields to the temptation of trifling immediate gain; and selling his birthright for a mess of pottage, becomes himself an instrument of monopoly.

The fair trade laws are thus a true and indispensable expression of our public policy against discrimination. As such they supplement the Robinson-Patman and Federal Trade Commission Acts. Historically, the legalization of price maintenance was closely associated with the statutory control of discriminatory tactics. Agitation for both appeared as a result of the failure of the Sherman Act to prevent monopoly and of the demonstrable need of small business for further protection against predatory tactics. The purpose of the Robinson-Patman Act was to protect the independent retailer from the unfair advantage gained by mass distributors in the form of price concessions from manufacturers. Standardization of selling prices among retailers through price maintenance is a step in the same direction and makes the elimination of discriminatory buying prices easier to achieve. The two policies are merely different parts of the same general program of eliminating unfair and discriminatory practices.

Fair Trade Tends To Equalize the Competitive Strength of the Independent Retailer With That of the Mass Distributor. Fair trade, it is claimed, further supports the competitive system by placing the independent retailer on a par with the mass distributor in respect to his ability to compete. Advocates of fair trade deny that the latter has any advantage in lower costs of operation. Their competitive strength lies in purely strategic weapons derived through unfair concessions in buying, ability to absorb local losses, and the sheer weight of massed capital.

Under the caption, "Small Business Needs Fair Trade to Survive," the Bureau of Education on Fair Trade presents the retailers' point of view as follows:

> The supporters of Fair Trade include thousands of manufacturers, many of them small, whose national brand products account for about 5% of U. S. retail sales. They include the vast majority of this country's 1,770,000 retailers, plus many thousands of wholesalers—who add up to the backbone of small business. They know from bitter experience that the pressure of superior dollar power, applied through such methods of unfair competition as "deliberate operations in the red" will permit retail monopolies to destroy them. Small business asks for competitive decency in the market place. It needs effective Fair Trade so that it can compete for the customer's favor on the basis of honesty, efficiency, services and skill.

Continuing in the same vein, the Bureau states:

> Fair trade is designed to give the small business man a chance to compete fairly and on equal terms with large distributors, and thereby to preserve for small enterprises the field in which they can function most efficiently—that of distribution.
>
> It is admitted that the mass-production manufacturing industries have become so big that no individual can command enough capital to engage in them successfully. But retail distribution is a business in which, as government findings show, the little fellow is fully as efficient as his corporate competitor. Unless we are welling to make practically all men hired-men and to deny to all but a few the opportunity to engage in businesses of their own, we should outlaw every unfair practice that gives the strong an unfair advantage over the weak.
>
> One of those advantages is the ability of massed capital to drive out competitors by selling temporarily below cost in one community, and thereafter to raise prices to the consumer and to use the profits so gained in carrying the process of extermination in other communities.

Large distributors have many devices at their command which do for them what fair trade does for the little fellow. They can distribute through agencies. Like the chain stores, they can control price all the way from producer to consumer. They can use informal methods. Fair trade merely equalizes these advantages.

It is claimed that court decisions had placed the small operator in a very precarious position. In the *Miles* case, the Supreme Court held that a seller could not maintain prices once he had transferred title. In the *General Electric* case, however, the Court held that price control through an assignment-agency system whereby General Electric distributed through 21,000 retailer-agents was perfectly legal. In the words of the counsel of the American Booksellers' Association:

> The effect was amazing—appalling. The Sherman Anti-Trust Act became a legal monstrosity—a breeder rather than a destroyer of trusts or quasi trusts. Only concerns of immense capital could protect their goods against ruinous price cutting; wealthy concerns became wealthier, poor concerns poorer. Only economic giants could survive in the deep seas thus charted out. Wholesaler and retailer alike became the hired servant of vast producers.

The Charge That Fair Trade Is Inherently Monopolistic in Character

Price Maintenance Means the Elimination of Price Competition Among Retailers. That systematic price maintenance is essentially monopolistic in character is the conclusion reached by most government agencies that have studied the problem. The Federal Trade Commission in its 1945 Report on Resale Price Maintenance, for instance, charges that "the essence of resale price maintenance is control of price competition."

Although the Commission recognizes that the movement to control prices originated among manufacturers as a device to protect the goodwill in their brand names, the Commission declares that it has become "a means of eliminating price competition both of dealers using the same methods of distribution and of dealers using new and different methods of distribution." The Commission concludes with the following comment:

> Both the results of the Commission's present special study of the operation of legalized resale price maintenance and information developed over a period of many years in connection with complaints strongly confirm these earlier conclusions and point to the further conclusion that in the absence of effective Government supervision in the public interest, resale price maintenance, legalized to correct abuses of extreme price competition, is subject to use as a means of effecting enhancement of prices by secret agreements and restraint of competition by coercive action on the part of interested cooperating trade groups of manufacturers, wholesalers, and retailers in such ways and to such an extent as to make it economically unsound and undesirable in a competitive economy.

A study made for the Temporary National Economic Committee led to substantially the same conclusion. The report states:

> In summary, it is sufficient to point out that resale price maintenance is not a fair-trade measure but a price-fixing, margin-setting measure that

injures consumers, reduces flexibility of output, restricts progress in marketing, and contributes to monopolistic prices and monopolistic action.

The Department of Justice as a result of its investigations of antitrust cases likewise has come to the conclusion that "the actual effects of resale price maintenance have been those which are to be expected from private price fixing conspiracies unregulated by public authority, whether or not they enjoy the sanction of law."

Fair Trade Indirectly Creates Conditions Favorable to the Growth of Monopoly. Fair trade is cited as an indirect stimulant to monopoly because it creates conditions favorable to the long-run growth of monopoly. The Antitrust Division of the Department of Justice thus found that the Miller-Tydings Act "sanctions arrangements inconsistent with the purpose of the antitrust laws, and becomes a cloak for many conspiracies in retraint of trade which go far beyond the limits established in the amendment."

The Federal Trade Commission has come to the same conclusion. Dr. Vernon Mund likewise believes that:

> In the operation of resale price laws, there is a tendency for various manufacturers—such as those of flour, cereals, soaps, canned milk, and vegetable shortenings—to make identical resale price agreements. This procedure serves to eliminate price competition at the manufacturing level, for all manufacturers will thereupon sell to the wholesalers or retailers at the same prices.

It is also contended that fair trade breeds monopoly because of the tendency to limit the number who may engage in a given field of business. High resale margins attract newcomers to the trade. It is said, for example, that high margins on price-fixed drug and pharmaceutical products have induced grocery stores, "dime" stores, and other retail outlets to establish medicine counters. As the fair trade field becomes crowded, it is feared that established firms will seek to restrict the number of these newcomers. In this connection, a statement in Fortune Magazine is pertinent. The statement reads:

> The specific granting to individuals of power to fix prices for all other individuals is bad enough. But it is only the first step. As shown by the record in England and Sweden, the exercise of this power tends to the creation of the further power to dictate who shall and who shall not sell the product. U. S. "fair" traders protest that this is not their intention, *yet they have already begun to move in this direction.* The minima that they have set on most drug prices yield such high margins of profit that other types of stores, notably groceries, have taken to stocking drugs. There has been a consequent outcry from the druggists that *only* druggists should be

entitled to handle these lucrative lines. The question then is raised as to who is a druggist, and this will inevitably lead to a demand for quotas . . .

The Statutory Guarantees of Competition Are Meaningless. Opponents of fair trade are quite skeptical of the effectiveness of the so-called statutory guarantees of free competition. They believe, for instance, that the requirement that commodities cannot be fair traded unless they are in free and open competition with other commodities of the same general type will in practice afford no real check on monopolistic practices. It is believed that manufacturers who utilize the price-maintenance privilege tend to regard the established price as more or less permanent and also expect their rivals to so regard it. No reduction in the minimum price is likely to be made by one manufacturer unless similar action is taken by his competitors. Margins on similar products tend to be uniform and any reduction will be opposed by retailers. This "pressure from distributors creates a strong resemblance to horizontal price fixing," as the Temporary National Economic Committee Report stated. In the same vein the Federal Trade Commission has declared:

> In practice . . . resale price maintenance serves as a focal point for dealer cooperative effort to bring pressure to bear on manufacturers to place products under price maintenance at prices yielding dealer margins satisfactory to cooperating organized dealer groups. In some lines of trade, where the individual manufacturer has faced strongly organized dealer group pressure, the extent of his freedom of choice as to whether he will place his brands under resale price maintenance has been extremely limited.

Both the Federal Trade Commission and the Department of Justice are concerned at the present time with the activities of several well-known associations which are bringing pressure on manufacturers to "fair trade" their products. Horizontal price fixing may not exist in name, but it is closely approached in fact.

Furthermore, the test of free and open competition is incapable of effective administration for the simple reason, to quote the Temporary National Economic Committee Report again, that "no adequate definition for 'free and open competition' exists." As a legal test it is meaningless. The same is true of the phrase, "commodities of the same general class." This has no significance in either law or economics.

When the Miller-Tydings bill was under consideration it was charged that the movement for fair trade in the drug industry was merely another step toward the perfection of monopoly in that industry. The counsel for the National Retail Dry Goods Association thus testified:

The development of this monopoly in the drug industry has been going on for some time and the industry lends itself peculiarly to such monopoly despite the huge number of items involved.

As evidence, he pointed out that in California the large drug manufacturers set the same prices on many of their products.

Fair Trade Laws Do Not Check Discriminatory Pricing. The critics of fair trade believe it to be a serious error to view fair trade as a significant deterrent to price discrimination and to associate fair trade laws and the Robinson-Patman Act in the same category of measures designed to eradicate the general evil of price cutting. Either is possible without the other and instead of being complementary, they frequently directly clash. Many of those who oppose the Miller-Tydings Act and the state fair trade laws are among the staunchest supporters of the Robinson-Patman Act.

It is pointed out that the fair trade laws are directed against price cutting *per se* whereas the Robinson-Patman Act is directed against price discrimination. There is a significant difference between the two targets even though at times they may appear to be the same. In the first place, fair trade affects the price the retailer receives. The Robinson-Patman Act affects the prices he pays. Fair trade prices can still be discriminatory as between retailers. Secondly, fair trade stops all price cutting whether it is discriminatory or not. A general policy of low prices based on low operating costs is not discriminatory by itself. It is the unfair advantage given to a particular distributor or the local price differential against all independents in a given community that produces discrimination. Fair traders insist that the legitimate low prices of a genuinely efficient retailer be prohibited as well as the low prices which are based on unfair concessions from the manufacturer.

Thirdly, the fair trade laws are designed to promote uniformity of prices whereas the Robinson-Patman Act may require specific variation in prices. If costs vary, then so should prices. To require all prices to be uniform in the absence of a similar uniformity of costs will frequently result in a violation of the basic principle of the Robinson-Patman Act. It was for this reason that the economist testifying on behalf of R. H. Macy Co. in 1937 referred to what he called the "strange inconsistency" in the views of those who advocated both price maintenance and anti-price discrimination laws. In the Robinson-Patman Act, he said, "you aim to conserve production economies for the consumer" whereas in the Miller-Tydings Act "it is proposed to prevent those and other economies from being passed on to the consumer."

For these reasons, it is believed that price maintenance is as much a stimulant to discrimination as it is a deterrent. Certainly, it cannot be relied upon to promote non-discriminatory treatment. Even if we placed all retail prices under control, discrimination would still persist. On the other hand, if the Robinson-Patman Act were properly enforced, the real evil of discriminatory price cutting would disappear. Thus, E. T. Grether believes that if the Robinson-Patman Act should destroy wide price variations between buyers it would remove one of the sore spots in trade conflicts which often receive the onus for price cutting in retailing. Consequently, one of the prime bases for the demand for resale price maintenance would be removed. And Dr. Vernon Mund states:

> There is abundant evidence indicating that the *real* and *continuing* price problem of local dealers is not sales below cost, as such, but rather discriminatory price cutting. In many cases, businessmen themselves do not realize that when a competitor is reducing prices locally, he is making up his losses in other localities where competition is weak or non-existent. . . . The solution for this problem is to make geographic price discrimination illegal, *per se*.

EFFECT OF FAIR TRADE PRACTICES ON RETAIL PRICES

A basic issue in the fair trade controversy is: What are the effects of resale price maintenance on retail prices? The initiative in this argument is taken by the opponents of fair trade who believe that the practice tends to make for higher prices, produces an undesirable uniformity of prices and introduces an objectionable element of rigidity into the retail price structure. The defenders deny that fair trade produces these results. We shall review first the indictment as drawn up by the opponents.

The Criticism of Fair Trade Prices

Fair Trade Prices Tend To Be High Prices. A large mass of data has been collected by the opponents of fair trade which, it is claimed, indicates that prices of fair trade commodities tend to be higher than prices on the free market. Typical of this evidence is the following:

(1) A number of actual cases in which fair trade apparently has had a substantial effect by way of raising prices are cited in the report to the Temporary National Economic Committee. The following are typical:

> In California fair trade prices in metropolitan cut-rate and chain-store institutions were raised, on the average, one-third above the prices for the same articles before the fair trade law became effective.

In a Los Angles cut-rate store, in October 1938, prices of five very popular nationally advertised drug items were 135 per cent higher than prices of their identical substitutes. Increases after the passage of the California act ranged up to 29 per cent. Some decreases also occurred.

In comparing Washington, which has no price-maintenance law, with Baltimore, where such a law exists, it was found that more than one-third of the Washington prices were lower and only one-tenth were higher than Baltimore prices.

This study concluded that "Such figures as are available show almost universally that price-maintained items sell for higher prices than non-maintained goods; that prices of contractual articles rose after the law was passed; that prices average higher in cities where maintenance is legal than in comparable cities where it is not legal."

(2) The Federal Trade Commission concluded from its survey that the most common effect of resale price maintenance was that "chain stores, department stores, and certain independent stores that were selling below the minimums set by resale price maintenance contracts in resale price maintenance territory were obliged to increase prices."

(3) E. T. Grether concludes that "All the evidence available and *a priori* theorizing point indubitably to the conclusion that the patrons of lower price, limited service firms are forced to pay higher prices for the goods under control than previously." Grether cites as a glaring example the fact that contractual prices in California in 1934 for products sold through drug stores were as much as one-third higher than the advertised prices in newspapers during the first six months of 1933.

(4) A study of comparative prices published in Fortune Magazine in 1949 found that:

Congressmen and lesser residents of the District of Columbia can lather up with a big tube of Barbasol bought for 29 cents; in fair-trade Maryland, the same tube would cost 39 cents. The Congressmen can regenerate the blood cells with Lilly's Lextron Pulvules (84's) for $2.29, instead of the fair-trade price of $3.15. A bottle of Old Grand-dad is $5.45 in Washington, $6.65 (before state tax) across the line. BC headache powders are a dime instead of 19 cents.

(5) In a later article Fortune Magazine declared that "this area of the argument can be removed from mere debate and placed on a basis of fact." In non-fair trade areas, "prices are consistently lower than where the same articles are 'fair' traded. How big a bill the American public is paying to give the retailer this protection no one has ever figured out. But to argue that there is no bill at all is simply disingenuous."

(6) A study of 117 branded drug items cited by Dr. Vernon Mund

showed that thirty-five cost about a third less in Washington than in Maryland, thirty-eight about a quarter less, and twenty-nine about a seventh less.

(7) An analysis of prices in free trade Missouri and fair trade Illinois reveals much the same situation. The St. Louis Star-Times reports that fifty-four fair trade drug items cost an average of 16.2 per cent more on the east bank of the Mississippi than on the St. Louis side. Dr. Mund concludes that the effect of price maintenance on trade-marked products "is to enhance prices and profits and deny consumers the benefits of lower prices made possible by differences in the productive efficiency, methods of sale, and scale of operations of the various sellers."

Fair Trade Produces an Undesirable Uniformity of Prices. The contention that price maintenance leads to an undesirable uniformity of prices is based first on the fact that the primary purpose of resale price control is the establishment of a price floor which must be observed by all retailers. Price maintenance decrees minima below which no seller can sell except in unusual circumstances. These minima are applicable to all stores regardless of individual costs and possible economies of operation. Furthermore, they tend to be uniform geographically and little adjustment is normally made for the special circumstances of individual communities such as costs of transportation. Frequently they are uniform throughout the nation. Price maintenance thus means uniform delivered prices regardless of costs of distribution.

It is further contended that the fair trade price normally is not merely the minimum; in practice it tends to become the actual price. It is recognized that it is theoretically possible for a manufacturer to establish a resale price below the price at which the bulk of the commodity is expected to sell. In this way stores could exercise a measure of freedom. The opponents of fair trade do not concede, however, that in practice this is what happens. To them the very nature of price maintenance seems to require that the minimum price should be the actual price. Experience, they claim, bears out this view and it is rare indeed that any retailer can afford to charge prices above the official prices advertised by the manufacturer.

This uniformity of prices is highly undesirable, according to the critics of fair trade, in that it works severe hardship on particular groups of customers. The contention is that customers of limited service, retailers such as cash-and-carry stores and super-markets are deprived of the opportunity to shop where their pocketbook directs them. As Grether points out, "the mal-effects of resale price control are concentrated upon consumers who patronized the dealers on the lower levels."

The blessings, "if any," fall upon those who already enjoy the conveniences of the smaller and full service firms. The Federal Trade Commission came to the same general conclusion.

When the Miller-Tydings Act was under consideration, numerous representatives of consumer groups protested the threatened injury to low income families. These families habitually patronize low-price stores which offer few services. They are willing to walk long distances and to carry packages to save a few cents. They rarely buy on credit. Fair trade means that they are deprived of these economies and are forced to pay for full services whether the latter are actually rendered or not. This, it was charged, is unfair, unreasonable and contrary to the public interest.

Fair Trade Makes for Objectionable Price Rigidity. A third major objection to fair trade prices is that they introduce an undesirable element of rigidity into the whole retail price structure. Once a price is established, the argument goes, it responds slowly to changes in economic conditions. Professor McNair has stated the case as follow:

> Keeping the price unchanged is the path of least resistance. It avoids potentially troublesome adjustments with wholesalers and retailers with respect to stocks of goods already in hand. It avoids also any difficulty which might be encountered in raising prices later in the event of a change in market conditions. Manufacturers frequently hesitate to make downward price changes for fear of "spoiling the market" in case demand proves to be inelastic. . . . As abundantly demonstrated during the depression, there are numerous manufacturers who will resort to many expedients before they will change prices; they will even in some instances reduce production and lay off labor first.

The Temporary National Economic Committee Report states that when prices are established by contract, "there can be no flexibility of prices." "Supply," the Report points out, "is determined by an artificially determined demand which itself is, in fact, a function of an administered price. There is created a rigid structure of prices that does not yield either to general or specific changes in economic conditions." It is believed that this rigidity removes one of the factors most essential to adjustments to economic change. It is all well and good for the advocates of fair trade to say that controlled prices resist inflation. It is true that in periods of rising prices, inflexibility is not serious. But during declines in price levels and particularly in periods of economic recession, rapid adjustment of prices to new and lower levels is necessary. Rigid prices merely serve to aggravate the reduction in output and employment in the controlled trades.

The Defense of Fair Trade Prices

Fair Trade Prices Are Fair Prices. The most elaborate statistical study made on behalf of fair trade is one conduced by Professor H. J. Ostlund of the School of Business Administration of the University of Minnesota and C. R. Vickland under the sponsorship of the Research Bureau of the National Association of Retail Druggists. It was an attempt to measure the movement of retail drug prices between the time that fair trade laws were adopted and 1939. The general conclusions were as follows:

(1) In the drug stores of the forty-two fair trade states covered by the survey, prices of leading fair trade items showed little change between the time they were placed under contract and 1939. Fifty leading trademarked items were included in the survey list and the weighted average price of these articles declined about one percent.

(2) Independent stores with from $20,000 to $30,000 annual volume of sales showed the greatest average reduction in prices, the index declining 3.5 points. Small stores showed a slightly smaller reduction with stores in the lowest group (less than $10,000 annual volume of sales) recording a decline of 2.5 points. Stores with sales above $50,000 showed a decrease of 0.4 points.

(3) Prices in chain stores increased, the index rising 4.9 points.

(4) In Missouri and Texas without fair trade laws, prices of the items surveyed decreased slightly more than in fair trade states. Between 1936 and 1939, the period comparable to that surveyed in the majority of the fair trade states, the index fell 2.7 points in Missouri and 2.8 points in Texas.

(5) The report concludes that inasmuch as price changes were too extensive to be attributed to ordinary market factors and could not be traced to other unusual factors, they must have been the result largely of fair trade.

A study made by the National Association of Chain Drug Stores shows that since 1939 prices of fair trade articles have restricted inflation better than prices of other goods. According to this study, the prices of 7,334 controlled drug products increased only 3.1 percent from 1939 to 1947, whereas food prices went up 93 percent and the over-all cost of living rose 59 percent. This has led the Bureau of Education on Fair Trade to claim, "If all prices had behaved like Fair Trade prices, we wouldn't be burdened today with such a high cost of living, and government price controls would not be needed."

Another oft-cited study is one made by an "independent research agency" for the Bureau of Education on Fair Trade and reported in an undated release of that Bureau. This survey covered the period from July through December, 1949. It included 26 top brands of headache marked goods sold through such standard pricing methods as consignment selling, exclusive dealerships and other legal forms of price maintenance. These standard pricing methods are used without recourse to fair trade and would continue to be used if all the fair trade laws were repealed.

It is pointed out that daily newspapers, magazines, automobiles, household appliances, gas and oil products, home furnishings, some wearing apparel, and many other products are sold at standard prices. We are thus constantly surrounded by standard prices in our daily lives. Ours is a standard price, a standard brand economy.

Standardization through fair trade is no worse than other forms of standardization. The Bureau of Education on Fair Trade asks, "If the practice of resale price maintenance is economically, legally and socially acceptable for a large group of producers who are able to use consignment selling or similar distribution techniques, then how can resale price maintenance under voluntary fair trade be opposed? The fair trade laws merely give manufacturers who are not able to use other forms of price maintenance the same right to protect their trade-marks and their distributive systems through resale price maintenance that everyone else is given."

Fair trade advocates deny the assertion that maintained prices cannot be easily adjusted to changes in economic conditions. Manufacturers, they believe, are as capable of adjusting their prices as retailers. If a price is too high, declining sales will force a reduction. The consumer in the last analysis is the real price fixer anyway and neither the manufacturer nor the retailer can pursue a policy for long that is contrary to the consumer's interests. In any event, flexibility does not require uncoordinated actions by individual retailers. It can be procured by simultaneous action with the initiative resting with the manufacturer.

---

10. ECONOMIC PRECONCEPTION AND THE FARM POLICY *

THE FEDERAL government policy of attempting to maintain farm income by means of price supports has received a full share of criticism from professional economists (see Selection 00 for a description of the development of the policy and some of the criti-

* John Kenneth Galbraith, "Economic Preconception and the Farm Policy," The American Economic Review, March, 1954, Vol. XLIV, No. 1, pp. 40-52. Reprinted by permission of the author and publisher.

The author (1908——) is Professor of Economics at Harvard University and remedies, dentifrices, shaving creams and other products sold 770 stores. A comparison was made between the prices in the trade states and the prices in the non-fair trade areas of M Texas, Vermont and the District of Columbia. It was claime the brands selected were the ones typically used as loss-leaders by cutters in the non-fair trade area. One would expect, therefore, their prices would be lower in the non-fair trade areas. According the Bureau of Education on Fair Trade the survey indicates, howev that on the average the American consumer is paying nothing for fa trade. Frequently he pays less. Twelve items sold for less in fair trade areas than in "free" areas. Only six sold for less in non-fair trade territory and the maximum difference in price on any of these products was only three cents.

The reason that fair trade does not raise prices is simple, according to fair traders. As expressed by the National Association of Retail Druggists, it is as follows:

> The manufacturer of a product determines the lowest price for which it can be sold to the consumer, covering its cost of production and yielding distributors a margin that will induce them to sell it. . . .
>
> A manufacturer establishing Fair Trade prices must set them low enough so that he will not be undersold by his competitors. Inasmuch as the minimums set must be uniform throughout a state, and generally are uniform throughout the nation, he runs the risk of losing *all* his business and being forced into bankruptcy if his prices are out of line. No manufacturer who has spent thousands, or perhaps millions, to establish his brands would take that risk. He will put his prices as low as possible, and those prices will be in effect everywhere.

Reply to the Charge That Fair Trade Prices Are Unduly Uniform and Inflexible. Advocates of fair trade seem to be inclined to recognize that price maintenance tends to introduce a measure of uniformity and inflexibility into the price structure. Where they differ with the critics is in respect to the consequences of this inflexibility. To them it appears to be a virtue. They take the position that fair trade pricing is merely one manifestation of standardization which is widely employed in all forms of production and distribution. We are told:

> Fair trade is only one form of this distribution technique and a less prevalent one at that. Over 35 million dollars' worth of trade-marked products were sold last year at standard retail prices established by manufacturers. This amounted to about 27 percent of the country's annual retail sales. Only five billion dollars' worth, or approximately four percent of total retail sales, represented national brands sold under voluntary fair trade. The other 30 billion dollars' worth of sales covered trade-

cisms). Professor Galbraith examines these criticisms for the purpose of determining whether they are theoretically sound and historically relevant.

ON FARM policy, in recent times, there has been a remarkable divergence between the weight of scholarly recommendation and the course of practical action. In the years since World War II, it seems clear, the policy of providing firm price guarantees for farm products has gained markedly in policial favor.[1] As recently as five years ago it was widely assumed that this policy would be discontinued as soon as the psychological transition to peacetime conditions had been completed and the opposition of some intransigent friends of the so-called "high and rigid" supports had been overcome. The policy can no longer be viewed as temporary. It has won the advocacy of a body of legislators of both parties who are formidable both in numbers and power. They clearly have on their side an important sector of farm opinion despite the formal opposition, so far, of two of the three national farm organizations.[2] During the presidential campaign of 1952 both candidates committed themselves, for the immediate future, to price supports at present levels and to the extension of protection to products not now covered. The popularity of price supports has clearly impressed a Secretary of Agriculture who has not concealed his personal distaste for the policy and his hope that it might be abandoned.[3]

---

a former member of the Board of Editors, *Fortune* magazine. Author of *Modern Competition and Business Policy, Economic Effects of Federal Public Works Expenditures,* and *American Capitalism: The Concept of Countervailing Power.*

[1] Under legislation expiring in 1954, support of prices at 90 per cent of parity is mandatory for six so-called basic commodities—corn, cotton, wheat, tobacco, rice and peanuts. Support is also mandatory but within a price range below 90 per cent of parity for a few more products, of which the most important are dairy products and wool and mohair. Other farm products may be supported at the discretion of the Secretary of Agriculture, and under this authority, which of late has been used rather sparingly, a limited number of other products (principally feeds and vegetable oil products) have been receiving formal support.

[2] The American Farm Bureau Federation and the National Grange have, so far, opposed the inflexible support prices at 90 per cent of parity. Only the smaller and more regional Farmers' Union supports the policy. However, it has been evident for some time that the Farm Bureau, especially in the South, does not have the full concurrence of its state units on this issue, and presidents of State Federations have appeared before Congressional committees in opposition to the position taken by the national organization.

[3] In his first press conference, in what may not have been the happiest choice of words, Secretary Benson expressed the belief that price supports should be used only to protect the farmer from "undue disaster." Amplifying this later at St. Paul, he said, "Price supports should provide insurance against disaster and help stabilize national food supplies. But price supports which encourage uneconomic production and result in continuing heavy surpluses and subsidies should be avoided."

In sharp contrast with the growing popularity of the policy has been the position of the economists who have spoken on this subject. Criticism of the policy would hardly be remarkable. What is remarkable is the unanimity with which this policy has been condemned by the professional students who have spoken on the subject. There have been almost literally no expressed partisans of the fixed guarantees. In the current climate of professional attitudes approval of the present farm policy, one senses, would be not alone exceptional but eccentric.

It follows that the literature in opposition to the present policy is nearly coextensive with the writing on agricultural policy. Thus toward the end of the war a committee designated by the Association of Land Grant Colleges and Universities urged the liquidation of wartime price guarantees, the precursors of the present support prices. Such fixed price guarantees were almost uniformly criticized and rejected by the prize-winning essays in the contest on postwar farm price policy conducted by the American Farm Economic Association.

More recently, in a strongly argued brief, the present policy has been unequivocally condemned by a committee of thirteen distinguished agricultural economists which included the present and seven past presidents of the American Farm Economic Association. The economists find the present policy inconsistent with general economic welfare, specifically damaging to low-income consumers and, among other faults to be mentioned presently, a threat to the freedom of decision of farmers. They urge its total abandonment and the re-establishment of "flexible prices based on open market demand and on free competition, not price controls."

I. THE CASE AGAINST THE POLICY

The economists who have spoken on the subject have not only been nearly unanimous in their objection to the present farm policy, but they have also been comprehensive in their criticism. The policy is credited with few or no good effects. To it is attributed a variety of unfavorable consequences all of them extremely serious.

The most common and probably the most telling criticism of the policy is that of its assumed effect on resource allocation and therefore on the efficiency with which economic resouces are employed.[4] There are two parts to this indictment: first, the support prices interfere with price movements and therewith, it is held, in a damaging way with

[4] This criticism will be recognized as implicit in the commonplace assertion that support prices prevent or retard needed adjustments in agriculture or stop desirable production shifts. *Cf.* the quotation from Secretary Benson above.

optimal resource allocation within the agricultural industry; and, second, they are condemned for interfering with the movement of resources between agriculture and nonagricultural enterprise and, in particular, for holding unneeded labor in farming. The effect on resource allocation within agriculture is regarded with particular alarm, an emphasis that may be attributed, at least in part, to the persuasive work of Professor Theodore W. Schultz. He has shown that price influences may not be dominant in the distribution of labor and capital between agricultural and nonagricultural enterprise and that "The movement of workers in and out of agriculture has been inconsistent with our economic *rationale* as to what people do (in the short run) in adjusting to changes in relative prices of products." But he has compensated for this seeming slight to the price system with a powerful exposition of the role of relative prices in adjusting resource use within agriculture. "Income-stabilizing programs are too heavy a burden for the pricing system to bear if it is to function efficiently in guiding agricultural production." However, alarm over the effect of support prices on resource movement in and out of agriculture has by no means disappeared. The committee of economists above cited (rather curiously with Schultz's concurrence) states that the subsidy, inherent in the use of support prices, inhibits the movement of resources and the equalization of factor returns between agricultural and nonagricultural enterprise and that "a support program above real market prices tends to tie down resources that should be moving out to non-agricultural uses. . . ." The consequences are clearly deemed to be grave.

Next to its effect on allocative efficiency, the most sharply articulated criticism of the present farm policy concerns its relation to foreign trade policy. For export crops, the support of prices above world levels must be offset by subsidies if the crop is to continue to move in international trade. Furthermore, the effect of support operations may be to attract imports which means in turn that foreign producers are sharing in the subsidies by the United States government to its domestic producers. Tariffs and quotas will almost inevitably be urged and quite likely be involked to prevent what would otherwise be an international distribution of domestic largesse. The prima facie inconsistency of such export subsidies, tariffs and quantitative restrictions with the professed goals of American foreign economic policy has been developed at length by Professor Johnson, and has commanded the attention of other scholars. Recent administrations, it is held, have promoted a liberal trade policy with one hand and in the farm policy have laid the foundation for economic nationalism with the other.

A third criticism of the policy is that the support prices contribute to a reduction of consumer welfare by restriction on the aggregate of resource use. For example, the economists hitherto cited assert that "A high-price program involving restriction of production hurts consumers, particularly in the lower-income groups, because they cannot satisfy their wants as adequately as they could if productive resources were used more fully." Similar allegations have been frequent. Thus, in addition to distorting the pattern of resource use, it is also charged that the policy results in an absolute withdrawal of resources from use.

While damaging the public at large, the gains to farmers from this policy are held to be transitory or illusory. Thus, while finding monopolization of resouce use damaging to consumers, the above-cited economists also warn farmers that ". . . monopolistic restrictions on farm production are much less effective than [they] have been led to suppose . . ." and that "This conclusion is based both on logic and the last three decades of agricultural experience."

The policy is also condemned as a cause of inflation and as a brake on recovery when deflationary forces are dormant. The above-cited economists conclude that it is dangerous on both of these grounds. Support prices "are among the factors which tend to put agriculture 'on the bandwagon' of a general inflationary movement" and "free-market clearing prices are likely to do a better job of pulling the economy out of business depression." Professor Brandt has been even more vigorous in his condemnation of the inflationary tendencies of the policy, while with considerable, although perhaps declining frequency, other scholars have held that, in seeking to stabilize farm prices, we may succeed only in unstabilizing the economy at large.

Finally, and beyond the range of economic values, the present policy is held to have the effect of destroying the freedom of choice, political independence, and moral character of the farmer. Thus the above-cited economists, in a passage italicized for emphasis, agree "that the evolution of national farm policies has now brought agriculture into a position of undue reliance on public financial assistance, on efforts to restrict market supplies, and into undesirable political involvement." Brandt has stated that "Our agricultural policy is now involved in the broad economic issue of western political democracy," and that "When millions of able [farm] entrepreneurs have regained the self-confidence to operate without the social harness of bureaucratic guidance and universal risk insurance, it is an event that may amount to a decisive victory in the free anti-collective world." It would seem to follow that political democracy both in the United States and abroad has been placed in jeopardy by the present farm policy.

If the economists who speak with the greatest authority on this matter are to be taken at their word—and it would be improper to do otherwise or to suppose that they are engaged in the poor scientific method of seeking emphasis through exaggeration—then our present farm policy profoundly threatens our national well-being. Inefficiency, economic isolation, monopolistic exploitation, inflation, depression, and the economic serfdom and political debasement of farmers are all abetted by the policy. The prospect, if all these tendencies are advanced, is disenchanting. Yet the policy which portends these afflictions is one on which Congress is launched and with increasing determination. If the economists are right, then we must brace ourselves for an unpleasant time for there is nothing in the present trend of affairs to suggest that their counsel will be heeded in time. The prospect is alarming unless, the seeming unanimity notwithstanding, there is a chance that the economists are wrong.

II. THE SETTING OF THE CRITICISM

It is the function and discipline of social scientists to concern themselves with consequences that lie beyond the eye of the politician. In the early 'thirties, with similar unanimity, the economists concerned with trade policy attacked the political advocacy of higher tariffs. In the later view, few would have argued that the politicians who, nonetheless, proceeded to enact the Hawley-Smoot tariff were following the course of wisdom. This may be the present case.

Yet, when any group of scholars finds itself strongly at odds with the current of practical policy it would seem important that it be sure of its case. This is especially true in the present instance for the farm policy under attack has now been in effect, in war and peace, for some thirteen years. Disaster or, at a minimum, grievous disorder has been predicted for much of this peroid. Yet during this time agriculture has shown, by common consent, a vigorous technological and managerial improvement and, on purely prima facie grounds, would seem to have conformed to high welfare criteria. As Brandt, in a statement that should be contrasted with his depressing view quoted above, has said:

> During the last few decades, a breath-taking technological evolution has been opening new frontiers in agriculture, and the progress has been most spectacular in the United States and Canada. Not only did it assist greatly in winning World War II, but it also kept millions of people in Europe and Asia alive after the war, while providing us at home with a better diet and lifting a large proportion of our farmers to a new level of income.

Moreover, there is a question whether the economists who have been speaking on farm policy have been bringing to bear all of the data which are relevant to a policy judgment. Without exception, the economists herein cited are offering recommendations for practical action. Such recommendations must be shaped not alone by economic and moral criteria, both of which have been liberally invoked, but also by the attitudes and desires of those who are affected. To assume that the economist should recommend only what farmers want or believe they want would reduce him to the role of a poll-taker. But to fail to take account of the farmer as a political entity, while making essentially political recommendations, can be an equal and opposite error. The theorist who, having reached the conclusion that such would be a socially meritorious course, urges union members to disband their organizations and to support the government in legislation to this end is not likely to have either a large influence on labor legislation or even a large reputation for political perspicacity and realism. Should he proclaim his desire to end all unions, willy nilly, he would appropriately be considered somewhat authoritarian in his attitudes. It seems possible that kindred recommendations are not only being made but are a commonplace in regard to farm policy.

If this is so, one antidote is a fuller appreciation of the history of the farm movement in the United States. By a fortunate accident of timing, the product of the mammoth labors of Professor Murray R. Benedict of the University of California has recently become available. This is the first comprehensive history of agriculture legislation in the United States and of the organization and agitation which gave rise to it. Benedict shows in a wealth of detail how long the present policy has been in the making. It is a story of much diversity in method and much inconstancy of both leaders and followers. Yet it also mirrors a remarkable and continuing determination by farmers to gain some control over market forces. The reader is left in little doubt that for a half century or more the free market has had little more appeal to the farmer than the unorganized labor market to the worker—or, for that matter, than an industrial market of atomistic purity would have for the modern corporation executive. Yet the free market is what is being urged on the farmer. Anyone is privileged to advocate revolution. He is perhaps better for knowing when he is a revolutionary.

III. RESOURCE ALLOCATION

Farm policy may still be a commitment to manifold disorders and disasters, and no less so because the commitment is deep. And even though the disasters have been predicted with increasing urgency for a decade or more without appearing, they may still be ahead. But it is possible that the analysis on which the prediction is based is incomplete or in error. This possibility also needs consideration in any re-examination of the grounds on which the economists' condemnation is based.

There is evidence that the analysis is at least partly in error. As noted, the most persuasive indictment of the farm policy to the economist is the effect of the policy on resource use efficiency. If prices must be a vehicle for sustaining income to farmers, they cannot be an efficient instrument for guiding resource use. For if prices are fixed they no longer command the movement of resources within agriculture or between agriculture and industry in accordance with the dictates of consumer choice.

Obvious though this may seem, further examination shows that some of the concern is ill-founded and more of it is subject to serious, if unconscious, exaggeration. As a broad tendency—to which I concede numerous exceptions—the support prices will be effective during times of low aggregate demand or depression. It is then that prices generally will be resting on the supports. At times of high demand—when the latter is sufficient to sustain high or "full" employment—some or most of the prices of supported commodities are likely to be above the support levels.[5]

When prices are above support levels there is no direct impairment of allocative efficiency as the result of the existence of these non-effective supports.[6] But when prices are at support levels as the result of a general deficiency in demand their effect on allocative efficiency is, to say the least, ambiguous. In this context—that of some degree of depression—some resources are idle. The use of resources in the "wrong" place may then be the alternative to no use at all. In any case, their use in one place need not deny resources to another employment since, by definition, there are idle resources on which those other uses may draw. This would appear to have been overlooked by Schultz, for example, who has stated:

> . . . during a depression, when consumer's purchasing power shrinks and prices drop . . . measures that keep farm prices from falling below the support price will disrupt both internal and external trade, unless it should happen that measures employed by the government create enough additional demand to equilibrate the supply at a price at least as high as the support price.
>
> . . . there are two primary objectives that appear to be appropriate in

[5] This has been the general postwar experience although during part of 1952 and most of 1953, mainly as the result of the rapid shrinkage of foreign demand, this has not been true. I discuss this case presently.

[6] There is a possible indirect effect through the reduction of uncertainty in price expectations. This, however, may have long-run investment consequences which would be generally approved.

pricing farm products: (1) to improve the allocation of resources in agricultural production, and (2) to maintain farm income. . . .[7]

The "disruption" of which he here speaks is plainly a disruption in resource allocation.

If support prices do not impair allocative efficiency within agriculture in periods of full employment and they do not worsen it in periods of unemployment, then apparently they do not impair it at all. And we have the impressive testimony of Schultz himself to show that relative prices and rewards to factors are a secondary consideration in the movement of resources between agriculture and other enterprise and specically that labor tends to move from agriculture to industry in times of high relative income rather than low.

However, I do not wish to overprove my case. Because the prices established by the parity formula are arbitrary and bear no necessary relation to equilibrium levels for individual products at full employment demand and because shifts in demand and supply schedules (of which the recent decline in exports and the recent growth in oleomargarine use provide notable examples) can sharply reduce consumption of particular products, price supports may be effective for some products even when aggregate demand is sufficient to sustain full employment. The conditions necessary for a distortion of resource use are then present.

However, here also an amendment to the conventional criticism is in order. In regard to allocative efficiency it seems plain that much comment is decidedly nonquantitative. If inefficiency can be demonstrated, it is *pro tanto* intolerable. There are no degrees of damage; a death sentence on the policy that produces it follows automatically. There is no need to inquire whether the loss of efficiency is serious—whether it warrants the desperate alarm that it induces. Moreover, an examination might, in fact, reveal a rather small cost. Under the relevant conditions—peacetime demand at full employment levels but with some support prices effective—the usual situation, at least in superficial view, tends to be one of fairly general abundance. The obvious manifestation of short-run inefficiency in resource allocation would be shortages and high prices for some products, while the supported products were impounding labor and other resources. This has not been obviously the case to date. At most, price supports have checked the movement of resources from production where the marginal utility of

[7] *Production and Welfare of Agriculture,* p. 96. *Cf.* also my comments, this *Review,* June, 1950, XL, 460-63. These views were expressed nearly four years ago, and it is my impression, based on conversation and correspondence, that Schultz, while still insisting on the absolute importance of free price movements for allocative efficiency might now be less insistent on the point in a depression context.

product, *e.g.*, for storage, is very low to others where marginal utility is also low or at least not spectacularly high. Thus a prominent alternative use for resources now held by supports in dairying would be in beef cattle production where there are no supports but where not all concerned would insist on the urgency of increased production.

It is possible, although by no means certain, that the supports have inhibited secular shifts, as from cotton to dairying in the South. Proof would require, however, a showing of the effect of the policy on long-run price relatives which is presently lacking. There seems to be little doubt that the tobacco programs have changed the ratio of land to fertilizer inputs. Even here, however, a case could be made that the distortion has been caused not by the support price but by the form of the resulting control.

IV. FARM AND TRADE POLICY

At first glance the inconsistency of the present support policy with a liberal trade program seems inescapable. Moreover, the desirability of such a trade policy—unlike the absolute importance of unimpaired allocative efficiency—is something which I am not disposed to question. Further, while the welfare consequences of an inefficiency in resource use are hardly matters of observation, the tariff adjustments and quotas that are required by the policy and their incongruity with our proclaimed trade policy are wholly visible.

Yet here again some qualifications, not commonly emphasized in attacks on the policy, are important. The products presently receiving the 90 per cent mandatory supports are either export crops or crops where there are normally no important imports. The general effect of the support prices is to create a market in the United States which would not otherwise exist. The quantitative restrictions and tariffs, to mention the most ostensibly illiberal consequences of the policy, thus protect a market which would not be attractive except for the support prices. Some qualifications are necessary with respect of certain qualities and staple lengths of cotton. There are more important qualifications with respect of wheat and competitive feed grain imports from Canada. (The impact of these restrictions is overwhelmingly on Canada.) But the general rule holds. The policy restricts imports that have first been made artificially attractive.

This is not a complete extenuation nor is it intended to be. As noted, the posture and integrity of American trade policy is inevitably weakened by any restrictions on imports and also by the counterpart subsidies on exports. On the other hand, there is surely a difference between a restrictive measure which offsets an increase in imports induced by another policy and one—like the classical tariff—which has the single aim and effect of inhibiting imports. To the extent that the farm policy is attacked as an original onslaught on a liberal trade policy rather than an unfortunate compensation the critics are not on strong ground.

V. RESTRICTIVE AND CYCLICAL EFFECTS

A measure of ambiguity or internal inconsistency has already been noted in the other common criticisms of the policy. In objecting to price supports both as a restraint on resource use and hence damaging to the consumer and also as a self-liquidating form of monopoly, the economists above cited have apparently contradicted their own arguments. It would be, however, that they have also drawn attention to a possible difference between the short- and long-run effects of the farm policy. During the years that the present policy has been in effect there has been a substantial expansion in farm output accompanied by a seemingly favorable rate of technological change. Stability in price expectations would normally be thought favorable to this expansion and change and to the requisite investment. Thus reduction in price fluctuations as the result of some monopolization in particular years *could* be the basis for a larger production and lower prices in the long run. Such considerations have played little part in the technical and scientific criticisms of the policy. The exclusion of price expectations as a factor in production responses (except only to show that they defeat monopolistic aims of farmers) would seem to be poor scientific method.

The attack on the policy as inflationary in inflation and deflationary in deflation also involves problems of internal reconciliation. Further, during the periods of acute postwar inflation the supports were effective only in rare instances for particular commodities.[8] Meanwhile there were counterinflationary effects from the liquidation of previously accumulated inventories. As one example, wartime and postwar cotton textile prices would have been far higher, both in the United States and abroad, had it not been for the large inventory carried over from the depression years of the 'thirties. It seems impossible that those who charge inflation against this policy have measured their argument against this history.

The argument that the supports accentuate or perpetuate deflationary tendencies is also weak. In the economists' report hitherto mentioned the case depends partly on the assertion that the restriction incident to the policy in time of declining demand introduces an "unstabilizing

[8] In 1946 and 1947, the years of most rapid increase in prices, the parity index averaged 113 and 115, respectively.

factor." It also rests partly on the claim that "free-market clearing prices" are more likely to arrest or reverse deflation than supported prices and associated production controls. Both of these propositions are coupled with the statement that for "many" farm commodities the price elasticity of demand is greater than unity so that to obtain a given increase in income a more than proportionate cutback in output is required.

These contentions do not stand scrutiny. The statement on price elasticity is flatly in conflict with the evidence. Indeed it is difficult to believe that the available information on the elasticity of demand for farm products could have been reviewed by the economists with markedly more care than a political advocate would normally bring to bear. But even more important, in the practical operation of the support policy in a period of declining demand, the control of production lags well behind—sometimes does not even follow—the pegging of prices. Income, accordingly, is maintained at the volume given by the support price times the full output. If no companion provision is made for taxes, the effect of government expenditures to maintain such income is surely counterdeflationary. In the approximate year and a quarter (to October 31, 1953) that farm prices have been at or near support levels, the Commodity Credit Corporation has committed 2.5 billion dollars to maintain income. There is at least a presumption that these expenditures have had an important effect in limiting the deflationary effects of the heavy decline in farm exports. Here again, the professional objection to the policy is on highly debatable grounds.

I shall pass quickly over the noneconomic objections to the policy. Whether the farmer has, in fact, been debauched or fettered is a matter of opinion, although it involves opinions that social scientists, when speaking professionally, should doubtless render with caution. On the most frequently cited charge—that policy threatens the farmer with a "substantial restriction [of their] freedom of choice," to quote the dry language of the economists above cited, or that they have placed him in "the social harness of bureaucratic guidance" in Brandt's more colorful figure—one observation must be made. This is a loss of freedom which is, by all appearances, much more disturbing to philosopher friends of the farmer than to the farmer himself. And it would be odd were men of some repute both for their intellectual alertness and their political determination, to have lost their freedom without more awareness and without protest.

VI. CONCLUSION

The foregoing is not intended to be a general exculpation of the present farm policy. On the contrary, the policy seems to me to have serious faults. The present price (parity) standards in my view are arbitrary. The discrimination in policy between the so-called basic commodities which are subject to mandatory support and the remainder of agricultural production—which is subject to the same market conditions and is of greater aggregate value—is impossible to defend. The present policy incorporates a design for acquiring large government stocks but none for their management and disposal. It benefits least the income of those farmers who receive least.

A strong case can also be made, if a given farm income is to be guaranteed, that the technique of supporting prices by loan and purchase operations is inferior, for many commodities, to measures which would allow prices to find their own level in the market and provide direct payments to sustain income at the guaranteed levels. Such a technique would go far to reconcile the agricultural with the national trade policy, and it would also elide many of the inventory and disposal problems inherent in the present policy by the admirable device of not acquiring the stocks in the first place. It is interesting that such a policy, in broad contour, has recently replaced fixed price guarantees in the United Kingdom.

Such proposals are not, however, the concern of this paper. Its purpose was to examine the present remarkable divergence between scientific prescription and practical farm policy. That some aspects of the latter are ill-conceived is hardly surprising. This is an area where imperfection is in the nature of things. But the standards of the scientist are less tolerant. He should, to cite the rules the afore-mentioned economists have laid down for themselves, "have technical competence to discover and explain the consequences of given economic actions" and he "should not be [among the] special pleaders for any group or any cause." Examination of the present criticism of farm policy leads me to question whether it is technically above reproach and also whether its weakness may not derive in part from predilections for a cause, which is not the less a cause because its goal is a seemingly traditional arrangement of economic life. If these are the reasons that economists in this field have lost touch with the present current of farm policy and are failing to influence its course there could be none more disturbing.

11. COTTONSEED PRODUCTS SURPLUS—A SERIOUS *Situation**

THE FOLLOWING selection might well be entitled "Problems in Supply and Demand." Certainly it is illustrative of several such problems. First, there is the case of the effect of government demand, added to other demand for cottonseed products, on the markets for cotton seed, cottonseed oil and soybeans. Then there is the changing demand for meal as compared with oil and the effect it has on the relationships between cottonseed products and soybeans. Third, there is the increased demand for margarine coupled with a decrease in the demand for cottonseed as an ingredient of margarine. The student will find several other demand-supply relationships illustrated in this article about the crisis in cotton seed.

THE HUGE cotton crop of 1949 prompted USDA to set up support prices for cotton seed. Shortly afterwards, the Korean War started. Then followed a period of good prices for seed—sometimes over $100 a ton. By 1951, however, surpluses were again in sight. So, starting with the 1951-52 season and continuing to date, the Government has provided these support prices for both cotton seed and soybeans:

Support Prices

(Per Cent of Parity)

Season	*Cotton Seed*	*Soybeans*
1951-52	90	90
1952-53	90	90
1953-54	75	90
1954-55	75	80

For the first two years both commodities were supported at 90 per cent of parity. The first year, surpluses didn't begin to show up until the season was well advanced. So the full effect of the support program on cotton seed was not felt. The second year (1952-53), however, products from about 50 per cent of entire cottonseed crop went into the loan. The USDA then realized that 90 per cent parity supports for both commodities would not work. Cottonseed oil and meal were not able to compete on that price basis. They lost many markets to competing soybean products.

In 1953-54, USDA dropped cottonseed supports to 75 per cent of parity, holding soybeans at 90 per cent. Even with a 15-point differ-

* *The Progressive Farmer,* December, 1954, pp. 124ff. Reprinted by permission of the publisher.

ential, about 20 per cent of the cottonseed crop went into the loan. Soybeans again sold freely on the market.

This year (1954-55) cottonseed supports are held at 75 per cent. But the soybean support price has been dropped to 80 per cent of parity. The USDA justifies this price support relationship by saying that more people wanted it that way—that is, all the soybean people plus the cotton growers. But if past experience is a good guide to the future, it will mean that probably 40 per cent of the cottonseed crop will go into loan.

It has been difficult for us to understand why soybeans should be able to drive cotton seed out of the market when both are supported at the same percentage of parity. We are not sure that we understand it now. We know that the products obtained from a ton of soybeans are more valuable than those from a ton of cotton seed, and that it costs less to process a ton of soybeans than a ton of cotton seed. But these differences in value of by-products and in processing costs have been reflected in prices for cotton seed and soybeans for a number of years. Parity is based on past prices. So, offhand it would seem that support prices based on the same per cent of parity would be fair to both.

The best explanation we have seen why it isn't fair has been given by Rhea Blake, executive vice president of the National Cotton Council. Mr. Blake explains it this way: Parity for the two products is based on prices during a period when the oil in the two products was more valuable in relation to the meal than at present. With the passage of years, the price relationship between oil and meal has shifted. Meal is now more valuable in relation to oil than was true when parity for the two products was established. Soybeans with 78 per cent meal compared with only 43 per cent for cotton seed have become more valuable relative to cotton seed. This means that in a free market, and without supports, soybeans would today sell at a higher percentage of parity than cotton seed. And when both are supported at the same percentage of parity, soybeans undersell cotton seed on the market.

Just how aggressive soybeans have been in pushing cotton seed out of former markets is shown by the margarine picture. Margarine consumption has been increasing. It is up from 862 million pounds in 1949 to 1,292 million pounds in 1953. In the past, this 430-million-pound increase in margarine consumption would have provided a bigger market for cottonseed oil. But the use of cottonseed oil in margarine has taken a huge slump—from 409 million pounds in 1949 to 275 million pounds in 1953. As the chart shows—cottonseed oil now supplies only 26 per cent of the oils used in margarine, compared with 57 per cent in 1949.

What does this mean to the cotton grower? The price paid the grower for cotton seed depends to a very large extent on the prices at which oil mills are able to sell oil, meal, linters, and hulls. When a competing product—soybeans—takes over markets that formerly belonged to cotton seed, it is a serious matter. Markets lost are often hard to recapture.

But perhaps even more serious is the huge supply of cottonseed products now held by the Government. Here are figures on the cottonseed oil and meal that have gone into CCC stocks during the last three years:

	Oil	*Meal*
1951-52	136.2 million pounds	175,000 tons
1952-53	874.4 million pounds	1,194,000 tons
1953-54	360.0 million pounds	498,000 tons
3-year total	1,370.6 million pounds	1,867,000 tons

The Government has put $365 million, exclusive of costs of administration and storage, into cottonseed products. Today CCC holds enough cottonseed oil to make more than a billion pounds of margarine. It still has $250 million tied up in cottonseed products.

So far the public hasn't taken much notice of the Government's huge stocks of cottonseed products. To date the Government's actual losses on cotton seed are not large. Last year's loss amounted to a sizable $20,300,000. Over a 21-year period, however, the net loss is only $5 million because of gains in earlier years. But with uncontrolled soybean production and soybeans crowding cotton seed out of its markets, the outlook is rather dismal.

There is imminent danger that cotton seed may be classed with butter as a sponge on the Government. Remember how the public condemned the butter program. And how the outcry against the program finally led to a reduction of the dairy farmers' supports from 90 per cent to 75 per cent of parity. Well, the Government now has more pounds of cottonseed oil on its hands than it has butter, although the value of the cottonseed oil is not as great. And it may lose heavily on these stocks. If this happens, we fear the cotton program as a whole will be publicly condemned—not only the cotton seed part of it, but the support program for lint as well. It would make the fight to continue lint supports at 90 per cent of parity still harder—perhaps a lost cause.

No cotton grower favors a lower price for cotton seed if there is any way to avoid it—and neither does The Progressive Farmer. But we should keep in mind that growers get five or six times as much from lint as from cotton seed. It would be foolish to allow the much less important seed loan to jeopardize our all-important lint program.

What can be done about it? First of all, something should be done about soybeans. Soybean industry leaders claim there is no surplus of soybean products. There is, however, a surplus of total oil seed products. And the only reason there isn't an actual surplus of soybean products is that price relationships under the support program have driven cottonseed products into the loan, leaving a much larger share of the domestic market to soybeans.

It now seems that the Government may drastically lower price supports on all oil seed crops—if not entirely drop them. This would allow cotton seed to compete with soybeans in the market on a more favorable basis. But it might also mean much lower prices for both commodities.

There is no easy answer to the problem. What we suggest here is that cotton producers take a good look at it—and try to find a solution. So far we have "swept it under the rug." Like Scarlett O'Hara in *Gone With the Wind,* when she met an unpleasant situation, we have said, "I'll think about that tomorrow." But we can't go along on the present basis much longer without serious consequences.

III

The Consumer

12. PECUNIARY CANONS OF TASTE *

OF ALL the works of Thorstein Veblen, *The Theory of the Leisure Class* is undoubtedly the most widely read. In it Veblen held up to penetrating examination the habits of consumption of those whose incomes enabled them to live above the subsistence level. He saw the wealthy ostentatiously spending their incomes to impress the poor, and the poor striving to emulate the wealthy. "Honorific expenditure" or "conspicuous consumption," with which he deals in this selection, is as much a part of our spending habits today as it was in the 1890's when this passage was written.

THE CAUTION has already been repeated more than once, that while the regulating norm of consumption is in large part the requirement of conspicuous waste, it must not be understood that the motive on which the consumer acts in any given case is this principle in its bald, unsophisticated form. Ordinarily his motive is a wish to conform to established usage, to avoid unfavourable notice and comment, to live up to the accepted canons of decency in the kind, amount, and grade of goods consumed, as well as in the decorous employment of his time

* From *The Theory of the Leisure Class* by Thorstein Veblen. Copyright 1899, 1912 by The Macmillan Company. Reprinted by permission of The Viking Press, Inc., New York.

The author (1857-1929) was a teacher of economics in many American colleges, including the University of Chicago, Stanford University and the New School for Social Research. Author of *The Theory of the Leisure Class, The Theory of Business Enterprise, The Engineers and the Price System,* and *Essays in Our Changing Order.*

and effort. In the common run of cases this sense of prescriptive usage is present in the motives of the consumer and exerts a direct constraining force, especially as regards consumption carried on under the eyes of observers. But a considerable element of prescriptive expensiveness is observable also in consumption that does not in any appreciable degree become known to outsiders—as, for instance, articles of underclothing, some articles of food, kitchen utensils, and other household apparatus designed for service rather than for evidence. In all such useful articles a close scrutiny will discover certain features which add to the cost and enhance the commercial value of the goods in question, but do not proportionately increase the serviceability of these articles for the material purposes which alone they obstensibly are designed to serve.

Under the selective surveillance of the law of conspicuous waste there grows up a code of accredited canons of consumption, the effect of which is to hold the consumer up to a standard of expensiveness and wastefulness in his consumption of goods and in his employment of time and effort. This growth of prescriptive usage has an immediate effect upon economic life, but it has also an indirect and remoter effect upon conduct in other respects as well. Habits of thought with respect to the expression of life in any given direction unavoidably affect the habitual view of what is good and right in life in other directions also. In the organic complex of habits of thought which make up the substance of an individual's conscious life the economic interest does not lie isolated and distinct from all other interests. Something, for instance, has already been said of its relation to the canons of reputability.

The principle of conspicuous waste guides the formation of habits of thought as to what is honest and reputable in life and in commodities. In so doing, this principle will traverse other norms of conduct which do not primarily have to do with the code of pecuniary honour, but which have, directly or incidentally, an economic significance of some magnitude. So the canon of honorific waste may, immediately or remotely, influence the sense of duty, the sense of beauty, the sense of ultility, the sense of devotional or ritualistic fitness, and the scientific sense of truth.

It is scarcely necessary to go into a discussion here of the particular points at which, or the particular manner in which, the canon of honorific expenditure habitually traverses the canons of moral conduct. The matter is one which has received large attention and illustration at the hands of those whose office is it to watch and admonish with respect to any departures from the accepted code of morals. In modern communities, where the dominant economic and legal feature of the community's life is the institution of private property, one of the salient features of the code of morals is the sacredness of property. There needs no insistence or illustration to gain assent to the proposition that the habit of holding private property inviolate is traversed by the other habit of seeking wealth for the sake of the good repute to be gained through its conspicuous consumption. Most offences against property, especially offences of an appreciable magnitude, come under this head. It is also a matter of common notoriety and byword that in offences which result in a large accession of property to the offender he does not ordinarily incur the extreme penalty or the extreme obloquy with which his offence would be visited on the ground of the naïve moral code alone. The thief or swindler who has gained great wealth by his delinquency has a better chance than the small thief of escaping the rigorous penalty of the law; and some good repute accrues to him from his increased wealth and from his spending the irregularly acquired possessions in a seemly manner. A well-bred expenditure of his booty especially appeals with great effect to persons of a cultivated sense of the proprieties, and goes far to mitigate the sense of moral turpitude with which his dereliction is viewed by them. It may be noted also—and it is more immediately to the point—that we are all inclined to condone an offence against property in the case of a man whose motive is the worthy one of providing the means of a "decent" manner of life for his wife and children. If it is added that the wife has been "natured in the lap of luxury," that is accepted as an additional extenuating circumstance. That is to say, we are prone to condone such an offence where its aim is the honorific one of enabling the offender's wife to perform for him such an amount of vicarious consumption of time and substance as is demanded by the standard of pecuniary decency. In such a case the habit of approving the accustomed degree of conspicuous waste traverses the habit of deprecating violations of ownership, to the extent even of sometimes leaving the award of praise or blame uncertain. This is peculiarly true where the dereliction involves an appreciable predatory or piratical element.

This topic need scarcely be pursued farther here; but the remark may not be out of place that all that considerable body of morals that clusters about the concept of an inviolable ownership is itself a psychological precipitate of the traditional meritoriousness of wealth. And it should be added that this wealth which is held sacred is valued primarily for the sake of the good repute to be got through its conspicuous consumption.

The bearing of pecuniary decency upon the scientific spirit or the quest of knowledge will be taken up in some detail in a separate chapter. Also as regards the sense of devout or ritual merit and adequacy in this connection, little need be said in this place. That topic will also come up incidentally in a later chapter. Still, this usage of honorific expenditure has much to say in shaping popular tastes as to what is right and meritorious in sacred matters, and the bearing of the principle of conspicuous waste upon some of the commonplace devout observances and conceits may therefore be pointed out.

. . . . .

These canons of reputability have had a similar, but more far-reaching and more specifically determinable, effect upon the popular sense of beauty or serviceability in consumable goods. The requirements of pecuniary decency have, to a very appreciable extent, influenced the sense of beauty and of utility in articles of use or beauty. Articles are to an extent preferred for use on account of their being conspicuously wasteful; they are felt to be serviceable somewhat in proportion as they are wasteful and ill adapted to their ostensible use.

The utility of articles valued for their beauty depends closely upon the expensiveness of the articles. A homely illustration will bring out this dependence. A hand-wrought silver spoon, of a commercial value of some ten to twenty dollars, is not ordinarily more serviceable—in the first sense of the word—than a machine-made spoon of the same material. It may not even be more serviceable than a machine-made spoon of some "base" metal, such as aluminum, the value of which may be no more than some ten to twenty cents. The former of the two utensils is, in fact, commonly a less effective contrivance for its ostensible purpose than the latter. The objection is of course ready to hand that, in taking this view of the matter, one of the chief uses, if not the chief use, of the costlier spoon is ignored; the hand-wrought spoon gratifies our taste, our sense of the beautiful, while that made by machinery out of the base metal has no useful office beyond a brute efficiency. The facts are no doubt as the objection states them, but it will be evident on reflection that the objection is after all more plausible than conclusive. It appears (1) that while the different materials of which the two spoons are made each possesses beauty and serviceability for the purpose for which it is used, the material of the hand-wrought spoon is some one hundred times more valuable than the baser metal, without very greatly excelling the latter in intrinsic beauty of grain or colour, and without being in any appreciable degree superior in point of mechanical serviceability; (2) if a close inspection should show that the supposed hand-wrought spoon were in reality only a very clever imitation of hand-wrought goods, but an imitation so cleverly wrought as to give the same impression of line and surface to any but a minute examination by a trained eye, the utility of the article, including the gratification which the user derives from its contemplation as an object of beauty, would immediately decline by some eighty or ninety per cent, or even more; (3) if the two spoons are, to a fairly close observer, so nearly identical in appearance that the lighter weight of the spurious article alone betrays it, this identity of form and colour will scarcely add to the value of the machine-made spoon, nor appreciably enhance the gratification of the user's "sense of beauty" in contemplating it, so long as the cheaper spoon is not a novelty, and so long as it can be procured at a nominal cost.

The case of the spoons is typical. The superior gratification derived from the use and contemplation of costly and supposedly beautiful products is, commonly, in great measure a gratification of our sense of costliness masquerading under the name of beauty. Our higher appreciation of the superior article is an appreciation of its superior honorific character, much more frequently than it is an unsophisticated appreciation of its beauty. The requirement of conspicuous wastefulness is not commonly present, consciously, in our canons of taste, but it is none the less present as a constraining norm selectively shaping and sustaining our sense of what is beautiful, and guiding our discrimination with respect to what may legitimately be approved as beautiful and what may not.

It is at this point, where the beautiful and the honorific meet and blend, that a discrimination between serviceability and wastefulness is most difficult in any concrete case. It frequently happens that an article which serves the honorific purpose of conspicuous waste is at the same time a beautiful object; and the same application of labour to which it owes its utility for the former purpose may, and often does, go to give beauty of form and colour to the article. The question is further complicated by the fact that many objects, as, for instance, the precious stones and metals and some other materials used for adornment and decoration, owe their utility as items of conspicuous waste to an antecedent utility as objects of beauty. Gold, for instance, has a high degree of sensuous beauty; very many if not most of the highly prized works of art are intrinsically beautiful, though often with material qualification; the like is true of some stuffs used for clothing, of some landscapes, and of many other things in less degree. Except for this intrinsic beauty which they possess, these objects would scarcely have been coveted as they are, or have become monopolised objects of pride to their possessors and users. But the utility of these things to the possessor is commonly due less to their intrinic beauty than to the honour which their possession and consumption confers, or to the obloquy which it wards off.

Apart from their serviceability in other respects, these objects are beautiful and have a utility as such; they are valuable on this account if they can be appropriated or monopolised; they are, therefore, coveted as valuable possessions, and their exclusive enjoyment gratifies the possessor's sense of pecuniary superiority at the same time that their contemplation gratifies his sense of beauty. But their beauty, in the naïve sense of the word, is the occasion rather than the ground of their monopolisation or of their commercial value. "Great as is the sensuous beauty of gems, their rarity and price adds an expression of distinction to them, which they would never have if they were cheap." There is, indeed, in the common run of cases under this head, relatively little incentive to the exclusive possession and use of these beautiful things, except on the ground of their honorific character as items of conspicuous waste. Most objects of this general class, with the partial exception of articles of personal adornment, would serve all other purposes than the honorific one equally well, whether owned by the person viewing them or not; and even as regards personal ornaments it is to be added that their chief purpose is to lend éclat to the person of their wearer (or owner) by comparison with other persons who are compelled to do without. The æsthetic serviceability of objects of beauty is not greatly nor universally heightened by possession.

The generalisation for which the discussion so far affords ground is that any valuable object in order to appeal to our sense of beauty must conform to the requirements of beauty and of expensiveness both. But this is not all. Beyond this the canon of expensiveness also affects our tastes in such a way as to inextricably blend the marks of expensiveness, in our appreciation, with the beautiful features of the object, and to subsume the resultant effect under the head of an appreciation of beauty simply. The marks of expensiveness come to be accepted as beautiful features of the expensive articles. They are pleasing as being marks of honorific costliness, and the pleasure which they afford on this score blends with that afforded by the beautiful form and colour of the object; so that we often declare that an article of apparel, for instance, is "perfectly lovely," when pretty much all that an analysis of the æsthetic value of the article would leave ground for is the declaration that it is pecuniarily honorific.

This blending and confusion of the elements of expensiveness and of beauty is, perhaps, best exemplified in articles of dress and of household furniture. The code of reputability in matters of dress decides what shapes, colours, materials, and general effects in human apparel are for the time to be accepted as suitable; and departures from the code are offensive to our taste, supposedly as being departures from æsthetic truth. The approval with which we look upon fashionable attire is by no means to be accounted pure make-believe. We readily, and for the most part with utter sincerity, find those things pleasing that are in vogue. Shaggy dress-stuffs and pronounced colour effects, for instance, offend us at times when the vogue is goods of a high, glossy finish and neutral colours. A fancy bonnet of this year's model unquestionably appeals to our sensibilities to-day much more forcibly than an equally fancy bonnet of the model of last year; although when viewed in the perspective of a quarter of a century, it would, I apprehend, be a matter of the utmost difficulty to award the palm for intrinsic beauty to the one rather than to the other of these structures. So, again, it may be remarked that, considered simply in their physical juxtaposition with the human form, the high gloss of a gentleman's hat or of a patent-leather shoe has no more of intrinsic beauty than a similarly high gloss on a threadbare sleeve; and yet there is no question but that all well-bred people (in the Occidental civilised communities) instinctively and unaffectedly cleave to the one as a phenomenon of great beauty, and eschew the other as offensive to every sense to which it can appeal. It is extremely doubtful if any one could be induced to wear such a contrivance as the high hat of civilised society, except for some urgent reason based on other than æsthetic grounds.

By further habituation to an appreciative perception of the marks of expensiveness in goods, and by habitually identifying beauty with reputability, it comes about that a beautiful article which is not expensive is accounted not beautiful. In this way it has happened, for instance, that some beautiful flowers pass conventionally for offensive weeds; others that can be cultivated with relative ease are accepted and admired by the lower middle class, who can afford no more expensive luxuries of this kind; but these varieties are rejected as vulgar by those people who are better able to pay for expensive flowers and who are educated to a higher schedule of pecuniary beauty in the florist's products; while still other flowers, of no greater intrinsic beauty than these, are cultivated at great cost and call out much admiration from flower-lovers whose tastes have been matured under the critical guidance of a polite environment.

13. CONSUMERS REPORT ON CHILDREN'S SHOES *

MANY words have been written about the plight of the consumer in a world where the commodities he buys are often of such complexity that he cannot intelligently evaluate their qualities. He does not know whether the very expensive sun glasses are any better than those sold in the five-and-ten-cent store, or whether the widely advertised "tonic" will bring a better tomorrow or merely a mild state of intoxication. He cannot expect much help from the seller of the product. Advertising all too often tends to be deceptive or superficial. There is, however, one source of information available to the consumer, the rating agencies. These concerns test various products in as objective a fashion as possible. They expose fake claims and wage perpetual warfare against false and misleading advertising. They compare rival products as to price, quality, and performance; then present the results of the tests to the consumer. The following on children's shoes is a good example of the work of one of these organizations.

TWO HUNDRED and thirty-eight children in four New England orphanages have given 238 pairs of shoes one of the largest actual performance tests in the history of Consumers Union.

Fourteen pairs of each of 16 different brands were worn by school boys and girls from 5 to 12 years old. Boys alone wore one other brand—the *Official Boy Scout* shoe. The first examinations of the shoes were made at the orphanages after three weeks and after six weeks. All the shoes were examined in the laboratory after seven weeks wear, then they were returned to the children for further punishment. At the end of the twelve-week test period the shoes went back to the laboratory for detailed analysis and final ratings. The results:

Eight brands stood up generally well, nine brands were not so good. No one brand, however, was excellent in every respect.

The 17 brands tested are, in the opinion of shoe experts, the largest selling children's shoes. Except for *Pediformes,* which are not made in this style, all shoes were moccasin-style brown oxfords. The *Pediforme* shoes were conventional oxfords with sharkskin toe caps. The prices range from about $4 to about $9. All of the shoes in the top group of eight brands cost at least $6.45 but a relatively high price tag does not always mean good wearing qualities. Four shoes selling for $6.45 or more did not win a place in the top group.

* Reprinted with permission from *Consumer Reports,* April, 1955, published by Consumers Union.

A KIDDIE'S HEEL

As might be expected, heels wore out oftener than any other part, repairs being called for before the end of the twelve weeks in 28% of all the pairs tested. Next most troublesome were the soles, with 23% replaced. Only ten pairs—a little more than 4%—of the shoes had such serious troubles with the insole, the box toe or the uppers that they had to be discarded before the test was finished.

Are leather or composition soles better? The U.S. Department of Agriculture in its *Farmers' Bulletin No. 1523,* "Leather Shoes: Selection and Care," says that leather generally gives better insulation and ventilation than composition soles. The better synthetics, according to the *Farmers' Bulletin,* show greater resistance to wear and water penetration than leather. CU's experience in part confirms this. The 113 leather-shod children succeeded in wearing through 28 pairs, or 25%. The 125 youngsters who walked on *Neolite, Avonite, Everlite, Searolite, Kinolite, Interflex* and rubber cord sent only 22% of these to the repair shop.

But these percentages don't prove that synthetic soles are necessarily better than leather. CU's laboratory staff found that the best leathers wore better than the best synthetics. For example, the only brand that didn't require a single resoling among the 14 pairs tested had leather soles—and the only two soles that earned a general rating of "Excellent," based not only on good wear, but also on lack of deformation and separation, were leather. Five of the top eight brands had leather soles. (According to the *Farmers' Bulletin,* chrome-tanned leather is the longest-wearing sole leather.)

All of the synthetics tested tended to spread slightly, changing their original dimensions. This enlargement of shoe soles is called creep. It is sometimes serious enough to break the stitches and loosen the sole, and it frequently causes the uppers to curl and lose their shape. Leather, on the other hand, is a fairly stable material.

One fact is beyond argument: The life of the average shoe depends mainly on the child. An inferior shoe on a young lady bookworm will outlast the finest on the far-ranging feet of the gang's best shortstop. CU's tests showed which of the test brands were likely to give longer wear under hard use.

WHAT MACHINES CANNOT DO

CU last reported on children's shoes four years ago. Laboratory machines were used then to test resistance to scuffing, and probable durability of the soles. The shoes were also taken apart and their construction studied.

No machine, however, can approximate the action of a child's foot, let alone a complete child. The typical child's shoe will experience more than the parents can recall or imagine when they have the first pair gilded. These jet-propelled leather casings may feel the dew of morning grass, the mud of city gutters, the bark of tree trunks, the impact of the tin can that asked to be kicked, the friction of the hard dirt where a circle is described for marbles or rectangles for hopscotch. The outer surface will collect toothpaste, soapsuds, soup, rain, snow, salt, manure, soda pop, ice cream, paint, oil and grease. The child's shoe is a diary of each day, and no two days are exactly alike. CU estimated that 84 days of this kind of wear would tell a good deal about the 17 brands of children's shoes.

The performance test was decided on after conferences with technical experts in federal agencies and private organizations. There was general agreement that actual wear by children was the only reliable way to test children's shoes. CU's first problem was to find groups of children of the right age to wear the shoes under controlled and observable conditions. In Massachusetts and New Hampshire, four private orphanages meeting the requirements of the test were found. They enabled CU to plan a balanced design for the test with nearly equal numbers of boys and girls, of young children and older ones, of city children and country children. All of the institutions welcomed the opportunity to participate in the tests.

The *Official Boy Scout* shoe is about twice as heavy as an ordinary child's shoe, and it is not intended for girls' wear, therefore the 14 test pairs of this brand were worn only by boys. Because boys are generally harder on their shoes than girls, the test results were adjusted accordingly. Three different manufacturers (International, Brown and General) make presumably identical shoes to specifications of the Boy Scouts. CU's test shoes all came from International (as shown by the label inside), the largest of the manufacturers of children's shoes making this brand.

FITTING THE CHILDREN

The 238 pairs of shoes and an extra pair of each brand to be preserved unworn for comparison, were bought at retail stores in Massachusetts, New Hampshire and New York. Because wear is materially affected by fit, CU took special pains in matching the shoes to the feet of the 238 children. Two veteran shoe fitters from independent shoe stores in Fitchburg, Massachusetts, and Manchester, New Hampshire, were employed for this work. The pair worked together and only when they agreed that the fit was correct, was the child given his test shoes to wear. The foot of the standing child was first measured for length and width. Several different brands of the proper size were then tried. There are slight but often significant differences in the lasts of different manufacturers which affect the volume and proportions of the shoe. For example, the 12C shoes of Manufacturer X might feel loose on a child's feet but the 12C made by Manufacturer Y might feel uncomfortably tight on the same child's feet. Another complication in fitting is that not all manufacturers furnish a complete range of widths.

Sometimes the fitters could not agree that any shoe on hand was a perfect fit. When that impasse occurred, a trip was made back to the store for more shoes.

One week after the test began the senior fitter returned to each of the four homes for a checkup. The initial fitting had been done so carefully that only about half a dozen children had any complaints about their new shoes, and these were easily remedied by the use of concealed pads.

Several other precautions were taken for the sake of uniformity. CU provided all of the children with nylon stretch socks at the time of fitting to insure that the way the shoes fitted would not be affected by differences in the kinds of sock worn. Matching laces for replacements were provided. Arrangements were made for a weekly polishing, with all of the children using the same polish.

THE SCORING SYSTEM

Three of CU's staff members were trained in the use of an elaborate scoring system that required some 200,000 recorded observations. Since there was no standard to follow, the scorers sought expert counsel in drafting their list of check-points and values. They consulted with government agencies, several manufacturers and custom shoemakers, a shoe trade journal editor and two orthopedists.

In the final evaluation of the worn shoes, 30 different items were judged as to the degree of failure, the major areas being the tread surface (outer sole, heel and shank), the upper structure, upper leather, insole, and midsole or bottom filler.

Interestingly, no failures were found in 6 of the 30 separate items in the scoring system. For example, none of the 238 pairs lost a rubber heel and in none did the insole crack or break.

Defects observed when the shoes were returned to the laboratory for a minute inspection after the seventh week were weighted to count more heavily than the same defects observed only at the end of the 12-week test. Even though many don't, children's shoes ordinarily should last for at least 12 weeks.

THE GENTLER SEX

The final scoring confirmed the expected—that boys are much harder on their shoes than girls are. Feminine vigor asserted itself comparably only at the heels, which were almost as much worn as the boys' were.

Eleven brands were of Goodyear welt construction, the generally preferred design in shoes. The other six were three-sole stitchdowns *(Sundial-Bonnie Laddie, Red Goose, Weatherbird, Sears, Thom McAn* and *Poll-Parrot).* The stitchdown design is commonly used in cheaper shoes. The simplest and cheapest stitchdown process makes resoling virtually impossible without affecting fit adversly, but the three-sole stitchdown does permit replacement, although not so easily as welt construction does.

The three-sole stitchdown has a full midsole of fiberboard or leather. With the support of these midsoles the shoes held their shape well during twelve weeks of wear. In Goodyear welt construction the space between the insole and the outsole is filled with granulated cork, bonded by an asphaltic or resinous adhesive. Under the weight of the body and the heat of the foot, the bottom filler forms depressions and ridges that correspond to the shape of the foot. Although some conformation is perfectly all right and even adds to shoe comfort, badly misshapen fillers can cause discomfort. No fillers in the CU test shifted enough to receive the maximum penalty but some were on the margin. The moral of this lesson is that very heavy children should wear the brands with the best fillers, *Pediforme, Official Boy Scout,* and *Stride-Rite,* or *Pied Piper* which has a unique welt construction which does not need a cork filler.

DURABLE SHANKS AND COUNTERS

Some methods of shoe construction, once regarded as relatively poor, made surprisingly good records. For instance, wooden shanks stood up quite well. However, some wooden shanks in individual shoes were found broken, whereas no steel shank was deformed in any way. The shank, made of steel or wood, supports the arch. It lies between the inner and outer soles. Only five brands *(Jumping-Jack Seniors, Little*

Yankee, Pied Piper, Stride-Rite and *Penney's)* had steel shanks. All others had wood, except *Kali-sten-iks.* As in CU's tests four years ago, *Kali-sten-iks* uses built-up rigid leather in place of the conventional shank.

An unexpected finding was the good performance of fiber board and impregnated paper counters, used in some shoes instead of leather. The counter, a vital part of the rear structure, is the concealed stiffener at the back of the heel and beneath the outer leather (called the quarter). Dissection revealed that nine brands, including all but *Kali-sten-iks* in the color check group, had paper or fiber-board counters. They did very well—in fact, there was very little back failure among any of the 17 brands. Of course the boy who jams his feet into shoes without loosening the laces is going to break down any material.

Probably as important as any other shoe part is the insole—the structure around which a Goodyear welt shoe is built. When the insole deforms by curling or by changes in dimension, the flat base which the insole should provide is destroyed, or the shoe is effectively made smaller, resulting in distortions of the foot and consequent discomfort. Generally the insoles of the Goodyear welt shoes performed their function very well except in the *Wards* and *Kinney's* where curl often occurred. In the case of the three-sole stitchdown shoes, where the insole is not stitched but rather is glued in place, considerable curl and deformation can occur when insoles get wet. In Goodyear welt shoes, the insoles are sewed down and resist this effect.

Although the box toes of *Official Boy Scout* and *Pediforme* shoes withstood heaven knows what and largely retained their youthful curves, most toes showed some effects of riotous living. Collapse of a box toe is not good for the foot. The pushed-down toe reduces the inside space of the shoe and thus changes the fit.

As experienced parents know, the best antidote for scuffed toes is the sharkskin cap. *Pediforme,* a toe cap style, and *Jumping-Jacks,* a moccasin style, had the only sharkskin toe caps in the test but several other brands can be purchased with sharkskin tip.

BUYING SHOES

Getting a correct fit is often difficult. The salesman can do his part if he is thoroughly experienced, unhurried, and not willing to sell a dubious size or last when he doesn't have the correct one. This kind of salesman will, unfortunately, be recognized as far from universal.

The manufacturer can help materially if he has provided a full range of lengths and widths and a variety of lasts to fit the many shapes and

Ratings of Children's Shoes

E = Excellent; G = Good; F = Fair; P = Poor

	Brand	Model Number	Size Range	Price	Sole	Heel	Shank	Insole	Midsole or Bottom Filler	Scuff Resistance	UPPER STRUCTURE Linings	Counter	Stitching	Bo Tol
√	*Pediforme,* Pediforme Shoe Co., NYC	E414	8½-12 A-EE 12½-3 A-EE 3½-4 A-EE	$7.95 8.95 9.45	G	P	E	E	E	E	E	G	E	G
√	*Jumping-Jacks Sr.,* Vaisey-Bristol Shoe Co., Monett, Mo.	212	8½-12 A-EE 12½-4 A-EE	6.45 7.45	G	G	G	E	G	E	E	G	G	G
√	*Little Yankee,* Yankee Shoemaker, Div. Sam Smith Shoe Corp., Newmarket, N. H.	1209 2209	8½-12 A-E 12½-3 A-E	6.50 6.95	E	P	E	E	G	G	G	E	G	G
√	*Kali-sten-iks,* Gilbert Shoe Co., Thiensville, Wis.	2913	8½-12 A-D 12½-3 A-D	7.95 8.95	G	F	G	E	G	G	G	G	G	G
√	*Pied Piper,* Pied Piper Shoe Co., Wausau, Wis.	4953 4954	8½-12 A-EE 12½-4 AA-E	7.95 8.95	E	P	E	G	E	F	G	G	E	G
√	*Official Boy Scout,* International Shoe Co., St. Louis	S-22	11-13½ A-E 1-6 A-E	7.45 8.45	G	E	E	G	E	F	G	G	P	E
√	*Buster Brown,* Buster Brown, Div. Brown Shoe Co., St. Louis	G810	8½-12 A-EE 12½-3 AA-EE	6.50 6.95	F	F	E	E	G	G	G	F	G	F
√	**Stride-Rite,* Green Shoe Mfg. Co., Boston	D4205 5200	8½-12 A-EEE 12½-3 A-EE	6.95 7.95	F	F	E	E	E	G	G	G	G	G
	Sundial-Bonnie Laddie Sundial Shoe Co., Div. International Shoe Co., Manchester, N. H.	7171	8½-12 A-E 12½-3 AA-E	6.45 6.95	F	G	G	P	G	G	G	G	G	G

Penney's J. C. Penney	20-8166	8½-12 A-E 12½-3 AA-E	5.50 5.90	P	E	E	E	G	F	G	G	F	G
Red Goose, Friedman-Shelby, Div. International Shoe Co., St. Louis	3560-2	8½-12 A-E 12½-3 AA-E	5.95 6.45-6.95	F	G	F	P	G	F	G	F	G	E
Weatherbird, Peters, Div. International Shoe Co., St. Louis	6975-2	8½-12 A-EE 12½-3 AA-EE	5.95 6.45-6.95	F	G	G	P	G	F	G	G	G	G
Sears 4-Star Feature Biltwell, Sears-Roebuck	1319	8½-12 B-D 12½-4 A-D	4.90 4.90	F	F	F	F	G	F	G	P	E	G
Thom McAn Melville Shoe Corp., NYC	MV655	8½-3 B-D	3.99	P	P	G	F	G	G	F	F	G	G
Poll-Parrott, Roberts, Johnson & Rand, Div. International Shoe Co., St. Louis	8133-3	8½-12 A-EE 12½-3 AA-EE	5.95 6.95	F	G	F	P	G	F	G	G	E	G
***Wards Best Quality,* Montgomery Ward	4620	8½-13½ B-D 1-4 B-D	5.79 plus postage	F	F	E	F	G	G	F	G	F	P
Kinney Educator, G. R. Kinney Co., mfd. by J. Landis Shoe Co., Palmyra, Pa.	2415 3415	8½-12 BC-DE 12½-3 BC-DE	4.99 4.99	P	P	G	F	G	F	F	G	F	G

* This brand is rated at the bottom of the check group because so many of the soles and heels had to be replaced relatively early in the test. If sole and heel durability is not considered important for a particular child, the shoe would rate among the best.

** Only C width is listed in some Wards catalogs.

In the table above, the 17 brands of shoes tested are listed in order of estimated overall quality. Checked (√) brands are of high overall quality. The 10 qualities which are letter-graded for each brand are the major factors scored; however, 20 other factors entered into the overall ratings. The individual qualities are listed to guide your buying. If your son is hard on soles, you may want to consider those brands which give particularly good sole performance, such as *Jumping-Jacks Sr., Pied Piper* or *Little Yankee*. If the child doesn't wear out soles and heels, then some other brand may be suitable. If he has an exceptionally wide or narrow foot, you should be most interested in the brands with wide size ranges. If scuffed toes is the problem, then ask for a model with a sharkskin-capped toe. If your child has a tendency to "pronation" or flat feet, then one of the several brands offering excellent shank performance may be desirable.

sizes of young feet. Unfortunately most brands are limited to a single last for a given model and a few to a narrow range of widths.

The child is not a reliable judge. Even adults make wrong judgments when choosing their own shoes.

What's more important is an unhurried decision. It is wise to inquire whether the child may test the shoes at home, on a rug, for half an hour two days in a row with the understanding that you may return the shoes if they are uncomfortable.

The long-established rule is to leave about ¾ inch of space in the toe of a new shoe. Plenty of width is essential—the foot should not be pushing against the sides. The inside of the shoe should be carefully explored to discover any rough edges or even heavy stitching that could cause discomfort or blisters.

According to the U.S. Dept. of Agriculture, shoes of correct shape are broad and round at the toe and straight along the inner edge. When the two shoes of a pair are placed together, side by side, the more the inner edges diverge or curve toward the outside of the shoe, the more unnatural the shoe's shape.

THE EVER-GROWING FOOT

Children's shoes are generally outgrown in three to five months. More than half the shoes in CU's test were judged to require replacement because of size after twelve weeks.

Shoes should be replaced when they no longer fit or are too badly worn to justify repair. If the end of the child's big toe is pushing near the leather, if the sides are bulging or if the heel is too tight, it's time for a new pair. By using a very small mirror and a flashlight, you can see on the insole the marks left by the child's toes. An even clearer check is provided if the inside of the shoe is lightly dusted with talcum and the child's sock toe dampened. Once the child puts on the shoe and stands, the position of the toes is recorded.

When shoes have become outgrown for regular wear, one orthopedist suggests that the forward half of the shoe's toe be sliced off. This creates a nicely ventilated auxiliary pair for indoor use.

If your child is likely to wear out his shoes before he outgrows them, you would do well to study the strong points of the eight top brands on pages 144-145 and try a brand that is rated highest where your children's shoes have proved weakest. For example, boys hard on soles might be fitted with *Little Yankee* or *Pied Piper* shoes.

PROLONGING LIFE

All the experts agree that it helps shoes if the soles are kept flat when the shoes are not being worn. Synthetic soles are particularly apt to curl. Some shoes emerged from the CU test with a stubby kinship to rocker-bottomed wooden shoes. The *Boy Scout* shoes, uniformly as a brand, developed a pronounced curl during the twelve weeks of test.

Admittedly the parent who has rarely bothered to tree his own shoes may not be the ideal instructor for his child, but maybe the old dog can still learn. A properly-shaped shoe tree is probably best, but a handful of tightly crumpled newspaper also works.

Wet shoes may be ruined if they are dried out on radiators or steam pipes, or in ovens. According to the Department of Agriculture, the right treatment is to wash off dirt with tepid water, wipe with a dry rag, apply castor oil lightly with cheesecloth and rub in. Then straighten the shoes, stuff them with newspaper, and let them dry slowly at room temperature. When they are dry they can be polished. Regular polishing is good for leather and virtually unheard of on the far side of puberty.

THE HEALTH ANGLE

The shoe industry has compiled and published a wealth of data on its operations and products. *Leather and Shoes,* an influential trade journal, has vigorously campaigned for a research organization sponsored by manufacturers and retailers to correct faults and to publicize facts. The Federal Trade Commission has issued many "cease and desist" orders against false, deceptive and misleading advertising of children's shoes; the National Shoe Manufacturers Association, in fact, published a pamphlet digest of the FTC rulings. Among other things, the FTC prohibited claims that certain shoes for children would "help insure the correct growth of their tender little feet" or would prevent flat feet, abnormalities and deformities.

One of the CU's orthopedic consultants recommends that shoes and socks be taken off at the end of the school day and the feet turned loose in play shoes, sneakers, sandals or nothing.

"Children's socks generally become damp or even wet from perspiration during the day," he explained. "But most youngsters keep wearing them until they go to bed. Can you imagine anyone keeping gloves on his sweating hands all day long, even in very cold weather? The feet, like the hands, should be allowed to breathe and cool off."

Once in a great while, the consultant said, pain in the foot may signal the start of a disease of the hip or knee in which early treatment is vital. If such pain hits a child who has not had trouble before, medical advice should be sought. Also meriting investigation is a child's tendency to push out one side of the shoe. Little things like a tendency to lopsided heels are no cause for concern.

---

14. FIXED COSTS OF LIVING *

THE FOLLOWING two selections are concerned with the relationship between income and consumer expenditures. Selection 15 reviews past experience in order to assess the predictability of this relationship. Selection 14 considers an important factor (fixed commitments) which may modify the effect of income changes on consumption expenditures.

SINCE the beginning of the year, merchants have been watching a strange phenomenon. Take-home pay is somewhat higher than a year ago, but retail sales are at a slightly lower level.

Salesmen get the blame when sales lag, especially when incomes are rising. This year, however, before blaming their salesmen, businessmen might take a closer look at consumers' income. Why? Because all money included as disposable income of consumers (personal income after taxes) is not currently available for spending. A good part of it is taken by "consumers' fixed costs."

WHAT ARE FIXED COSTS?

No clear line can be drawn to separate consumers' fixed expenditures from other outlays. Spending patterns can be rigid without contracts to make them rigid. For example, the urge to keep up customary living standards makes a lot of expenditures seem fixed. So it is impossible to set up clear-cut boundaries for fixed spending. Some fixed expenditures, however, can be measured because they involve actual commitments or contracts.

The largest item among the contractual expenditures is debt service. Scheduled repayment and interest charges on installment and mortgage debt are fixed claims against income. Over the early part of 1954, it is estimated that on a yearly basis these claims on income totaled

* John R. Bunting, Jr. Reprinted with permission from the *Business Review* of the Federal Reserve Bank of Philadelphia.

The author (1925——) is Associate Economist of the Federal Reserve Bank of Philadelphia. Mr. Bunting is also a Lecturer in economics at Temple University. Author of numerous articles published in the monthly *Business Review* of the Federal Reserve Bank of Philadelphia.

$34.5 billion—more than three times the level at the end of World War II. Payments on instalment debt, principally for automobiles and major home appliances, have been running at about $28 billion, and scheduled payments on residential mortgage debt come to around $6.5 billion. Actually, mortgage repayment has been much larger, but only a fraction of the total represents regular payments. A big portion is prepayment and "roll over"—sell one home, pay off mortgage, then buy another home.

Contractual repayment of debt is not the only fixed claim against consumer incomes. Consumers have commitments for rents,[1] insurance, and property taxes. (Property taxes are not included as personal taxes in the calculation of disposable income by the Department of Commerce.) The total of all these claims has increased rapidly in the post-war period. So far in 1954 these costs total about $46.3 billion at an annual rate. The rise has been held down by the continued existence of rent controls in some areas; however, total payments on rents, insurance, and property taxes are at least double what they were in 1946.

FIXED COSTS ARE TAKING A LARGER SLICE OF INCOME

Of course, contractual payments would be expected to increase in the post-war period. Prices and incomes are both higher, so that the dollar total of fixed costs is not too meaningful. What is significant is that the proportion of income taken by contractual payments has also been rising. This means that consumers are giving themselves less leeway in the use of current income.

In 1946, only about 20 cents of the consumer's dollar was tied up in contract payments. This year the part that consumers have committed has climbed to 32 cents. Debt service charges alone took 14 cents out of their dollar for the first half of this year as compared with 6 cents at the end of the war. What this means to the consumer, of course, is that he has a lesser proportion of his disposable income available for the purchase of other goods and services. It is interesting, too, that this year is the first time that fixed costs absorbed as large a proportion of disposable income as in pre-war 1939.

UNCOMMITTED INCOME IS BELOW YEAR-AGO LEVELS

Consumers' fixed costs have increased actually and in relation to income each year since 1946. Generally, however, the yearly increase in

[1] In addition to contract rent payments, estimated rent of homeowners is included since this is an imputation and does not represent funds available for spending.

income has been larger in dollars than the rise in contractual payments. Therefore uncommitted income has tended to increase each year. This is illustrated in the chart below. The black portion above the line represents uncommitted income. It shows a rise in every year except 1949 and so far in 1954. The white portion below the zero line represents contract payments. These have gained each year. The black and white parts together equal disposable income for each year.

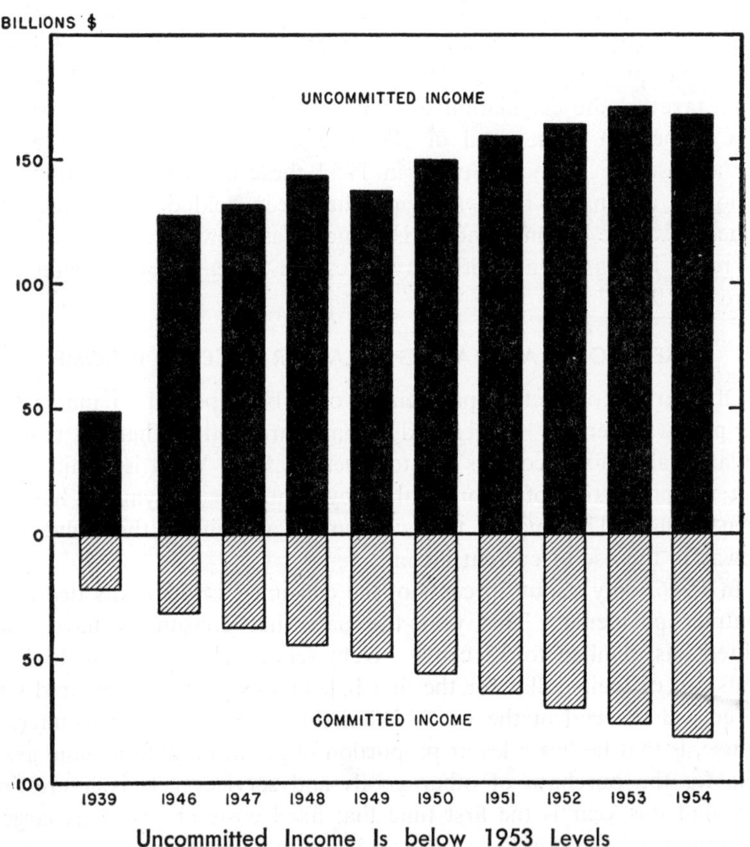

Uncommitted Income Is below 1953 Levels

The fact that fixed costs are rising more, dollarwise, than income in 1954 is important. It has special meaning for companies that relate their sales to general business conditions affecting them. If a company's product sells directly to consumers, purchasing power—as reflected in total disposable income—is usually the factor most closely associated with sales. This year, particularly, many firms comparing sales and income are faced with a discouraging trend. Sales are down and income is up. But does this indicate they are losing their share of the market?

UNCOMMITTED INCOME—A BETTER GUIDE?

Uncommitted income is possibly a better indication of ability to buy and therefore a more appropriate guide to the success or failure of a company to hold its share of the consumer market. Certainly, the fact that fixed commitments are rising faster than income must influence consumers' spending patterns.

Food merchants, especially, find a changed picture when their sales are compared with uncommitted income. So far in 1954, retail sales of food represent a smaller part of income than in 1953; however, when fixed costs are subtracted from income in each year the sales of food products takes a larger slice of the consumers' uncommitted dollar this year. On the other hand, automobile purchases are not taking so large a part of income this year by either standard. Department stores have nearly as much of the market in 1954 as in 1953, if consumers' uncommitted income is used. Furniture and major appliances are running ahead of last year's relationship with uncommitted income.

SUMMARY

Since the end of World War II, consumers have shown an increasing willingness to commit their incomes. Total contractual payments on mortgages and instalment debt, life insurance policies, property taxes, and rent have absorbed an increasing share of income in each successive year. Usually, however, income increased more than contractual payments; so that uncommitted income tended to rise. This year uncommitted income has declined, even though total income is slightly higher than a year ago. In other words, the rise in contractual payments is larger than the gain in income. Here at least is a partial explanation of the paradox that has been worrying businessmen—why sales have declined in the face of increased disposable income.

15. THE CONSUMER—PERVERSE OR PREDICTABLE *

For an introductory statement to this selection, see the headnote for Selection 14 on page 148.

The spending spurts and lags in 1950 and 1951 focused attention on the unpredictability of the post-war consumer. Furthermore, since 1947 evidence has been accumulating that consumers have been spending more than would be expected on the basis of the pre-war spending-income pattern. An upward shift in spending as related to disposable income has occurred since the war. But despite the considerable attention given the erratic changes in consumer spending, the data indicate a new spending-income pattern may be forming with aberrations from it thus far no greater than pre-war. Surprisingly, the relation between changes in income and changes in expenditures is nearly the same as before the war.

Time was when the level of consumer spending was not considered so difficult to predict; indeed, until fairly recently the subject of consumption was to some virtually closed. Consumer spending, it was believed, depended mainly upon the amount of disposable consumer income, and consumer income was dependent on what happened in the business and Government sectors of the economy. In other words, spending was a function of income. Consumer behavior, therefore, was not an independent force; individuals' spending responded to changes in income.

Recently all of this has changed. Consumer spending is no longer relegated to a passive role; instead it is emphasized that consumer spending is a most uncertain factor. Few any longer question the ability of the consumer to change his rate of spending irrespective of shifts in income.

THE CONSUMER HAS ASSERTED HIMSELF

The reasons for the new respect accorded the consumer are based broadly on the obvious effect that consumer actions have had on business activity at and subsequent to the outbreak of fighting in Korea and on the changed pattern of spending that has prevailed in post-war years.

The buying waves touched off by the invasion of South Korea in June

* John R. Bunting, Jr. Reprinted with permission from the *Philadelphia Federal Reserve Bank Business Review*, February, 1954, pp. 7-12.

For a brief biographical sketch of the author, see Selection 14 on page 148.

1950 and by the entry of the Chinese in the northern armies early in 1951 provided a dramatic illustration of the ability of consumer spending to change direction and to greatly influence economic activity.

The consumer stirred up quite a fuss, and more was coming. As if to show his capricious nature, he followed each spending spree with a saving spree. In the months following the buying wave in 1951, consumer spending declined noticeably despite a steady rise in personal income. As a consequence, inflationary pressures eased and stable conditions prevailed over the balance of the year. These changes in consumer spending had such a pervasive influence on business activity in 1951 that the instability of consumer spending became the subject of many year-end reports.

Less dramatic but equally significant evidence of the emergence of the consumer as an independent economic factor is illustrated in the

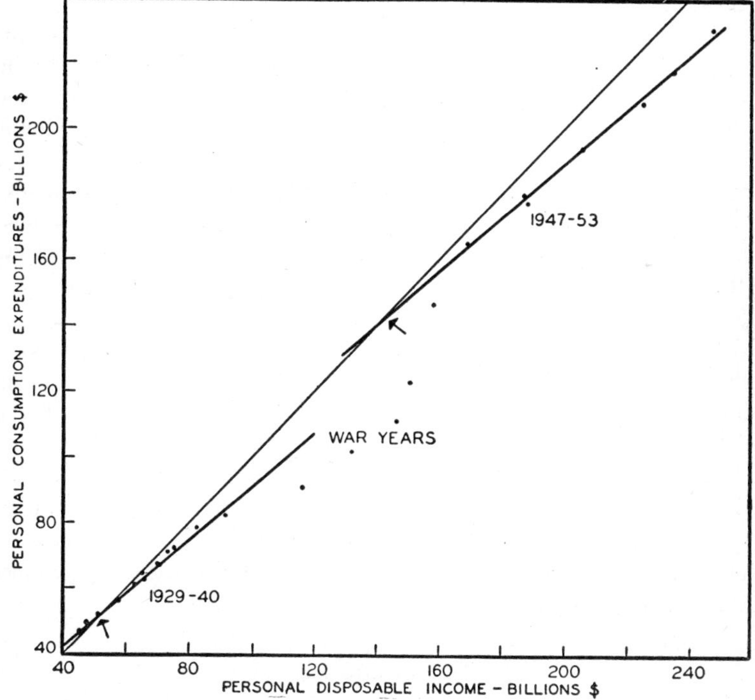

Relation between Consumer Spending and Disposable Income

graph. In this chart the amount of consumer spending is plotted against the amount of personal disposable income for each year from

1929 to date. The solid black line drawn through the pre-war years 1929-1940 plotted in the lower left area is called a line of regression. This line expresses a pattern of spending at different levels of income. If all of the dots on the chart from 1929 to 1953 fell on this straight line, it would indicate a perfect and unchanged relationship between spending and income over the entire period. The grouping of the pre-war points very near to the line indicates how closely the spending habits of consumers in 1929-1940 conformed to this pattern. The war years 1941-1946, during which shortages, price controls, and rationing were paramount, could hardly have been expected to fall on this line. The fact that the years since 1947 do not fit on an extension of the pre-war line indicates a shift in the relation has occurred.

The thin line drawn diagonally across the chart expresses a 100 per cent consumption function; that is, it shows how the pattern would look if consumers continuously spent all of their incomes. It intersects the pre-war regression line at an income level of about $52 billion. This indicates that at income levels below the intersection in the years before the war, consumer spending exceeded current disposable income. (Consumers made net withdrawals from liquid assets and went into debt when incomes fell below this point.) When incomes were above $52 billion, consumers spent less than they received.

The slope of the pre-war line shows that when income rose, spending increased, but not commensurately. The same is true of declines in income and spending. To put it more precisely, the line shows that, on the average, a 10 per cent change in income was associated with an 8½ per cent change in spending.

Many reasons are given for the changes that have occurred in consumer spending. The reason relevant to the alternate buying and saving sprees, following the outbreak in Korea, has to do with discretionary spending power of individuals. According to this theory, the much higher level of income, as compared with pre-war, has left people with a larger margin between income and essential expenditures. With the larger proportion of optional expenditures, willingness to spend has become a more important factor and the volume of spending is influenced more by psychological forces, it is argued.

BUT OLD HABITS PERSIST

The essential truth of the theory that the consumer has the power to change his spending irrespective of short-run changes in incomes and the obvious shift away from the pre-war spending-income pattern have tended to complicate studies of the post-war consumption function; or perhaps it is because there are not enough years to provide conclusive evidence that little attention is given the post-war consumption function. Nevertheless, there are some indications that consumers are tending to establish a new spending-income pattern.

The chart indicates a shift away from the pre-war spending schedule. The fact, however, that a regression line—the solid black line in the upper right of the chart—can be successfully fitted to post-war years suggests a new relationship is forming. Two significant observations may now be made from this chart. One is that the level of consumer expenditures in relation to income has shifted upward in the period since the war. Consumers spend a larger proportion of the same income than before the war. This means that the level at which consumer spending would be expected to exceed income is much higher now. The post-war regression line intersects the thin diagonal line expressing a 100 per cent consumption function at an income level of $143 billion as compared with $52 billion before the war.

The other observation is (given this upward shift) the slope of the post-war regression line indicates that the same relationship exists between *changes* in income and *changes* in spending as in the 1929-1940 period. A 10 per cent change in income is still associated, on the average, with an 8½ per cent change in spending. Thus, despite the difference in spending in the two periods, a given change in disposable income resulted in the same proportionate change in expenditures.

CONCLUSIONS

While it is true that post-war consumer spending has fluctuated considerably on a quarterly basis the relationship between spending and income, annually, has been no more erratic than pre-war. This suggests that the whimsical nature of post-war consumer spending may be exaggerated. It suggests, too, that the most important cause of the upward shift in the consumption function may have to do with factors other than increased discretionary spending power. A long period of rising prices; a shift in the distribution of income, with a smaller proportion going to the upper-income groups; an increasing proportion of older people in the population; a widening of the Social Security coverage; a more progressive income-tax structure; and an upward secular drift in the standard of living, are all institutional or long-run changes which have probably tended to increase spending out of given levels of income.

16. ECONOMIC PSYCHOLOGY *

PRICE theory is based upon only the most general assumptions as to human behavior, but Professor Katona's study, described in this selection, indicates that man's free will may make him so capricious as to render even these generalizations invalid.

IN 1923, the year of the great inflation in Germany, when the price of a loaf of bread rose to 214,000 million marks and one could make a living by buying cigarettes in a retail store in the morning and selling them in the evening, I was a young psychologist engaged in experiments on visual perception at a university. Like many of my colleagues, I had to leave my work and get a job in a bank, where we were paid daily at noon so that we could spend the money right away. I also began to read economics to try to find out what was going on.

I read that inflation is the result of an increase in the money supply—of more purchasing power competing for the available goods. Observing that hardly anybody had ready cash, and finding out from statistical tables that the German note circulation was exceedingly small when expressed in real purchasing power, I wondered. Then I discovered in the literature a second vicious character, called "velocity of circulation," which joined forces with the major culprit, the "quantity of money." But naming the phenomenon did not seem to explain it. I pondered whether the explanation should not have been looked for in the psychological factors that induced the German people to get rid of their money as fast they received it, rather than in the high rate of turnover itself.

During the mild inflation in the U. S. that followed the outbreak of the Korean War in 1950, I was again impressed by the disagreement between actual events and what I had read in economic textbooks. Prices rose rapidly before there was any appreciable increase in Government spending or money supply. But when, in the spring of 1951, rearmament expenditures really got under way, prices stopped rising. U. S. families ceased their rush buying and began to hold on to their money.

It seemed that here again, as in Germany in 1923, the answer must

* George Katona, *Scientific American,* October, 1954. Reprinted by permission of the author and the publisher.

The author (1901——) is Associate Professor of Psychology and Program Director of the Survey Research Center at the University of Michigan. Fellow of the Guggenheim Memorial Foundation, 1940-1942. Author of *Organizing and Memorizing* and *War Without Inflation.*

lie in psychology; the people's economic behavior appeared to be governed more by their expectation of what was going to happen than by the situation of the moment. And so in 1950-1951 at the Survey Research Center of the University of Michigan we undertook to examine the developments with a new approach, that of economic psychology. There were available then, as there had not been in 1923, conceptual tools and measuring sticks, such as sample interviewing, for investigating changes in mass behavior.

Let us consider first the theoretical background of economic psychology. In traditional economics the term "economic behavior" has been used in three different ways. In one sense it has purported to explain the behavior of businessmen and consumers in terms of a norm: how rational men should seek a maximization of profits or of utility, on the assumption that they have full knowledge of and control over all means of achieving the postulated economic end. In a second sense economic behavior has been used to mean the behavior of prices, of incomes and of the economy of a nation. Economists with this outlook have been concerned with the relationships that exist between changes in supply, prices, incomes, consumption, saving and investment.

These two approaches have been of great value. But they disregard the fact that it is human beings who supply the goods, make prices, strive for incomes, spend, save and invest money. They leave out of the equation human needs and desires, hopes and fears, opinions, prejudices and misinformation.

Traditional economics has, to be sure, done some exploration of economic behavior in the third sense of the term—the behavior of businessmen and consumers as people. It has made case studies of business behavior, statistical studies of business cycles and theoretical studies of mass behavior. But the information obtained was of a general natrue. It was known, for instance, how national income changed from one year to the next, but it was not known how many families had an increase and how many a decrease in income, what kinds of families these were or how they reacted to their income development. Nor were there any data on changes in attitudes and expectations, the frequency of such changes or their causes and effects.

In recent years the development of the sample interview survey has made it possible to investigate these matters. Economics psychology maintains that businessmen and consumers are not marionettes pushed around by the law of supply and demand; they have some discretion and latitude, within limits. We shall illustrate both the latitude of the actors on the economic scene and its limits with reference to consumer behavior. We select the consumer because the influence of his psychology on employment and business conditions has not been generally recognized.

In our studies of consumer behavior we distinguish five sets of variables. First there are the *enabling conditions* that set the limits to the consumer's discretion: his income, assets and access to credit. Second, his economic behavior is influenced by *precipitating circumstances:* an increase or decrease in purchasing power, a change in family status, the birth of a child, a move to a new house or locality, the wearing out or breakdown of possessions, and so on. Third, there is the important factor of *habit:* the set patterns of behavior that operate, for instance, in such matters as the purchase of groceries. Fourth, we have to take into account *contractual obligations:* for example, rent, repayment of debt, life insurance premiums, taxes, dues and the like. Previous actions, such as the purchase of an automobile on installments, make both for contractual obligations (repayment of debt) and for consequent actions (purchase of gasoline). Finally, we must deal with the consumer's *psychological state*. Whether a rise in income, a transfer to a new locality, the breakdown of an old refrigerator or any other event will result in important changes in spending depends on the prevailing motives and attitude. If the attitude is conducive to spending, one kind of decision will be made; if it is not, another decision.

How does all this affect the economy as a whole? Can the actions of individuals, influenced by these variables, produce a general economic trend? Sometimes it has been assumed that the attitudes of different people, their optimism and pessimism, for instance, should cancel out. Our studies, however, show that trends do appear. As a result of group identification and mass communication, similar changes in attitudes often occur among very many people at about the same time. This proposition serves as the starting point for quantitative studies of the origin of changes in attitudes and their influence on economic fluctuations.

The power of consumers to influence economic fluctuations will not be the same in different economies. In a subsistence economy, in which the entire income of most consumers is devoted to the acquisition of minimum necessities, the consumer and his attitudes may perhaps be disregarded. But today in the U. S. we find substantial discretionary income in the possession of broad groups of people, and also widespread ownership of liquid assets and easy access to credit. Moreover, the things that people consider necessities now include numerous durable goods (automobiles, television sets) the purchase of which can be postponed or advanced. Therefore economic psychology is particularly important in this country at this time.

The sample interview survey offers a bridge between individual attitudes and aggregate behavior, as measured by national statistics on income, spending, saving and so on. Individuals are interviewed, and for each individual respondent who falls in the sample three kinds of measures are obtained: (1) demographic data, such as occupation, education, age, marital status and the like; (2) economic data, such as income, expenditures, assets and debts; (3) psychological data, such as motives, expectations and intentions. From representative samples it is possible to determine the frequency of each type of measure at successive time points; for instance, we may find that one year 25 per cent and the next year 30 per cent of U. S. families had annual incomes over $5,000; or that one year 20 per cent expected their incomes to go up and the next year 30 per cent. We can also measure functional relations between different variables. We may find, for instance, that of those who say they feel better off, 50 per cent buy durable goods in a given year, while of those who say they feel worse off, only 25 per cent buy such goods. By repeating such measurements under different circumstances the sample interview survey may serve to test hypotheses.

What insights were obtained from such surveys in 1950-1951? They disclosed dramatic shifts in attitudes which were connected with the shifting fortunes of the Korean War. When military reversals came in the summer of 1950 and again a few months later after the intervention of the Chinese Communists, many people feared that World War III was imminent. Fear of war evoked not-too-distant memories of shortages of goods and of rapid and substantial price increases. The buying sprees of consumers in 1950 occurred in two waves, coinciding with the two periods of adverse military news.

Early in 1951 the situation changed completely. When the military front in Korea was stabilized, the expectation of World War III gave way to the notion that we were living in a period of cold war. Acute fear gave way to uneasy anxiety. The expectation of shortages disappeared; people learned that the U. S. economy could supply both butter and guns (for a cold war). By the summer of 1951 many experts spoke of a buying lull and attributed it to saturation due to previous extensive purchases. But it appeared to us who studied people's opinions and feelings that this was not an adequate description of the developments. "Lull," says Webster, means "temporary cessation," but there was nothing temporary in people's attitudes. We found that in many cases money was not lacking, and on the whole needs and desires for new and better things were expressed as frequently as before. But "this is not a good time to buy" was a frequent comment. The business outlook did not appear favorable; people complained of high taxes and high prices. Many decided to postpone the purchase of automobiles, television sets and furniture. The prevailing attitudes resulted in a low rate of spending and a correspondingly high rate of saving during 1951 and most of 1952. It is not money in the possession of consumers that moves goods off the shelves; it is people who decide to spend their money. In order to predict the trend of consumers' spending, it is necessary to obtain data both on the resources of consumers and on the motives that tend to encourage or discourage the spending of money.

What generalizations can we draw from the recent research in economic psychology?

The economic theory of Lord Keynes, which has dominated the thinking of economists in recent decades, put great stress on the effects of changes in income on spending and saving. We have found that in a period of good business, those who suffer declines in income reduce their rate of saving so as to maintain their accustomed standard of living, as the Keynes theory predicts, provided they expect the decline to be temporary and have liquid assets. On the other hand, with an increase in income, spending often rises faster than the income if the economic trend is upward. That is to say, an increase in income often leads people to reduce saving, contrary to the Keynes theory. If an economist were asked which of three groups borrows most—people with rising income, stable income or declining income—he would probably answer: those with declining income. Actually in the years 1947-1950 the answer was: people with rising income. People with declining income were next and those with stable income borrowed least. People's readiness to step up their level of living in response to their feeling that their situation has improved contributes to the dynamic nature of American society. Similiar investigations carried out in Great Britian at the same time yielded different results, more in accord with traditional assumptions about saving and spending.

Another traditional assumption is that if people expect prices to go up, and have money, they will hasten to buy; if they expect prices to go down, they will postpone buying. But our surveys showed that this is not always true. Often the expectation of price increases does not stimulate buying. One typical attitude was expressed by the wife of a mechanic in an interview at a time of rising prices. "In a few months," she said, "we'll have to pay still more for meat and milk; we'll have less to spend on other things." Her family had been planning to buy a new car, but they postponed this purchase. Furthermore, the rise in prices that has already taken place may be resented and evoke buyers' resistance. For example, there is this typical comment of a teacher in 1951: "I just don't pay these prices, they are too high. Prices will go up still more. Nobody will be able to buy anything." To be sure, as we have seen, expectations of war, shortages and very large price increases may result in different behavior.

The effect of price reductions varies. If people believe them to be the beginning of a downward trend, buying may freeze up. If they feel that they are being offered a bargain which will last only a short time, they hurry to buy.

The condition most conducive to spending appears to be price stability. If prices have been stable and people have become accustomed to consider them "right" and expect them to remain stable, they are likely to buy. Thus it appears that the common business policy of maintaining stable prices with occasional sales or discounts is based on a correct understanding of consumer psychology.

Finally, consumers' spending is influenced by the general economic outlook as well as by their personal circumstances and the immediate price picture. Even though a family head does not expect a cut in his own income, if he fears a general recession he may say no to the family demand that he trade in the old television set for a new one with a 21-inch screen. It appears that many people feel vaguely that their own income is an insensitive indicator; that sooner or later economic trends prevailing in the country will affect them personally. Group influences, experiences shared with neighbors and friends, also shape people's attitudes. Most U. S. families have an abundance of unsatisfied needs. (The rich are no exception.) Under what conditions are needs most likely to be transformed into effective demand? When people are confident about the future of the economy. They are most likely to postpone such satisfactions when they feel uneasy about the future course of economy.

The notion of "saturation" of the market is based on old-fashioned psychological assumptions which in turn rest on the analogy of biological drives: for example, if an animal is hungry, it is motivated to search for food; after it has eaten, the motive disappears or becomes weak. The saturation concept has resulted in dire predictions about the future of the U. S. economy. Some people point to the large proportion of U. S. families that already possesses major goods, such as refrigerators (over 80 per cent) or automobiles (about 70 per cent), and they argue that in the future sales will be limited largely to replacement needs.

But social motives are different from biological ones. Levels of aspiration—in sports, for school grades, for position, for income and for goods—most commonly rise with achievement. A beginner in golf, for instance, may strive hard to achieve a score of 100; when he has achieved his goal, he invariably raises his sights. We give up aspirations when we have failed, not when we have succeeded.

In the economic field, a family that has saved enough to buy a home usually sets out on a new objective, such as college education for the children; fulfillment of one aim leads to striving for another. Indeed, in a recent survey it was found that this applied to goods already owned; families with a refrigerator in good operating condition often were preparing to buy a larger one, or one with shelves on the door and a better freezing compartment.

We translate our needs into demand when we are optimistic, confident and secure. We are "saturated," on the other hand, when we are pessimistic, insecure and especially when our past endeavors have been unsuccessful.

America is prosperous. Prosperity means that many more people than ever before own houses, automobiles, refrigerators, TV sets and the like. Is prosperity its own gravedigger; must a few years of high rates of purchasing inevitably be followed by saturation and slump? The answer is no: it is not automatic or inevitable that prosperity be followed by depression or that cyclical movements occur. This, of course, does not mean that we already know how to avoid depressions. But an understanding of what motivates people, and of how motives change, should contribute to this goal.

The few generalizations derived from recent surveys of consumer attitudes and expenditures represent a promising beginning. As yet we know far too little about the origin of mass attitudes, their spread among people and the effects of different attitudes on action. But what we do know is that economic psychology may usefully supplement the theoretical and statistical approach of traditional economics. It contributes to the understanding and prediction of economic fluctuations, and thereby promises to provide policy makers with better tools which they may use to combat the recurrence of periodic depressions and inflations. It should also contribute toward the attainment of the ultimate goal of the behavioral sciences—the development of the theory of social action.

IV

National Income, Business Cycles, and Stabilization Policy

17. CHANGES IN NATIONAL INCOME: 1929-53 *

THE GRAPHIC account of the collapse of the Bull Market in 1929 (Selection 19) leaves the student at the threshold of the depression of the 1930's. What happened next? The answer to this question, insofar as it relates to changes in the size and distribution of the national income until the mid 1950's and the major factors influencing such changes, is set forth in this section from a national income study by the United States Department of Commerce.

The year 1929 marked the end of an era of relatively full employment, business confidence, and general prosperity. Economic activity had been advancing strongly, with only minor interruptions, for eight years.

BUSINESS DECLINE: 1929-33

The 1929 downturn, the ultimate causes of which are still a matter of controversy, was most clearly reflected in the collapse of investment demand. Gross private domestic investment dropped about one-third from 1929 to 1930, as new construction and producers' purchases of durable equipment were cut sharply and the accumulation of nonfarm business inventories ceased. Foreign purchases also declined in 1930, although the drop was not reflected in net foreign investment because of a matching reduction in import demand.

With employment and incomes adversely affected by the sharp re-

* *National Income, 1954 Edition,* A Supplement to the *Survey of Current Business,* U. S. Department of Commerce, Office of Business Economics (Government Printing Office, 1955), pp. 15-26.

duction of investment, consumer purchases also decreased, contributing to the general contraction and inducing still further cuts in outlays for investment.

Consumer purchases, however, held up much better in 1930 than investment demand. The aggregate income flow to individuals shrank less than production and the incomes generated by it, as undistributed corporate profits absorbed a disproportionate share of the over-all decrease in earned income. Also, consumers tended to spend a higher proportion of current income or to dissave in the attempt to preserve previous living standards.

Essentially the same pattern of cumulative decline persisted, and in fact accelerated, during 1931 and 1932. By the latter year, gross private domestic investment had fallen to the very low level of less than $1 billion, as contrasted with $16 billion in 1929. The further moderate decline of the gross national product in 1933 was in consumer purchases, where it reflected primarily lower average prices rather than a further decrease in volume.

National Product Halved in Value

Over the entire period of contraction from 1929 to 1933, the gross national product dropped by nearly one-half, from $104 billion to $56 billion. At the bottom of the depression less than 3 percent of the Nation's output went into business investment, as compared with 15½ percent in 1929. Conversely, consumer purchases rose from three-fourths of the total in 1929 to five-sixths in 1933. Government purchases, although little changed in absolute dollar volume, were considerably increased in relative importance by the collapse of private demand.

More than half of the 1929-33 decline in the market value of the national product stemmed from lower prices. As measured by the gross national product in constant (1947) dollars, real output fell by three-tenths.

Foremost among the factors underlying the shrinkage of real output was the reduction of employment. At the depth of the depression, the number of persons engaged in production was almost one-fifth lower than in 1929, and unemployment was almost 13 million—close to one-fourth of the Nation's labor force. Moreover, average hours worked per week by those who remained employed were considerably reduced.

RECOVERY: 1933-37

Some of the most serious deflationary forces underlying the post-1929 collapse were by 1932 beginning to spend themselves. Installations of new plant and equipment had virtually ceased in most segments of the economy, and such gross fixed business investment as did persist represented primarily the fulfillment of minimum replacement needs. As replacements had been cut to the bone for several years, the feasibility of further postponing them was rapidly diminishing by the end of 1932. Business purchases of durable equipment, accordingly, fell no lower in 1933. Private construction activity did continue downward, but the drop was smaller than in any of the three preceding years.

Sizable inventory liquidation continued in 1933, but as it had already carried working stocks close to a minimum even in relation to the low current volume of sales, the rate of liquidation was considerably reduced. It had previously been possible for businesses to meet the sagging volume of sales partly out of relatively excessive existing inventories, with the consequence that production—and hence total income—was reduced even more than consolidated business sales. Now, however, this possibility was vanishing, and it became necessary to keep output at least on a par with current demand. Here too, then, a weighty deflationary force was exhausting itself.

With the marked retardation of income declines stemming directly from reduced investment expenditures, the fall in consumer demand was measurably slowed in 1933. The stage was thus finally set for recovery. It was evidenced in a few industries as early as the fall of 1932, but appears to have dated generally from the spring of 1933. Monthly personal income data show the low point in March, after which there was a slow and uneven rise during the remainder of the year.

With its decline arrested in 1933, fixed business investment turned up moderately in 1934, when both construction and equipment outlays began to expand again. Nonfarm inventory liquidation ceased, and a general trend toward rebuilding of stocks depleted during the depression set in. It was stimulated not only by the emerging recovery of sales, but by the rise in prices already under way during 1933.

Government Supplements Private Recovery

In the meantime, the Federal Government had assumed an active role in the economy, and was making strenuous efforts to promote recovery. Along with the adoption of other measures, it entered the market directly on an expanding scale, especially in its work relief activities, and also provided substantial aid to State and local governments.

With the increase of incomes generated by the pick-up of business investment and the growth of government purchases, personal consumption expenditures also rose in 1934. Their expansion, in turn, fed the income stream and provided stimulus for a further upsurge of investment. This was at first mainly confined to long-deferred replacement of capital facilities which had deteriorated during the depression; but as profits reappeared and business confidence in future prospects was gradually restored, an increasing proportion went into wholly new plant and equipment, and inventories were expanded to meet the rising volume of sales. Residential building, spurred in part by Federal aid to homeowners, moved ahead once more, and total gross private domestic investment advanced steadily from $1½ billion in 1933 to 11½ billion in 1937.

Consumer purchases also continued to rise. At $67 billion in 1937, they were 45 percent above the low mark of 1933. Although their rate of increase was proportionately smaller than that of domestic capital formation, they represented quantitatively the largest element in the upward spiral of employment, production, and incomes.

Apart from the newly expanded role of government, the whole mechanism of the recovery was thus very similar to that of the downswing, except that it operated in reverse and also more slowly. Of the $35 billion increase in gross national product from 1933 to 1937, about 30 percent was in private domestic investment, raising it from 2½ to 13 percent of the total. Consumer outlays accounted for about 60 percent of the change—substantially less than their share of total output—and government purchases, dropping slightly in relative importance, absorbed the remaining 10 percent of the increment.

The Recession of 1938

Incomplete as was the recovery of the economy by 1937, it was interrupted by a downturn beginning in the latter part of that year and extending through mid-1938. Although of brief duration, this downturn was relatively severe. Within a few months, unemployment rose sharply. Industrial production fell by over one-fourth from August, 1937 to January, 1938, and personal income dropped at a pace comparable to that prevailing in 1931-32. The decline tapered off thereafter, however, and production began to pick up again in the second half of 1938. For the year as a whole, the decrease in gross national product was about 6 percent.

The 1937-38 recession was much steeper in its initial descent than the previous downswing, but it was of a less basic character. Of the $5½ billion decline in gross national product from 1937 to 1938, almost three-fifths was attributable to a shift from accumulation to liquidation of business inventories. Inventory shifts accounted for only 16 percent of the drop in output from 1929 to 1930.

Business plant and equipment expenditures contracted about as sharply in 1938 as in 1930, but residential construction activity, contrastingly, continued to rise, and consumption expenditures, despite the drop in employment and personal income, declined by only 4 percent, as compared with 10 percent in 1930. The consuming public as a whole sustained its spending close to the 1937 rate by a $3 billion cut in personal saving. Moreover, the moderate decline in consumer outlays which did occur was very largely counterbalanced by increased government buying and net foreign investment.

Altogether, purchases of goods and services by final users of the Nation's output declined by less than 3 percent in 1938, as compared with 11 percent in 1930, and the major portion of the swing in production was absorbed by the change in inventories. Curtailment of production ceased as soon as the strength of final demand became apparent. The drop in fixed business investment proved to have been instigated by short-run considerations, rather than by any fundamental lack of investment opportunities. The basic underlying situation, in fact, was that large capital requirements accumulated during the depression still remained to be fulfilled, and that many new investment opportunities stemming from technological advances remained to be exploited.

Renewed Recovery: 1938-41

Following the jar of the 1938 recession, the recovery was renewed and continued steadily into 1941, when it was merged with the first stages of military preparation for World War II.

All forms of business investment were expanding steadily during this period. Purchases of producers' durable equipment nearly doubled in dollar volume from 1938 to 1941, and private construction activity also rose strongly. Inventory liquidation ceased in 1939, when production was brought back in line with current sales, and inventories were accumulated on a mounting scale in the next two years.

By 1941, total gross private domestic investment was not far from three times as large as in 1938. For the first time, it surpassed the 1929 total, both in value and in physical volume. Net foreign investment was also sizable in the three years following 1938, being especially stimulated in 1940 and 1941 by foreign demand for munitions and other supplies required for the Allied war effort.

Responding to the increased incomes generated by expanding employment—and contributing, in turn, to the advance of profits, business investment, employment, and incomes—personal consumption expenditures rose from $64½ billion in 1938 to $82 billion in 1941. The relative rise was particularly marked—about two-thirds—in outlays for durable goods. Higher prices figured in the advancing rate of consumer spending, but the major portion represented enlarged quantities of goods and services. The real volume of personal consumption per capita increased 16 percent from 1938 to 1941, and exceeded the 1929 figure from 1939 on.

Military Requirements Become Dominant

Government purchases were approximately stable until the latter part of 1940. After the fall of France, the national defense program got under way on a rapidly expanding scale with progressively greater influence upon economic conditions. Throughout 1941 and thereafter it was the dominant factor in the economy.

In this second stage of recovery from the depression, from 1938 to 1941, the dollar value of the Nation's output advanced by almost 50 percent, to $126 billion. With a general price rise in the neighborhood of 9 percent, the increase in the physical volume of production was close to two-fifths.

The year 1941 was one of marked expansion, and on the average did not represent full peacetime capacity. During much of the year, there were idle manpower resources, as is attested by the fact that the proportion of the labor force unemployed was slightly higher than in 1930, the first year of the depression.

Nevertheless, the degree of recovery evidenced by 1941 was impressive. In constant dollars, the gross national product stood one-third higher than in 1929. This expansion of real output was achieved with an increase of only 15 percent in the total number of persons engaged in production. Moreover, average hours worked per week were reduced considerably over the 12 years. In the private sector, where the increase in output was about 30 percent, total man-hours utilized differed but little from those in 1929.

That so large an increase in the volume of output was nonetheless accomplished was attributable to the rise in real product per man-hour worked in the private economy. Although lagging in the depression, productivity had advanced rapidly after 1934, and by 1941 was near the level indicated by its long-term trend.

The larger output of 1941 was being distributed to major economic groups in a somewhat different fashion from that of 1929. The most noteworthy change was in the share bought by government. With substantial military preparations getting under way, this share—including a slightly smaller portion for State and local governments—amounted to roughly one-fifth of the gross national product as compared with less than one-tenth in 1929. The proportion purchased by consumers, on the other hand, was reduced from 76 to 65 percent, while the percentages going into gross private domestic and net foreign investment were little changed.

THE WAR ECONOMY: 1942-45

Preparations for war began at a time when the economy was operating at less than full capacity, with unemployed labor, plant, and equipment, and an abundance of raw materials. At first, because of the availability of these unused economic resources, war production could be superimposed upon the civilian economy. It acted as a stimulant, and civilian production increased concurrently. Gross private domestic investment proceeded at a high rate, and consumer purchases—especially of durable goods—were buoyant.

During most of 1941, the needs of the war program were thus compatible with expanding civilian production. Moreover, much of the capital equipment acquired during this period later proved to be readily convertible to war production. Also, the additions to the stock of capital, along with additions to the stock of durable consumer goods, subsequently permitted the diversion of more productive resources from civilian use than would otherwise have been possible except with sharper cuts in living standards.

Emergence of War-time Problems

As the dimensions of the war effort expanded, however, serious problems emerged. Although the rising volume of war production generated a rapid expansion of incomes, it provided no goods and services to satisfy the resultant growth of civilian demand. Instead, it impinged upon their availability as soon as the slack in the economy had been taken up. Shortages of specific labor skills, capital facilities, and raw materials began to be more and more frequently encountered. After Pearl Harbor, it became obvious that the war program would take proportions of output so huge that they could not be provided by enlarged production alone, and that civilian demand would have to be restricted.

During the period of transition to a full war economy, accordingly, a succession of measures was adopted with a view to ensuring maximum war production together with the optimum functioning of the civilian economy. Rates of taxation were steeply increased, not only to help finance Government war expenditures, but also to restrict the amount of civilian purchasing power avaliable to bid for the limited volume of goods and services remaining after military requirements had been met. Fiscal measures were supplemented by the imposition of direct controls, including priorities, inventory limitation orders, allocations, manpower regulations, price and wage controls, and rationing. In addition, individuals were urged to restrict consumption voluntarily and to invest their surplus purchasing power in Government bonds.

On the whole, the flexibility of the economy in the transition to full-scale war production proved great and total production continued to rise rapidly despite conversion.

War Peak Reached in 1944

In 1944, the peak year of war production, the dollar value of the Nation's output was $211 billion—$85½ billion higher than in 1941. Because of the extreme changes in the nature and composition of output, it is difficult to measure how much of this dollar increase reflected physical volume. According to the constant-dollar gross national product series, the expansion of real output from 1941 to 1944 was more than one-third. Whatever the precise figure, it is clear that there was a large rise in physical production during World War II. The major underlying factors were an extraordinary expansion of the labor force and employment, an increased stock of capital equipment, large-scale operations and technological progress in war production, and a better utilization of labor and productive capacity in many civilian industries.

The increase in physical output was by far the most important source of war output. Next in importance were reductions in gross fixed investment, consumer durables, and government non-war purchases. According to available evidence, real consumption of nondurable goods and of services was more than maintained in total. While the wartime level of personal consumption is somewhat exaggerated in the constant dollar figures because of the impossibility of measuring fully the actual price rise which occurred during the war, it is evident that, in the aggregate, real consumption was not curtailed.

Although personal consumption held up during the war, it was much lower in relation to income than it would have been in ordinary peacetime years of high economic activity. An unprecendented proportion of wartime incomes was absorbed by taxes, and the saving rate was abnormally high. The latter reflected a combination of restricted civilian supplies regulated by price control and rationing and the response to patriotic appeals for investment in war bonds.

War Changes Distribution of Output

As a result of these wartime changes, the composition of gross national product in 1944 differed drastically from that in 1941. Government purchases amounted to 46 percent of the total in 1944. The comparable figure for 1941 was only 20 percent, including twice as large a proportion for civilian programs of Federal, State, and local governments.

All other major uses of output were reduced far below their usual relative importance, with the sharpest cuts being those in domestic and net foreign investment and in consumer durables. Private fixed capital formation fell to about 4 percent of the national product as compared with 11 percent in 1941; and requirements were also met in part through a net drain upon both business inventories and foreign sources of supply. The proportion representing consumer outlays for durable goods was more than halved as compared with that of 1941, and the relative share of personal consumption expenditures for nondurables and services also decreased—though by a much smaller margin.

RECONVERSION AND POSTWAR BOOM: 1945-48

At the end of World War II, the Nation faced a set of economic problems which in some ways were the counterpart to those of the original mobilization. It was widely recognized that the transition from a situation in which roughly two-fifths of economic resources were being employed in war production to one in which most of the resources would again be devoted to civilian output could only be accomplished in an orderly fashion by widespread cooperation among all major groups in the economy. As in the mobilization itself, the striking flexibility of the economy was demonstrated.

A broad Government program designed to speed reconversion, and to ease its impact upon the returning soldier and upon business, was enacted. With the quick resurgence of business, personal, and foreign demands, as well as the vast Government programs undertaken to aid in the rehabilitation of war devasted areas, the immediate postwar economic decline was held to moderate proportions.

Although war purchases of the Federal Government were cut back with great speed—from an annual rate of $90 billion in the second quarter of 1945 to $28 billion in the first quarter of 1946—much of the slack was quickly taken up by the rapid expansion of private spending. Total gross national product dropped 12 percent over these three quarters, or by $27 billion at annual rates; thus more than half of the drop in war expenditures was offset. Discharged servicemen and war plant workers were speedily absorbed in civilian pursuits, and at no time did unemployment rise appreciably above 2½ million.

After the first quarter of 1946, the buoyancy of private demand more than offset the moderate further declines in government purchases. Strong inflationary pressures characterized the 1945-46 reconversion, even before controls were eliminated, and continued to dominate the economic scene for the next two years.

Influence of Liquid Saving and Backlog Demands

Several key factors underlay the strength of private demand. During the war, both consumers and businesses had accumulated an enormous volume of savings—much of it in liquid form. At the same time, they had built up a backlog of urgent demands for all types of civilian goods, and especially for durables.

As regards the purchasing power of consumers, it may be further noted that in the brief contraction from mid-1945 to early 1946 the flow of disposable personal income was maintained. Undistributed corporate earnings absorbed a large share of the swing in total income arising from production, and the Government disbursed mustering-out payments and other veterans' benefits in large volume and lowered the wartime tax rates. Not only did the pent-up demand for durable consumer goods materialize as expected, but an insistent consumer demand for nondurables and services also became an active and powerful force in the economy.

Business Speeds Investment

At the same time, business plant and equipment investment programs were pushed ahead fast in the immediate reconversion period and continued to expand strongly thereafter. Inventories, very low at the close of the war, had to be accumulated rapidly to bring working stocks into line with the heavy volume of business. The pace of residential building activity also accelerated steadily.

Moreover, net foreign investment assumed a relative importance far beyond its usual role. With financial support provided both by wartime accumulations of gold and dollar balances and by a large volume of United States Government loans, and under the stimulus of worldwide shortages stemming from the impairment of productive facilities abroad, net foreign purchases of American output reached unprecedented proportions.

In combination, these heavy demands placed a severe strain upon the productive capacity of the economy, which was reduced considerably below the wartime peak. Despite low unemployment, the number of persons engaged in production was 7 million, or 11 percent, lower in 1946 than in 1944. This was due to the withdrawal from the labor force of sizable classes of individuals—such as adolescents, housewives, and persons past the normal retirement age—who are not ordinarily employed, but who had been induced by special wartime circumstances to accept employment. In addition, average hours worked per week fell off as overtime schedules were abandoned, and there appears to have been some loss during the reconversion period in real output per man-hour worked in private industries.

Rapid Price Rise Until 1948

With the physical volume of production thus pressing against capacity, much, if not most, of the pressure exerted by intensive consumer, business, and foreign buying was reflected in price movements. Prices were already advancing, though often in covert fashion, in the early reconversion period. After the termination of wartime controls in the latter half of 1946, they spurted up very sharply, and, except for a brief interlude of hesitation in the spring of 1947, serious inflationary tendencies accompanied the postwar boom until 1948.

In that year a better balance between supply and demand emerged, and the price rise tapered off. This was brought about partly through an appreciable expansion of real output and partly through a diminution in the intensity of some of the demands, including those from abroad, from which the greatest pressures had emanated.

There was a break in agricultural prices early in 1948. Although these recovered briefly, their downward slide, influenced by the prospect of excellent domestic harvests and an improved crop situation abroad, was resumed after midyear. Agricultural prices are a substantial element in the total price picture, and their decline was an important factor shaping the course of economic developments during 1948.

More notable, however, was the increasing stability in consumer markets. The upsurge in personal consumption expenditures, stimulated by backlog demands and reinforced by large holdings of liquid assets and a low volume of consumer debt oustanding, had constituted one of the main foundations of the boom. As the more urgent backlog demands were satisfied, and as the abnormally high spending rate of 1947 made inroads into the net liquid asset positions of many consumers, the rising trend of consumption flattened out in the latter part of 1948.

Closely allied with this tapering-off was the appearance of substantial inventory accumulations, prevented in 1947 largely by the intensity of consumer demand. These related developments, more than any others, slowed the price rise and brought the inflationary spiral to an end during 1948. Late that year, there came a general downturn in prices, and the postwar economy entered a new phase.

BUSINESS READJUSTMENT AND RECOVERY: 1949-50

Businessmen adopted more cautious buying policies toward the end of 1948, and the large inventory accumulations of that year were sharply reduced in the first quarter of 1949. Substantial inventory liquidation emerged in the next quarter, and the drain upon stocks persisted during the remainder of the year. The shift in the inventory position was reflected in a curtailment of production mainly in the manufacturing industries, where the bulk of all inventories held in the economy is produced.

By contrast, total final purchases—that is, elements of the gross national product other than the change in inventories—held up extremely well during 1949. Consumer spending in the first quarter dropped but slightly below its dollar volume at the crest of the postwar boom, then climbed slowly upward again during the remainder of the year. Residential building activity decreased from a peak in the second quarter of 1948 but picked up again in the spring and advanced strongly thereafter. And government purchases, chiefly because of the expanding Federal foreign aid and farm price support programs, more than offset the moderate declines which occurred in business outlays for plant and equipment. For the year as a whole, total final purchases actually exceeded those of 1948.

That the curtailment of employment and payrolls in the manufacturing sector had no greater impact upon consumption expenditures in 1949 was attributable in part to the payment of sizable unemployment compensation benefits, and also in some degree to the cushioning effects upon disposable personal income of lower Federal income taxes as a result of the previous year's Revenue Act. It may also be noted that dividends were sustained, notwithstanding the sharp fall in profits. Perhaps more important than any of these factors, however, was the apparent willingness of the consuming public as a whole to spend increasing proportions of current income to maintain living standards during the recession.

It became apparent in the second half of 1949 that the curtailment of output had been excessive in relation to the existing stable volume of business sales. Accordingly, production was stepped back up, and the accumulation of inventories was resumed. Meanwhile, the recovery of residential construction had grown into a sustained building boom, and consumer demand, already strong, was being bolstered by large Government payments to veterans. These factors, moreover, were being reinforced by a renewed upturn in fixed business investment.

This widening resurgence of production generated increases in employment and incomes, adding further impetus to consumer purchasing. Before mid-1950, a business upswing of substantial dimensions was under way and was carrying the economy close to full-capacity operation.

KOREAN WAR PERIOD

It was upon this expansionary situation that the urgent demands resulting directly and indirectly from the outbreak of hostilities in Korea were superimposed, as the Nation decided upon a defense program encompassing a sharp step-up in direct military potential as well as the establishment of a broad base of productive facilities to permit quick economic mobilization in case of full-scale war.

The ensuing rise in national output continued without interruption for three years, until the second quarter of 1953, when gross national product reached a peak of $370 billion at seasonally adjusted annual rates, one third above the rate of $276 billion in the second quarter of 1950. About half of this rise represented expansion in physical volume while the remainder reflected the sharp advance in prices which occurred in large part during the first nine months of the period.

In terms of current dollars, Federal Government purchases, mainly for national security purposes, accounted for more than two-fifths of the increase in national output. These purchases tripled over the three-year period, and their share of total output rose from 8 to 17 percent. All other types of national expenditure combined rose by about one-fifth, with consumption, investment, and State and local government outlays each registering substantial gains.

In real terms the shifts in the use of output were more pronounced, with the Federal Government absorbing about two thirds of the increase in constant-dollar gross national product. But on this basis also a margin was left which permitted an expansion in other purchases in spite of the increased demands of national security. Total real consumption was about 9 percent higher in mid-1953 than three years earlier, reflecting mainly a larger volume of nondurable goods and services. On a percapita basis the increase amounted to more than 3 percent. Real purchases of State and local governments showed a similar movement. The rate of aggregate investment decreased somewhat in real terms, although fixed investment was higher, due to a larger volume of producers' durable equipment.

Inflationary Upsurge

While the defense buildup was the dominant factor in the economic situation throughout the three years following mid-1950, its character and impact varied considerably during this period.

In the initial stage the increase in national security expenditures was heavily concentrated in military payrolls, food, clothing, and other related outlays which were capable of rapid expansion in a comparatively short time. The strength of the Armed Forces increased by 1¾ million persons in the first year of the defense effort—about four-fifths of the ultimate total increase—and national security outlays mounted from 6 percent to 11 percent of the gross national product.

At the same time there was a strong advance in investment by businesses that were participating in the growing volume of defense orders. This included investment in inventories and in plant and equipment, the latter receiving a special stimulus from the rapid amortization provisions that had been granted for emergency facilities.

Although the demands stemming directly from the defense program contributed to expansionary developments, it was the waves of anticipatory buying, set in motion by the expectation of commodity shortages and price increases, that determined the tone of the business situation in this period. Consumer buying spurted in the third quarter of 1950 and again in the first quarter of 1951, following the further extension of the Korean conflict. Responding to sharply rising sales, as well as to the same expectations that motivated consumers, businessmen added greatly to their inventories, and fixed investment not related to the defense program was also stimulated.

Although production continued to rise briskly, demand outstripped the supply of goods, and prices bounded upward.

Shift to Defense Production

By mid-1951 the situation had changed significantly. Output was expanding at a rapid rate, and it became apparent that the productive capacity of the economy had been underestimated. Taxes had been raised, and the establishment of price and wage controls gave some assurance to the public that inflation would be kept in check. Other measures, including controls on credit and on the flow of strategic materials, had been introduced to ensure that the necessary resources would be channeled in an orderly fashion into the defense program.

As a consequence of these developments, and the well-stocked position of consumers after several months of extraordinarily heavy buying, spending propensities eased markedly during 1951. The rate of consumer spending out of disposable income, which had risen to 96 percent during the buying surge in the first quarter fell to about 91 percent in the succeeding quarters of the year. Since the trend of income was strongly upward, the absolute dollar value of consumption in the final quarter of the year exceeded the first-quarter rate in spite of this decline in the spending rate.

The easing in the urgency of consumer demand was paralleled by a curtailment of business buying, which had been geared to the same sort of anticipations and to the resultant abnormal volume of sales. The shift entailed a very substantial inventory readjustment—with a notable scaling down in the accumulation of civilian goods.

In the setting of rapidly increasing physical production, of Government measures designed to minimize the disruptive effects of economic mobilization upon the economy, and of less urgent private demand, it was possible to achieve a substantial expansion in national defense expenditures and allied fixed capital outlays concurrently with a high rate of civilian consumption and a diminution of inflationary pressures.

The absolute increase in national security expenditures in the second year of the defense buildup was nearly as large as in the previous year although the percentage increase was smaller. It was concentrated in hard goods, such as planes, tanks, and electronic equipment. Deliveries of these items were reaching a high volume, after design difficulties had been overcome and the long lead-time involved in their production had elapsed. Defense-connected fixed investment also expanded rapidly in this period. In contrast, the advance in total fixed investment was limited by offsetting declines in investment not related to the defense effort.

General Expansion

In the third year of the defense effort—from mid-1952 to mid-1953—the Nation's capacity to produce continued to expand substantially while the rate of growth of national security outlays tapered off. This shift in the relation of supply and demand permitted the relaxation and subsequent removal of economic controls.

Civilian demand proved strong, particularly in the durable goods lines previously restricted by controls and material shortages. Residential, instititutional, and State and local construction, business investment in plant and equipment other than in defense-connected industries, and consumer and inventory demand for automobiles and other durable goods became major factors supporting further economic growth. Together with the still rising military demand they provided the basis for a balanced economic expansion which, unlike that of the previous year, was shared by most industries.

Agriculture was the principal sector of the economy that ran counter to the generally favorable trend. As a consequence of lower farm prices, income originating in agriculture was reduced substantially during 1952 and 1953. The steady downward pressure on prices reflected the unusually heavy output of farm products—which reached successive highs in the 2 years—and the appreciable decline in foreign sales. Domestic consumption remained firm, however, and the full force of the other developments was not reflected in farm income, as large quantities of the chief crops and dairy products were placed under loan to the Commodity Credit Corporation, both in 1952 and 1953.

The restoration of civilian durable goods production was retarded by the steel strike which occurred in the second quarter of 1952 and affected end products mainly in the third. As a consequence final purchases and inventory accumulation of durables were particularly heavy in the fourth quarter of 1952 and were probably raised also in the opening half of 1953.

National Output Reduced

Total production reached a peak in the second quarter of 1953 and receded moderately in the latter half of the year. The major change occurred in the net flow of goods into the inventories of durable goods industries. These inventories had been replenished and the immediate need for further accumulation had thus been removed. In addition, sizable liquidations were made when it became apparent that, relative to actual and prospective demand, some of the earlier build-up had been excessive.

National security expenditures, entering a new phase, registered moderate declines, mainly in the procurement of hard goods, and consumer purchases of commodities, particularly durables, also drifted downward. The effect of these reductions on total final purchases was offset, however, by advances in other components of national expenditures, notably consumer expenditures for services, State and local government purchases, and the agricultural price support outlays of the Federal Government. Hence final purchases were maintained in the aggregate in the latter half of 1953.

While the percentage decline in total national output was small, it was heavily concentrated in durable goods and thus had a disproportionate impact upon the durable goods manufacturing industries where it led to substantial reductions in production, employment, wages, and profits. The year 1954 opened with these developments still in progress.

---

18. IF PEACE BREAKS OUT *

IF PEACE breaks out, so may a depression, suggests Mr. Chase. The economy is being supported by large government purchases for overseas relief and rehabilitation and for war. If the "cold war" ceases and these expenditures are terminated, what will happen to national income? The author gives an imaginative description of the economic crisis that would shortly face the country if Peace Day finds it unprepared. To avoid this development, he proposes a program of planned expenditures that would be initiated as rapidly as conditions demand.

ON PEACE day the New York *Times* carried an eight-column streamer: "Russians Sign Lilienthal-Acheson Plan: Amended Pact Ends Atomic War Threat." The story tells of crowds cheering, singing, praying, in Pennsylvania Avenue, Herald Square, Pall Mall, Place de la Concorde, even the Red Square. Years of nightmare tension are suddenly released. The world goes wild with joy.

Not quite all the world. The *Times'* special jumbo edition includes several dissenting opinions: "More Squandered Billions—Wheery"; "Communist Plot—McCormick." Mr. Hearst is not pleased, either, while Westbrook Pegler is quoted as saying that the entire Administration ought to be shot. "I'm the only American left in America." Still, most of the 2.2 billion members of the human race who hear the news are very happy.

Three days earlier the Federal Reserve Board released a financial summary of the United States. It too made happy reading in its way. The post-war inflation of course had long since come to an end, but after a salutary shakedown in prices and costs, gross national income had leveled out at $250 billion and unemployment at two million.

* Stuart Chase. Reprinted from *The Nation,* June 11, 1949, p. 655-57. By permission of the author and the publisher.

The author (1888——) is an economic consultant. Formerly with the Securities Exchange Commission and the Tennessee Valley Authority. He is a prolific writer, his better known books being *The Tragedy of Waste, Men and Machines, A New Deal, The Proper Study of Mankind,* and *Tomorrow's Trade.*

Prosperity seemed assured for some time to come. Consumers, the story went on, had given up their buyers' strike and flocked to the stores again, now that prices were at levels which they considered reasonable. The stock market was having a little rally of its own. Strikes were at a ten-year minimum in man-days lost.

Federal expenditures were running close to $45 billion a year, more than half of it for military and power-politics outlays. Costs of the Atlantic Pact, much of the Marshall Plan, subsidies to Germany and Japan and elsewhere, when added to straight outlays for guns, aircraft, tanks, and atomic bombs, totaled $25 billion. Federal income did not reach $45 billion at current tax rates, and the Treasury was running a deficit again, though not a great one.

Many people still believed that dollars voted for foreign aid in some mysterious way disappeared. Nothing of the kind was happening. Foreigners do not use dollars abroad; try paying a Paris taxi driver with a dollar bill. Foreigners send the dollars back for American goods, and thus make jobs for American workers and farmers. Every cent is finally spent right here; indeed, most of the dollars appropriated for foreign aid never leave the country at all. The *stuff* goes—the wheat, tractors, machine tools, generators—but the dollars stay.

At the time of the Federal Reserve Board's report, the United States economy had in effect a gigantic "public-works" program totaling $25 billion in operation, underwriting its prosperity. This was five times greater than anything Mr. Roosevelt had ever been able to batter through Congress in New Deal days. The famous "lend-spend" bill only called for some $4 billion.

In brief, said the Federal Reserve Board, everything was fine. Then followed the signing of the Lilienthal Plan and days of rejoicing. Amended so that the Soviet government was satisfied with inspection procedure, and with the rapid release of atomic power for industry, the plan overcame all serious objections. The United States Atomic Energy Commission had succeeded in developing a practicable atomic prime mover, and this is probably what won the Russians and the Chinese over. They needed such an engine to build up local industry and standards of living—one in which a few pounds of fuel released thousands of horse-power. The engine was theirs by signing the pact. The know-how and techniques, under proper safeguards, were to be placed at the disposal of the peoples of the world.

The farsighted saw another cause for rejoicing. The creation of the World Atomic Authority offered at last a *functional* basis for a world state. Other functions—conservation, communication, world airways, world food supply, epidemic control, displaced persons, the World

Bank—could be tied on to it in due course. This was a sounder way to build One World than trying to create it *de novo* by a paper constitution.

The sky was blue as the bells rang out. At formal ceremonies in every capital decorations were awarded, toasts drunk, speeches delivered, flowers strewn. Lower Broadway was a foot deep in torn-up telephone books. The Iron Curtain was lifted and celebrations were held at the frontiers. Shostakovich and Copland composed anthems to Russian-American friendship.

And then—. Doubts and disillusionment came first in financial circles. Operators in Wall Street and in the United States commodity markets, the members of the N. A. M., big wholesalers, and big department-store executives began to do some figuring. At night, after their wives were sound asleep, they lay awake figuring. Twenty-five billion dollars knocked out of the United States economy in the coming year! That's a lot of jack. That's between five and ten million jobs knocked out. How will it affect my business? Less demand for steel, coal, aluminum, rubber, oil, cement, lumber, cotton, wool, wheat, canned goods, tractors, machine tools, chemicals—all the supplies which sustain armies, navies, and air forces. Twenty-five billion dollars of orders wiped off the books, practically overnight!

That means trouble, plenty of trouble. The tycoon trembles on his beauty-rest mattress. I'd better start retrenching, he thinks. That new wing on the factory, that order for sheet steel, that branch in Tuscaloosa, those new delivery trucks. The beauty-rest shakes again. He reaches the office next morning with his face set. The retrenchment is conducted with our traditional American efficiency.

Within a month of the day when peace broke out, the United States economy begins to slide. Headlines like these appear: Market Breaks Wide Open; Ticker Forty Minutes Behind—Wheat, Corn, Oats Drop Limit; No Bids at Bottom—New Investment at Standstill—Jobless Cross Four Million Mark—Lawrence Mills Lay off 5,000—Construction Slumps—Steel Output Off—New Bank Loans Drop Third Week in Row—Used-Car Market Caves in—Retail Sales Down 12 Per Cent.

Another month goes by, and even the President's Advisory Committee is forced to admit that business is in a corkscrew descent rivaling that of December, 1929. As it swings, the rest of the Western world, and large sections of the Eastern, begins to gyrate, too.

Joy and ruin simultaneously! One remembers the "peace scares" which shook the market in 1944; one remembers the bitter "paradox of plenty." Must prosperity depend upon disaster? World War I took us out of the depression of 1914. World War II ended the chronic unemployment of the 1930's. The cold war sustained the post-war boom. Is peace intolerable in the era of mass-production?

President Truman calls a bipartisan conference to answer these questions, before the situation gets completely out of hand. The Kremlin is smiling broadly and saying to the world: "What did we tell you about those capitalists? One puff, and their system explodes from its inner contradictions!"

The President calls the meeting to order. Practically everybody is there—Bernard Baruch, Herbert Hoover, Beardsley Ruml, Chester Bowles, Raymond Fosdick, Henry Luce, Evans Clark, Paul Hoffman—everybody. What is the agenda? what will the subcommittees report? what will be the grand conclusions? Even Drew Pearson quails at this assignment. His prediction rate falls from a steady 81 per cent accurate to 74.

This, friends, is about as far as my imagination will carry me. I have imagined one result of Peace Day, based on the thesis of the disaster economy—the bigger the disaster, the greater the prosperity. It fits the last decades pretty well. That other, and happier, results are possible I would not deny.

Let us return to 1949 and think about what Congress, the Administration, labor leaders, farmers, business men, might do to get ready for that momentous day when peace breaks out. They might take a hint from a question which a G. I. tank driver once asked me in a discussion of post-war problems at Fort Hamilton. He was to sail very soon for the battlefields of France. He got to his feet and hesitated a moment. "Well," he said, "if the country can keep prosperous making tanks for men like us to die in, why can't it keep prosperous making houses for people to live in?" Everyone who cares about the future of America and the world should have this question pasted under the glass top of his desk, or over his work bench, or over the sink in the kitchen.

If $25 billion for tanks goes out of the economy, something must come in—or else. What can the something be? It could be a great housing program, as the soldier said. It could be a health program for all Americans; it could be more highways, schools, hospitals. In place of $25 billion of "illth"—as Ruskin once called waste, loss, and lethal weapons—an equal amount of wealth. This is what we have to do; shift some eight million jobs from illth to wealth. If we just cancel the illth, the economy will drop like a plummet, and soon both consumers and business men will be so alarmed that even the remaining output of "goods" will be seriously reduced, as it was between 1930 and 1933.

Someone inquires, "Where's the money coming from?" That is a fair question, if somewhat shopworn. If we can finance $25 billion of waste without undue strain, why can't we finance an equal amount of wealth? A modern state, according to the London *Economist,* "can finance anything it can produce."

During the war nobody asked where the money was coming from; they asked where the raw materials and man-power were coming from. One could name a score of men who have the technical ability to arrange the financing of the shift from illth to wealth. It is small potatoes compared with what these same men accomplished in financing a $300-billion war.

War finance demolished the arguments and warnings of the "money-first" school of economic philosophers, who promised dire ruin all through the 1930's if the national debt should ever reach $50 billion. Well, it reached $279 billion without ruin. Now it is $252 billion.

Nobody can guarantee that such a transfer will succeed. Economics is not yet an exact science. By the same token nobody can guarantee that it will fail. The probability of success based on past experience is encouraging; and it is better to take what risk remains than go to hell in a hack. We tried that from 1929 to 1933.

Houses instead of tanks are fine, but for long term outlays to balance the business cycle there is, I believe, something even better. Houses ought to be built anyway, together with hospitals and schools, when currently needed. A Fifty-Year Plan—keep calm, Mr. Pegler, just try to hold on—*to restore the resource base* of America would have the advantage of being flexible. The appropriations could be turned on and off within wide limits. Suppose we list the major tasks:

1. The water table of the whole Far West is sinking, and unless we come to terms with the hydrologic cycle, about half our country ultimately will become a desert.

2. Equally important is erosion control on that half of America east of the twenty-inch rainfall line.

3. Expanded programs are needed to restore forests, grasslands, wild life, so mercilessly demolished on our triumphal march from Atlantic to Pacific. Europe has been bombed and devastated, yes, but the soil of Western Europe is still securely in place, and richer than it was in Caesar's time. The way things are going, Europe may some day have to raise a Marshall Plan for us.

4. A series of multiple-purpose river developments, like the TVA.

5. Allied to the foregoing is a great project for halting stream pollution, which now poisons practically every river in the Republic. We can spend billions on this over the years with great advantage to the health, sanitation, scenery, and recreation of America.

These five items are, for the long run, as fundamental forms of wealth as one can imagine—water, soil, minerals, forests, grasslands. They tend to restore the assets most depleted by war and foreign relief. Techniques are available in the Soil Conservation Service, the Forest Service, the TVA, and elsewhere to design such a Fifty-Year Plan with a minimum of loss, leak, and friction. The Public Affairs Institute in Washington has prepared a very fine program in "Our Conservation Job." Much research is still needed, of course, and should be part of the plan. Conservation, furthermore, encounters a minimum of vested interests.

Well, let us tuck this thought under the door of Mr. Truman's conference imagined earlier. With such a program in operation, the Federal Reserve Board could continue its cheerful reports. The United States could not go down in a financial maelstrom, dragging the planet with it. Here is one way to keep a world made happy by Peace Day, happy after Peace Day.

---

19. THE STOCK MARKET CRASH OF 1929 *

LIKE the shots on Lexington Green, the crash of security prices in 1929 was heard around the world, and its echoes are still ringing in the ears of many a sadder and wiser American. Mr. Allen writes of the events that took place before and during those fateful days in October, 1929. He recounts what the people were saying and what they were doing as the big bull market roared upward to dizzying heights—and then crashed. This article is a description rather than an explanation, a description of the beginning of the end of the short-lived prosperity period of the middle and late twenties.

THE MADNESS OF 1929

BY THE summer of 1929, prices had soared far above the stormy levels of the preceding winter into the blue and cloudless empyrean. All the old markers by which the price of a promising common stock could be measured had long since been passed; if a stock once valued at 100 went

* Frederick Lewis Allen, *Only Yesterday* (Harper & Brothers, 1931), pp. 309-11, 314-16, 320-21, 325-37. Copyright, 1931, by Frederick Lewis Allen. Reprinted by permission of the author and the publisher.

For a brief biographical sketch of the author, see Selection 3 on page 5.

to 300, what on earth was to prevent it from sailing on to 400? And why not ride with it for fifty or a hundred points, with Easy Street at end of the journey?

By every rule of logic the situation had now become more perilous than ever. If inflation had been serious in 1927, it was far more serious in 1929, as the total of brokers' loans climbed toward six billions (it had been only three and a half billions at the end of 1927). If the price level had been extravagant in 1927 it was preposterous now; and in economics, as in physics, there is no gainsaying the ancient principle that the higher they go, the harder they fall. But the speculative memory is short. As people in the summer of 1929 looked back for precedents, they were confronted by the recollection that every crash of the past few years had been followed by a recovery, and that every recovery had ultimately brought prices to a new high point. Two steps up, one step down, two steps up again—that was how the market went. If you sold, you had only to wait for the next crash (they came every few months) and buy in again. And there was really no reason to sell at all: you were bound to win in the end if your stock was sound. The really wise man, it appeared, was he who "bought and held on."

Time and again the economists and forecasters had cried wolf, wolf, and the wolf had made only the most fleeting of visits. Time and again the Reserve Board had expressed fear of inflation, and inflation had failed to bring hard times. Business in danger? Why, nonsense! factories were running at full blast and the statistical indices registered first-class industrial health. Was there a threat of overproduction? Nonsense again! Were not business concerns committed to hand-to-mouth buying, were not commodity prices holding to reasonable levels? Where were the overloaded shelves of goods, the heavy inventories, which business analysts universally accepted as storm signals? And look at the character of the stocks which were now leading the advance! At a moment when many of the high-flyers of earlier months were losing ground, the really sensational advances were being made by the shares of such solid and conservatively managed companies as United States Steel, General Electric, and American Telephone—which were precisely those which the most cautious investors would select with an eye to the long future. Their advance, it appeared, was simply a sign that they were beginning to have a scarcity value. As General George R. Dyer of Dyer, Hudson & Company was quoted as saying in the *Boston News Bureau,* "Anyone who buys our highest-class rails and industrials, including the steels, coppers, and utilities, and holds them, will make a great deal of money, *as these securities will gradually be taken out of the market.*" What the bull operators had long been saying must be true, after all. This was a new era. Prosperity was coming into full and perfect flower.

Still there remained doubters. Yet so cogent were the arguments against them that at last the great majority of even the sober financial leaders of the country were won over in some degree. They recognized that inflation might ultimately be a menace, but the fears of immediate and serious trouble which had gripped them during the preceding winter were being dissipated. This bull market had survived some terrific shocks; perhaps it was destined for a long life, after all.

On every side one heard the new wisdom sagely expressed. "Prosperity due for a decline? Why, man, we've scarcely started!" "Be a bull on America." "Never sell the United States short." "I tell you, some of these prices will look ridiculously low in another year or two." "Just watch that stock—it's going to five hundred." "The possibilities of that company are *unlimited.*" "Never give up your position in a good stock." Everybody heard how many millions a man would have made if he had bought a hundred shares of General Motors in 1919 and held on. Everybody was reminded at some time or another that George F. Baker never sold anything. As for the menace of speculation, one was glibly assured that—as Ex-Governor Stokes of New Jersey had proclaimed in an eloquent speech—Columbus, Washington, Franklin, and Edison had all been speculators. "The way to wealth," wrote John J. Raskob in an article in the *Ladies Home Journal* alluringly entitled "Everybody ought to be Rich," "is to get into the profit end of wealth production in this country," and he pointed out that if one saved but fifteen dollars a month and invested it in good common stocks, allowing the dividends and rights to accumulate, at the end of twenty years one would have at least eighty thousand dollars and an income from investments of at least four hundred dollars a month. It was all so easy. The gateway to fortune stood wide open.

Gradually the huge pyramid of capital rose. While supersalesmen of automobiles and radios and a hundred other gadgets were loading the ultimate consumer with new shining wares, supersalesmen of securities were selling him shares of investment trusts which held stock in holding companies which owned the stock of banks which had affiliates which in turn controlled holding companies—and so on *ad infinitum.* Though the shelves of manufacturing companies and jobbers and retailers were not overloaded, the shelves of the ultimate consumer and the shelves of the distributors of securities were groaning. Trouble was brewing—not the same sort of trouble which had visited the country in 1921, but trouble none the less. Still, however, the cloud in the summer sky looked no bigger than a man's hand.

How many Americans actually held stock on margin during the fabulous summer of 1929 there seems to be no way of computing, but it is probably safe to put the figure at more than a million. (George Buchan Robinson estimated that three hundred million shares of stock were being carried on margin.) The additional number of those who held common stock outright and followed the daily quotations with an interest nearly as absorbed as that of the margin trader was, of course, considerably larger. As one walked up the aisle of the 5:27 local, or found one's seat in the trolley car, two out of three newspapers that one saw were open to the page of stock-market quotations. Branch offices of the big Wall Street houses blossomed in every city and in numerous suburban villages. In 1919 there had been five hundred such offices; by October, 1928, there were 1,192; and throughout most of 1929 they appeared in increasing numbers. The broker found himself regarded with a new wonder and esteem. Ordinary people, less intimate with the mysteries of Wall Street than he was supposed to be, hung upon his every word. Let him but drop a hint of a possible split-up in General Industries Associates and his neighbor was off hot-foot the next morning to place a buying order.

The rich man's chauffeur drove with his ears laid back to catch the news of an impending move in Bethlehem Steel; he held fifty shares himself on a twenty-point margin. The window-cleaner at the broker's office paused to watch the ticker, for he was thinking of converting his laboriously accumulated savings into a few shares of Simmons. Edwin Lefevre told of a broker's valet who had made nearly a quarter of a million in the market, of a trained nurse who cleaned up thirty thousand following the tips given her by grateful patients; and of a Wyoming cattleman, thirty miles from the nearest railroad, who bought or sold a thousand shares a day—getting his market returns by radio and telephoning his orders to the nearest large town to be transmitted to New York by telegram. An ex-actress in New York fitted up her Park Avenue apartment as an office and surrounded herself with charts, graphs, and financial reports, playing the market by telephone on an increasing scale and with increasing abandon. Across the dinner table one heard fantastic stories of sudden fortunes: a young banker had put every dollar of his small capital into Niles-Bement-Pond and now was fixed for life; a widow had been able to buy a large country house with her winnings in Kennecott. Thousands speculated—and won, too—without the slightest knowledge of the nature of the company upon whose fortunes they were relying, like the people who bought Seaboard Air Line under the impression that it was an aviation stock. Grocers, motormen, plumbers, seamstresses, and speak-easy waiters were in the market. Even the revolting intellectuals were there: loudly as they might lament the depressing effects of standardization and mass production upon American life, they found themselves quite ready to reap the fruits thereof. Literary editors whose hopes were wrapped about American Cyanamid B lunched with poets who swore by Cities Service, and as they left the table, stopped for a moment in the crowd at the broker's branch office to catch the latest quotations; and the artist who had once been eloquent only about Gauguin laid aside his brushes to proclaim the merits of National Bellas Hess. The Big Bull Market had become a national mania.

CRASH!

Early in September the stock market broke. It quickly recovered, however; indeed, on September 19th the averages as compiled by the *New York Times* reached an even higher level than that of September 3rd. Once more it slipped, farther and faster, until by October 4th the prices of a good many stocks had coasted to what seemed first-class bargain levels. Steel, for example, after having touched 261¾ a few weeks earlier, had dropped as low as 204; American Can, at the closing on October 4th, was nearly twenty points below its high for the year; General Electric was over fifty points below its high; Radio had gone down from 114¾ to 82½.

A bad break, to be sure, but there had been other bad breaks, and the speculators who escaped unscathed proceeded to take advantage of the lesson they had learned in June and December of 1928 and March and May of 1929: when there was a break it was a good time to buy. In the face of all this tremendous liquidation, brokers' loans as compiled by the Federal Reserve Bank of New York mounted to a new high record on October 2nd, reaching $6,804,000,000—a sure sign that margin buyers were not deserting the market but coming into it in numbers at least undiminished. (Part of the increase in the loan figure was probably due to the piling up of unsold securities in dealers' hands, as the spawning of investment trusts and the issue of new common stock by every manner of business concern continued unabated.) History, it seemed, was about to repeat itself, and those who picked up Anaconda at 109¾ or American Telephone at 281 would count themselves wise investors. And sure enough, prices once more began to climb. They had already turned upward before that Sunday in early October when

Ramsey MacDonald sat on a log with Herbert Hoover at the Rapidan camp and talked over the prospects for naval limitation and peace.

Something was wrong, however. The decline began once more. The wiseacres of Wall Street, looking about for causes, fixed upon the collapse of the Hatry financial group in England (which had led to much forced selling among foreign investors and speculators), and upon the bold refusal of the Massachusetts Department of Public Utilities to allow the Edison Company of Boston to split up its stock. They pointed, too, to the fact that the steel industry was undoubtedly slipping, and to the accumulation of "undigested" securities. But there was little real alarm until the week of October 21st. The consensus of opinion, in the meantime, was merely that the equinoctial storm of September had not quite blown over. The market was readjusting itself into a "more secure technical position."

The expected recovery in the stock market did not come. It seemed to be beginning on Tuesday, October 22nd, but the gains made during the day were largely lost during the last hour. And on Wednesday, the 23rd, there was a perfect Niagara of liquidation. The volume of trading was over six million shares, the tape was 104 minutes late when the three-o'clock gong ended trading for the day, and the *New York Times* averages for fifty leading railroad and industrial stocks lost 18.24 points—a loss which made the most abrupt declines in previous breaks look small. Everybody realized that an unprecedented number of margin calls must be on their way to insecurely margined traders, and that the situation at last was getting serious. But perhaps the turn would come tomorrow. Already the break had carried prices down a good deal farther than the previous breaks of the past two years. Surely it could not go on much longer.

The next day was Thursday, October 24th.

On that momentous day stocks opened moderately steady in price, but in enormous volume. Kennecott appeared on the tape in a block of 20,000 shares, General Motors in another of the same amount. Almost at once the ticker tape began to lag behind the trading on the floor. The pressure of selling orders was disconcertingly heavy. Prices were going down. . . . Presently they were going down with some rapidity. . . . Before the first hour of trading was over, it was already apparent that they were going down with an altogether unprecedented and amazing violence. In brokers' offices all over the country, tape-watchers looked at one another in astonishment and perplexity. Where on earth was this torrent of selling orders coming from?

The exact answer to this question will probably never be known. But it seems probable that the principal cause of the break in prices during that first hour on October 24th was not fear. Nor was it short selling. It was forced selling. It was the dumping on the market of hundreds of thousands of shares of stock held in the name of miserable traders whose margins were exhausted or about to be exhausted. The gigantic edifice of prices was honeycombed with speculative credit and was now breaking under its own weight.

Fear, however, did not long delay its coming. As the price structure crumbled there was a sudden stampede to get out from under. By eleven o'clock traders on the floor of the Stock Exchange were in a wild scramble to "sell at the market." Long before the lagging ticker could tell what was happening, word had gone out by telephone and telegraph that the bottom was dropping out of things, and the selling orders redoubled in volume. The leading stocks were going down two, three, and even five points between sales. Down, down, down. . . . Where were the bargain-hunters who were supposed to come to the rescue at times like this? Where were the investment trusts, which were expected to provide a cushion for the market by making new purchases at low prices? Where were the big operators who had declared that they were still bullish? Where were the powerful bankers who were supposed to be able at any moment to support prices? There seemed to be no support whatever. Down, down, down. The roar of voices which rose from the floor of the Exchange had become a roar of panic.

United States Steel had opened at 205½. It crashed through 200 and presently was at 193½. General Electric, which only a few weeks before had been selling above 400, had opened this morning at 315—now it had slid to 283. Things were even worse with Radio: opening at 68¾, it had gone dismally down through the sixties and the fifties and forties to the abysmal price of 44½. And as for Montgomery Ward, vehicle of the hopes of thousands who saw the chain store as the harbinger of the new economic era, it had dropped headlong from 83 to 50. In the space of two short hours, dozens of stocks lost ground which it had required many months of the bull market to gain.

Even this sudden decline in values might not have been utterly terrifying if people could have known precisely what was happening at any moment. It is the unknown which causes real panic.

Suppose a man walked into a broker's branch office between twelve and one o'clock on October 24th to see how things were faring. First he glanced at the big board, covering one wall of the room, on which the day's prices for the leading stocks were supposed to be recorded. The LOW and LAST figures written there took his breath away, but soon he was aware that they were unreliable: even with the wildest scrambling, the boys who slapped into place the cards which recorded the last prices shown on the ticker could not keep up with the changes: they were too numerous and abrupt. He turned to the shining screen across which ran an uninterrupted procession of figures from the ticker. Ordinarily the practiced tape-watcher could tell from a moment's glance at the screen how things were faring, even though the Exchange now omitted all but the final digit of each quotation. A glance at the board, if not his own memory, supplied, the missing digits. But today, when he saw a run of symbols and figures like

R 　　　　　　　　 WX
6.5½.5.4. 　　　　 9.8⅞¾½¼.8.7½.7.

he could not be sure whether the price of "6" shown for Radio meant 66 or 56 or 46; whether Westinghouse was sliding from 189 to 187 or from 179 to 177. And presently he heard that the ticker was an hour and a half late; at one o'clock it was recording the prices of half-past eleven! All this that he saw was ancient history. What was happening on the floor now?

At ten-minute intervals the bond ticker over in the corner would hammer off a list of selected prices direct from the floor, and a broker's clerk would grab the uncoiling sheet of paper and shear it off with a pair of scissors and read the figures aloud in a mumbling expressionless monotone to the white-faced men who occupied every seat on the floor and stood packed at the rear of the room. The prices which he read out were *ten or a dozen or more points below those recorded on the ticker.* What about the stocks not included in that select list? There was no way of finding out. The telephone lines were clogged as inquiries and orders from all over the country converged upon the Stock Exchange. Once in a while a voice would come barking out of the broker's rear office where a frantic clerk was struggling for a telephone connection: "Steel at ninety-six!" Small comfort, however, to know what Steel was doing; the men outside were desperately involved in many another stock than Steel; they were almost completely in the dark, and their imaginations had free play. If they put in an order to buy or sell, it was impossible to find out what became of it. The Exchange's whole system for the recording of current prices and for communicating orders was hopelessly unable to cope with the emergency, and the sequel was an epidemic of fright.

In that broker's office, as in hundreds of other offices from one end of the land to the other, one saw men looking defeat in the face. One of them was slowly walking up and down, mechanically tearing a piece of paper into tiny and still tinier fragments. Another was grinning shamefacedly, as a small boy giggles at a funeral. Another was abjectly beseeching a clerk for the latest news of American & Foreign Power.

And still another was sitting motionless, as if stunned, his eyes fixed blindly upon the moving figures on the screen, those innocent-looking figures that meant the smash-up of the hopes of years. . . .

GL. AWW. JMP.

8.7.5.2.1.90.89.7.6. 3.2½.2. 6.5.3.2½

A few minutes after noon, some of the more alert members of a crowd which had collected on the street outside the Stock Exchange, expecting they knew not what, recognized Charles E. Mitchell, erstwhile defender of the bull market, slipping quietly into the offices of J. P. Morgan & Company on the opposite corner. It was scarcely more than nine years since the House of Morgan had been pitted with the shrapnel-fire of the Wall Street explosion; now its occupants faced a different sort of calamity equally near at hand. Mr. Mitchell was followed shortly by Albert H. Wiggin, head of the Chase National Bank; William Potter, head of the Guaranty Trust Company; and Seward Prosser, head of the Bankers Trust Company. They had come to confer with Thomas W. Lamont of the Morgan firm. In the space of a few minutes these five men, with George F. Baker, Jr., of the First National Bank, agreed in behalf of their respective institutions to put up forty millions apiece to shore up the stock market. The object of the two-hundred-and-forty-million-dollar pool thus formed, as explained subsequently by Mr. Lamont, was not to hold prices at any given level, but simply to make such purchases as were necessary to keep trading on an orderly basis. Their first action, they decided, would be to try to steady the prices of the leading securities which served as bell weathers for the list as a whole. It was a dangerous plan, for with hysteria spreading there was no telling what sort of *débâcle* might be impending. But this was no time for any action but the boldest.

The bankers separated. Mr. Lamont faced a gathering of reporters in the Morgan offices. His face was grave, but his words were soothing. His first sentence alone was one of the most remarkable understatements of all time. "There has been a little distress selling on the Stock Exchange," said he, "and we have held a meeting of the heads of several financial institutions to discuss the situation. We have found that there are no houses in difficulty and reports from brokers indicate that margins are being maintained satisfactorily." He went on to explain that what had happened was due to a "technical condition of the market" rather than to any fundamental cause.

As the news that the bankers were meeting circulated on the floor of the Exchange, prices began to steady. Soon a brisk rally set in. Steel jumped back to the level at which it had opened that morning. But the bankers had more to offer the dying bull market than a Morgan partner's best bedside manner.

At about half-past one o'clock Richard Whitney, vice-president of the Exchange, who usually acted as floor broker for the Morgan interests, went into the "Steel crowd" and put in a bid of 205—the price of the last previous sale—for 10,000 shares of Steel. He bought only 200 shares and left the remainder of the order with the specialist. Mr. Whitney then went to various other points on the floor, and offered the price of the last previous sale for 10,000 shares of each of fifteen or twenty other stocks, reporting what was sold to him at that price and leaving the remainder of the order with the specialist. In short, within the space of a few minutes Mr. Whitney offered to purchase something in the neighborhood of twenty or thirty million dollars' worth of stock. Purchases of this magnitude are not undertaken by Tom, Dick, and Harry; it was clear that Mr. Whitney represented the bankers' pool.

The desperate remedy worked. The semblance of confidence returned. Prices held steady for a while; and though many of them slid off once more in the final hour, the net results for the day might well have been worse. Steel actually closed two points higher than on Wednesday, and the net losses of most of the other leading securities amounted to less than ten points apiece for the whole day's trading.

All the same, it had been a frightful day. At seven o'clock that night the tickers in a thousand brokers' offices were still chattering; not till after 7:08 did they finally record the last sale made on the floor at three o'clock. The volume of trading had set a new record—12,894,650 shares. ("The time may come when we shall see a five-million-share day," the wise men of the Street had been saying twenty months before!) Incredible rumors had spread wildly during the early afternoon—that eleven speculators had committed suicide, that the Buffalo and Chicago exchanges had been closed, that troops were guarding the New York Stock Exchange against an angry mob. The country had known the bitter taste of panic. And although the bankers' pool had prevented for the moment an utter collapse, there was no gain-saying the fact that the economic structure had cracked wide open.

Things looked somewhat better on Friday and Saturday. Trading was still on an enormous scale, but prices for the most part held. At the very moment when the bankers' pool was cautiously disposing of as much as possible of the stock which it had accumulated on Thursday and was thus preparing for future emergencies, traders who had sold out higher up were coming back into the market again with new purchases, in the hope that the bottom had been reached. (Hadn't they often been told that "the time to buy is when things look blackest"?) The newspapers carried a very pretty series of reassuring statements from the occupants of the seats of the mighty; Herbert Hoover himself, in a White House statement, pointed out that "the fundamental business of the country, that is, production and distribution of commodities, is on a sound and prosperous basis." But toward the close of Saturday's session prices began to slip again. And on Monday the rout was under way once more.

The losses registered on Monday were terrific—17½ points for Steel, 47½ for General Electric, 36 for Allied Chemical, 34½ for Westinghouse, and so on down a long and dismal list. All Saturday afternoon and Saturday night and Sunday the brokers had been struggling to post their records and go over their customers' accounts and sent out calls for further margin, and another avalanche of forced selling resulted. The prices at which Mr. Whitney's purchases had steadied the leading stocks on Thursday were so readily broken through that it was immediately clear that the bankers' pool had made a strategic retreat. As a matter of fact, the brokers' who represented the pool were having their hands full plugging up the "air-holes" in the list—in other words, buying stocks which were offered for sale without any bids at all in sight. Nothing more than this could have been accomplished, even if it could have been wisely attempted. Even six great banks could hardly stem the flow of liquidation from the entire United States. They could only guide it a little, check it momentarily here and there.

Once more the ticker dropped ridiculously far behind, the lights in the broker's offices and the banks burned till dawn, and the telegraph companies distributed thousands of margin calls and requests for more collateral to back up loans at the banks. Bankers, brokers, clerks, messengers were almost at the end of their strength; for days and nights they had been driving themselves to keep pace with the most terrific volume of business that had ever descended upon them. It did not seem as if they could stand it much longer. But the worst was still ahead. It came the next day, Tuesday, October 29th.

The big gong had hardly sounded in the great hall of the Exchange at ten o'clock Tuesday morning before the storm broke in full force. Huge blocks of stocks were thrown upon the market for what they would bring. Five thousand shares, ten thousand shares appeared at a time on the laboring ticker at fearful recessions in price. Not only were innumerable small traders being sold out, but big ones, too, protagonists of the new economic era who a few weeks before had counted themselves millionaires. Again and again the specialist in a stock would find himself surrounded by brokers fighting to sell—and nobody at all even thinking of buying. To give one single example: during the bull market the common stock of the White Sewing Machine Company had gone as high as 48; on Monday, October 28th, it had closed at 11⅛. On that black Tuesday, somebody—a clever messenger boy for the Exchange, it was rumored—had the bright idea of putting in an order to buy at 1—and in the temporarily complete absence of other bids he actually got his stock for a dollar a share! The scene on the floor was chaotic. Despite the jamming of the communication system, orders to buy and sell—mostly to sell—came in faster than human beings could possibly handle them; it was on that day that an exhausted broker, at the close of the session, found a large waste-basket which he had stuffed with orders to be executed and had carefully set aside for safe-keeping—and then had completely forgotten. Within half an hour of the opening the volume of trading had passed three million shares, by twelve o'clock it had passed eight million, by half-past one it had passed twelve million, and when the closing gong brought the day's madness to an end the gigantic record of 16,410,030 shares had been set. Toward the close there was a rally, but by that time the average prices of fifty leading stocks, as compiled by the *New York Times,* had fallen nearly forty points. Meanwhile there was a near-panic in other markets—the foreign stock exchange, the lesser American exchanges, the grain market.

The next day—Wednesday, October 30th—the outlook suddenly and providentially brightened. The directors of the Steel Corporation had declared an extra dividend; the directors of the American Can Company had not only declared an extra dividend, but had raised the regular dividend. There was another flood of reassuring statements—though by this time a cheerful statement from a financier fell upon somewhat skeptical ears. Julius Klein, Mr. Hoover's Assistant Secretary of Commerce, compose a rhapsody on continued prosperity. John J. Raskob declared that stocks were at bargain prices and that he and his friends were buying. John D. Rockefeller poured Standard Oil upon the waters: "Believing that fundamental conditions of the country are sound and that there is nothing in the business situation to warrant the destruction of values that has taken place on the exchanges during the past week, my son and I have for some days been purchasing sound common stocks." Better still, prices rose—steadily and buoyantly. Now at last the time had come when the strain on the Exchange could be relieved without causing undue alarm. At 1:40 o'clock Vice-President Whitney announced from the rostrum that the Exchange would not open until noon the following day and would remain closed all day Friday and Saturday—and to his immense relief the announcement was greeted, not with renewed panic, but with a cheer.

Throughout Thursday's short session the recovery continued. Prices gyrated wildly—for who could arrive at a reasonable idea of what a given stock was worth, now that all settled standards of value had been upset?—but the worst of the storm seemed to have blown over. The financial community breathed more easily; now they could have a chance to set their houses in order.

It was true that the worst of the panic was past. But not the worst prices. There was too much forced liquidation still to come as brokers' accounts were gradually straightened out, as banks called for more collateral, and terror was renewed. The next week, in a series of short sessions, the tide of prices receded once more—until at last on November 13th the bottom prices for the year 1929 were reached. Besides the figures hung up in the sunny days of September they made a tragic showing:

	High price Sept. 3, 1929	*Low price Nov. 13, 1929*
American Can	181⅞	86
American Telephone & Telegraph	304	197¼
Anaconda Copper	131½	70
General Electric	396¼	168⅛
General Motors	72¾	36
Montgomery Ward	137⅞	49¼
New York Central	256⅜	160
Radio	101	28
Union Carbide & Carbon	137⅞	59
United States Steel	261¾	150
Westinghouse E. & M.	289⅞	102⅝
Woolworth	100⅜	52¼
Electric Bond & Share	186¾	50¼

The *New York Times* averages for fifty leading stocks had been almost cut in half, falling from a high of 311.90 in September to a low of 164.43 on November 13th; and the *Times* averages for twenty-five leading industrials had fared still worse, diving from 469.49 to 220.95.

The Big Bull Market was dead. Billions of dollars' worth of profits —and paper profits—had disappeared. The grocer, the window-cleaner, and the seamstress had lost their capital. In every town there were families which had suddenly dropped from showy affluence into debt. Investors who had dreamed of retiring to live on their fortunes now found themselves back once more at the very beginning of the long road to riches. Day by day the newspapers printed the grim reports of suicides.

20. DEFENSE AGAINST RECESSION *

Deliberate (Non-Automatic) Measures To Prevent or Check a Recession

THE FOLLOWING selection is from a policy statement, *Defense Against Recession,* by the Research and Policy Committee of the Committee for Economic Development. In this policy statement the committee discusses and recommends three lines of defense against recession: 1) public and private measures to prevent the emergence of recessionary tendencies by sustaining the growth of demand as the productive capacity of the economy grows, 2) public and private measures to strengthen the automatic tendencies of the economy to withstand and check recessionary movements, and 3) discretionary measures to be taken in the event that the first two lines of defense prove to be inadequate. The pages reprinted below deal only with the third part of this three-part program.

THE SPONTANEOUS reactions of the economic system will not multiply a deflationary impact nearly as much as they did in the past. It is necessary, however, to consider what additional measures might be deliberately undertaken to resist a decline or promote recovery. This is mainly a matter of *governmental* measures. The important contribution of private businesses, individuals and organizations to the maintenance of high employment is in the two areas already discussed—the creation of a large flow of new demand and the spontaneous, stabilizing reaction to a decline of demand.[1]

INSTRUMENTS OF POLICY

The available instruments are, in general, measures to add to total demand, which the government can do in several ways. By increasing its own expenditures (without increasing taxes) the government can either add to demand directly or increase the income that others have available to spend. Government can also increase the available incomes

* An extract from *Defense Against Recession,* a statement on National Policy by the Research and Policy Committee of the Committee for Economic Development, March, 1954.

[1] *Footnote by Leroy A. Lincoln:* Although I approve this policy statement in general, I feel that it might be interpreted to advocate 'too much too soon' with respect to government action. In my view, strong anti-recession governmental action is not needed now, and is unlikely to be needed in 1954. I believe that there is grave question whether government can determine better than the forces of the free market what corrections should be applied or when they should be applied."

of individuals and businesses by cutting taxes (without cutting expenditures). It can increase the availability of credit by its banking policy and it can, by guaranteeing or making loans, assume some of the risks of credit extension.

In listing these instruments we do not mean to suggest that all of them should be used to deal with all economic declines, actual or forecast. Some instruments should be reserved for serious situations and in general the use of each instrument should be attuned to the particular circumstances.

Tax Reduction

By cutting the present high tax rates, it would be possible to reduce tax collections by billions of dollars on very short notice, and thus offset a large part of the decline in private after-tax incomes that occurs in a recession. Nothing like this was possible in, say, 1930 or 1938, because there were not large amounts of taxes to cut. Also, before current tax payments and withholding were introduced there was no way in which a tax cut could have a *quick* effect on individuals' available incomes.

The purpose of cutting taxes would be to increase private expenditures. While not all of the increased incomes provided by tax relief would be spent, a large proportion almost certainly would be, and since the amount of tax relief possible is very large, a large increase in private expenditures could be achieved.

Government Expenditures

The possibilities of adding to total expenditures *quickly* by increasing government expenditures are more limited. However, advance plans and preparations have been made that would appear to permit an increase of about $1.5 billion in Federal construction expenditures within one year after the decision to undertake the expansion. This is not a large figure in relation to the size of the American economy, but it could, under some circumstances, be a valuable ingredient in an anti-recession program. There are urgent backlogs of need for state and local construction. As of today, the possibility of using a quick acceleration of state and local construction as an anti-recession measure is limited by inadequacy of advance preparation and by financial difficulties. But these limitations are not insuperable.

Some government expenditures other than those for public works may also lend themselves to increase as part of an anti-recession program without serious loss of efficiency. The stockpiling program and some aspects of the military program—particularly military construction—may be cases of this sort. We have not examined these possibilities and are unable to offer recommendations on them except to say that they deserve consideration.

Monetary Policy

By purchasing government securities and by reducing reserve requirements the Federal Reserve can help to stimulate or sustain demand in several ways.

Banks can be provided with reserves in excess of their legal requirements. Thus banks will not be limited by their reserve positions in making loans, and in fact will be induced to look for loans to put their reserves to work. Also, an easy money policy will tend to raise the market prices of government bonds and other gilt-edged securities, to reduce the interest yield per dollar of such assets (at market prices), and to increase the public's holdings of money. All of these effects will tend to encourage holders of such assets to make additional investments and expenditures.

The mere availability of funds will not, and should not, make financial institutions extend credit on loans they regard as unsafe, nor make businesses borrow if they do not see profitable investment opportunities. This does not mean, however, that banking policy has no positive contribution to make to preventing or moderating a recession. Banking policy can help to *prevent* a recession by restraining a previous boom and at the same time avoiding the acute credit stringency that might bring the boom to a precipitate end.

Once a recession has started, investment opportunities decline, but they do not fall to zero. Especially if there is a general program to keep recessions moderate, there will be active investment opportunities that are more likely to be exploited if credit is available on easy terms than if it is not. It seems clear that the influence of an easy money policy in a recession would be in an expansionist direction. The size of the influence, however, is difficult to appraise.

Federal Loans and Loan Guarantees

Through its operations as lender or guarantor of loans, the government can go beyond the indirect influence of banking policy in assuring or stimulating the flow of credit. Through these operations it can assume risks that private lenders may be unwilling to assume.

The most important continuing activity of the Federal government as a lender or guarantor is in the housing field. The terms—especially the down payment requirements—set by the Federal agencies (FHA and Veterans' Administration) for guaranteeing or insuring loans have proved an important influence upon the volume of residential construction. It should be possible to use this influence to maintain or stimulate housing construction in a recession. This possibility is limited if we have relied on the stimulus of easier credit terms too much before it is really needed.

At various times in the past the government, through the RFC and to some extent the Federal Reserve, has been actively engaged in making direct loans to business or in guaranteeing such loans. Such programs raise difficult problems of standards and of government control of business operations. For this reason large scale direct lending to business should, in our opinion, be regarded as an emergency measure.

. . . . .

Despite the limitations mentioned, these instruments add up to a powerful package, more powerful than has previously been available, chiefly because of the potentialities of tax reduction. These instruments are not so flexible, their effects are not so predictable, that they can be combined into a program for precise control of the level of economic activity. But if used with determination and skill they can help protect us against serious, prolonged recessions.

THE MANAGEMENT OF AN ANTI-RECESSION PROGRAM

The big problem is to manage the use of these instruments in a way that will get the most out of them, with the least danger of inflation or other undesirable consequences. In what amounts, at what times, and in what combinations should the instruments be used? This raises one of the most difficult questions in the field of stabilization: how far can we protect the economy against declines without stimulating long-run inflation? There is a danger of doing too much too soon and causing inflation, as well as a danger of doing too little too late. Also, there is danger of using the wrong combination of instruments which, while stimulating employment, might stimulate it in less efficient directions. We believe these dangers can be avoided, by wise and cautious policy, but they must not be ignored.

It is not possible to develop a blueprint in advance that will meet all circumstances. Decisions will have to be made by responsible officials applying their best judgment to the facts of the time. There are, however, certain general principles that will be helpful in the management of an anti-recession program.

Much of the difficulty in the management of a program for economic stabilization results from inability to forecast economic changes. For all of the non-automatic measures being discussed here, there is a lapse of time between the decision to act and the effects of the decision. The appropriateness of the action will depend upon how well it fits the situation existing when it takes effect, not how well it fits the situation when the decision is made. But when the decision is made no one knows what the situation will be when the action takes effect.

The possibility of error can be reduced in two ways: by improving the quality of forecasts and by increasing the flexibility of action.

Improving Forecasting

The art of economic forecasting is a large and technical subject that cannot be adequately covered in this paper. We do not suppose that it will ever be possible to predict economic conditions, particularly turning points in economic conditions, with great accuracy and precision. But we believe that every effort should be made to improve the quality of forecasts and that some progress can be achieved by collecting more information more quickly.

One of the most important advances of recent years in economic forecasting has been the development of the survey of anticipations. One example is the survey of business plans for expenditure for new plant and equipment in the ensuing year. Another is the survey of consumers' plans and attitudes toward expenditure, particularly for durable goods. The reliability of these surveys has not been tested in a variety of circumstances, but the results so far have been sufficiently encouraging to justify further work. The feasibility of prompter and more frequent reports and of expanding the samples to permit more detailed classification of the responses should be investigated. The possibility of applying similar techniques to business plans for increasing or decreasing inventories, to farmers' investment plans, and to state and local government expenditure plans should also be tested.

We need quicker reporting to find out where we are, economically, at any time. Prompter information should be obtained on new and unfilled orders and on inventories and their composition. More accurate, detailed and current savings statistics would be an important aid to the interpretation of economic developments. A more complete and prompt flow of information from business to government economic and statistical agencies about the situation and outlook of particular industries would also help to improve the quality of forecasts.

Increasing Flexibility

Whatever progress may be made in the art of economic forecasting we shall have to contend with the probability of errors. Therefore, we cannot emphasize too strongly the importance of making action more flexible, of shortening the interval between the decision to act and the effects of the action, in order to reduce reliance on long period forecasting. Flexibility also involves assuring that action, once taken, will be changed if economic conditions call for a change. Such flexibility is, in our opinion, the key to successful stabilization policy.

Taxes as a Flexible Instrument. If reduction of tax rates is to be an important anti-recession instrument, preparation should be made in advance for its flexible use. The time that is administratively and mechanically necessary between a government decision to change tax rates and the first effects of that decision on taxpayers is short. With a small amount of advance preparation, for example, a decision to cut income tax rates could be felt in withholding and therefore in take-home pay within two months.

The main problem is the length of time needed to make the decision. This process would involve an Administration decision to recommend a tax reduction of a particular kind and a Congressional decision to approve, modify or reject the Administration recommendation. In principle it might be possible to short-cut this process by legislation providing for a tax cut to go into effect automatically under certain conditions, or by giving the President authority to reduce certain taxes under specified conditions. There are, however, difficulties, in the way of either procedure. To make the present procedure more flexible, it would be helpful for the Administration to decide: (a) whether in the event of a recession (actual or forecast) it would recommend tax reduction; (b) in what kinds of situations, on the basis of what facts, it would take such action; and (c) what kind of tax reduction it would recommend. The Administration should discuss these plans with Congressional leaders and attempt to reach general agreement, by mutual adjustment. These, it should be noted, would be plans, not binding commitments. The plans could be changed. But laying this kind of groundwork in advance will save much valuable time.

The possibility of prompt action to cut tax rates to counter a recession will depend upon the kind of tax cut that is recommended. When everyone agrees about the desirability of cutting taxes, action should not be delayed by disagreement about whose taxes get cut the most. A general income tax rate reduction not only would be economically beneficial but also would be more likely to command general agreement than any other kind of tax reduction.[2]

There are other reasons for suggesting that anti-recession tax cuts be made in the income tax rather than in excises or corporate taxes.

[2] *Footnote by Beardsley Ruml, Wayne C. Taylor and James F. Brownlee:* "In some circumstances an increase of exemptions should be considered."

The anticipation of excise tax cuts may lead purchasers to stay out of the market until cuts go through and prices come down—a result not desired in a recession. While corporation expenditures are significantly influenced by corporation taxes, a *temporary* tax change will have little effect on investment intended to pay off over a longer period.

There may be some circumstances in which anti-recession tax cuts should be made in other taxes as well as in the personal income tax. For example, if there are agreed upon tax reductions of other kinds that should and would be made within a year or two anyway, the need to stimulate the economy may be a reason for advancing the date of such reductions.

The greater the possibility of ending the tax cut when it is no longer justified by the economic situation, the safer it will be to use tax reduction as an anti-recession measure. For obvious reasons, it will be easier to get tax rates cut than to get them restored. This difficulty cannot be entirely eliminated, but provision for automatic termination of the emergency tax cut after a definite period, say a year, would help. Of course, such automatic expirations do not always take effect. There may be situations in which they should not take effect. But the automatic expiration forces reconsideration and positive action if the lower tax rates are to be retained.

Preparing for Public Works. The Federal government is now in a much better position than it was in the 'thirties to increase its public works expenditures rapidly. The Federal agencies maintain continuously revised six-year plans, listing the projects they would want to construct in the next six years, and indicating their priorities and state of readiness. In an emergency it would be possible to increase construction by accelerating work on the projects that are most urgent and ready from the standpoint of plans, funds, site acquisition and other prerequisites. It has been estimated that these reserves of projects would permit an increase of about $1 billion in the annual rate of non-military public works within one year and about $1.5 billion in total Federal construction (including military construction).

While this is encouraging, we are not sure that it fully exploits the possibility of preparation for rapid expansion. The total reserve of listed projects seems large enough, but it may be desirable to have a larger proportion of the projects authorized, financed, blueprinted and ready to go. This would offer a wider range for the selection of projects best adapted to the particular situation, even if it never became necessary to increase expenditures by more than $1 billion or $1.5 billion.

If an anti-depression Federal public works program ever becomes necessary, it should be coordinated and expedited by an agency centrally located in the Administration. Plans for the establishment of such an agency should be made in advance.

Flexible use of state and local construction as an anti-depression instrument involves two interrelated problems, planning and finance. Apparently there is on hand a sufficient backlog of plans to keep the current rate of construction running for about a year. If state and local governments should encounter financial difficulties, however, appropriations for the preparation of drawings and specifications would be sharply cut, especially in view of the expectation, based on past experience, that at some point the Federal government will step in and provide funds for planning. The interruption of the planning function at the outset of a recession would mean an interruption in actual construction after a year or so.

The development of long-run capital budgets by many cities and states and the growth of metropolitan planning techniques and staffs will help to maintain the continuity of state and local construction. These institutions could well be adopted more widely, not only for this reason but also because of their contribution to government efficiency.

At the end of World War II, and again in 1949, the Federal government arranged for loans to enable state and local governments to prepare plans in advance of need. Such a program should be revived. There would probably be little activity under the program in prosperous times, but the funds would be drawn upon in time of recession and would help to sustain the volume of state and local construction.

To sustain the total volume of state and local construction in a serious recession, and, even more, to bring about an increase, is likely to require Federal financial aid. At least, the question of such aid will arise, and it will be important to have a Federal policy to deal with the situation formulated in advance. Uncertainty about Federal policy in this respect would be a major obstacle to the prosecution of local projects, including projects that the local authorities could and would carry on by themselves if they were confident that no aid would be forthcoming.

Flexible Loan and Loan Guarantee Policies. The terms of Federal loans and loan guarantees should be adjusted flexibly as an instrument of economic stabilization, insofar as many be consistent with the other purposes of the programs. The Administration should have clear authority to make such adjustments within limits set by Congress. To promote flexible and consistent adjustment of these terms a Federal Loan Council, including the chief agencies involved, should be established.

At present the possibility of easing Federal credit terms is restricted by the generally easy terms already in force. There is some room now, however, to make terms easier, especially for modernization loans and for mortgages on higher priced homes. And more room will exist in the future if maximum ease is not maintained during prosperity.

THE BALANCED COMBINATION

Despite advance preparations that may be made to increase their flexibility, tax reductions or public works programs will not be sufficiently flexible to deal with small, short and uncertainly forecast recessions. The attempt to use such instruments to deal with such economic movements would sometimes turn out to be correct—in those cases when the small decline is the forerunner of a more serious and protracted depression. But in most cases it would turn out to be wrong—the stimulating effect would probably not start until the need for it had passed and would continue even though it created a danger of inflation. In addition, the attempt to lower and raise tax rates frequently, or to turn public works programs on and off, would be a source of inefficiency and disturbance.

In the early stages of a decline, unless there is strong evidence of a serious recession, we must rely on more flexible instruments, particularly upon monetary policy supplementing the automatic stabilizers discussed in the preceding section. These have the great advantage that they can come into play quickly and be stopped or reversed quickly when the situation changes.

Such measures as tax reductions and public works programs should be reserved for more serious situations—either for an existing recession of some severity or for a recession that is forecast with a high degree of certainty. In such cases there is little danger that the net effect will be inflationary, and the costs of inaction are so serious as to make the risk of inflation worth taking.

A number of factors are relevant to appraising the seriousness of the situation—how many people are without jobs and looking for them, how many have jobs but are not at work because of layoffs, the average duration of joblessness, average hours of work per week, the degree to which declines of employment are geographically and industrially localized or general, the age and sex of those without jobs and so on. One implication of this is that the seriousness of an economic decline cannot be simply measured by one figure—the number of unemployed.

It will also be important to distinguish between declines that are largely confined to inventory movements and declines that include a large element of cutback in construction and equipment expenditures. The latter are more likely to call for strong counter-measures.

In suggesting that tax reductions and public works programs be reserved for more serious declines we do not mean to imply that less serious declines should be viewed with equanimity. On the contrary, strenuous efforts should be made to prevent smaller declines by means appropriate to that task. We are confident that the steps discussed in earlier sections[3] of this report would be effective in doing this except in very unusual circumstances. But we would warn that the attempt to use relatively inflexible instruments to confine fluctuations within relatively minor limits is more likely to be destabilizing than stabilizing.

When used, the less flexible but more powerful instruments should be used with vigor and determination. Their goal should be not merely to moderate an economic decline but to stop it and promote recovery.

---

21. A YEAR OF ECONOMIC TRANSITION *

THE PRESIDENT of the United States is obliged, by the Employment Act, to report to the Congress on the present and prospective economic health of the nation and to suggest policies designed to maintain or improve it. The following article is interesting as an example of the analysis performed by the President's economic advisors. It has additional interest in that it assesses the extent to which our tax system automatically promotes economic stability.

AT THE TIME last year when the Economic Report was submitted to the Congress, our economy was undergoing a contraction, partly as a result of readjustments forced by the ending of the Korean conflict, partly for other reasons. Today, after a small and brief over-all decline, though one that affected individual industries and localities unevenly, production and employment are again increasing on a broad front. The recovery has already carried economic activity to the highest level of the past twelve months. And although aggregate production and employment during 1954 fell somewhat short of the levels reached in 1953, the year just concluded will go down in history as one of our most prosperous years.

THE ONSET OF CONTRACTION

In our economy, or in any other of which we have definite knowledge, occasional imbalances between production and sales are virtually bound

[3] Not reprinted in this selection.

* *Economic Report of the President,* January, 1955 (Government Printing Office, 1955), pp. 11-25.

to occur. Such a condition developed in 1953. After the steel strike in the summer of 1952 was settled, production, employment, and incomes increased sharply. So too did consumer spending, though at a somewhat lower rate than the increase of personal incomes. The rate of general economic expansion was reduced, but continued to be fairly rapid, during the early months of 1953. Total spending by consumers roughly kept pace with their rising incomes during these months; however, spending on commodities, as distinct from services, tapered off. Inventories therefore kept rising, particularly those held by retailers. About the same time the flow of new defense contracts, which tie up inventories of factories on a larger scale than civilian production, diminished sharply. In view of these developments, as well as the general quickening of deliveries, many business firms deemed it prudent to bring their inventories into better balance with sales and incoming orders. The effort to adjust inventories led to scattered declines in production, which became visible in the Nation's aggregate of industrial production after July 1953. Within a few months, total production fell short of consumption, just as it had previously exceeded consumption. An inventory recession, of the sort that occurred in 1948-49 and earlier times in our history, was under way.

This economic readjustment was complicated and aggravated by the close of hostilities in Korea. With the war at an end, the need for many types of defense goods diminished. At the same time, basic defense plans were being modified to strengthen our economy for what might prove a very long period of "cold war." The changed situation in Korea, the revisions of military programs, and improvements in the administration of our defense establishment brought about a sizeable drop of military and related expenditures. A larger reduction was carried through during 1954 than had been anticipated, and it called for further readjustments by the economy. For the decline of defense spending not only reduced the Nation's stream of expenditures for final use; it also accentuated the efforts of businessmen to cut inventories.

The primary contractive factor during the latter part of 1953 was the adjustment of inventories. This role shifted to defense spending after the turn of the year. In the second quarter of 1953 businessmen added to their inventories at an annual rate of 5.4 billion dollars. In the first quarter of 1954 they reduced their inventories at a rate of 4.2 billion. In the meantime, expenditures on national security fell from an annual rate of 54.3 billion dollars to 46.9 billion, while total Federal spending on goods and services fell from 62.2 billion to 55.0 billion. Thus the combined decline of inventory and defense spending over this nine-month interval was at an annual rate of 17 billion dollars.

This reduction of expenditures was reflected rather promptly in production, employment, the flow of incomes, business loans, imports, and other phases of the Nation's economic life. The over-all decline of economic activity was small, but its impact was very uneven, and some industries and localities suffered seriously. The impact of inventory liquidation and of the cuts in defense expenditures was heaviest on those engaged in the manufacture of durable goods. Other factors added to the downward pressure on this sector of the economy. Although total spending by consumers was virtually unchanged between the second quarter of 1953 and the first quarter of 1954, their outlays on durable goods were considerably reduced. Investors in fixed capital likewise reduced their outlays on equipment, though not on construction. In consequence, while the physical volume of nondurable manufactures declined 6 percent between July 1953 and March 1954, the production of durables declined 14 percent and manufacturing production as a whole, 10 percent. About 1¼ million men and women lost their jobs in manufacturing during this period, nearly a million of them in steel mills, ordnance establishments, shipbuilding yards, automotive plants, locomotive works, and other durable goods factories. In the meantime, overtime work was curtailed and the average length of the workweek declined. Wage rates continued to rise, but their influence was swamped by reduced employment and working hours, and the annual rate of wage income in manufacturing fell by 5½ billion dollars, or 11 percent. As is usual at such a time, profits fell more sharply; dividend payments, on the other hand, were maintained or even increased.

Economic contraction was not confined to manufacturing industries. Sizable reductions of activity occurred also in the mineral and transportation industries, particularly in coal mining and railroading, whose long-standing difficulties in maintaining a satisfactory market position were accentuated. Agriculture continued to be characterized by large surpluses, inadequate exports, and lower prices received by farmers relative to those paid by them. Other branches of industry—notably, construction, the electrical utilities, and the great range of service industries—were successful in resisting the forces of contraction and even continued to grow. Nevertheless, by early March 3¾ million persons were unemployed, an increase of about 2 million from the preceding July. Another ¼ million were temporarily laid off, and a large number were working only part time. A cry of impending depression was raised.

GATHERING FORCES OF RECOVERY

The depression that so many feared or expected did not, however, develop. Toward the end of 1953 signs of improvement began to appear in financial and investment markets, and these indications multiplied after the turn of the year. Stock prices started rising in September 1953. Contracts for residential building resumed their advance at about the same time. Contracts for commercial and industrial building joined the advance at the beginning of the new year, as did new business incorporations and orders placed with manufacturers of durable goods. The liabilities of business firms forced into failure reached a peak in February, then declined irregularly. Meanwhile, money rates, which had been falling since June 1953, continued to move downward. Credit became more readily available at progressively cheaper rates. The terms of mortgage financing, which had already been extensively liberalized by the fall of 1953, continued to ease during 1954, and a buoyant market developed for new mortgages. Also the market for capital issues, especially for State and local government bonds, became increasingly active and confident.

The early recovery was most dramatic in the financial and investment spheres, but it was not confined to them. After the turn of the year, retail sales began to increase, despite a substantial drop of outstanding consumer credit. Exports rose above the preceding year's level, despite a drop of imports. Inventories of manufacturers continued to decline, and sales therefore continued to exceed production. But by the spring of 1954, the decline in production had abated and the economy stabilized. The combined output of manufacturing and mining industries traced an even course between March and August. The gross national product, which expresses the dollar value of the Nation's total output of goods and services, was virtually the same for the second and third quarters of the year as for the first. Employment in nonagricultural establishments continued to fall; but the rate of decline in employment diminished appreciably and the average length of the workweek in manufacturing actually increased somewhat. The flow of total personal income, as well as of labor income, reached a low point in April and then began to rise gradually.

Meanwhile, investment preparations, especially of home builders, proceeded on an expanding scale. Businessmen also continued their efforts to win better control over inventories. These efforts met with success. Around the turn of the year, the ratio of inventories to sales had ceased rising in most lines of industry. The ratio for manufacturing as a whole, which was 1.95 in January 1954, fell to 1.88 in May and to 1.85 in September. For retailers the ratio moved from 1.66 in January to 1.62 in May and 1.58 in September. These readjustments were largest in the case of durable goods, which had felt the impact of contraction most keenly. With inventories under better control, the gap between the orders received by manufacturers and their current sales became progressively narrower, while commodity prices at wholesale and retail changed very little on the average. Wage rates continued to move upward, but most adjustments were of moderate proportions and some decreases occurred. In these circumstances the retirement of marginal units of equipment, reductions of overtime work, and other economies resulted in lower unit costs for many businesses. By the late summer of 1954, a broad foundation had thus been laid for industrial recovery.

The transition from contraction to recovery is an intricate economic process, worked out over time, whose character is never disclosed by over-all measures of economic activity. The virtual stability of the gross national product over a good part of the past year concealed the fact that, after the turn of the year, the number of declining industries in the area of manufacturing progressively diminished. It also concealed the vital transformation that was taking place in the Nation's stream of expenditure. Between the first and third quarters of 1954, total Federal spending on goods and services declined at an annual rate of 7 billion dollars. Meanwhile, other major categories of expenditure—that is, consumer spending, private domestic investment, foreign investment, and State and local expenditures—increased, in the aggregate, at approximately this rate. Not only that, but each of these four broad classes of expenditure expanded. Thus, while the gross national product stood still, the civilian part of the economy kept moving forward, enlarging its outlays, taking up the slack caused by the continued decline of Federal spending. This adaptive power of the economy during a difficult period of readjustment from war to peace supported and strengthened a widespread feeling of confidence.

By the early autumn of 1954, the forces of recovery had gathered sufficient strength to lift total production and employment, despite a continued drop of Federal spending. Total industrial production began rising gently in September, then gained momentum as the virtual shutdown of automobile plants for model change-overs ended. Employment in nondurable goods manufactures reached a trough in July, in durable goods manufactures in August, in nonagricultural establishments as a whole in the same month. In early October unemployment fell below the 3 million mark for the first time in 1954. By November economic improvement had again pushed the average length of the workweek in manufacturing above 40 hours. The recovery was largest in the steel, automobile, household appliance, and textile industries. It was felt also in coal mining, railroad freight movements, and a host of other activities. In the meantime, the construction industry, which had stubbornly defied the recession, continued to advance. The flow of personal incomes, reflecting all these improvements, expanded at a more rapid rate. Weekly earnings in manufacturing reached a new record. Bank loans increased again and interest rates stopped declining. Commodity markets generally kept steady, but rising demand for industrial raw materials pushed up their prices. Some tendency to lengthen inventory commitments developed, and the flow of orders to manufacturers again exceeded their sales. When the year ended, the traces of contraction had not yet been erased, but a general economic recovery was in process.

WHY THE CONTRACTION PROVED MILD

The course of the recent contraction raises important questions for all students of public affairs, namely: Why did the economic setback of 1953-54 prove so mild on an over-all basis? Why did our total national output of goods and services decline no more than 4 percent? Why did not the decline turn into the cumulative, spiraling depression that many feared and some expected? Why, to put a still more exacting question, did the gross national product decline from an annual rate of about 370 billion dollars in the second quarter of 1953 to 356 billion in the third quarter of 1954, or by 14 billion dollars in all, when the primary contracting factors—inventory spending and Federal spending—declined between them as much as 24 billion dollars?

These are difficult questions and they will doubtless engage the attention of scientific investigators for a long time to come. Nevertheless, some of the factors that contributed to the result are clear even today. Consumers not only maintained their spending at a consistently high level, but reduced their rate of saving during 1954. Businessmen kept up their capital expenditures at a high rate, increased the flow of dividends to stockholders, and intensified their selling efforts. Builders and real estate developers stepped up their operations. Trade unions conducted their affairs with an eye to basic conditions and with a sense of responsibility. Farmers and their organizations recognized the danger of piling up ever larger surpluses. Commercial banks and other financial institutions made ample supplies of credit available on liberal terms. States and localities carried out large and expanding programs of school, hospital, and road construction. And the continuing recovery of Western Europe helped to augment our exports and to bolster the prices of internationally traded raw materials.

Clearly, many people had a part in stemming the economic decline and easing the readjustment from war to peace. The Federal Government also contributed significantly to the process of recovery. It influenced the economy in two principal ways, first, through the automatic workings of the fiscal system, second, by deliberately pursuing monetary, tax, and expenditure policies that inspired widespread confidence on the part of people and thus helped them to act in ways that were economically constructive.

ROLE OF FEDERAL GOVERNMENT

It is well to recall that we have developed in our country a fiscal system that tends to cushion or offset a decline in private income. When employment and income decline, tax receipts decrease and certain expenditures, such as unemployment insurance payments, automatically increase. These offsets cannot be counted on to prevent a depression, but they can be of very material assistance, as recent experience indicates.

Between July 1953 and July 1954 total personal income derived from production decreased at an annual rate of 4.4 billion dollars. In the meantime, unemployment insurance and other social security payments to the public increased at a rate of 2.2 billion dollars, while tax payments by the public—quite apart from the change in rates that became effective in January 1954—fell at the rate of another billion. These two factors alone served, in very large part, to offset the over-all decline of personal income from production, and their effects were augumented by the operations of the farm price-support system.

The experience of corporations was similar to that of individuals. While corporate income decreased at an annual rate of 7.4 billion dollars between the second quarter of 1953 and the second quarter of 1954, the tax liability of corporations was cut by 4.5 billion dollars merely as a result of the decline in income and quite apart from any change in the tax law. Once again, therefore, our taxing machinery automatically cushioned the impact of a declining income on the sums available to corporations for paying dividends or adding to their assets.

The Government was not content, however, to play merely a passive role in the economy. On the contrary, definite and deliberate steps were taken to promote a stable prosperity. One of the earliest acts of the new Administration, after taking office in January 1953,, was to remove price and wage controls, in order to restore the functions of competitive markets. With a boom psychology existing at the time and unemployment at a vanishing point, this reform carried the danger of inducing fresh inflation. A precautionary policy of restricting credit expansion was therefore adopted. The aim was to prevent a reckless increase of investment and a deterioration in the quality of new credits, such as had often characterized the closing stages of economic booms in our history.

By May of 1953 it became clear that a policy of credit restraint had already accomplished this purpose, and that its further continuance might incite an anxious scramble for cash. The Federal Reserve authorities therefore proceeded promptly to ease credit conditions, first, by expanding the reserves of commercial banks, second, by reducing the reserves that the banks were required to hold against their deposits. In line with these actions, the Treasury arranged its financing so as not to compete with mortgages and other long-term issues. These steps were initiated before the peak of business activity had been definitely passed.

Later, in September 1953, when it was not yet generally appreciated that an economic decline had already begun and that the curtailment of defense spending might carry it further, the Secretary of the Treasury announced that the Administration, besides relinquishing the excess-profits tax, would not seek to postpone the reduction of the personal income tax, scheduled for January 1, 1954. The cuts served to reduce taxes during the next six months by 1.1 billion dollars, and it has been estimated that they will reduce taxes from July 1954 to June 1955 by 4.7 billion dollars. Although the tax reductions were partly offset by increases in social security contributions that also became effective in January 1954, the net effect was to increase substantially the money available to people for spending or investing.

In January 1954 the Economic Report of the President developed a comprehensive program to stimulate competitive enterprise, to strengthen the floor of security for the individual, and to curb tendencies toward either depression or inflation. The program called for structural tax changes to encourage economic growth, in particular, for more liberal treatment of depreciation allowances, for treating research and development outlays as a current expense, for reducing the double taxation of dividends, and for lengthening the period over which business losses could be carried back in reckoning the income tax. The program called also for tax adjustments to ease personal hardships, an enlargement of the credit facilities for housing, the speeding of slum clearance, extension of the protective scope of old-age and unemployment insurance, improvement of the highway system, systematic planning of public works, a realistic agricultural policy, and an extension of the President's authority to control the terms on which the Federal Government would underwrite housing loans and mortgages. The announcement in January of these legislative proposals, nearly all of which were subsequently enacted by the Congress, helped to inspire confidence in the economic policies of Government.

In later months, additional steps were taken by the Government to stimulate the economy. Federal Reserve banks lowered their rediscount rates. The reserves that member banks are required to hold in support of their deposits were reduced once again. Excise taxes were cut, carrying a revenue loss of about 1 billion dollars in the fiscal year 1955, in addition to the loss of 1.4 billion dollars as a result of enacting structural tax changes. Some of our hard-pressed industries were aided—notably shipbuilding through a new construction program, and zinc and lead mining as a result of a revised stockpiling program. The Executive Branch attended to its housekeeping duties by expediting actions that involved the private economy, as in the case of refunds of overpaid taxes, and by announcing promptly its own commitments, as in the case of grants to the States for road building. The Government also attempted to assist localities suffering from unemployment by channeling contracts to them as far as feasible, by boosting the allowable rate of accelerated amortization on facilities needed for the mobilization base, and by expanding the activities of the Area Development Division of the Department of Commerce.

EFFECTS OF GOVERMENTAL POLICIES

This, in broad outline, is the record of recent actions of the Federal Government to stimulate the economy. What gave them a special character was their promptness and the heavy reliance on momentary policies and tax reductions. The shift from credit restraint to credit ease before an economic decline had begun, the announcement of sizable tax reductions before it was generally appreciated that an economic decline was actually under way, the submission to the Congress of a comprehensive program for encouraging the growth of the economy through private enterprise—these early measures to build confidence were by far the most important. For they strengthened confidence when it was most needed, and thereby rendered unnecessary any later resort to drastic governmental programs in an atmosphere of emergency.

The basic policy of the Government in dealing with the contraction was to stimulate business firms, consumers, and States and localities to increase their expenditures, rather than to expand existing Federal enterprises or initiate new spending programs. The success of this policy is evident in the present recovery. It is evident also in some of the unusual, and at first blush puzzling, characteristics of the recent contraction—the steady increase of disposable personal income, the almost uninterrupted rise of consumer spending, the expansion of State and local improvements, the maintenance of private investment in fixed capital close to peak levels, the expansion of the money supply, and the steadiness of the price level.

Tax reductions, along with unemployment insurance benefits and other social security payments, supported powerfully the income at the disposal of individuals and families. This can be seen from a simple calculation for the interval from July 1953 to July 1954. If we combine the effects, first, of the automatic reduction of tax payments resulting from reduced incomes, second, of the deliberate changes of tax rates that occurred in January 1954, third, of the expanded flow of unemployment insurance and related payments, we get a sum of offsets to a declining production income that comes to 5.2 billion dollars. Since the income derived from production declined by an annual rate of only 4.4 billion dollars, the income available to the public for spending or saving actually increased by nearly 1 billion dollars. This remarkabe result—namely, a rise in disposable personal income accompanying a 10 percent decline of industrial production—has no parallel in our recorded economic history.

Tax reductions not only offset reductions from production income; they also helped to make production income itself larger than it would otherwise have been. As noted previously, corporate profits before taxes fell at an annual rate of 7.4 billion dollars between the second quarter of 1953 and the second quarter of 1954. Meanwhile, the reduction of taxes that automatically accompanied the decline of income, coupled with the removal of the excess-profits tax, reduced the tax liability of corporations at an annual rate of 5.5 billion dollars, and thus offset the greater part of the reduction of corporate income. Had it not been for this reduction of taxes, it is unlikely that corporations would have increased their dividend payments at an annual rate of 300 million dollars during this period, thus bolstering the flow of personal income. Nor is it likely that they would have maintained their capital expenditures at so high a rate, thereby supporting the Nation's income base. And if this is true of corporations, it is not less true of individuals and families. With their disposable income increasing, people spent money rather freely and thus supported employment and the flow of income to themselves, their neighbors, and others.

The effects of monetary and debt management policies on the community's income stream are harder to trace than the effects of lower taxes, but there can be no doubt of their significance or pervasiveness. These policies were adjusted swiftly to changing conditions, and helped materially, first to prevent inflation, later to check contraction. Before the recession of economic activity in 1953 had commenced, interest rates were already declining. Later in the year, the easing of credit terms became general, and extended from prime issues to those involving larger risks. Financial institutions, amply supplied with reserves or cash, sought opportunities to put their resources to use. With the demand for business and consumer loans relatively low, they eagerly took up mortgages, municipal bonds, corporate issues, and Treasury obligations. As a result, the loans and investments of commercial banks increased by about 10 billion dollars during 1954 and the money supply increased further—especially in the second half of the year. Had it not been for the increased availability of credit and the easing of terms, the fast pace of residential, commercial, and State and local construction, which did so much to stablize the economy during the past year, would not have been attained. Nor would consumers have been able so easily to arrange financing for a part of their expenditure. Nor would the liquidation of inventories have proceeded with so little disturbance to markets or general economic activity.

It is well to recognize, however, that the reasons for the success of recent policies are not to be found in them alone. Tax reductions, however attractive they may seem when the economy is declining, will not necessarily lead to an increase of spending or investing. Easier credit conditions, larger bank reserves, even a larger money supply will not necessarily put new money to work in industry. Management of the public debt so as to avoid competition with mortgages and other capital issues will not necessarily increase private capital formation. If such policies are to be of material help in stemming a contraction, there must be a pervasive feeling of confidence on the part of people. The effectiveness of a particular policy, whatever be its sphere or expression, is conditioned by the mood of the time, and this is bound to reflect people's attitudes toward governmental policies at large. It is not merely the intrinsic merit of the individual policies that were pursued, but also the fact that each was part of a cohesive program for strengthening the confidence of people in their own and their country's economic future, that accounts for our recent success in curbing economic contraction.

LESSONS FROM EXPERIENCE AND GUIDES TO THE FUTURE

In the course of our latest encounter with the business cycle we have learned or relearned several lessons. First, that wise and early action by Government can stave off serious difficulties later. Second, that contraction may be stopped in its tracks even when governmental expenditures and budget deficits are declining, providing effective means are taken for building confidence. Third, that monetary policy can be a powerful instrument of economic recovery, so long as the confidence of consumers and businessmen in the future remains high. Fourth, that automatic stabilizers, such as unemployment insurance and a tax system that is elastic with respect to the national income, can be of material aid in moderating cyclical fluctuations. Fifth, that a minor contraction in this country need not produce a severe depression abroad. Sixth, that an expanding world economy can facilitate our own readjustments. These teachings of experience should serve us well in the years ahead, though we must always be alert to the special needs of every new situation.

As our minds turn from the past to the future, the basic fact to keep before us is that, while the groundwork for the recent recovery was laid by the Government, the recovery itself was brought about by the American people. A mood of confidence about the economic future has been gradually developing in recent years, and the strength exhibited by our economy last year has reinforced this trend.

A large and increasing number of business managements have become accustomed to thinking in ambitious, long-range terms. Expecting our economy to grow and prosper, they do not permit minor variations in sales to divert them from the objective of strengthening, or at least maintaining, their competitive position five or ten years later. Hence they boldly allot large sums to research, plan capital expenditures well beyond immediate needs, launch extensive investment projects, and even judge one another by these yardsticks no less than by profit-and-loss statements.

The economic horizons of consumers are also widening. One of the marvels of our generation has been the growth of consumer capital—modern homes, automobiles, radios, television sets, washing machines, air conditioning units, electric dryers, food freezers, and so on in an ever longer list. Perhaps at no time in the past has the desire for material improvement played so large a role in the economy as it does today. Consumers continue to visit bargain basements but their preferences run strongly toward the latest contrivances, newest conveniences, and premium grades. And if people are no longer timid about borrowing to expand their current spending, they are also willing to work hard to acquire the incomes needed to live as they feel they should.

With the business cycle apparently under reasonable control, with the size of population growing rapidly, with science and technology adding new wonders each day, with incomes distributed widely, with mass markets expanding to match mass production, and with governmental policy steering a middle course between the political extremes, both material and psychological factors are peculiarly favorable to economic progress. Hence, the business recovery now under way is powerfully supported by underlying forces of economic growth. While only of very recent date, the recovery is widespread and has already made up half of the decline that had occurred in industrial production. The rate of inventory liquidation has sharply abated and we are soon likely to experience some rebuilding of inventories. The projected decline of Federal spending is less than in the past two years. State and local expenditure will probably continue to expand and more than offset any further decline that may occur in Federal expenditure. The recent increase of housing starts and the rush of applications to Federal agencies for mortgage insurance or guarantees promise that home building will continue to mount for some time. The recent high level of commercial building contracts is practically sure to mean a high level of expenditure for this type of construction over coming months. The prospects for plant and equipment expenditure are more uncertain; however, rising orders for machinery, to say nothing of the new plans and revisions of old plans that are likely to accompany continued recovery, give a basis for expecting that the broad category of expenditure will soon join, though perhaps only modestly at the start, the general economic advance. In view of the resurgence of the economy of Western Europe and the reduction of restrictions against dollar trade, it seems likely that our exports will continue to increase. The spirited behavior of retail sales in recent months has borne out earlier surveys of consumer attitudes. Further expansion of consumer spending may be expected as economic recovery cumulates.

Beyond these indications of immediate or short-run prospects is the fact that new firms are being established at an increasing rate, and that the offices of architects are reported to be bursting with plans for new homes, schools, and all sorts of commercial and industrial projects. Still further in the future, but already a factor in business thinking, is a new national highway system, which will create great economic opportunity in many directions, and of which something will be said later in this Report.

In the course of the current year, the economic situation may therefore be expected to continue to improve. The gross national product increased from an annual rate of about 355 billion dollars in the third quarter of 1954 to about 360 billion dollars in the fourth quarter. With economic activity continuing to expand, it is reasonable to expect that the Nation's output within the coming year will approximate the goals of "maximum employment, production, and purchasing power" envisaged by the Employment Act. At this juncture of our economic life, when confidence is running especially high, it is well, however, to keep in mind the sobering fact that there is no way of lifting more than a corner of the veil that separates the present from the future. How long the current phase of expansion will continue before the new international trouble or a cyclical reversal of business occurs, or how far the expansion will carry, it is impossible to say with great assurance. The uncertainty of economic predictions requires that the Federal Government be prepared to adjust its policies promptly if economic events should not bear out current expectations. Over coming weeks or months we should, however, be careful not to confuse seasonal fluctuations in employment or special fluctations of individual industries or markets with over-all economic trends. It will prove helpful to keep in mind that a business recovery never retraces the precise path of the preceding contraction, and that this divergence is apt to be sharpest in postwar movements. The prosperity that some industries and localities attained during the Korean conflict, and which they have now lost, will not be regained quickly in all instances. Here and there the process of readjusting to reduced markets may be prolonged, although it will be greatly eased as general economic expansion continues.

We must also remember that, just as economic expansion resolves old problems, so it often brings new ones in its train. History tells us that industrial disputes have usually been more frequent in periods of expansion than in periods of contraction, and that industrial disputes sometimes have serious economic repercussions. History also warns us that activities which involve the discounting of a long future, as in the case of home purchases or the pricing of corporate shares, may be carried to excess in the course of a business expansion. Fortunately, when speculative trends develop, they usually become self-corrective before they become excessive. It is highly desirable that corrective movements, testing the soundness of various parts of the economy, be scattered over a period of time rather than culminate at the same time. As the recent increase of stock margin requirements by the Federal Reserve Board has demonstrated, the Government is mindful of its great responsibility to help assure balanced economic growth. It is essential to keep a close watch on financial developments. Continued economic recovery must not be jeopardized by overemphasis of speculative activity.

V

Big Business

---

22. THE CONCENTRATION OF PRODUCTIVE FACILITIES *

IN 1947 the Federal Trade Commission made a study of the concentration of productive facilities in the American economy. One index of concentration used by the Commission was the percentage of the net capital assets of an industry owned by each of the major companies in that industry. The findings of the Commission are presented in part in the article below. These findings are now almost ten years old and some of the data will no longer be correct. However, the method used in classifying industries and the conclusions of the study are still important and generally applicable to the economy. The reader may find it helpful in this respect to read the comments on classification of industries found in Selection 24, page 239.

SUMMARY OF DATA BY INDUSTRIES

THE DIFFERENCES in the degree and character of concentration are revealed in greater detail in Tables 1 and 2. Here the same basic data are presented in two different ways. Table 1 shows varying degrees of control (expressed in terms of class intervals) reached by different numbers of companies. At the top are the tin can, aluminum, and linoleum industries; in each of these, from 50 to 59 per cent control is reached with only one company. At the bottom is the drug and medicine industry in which less than 25 per cent control is reached with

* *Report of the Federal Trade Commission on the Concentration of Productive Facilities, 1947* (Government Printing Office, 1950), pp. 20-22, 43-45, 53-57, 70-71.

TABLE 1

26 Selected Manufacturing Industries, Number of Corporations Owning Selected Proportions of Total Net Capital Assets of Industry, 1947

(Number of corporations)

Industry	*Per Cent of Net Capital Assets of Industry*							
	10-24	25-32	33-49	50-59	60-69	70-79	80-89	90 and over
1. Tin cans and other tinware	—	—	—	1	—	—	—	2
2. Aluminum	—	—	—	1	—	—	2	3
3. Linoleum	—	—	—	1	—	—	2	3
4. Copper smelting and refining	—	—	1	—	—	2	3	4
5. Plumbing equipment and supplies	—	—	1	—	2	3	—	—
6. Cigarettes	—	—	1	—	2	3	4	5
7. Motor vehicles	—	—	1	—	2	4	13	—
8. Agricultural machinery	—	—	1	2	3	4	6	—
9. Office and store machines and devices	—	—	1	2	3	4	6	15
10. Biscuits, crackers, and pretzels	—	—	1	2	3	4	—	—
11. Rubber tires and tubes	—	1	—	2	—	3	4	5
12. Distilled liquors	—	1	—	2	—	3	4	6
13. Electrical machinery	—	1	—	2	3	5	10	—
14. Meat products	—	1	2	2	3	5	10	—
15. Glass and glassware	—	1	2	3	4	7	—	—
16. Dairy products	—	1	2	3	5	8	—	—
17. Industrial chemicals	—	1	2	4	5	7	11	—
18. Primary steel	—	1	2	4	5	9	—	—
19. Carpets and rugs	1	—	2	4	5	—	—	—
20. Footwear (except rubber)	1	2	2	6	—	—	—	—
21. Aircraft and parts	1	2	3	5	6	8	11	—
22. Canning and preserving	1	3	4	8	—	—	—	—
23. Grain-mill products	1	3	4	9	—	—	—	—
24. Bread and other products (except biscuits and crackers)	1	3	5	—	—	—	—	—
25. Woolen and worsted goods	1	3	6	—	—	—	—	—
26. Drugs and medicines	2	4	5	10	—	—	—	—

two companies. The ranking of the industries shown on the table is thus a measure of their relative concentration. The analysis of the table may be illustrated by the following example. Reading from left to right across the table, it may be noted that in the case of motor vehicles the proportion of the industry's net capital assets owned by its single largest company falls between 33 and 49 per cent, the proportion owned by the 2 largest falls between 60 and 69 per cent, by the 4 larg-

TABLE 2

26 Selected Manufacturing Industries, Proportion of Net Capital Assets Owned by Leading Concerns, 1947

Industry	*Per Cent of Net Capital Assets Owned by—*						
	1 Company	2 Companies	3 Companies	4 Companies	8 Companies	15 Companies	All Companies
1. Linoleum	57.9	80.8	92.1	93.6	—	—	100.0
2. Tin cans and other tinware	55.2	92.1	95.3	96.4	—	—	100.0
3. Aluminum	55.0	85.0	100.0	—	—	—	100.0
4. Copper smelting and refining	46.8	73.5	88.5	94.6	100.0	—	100.0
5. Biscuits, crackers and pretzels	46.3	57.0	67.7	71.4	—	—	100.0
6. Agricultural machinery	45.3	56.8	66.6	75.4	82.1	—	100.0
7. Office and store machines and devices	42.0	56.3	69.5	74.3	85.3	89.6	100.0
8. Motor vehicles	40.9	62.8	68.7	70.7	77.3	86.1	100.0
9. Cigarettes	36.6	64.4	77.6	87.8	—	—	100.0
10. Plumbing equipment and supplies	33.2	64.9	71.3	74.3	—	—	100.0
11. Distilled liquors	29.0	53.3	72.4	84.6	94.3	—	100.0
12. Meat products	28.8	54.7	64.0	69.3	77.6	81.6	100.0
13. Primary steel	28.6	42.0	49.2	54.5	69.3	77.2	100.0
14. Rubber tires and tubes	27.8	49.9	70.3	88.3	94.8	—	100.0
15. Dairy products	27.5	48.9	55.8	59.6	71.3	—	100.0
16. Glass and glassware	24.9	49.1	57.4	62.2	73.9	—	100.0
17. Carpets and rugs	24.1	36.8	48.9	57.9	—	—	100.0
18. Footwear (except rubber)	23.6	39.6	43.4	46.8	53.1	57.5	100.0
19. Industrial chemicals	21.5	36.5	45.5	51.8	70.2	80.2	100.0
20. Woolen and worsted goods	16.7	23.5	28.1	30.3	36.4	—	100.0
21. Electrical machinery	15.8	28.8	41.7	47.5	55.2	60.7	100.0
22. Grain-mill products	15.6	23.5	30.2	36.3	48.6	56.6	100.0
23. Aircraft and parts	13.6	25.4	35.2	44.0	73.7	86.2	100.0
24. Bread and other products (excluding biscuits and crackers)	13.0	20.0	25.4	30.6	38.2	—	100.0
25. Canning and preserving	10.7	21.4	32.0	39.4	51.0	59.2	100.0
26. Drugs and medicine	8.4	16.5	23.5	30.0	47.7	—	100.0

est between 70 and 79 per cent, and by the 13 largest between 80 and 89 per cent.

In all the industries shown, 6 or fewer corporations control at least one-third of the total net capital assets of their respective industries; in almost half of the industries shown, 4 or fewer companies control 70 per cent or over; and in 14 of the 26 industries, 3 or fewer companies account for at least 60 per cent of the net capital assets.

The data in Table 2 reveal in a slightly different way much the same picture of concentration. Here, the industries are ranked according to the ownership of assets by the single leading corporation in each industry, and the increments to concentration are indicated as the second, third, etc., corporations are added thereafter.

This table emphasizes the contribution of the leader to the over-all degree of concentration in the various industries. In most cases the rankings of the industries in terms of over-all concentration are not substantially altered as the remaining corporations are added. The principal difference in the rankings between Table 1 and Table 2 is electrical machinery, which stands much higher in the former, owing to the very substantial size of the second leading corporation. The general similarity in the rankings shown by the two tables would thus suggest that a significant clue to the degree and character of concentration is provided by the relative importance of the single largest corporation.

While these summary tables serve a useful purpose in indicating differences in concentration among the various industries, in order to obtain a better understanding of the significance of the data for a particular industry, it is necessary to note certain characteristics of the individual industries that affect the interpretation of the data, as will be brought out in the following discussion of [some of] the industries included in the report.

ALUMINUM

In the case of the aluminum industry—and only in this field—it has been decided not to use net capital assets owned by the three corporations as the measure of concentration. In terms of ownership of such assets, Aluminum Co. of America accounts for 82 per cent; Reynolds Metals Co., 16 per cent; and Permanente Metals Corp., slightly in excess of 2 per cent. But these are unrealistic figures in view of (*a*) the peculiar importance of war-built plants in the industry which are leased to both Reynolds and Permanente; and (*b*) the improbability, in view of the court's decision in the *Aluminum* case and an adverse ruling of the Attorney General, that these Government-owned plants will come under the ownership of Alcoa. If account is taken of the assets leased to, as well as owned by, Reynolds and Permanente, the proportion of estimated net capital assets operated by the aluminum companies would be roughly as follows:

	Per Cent
Alcoa	55
Reynolds	30
Permanente	15

These proportions, it may be noted, are about the same order of magnitude as the relative shares of primary aluminum capacity controlled by the three aluminum corporations.

TABLE 3

Total Sales and Virgin Pig Aluminum Production in the Aluminum Industry, 1947

	Total Sales		*Virgin Pig Output*	
	Thousands of dollars	Per Cent of Total	Thousands of pounds	Per Cent of Total
Alcoa	292,640	62.2	637,951	57.8
Reynolds	128,279	27.3	281,359	25.5
Permanente	49,605	10.5	184,919	16.7
Total	470,524	100.0	1,104,229	100.0

Source: Material submitted in evidence, *United States* v. *Aluminum Company of America,* equity 85-73 U.S. District Court of the Southern District of New York, 1949.

This general picture of the distribution of the industry among the three companies is corroborated by data secured by the Department of Justice in connection with the Aluminum case. As shown in Table 3, Alcoa in 1947 accounted for slightly more than 60 per cent of the industry's sales and approximately 58 per cent of the virgin pig aluminum output. The corresponding figures for Reynolds are 27 per cent and 26 per cent.

TABLE 4

Cumulative Per Cent of Net Capital Assets Owned by Largest Corporation, 1947

Rank	*Company*	*Per Cent of Net Capital Assets Owned by Each Corporation*	*Cumulative Per Cent Owned*
1.	Aluminum Co. of America	55.0	55.0
2.	Reynolds Metal Co.	30.0	85.0
3.	Permanente Metals Corp.	15.0	100.0

Source: Federal Trade Commission, Securities and Exchange Commission, and Moody's Investors Service.

Until 1949, the Kaiser Co. [Permanente] engaged in no aluminum fabricating activity other than sheet production. Moreover, at the basic raw material stage, Permanente obtains most of its bauxite requirements from an Alcoa subsidiary under terms of a lease now in force, and according to a statement of Permanente the costs of this bauxite are somewhat less favorable to it than bauxite costs to Alcoa from the same source.

MOTOR VEHICLES

The motor vehicles industry presents a study in the problems of measuring concentration. In some studies concentration has been measured in this field by determining the proportion of the industry's output of its principal finished products, automobiles and trucks, which is produced by the largest single company, by the "Big Three," etc. This type of measure for the year 1948 is shown below:

TABLE 5

Concentration of Production of Automobiles and Trucks, 1948

	Automobiles		*Trucks*		*Total*	
Company	Thousands	Per Cent of Total	Thousands	Per Cent of Total	Thousands	Per Cent of Total
General Motors	1,565	40	483	35	2,048	39
Chrysler	825	21	172	13	997	19
Ford	747	19	302	22	1,049	20
Big three	3,137	80	957	70	4,094	78
All others	771	20	419	30	1,180	22
Total	3,908	100	1,376	100	5,274	100

Source: *Ward's Automotive Reports,* Jan. 10, 1949, p. 16.

This measure, while useful for some purposes, has the disadvantage that it is focused entirely upon the end-product stage of the industry and in effect ignores the vast amount of productive resources at the industry's lower stages of production. It happens that there is a large amount of facilities in the industry owned by parts-makers, who sell various parts and components to the automobile producers. Thus, no matter how important a parts-maker and no matter how large his productive facilities, he is ignored by this measure of concentration.

As a consequence, it is to be expected that a measure such as net capital assets, which reflects the productive facilities of all corporations classified in the industry, whether automobile producers, parts-makers, or anything else, will show a somewhat lower degree of concentration than is indicated at the end-product stage. And the less integrated is an automobile producer, that is, the greater is his dependence on independent companies for the parts and components which go into his finished product, the lower would be a measure of his production facilities, as compared to a measure of his end-product production.

The facts tend to confirm this expectation. The concentration of the industry in the hands of the "Big 3," as measured by net capital assets, is substantially below that indicated by the figures on the production of automobiles and trucks. Thus, General Motors, Chrysler, and Ford own only 69 per cent of the industry's net capital assets, whereas they account for 78 per cent of the production of automobiles and trucks. Moreover, nearly all of this difference is traceable to the Chrysler Corp., which is much less integrated than the other two major companies.

	Per Cent of Industry's Net Capital Assets, 1947	*Per Cent of Automobiles and Trucks Produced, 1948*
General Motors	41	39
Ford	22	19
Chrysler	6	20
	—	—
Total	69	78

In using the asset figures for this industry, it should be borne in mind that the activity of the leaders, principally General Motors, in fields outside the motor vehicle industry distorts the figures. Although it is impossible to provide any quantitative measure of the extent of this distortion, it is not believed that this factor invalidates the conclusion as to the concentration of over-all productive strength. The reasons

TABLE 6

Cumulative Per Cent of Net Capital Assets Owned by Largest Corporations, 1947

Rank	*Company*	*Per Cent of Net Capital Assets Owned by Each Corporation*	*Cumulative Per Cent Owned*
1.	General Motors Corp.	40.9	40.9
2.	Ford Motor Co.	21.9	62.8
3.	Chrysler Corp.	5.9	68.7
4.	Budd Co., The	2.0	70.7
5.	Borg-Warner Corp.	1.7	72.4
6.	Nash-Kelvinator Corp.	1.7	74.1
7.	Kaiser-Frazer Corp.	1.6	75.7
8.	Hudson Motor Car Co.	1.6	77.3

Source: Federal Trade Commission, Securities and Exchange Commission, and Moody's Investors Service.

for this supposition are threefold: (1) As compared to the total size of General Motors, it is believed that the amount of General Motors assets engaged in outside fields is relatively minor; (2) Many of the facilities so engaged are readily convertible to the production of motor vehicles; and (3) Significant proportions of the assets of the industry's smaller companies, particularly the parts makers, also are engaged in producing items in "outside" fields.

There are five smaller independents in the automobile assembling business—the makers of "Hudson," "Packard," "Nash," "Studebaker" and "Kaiser" automobiles.* The combined net capital assets of these independents represent less than 10 per cent of the net capital assets of the industry. That this proportion is somewhat less than their percentage of the production of automobiles and trucks is again due to the inclusion of the parts manufacturers in the industry group.

MEAT PRODUCTS

. . . The combined net capital assets of the first two producers [in the meat products industry—that is, Armour and Swift] amounts to almost 55 per cent of the total of all corporations engaged primarily in meat-packing, with Armour owning almost 29 per cent. Smaller than these two giants, but still significant factors in the industry, are the "second-line" companies, Wilson & Co., Inc., with 9 per cent, and Cudahy Packing Co., with 5 per cent of the total.

Below these firms is a third group of packers composed of such firms as John Morrell & Co., Rath Packing Co., George A. Hormel & Co., Oscar Mayer & Co., Inc., Hygrade Food Products Corp., and Kingan & Co., Inc., each of which owns from 1 to 3 per cent of the industry's productive facilities. The combined assets of this "third line" are just about equal to those of Wilson & Co., third largest of the Big Four. These concerns have more localized distribution than the national meat packers, and for the most part confine their business mainly to pork processing.

Almost all other corporations in the industry are local in character, buying and selling in nearby markets. Altogther, they account for less than 20 per cent of the industry's facilities, or less than the amount held by the industry's second largest firm, Swift & Co.

The leading companies in this field are engaged in a number of activities outside of the meat-packing industry, such as the production of fertilizer, hides and leather, and similar products. This ownership of assets engaged in other fields tends to result in an over-statement of

* "Hudson" and "Nash" are now manufactured by American Motors Corporation, "Studebaker" and "Packard" by the Studebaker-Packard Corporation.—Eds.

concentration in meat packing. However, that tendency is offset to a considerable extent by the fact that (*a*) many of the smaller companies, particularly the second- and third-line companies, are also engaged in such "outside" activities and (*b*) the production of many of these "other" items is in the nature of a byproduct operation, requiring relatively small additions to the productive facilities required for meat packing.

The following table presents figures showing the proportion of the output of the industry's principal products accounted for in 1937 by the four largest producers of these products. Except for some of the pork products, the levels of concentration for the individual products are not appreciably below the net capital assets figure.

Product	*Per Cent of Value of Product Produced by 4 Leading Companies in 1937*
Meat, canned, vacuum cooked	70.0
Meat, cured; hams, cooked	44.4
Meat, cured; pork, dry salted, not smoked	54.6
Meat, cured; pork, smoked	45.9
Meat, cured; pork, not smoked	70.1
Meat, fresh; beef	58.2
Meat, fresh; mutton and lamb	74.5
Meat, fresh; pork	45.5
Meat, fresh; veal	59.4
Meat, fresh; edible organs, tripe, etc.	63.5

TABLE 7

Cumulative Per Cent of Net Capital Assets Owned by Largest Corporations, 1947

Rank	*Company*	*Per Cent of Net Capital Assets Owned by Each Corporation*	*Cumulative Per Cent Owned*
1.	Armour & Co.	28.8	28.8
2.	Swift & Co.	25.9	54.7
3.	Wilson & Co., Inc.	9.3	64.0
4.	Cudahy Packing Co.	5.3	69.3
5.	Morrell, John & Co.	3.2	72.5
6.	Rath Packing Co.	2.2	74.7
7.	Hormel, George A., & Co.	1.5	76.2
8.	Mayer, Oscar, & Co., Inc.	1.4	77.6

Source: Federal Trade Commission, Securities and Exchange Commission, and Moody's Investors Service.

CANNING AND PRESERVING

With the exception of drugs and medicines, the concentration curve starts at a lower point in canning and preserving than in any of the other fields covered in this report, the largest firm owning only 11 per cent of the industry's net capital assets. The curve than rises rather steadily, however, with the next three companies adding an average of about 10 per cent each, the four firms thus holding 39.4 per cent of the industry's facilities.

Because of specialization in particular fields, the degree of concentration for many of the industry's individual products is considerably higher than is indicated by the figure for the industry as a whole. Thus the industry may be divided into those firms which specialize in canning of soups and baked beans and those which process and can a more general line of fruits and vegetables. Among the former group, the leading corporations are H. J. Heinz Co., with 10.7 per cent of the whole industry's net capital assets, and Campbell Soups, with 10.6 per cent. In the latter group, the principal firms are California Packing Corp., with 10.7 per cent, and Libby, McNeill & Libby, with 7.4 per cent.

Within this broad division there is a further degree of specialization. It frequently happens that one or two firms dominate the canning of certain fruits and vegetables, and do not participate at all or only slightly in canning other products, which in turn are dominated by other large companies.

The effect of this specialization on the degree of concentration for the individual products is clearly apparent from the following table which shows the proportion of the output of the industry's principal products accounted for in 1937 by the four largest producers of each product. It will be noted that of the seven items which come within the standard of "principal product" used in this report, the degree of concentration in all but two, canned corn and canned peas, is higher

Product	*Per Cent of Value of Product Produced by 4 Leading Companies in 1937*
Fruit salad and cocktail	48.8
Peaches	40.6
Beans, baked	58.2
Corn	23.6
Peas	24.0
Tomato juice and cocktail	45.4
Tomato ketchup	46.6

than the proportion of the industry's net capital assets held in 1947 by its four largest companies (39.4 per cent).

TABLE 8

Cumulative Per Cent of Net Capital Assets Owned by Largest Corporations, 1947

Rank	*Company*	*Per Cent of Net Capital Assets Owned by Each Corporation*	*Cumulative Per Cent Owned*
1.	Heinz, H. J., Co.	10.7	10.7
2.	California Packing Corp.	10.7	21.4
3.	Campbell Soups	10.6	32.0
4.	Libby, McNeill & Libby	7.4	39.4
5.	Hawaiian Pineapple Co., Ltd.	4.8	44.2
6.	Stokely-Van Camp, Inc.	3.1	47.3
7.	Alaska Packers Association	2.0	49.3
8.	Deerfield Packing Corp.	1.7	51.0

Source: Federal Trade Commission, Securities and Exchange Commission, and Moody's Investors Service.

CIGARETTES

The cigarette industry is one of the most highly concentrated fields in American industry, with the American Tobacco Co. ("Lucky Strikes" and "Pall Mall"), Liggett & Meyers Tobacco Co. ("Chesterfields"), R. J. Reynolds Tobacco Co. ("Camels"), and P. Lorillard Co. ("Old Golds") owning 87.8 per cent of the industry's net capital assets. The concentration curve for the industry starts at the high point of 36.6 per cent for the American Tobacco Co., and rises precipitously, with the second company bringing the curve to 64.4 per cent, and the third to 77.6 per cent.

Of the few smaller companies sharing the remaining 12 per cent of the industry, the largest is Philip Morris, with 7.6 per cent of the assets. Other small companies are Benson & Hedges, Flemming-Hall Tobacco Co., Inc., Brown & Williamson, etc.

Because of the fairly narrow definition of the industry and the comparative lack of diversity of operations on the part of the leading companies, the degree of concentration for the industry as a whole should be quite close to that for its principal, and indeed only product. It happens that this supposition is correct. In 1937 the four largest companies accounted for 84.8 per cent of the value of output of cigarettes, which compares with the figure of 87.8 per cent representing the proportion of the industry's net capital assets owned in 1947 by its four largest companies.

TABLE 9

Cumulative Per Cent of Net Capital Assets Owned by Largest Corporations, 1947

Rank	*Company*	*Per Cent of Net Capital Assets Owned by Each Corporation*	*Cumulative Per Cent Owned*
1.	American Tobacco Co.	36.6	36.6
2.	R. J. Reynolds Tobacco Co.	27.8	64.4
3.	Liggett & Meyers Tobacco Co.	13.2	77.6
4.	P. Lorillard	10.2	87.8
5.	Philip Morris, Ltd. Co.	7.6	95.4

Source: Federal Trade Commission, Securities and Exchange Commission, and Moody's Investors Service.

23. BIGNESS AND MONOPOLY *

Why Penalize Success and Efficiency?

IN THIS article the President of the Du Pont Corporation cites the magnitude of the expenditures necessary to the research and development of such products as "nylon" and "orlon." Through examples he demonstrates that expenditures are practical and practicable only under the aegis of big business. However, bigness does not necessarily mean monopoly, states Mr. Greenewalt, and as evidence he cites the competition in the markets for the products sold by his firm.

BEFORE I try to deal with the problems of bigness and monopoly—both very controversial subjects—let me see if I can define the economic area in which there is agreement. I think we can all get together on the desire for economic progress. We all want a stronger America—a more prosperous America—an ever better place in which to live. We have won for ourselves the highest living standard in the world, and the benefits of our economy are spread among all our people, perhaps not so widely as we would like, but nevertheless more widely than in any other country.

* Crawford H. Greenewalt, *Vital Speeches,* December 1, 1949, pp. 118-121. Reprinted by permission of the author and the publisher.

The author (1902——) is President of E. I. du Pont de Nemours and Company.

As a nation we are not content to stay put. We are eager to push ahead—to reach ever higher—to spread the benefits of our productive genius ever farther.

The quarrel comes not in what we want to accomplish but how best we can get at it.

That is where the problem of bigness in business first rears its head. We have big business—we have always had it.

But many people now seem to regard big business as in some way inimical to the public interest. They look upon large corporations as "monopolies," "concentrations of economic power," selfish and heartless, seeking economic aggrandizement for themselves at the expense of the rest of the people. Believing that, it is a natural consequence to favor the use of political power to restrict corporate activities, to bring their operations under the control of the government, and in some cases to break them up.

Any one who has studied the economic problems of the nation must know that these premises are wrong. A business, whether it be big or little, to be successful must serve the public interest; and if a business grows it does so because the quality and price of its products win public confidence. Its ultimate size is then dictated only by the aggregate demand of its satisfied customers. There is a clear difference between protecting competition and protecting competitors, and true and lasting economic progress lies in encouraging the most efficient producers so that all people may have more and better things for their money.

Actually growth in an industrial enterprise has only one connotation —and that is success in pleasing three groups of people—its customers, its employees, and its stockholders. That is no easy task. The record also shows that there is nothing static in that success once it is achieved. If you will look at the lists of the largest industrial corporations in this country year by year since the beginning of the century you will see that success in business, as in any other endeavor, is indeed a fugitive thing. Most of us have forgotten that some of the leaders of a generation ago ever existed, and that is because the decision that led to their downfall or shrinkage was taken, not by government, but by the most powerful body in this country—the customers with dollars in their hot hands searching eternally for lower costs and better quality.

The Du Pont Company *is* successful and it *is* big, and in saying that I am merely reciting cause and effect. Those of us who are responsible for its management are thoroughly and painfully aware that that success comes about through public acceptance of the goods and services we offer. Should we ever fail in maintaining that acceptance, we will lose business and someone else will gain it. And that, gentlemen, will bring about a breakup of what has been called the "Du Pont industrial empire" far more quickly and far more devastatingly than any outside attack.

"Monopoly" is a word in the glossary of modern terminology which is much used, and much abused. We now have a legal interpretation that says "monopoly" is the manufacture of a large share of any product by any one company regardless of how competitive that product may be with other materials doing the same job. To add to the legal confusion, the word "share" appears to mean anything between 30% and 100% depending upon circumstances which are also as yet undefined.

The political interpretation of "monopoly" seems to be that anyone who is big has it, and very recently we have been given the concept that if as many as three or four companies have a majority of a market they are said to be monopolists, or "oligopolists" as the erudite call it, regardless of how intense the competition be between them.

Actually monopoly means "one seller," and the test of monopoly is whether the buyer of any article has freedom of choice in fulfilling his requirements. If he can make his purchase from only one source, then a monopoly exists, even though that monopoly may be a perfectly legal one, such as the purchase of electric power in many of our communities. But if he can select from among several materials, each of which will to a greater or less extent relieve his need, then no monopoly in any real sense exists. The choice becomes that of the customer and he can buy or refuse to buy without compulsion and according to his best judgment.

The term "monopoly" has also been given the implication that it is intended to smother or to exclude competition. The chemical industry is popularly depicted as a haven of monopoly, yet it is in fact one of the most competitive industries in the world.

There are something like 9,000 companies engaged in the manufacture of what the Census Bureau describes as "chemical and allied products." As a corporation, the Du Pont Company is the largest of these and has roughly 8% of the trade in this segment of American industry. Individually, however, few of our products lead their fields. In most instances our leading competitors are more important factors than we in many of our markets.

In the paint field, Sherwin-Williams is bigger than Du Pont and both of us fight for business among nearly 1,200 active competitors. American Viscose is larger than we in viscose rayon; Celanese in acetate rayon, and there are about 15 other important companies in those fields.

Union Carbide is bigger than we in plastics; Allied Chemical in nitrogen products; Eastman Kodak in photographic film; Dow in chlorine products and also in insecticides.

I say that without shame, because it comes about as a matter of deliberate policy—a policy of diversification which I believe has operated in the interests of the consumer, of the Du Pont Company, and of the public at large. With limited resources for capital expenditure, we have no wish to strive for a fixed percentage of any market. To do so would prevent us from exploiting to the full the new developments produced in our research laboratories, and that I think is our greatest challenge and our greatest responsibility. Any success we might have in excluding competition in viscose rayon, in paint, or in sulfuric acid might very probably make us miss a neoprene synthetic rubber, a cellophane, or a nylon, and that would be advantageous neither to us nor to the public.

For the Du Pont Company, and I believe this is also true for the chemical industry, I can say categorically that our present size and our present success have *not* come about through a process of stifling competition by absorbing competitors.

It has come about through the new products and new processes that have been developed in our laboratories, and the proof of that statement is in our sales figures. Sixty per cent of Du Pont sales in 1948 consisted of products that were not in commercial production in 1928—just two decades ago.

Experience in other countries has shown that the hand of monopoly is a dead hand indeed. It profits no one, least of all the company that attempts to practice it.

The Du Pont Company has existed for nearly one hundred and fifty years in an atmosphere of free and vigorous competition. We have done well under that system and we like it. Competition is a prod that keeps us continually on our toes. We think we are stronger because of it; we think we would be weaker without it. The opportunities for growth and service in our industry through the development of new things are limitless. It is utter foolishness to think that growth in any of its varied phases can be brought about only by the elimination of other manufacturers.

It should be obvious to anyone that big businesses are essential in the complex economy in which we live today. A business is simply a pool of people's resources—the resources of a group of employees, of a group of investors to accomplish a given task. Since there is a limit to what any one man will risk, the larger the task the bigger the pool must be. If we want low-priced automobiles, low-priced radios, low-priced television sets, we must have a large team of people to work and venture so that the benefits of mass production can be applied to those products.

It follows also that big business has its own peculiar responsibility—that is to devote itself to those tasks that require its full resources of manpower, of finance, of talent. So far as Du Pont is concerned we have endeavored over the years to tackle the difficult projects that make full use of the resources we enjoy. I would like to cite a few examples out of many in which that policy has been successfully employed.

The United States had no dyestuffs industry worthy of the name prior to the First World War and was dependent on Germany even for the dyes with which to print stamps and money. Du Pont was one of the pioneers in instituting dyestuffs manufacture in this country. What that venture cost like-minded chemical manufactures I do not know. I do know that for Du Pont it was eighteen years and 43 millions of dollars before profits offset losses.

In the early twenties we built a plant in West Virginia to manufacture ammonia and other chemicals by the application of pressures unheard of commercially up to that time. That was another long and expensive trip since it was more than ten years and many millions of dollars before that department began to show black ink on its profit and loss statement.

Nylon is at the same time one of our greatest successes and one of our greatest gambles. Basic research leading to this development was started in 1928 but it was not until 1940 and the expenditure of about 27 millions of dollars that we were able to sell the first pound made in a commercial unit.

Some of you may have heard that we have a new textile fiber in the making which we have called "Orlon" acrylic fiber. We are building the first commercial unit for its manufacture at Camden, S. C. We have hopes for that new product but I must admit that we do not yet know whether it will be a sheep or a goat. Before we find out, sometime in 1950 or 1951, we will have gambled $7 million in research and $15 million in plant investment.

Nylon, ammonia, dyestuffs have been profitable items for Du Pont. But don't think for a minute that Du Pont stockholders were the only gainers. There were thousands of men and women who got jobs that never existed before. There were millions of consumers whose standard of living was raised by each such success. There is the country itself, stronger both in peace and in war. When these gambles pay off, *everybody* benefits.

And research itself is perhaps the greatest gamble of all. You gentlemen see only the successes described in high-sounding releases from our Public Relations Department. What you do not see is the long list of failures—the brave new ideas that don't pan out. I speak with deep feeling because as a research man I had lots of those brave new ideas myself that ended in the trash can.

Statistics on failures are difficult to come by but it is a fair approximation to say that not more than one out of five research dollars pays off. That means simply that if the direct cost of nylon research is say five million dollars, there is perhaps twenty-five million dollars worth of unsuccessful research that has to be paid for by that one successful development. We are playing with very blue chips indeed.

And our success in the future, if we are fortunate enough to have it, will come not because we have taken business from someone else, but because we are able to keep that stream of new products and improved processes continually flowing.

On many of these developments we have for seventeen years the sole right of manufacture by virtue of patents granted us under the laws of the United States. Nylon is one of those developments. But let me assure you that while we are the only manufacturer of nylon, we have in no sense a monopoly of the applications for that product. Nylon competes for the customer's dollar with every synthetic and natural textile fiber. Your wives may have their stockings, dresses and lingerie made of nylon, but you may be very sure that if price and quality are not competitive, the ladies will turn to silk, rayon, or in fact anything that better suits their fancy and their purse. If we are not successful in meeting the competitive requirements of the market place we may continue to be the only manufacturer, but we will have nothing but red figures on the balance sheet to show for it. And that is cold comfort indeed.

With our new products it is essential that we strive for the largest market, not for the highest price or the highest profit. We introduced cellophane many years ago and costs of manufacture by the methods used then forced us to sell it at $2.65 a pound. It was used initially only in wrapping luxury items, such as perfumes, bath salts, and fancy candy boxes. Some purchasers even thought it valuable enough to keep in their safes. Today, as a result of technological improvements and increased volume, cellophane sells for around 50 cents a pound. Because of that low price, cellophane now protects the most commonplace articles and saves millions of dollars annually in eliminating waste and spoilage of food.

And so to strive for the largest market, at the lowest price that yields a reasonable return on our investment, is a policy which serves many ends. It is beneficial to the public in making available to them an ever-increasing flow of the goods and services they desire. It is beneficial also in creating new opportunities for employment, and, finally, it is profitable to us as a corporation and so provides our 100,000 stockholders with a return on their capital.

There is much misconception also about the relationship between big and little businesses. The idea has been put forward that big businesses grow by swallowing little businesses or by limiting their growth. Nothing could be farther from the truth. No little business could compete with us in nylon for the reason that no such business could bring together the capital and technical resources required for an efficient producing unit. We, on the other hand, have no interest in competing in spheres where we can make no substantial technical contribution, and there are many activities, particularly in fields of marketing and distribution that small businesses can do better than we. It is, in addition, essential for us to pursue a cooperative relationship with those small businesses since they are the suppliers of our raw materials and the primary consumers of our finished products.

Let me cite an example. We make nylon yarn and sell it to whoever will buy. Your wife buys, let us say, a nylon blouse. Between the sale of that yarn and that blouse are the throwster who twists the yarn, the weaver who weaves it, the finisher who finishes and dyes it, the cutter who makes the garment, and the retail store that sells it. For the most part those are small businesses. They need us; we need them. We thrive together by virtue of a cooperative relationship. Perhaps I can put it for you quantitatively. Your wife pays about $1.50 for her nylon stockings. We get about 10 cents for the yarn that goes into them, and the difference represents the contribution, the opportunity, and the profit of the many smaller businesses that lie between us and the final consumer.

Had we the power and the desire,—which we do not,—to swallow these businesses or to drive them out of existence, we would indeed be killing the goose that lays the golden egg.

I have spoken about big business and about monopoly. Let me say a word about the laws that regulate them. We have had on our books for many years the Sherman anti-trust law. The Du Pont Company is now and has always been heartily in favor of that law and the safeguards it provides for our system of free, competitive enterprise. Unfortunately that law states an objective and prescribes no rules so that the ideology of enforcement is left to the shifting winds of political thought. This had led to continuing changes in interpretation as one court decision succeeds another. Unfortunately also, no practical statute of limitations applies,—so business frequently finds itself attacked for acts done many years ago in all good faith and with the best legal advice available.

I do not want to leave the impression that business, whether large or small, has never made mistakes. A business is a group of people, subject to the same human frailties as people in any sphere of activity. We must not let the occasional error blind us to the overriding benefits our industrial system has brought. That system has made America the strongest nation on earth, and its free development will carry us to new heights.

The controversy which is rising to a climax in this country over so-called "monopoly" and big business is a matter of vital interest to all of its citizens.

This nation has grown strong by allowing the forces of the market place to rule—the business laurels falling to whoever is able enough to win them, the law present to insure fair play. I do not see that there is any tenable alternative. In the national interest no steps must be taken that penalize success and efficiency. We dare not hobble the willingness of a business to venture by refusing it the fruits of its success or by holding out the doubtful privilege of government regulation when that success has been achieved. We can preserve competition only by allowing it to operate, and so to make effective the votes of thousands of satisfied customers.

It is vital to the strength, happiness and future standard of living of the people of this country that we permit the free growth and development of large businesses capable of taking the great risks involved in the difficult industrial tasks, for we cannot have what we do not produce.

I have spent many of my working years in the fields of science. I learned there a fundamental principle—never to discard the results of a well-demonstrated experiment in favor of an untried hypothesis. I would urge that that principle never be forgotten in dealing with these vital problems.

24. CONCENTRATION OF POWER IN THE AMERICAN ECONOMY *

THE STUDENT who thinks that monopolistic activity by "big business" constitutes a serious threat to the consumer and to other elements in the economy will find this article by Professor Wilcox enlightening. The author describes the problems confronting our economy because of pressures exerted by "little business," labor, and agriculture in the struggle among these groups to control the distribution of the products of industry. Further, he points out the economic and political power held by these three groups and the checks and limits upon that power.

THE DECISIONS that are vital in any economy are those that determine what goods and services are to be produced, and where, how, when, and by whom; and also what people are ultimately to receive the products of industry and in what proportions.

The power to influence these decisions, though theoretically it may be widely dispersed, actually is likely to be concentrated in greater or lesser degree. Such concentrated power may exert itself (1) through *economic* channels, by monopolizing demand or supply in the markets where goods and services are bought and sold, or (2) through *political* channels, by forcing the enactment of legislation and the adoption of public policies that serve its ends. The distinction is not important; economic power carries with it the means of influencing government, and political power can be employed to bring markets under control. No matter how it may be exerted, concentrated power will influence the allocation of resources and the distribution of income.

In whose hands and to what extent is the power to influence vital economic decisions seriously concentrated in our community? In almost all the discussion of this question—by journalists, before committees of Congress, and even among academicians—attention has been centered on big business. And in the popular mind it is the symbol of big business that is usually evoked by references to the "concentration of economic power." Is the influence exerted by big business as pervasive and as compelling as we have been led to believe? Is it unique in

* Clair Wilcox, *Harvard Business Review,* November, 1950, pp. 54-60. Reprinted by permission of the author and the publisher. Material for this article was drawn from an address by the author before the Occidental Institute of Economics and Finance at Occidental College.

The author (1898——) is Professor of Economics at Swarthmore College. Author of *Competition and Monopoly in American Industry* and *A Charter for World Trade.*

character; or is it but one among many manifestations of concentrated control, and, if so, what is its relative significance?

BIG BUSINESS

A number of studies published during the past 20 years have revealed the existence of substantial concentration of the assets and income of all nonbanking corporations in the hands of a few large firms; of the assets, income, employment, and output in manufacturing as a whole and industry by industry; and of the output—product by product—of manufactured goods. They have also revealed a marked concentration in the ownership of corporate securities and have shown an even greater concentration of corporate control in the hands of minority interests and self-perpetuating managements. It has frequently been said, too, that control over corporate activity is still further concentrated—through stock ownership, interlocking directorates, common affiliations with investment banks, and intangible personal relationships—in the hands of a small number of financial interest groups.

This is the evidence that is usually cited in support of generalizations concerning the concentration of economic power. On the surface it is impressive. But on examination it is less conclusive than it seems.

The concentration figures for all nonbanking corporations apply to a heterogeneous group that includes some enterprises that may be able substantially to control important markets, others that are subject to regulation by public authorities, and still others that face effective competition; they tell us little or nothing about the incidence of economic power. The figures for manufacturing as a whole apply, likewise, to an undifferentiated group ranging all the way from industries that are highly competitive to those that are virtually monopolized; they throw no light on the markets for the particular products of particular industries.

All the studies of concentration in manufacturing, moreover, are confined to an area that accounts for less than three tenths of the income produced in our economy; they afford no data concerning the situation that may exist in agriculture, forestry, fisheries, mining, building construction, wholesale and retail distribution, and the service trades, accounting for more than seven tenths of income produced.

Nor is this the only limitation of such studies. The concentration ratios for particular industries are based on a classification (employed by the Census of Manufactures) in which industries are defined in part according to the raw materials they use and the processes that they employ. Data on concentration within such categories can afford little insight into the structure of the markets for particular goods.

There is only one study that presents concentration ratios product by product,[1] but this, similarly, is based upon a Census classification developed for other purposes, which defines products in part according to the materials from which they are made, the processes employed in their fabrication, and the degree of integration obtaining in the establishments where production is carried on; as a result, there may be many listings for a single commodity. In some cases, the degree of concentration is understated because the output figures are nationwide and markets are regional, or because dissimilar goods are lumped together in a common category; in others, the degree of concentration is seriously overstated because products directly in competition with one another are listed in unrelated categories.

It should be clear that generalizations based upon such a classification cannot be said to afford an accurate index of the concentration of *power over markets.* For this purpose it would be necessary to devise a series of definitions that would group goods according to the readiness with which one can be substituted for another and to determine the spatial limits of the market areas within which goods compete for sale. Until this is done, precise measurements of such concentration are not to be obtained.

Power over markets. Where there is evidence of substantial concentration of output in the hands of a few producers, this fact suggests that such firms possess the power to increase their profits, at the expense of the community at large, by curtailing production, worsening quality, and raising prices. But this will not always and may not often be the case. Competition may sometimes be more effective among a few large enterprises than among many smaller ones. Great power among sellers is frequently diluted by the possibility of changes in technology, the multiplication of substitutes, the emergence of new competitors, and shifts in demand. It may also be offset by the existence of similar aggregations of power on the buyers' side of the market.

The markets for consumers' goods in the United States are more competitive than any study of concentration of output can be expected to reveal. The boundaries of these markets are being steadily extended by the growth of transportation and communication. And the boundaries of products are constantly being pushed outward as industrial research provides us with an increasing variety of ready substitutes. New goods must frequently compete with secondhand goods that must be counted as a part of the available supply. New cars are produced by a few firms and offered at fixed prices, but many dealers normally compete in the

[1] Willard Long Thorp and Walter Frederick Crowder, *The Structure of Industry,* Temporary National Economic Committee, Monograph No. 27 (Washington, D. C., Government Printing Office, 1941).

allowances they offer on old cars given in trade. Giant corporations, operating mail-order houses and chain stores, act as purchasing agents for the consumer, using their mass buying power, in his behalf, to force down the prices that highly concentrated producers might otherwise be disposed to charge.

In the markets for producers' goods, likewise, concentration of power does not obviate competition as much as might otherwise be expected. Here the possibilities of substitution are systematically explored. And here, quite typically, a few salesmen representing oligopolists may deal with a few skilled purchasing agents representing oligopsonists. Iron ore is sold to the steel mills; steel mill products to the manufacturers of locomotives, railway cars, automobiles, and machinery; locomotives and railway cars to the railroads; machinery to factories and the public utilities; chemicals to industrial users; tire fabrics to the rubber companies; tires and plate glass to the automobile companies; newsprint to the urban dailies; and milk bottles to the big milk distributors. In each of these cases the purchaser is abundantly able to take care of himself. When size among buyers is arrayed against size among sellers, it serves as an effective check on market power.

High concentration of output, however, is by no means characteristic of all industries in the United States. Outside the field of the regulated utilities, as a matter of fact, it is confined to minerals and metals, machinery and equipment, chemicals, rubber, glass, newsprint, and and cement. The great bulk of productive activity is to be found in industries where the degree of concentration is low and large numbers of producers occupy the field.

This is not to say that concentration of power over markets in the hands of big business is not a problem. There are, indeed, a number of cases in which the output and sale of a commodity are virtually monopolized by one or more large firms. But such cases are not so numerous as has sometimes been supposed. And they are not the only ones in which concentrated power has been employed to bring markets under control.

Power over corporations. It is true that power to control the affairs of any large corporation is likely to be concentrated in the hands of a minority of its owners or a self-perpetuating management. The danger inherent in this sort of concentration is that corporate insiders may divert to their own pockets earnings to which the shareholders have a legal claim. It may be said that this is now somewhat more difficult to do than it was before 1933.

But in any event the issue would appear to be irrelevant. For even if the control of corporations were really democratic and managements were held strictly accountable to the shareholders, the problem of concentration of power over markets would still exist. Indeed, the danger that such power would be abused might well be increased. For the relative impotence of the shareholder affords the corporate manager a measure of independence that enables him to give greater weight to the interests of the worker, the consumer, and the state than would otherwise be the case. Undoubtedly a good bit of nonsense has been spoken and written about the professionalization of management, yet there is still something in it, and the community would probably stand to lose if it were to be destroyed.

The material that is available on the subject of so-called "interest groups" in big business is too nebulous to permit an appraisal of its possible significance. There is some concentration of control over investment funds in the hands of insurance companies and other financial institutions. But it would appear that the increasing importance of reinvested earnings as a source of corporate capital may have diminished the power of banker control. Certainly the notion that Wall Street holds the reins of government, though it may still be encountered in the folklore of Communism, is at least 20 years out of date.

RIVAL CONCENTRATIONS OF POWER

So much for big *big* business. But this is not the end of the problem of concentrated power. There is also big *little* business, big labor, and big agriculture. And each of them merits some attention.

We shall not concern ourselves here with big government. Government is big enough, certainly. But government, in a democracy, is not to be envisioned as an independent locus of power. It is but an instrument through which those who possess power may bring it to bear. And it is by organizing to exert political pressure that those who may be small in size have nonetheless grown large in power.

Big little business. Little business often seeks to control markets through the activities of national and regional trade associations and local bidding rings. But some of these activities are clearly illegal and others, lacking legal sanction, are difficult to enforce. Little business has therefore turned to the legislatures to obtain legal sanctions for its restraints and aid in their enforcement.

A striking example of the political power of little business is afforded by the story of the enactment of the laws that permit the maintenance of resale prices on branded goods. Under this legislation the signing of a contract by a single retailer makes it impossible for any other retailer in the state to pass on to consumers, in a lower price, any of the gains that may result from simplified service, enhanced efficiency, or lowered cost. The laws, beginning in California in 1931, were whipped through 45 legislatures and the Federal Congress by the National Association of Retail Druggists at such breakneck speed that—in 11 states—the House and the Senate passed and the Governor signed a draft containing an obvious boner committed by an association stenographer when she transcribed her notes.

Nor is this an isolated example. At the behest of the grocery trade, no-sale-below-cost laws have been enacted and discriminatory taxes imposed on chain stores by more than half of the states. Again, in the Robinson-Patman Act, Congress has forbidden suppliers to pass on to distributors savings that result from the elimination of brokerage services in making a sale and has authorized the Federal Trade Commission to establish quantity limits beyond which differences in price may be forbidden even though they can be justified by differences in cost.

To these there must be added a multitude of statutes designed to exclude competitors from other states, ordinances adopted to prevent outsiders from competing in local markets, and licensing systems so administered as to bar the entry into privileged trades. All these measures, like the restrictive practices of big *big* business, affect the allocation of resources, the costs of production, and the quantity, quality, and price of output. All of them are deliberately designed to influence the distribution of income. And all of them have come into being through a conscious exercise of concentrated power.

Big labor. Labor is now effectively organized in all the major industries in the United States. And it is organized primarily for the purpose of influencing the distribution of income. The method employed is that of monopolizing the supply of labor services, industry by industry, and withholding or threatening to withhold them from use until the rate of wages is increased. This process is usually defended as a means of insuring equality of bargaining power. But it is now evident that the scales, instead of being balanced, have sometimes been tipped the other way. Even if this were not the case, it cannot be concluded that equality of bargaining power would serve the common interest. For there is one party at interest—the ultimate consumer—who is not represented at all in the conclusion of the wage bargain.

The influence of labor monopoly is felt not only in the market for labor itself but also in the markets for other goods and services. It manifests itself sometimes through measures which operate directly to exclude outsiders from participation in a trade, sometimes through connivance with employers in the cartelization of an industry. It is employed more often to establish for all the firms competing in a market a standard rate of wages that operates to check such competition as might be based on lower labor costs and to promote industrial concentration by eliminating marginal firms and obstructing the entry of new competitors.

The organization of labor carries with it political as well as economic power. Moreover, this power has been used, not only to establish and maintain the institution of collective bargaining, but also to preserve labor's exemption from the antimonopoly laws and to enlist the support of government in the settlement of wage disputes. The price of labor is the only price that has ever had to be determined in the White House by the President himself. In action at this level political considerations are likely to receive a heavy weight.

There is a possibility not to be ignored that labor monopoly, by forcing wages to levels that cannot be justified by gains in productivity, may operate (1) either to impair incentives to investment, restrain expansion of output, and create unemployment or (2) to induce continuous inflation throughout the whole economy. It is difficult to understand the point of view that can discern a dangerous concentration of power in the hands of a grocery chain that accounts for less than 7% of the foodstuffs sold in the United States and not in the hands of a labor leader who, through his command over 100% of the men employed in the coal industry, can cut the operation of the mines from five days a week to three—or none.

We have in labor's drive for higher wages a force that influences the allocation of resources, the volume of output, the costs of production, the level of prices, and the distribution of income. And this force too, as in the case of the big little business, is made effective through the conscious exercise of concentrated power.

Big agriculture. Agriculture, which like labor was until 1933 an underdog, is now conspicuous among the upperdogs. Its power, exerted through the channels of politics, is felt in every election and at every session of Congress and of the legislatures of the several states. And it has produced some striking results.

For nearly 20 years the national government has sought to divert income from the consumer and the taxpayer into the pocket of the farmer, by boosting the prices of foods and fibers and subsidizing the restriction of output and sales. "Parity"—introduced as a statistical expression of distributive justice—has been raised again and again by shifting the base dates for particular crops and by adding new components to the parity index. Inaugurated as a goal to be approached in the fullness of time, it has become a floor below which prices must never be allowed to fall. Curtailment of output has spread from crop to crop. At first voluntary, it has become compulsory, and a two thirds vote to boost prices by withholding supplies has come to be defended as a fine expression of democracy in action.

In many of the markets for fruits and nuts and vegetables and in most urban markets for fluid milk, sales are limited and prices fixed, at the expense of the consumer, and the profits of monopoly are shared among producers, processors, and distributors belonging to compulsory cartels. This is done under state and federal laws, with the blessing and the backing of public authority.

Here, again, the allocation of resources, the volume of output, the efficiency of production, the level of prices, and the distribution of income are influenced through the conscious exercise of concentrated power.

STRUGGLE OF POWER GROUPS

The class struggle in America is not a struggle between the proletariat and the bourgeoisie. It is a struggle among functional groups possessing concentrated power—a struggle to control the distribution of the products of industry. It is this struggle that confronts us with the greatest economic, political, and moral problem of our time. We are attempting, many of us, to seek salvation, not through measures that will produce a larger national product in the interest of all, but through measures that will obtain a larger share of the product for the members of our particular group. The "gluttons of privilege" in our community are to be found not exclusively among the "economic royalists" but also among the owners of small business, the ranks of labor, and the sturdy individualists who till the soil.

Whether concentrated power is brought to bear in the interest of big business, little business, labor, or agriculture, the economic consequences are much the same. The allocation of resources is distorted. Inefficiency is protected; efficiency is handicapped. Technological progress is retarded; innovation is obstructed. Standards of living for the community as a whole are lower than they otherwise could be. Group scarcities do not bring general plenty.

But though the *consequences* of power when employed by big business, by little business, by labor, and by agriculture may be the same, the *respectability* of such action is subject to striking differences. When big business restricts output and boosts prices to increase its income, it is said to be engaging in a "conspiracy in restraint of trade" and is subject to punishment by fine and imprisonment. When little business does the same thing, it is said to be practicing "fair trade" and is given official blessing. When labor restricts output and boosts prices to increase its income, it is said to be participating in "collective bargaining," which is shown in any elementary text to be a highly desirable process. When agriculture does the same thing, it is said merely to be seeking "parity," which is known by all right-thinking men to be no more than an expression of essential justice.

As among these four—big business, little business, labor, and agriculture—where lies the greatest power?

For the exertion of *economic* pressure, the greatest power probably lies with labor, already strong and growing in numbers and in strength, its command of monopoly more complete and more effective than that enjoyed by any other group.

As for the real *political* power, certainly it does not lie with big business, which must watch its step if it is to avoid antitrust prosecution or administrative regulation. To a great extent, perhaps, it lies with little business, which is found at every crossroads where legislators turn for votes. To an even greater extent it lies with labor, numerous enough to influence the outcome of an election but not yet strong enough, it should be noted, to force the repeal of the Taft-Hartley Act. To the greatest extent of all it lies with agriculture, as is evidenced by the fact that no political party has the courage to question a policy that employs a battery of artificial devices to divert a sizable portion of the nation's income to its farms. And this is true because our founding fathers, in their infinite wisdom, provided that agriculture should be overrepresented in our elections, in our state legislatures, and in the halls of our Congress. The least assailable center of political power in the United States is located, not in Wall Street, not on Main Street, not even on the picket line, but somewhere between the haystack and the barn.

Group responsibility. Given the concentration of power—economic and political—in the hands of special-interest groups, how is the general interest to be served? It has sometimes been suggested that group power may come to be exercised in time with a greater sense of social responsibility. But it would not appear that the prospects for such an outcome are any too bright.

In the case of big business, to be sure, conditions that may make for such an assumption of responsibility are frequently found to obtain. The business manager in the large corporation has three masters rather than one: the owners and directors, the labor union, and the state. The shareholders in such an enterprise may be relatively impotent; labor and the government are both comparatively strong. The manager finds himself in the position of an intermediary between conflicting pressures. He is driven perforce to compromise in order to achieve a balance that will stand.

Within associations representing little business, however, the position of the manager is quite a different one. The only pressure that he feels is that exerted by the members of his trade. If he is to retain his office, it is their interest—however they may see it—that must be served.

This applies also to the labor leader. He is a general rather than a judge. He has learned and taught that victories are won through conflict. He holds his army together by demonstrating his determination to improve its relative position, here and now. He is constantly demanding something more—higher wages in prosperity to realize the gains in productivity; higher wages in depression to distribute purchasing power; social security for the community, perhaps, but higher pensions for his constituents. Out of this conflict it is possible that labor statesmanship may yet emerge. But there are no forces now in sight that would surely lead to this result.

In agriculture the situation is the same. The organizations that represent the farmer are dedicated to the task of obtaining differential advantages for their membership. The structure of government and the climate of politics conspire to crown their efforts with success: the constitutional deck is stacked in favor of the rural areas; legislators are pliable; public opinion is acquiescent. And so long as this is the case, there is no reason to suppose that agriculture will moderate its demands.

To expect the leaders of pressure groups to become farsighted, to embrace altruism, or to be guided by the precept of the Golden Rule is to expect the leopard to change his spots. It would be unwise, therefore, to bank too heavily upon the development of group responsibility. The community, instead, must look for its defenses to those forces, both economic and political, that operate to check abuse of power.

Limits to power. There are *economic* checks to power in elasticity of demand, in continuous innovation, in the increasing availability of substitutes, and in the possible emergence of new competitors. The taxation of chain stores gives rise to the supermarket. The antidiscrimination laws induce the integration of mass distributors. The fair trade laws increase the sale of private brands. Wage rates placed too high speed mechanization and reduce employment. The railway brotherhoods encourage the development of the trucking industry. The United Mine Workers stimulate the sale of oil-burning equipment.

Agriculture, too, prices itself out of the market. The rigged price of cotton creates new customers for paper and rayon. The rigged price of fluid milk checks consumption and reduces the farmer's average return by forcing him to sell an increasing portion of his output to processors for whatever it will bring.

In all of these cases the strength of the underlying competitive forces in a relatively free economy prevents the restrictive practices that originate in group pressures from doing the harm that they were intended to do.

There are also *political* checks to power. For finance, transportation, and the public utilities, administrative regulation is an actuality. For other large enterprises, the ever-present possibility of prosecution or regulation induces a certain circumspection in matters of business policy. In the case of labor, there is always the danger that the disturbance of the peace and the interruption of essential services may overstep the bounds of public tolerance. With agriculture, there is the prospect—as yet remote—that the burden of financing increasing surpluses may finally become so heavy that the taxpayer will lose his enthusiasm for footing the bill.

Whatever the concentration of power in the American economy, it should be noted that it has not prevented a repeated reformation of the patterns of production and distribution, a progressive development of technology, a steady flow of new products, a continuous cultivation of new tastes, a constant improvement of quality, and an ever-widening provision of goods and services. It is an impressive fact that, no matter how valiant the efforts that we have made throughout our history to check the production of wealth, our national income has risen steadily—from \$2 billion to \$20 billion in the last half of the last century from \$20 billion to more than \$250 billion in the first half of this century. And it is not improbable that, in spite of all our efforts to prevent it, we shall reach the trillion dollars that the President has promised before the year 2000 rolls around.

---

25. THE CASE AGAINST BIG BUSINESS *

LIKE THE critical mass of an atomic bomb the great danger of big business to free enterprise may be the chain reaction which it is capable of starting. We think primarily of the monopoly aspects of big business as direct limitations upon free enterprise. In the following article Professor Stigler points to the "trigger effect" of big business on our economic life. Labor has organized and

* George J. Stigler. Reprinted from the May, 1952, issue of *Fortune* Magazine by Special Permission of the Editors; Copyright Time Inc.

The author (1911——) is Professor of Economics at Columbia University and a member of the research staff of the National Bureau of Economic Research. Author of *Production and Distribution Theories, The Theory of Price,* and *Trends in Output and Employment.*

consolidated in response to the growth of the business unit. Government, in turn, has justified the expansion of the area of its control over the economy because of the growth of both business and labor. This control has not been limited to the firms exercising monopoly power or even to the industries under monopoly influence; rather it has extended over the whole economy.

UNTIL THE Korean hostilities began, bigness in business was in a fair way to becoming an important issue in America. For almost two years now, however, it has been overshadowed by the economic and political problems growing out of rearmament at home and abroad, and few antitrust actions have been initiated in industries important to rearmament.

Perhaps our traditional suspension of antitrust laws in periods of acute national emergency is sound—it may be that we would impair our short-run efficiency more by the diversions of prosecution and defense in antitrust actions than it is impaired by monopolies acting for a time, we hope, only in the national interest. But it is not sound to suspend our discussions of the problem of bigness even if we are doomed to a long period of international tension and recurrent emergencies.

A suspension of discussion is not sound because it leaves us unprepared for positive, informed action when we emerge into a period when we shall be free to move toward the type of economic system we want. It is not sound because we cannot put the issue of bigness in business aside even during an emergency. It will insist upon presenting itself from day to day: we shall continuously encounter situations in which we can affect the structure of business without a clear or important effect on immediate efficiency. The procurement policies of the armed forces, for example, teem with choices of this sort. And finally, it is not sound to postpone discussion because the problem of bigness is present in many industries whose connection with the rearmament program is negligible. So, let us look at bigness.

WHAT IS BIGNESS?

Bigness in business has two primary meanings. First, bigness may be defined in terms of the company's share of the industry in which it operates: a big company is one that has a big share of the market or industry. By this test Texas Gulf Sulphur is big because it produces more than half the sulfur in America, and Macy's (whose annual sales are much larger) is small because it sells only a very small fraction of the goods sold by New York City retail stores. By this definition, many companies that are small in absolute size are nevertheless big—the only brick company in a region, for example—and many companies that are big in absolute size (Inland Steel, for example) are small. Second, bigness may mean absolute size—the measure of size being assets, sales, or employment as a rule. Then General Motors and U.S. Steel are the prototypes of bigness.

These two meanings overlap because most companies that are big in absolute size are also big in relation to their industries. There are two types of cases, however, in which the two meanings conflict. On the one hand, many companies of small absolute size are dominant in small markets or industries. I shall not discuss them here (although they require attention in a well-rounded antitrust program) for two reasons: they seldom have anywhere near so much power as the companies that are big relative to large markets and industries; and they raise few political problems of the type I shall discuss below. On the other hand, there are a few companies that are big in absolute size but small relative to their markets—I have already given Macy's as an example. These companies are not very important in the total picture, and I shall also put them aside in the following discussion.

For my purposes, then, big businesses will mean businesses that are absolutely large in size and large also relative to the industries in which they operate. They are an impressive list: U.S. Steel, Bethlehem, and Republic in steel, General Electric and Westinghouse in electrical equipment, General Motors, Ford, and Chrysler in automobiles, du Pont, Union Carbide, and Allied Chemical among others in chemicals, Reynolds, Liggett & Myers, and American Tobacco in cigarettes.

What bigness does not mean is perhaps equally important. Bigness has no reference to the size of industries. I for one am tired of the charge that the critics of the steel industry vacillate between finding the output too large and too small: at various times the industry's output has been too small; for fifty years the largest firm has been too large. Concerted action by many small companies often leads to over-capacity in an industry: it is the basic criticism of resale price maintenance, for example, that it encourages the proliferation of small units by fixing excessive retail margins. Industries dominated by one or a few firms—that is, big businesses—seldom err in this direction. Nor does bigness have any direct reference to the methods of production, and opposition to big business is usually compatible with a decent respect for the "economies of large-scale production," on which more later.

The fundamental objection to bigness stems from the fact that big companies have monopolistic power, and this fundamental objection is clearly applicable outside the realm of corporate business. In particular, big unions are open to all the criticisms (and possibly more) that can be levied against big business. I shall not discuss labor unions, but my silence should not be construed as a belief that we should have a less stringent code for unions than for business.

THE INDICTMENT OF BIGNESS

There are two fundamental criticisms to be made of big businesses: they act monopolistically, and they encourage and justify bigness in labor and government.

First, as to monopoly. When a small number of firms control most or all of the output of an industry, they can individually and collectively profit more by cooperation than by competition. This is fairly evident. since cooperatively they can do everything they can do individually, and other things (such as the charging of non-competitive prices) besides. These few companies, therefore, will usually cooperate.

From this conclusion many reasonable men, including several Supreme Court Justices, will dissent. Does not each brand of cigarettes spend huge sums in advertising to lure us away from some other brand? Do not the big companies—oligopolists, the economists call them—employ salesmen? Do not the big companies introduce constant innovations in their products?

Competition of a Kind

The answer is that they do compete—but not enough, and not in all the socially desirable ways. Those tobacco companies did not act competitively, but with a view to extermination, against the 10-cent brands in the 1930's, nor have they engaged in price competition in decades (*American Tobacco* vs. *United States, 328 U.S. 781*). The steel companies with all their salesmen, abandoned cartel pricing via basing-point prices only when this price system was judged a conspiracy in restraint of trade in cement (*Federal Trade Commission* vs. *Cement Institute, 333 U.S. 683*). The plain fact is that big businesses do not engage in continuous price competition.

Nor is price the only area of agreement. Patent licensing has frequently been used to deprive the licensees of any incentive to engage in research; General Electric used such agreements also to limit other companies' output and fix the prices of incandescent lamps (*U.S.* vs. *General Electric, 82 F. Supp. 753*). The hearings of the Bone Committee are adorned with numerous examples of the deliberate deterioration of goods in order to maintain sales. For example, Standard Oil Development (a subsidiary of the Jersey company) persuaded Socony-

Vacuum to give up the sale of a higher-potency commodity (pour-point depressant) whose sale at the same price had been characterized as "merely price cutting."

Very well, big businesses often engage in monopolistic practices. It may still be objected that it has not been shown that all big businesses engage in monopolistic practices, or that they engage in such practices all, or even most of, the time. These things cannot be shown or even fully illustrated in a brief survey, and it is also not possible to summarize the many court decisions and the many academic studies of big business. But it is fair to say that these decisions and studies show that big businesses usually possess monopolistic power, and use it. And that is enough.

For economic policy must be contrived with a view to the typical rather than the exceptional, just as all other policies are contrived. That some drivers can safely proceed at eighty miles an hour is no objection to a maximum-speed law. So it is no objection to an antitrust policy that some unexercised monopoly power is thereby abolished. (Should there be some big businesses that forgo the use of their dominant position, it is difficult to see what advantage accrues from private ownership, for the profit motive is already absent.)

Second, as to bigness in labor and government. Big companies have a large—I would say an utterly disproportionate—effect on public thinking. The great expansion of our labor unions has been due largely to favoring legislation and administration by the federal government. This policy of favoring unions rests fundamentally upon the popular belief that workers individually competing for jobs will be exploited by big-business employers—that U.S. Steel can in separate negotiation (a pretty picture!) overwhelm each of its hundreds of thousands of employees. In good part this is an absurd fear: U.S. Steel must compete with many other industries, and not merely other steel companies, for good workers.

Yet the fear may not be wholly absurd: there may be times and places where big businesses have "beaten down" wages, although I believe such cases are relatively infrequent. (In any event, the reaction to the fear has been unwise: for every case where big business has held down workers there are surely many cases where big unions have held up employers.) But it cannot be denied that this public attitude underlies our national labor policy, the policy of local governments of condoning violence in labor disputes, etc.

Big business has also made substantial contributions to the growth of big government. The whole agricultural program has been justified as necessary to equalize agriculture's bargaining power with "industry," meaning big business. The federally sponsored milkshed cartels are defended as necessary to deal with the giant dairy companies.

Business Across the Board

Big business is thus a fundamental excuse for big unions and big government. It is true that the scope and evils of big business are usually enormously exaggerated, especially with reference to labor and agriculture, and that more often than not these evils are merely a soapbox excuse for shoddy policies elsewhere. To this large extent, there is need for extensive education of the public on how small a part of the economy is controlled by big business. But in light of the widespread monopolistic practices—our first criticism of bigness—it is impossible to tell the public that its fears of big business are groundless. We have no right to ask public opinion to veer away from big unions and big government—and toward big business.

EFFICIENCY AND BIG BUSINESS

Are we dependent upon big businesses for efficient methods of production and rapid advances in production methods? If we are, the policy of breaking up big businesses would lower our future standard of living and many people would cast about for other ways than dissolution to meet the problems of bigness.

A company may be efficient because it produces and sells a given amount of product with relatively small amounts of material, capital, and labor, or it may be efficient because it acquires the power to buy its supplies at unusually low prices and sell its products at unusually high prices. Economists refer to these as the social and the private costs of production respectively. Big businesses may be efficient in the social sense, and usually they also possess, because of their monopoly position, private advantages. But the ability of a company to employ its dominant position to coerce unusually low prices from suppliers is not of any social advantage.

It follows that even if big companies had larger profit rates or smaller costs per unit of output than other companies, this would not prove that they were more efficient in socially desirable ways. Actually, big businesses are generally no more and no less efficient than medium-sized businesses even when the gains wrung by monopoly power are included in efficiency. This is the one general finding in comparative cost studies and comparative profitability studies. Indeed, if one reflects upon the persistence of small and medium-sized companies in the industries dominated by big businesses, it is apparent that there can be no great advantages to size. If size were a great advantage, the smaller companies would soon lose the unequal race and disappear.

When we recall that most big businesses have numerous complete plants at various points throughout the country, this finding is not surprising. Why should U.S. Steel be more efficient than Inland Steel, when U.S. Steel is simply a dozen or more Inland Steels strewn about the country? Why should G.M. be appreciably more efficient than say a once-again independent Buick Motors? A few years ago Peter Drucker reported:

The divisional manager . . . is in complete charge of production and sales. He hires, fires and promotes; and it is up to him to decide how many men he needs, with what qualifications and in what salary range—except for top executives whose employment is subject to a central-management veto. The divisional manager decides the factory layout, the technical methods and equipment used. . . . He buys his supplies independently from suppliers of his own choice. He determines the distribution of production within the several plants under his jurisdiction, decides which lines to push and decides on the methods of sale and distribution. . . . In everything pertaining to operations he is as much the real head as if his division were indeed an independent business.

If big businesses are not more efficient as a rule, how did they get big? The answer is that most giant firms arose out of mergers of many competing firms, and were created to eliminate competition. Standard Oil, General Electric, Westinghouse, U.S. Steel, Bethlehem, the meat packers, Borden, National Dairy, American Can, etc.—the full list of merger-created big businesses is most of the list of big businesses. A few big businesses owe their position to an industrial genius like Ford, and of course future geniuses would be hampered by an effective antitrust law—but less so than by entrenched monopolies or by public regulatory commissions.

We do not know what share of improvements in technology has been contributed by big businesses. Big businesses have made some signal contributions, and so also have small businesses, universities, and private individuals. It can be said that manufacturing industries dominated by big businesses have had no larger increases in output per worker on average than other manufacturing industries. This fact is sufficient to undermine the easy identification of economic progress with the laboratories of big businesses, but it does not inform us of the net effect of monopolies on economic progress.

At present, then, no definite effect of big business on economic progress can be established. I personally believe that future study will confirm the traditional belief that big businesses, for all their resources, cannot rival the infinite resource and cold scrutiny of many independent and competing companies. If the real alternative to bigness is government regulation or ownership, as I am about to argue, then the long-run consequences of big business are going to be highly adverse to economic progress.

REMEDIES FOR BIG BUSINESS

Let me restate the main points of the foregoing discussion in a less emphatic—and I think also a less accurate—manner:

1. Big businesses often possess and use monopoly power.
2. Big businesses weaken the political support for a private-enterprise system.
3. Big businesses are not appreciably more efficient or enterprising than medium-size businesses.

Few disinterested people will deny these facts—where do they lead?

A considerable section of the big-business community seems to have taken the following position. The proper way to deal with monopolistic practices is to replace the general prohibitions of the Sherman Act by a specific list of prohibited practices, so businessmen may know in advance and avoid committing monopolistic practices. The proper way to deal with the declining political support for private enterprise is to advertise the merits of private enterprise, at the same time claiming many of its achievements for big business. Much of this advertising has taken literally that form, apparently in the belief that one can sell a social system in exactly the same way and with exactly the same copywriters and media that one sells a brand of cigarettes.

Guard the Sherman Act

The request for a list of specifically prohibited monopolistic practices will be looked upon by many persons as a surreptitious attack upon the Sherman Act. I am among these cynics: the powerful drive in 1949 to pass a law legalizing basing-point price systems is sufficient evidence that large sectors of big business are wholly unreconciled to the law against conspiracies in restraint of trade. Even when the request for a specific list of prohibitions is made in all sincerity, however, it cannot be granted: No one can write down a full list of all the forms that objectionable monopoly power has taken and may someday take. Moreover, almost all uncertainties over the legality of conduct arise out of the Robinson-Patman Act, not the Sherman Act, and I would welcome the complete repeal of the former act.[1]

[1] The prohibition against price discrimination was partly designed to cope with a real evil: the use by a large company of its monopoly power to extort preferential terms from suppliers. This exercise of monopoly, however, constitutes a violation of the Sherman Act, and no additional legislation is necessary if this act can be made fully effective. The Robinson-Patman Act, and certain other parts of the so-called "antitrust" amendments, also have another and objectionable purpose: to supervise and regulate the routine operations of businesses in order to ensure that they will display the symptoms of competitive behavior.

We must look elsewhere for the solution of the problems raised by big business, and a satisfactory solution must deal with the facts I listed at the head of this section. Our present policy is not a satisfactory solution. The Sherman Act is admirable in dealing with formal conspiracies of many firms, but—at least with the Supreme Court's present conception of competition and of the proper remedies for demonstrated restraint of trade in oligopolistic industries—it cannot cope effectively with the problem posed by big business. In industries dominated by a few firms there is no need for formal conspiracies, with their trappings of quotas, a price-fixing committee, and the like. The big companies know they must "live with" one another, and the phrase means much the same thing as in the relationships between man and woman. Any competitive action one big company takes will lead to retaliation by the others. An informal code of behavior gradually develops in the industry: Firm X announces the new price, and except in very unusual circumstances Y and Z can be relied upon to follow. So long as there are a few big businesses in an industry, we simply cannot expect more than the tokens of competitive behavior. Antitrust decrees that the big businesses should ignore each other's existence serve no important purpose.[2]

This conclusion, I must emphasize, is not merely that of "economic theorists," although most (academic) economists will subscribe to it. It is also the conclusion our generation is reaching, for our generation is not satisfied with the behavior of big business. More and more, big businesses are being asked to act in "the social interest," and more and more, government is interfering in their routine operation. The steel industry, for example, what with congressional review of prices and presidential coercion of wages, is drifting rapidly into a public-utility status. And the drift will not be stopped by slick advertising.

Dissolution the Remedy

No such drastic and ominous remedy as the central direction of eco-

[2] In the National Lead case (67 Sup. Ct. 1634, 1947) this company and du Pont were convicted of violating the Sherman Act. The two companies produced about 90 per cent of all titanium, but the Court refused to order divestiture of plants. The Court documented the "vigorous and effective competition between National Lead and du Pont" with the fact that "The general manager of the pigments department of du Pont characterized the competition with Zirconium and Virginia Chemical as 'tough' and that with National Lead as 'plenty tough.'" Economists will always find such testimony an inadequate demonstration of competition. Even more unfortunate was the refusal of the Court to order divestiture of foreign holdings of the Timken Roller Bearing company, which had also been convicted under the Sherman Act (71 Sup. Ct. 971, 1951). Here Mr. Justice Reed, the Chief Justice concurring, argues that so "harsh" a remedy as divestiture should be invoked only in extreme cases, perhaps forgetting that inadequate remedies for monopoly are "harsh" treatment of the public interest.

nomic life is necessary to deal with the problems raised by big business. The obvious and economical solution, as I have already amply implied, is to break up the giant companies. This, I would emphasize, is the minimum program, and it is essentially a conservative program. Dissolution of big businesses is a one-for-all measure in each industry (if the recent anti-merger amendment to the Clayton Act is adequately enforced), and no continuing interference in the private operation of business is required or desired. Dissolution involves relatively few companies: one dissolves three or four big steel companies, and leaves the many smaller companies completely alone. Dissolution does not even need to be invoked in a large part of the economy: some of our biggest industries, such as textiles, shoes, and most food industries, will require no antitrust action.

A policy of "trust busting" requires no grant of arbitrary powers to any administrative agency; the policy can be administered by the Antitrust Division acting through the courts. It is sufficient, and it is desirable, that the policy be directed against companies whose possession of monopoly power is demonstrated, and that dissolution be the basic remedy for the concentration of control in an industry that prevents or limits competition. Indeed, the policy requires new legislation only to the extent of convincing the courts that an industry which does not have a competitive structure will not have competitive behavior.

The dissolution of big businesses is only a part of the program necessary to increase the support for a private, competitive enterprise economy, and reverse the drift toward government control. But it is an essential part of this program, and the place for courage and imagination. Those conservatives who cling to the status quo do not realize that the status quo is a state of change, and the changes are coming fast. If these changes were to include the dissolution of a few score of our giant companies, however, we shall have done much to preserve private enterprise and the liberal-individualistic society of which it is an integral part.

---

26. CORPORATIONS AND DEMOCRACY *

"It is the object of this paper to examine the theory that there is an antithesis between the large corporation and the institution of democracy," states the author who, by virtue of his wide experience with

* Adolf A. Berle, Jr. "The Corporation and the Modern States," in Thurmand Arnold and others: *The Future of Democratic Capitalism* (University of Pennsylvania Press, 1950). Reprinted by permission of the publisher.

The author (1895——) is a lawyer and Professor of Corporation Law at anti-trust laws and corporate business practices is well qualified to make such an analysis. He concludes that . . . "The corporation is not the force which will determine whether the democratic state lives or dies." The reasoning by which Mr. Berle reaches this conclusion will be found in this excerpt from his paper.

WE ARE dealing with the corporate institution at a point in its development which poses new problems in the evolution of the American political structure. We have passed from the period in which the problem was chiefly financial to a period in which the next set of problems involves the economic and sociological structure of the modern state.

Does this development threaten democracy? And does it forecast the end of capitalism?

Our ancestors feared that it might do both. Justice Brandeis feared the growth of large corporations, and stated his fears in an essay on corporate developments, his famous dissent in the Florida chain store case:

> Through size, corporations, once merely an efficient tool employed by individuals in the conduct of private business, have become an institution—an institution which has brought such concentration of economic power that so-called private corporations are sometimes able to dominate the State. The typical business corporation of the last century, owned by a small group of individuals, managed by their owners, and limited in size by their personal wealth, is being supplanted by huge concerns in which the lives of tens or hundreds of thousands of employees and the property of tens or hundreds of thousands of investors are subjected, through the corporate mechanism, to the control of a few men. Ownership has been separated from control; and this separation has removed many of the checks which formerly operated to curb the misuse of wealth and power. And as ownership of the shares is becoming continually more dispersed, the power which formerly accompanied ownership is becoming increasingly concentrated in the hands of a few. The changes thereby wrought in the lives of the workers, of the owners and of the general public, are so fundamental and far-reaching as to lead these scholars to compare the evolving "corporate system" with the feudal system; and to lead other men of insight and experience to assert that this "master institution of civilized life" is committing it to the rule of a plutocracy.

And if fear of the giant corporation exists, apprehension of the leviathan state is surely no less. A generation which has watched the extreme of police-state organization in Soviet Russia and its equally frightening off-shoot "sport," the Nazi and Fascist organizations in Germany and Italy, is not likely to underestimate the possibility that

---

Columbia University. Assistant Secretary of State, 1938-44. Ambassador to Brazil, 1945-46. Author of *The Modern Corporation and Private Property*.

an overmastering state likewise can become a tyrant. Though the more vocal opponents of big business, on the one hand, and of statism, on the other, appear to start from opposite premises, they are really fearing (and saying so) a similar threat. They are also struggling against the same thing, as they see it, in different forms, namely, the power that comes from expansion in size with concentration of control.

It is questionable whether either side has fully appreciated the development of faith and force in American democracy during recent years, and the strange and absorptive quality of American thought. One is reminded, for example, of the debate when New York took over its water supply—theretofore a private enterprise. New York City politics are of anything but the "kid-glove" variety. The possibility that a political government could misuse its control of a vital necessity like water to make life miserable for its enemies was certainly present. Public ownership, of course, occurred; yet in a century of violent political history the water development in New York has never been used, as a weapon of politics. Even the most unscrupulous city governments have not dared to use it for political control.

On the other hand, one may contemplate the American Telephone & Telegraph Company, a private monopoly of huge proportions which is clearly capable of unlimited abuse in evil hands. Yet, through the years, there has grown up a tradition of impartiality, carried out through the medium of that particular company—the quality of whose communications service is foremost in the world, and the fair handling of which has never been questioned. When one abandons theory and gets down to cases, the problem assumes a different aspect. The United States is no less a democracy because its water supply is in public hands or because its telephone service is in corporate hands. Only a lingering crackle of rear guard action maintains that the Tennessee Valley Authority is an instrument of public tyranny; the cry that public social security insurance threatened the commencement of a nondemocratic state has completely subsided; but so also has the agitation for public ownership of railroads.

This leads us to wonder whether democracy under any particular organization is a matter of mechanics turning on economic structure, or whether it is a matter of philosophical faith which guides the people of a country. To put it differently, will not democracy continue to be a democracy under any form of economic organization, and, conversely, may not tyranny constitute itself no matter how free and fair the economic situation may be? Certainly, revolts alleged to be against capitalism in the period between the wars led to tyranny and not to freedom. Despite this question, it remains, of course, a proper concern of prudent men to deal with economic organization in such a way as to place the least strain on democratic institutions.

Capitalism appears to be a singularly malleable institution. It changes constantly to a point where the word scarcely has definable meaning. Capitalism has changed, and no doubt it will change further, but the changes seem natural and, on the whole, healthy.

It is factually clear that the giant corporation, as it increasingly becomes a necessary part of economic structure, does inevitably meet the state, and must necessarily find common ground with it. A series of illustrations suggests the development.

Banking, since Andrew Jackson ended the Second United States Bank, has been carried on by up to twenty-five thousand organizations, some extremely large, but none of which really dominates the field of commercial banking. There is concentration, but not control. Sheer force of necessity has created a central organization in the Federal Reserve Bank System and a central planning agency carried out through its Board of Governors. A series of cataclysms compelled this result; there is no likelihood that it will be reversed. At top level, privately-owned banking and the state meet in a white building in Washington.

Shipping is considered a national necessity for various reasons, be they good or bad. The shipping corporations have generally been unable to make profits in a competitive world market, with the result that a plan has been worked out through the Maritime Commission by which the national government, in large measure, routes and finances lines; it even builds ships with the private company becoming merely a contractor for the government.

The steel industry, basic, concentrated, and requiring a huge organization, is nominally private. Yet when an underproduction of steel developed after the close of World War II and the central planning function formerly exercised through the Office of Price Administration had been relaxed, the crisis required some means of allocating the steel in order to meet national necessities. In consequence, partly at the instance of the steel companies themselves, the Voluntary Allocation Act was passed, and perhaps 15 per cent of steel products are covered by government approved allocation agreements. The experiment is not wholly successful; the impressive fact is that the necessity for some means of assuring community needs was met by establishing a priority system and assuring supply.

Electronics, particularly in the radio field, represents a new, private and, in many respects, highly competitive industry, heavily concentrated on the manufacturing side. Cartel organizations being interdicted in the United States, a variety of controls appear in different forms, running all the way from the method by which defense orders are allocated through the armed services to the handling of frequencies through the Federal Communications Commission.

One can go steadily through the list discovering pragmatically that concentrated industry inevitably collides with the state at certain points. Where dire need exists and private capital is unable to supply it, as in the case of such regional developments as those in the Tennessee Valley and the Colorado River Basin, the state acts. Where lesser problems exist, they are met in different ways by such state action as is needed. Consequently, the United States has developed a spectrum of economic organization, running all the way from methods which a doctrinaire European would call socialist to methods which a British Conservative would recognize as laissez-faire capitalism. We do this with a minimum of shock to our economic and political systems; we soon recover our balance and go on our way with rejoicing or recriminations. Life in the Tennessee Valley, for example, is still democratic and capitalist, though the central planning is done by an agency of the federal government. Probably there is more of socialism in highly unionized mining towns where the loose framework is that of unregulated private companies. Yet in neither case does the individual feel that democracy is seriously threatened, or that the private ownership system is likely to disappear.

It is suggested that democracy is not in any danger and that wise measures can reduce such dangers as do, and clearly, inhere either in a concentrated corporate system or in concentrated statism.

The impulse to democracy resides not in an economic organization but in the minds and hearts of men. The modern corporation and the modern state alike will be turned to the uses exacted by the controlling public opinion.

It would be absurd, for instance, to say that the socialist state in England has ceased to be democratic. Many of their socialized practices result directly from an attempt, even under adverse conditions, to give greater consideration to the individual, his personality, his views, and his fundamental right to live.

It would be equally absurd to say that industrialist United States had ceased to be democratic, in view of the plain indication that through the years its free public opinion has been capable of controlling, as far as necessary, the system of concentrated corporate production. Democracy did not depend on the existence of small-scale production, described by Adam Smith, but on the philosophical realization of men that the end and aim of both economics and government is the fostering of individual dignity and worth, combined with the greatest attainable opportunity for self-reliance.

Nonetheless, wise measures can reduce strain and avoid crises. It is undeniable that power in any form reacts ultimately on its wielders, in either government or economics. The anthropology of men in plants or in governmental organizations does differ from that of the men at forges, farms, and small shops a century ago. New times do call for new measures. Four fields of consideration are suggested here as worthy of careful study.

First should come a conscious attempt to make size correspond to the greatest productivity, rather than to the possibilities of stock promotion or financial interests. Size must be justified, and its justification must rest on actual operating economies in production and distribution. Concentration or expansion beyond that point is unsound business. Many wise business men attempt to follow this rule today. But there have always been, and probably always will be, the financial empire-builders who seek power for its own sake through the route of stock pyramids, and who hope to cover, for a time at least, loss of efficiency by control of market price. Here is a task for business men, business schools, business research, and economists, advised by good engineers.

Next, sound business practice should seek the greatest decentralization possible within any given unit and attempt to distribute individual responsibility and recognition as widely as possible. Peter Drucker wrote of one such experiment in *The Concept of the Corporation*—a study of General Motors. It was interesting that such a study of a great corporation should have occurred only shortly after a famous debate between David Lilienthal, then of the Tennessee Valley Authority, arguing for decentralization in governmental operations, and Harold Ickes, then Secretary of the Interior, who sought centralized control in Washington. There was the same problem in both cases. Some followers of the debate considered Lilienthal's advocacy of decentralization to be unanswerable, and quite as applicable to corporations as to government. Bureaucracy in business works out much the same way as bureaucracy in government.

Third, relevance of productive units to the public need must be obtained through some method of planning. Planning is an unpopular word, but search for a method of rationalization has persisted in American industry. Private concerns are forbidden to do it—and rightly so—under the antitrust acts, since planning motivated chiefly by search for the greatest possible profits would lead to sheer exploitation. Public planning is still in its infancy; though in specialized fields—such as banking, railroad and air transport, shipping, the growing use of river valleys, public power, and regional development—it is already present. Absence of it indeed may lead to such strain as to force private enterprise to demand it; hence the Voluntary Allocation Act we observed a moment ago.

Finally, the sheer irrationalities by which employment may be interrupted without cause on the part of the worker must be avoided or, if not avoided, compensated, so that men do not live in perpetual hazard of economic forces beyond their control, subject to economic misfortune and degradation regardless of their industry, ability, and character.

It may be, in the rapid sweep of history, that fifty years from now a commentator looking back to our present age will wonder what we have been discussing. He may well live in a world from which engineers have abstracted the large corporation. Science may have substituted for it a tremendously dispersed system of craft production based, say, on atomic energy or the sun's radiation. In our time the ways of mechanics have been transformed beyond belief. But I think he would find that the philosophical faith which motivates men changes very slowly. Students of history might tell us that faith in individual development, responsibility, and consideration has existed in this world for centuries, whereas giant corporations appeared in the seventeenth century, disappeared in the eighteenth, and reappeared in the nineteenth century, only to disappear again perhaps, for all we know, in the twentieth. The historian would stress the fact that the great conceptions on which nations have been built and life has been lived have lasted for millennia. Russia was a tyranny under the Czars and is so under the Communists, no individualist philosophy ever having penetrated that great population. Much of Europe, he would point out, is an aristocracy or an oligarchy because for centuries the people accepted the philosophical thesis that such an organization was the most logical, advantageous, and satisfactory. America, in large measure a product of the Protestant Reformation, he would observe, was settled by a screened population, practically all of whom rebelled against authoritarianism and came here because of their belief in liberal democracy based on individual freedom, a belief only incidentally related to any form of economic organization.

We might call to the historian's attention a book published in 1899, exactly fifty years ago, *When the Sleeper Wakes* by H. G. Wells. In fantasy, this famous prophet forecast concentration in England of wealth, ownership, and production to a point at which the sleeping owner became the symbol of government and power combined. A Fascist managerial group (we should call it today) in his name attempted to rule the world by controlling a predicted mechanization and production schedule. Our historian would point out that H. G. Wells' mechanical prophecy of airplanes, radio, concentrated transport, giant industry, unlimited electronics, and huge cities actually came true with surprising accuracy; but that the British people declined to behave in any respect as his fantasy suggested. They stuck to their Parliament and representative government, to free elections and full civil rights.

The modern corporation, an instrument with greatness and dangers, is leaving its mark on the social organization of our own time. But it is not the force which will determine whether the democratic state lives or dies. Democracy lies deeper—in the philosophical fortresses of the minds of millions of men.

VI

Labor and Enterprise

---

27. NEW LIGHT ON LABOR MANAGEMENT *

THE APPLICATION of scientific method of the field of labor management is a relatively new development. Startling discoveries have recently been made in this hitherto almost unexplored region. Old ideas about the effects of working conditions on the productivity of workers are being replaced by positive, empirical knowledge of the group behavior of individuals in industry. The Hawthorne experiment, described by Mr. Chase in the article below, is but one example of the research into the psychological factors influencing labor productivity.

NEW LIGHT ON LABOR MANAGEMENT

FOR MANY thousands of years men have worked at the bidding of other men, sometimes as kinsmen, sometimes as slaves, sometimes as freemen. An unequal relation between manager and worker is nothing new in human affairs—think of the building of the Pyramids. But it is hard to realize that the factory system, especially in its mass production phase, is something never known in any earlier society. We can say this without fear of contradiction because there never was a practical prime mover to power factory machines until Watt invented his steam engine in 1776.

The master-servant relation which crystallized in the early factories

* Stuart Chase, *The Proper Study of Mankind* (Harper & Brothers, 1948), pp. 137-46. Copyright, 1948, by Stuart Chase. Reprinted by permission of the author and the publisher.

For a brief biographical sketch of the author, see Selection 18, page 179.

was derived in part from the old family system, in part from the apprentice-craftsman system, in part from the lord-of-the-manor system. It worked, in the sense of getting out the goods—at least in fits and starts—but it seldom worked in the sense of willing human cooperation. Karl Polanyi, in *The Great Transformation,* demonstrates that the chief trouble with the early factory system was not that it exploited people economically, but that it destroyed immemorial culture patterns and put nothing in their place.

The factory was a crippled institution from the beginning. From its maladjustment rose the "labor movement," trade unionism, industrial unionism, socialism, communism, the IWW, and various short-tempered ideologies. From it arose concrete physical effects as well—strikes, lockouts, sabotage, slowdowns, sitdowns, riots, goon squads, barricades, and untold destruction and violence.

Explanations of the failure of labor and management to cooperate in using the machine have been loud and dogmatic. Spokesmen for the workers have said that the bosses exploited them shamelessly, piling up fabulous profits while men starved. The bosses, angry at this charge, have said that workers were inefficient, lazy, ignorant, unreliable, and easily misled by agitators—mostly foreign. For a century and more the chorus has thundered back and forth, with little reduction in the volume and violence of strikes, bad blood, and bad language.

The principal attempts to understand or at least explain the "labor problem" occurred in two directions: in the elaboration of the aforesaid ideologies, largely variations on the "class struggle"—which infuriated the managers; and in time studies of physical movements by stop-watch engineers—which infuriated the workers. The scientific method as we have defined it was not applied anywhere to the real problem of labor-management relations. Frederick W. Taylor's *Scientific Management* applied the scientific method to the working technique but not to the worker. Here and there, good relations were maintained by intuition on the part of a wise employer. No one knew how he did it, least of all himself.

If you started a nice little business—say the production of aluminum wheelbarrows—you could get all kinds of scientific advice about your machines and materials, but very little on how to handle your men. You could buy payroll books, of course, and fine chromium-plated time-clocks, but no information about the characteristics, temperatures, and boiling points of the men and women who came to work for you. So some days the wheelbarrows came off the line per schedule, and some days they did not. You began to wonder what you could have done to be hated so. Presently you joined the National Association of Manufacturers and began to hate back in orchestrated union with other employers.

This dreary round continued with hardly a break until a group of social scientists, under the guidance of Elton Mayo, performed a series of experiments in a factory and discovered some of the basic theory involved. The publication in 1940 of *Management and the Worker* by Roethlisberger and Dickson was a landmark in the history of both labor relations and social science. It made obsolete a century of assumptions, assertions, and dogma about "labor." In effect it reported "no such animal." Let us look at two of the most famous experiments in the book.

THE HAWTHORNE EXPERIMENTS

Six girls are sitting in a small room in a large factory in the town of Hawthorne, near Chicago. On the bench before them are small metal parts in trays to be assembled into a telephone "relay"—which looks something like a pocket whistle. Their nimble fingers fly. When a relay is completed, every minute or so, it is dropped into a chute where it is automatically counted. The production rate of each girl, and of the group, can thus be figured per hour, per day, per year.

In the back of the room sits a man with a notebook, watching everything that happens, day in, day out for five years, beginning in 1927. (He has substitutes from time to time.) The girls do not resent him, they come to like and often tell their troubles to him. They learn to trust him as a kind of father confessor, and he respects their confidence. He represents the company, the Western Electric, and the Harvard School of Business Administration, which are jointly making the experiment under Dr. Mayo's general direction.

In experiments for the Fatigue Institute in England during World War I, Mayo had worked with factory women before. He proved that sometimes they produced more munitions in a ten-hour day than in a twelve-hour day. This was contrary to common sense, but not to human nature—which may tire and run down when worked too long. The girls at Hawthorne were a test group, being compared with a control group assembling relays in a larger room. The object of the experiment was to determine the effect on output of various changes in hours, in wages, rest periods, piecework, and so on. The assumptions were that higher wages would increase output while shorter hours might decrease it—the usual common sense assumptions.

Before the experiment was a year old, all preconceptions had been seriously upset. What was the matter with these girls? Why didn't they behave the way they were expected to behave? Being scientists, the inevstigators continued to keep a faithful record of what happened even if they were in the dark as to what caused it. The mystery story developed like this:

The first seven weeks were devoted to establishing a base period. The girls averaged 2,400 relays a week each, and worked a regular 48-hour week, including Saturdays.

They were then put on a piecework basis for eight weeks. Output went up.

They were given two rest pauses, morning and afternoon, for five weeks. Output went up again.

The rest pauses were lengthened. Output went up sharply.

Six rest pauses were tried and output fell off slightly. The girls complained that their rhythm was broken.

Then back to two rest pauses. Output went up again.

Hours reduced for a seven-week period. Output went up.

So it continued, trial after trial, each one lasting for some weeks. Whatever new factor was introduced, the number of relays coming through the counters increased, with the one exception noted. The research staff began to lose sleep as their assumptions disintegrated. Some force they could not measure was pushing output up no matter how they shifted hours, wages, rest pauses.

They prepared then for a supreme test. Take away *everything* given to the girls over all the periods, and go back to where the experiment started—forty-eight hours, no rest pauses, no hot lunch on the company, no piecework, no Saturday holiday, nothing. The supreme test lasted twelve weeks. Output jumped to an all-time high—3,000 relays a week!

The social scientists were as disorganized as their assumptions. They had tried to return the girls to the original conditions of the experiment but the original conditions had disappeared. The experiment had transformed the group; the girls no longer possessed the characteristics they had started with. What was this mysterious X which had thrust itself into the experiment? The staff began looking for it all over the factory but it was not there.

They finally found it in the girls themselves. The workers' attitudes had changed. The mysterious X was the way the girls now felt about their work. By putting them in a little friendly world of their own, by consulting them often, the scientists had caused a psychological change in these young women and given them a new sense of their status and value. The girls were no longer separate cogs in an impersonal, pecuniary machine; they were helping in a small way to direct the machine. So their output went up no matter how conditions were changed under them.[1] The investigators concluded that this happened because the girls were recognized, because they felt *important*. They had found work whose purpose they could clearly see. So they performed their tasks faster and better than ever before in their lives.

Since the invention of the steam engine most factory managers had regarded workers as "hands"—a part, and on the whole an unreliable part, of the cost of production. "Labor" was a commodity, to be bought and sold like pig iron. Sometimes, by way of contrast, a paternalistic manager treated his workers like little children, to be given candy and petted. The Hawthorne experiment broke down these illusions and proved that the way to make workers work hard and willingly lay in two basic and allied principles:

First, make the worker realize that his work is important, and that he is important.

Second, accept the fact that a factory is part of society, and under its roof society must function in its accustomed ways. Bands and teams and groups will form. They must be allowed for, utilized, and respected.

FOURTEEN MEN

The research staff then proceeded to set up their instruments in another room in the Hawthorne plant. Here were fourteen men engaged in "bank wiring," which means attaching wires to switches for certain kinds of telephone equipment. Nine men are wirers, three are solderers, two are inspectors. In another frame of reference, four are Czechs, three Germans, three Yankees, two are Poles, one is Armenian, and one Irish—an average Chicago ethnic cocktail.

These men have somehow become a team, a little society, inside the Hawthorne plant of 20,000 workers. Unlike the group of relay girls, however, this society does not increase output which is one of the reasons it is being studied. Not only has a team been formed spontaneously, but natural leaders have risen to the top. The managers of the plant are sublimely unaware of the strength and toughness of this outfit. The fourteen-man team is not opposed to management but comparatively indifferent to it, having more important matters to attend to. It is strictly a cultural phenomenon, not an economic one. The men are not concerned with the amount of money they get nearly as much as they are concerned with how their wages compare with Tom's and Jerry's. The *relative* factor is what counts with them.

[1] Of course, if physical conditions had been changed beyond tolerable limits, output would have been affected.

The company has recently adopted an "incentive pay plan," whereby the more work an employee does, the more he earns. It is a fair plan, and contains no speed-up provision, and management assumes it will increase production. It does nothing of the kind. The team members hold to a flat 6,000 units a day, no more, no less—though they could readily turn out 7,000 units without fatigue. If some member gets ambitious, the gang slaps him down. There is no apparent relation between an individual's ability and his output. The team does not act in accordance with its pecuniary interests at all. Why?

More brain racking for the research staff. Why don't workers earn more money when they have a fair honest chance to do so? The answer seemed to be that the men in the bank wiring room were more interested in maintaining their group than in hard cash. This was a result which neither the incentive plan nor the management was prepared to cope with. Yet any management which leaves out the feelings, sentiments, belief systems of the workers is operating in the dark.

The whole great plant at Hawthorne was found to be full of similar informal groups and teams, powered by leaders whom nobody in authority had ever selected. They exerted a rigid control over "rate busters"—who turned out too much work; over "chiselers"—who turned out too little; over "squealers"—who told on group members. The life of a squealer could be made very unhappy indeed.

It was further found that the efficiency engineers had tried in the past to break up informal groups, hoping to free individuals for greater production. This policy looked well on paper but time and again production went down when it was put into effect. The stop-watch men had unwittingly deprived the worker of the thing which chiefly gave meaning to his work and without which his full cooperation was impossible.

AIRCRAFT PLANT TEAM

During the war, other social scientists from the Harvard Business School studied labor-management relations in California aircraft factories for the government. Why were labor turnover and absenteeism so high? Here is a case which helps explain it.

John Briggs is a team leader in Department Z. Nobody appointed him, he just is, and every worker in that end of the shop knows it. One day John goes to the supervisor to present a grievance for one of his team members—a little matter, easily straightened out. The supervisor, who is having an off day and dislikes John anyway, offers him his time before the grievance is even heard. Maybe it was about the lights, maybe the washroom. Whereupon a team leader is lost who the management did not even know existed. John had been building up production the way a good football coach builds a random collection of rookies into a striking force.

The research men discovered he was boosting morale at his end of the plant, and was in a position to relieve the foreman of many problems of minor discipline—a real tower of strength. And now he is walking out the gate, burning with resentment at the supervisor and the company. The team he had led has lost its structure. In the front office, the chartmakers will presently begin to wonder why output in Department Z has gone all to pieces.

The social scientists found three kinds of groups in aircraft factories: (1) a "natural" team, with rarely more than seven members; (2) a "family" group, with up to thirty members, where leaders guided the newcomers and the less experienced; (3) an "organized" group deliberately set up by management to take advantage of this human urge. It is useless for management to ban informal groups. They will form anyway; they seem to be as natural as falling in love. So intelligent managers now are utilizing the drive behind them and even organizing them deliberately.

It was found in this California experiment that most absenteeism and labor turnover came from the ranks of workers who did not make a team, who perhaps had no chance to do so. Thus they had no social life in the factory, nothing to hold their interest and loyalty. Again and again the path comes back to that first principle of the anthropologists: man is a social animal.

You cannot fail to see what has happened in these experiments. Social scientists are at least getting at the basic theory underlying human realtions in factory and office. Prior to Hawthorne, we had nothing but guesses, some expert know-how with no underlying theory, a little common sense, and a great deal of plain loud dogma from management and men. Now we are beginning to know what makes workers work and testing the knowledge in controlled experiments. As Roethlisberger says:

> I should like to suggest that the manager is neither managing men nor managing work, but that he is managing a coordinated set of activities; he is administering a *social system*. That is the human relations approach as contrasted with any approach which implies that people at work can be considered separately from their work.

The big story is that when a factory is studied as a social system—a functioning community like Middletown or Plainville—the behavior of workers makes sense. When it is regarded as an exhibit in the class struggle, or in paternalism, or as a kind of zoo for Economic Men —what workers do makes no sense at all most of the time. About all the investigator can do is to cuss human nature. It goes without saying that union leaders need this new knowledge as much as company managers.

Mayo deserves credit for opening up this fruitful research more than any other one man. But some anticipated him, like Carleton Parker and Clarence J. Hicks. Many cooperated with him at Hawthorne and other experimental stations, like Roethlisberger. Many more, indeed a growing army, are refining theory and techniques at Yale, MIT, and other universities, while young men trained at these centers are applying the new knowledge in industry and government all over the country.

A MILLION FOREMEN

Perhaps the most ambitious of recent applications was the Training Within Industry programs initiated by the War Manpower Commission during the war. More than a million foremen in war industry were taught new methods for handling the group under them, based on the recognition that they were human beings in a social structure. In one simple technique the foreman may straighten out a situation in the factory by letting Bill tell him about the trouble at home. This is a long way from the old-time foreman who was asked:

"How do you handle a new employee?"

"I jest stand there . . . and stare him down to kinda show him how dumb he is."

"And then?"

"Then I spit. . . ."

The Job Relations Course in the TWI programs gave every foreman a little blue card with these principles to be constantly referred to:

Let each worker know how he is getting along.

Give credit when due; tell him while it's "hot."

Tell people in advance about changes that will affect them. Tell them why.

Look for ability not now being used.

People must be treated as individuals, not members on the payroll.

In any given problem, *first* GET THE FACTS, then weigh and decide and only then TAKE ACTION. Afterwards be sure and check results.

This problem-solving technique for foremen is not merely a common sense approach, it is based squarely on scientific method.

Another interesting application is a project of the National Planning

Association, under the direction of Clinton Golden, trade union leader and teacher at the Harvard Business School. A score of plants all over the country with especially good labor relations are being studied on the spot by social scientists. Both unions and managements are actively cooperating. If characteristics are found common to *all* successful programs, scientific conclusions can be drawn and made available to managers, government officials, and unions everywhere.

Benjamin M. Selekman, long a co-worker with Mayo at Harvard, in his book, *Labor Relations and Human Relations,* makes this cogent summary.

> In exploring the hostilities implicit in modern industry, we must be careful not to idealize the human satisfactions in earlier societies. Man proverbially has had to earn his bread by the sweat of his brow, and nothing in the historic record justifies the belief that he ever found the toil and sweat in themselves deeply desirable. The reduction in back-breaking human costs of labor by the development of modern industrialism has long been accounted one of its outstanding benefits. Nonetheless, from the beginning of human experience, work has been part of the whole effort of man to master and control his environment. . . . Its emotional satisfactions stem normally, therefore, from the sense of effectiveness the individual derives from the daily round of labor. The average worker no longer draws this basic satisfaction from his job.

How can he recapture it? This is the fundamental question in the labor problem of today.

---

28. UNION WAGE DECISIONS AND EMPLOYMENT *

THE LABOR leader must be concerned with both the level of wages and the quantity of employment of the members of his union. However, the objective of high and rising wage rates and the objective of full employment of members may, at times, be inconsistent. Demands for higher wages (or resistance to wage reductions in periods of recession) may reduce the employment

* George P. Shultz and Charles A. Myers, *The American Economic Review,* June, 1950, pp. 362-79. Reprinted by permission of the authors and publisher.

George P. Shultz (1920——) is Assistant Professor of Industrial Relations at Massachusetts Institute of Technology. Author of *Pressures on Wage Decisions* and (with Charles A. Myers) of *The Dynamics of the Labor Market*. Charles A. Myers (1913——) is Professor of Industrial Relations at the same school. He is author of *Industrial Relations in Sweden: Some Comparisons with American Experience* and (with W. R. McLawrin) of *The Movement of Factory Workers.*

of members. Some economists have come to the conclusion that the leader is concerned primarily with the wage rate—if he does not provide increases (or does not resist cuts), the membership may become dissatisfied with his leadership and he may lose his position—and only secondarily with employment. The following article is the result of an empirical investigation of this question.

THE END of a seller's market in many unionized industries and the strategic importance of union wage decisions in the economy underline the significance of a question which has increasingly concerned economists: are a union's wage decisions influenced by the possible effects of those decisions on the employment opportunities of its members? Until recent years there was more or less general agreement in the literature of labor economics that many unions took into account the relation between wage demands and employment in the particular firm or industry. But in 1947, in a series of articles, one of which appeared in this *Review,* Arthur M. Ross argued: "The volume of employment associated with a given wage rate is unpredictable before the fact and the effect of a given rate on employment is undecipherable after the fact. The employment effect cannot normally be the subject of rational calculation and prediction at the time the bargain is made, and union officials are normally in no position to assume responsibility for it."

This latter view rests upon the conception of a trade union as a political institution, whose leaders must continually balance the pressures from the rank and file, rival factions in the union, rival unions, employers, and government. Such a "model" is consistent with the postwar emphasis on "rounds" of wage increases emanating from "key bargains" and would, in fact, help explain assertions, like the one by Dunlop, which follows:

> We have reached the stage where a limited number of key bargains effectively influence the whole wage structure of the American economy. When these strategic wages have been determined, for all practical purposes wage rates are determinable throughout the rest of the system within narrow limits.

The same line of thinking, which would reorient explanation of wage changes from economic to political forces, is, in effect, supported by recent discussions of the theory of the firm, especially the firm's short-run reactions to changes in costs. Reynolds, for example, develops the importance for the determination of price of a "firm's long-range market strategy *vis-a-vis* competing firms." He then observes,

> Once the price has been set, output is determined solely by the firm's estimate of how much can be sold at this price. Cost considerations are not directly involved in the output decision.

It follows that there is no reason why a wage increase (or any other cost increase) confined to the firm in question should have any effect on output, unless a level of costs is reached which forces the firm to suspend operations entirely.

Thus, with no compelling economic forces operating in the short run—no "employment effect" of a wage increase—the stage is set for the determination of wages by political pressures.

Are the output and employment decisions of an individual firm unresponsive, within a reasonably short period of time, to change in wages (or other) costs? If there were a response, would unions always and inevitably ignore it? Evidence which we have recently collected suggests that the answer to these questions may, for many situations, be "no." This evidence, in its broad outline, will be presented in this paper. Two subsidiary, though important, questions must also be raised, if this discussion of union reactions to an "employment effect" is to prove constructive. First, what are the sources of pressure which may compel union decision-makers to recognize a possible "employment effect"? In what way are these pressures expressed? Second, what are the types of situations in which wage decisions are most likely to be influenced by the volume of work available to union members?

The new evidence on which we base our analysis is drawn from two recent field-research projects. The first was a study of the highly competitive and only partially unionized men's shoe industry, and more intensively, of that portion of the industry centered in southeastern Massachusetts. In this region, a strong independent union, a "brotherhood" of fourteen craft units, bargains with some thirty firms, many of which are members of a manufacturers' association. The second study was directly concerned with the effects of unemployment in another New England industrial community, where the partial shutdown of a large textile mill contributed substantially to a peak unemployment of about 13 per cent of the labor force in April, 1949. Here we were interested, in part, in the effects of unemployment on wage settlements made under collective bargaining.

Wage decisions are made on many other occasions than at the time of a general wage settlement. For example, union leaders must take a position on individual piece rates and work loads; they must decide when to enforce the union scale and when not to; they must adjust to new products constantly being introduced; they must make decisions on questions involving technological changes and on proposals to "rationalize" the plant wage structure, as in job evaluation; and, in some industries, they must decide what "grade" of merchandise is being produced in order to determine what scale of wages is appropriate.

Finally, programs of union-management cooperation are often motivated, initially at least, by a need to adjust costs to lower levels when this is not possible through general reductions in wages.

Taking, as we must, then, the whole gamut of wage decisions for examination, we turn now to the shoe study for evidence that employment opportunities can effect wage decisions. The discussion will center upon these points: (1) the existence and function of the "grade system" of relating labor costs to product prices, (2) the flexibilities within the piece-rate structure, and (3) the general wage movements. Following this discussion, we shall take up the findings in the second study, as they relate to wage decisions and employment.

The grade system, as it exists in the Massachusetts shoe industry, is a method of determining the labor cost on a pair of men's shoes: the higher the selling price, the higher the labor costs, with piece rates on individual operations varying proportionately. Though the system is objectionable from many points of view,[1] it has persisted for at least thirty years as the basis for the industry's rate structure. This can be explained only by relating the union's wage decisions to employment opportunities of the membership. For over two decades, a great shift down in the price preferences of footwear consumers has resulted in a smaller and smaller potential market for higher-priced shoes, and, as a result, a constantly dwindling volume of business for the quality-minded manufacturers in this region.[2] In turn, consequent unemployment and underemployment of local shoeworkers placed great pressure on the established level of piece prices, and the grade system represented a more acceptable adaptation to that pressure than a general wage reduction. As the *Shoe Workers' Journal* stated with resignation in 1928, "As long as shoes are sold at different price levels, they will be made at varying labor cost."

The grade system was started, then, and has continued in operation as an adaptation to the declining volume of business available on established lines of shoes. Thus, the very existence of the differentiated labor costs which the "system" implies provides a striking example of the importance of the "quantity axis" in wage bargains. Furthermore, the

[1] The worker is dissatisfied when he receives a different return for doing substantially the same operation on two "racks" of shoes, simply because one carries a "pink tag" and the other an "orange tag." The manufacturer finds it difficult, if not impossible, to get superior workmanship on his better shoes. The union finds the system difficult to police, always being suspicious that some manufacturer is "juggling tags," in order to make his high-grade shoes on a lower labor cost.

[2] For example, shoe production in the region declined from 20.3 million pairs in 1920 to 9.3 million in 1940. Wages paid shoeworkers in the region's largest city fell from $14.5 million to $3.8 million over the same period, while employment declined by a little over 50 per cent.

grades have functioned as the mechanism through which the union and individual manufacturers have worked out their season-to-season and year-to-year problems. The sorts of adjustment for which the grade system has proved an appropriate mechanism all relate to the stimulation of local employment through wage decisions. They may be classified into three general types: (1) a means for making general wage reductions without giving the appearance of having done so; (2) a means for discriminating between the "ability to pay" of the various price-grades of shoes; and (3) a means for discriminating between the "ability (or willingness) to pay" of various companies. In each of these types of adjustment, the primary orientation has been toward increasing the volume of production by changing piece rates (labor costs) in particular factories.

In 1935, as a result of discussions between the union and the manufacturers, a 10 per cent reduction in wages seemed in prospect, in order "to stop the loss of business and get new business." Discussing the possibilities presented by this situation, however, some of the manufacturers expressed doubt as to whether such a reduction in wages would be of much help to them: "10% won't help long. It will affect other Districts; they will try to get 10% off . . . I can't see it, when you talk percentages; I think it is very dangerous." As a result of this feeling, no general wage cut was made. But what was done amounted to the same thing: while manufacturers in the lowest grade were granted a reduction, those in other grades were "given" the next lowest piece rate "list," though no real change was made in the quality of shoe which they produced. A *de facto* reduction was achieved without creating a "pattern" for competing production centers to follow, thereby enabling local manufacturers to attract some additional business. Further, by making the change through the mechanism of the grade system, the union was able to refuse an adjustment on the highest-priced shoes, where, they reasoned, their small concession (percentagewise to selling price) could not become an effective stimulus to increased sales.

The series of events which took place early in 1938 were similar to the 1935 experience recounted above. In addition, the grade system became the vehicle for further company-by-company arrangements which had as their central referent a specific wage-employment bargain: the union agreed to "submit a stated labor cost" in return for a guarantee of daily production. For example, late in 1938, union officials signed an agreement providing, in part, as follows:

1. The Company agrees that from the period of November 15th, 1938, until April 30th, 1939, they shall produce 140 dozen pairs of shoes daily for a period of five days each week. It is understood that the production

of $5.00 shoes shall not exceed 40 dozen pairs daily during this period.

2. In consideration of the above commitments on the part of the Company, it is agreed by the Union that they shall furnish the Company with a new price list to apply to $5.00 shoes, this price list not to exceed 60¢ per pair on a plain black oxford commonly referred to as a base shoe.

In another case, a manufacturer who also operated successful selling outlets stated, in response to questions from union officials, that he was buying shoes "outside" cheaper than he could make them in his own factory. He presented the union with invoice and cost slips and, after some independent investigation by the union, a contract similar to the one just cited was signed. These bargains were not infrequent and exceptional; on the contrary, they represent the dominant theme of wage activity in this section of the industry: the adjustment of wages to the realities of business and employment conditions.

A second area, which may be disposed of briefly, where wage decisions have reflected the level of employment is the settlement of individual piece rates. It must be apparent now that the orientation of these rates is, basically, toward the product market, rather than toward working conditions in particular factories. It would, in fact, be difficult or impossible to administer a set of rates strictly in accordance with variations in job requirements.[3] As a result, the piece-rate system is "administered" in accordance with bargaining power, the basic element of which is the employment prospect. With new styles constantly working their way through the factory, the union has obtained high rates and many "extras" during times of high-level employment, especially in the period immediately following World War II. On the other hand, "quality drives" in the periods of low business activity and variations in the number of work steps required,[4] without demands for changes in piece rates have had the effect of adjusting wage costs downward. Even though this may take place in the absence of a positive union decision, a wage decision is nevertheless implicit. Altogether, then, piecemeal changes in the rate structure and in work requirements have been an additional and important source in the adjustment of wages and labor costs to employment conditions.

During the years between 1933 and 1948, there were four periods

[3] The difficulty results from the great number of types of shoes produced in a single factory, from the infinite variations between pieces of leather, and from constant change in the quality of work demanded.

[4] For example, a good job of edgesetting requires the performance of all the work steps twice, though the improvement over a "one-set" edge is not apparent until the shoe has been worn for several weeks. In many shoe factories during the war, the foremen "looked the other way" while the workers collected a "two-set" piece price for doing a "one-set" job. After the war, the "two-set" requirements were again enforced.

involving general wage movements in this region. Though there is not space here to describe all these events, conclusions from them will be summarized and a few of the episodes from which these conclusions are drawn will be described.

First of all, political forces have sometimes been quite potent in the determination of a general movement in wages. The shoeworkers' union in this region has been particularly subject to these pressures since it is (1) a democratic organization, allowing the membership considerable freedom to criticize action of the leaders and providing for secret-ballot referenda for the election of officers every two years, and (2) a bona fide independent union, faced, on the one hand, with the Boot and Shoe Workers' Union (AFL) from which it seceded in 1933, and, on the other, with an aggressive CIO affiliate, the United Shoe Workers of America, which has considerable strength in New England. Thus, union leaders have stated that they need to "get 10 per cent and get it quick to stop this agitation" and the manufacturers have been impressed by the argument that they must "make some move in a hurry."

But, to test the thesis that employment considerations have no place in the decision-making process of unions, situations must be found where the "political" and "economic" forces push in opposite directions. We need go back no further than 1947, 1948, and 1949 to find such a situation in the Massachusetts men's shoe industry. These were years of generally rising living costs and widely publicized "rounds" of general wage increases. During this period, furthermore, the rival USWA conducted a strong though unsuccessful campaign to discredit the Brotherhood and win an NLRB election; and two close contests for president, vice president, and secretary-treasurer of the BSAC were held. In the first of these, the incumbents held their positions by narrow margins, but in the second, they were defeated. Despite all these circumstances, there were no general wage increases in the district. Several half-hearted requests were made by the former officials; however, the new ones passed up an opportunity to reopen the wage question, signing a contract effective until January, 1951. Why were the Brotherhood officials not forced to press demands for a general wage increase? Certainly they would have been if political considerations were controlling. But employment and payrolls in the region's shoe industry both declined from their 1946 level during this three-year period. Many of the union's members were unemployed and others were working only part time. As one of the union's officers explained, "Our problem right now is shoes not wage rates."

An even more dramatic example of the relationship between employment and this union's wage decisions occurred in 1940, and involved a piece price list (labor cost) submitted by the union and used by the manufacturers in bidding on a large order of Army shoes. The background for this bid was one of generally depressed conditions in the region's shoe factories, unsuccessful attempts to obtain a share of three previous government orders, and a union election campaign culminating three days after the bids were to be opened. After some controversy in the local papers as to who was responsible for the inability of local firms to get government business, the union announced that it had "available a price list which is comparable item for item with prices now being paid by the largest manufacturer of service shoes in the country." Under the stimulus of this general reduction in piece prices on service shoes, several manufacturers pared their other costs to the bone and bid successfully for the business against the country's largest shoe companies.

Here union officials had made a considerable wage concession in order to gain employment opportunities for the membership. Further, if the results of the secret-ballot election held a few days after these bids were opened is an indication of the feelings of the rank and file, this action must be judged a political success: all the union's incumbent officials were re-elected by landslide margins.

Altogether, then, the record in this section of the industry indicates that "political" forces have been more important as a pressure on general wage movements, than on piece rates under the "grade system." Even with respect to general wage movements, they have been dominant considerations only when accompanied by the permissive condition —an encouraging employment prospect. In more adverse circumstances, however, general wage decisions have been more strongly influenced by the possible "employment effect" despite concurrent and important election campaigns; and when all types of wage activity are considered, the influence of employment prospects on wage decisions must be regarded as decisive.

Our findings in the other study tend to confirm these conclusions. In this case, the permanent layoff of large numbers of textile workers between September, 1948, and February, 1949, precipitated a local employment crisis, which was aggravated by further layoffs in almost all of the city's other industries by the spring of 1949. During the period, general wage negotiations were conducted with most of the unionized firms and, in many of them, questions were raised as to the appropriate piece rate on new jobs, the work loads on standard operations, or the productivity on hourly-rated jobs. All these questions involve wage decisions of one sort or another, which provide information relevant to the issues raised in this article.

In all the firms where negotiations were conducted during the period of our study, the drop in local and, often, company employment was judged to have affected wage negotiations, and, in about 80 per cent of the cases, this factor was the dominant influence on the settlement. Union officials felt that local union members did not have the necessary enthusiasm for pressing wage demands. This they attributed in turn to these fears of their members: (1) that a strike might develop, causing hardship where unemployment had already reduced the family income, and costing jobs if the employer proved strong enough to win the strike by replacing part of his present work force; and (2) that higher labor costs forced on the employer might cause him to lose more of an already scarce item: business. Examples follow.

1. One company operating in a competitive industry settled for no wage change, despite large company profits for the preceding year. Union officials were apparently concerned about the impact of a wage change on job opportunities within the company, for they pointed out to the membership in a mimeographed statement that "in our own area and in other areas . . . factories are being permanently closed," and "the important thing for the employees of the company is to keep production at a good level and to keep the factories going at the maximum number of full weeks of work." The membership apparently agreed, for the rank-and-file voted in favor of this settlement registered a 4-to-1 majority.

2. In two other cases, not in the same industry, the AFL and CIO unions involved had usually made large wage demands and had obtained several sizable increases during preceding years. At this time, however, the unions asked for two additional paid holidays. But after one bargaining session, this demand was dropped and the contract settled with no change. Employee representatives on the negotiating committees had been on "short time" for several weeks and were impressed with employer arguments that increased costs at this time threatened his ability to attract orders. In still another company, a union leader explained his failure to press for wage demands with his statement: "You can't push that guy anywhere except out of business."

3. In another case, a six-cent general increase was given by the company in exchange for acceptance of a job evaluation and time study plan which, by raising work standards without major changes in plant layout, brought labor costs to their original level. Why didn't the union insist on more pay for more work? The CIO International officer stated that he could not work up any "steam" in the local people, who were "scared for their jobs and wanted their weekly income."

4. In a company where employees were organized into several craft

unions affiliated with the AFL, the International representative of a small but strong group told this story:

> I wish I could think only in terms of the added costs to the company of our demands. They don't amount to anything since we have so few members. However, I have to think of the effect of my increase on the whole plant because the other unions will insist on parity of treatment. But the company can contract out for the work of our local. If our actions cost them too much in terms of total plant payroll, they will do just that; then our men will be out of some very good jobs.

Here the apparent inelastic demand for the labor of a small group was not real, since special circumstances made the effects on total wage costs of primary consideration.

5. Several union representatives, generalizing on their experience in this community and elsewhere, made the following statements in interviews:

> In the past seven years, there has been no question that we could get pattern wage adjustments in many plants. Business had the money to pay. But now things are getting different. We have to consider whether, if we get a wage increase now, there will be as much work for our members. If a plant is operating forty hours a week, they may be able to continue to give that much work if we take no increase and just settle for a wage reopening clause. But if we demand and get an increase, the men may get only four days' work a week. Those are the things we take into account now.
>
> We may settle for a reopening with no increase, in hopes that things are better later. We know there have been substantial layoffs at the company and in the community.
>
> When I am called in by local people to help prepare contract demands, I ask them: "How many days are you working a week? How much backlog of orders is there? How does business seem? What is happening in the other plants in the area? Is there much unemployment?" (If they say, yes, as they are saying now, I tell them, "Well, there's your answer."

The day-to-day types of wage decisions also present several interesting examples of responses to depressed conditions in this community. In one small, job-lot plant, organized by an AFL affiliate, most of the work is performed by the piece, with rates set by bargaining rather than by more "scientific" techniques. Labor costs amount to almost half the total costs. The plant, along with the rest of its industry, had been operating on a four-day week. When, on several occasions, the possibility of bidding in additional orders at reduced prices was presented, union representatives (who were, at the same time, workers in the plant) made concessions as they set their prices for the prospective work. In this way, by reducing their wage per unit, they increased their depleted weekly income.

Another small textile company, making a fairly well standardized product, had been forced to curtail operations by 50 per cent and the prospect for future business did not seem bright. The employer raised the question of work loads with the union, recalling that his factory was popularly known as an "old ladies' home." After several negotiating sessions, work loads were increased by about 25 per cent on almost all operations performed in the plant, without any change in the hourly rates.

The influence of actual or potential employment conditions on wage decisions is illustrated, then, by events which took place in both labor markets we studied. In some of these cases, of course, unemployment affected wage decisions simply by reducing the union's control over its membership. The great majority of instances cited, however, cannot be reconciled with the view that union wage decisions do not take into account the "employment effect." Instead, these wage decisions were based on a probable or an assured effect on employment. But, perhaps these illustrations could be dismissed as inconsequential, as "the exceptional case which is so widely celebrated in the literature of labor economics." To meet this criticism squarely we must explore two additional problems. First, the way in which the "employment effect" exerted its pressure must be examined; and, second, the types of situation where union decisions respond to employment prospects must be identified. Then we can consider whether such situations are the "exceptional case."

An understanding of union wage decisions must, if it is to have any predictive value, be based on an understanding of the union itself. Fortunately, Ross has provided an acceptable "model" of the trade union as a "political agency," though we differ with him as to the range of possibilities which this "model" admits. He stresses, correctly for many situations, the institutional and personal needs which union activity must satisfy, emphasizing the "distinction between the union and its members." For other cases, though, he may be inaccurate in relegating the provision of benefits for the rank and file to the role of "formal rationale," just "an incident to its [the union's] activities." Let us see what these variations in emphasis, all within the "political" model of the trade union, mean with respect to the process and pressures involved in the making of union wage decisions.

There are at least four possible lines of pressure which might lie behind a union's wage decision in a contest of concern over present or prospective job opportunities. First of all, as a result of pressure to build their own reputations as "militant fighters" and to uphold the prestige of their own union *vis-à-vis* rival institutions, union officials could refuse to make any wage concessions. They could probably make an appealing case for their position before the rank and file, maintaining their own status at the top of the union's hierarchy. Ross takes the position that this is, in fact, the typical case. An excellent illustration supporting his point of view was presented by Gladys L. Palmer in her study of the tactics of three Philadelphia textile unions, as they faced serious economic changes. In her description of the Tapestry Carpet Workers' struggles, she states:

> Although over a period of years, numerous occasions were offered when they might, by concessions in rates, have saved the union or salvaged some employment for their members while unemployment was steadily increasing in the trade, they steadfastly refused to do so. They "went down fighting."

Ross does concede, however, a second alternative: that the economic environment may "generate political pressures which have to be reckoned with by the union leader." But what are these pressures? Apparently, the principal motivating force is the employer, making full use of the union's survival needs to attain his concessions:

> Thus it is the employer rather than the unemployed or potentially unemployed worker who forces the decision in the normal case. From the standpoint of the union, the purpose of agreeing to the cut is to maintain the bargaining relationship on as satisfactory a basis as possible. What appears as a danger is not that unemployment will fall off but that the employer will become hostile. It is the loss of friendly relationships, bargaining units, and collective agreements, rather than the loss of jobs, which is most to be avoided.

This is undoubtedly an accurate description of what happens in some cases; but it is hazardous, for the Boot and Shoe Workers' Union was overthrown in southeastern Massachusetts for just such behavior.

These two lines of pressure, one oriented to the needs of the union's leaders and of the union as an institution and the other emanating from the employer, both seem to envisage the rank and file in a more or less passive rôle. Is it conceivable, though, that loss of jobs and lowered income through underemployment could become a matter of grave concern to workers? Two additional lines of pressure on union decisions could result from such concern. First, the union's bargaining power may be impaired by rank and file unwillingness to go out on strike. As we have pointed out in connection with our second field study, workers have held negotiators back because of (1) inability or unwillingness to forego income when other members of the family are already unemployed, and (2) fear that the employer might defeat a strike and replace part of his present work force.

Second, many occasions have been noted where rank and file pressure has oriented union wage activity primarily toward a consideration for employment, toward incomes rather than wage rates. A particularly striking example, taken from the shoe study, occurred just after the present independent union had won recognition from the manufacturers. The union was in the throes of wage negotiations with the manufacturers' association. One of the district's largest companies, however, was not in on these negotiations, having refused to recognize the new union. This company had even granted a 10 per cent increase in pay as an inducement to get men back to work under jurisdiction of the union to which they had formerly belonged. Upon recognizing the new union, the company wished to withdraw its offer of a 10 per cent increase. The union's officials, understandably under such circumstances, refused to consider the request. The company then threatened to do what it had done on past occasions—buy large quantities of shoes from other companies for sale in its own stores. After two union meetings in which representatives of the factory's crew pleaded for consideration of their jobs, restoration of the former wage scale was reluctantly agreed to, on condition that the company would "keep the business of the cheaper grade of shoes that they had planned to purchase outside the city." In this case, then, a wage concession designed to stimulate employment resulted from strong rank and file pressure, despite strong "political" forces in opposition.

We have previously cited several other instances where concern over the volume of work has forced union leaders to modify demands or look for ways to grant concessions. More often than not, as indicated earlier, these concessions have been made outside the context of general wage bargaining, in ways which were more attractive politically. The operation of the grade system in the men's shoe industry, of course, is a case in point.

The meaning of this section to our central question may be summarized in three statements: (1) the model of a trade union as a "political agency" is congenial to the explanation of union wage decisions; (2) the concept of a "political agency" admits a wide range of pressures applied to union leaders, including the four possibilities outlined above; (3) rank and file pressure for wage decisions oriented toward the effect on employment is an important alternative among the possible lines of pressure arising in a context where work is relatively scarce.

The case against a relationship between wage decisions and the volume of employment in a given company does not rest, however, with the assertion that "union officials are normally in no position to assume responsibility for it [employment]." We have quoted Reynolds earlier as arguing that "there is no reason why a wage increase (or any other cost increase) confined to the firm in question should have any effect on output, unless a level of costs is reached which forces the firm to suspend operations entirely." Similarly, in discussing the "fiction of the 'wage-employment' bargain," Ross identifies four links by which the wage rate is connected with the demand for labor: wage rate to labor costs; labor cost to total cost; total cost to price; and price to volume of sales and production. He finds that there is "a great deal of free play at each link in the chain" and that "as a result, the initial and final links are so loosely connected that for practical purposes they must be regarded as largely independent."

But after arguing the looseness at each link, though not always in a convincing way, Ross takes up certain instances in the textile and garment industries where "wage-cost-price-employment relationships were relatively clear and predictable." He explains these "exceptional" cases by noting the following conditions: (1) the piece-rate method of compensation, under which "wage rates were closely linked with unit labor costs"; (2) "labor cost was a fairly substantial proportion [23.1% and 19.7%, respectively] of total cost; moreover, at the same time that wages were cut, the employers agreed to take other measures to reduce overhead and material costs"; (3) the "competitiveness of the industry" meant that "selling prices were closely related to total costs"; and finally (4) prices and volume were associated because of the existence of non-union competition.

We agree that these are conditions under which an "employment effect" might be expected. At least three other conditions, which might sometimes be important, should be added, however. First, the distinction made by Gordon is useful, between "the 'job shop' type of business, which quotes on individual orders to particular specifications and produces only after the sale is made, and the type of business which is geared to continuous production of one or more products, for which production plans are made and prices are quoted in advance of sales." Reynolds seems to have thought only in terms of the latter type of business. Second, important pressures may develop where the work force is underemployed; thus, cases where the number of jobs is involved should be distinguished from cases where the quantity of work available to those already employed is the issue in question. The chances for a concession of some sort might be greater, of course, in the latter case, since those making the "sacrifice" would be the direct beneficiaries.

Finally, whenever a real threat develops of the discontinuance of a group of jobs or all jobs in a plant, the people involved may consider the possibility of altering labor costs in an attempt to retain their positions.

Given these various conditions, which, sometimes singly but probably more often in combination, may give rise to a wage change oriented toward an "employment effect," the question really becomes, "Are these conditions so 'exceptional' that they may be ignored in the search for the forces important in wage determination?" We think not.

First of all, incentive methods of wage payment are not uncommon in American industry, despite the widely publicized opposition of some unions to them. A postwar survey made by the Bureau of Labor Statistics, for example, estimates that 30 per cent of the plant workers in the manufacturing industries sampled were paid on an incentive basis. The "substantial proportion" of labor cost to total cost in textiles and clothing does not seem particularly high; in fact Ross cites a Federal Trade Commission analysis which reports over half the industries studied to be in this "substantial" category, or higher. It is impossible to classify all American business into "continuous production" or "job shop" categories; but "job shop" conditions do exist in such diverse industries as men's and women's clothing, independent foundry operation, and the manufacture of specialized machinery, to name a few. Under these conditions, especially, pressure from an underemployed work force may be strong.

At the national level in well-organized industries, furthermore, concern over industry employment may have important effects on union policies. The International Fur and Leather Workers' Union, for example, recently agreed to return to the prewar "two-price" system, as a means of stimulating employment in the slack season. This agreement, the result of "rotten" business in 1949, specified an 11 per cent reduction in wages from January through June. And the unions in both the men's clothing and ladies' garment industries are well known for their willingness to cooperate with management in reducing costs, including labor costs, by more efficient production methods. This is their method of protecting the jobs and wages of union members.

Finally, the experience of war and postwar years should not form the basis for general statements on the question of union responses to employment problems. When job opportunities equal or exceed the number of available workers, why should anyone worry about the amount of labor employed as a result of a particular wage level? Union leaders, "judging their market," could make the wage rate their sole concern. In the spring of 1949, however, *Labor's Monthly Survey* advised AFL unions, "Perhaps your employer's prospects are excellent;

but if his profit margin is being squeezed by price declines, your future will be more secure if you help him improve his competitive position." In a similar vein, Taylor writes, "We now have industries where this second criterion of whether a union will take a wage increase if it means a significant loss of jobs or of work opportunity is of tremendous importance."

---

29. THE UNIONS' INFLUENCE ON WAGES *

Trade Unionism and Distributive Shares

LABOR economists have long been at odds as to the effect of trade unionism on the general level of wages. Some have insisted that union pressures have, in effect, substituted monopolistic supply for competitive supply with a resulting increase in labor's share of national product at the expense of the other factors. Others have felt that labor's share in distribution remains relatively constant in spite of union activity. This latter point of view is here presented by Mr. Kerr.

UNDER what circumstances, if any, will trade unionism affect distributive shares [in percentage terms] and in what fashion? Unionism [for present purposes] may be categorized into six types according to their attempted depth of penetration into economic processes and according to their reliance on economic or political methods. Depth of penetration is shown by three levels: (a) bargaining over the money wage, (b) bargaining over the real wage, and (c) bargaining over distributive shares. These three levels of penetration, taken together with the two kinds of methods—collective bargaining and political action—yields us our six types.

1. "Pure and simple unionism" [where the emphasis is on collective bargaining to raise the money wage]. It is relatively easy for employers not to be caught by the economic program of "pure and simple unionism." To begin with, union wages may not be raised above the rates which otherwise would have prevailed. If they are, there are two important links between wages and profts, and employers may elude pursuit at either or both of these two points. First, they may raise

*Clark Kerr, *Monthly Labor Review,* February, 1954.

The author (1911——) is Chancellor of the University of California at Berkley and author of *Migration of the Seattle Labor Market Area* and *Unions, Management and the Public.*

prices (and this is particularly easy to do if the union covers the whole industry); and, second, they may introduce labor-saving devices or otherwise raise productivity. Thus one would expect this kind of program to result in a [usually temporarily] higher share for labor only when unionism was particularly aggressive, as perhaps in its organizing period; when the market was "hard," i. e., when it was pressing down on prices; and when laborsaving innovations or other improvements in the use of labor were not available.

"Pure and simple unionism" may, under some circumstances, actually reduce labor's share and raise the share of profits, although I do not wish to imply that it is a very normal occurrence. With the introduction by unionism of the "standard rate," the natural spread of rates over a wide range from firm to firm is greatly reduced or even eliminated. Some firms may be forced out of business, although this seldom occurs, and others may have their profit margins reduced, but for others the "standard rate" preserves for the firm itself that portion of profits it otherwise would have shared with labor.

2. "New Deal unionism." Under a program emphasizing the achievement of full employment through governmental policy, unions can chase employers faster with higher money wages than in periods marked by less than full employment, but employers can run still faster. The profit share rises and, even though the shares for rent and interest are reduced, labor's relative share of national income falls. In a depression, exactly the reverse happens and labor's share rises. Thus, over a period of time, a permanent full employment economy will show a lower average share for labor than one where prosperity and depression alternate.

While we are inclined to agree with Morton that union wage pressures do not cause inflation, still the governmental policies associated with "New Deal unionism" may, and inflation does cut labor's share. In fact, the chief beneficiary of "New Deal unionism," in terms of shares, is entrepreneurial income. With their policies of the "standard rate" and full employment, unionism of our first two types might be viewed as the protector of profits.

3. "Improvement unionism." The policy of improvement unionism seeks to tie wages closely to the cost of living and to the increase in physical productivity. Wages tend to follow the cost of living and productivity in any event. This policy, by calling for quick and automatic adjustments, reduces the lag. Thus labor's share would tend to fall slightly less than it otherwise would on the upswing and rise slightly less (assuming the escalator clause is allowed to work downward as

well as upward) on the downswing. Assuming, however, a full employment economy without inflation, the net results, as compared with what otherwise might happen, would probably be negligible.

The policy probably, on balance, slightly favors chronic inflation by reducing lags, although Ross and Reder have suggested that it will make the swings in both directions more violent.

More generally, however, this is a policy designed not so much to catch the employers as to prevent them from running farther away. Individual employers, of course, can run away farther by having their prices advance faster than prices generally or by raising the productivity of their workers more than the general rise in productivity, but employers in totality cannot.

4. "Direct controls unionism." The essence of this policy is direct price control by government. [This is a counterpart of "improvement unionism" with a national bargain at the parliamentary level taking the place of a plant or industrywide or even nationwide bargain across the conference table.] At least in the short run, profit margins can be held steady in an inflationary period or even squeezed, if enforcement is adequate, and the share of labor maintained or raised. By holding down rents, the share of labor can further be advantaged. Under this policy, with the government holding on to him, unionism can catch the employer and take some profits from him, although there may be some cost in volume of employment or size of total output.

5. "Managerial unionism." [Unions adopting this approach try to affect distributive shares at the plant or industry level through such devices as the "all-or-none" contract, profit-sharing schemes, union-management joint control of the industry with the union participating in price setting, control of entry of firms, and so forth.] The employer, however, may be able to escape the impact of the "all-or-none" bargain by raising prices or by increasing the output of his labor force.

[Under] direct profit sharing, the employer can only regain the original amount of profit he obtained by increasing the total amount since some of the profit must be shared with his employees. [With] partial or complete [union] participation in the direction of the industry, the incentive for efficiency lies more with the employees than with the employers.

This kind of policy is very limited in its actual application, but there is no doubt that under it, given enough power to the union, shares can be affected; labor can receive more than its marginal revenue product.

6. "Labor Party unionism." This policy relies on taxation and on subvention to affect not the income received in the primary distribu-

tion, which we have been discussing up until now, but rather the income retained after secondary distribution has taken place. Through progressive taxation and subsidies the real income available to labor can be raised as compared with that of originally more highly rewarded elements in the population. Here at last the employer can really be caught, although perhaps not as much as might first appear. Goods and services are taken out of the market place and given to wage and salary earners with the cost financed by taxes bearing heavily on other segments of the population.

American historical experience is consistent with the suggested impacts of these different union programs:

1. Employee compensation as a share of income originating within the business sector of the economy, after allowing for interindustry shifts in weights, has been quite stable over substantial periods of time. It was virtually unchanged from 1929 to 1950.
2. This share was higher in depression (1930-33) and recession (1938) than in more prosperous periods.
3. During wartime inflation this share sank a bit but rose later in the one area where price control was most effective—nonfarm corporations.
4. This share rose in 1945-47 when corporation profits were depressed by reconversion and when unions were unusually aggressive.
5. After adjustments for allocable taxes on income, compensation of employees rose more comparatively than did other shares. The great loser, after taxes, was the share going to corporate profits.
6. Labor's share of income has fared no more favorably in unionized industries than in nonunion. [*Editor's Note:* Dr. Kerr based his statement on research at the University of California's Institute of Industrial Relations in which analyses were made of income distributions for 1929 and for several postwar years. Dr. Kerr believes that two other economists who reached contrary conclusions may have been misled by their selection of a terminal year.]
7. Degree of unionization by metropolitan area is not significantly related to labor's share of manufacturing income in these same areas according to our own calculations.

The conclusion from this record is that trade unionism in the United States to date has had no important effect on labor's share of national income except as (1) it has encouraged an employee-oriented national economic policy with heavy emphasis on full employment (which has served to reduce the share of labor), (2) it has supported effective price control, (3) it has put wage pressure on employers temporarily unable to recapture profits (the special case of the reconversion period when output was limited and the "administered prices" for durable consumers' goods were rising comparatively slowly), and (4) it has furthered progressive income taxes. There is no evidence of any significant effect through normal collective bargaining.

The British history is different in detail but not in essentials. [It] suggests two modifications of the conclusions drawn from the American record. First, wage earners may gain at the expense of salaried workers. Second, full employment probably reduces the share of wages much less than the share of all employees, and unions are particularly concerned with the share of wages.

Can trade unionism affect distributive shares? Part of the answer is that, under certain conditions, it can. It can reduce labor's share through the furtherance of a policy of continuing full employment and perhaps also through the application of the "standard rate." It can raise labor's share, in particular, through standard collective bargaining when employers cannot quickly escape; or through support of the application of effective price controls; or, in terms of "kept" income, through the encouragement of progressive taxation and subventions.

The other part of the answer is that, while it can raise labor's share, it cannot raise it by very much. The power of trade unionism has been apparently "countervailing" and not "original." One can only speculate about what might have happened if this "countervailing" power had not developed. In Great Britain, on the other hand, through what might be viewed as "original" political power, a significant redistribution has taken place.

Now it might be concluded that all this union pursuit of the employer is much ado about very little; that unions are relatively powerless institutions in a market which responds to other, more persuasive forces. This may well be. However, this could not be known surely in advance and it is worth knowing. Workers could not be expected to accept the broad allocation of income between and among distributive shares without having their organizations explore the possibilities of major shifts.

To the extent that distributive shares are affected, this comes about only from a significant shift of decision-making power away from the employer to trade-union leaders and government representatives [and] requires that they enter a long way into the direction of economic processes at the plant or industry or national level. The avenues for escape by employers must be narrowed or closed, if labor's share is to rise at the expense of profits. Knowledge of this fact may, of course, serve to sharpen labor's drive to deepen its control, directly or indirectly, and management's desire to resist.

This brings us up against the problem of absolute shares. They may move in an opposite direction from relative shares. For example, in moving toward full employment, the absolute share of labor (whether in real or money terms) will rise with the expansion in the number of jobs, yet the relative share will fall.

It is the size of the absolute share which is the more important, even in the short run; and, so, the significance of what is happening to relative shares can be understood only by reference to the much greater significance of the trend in the magnitude of absolute shares.

---

30. THE ECONOMIC EFFECTS OF THE FRENCH MINIMUM WAGE LAW*

LEGISLATION which does not take full account of economic theory is often repealed by the law of supply and demand. The following article describes an attempt to alter real income distribution by legislation, and the consequences of that attempt.

RECENT French experience throws some light on the effects of a minimum wage law. The classical economic tenets lead us to suppose that a minimum wage fixed at a level higher than that of the lowest paid workers will cause unemployment. Optimists believe that a minimum wage law will offset the monopsonistic power of buyers of labor and that, in this or more mysterious ways, higher wages will come out of profits. The common view in France is that a rise in the minimum wage will provoke a proportional rise in prices and not in real wages. Causal connections cannot be found in statistics, but it is manifest that in France from 1950 to 1952 movements in the minimum wage and in prices have been closely related. The minimum wage was established, and its level subsequently raised, only in a period of vigorous economic expansion during which increases in military expenditures and in private investment would have caused increases in output, money supply, and prices even in the absence of an inflationary wage policy. Hence, conclusions cannot be drawn from this experience about the influence of a rise in the minimum wage under stable economic conditions.

In February 1950 wages in France were freed after eleven years of government control. At the same time, provision was made for a *salaire minimum national interprofessionel garanti* to protect the lowest paid workers from a socially unacceptable standard of living. On

* Harry C. Eastman, *The American Economic Review,* March, 1954, vol. XLIV, no. 3, pp. 369-376.

The author is a Lecturer in Political Economy at the University of Toronto.

August 23, 1950, the government set this minimum wage. On the assumption that an individual's real income is closely connected to the hourly wage he receives, the decree fixed a minimum hourly wage for each of the twelve geographical zones that had existed under the previous system of wage control. These ranged from 78 francs an hour in the Parisian zone to 64 francs an hour in the lowest wage zone, the maximum differential being 18 per cent, and applied alike to workers of both sexes and of all industries. Lower wages could be paid to young or handicapped workers.

In order to protect its real value, the minimum wage was increased on March 24, 1951, to 87 francs an hour in Paris and on September 8, 1951, to 100 francs. The latter increase not only maintained but also increased the real value of the minimum wage, at least temporarily, for it made allowance for an expected future rise in prices. In the middle of 1952, the minimum wage was tied to the cost of living index. Since that date the cost of living has not risen sufficiently to cause a rise in the minimum wage.[1]

Only a very rough estimate can be made of the number of workers whose wages had to be increased to conform to the minimum established in August 1950. On July 1, 1950, perhaps 30 per cent of the labor force received wages lower than the minima that were established in the several zones by the decree of August 23. The immediate application of these minima would have swollen the wage bill by approximately 1½ per cent. After July 1 prices began to rise, so that at the time of the application of the minimum wage the level of wages undoubtedly exceeded that of the earlier date. Nevertheless, the minimum wage affected directly the wages of the less skilled workers. This can be seen in the substantial contraction in occupational wage differentials between July 1 and October 1, 1950. In the Parisian zone the wage of a highly skilled worker was 68 per cent higher than that of a common laborer in July; it was only 59 per cent higher in October.

Women, whose wages are normally lower than men's, were even more affected by the minimum wage. In Paris on July 1, the only men who received wages of less than 78 francs were common laborers in a few industries, whereas amongst women the average wage of common laborers in all industries, of specialized laborers in most industries, and of semiskilled workers in a few industries was below this level. The differential between male and female wages narrowed when the minimum wage was set and each time it was raised.

The government followed a policy of reducing the differential between wages in Paris and in the provinces. In July 1950 the average

[1] This was written in September 1953.

wage of common laborers in the lowest zone was 24 per cent less than in the Parisian zone, whereas the minimum wage set in the lowest zone was only 18 per cent below that of Paris. Thus the minimum wage narrowed the differential between the wages of unskilled labor in Paris and in the provinces. Occupational wage differentials contracted more in the provinces than in Paris.

Immediately following the introduction of the minimum wage law the wages of skilled workers rose, though proportionately less than those of unskilled workers. The rise in the wages of skilled workers was stimulated by the general rise in prices and in industrial activity that began in the second half of 1950 after a year and a half of fairly stable production and prices. It was also provoked by the necessity of preventing the abolition of certain occupational wage differentials and the undue compression of others. That this mechanism must have operated is suggested by the narrowing of geographical wage differentials for skilled workers as well as for common laborers.

The legally enforced increase in all wages below the minimum did not give rise to unemployment. On the contrary, employment of all grades of labor continued to rise, but so did prices and wages. By January 1, 1951 the compression of geographical wage differentials was no longer evident amongst male workers and was rapidly disappearing amongst female workers. Occupational wage differentials, though not restored to the position of July 1950, were expanding. Inflation was obliterating the effects of the minimum wage.

The index of consumer prices in Paris rose by 12 per cent between August 1950, when the minimum wage was announced, and March 1951, when the minimum wage was raised by the same percentage. The number of wages below this new higher minimum was considerably smaller than the number that had been below the original minimum. This increase in the minimum wage had no noticeable effect on occupational wage differentials amongst female workers, and amongst male workers occupational differentials actually continued to increase. Nor did the increase in the minimum wage appear to affect geographical wage differentials.

On March 24, 1951 the differential between the minimum wage applicable in the lowest wage zones and in Paris was reduced to 15 per cent, and on June 13, 1951 a reduction of 25 per cent was made in the differentials of all zones as they had existed before March. The differential in average wages between the two lowest zones and Paris was noticeably reduced between January and July, for the wages of common labor were not above the minima in the lowest wage zones and the wages of skilled workers rose with those of the unskilled. The wages of female labor in the higher wage zones were also affected by the change in the minimum wage, but male wages in these zones were sufficiently above the minimum to be unaffected.

From March to September 1951 retail prices increased more slowly than at the beginning of the year, but by September the index of consumer prices in Paris had nevertheless risen by 7½ per cent. In the same month the minimum wage was raised by 15 per cent. The number of workers having wages lower than the new minimum at the time of its application was at least as great as in August 1950.

The trimestrial survey of wages revealed that between July 1 and October 1, 1951, the contraction in geographical wage differentials was as large as in 1950 at the time of the fixing of the first minimum wage. But occupational wage differentials amongst female workers remained stable and amongst male workers they actually expanded in the case of more than half the grades of labor in the five zones. The increase in the minimum wage was interpreted as the signal for a general wage increase. Employers applied to all their workers the same percentage increase in wages as they gave their unskilled laborers, but, quite naturally, they did not take into consideration the increase in the wages of unskilled workers in other zones. Since the minimum wage affected proportionately more workers in the lower than in the higher wage zones, it forced a larger ultimate increase in the former zones and a contraction of the geographical differential.

The wholesale price index for domestic products, which had declined since May 1951, rose from 130 in August to 148 in November 1951 (1949 = 100). By the end of 1951, prices had risen so rapidly that only in the two lowest zones were wages still affected by the minimum, and geographical wage differentials had returned to the position of July 1, 1951. The price level ceased to rise early in 1952 and remained roughly stable thereafter. Occupational and geographical wage differentials gradually widened toward the position in which they had been before the introduction of the minimum wage.

The minimum wage law does not appear to have affected the forces that distribute the national income between the several factors of production. Real income from wages rose following the introduction of the minimum wage, but this rise was a concomitant of a rise in the gross national product, in real terms, from 100 in 1949 to 102 in 1950, 109 in 1951, and 112 in 1952. The compensation of employees, including employers' contributions to social insurance as well as wages and salaries, remained a constant percentage of the gross national product.

In temporarily affecting the structure of wages and their real value, the minimum wage law intensified the upward movement of prices and money wages. A distinction must be made between the establishment of the minimum wage in August 1950 and the increases in the minimum wage in March and September 1951. In the first case, the wages of unskilled workers increased sharply, while prices and the wages of skilled workers took no such jump, but increased more gradually. In the others, all wages and prices sprang up together.

In the summer of 1950 industrial production was only beginning to rise after the outbreak of the Korean war. There was considerable unused capacity and little upward pressure on wages. The decree of August 1950 establishing the minimum wage stated that it was not to be a signal for a general wage increase, and Frenchmen did not expect such an increase. The wages of skilled workers increased steadily with the general inflation over the next few months until the contraction of occupational wage differentials, caused by the abrupt rise in the wages of unskilled workers, had in large part disappeared.

After the March 1951 increase in the minimum wage, occupational wage differentials did not contract, for all wages rose together. Nor did geographical wage differentials appear to change appreciably. The monthly wage statistics of the metal-working industry in Paris show an abrupt increase in the wages of both unskilled and skilled workers. The intention of the draftsmen of the law had been to guarantee workers a certain minimum real income, while leaving the general pattern of wages to be freely determined by collective bargaining. In practice, employers were reluctant to grant wage increases while the minimum wage was stable for fear of being obliged to give further increases should the minimum wage rise. Thus the minimum wage legislation became the primary determinant of the timing of wage increases.

In September 1951 when the minimum wage was increased by 15 per cent, wholesale prices and wages sprang up sharply. The difference between the effects of the minimum wage of August 1950 and of September 1951 was, in part, the result of changed economic conditions. The index of industrial production had increased steadily from 125 in September 1950 to 137 in September 1951 and it was to rise to 147 in November 1951 (1938 = 100). By September 1951 unemployment was at an unprecedently low level. A change in the minimum wage was now interpreted as a sign of official sponsorship of a general wage increase, and the wages of all workers were increased in approximately the same proportion as the minimum wage. The rise in wages affected all firms at the same time, thus facilitating the increase in prices each wished to make to cover increased costs. Buyers did not resist price increases, for recent experience had made them anticipate further price rises and they bought goods to safeguard the real value of their assets.

Thus, the minimum wage, fixed in terms of money, became in effect a *numéraire* placing a lower limit on other prices.

In sum, the minimum wage legislation in France did not influence the real wages of workers. Its principal effect was to worsen the economic position of groups with fixed incomes.

---

31. THE FUNCTION OF PROFITS *

THE TITLE to the article below might well be "The Function of Profitability under Capitalism, Socialism, and Communism." Professor Drucker makes a distinction between profitability and profits, and discusses profitability as a determinant of business policy and as the goal toward which enterprises are striving in any industrial society.

THE BIG industrial enterprise is the dominant or "socially constitutive" organ of everyday life in all industrial countries: the modern corporation in the U.S., the Public Board in Britain, the trust in Russia. Like any other institution, the enterprise must first serve its own survival; this means it must operate at a profit. But this law of its being must be consonant with the aims of the society in which it exists. Many Americans today, both in and out of the labor movement, believe that the aims of society and the corporation's focus on profit are somehow incompatible. This conflict provides the theme of much high-minded palaver: "production for use" versus "production for profit," "pecuniary versus social accounting," "private greed versus public interest," and the like.

I propose to show that the conflict is more literary than real. Profit discharges a function essential to the success if not the survival of any industrial society, and profitability must be the criterion of all responsible business decisions, whether the society is organized along free-enterprise, socialist, fascist, or communist lines. There are serious conflicts within any industrial system, but there is also an overriding harmony, which may be expressed thus:

1: The survival of the corporate enterprise depends on its economic performance; and
2: The overriding demand of society is for economic performance; and

* Peter F. Drucker, *Fortune,* March, 1949, pp. 110 ff. Reprinted by permission of Harper and Brothers, copyright assignee.

For a brief biographical sketch of the author, see Selection 4 on page 25.

3: The criteria of economic performance, both from society's standpoint and from the standpoint of the survival-seeking corporation, are *cost* and *increased productivity*. Both are measured and expressed by profitability.

THE DUTY OF ECONOMIC PERFORMANCE

It is fashionable nowadays to think of the modern corporation as a political rather than an economic institution. So it is; there is even some merit in the claim of ultraprogressive managements that their purpose in life it not to make profits, not even to make goods, but to make people happy. As Dean David of the Harvard Business School puts it, "Business leaders must assume the responsibility for increasing all the human satisfactions of the group with which they are associated." But they will fall the shorter of this aim the more they forget the purpose for which corporate enterprise developed. Its original purpose, and its first duty to society still, is economic performance.

In the discharge of this duty, its first objective must be to preserve intact the productive capacity of the resources entrusted to it. Never mind how it got these resources; consider them—as many managements today consider them—as a public trust. The resources consist of machinery, land, skills, know-how, men, money, and, not least, the productive unit into which these elements are joined. The preservation of these resources is the corporate enterprise's first obligation to itself and to society. If it fails in this, it not only weakens its own power to survive, but impoverishes the whole of society.

To keep its resources intact, the corporation must be able to cover costs out of current production. But "cost" and "current production" are misleading terms. The cost of doing business, for example, by no means covers the cost of staying in business. Industrial production focuses on the future; the loss it seeks to avoid is future loss, the costs to be met from current production are future costs; and one of these future costs is risk.

RICARDO'S IMAGE

If this sounds too simple, compare it with orthodox economic thinking, whether Marxist, liberal, or conservative. All these schools still bear the stamp of Ricardo, who gave orthodox economics its terms, tools, and mood. Ricardo was a London stockjobber, and he built his system in that image. No other vocation could have furnished so pure a model of "economic man in the market." The stockjobber works without employees and without organization. The time element does not enter into his activity. He turns over his entire capital immediately; for the first rule of the stockjobber's profession is to clear the books and liquidate all positions every day. Every morning, therefore, the stockjobber starts business anew, as it were from scratch. Every evening he liquidates his business completely. His is an almost timeless world—very much like the universe of the Newtonian physicists.

In this trading economy all costs are in the past. The surplus of current income over past costs is profit. It is measured by comparing the present income with the past outlay; it is a projection of the present on the past. Its explanation must, therefore, lie in the past. In this traditional system the role of "profit" is not so much a function of production as it is an individual motive.

The structure of a modern industrial economy is radically different from that of a trading economy. In the first place, the economic subject of an industrial economy is not an individual but an enterprise, which means an organization of a great many people and a heavy fixed investment of capital. Second, the economic activity of an industrial economy is not the "trade" taking place in the instant of exchange, but production over a very long period. Neither the organization (the human resources) nor the capital investment (the material resources) is accountably productive in the "here and now" of the present. It will take years before the organization or the investment begins to pay for itself.

This shift in economic facts is beginning to make itself felt in our economic theory. A sure sign is the revival of pre-Ricardian mercantilist ways of thinking with its implicit sanctification of the "going concern." The very idea of a war economy, with its emphasis on "flow" and "bottlenecks," as well as the whole theory of national-income analysis on which our financial and fiscal policies are increasingly based, suggest not Ricardo but the thinking of the eighteenth-century physiocrats whom Adam Smith and Ricardo were supposed to have killed forever. The resemblance between Quesnay's once celebrated *Tableau Economique* and a national-income table is much more than superficial. The mercantilists and the cameralists of the seventeenth century, whom Keynes and others have revived, thought in terms of economic institutions rather than in terms of the "isolated individual in the market." Their institution, however, was the state rather than the enterprise; and their mere revival cannot give us an adequate theory of industrial economics. Though a good deal of preparatory work has been done, the big job is still ahead.

So far we can state these propositions:

1. Where a trading economy focuses on the past, with difference between

past costs and current income a "profit," an industrial economy focuses on the future, with difference between current cost and current production a "premium" for the future costs of staying in business.

2. But the future is always unknown and unknowable, unpredictable and uncertain; hence these future costs are "risks."
3. Coverage of these "risks" of the future out of current production is a law of the industrial enterprise. It is its responsibility toward itself and also toward society. And this coverage can come only out of current production.

FOUR KINDS OF RISK

The future costs of staying in business can be divided into four major risks. They are: replacement, risk proper, uncertainty, and obsolescence. Replacement and obsolescence refer to the industrial process; they affect the organization's capacity to produce physically. Risk proper and uncertainty refer to the industrial product; they affect the organization's capacity to produce economically—that is, to produce something accepted by society as worth its price.

Of the four risks, only one—*replacement*—is calculable in advance. And the fluctuating value of money makes even this calculation inexact (which is why U.S. Steel and others have recently had to set up special inflation reserves). Replacement is also the only one of the four risks that is commonly accepted as a cost by our laws and mores. The tax collector allows it as depreciation, though he is vigilant against its imaginative use. The costs of replacing a good labor force, for example —and a good labor force is the most perishable of all assets—may go well beyond the standard pension plans approved as costs by the Treasury.

Like replacement, *obsolescence* is generally understood as a fact of industrial life and accountants rarely make advance provision for it. General Motors recently set up a special obsolescence reserve, but of the four kinds of risks obsolescence is probably the least calculable in advance. It means simply that the economic life and the physical life of equipment are not necessarily of the same duration. Virtually new equipment may become obsolete through a sudden advance in the art. During the depression millions of dollars worth of steel rolling equipment, although well protected against replacement, were made obsolete almost overnight by the development of the continuous-strip mill.

In contrast with replacement and obsolescence, risk proper and uncertainty (which relate to the product rather than the process) are not considered costs at all, but rather charges against "profit." Nevertheless they are part of the cost of staying in business.

Risk proper is the cost of management's inability to foresee the economic future of its product. In pre-industrial economies the proper risks were mostly physical ones. The husbandman ran the risk of an epidemic among his sheep, the farmer the risk of a hailstorm. What was produced, in other words, was practically always marketable; the only question was whether there would be anything to market. One of the greatest achievements of the mercantile age was the conversion of many of the physical risks into something that could be predicted and provided against. It is no exaggeration to say that without the eighteenth-century development of insurance, which subjected physical risks to the laws of probability, industrial society could never have been born.

RISK AND PLANNING

But in the place of physical risks, the industrial system is subject to genuine economic risks, risks of marketability of the product. Risk proper stems from unforeseeable shifts in demand. It may be a change in fashion or a change to a genuinely improved product. In any case this risk is inherent in any industrial system, not just a free-market economy. For example, that seemingly least competitive of services, the interurban streetcar, has in two decades been erased by the automobile from the face of the U.S.

The advocates of a planned economy claim that they can control this risk: i.e., if strawberries and cream are produced, people will eat them and like it. Under unusually favorable circumstances this may be true. Risk proper may be controlled in an industrial economy—whether planned or unplanned—when it operates under extreme scarcity conditions, when any product is eagerly bought at any price, as in Russia since 1917 or in the U.S. from 1945 to 1948. Risk proper may also be controlled in part as long as the planned economy is backward; for then it will confine itself to imitating by and large products and services successfully tried out elsewhere. But if ever a planned economy reaches the stage of technological leadership, it will have the same problem of risk proper in deciding what new products to make and what old ones to continue making. Shifts in demand stemming from fashion are even harder to control than those stemming from real improvement. When the Nazis tried to control the fashion market just before the war, the black market in non-standardized buttons upset all their calculations. As for the next risk—uncertainty—it becomes actually greater under planning, as we shall see.

Uncertainty is the time factor in risk proper. How long must the new product stay in the laboratory, or compete in jeopardy, before it establishes its marketability against the old? This is a new contingency hardly known to pre-industrial producers. The farmer always knew that if he did not have a corn crop by frost time, he would not have a corn crop at all. But an industrial producer, even if he has a sure-fire product, cannot say with certainty when it will be successful. Ever since the development of the polymerization process during World War I, it was clear that natural-rubber tires would someday have a synthetic substitute. The laboratory man-hours piled up, first in Europe and then in the U.S., and the product was good enough for war. But not until a year ago was nature actually improved upon. This was the result of concentrating on the special purposes for which the synthetic was wanted, and also of the adaptation of low-temperature processes used in oil refining. The date of this solution could not possibly have been predicted in advance. The "bugs" in any new process or product are by definition unforeseeable.

NO TELLING WHEN

The importance of this risk can be seen from the fact that modern research engineers estimate from five to twenty years for the successful development of a new product or process, from laboratory to sales. Indeed, in our larger industrial research laboratories, uncertainty is considered so basic that little attempt is made to focus research directly on the production of a marketable product. Companies like General Electric and the American Telephone Co., as well as the major chemical companies, have gone in for pure research and expect the marketable product to come out as a byproduct; and experience has proved the soundness of this policy of "serendipity." It is based on the realization that the time factor is so unpredictable and incalculable as to make it more profitable not to try to predict or calculate it at all.

"Uncertainty" usually occurs together with risk proper, and it is difficult in any concrete situation to separate the two. As a concept, however, "uncertainty" has to be kept separate. For one important characteristic of industrial production is that every single advance in productivity increases the "uncertainty" under which production operates.

Such are the four risks faced by each individual enterprise in its battle for survival in a modern industrial economy: replacement, obsolescence, risk proper, uncertainty. The enterprise must cover these risks out of current production as a duty to itself. But the *successful* enterprise also owes two additional duties to the industrial society of which it is a part. And these duties, though they are not so represented in the average balance sheet, are also necessary charges against current production.

THE DRY HOLES

First, the successful enterprise must carry a share of the losses that unsuccessful enterprises will sustain in the future. Just as a productive oil well must pay for the pipe and labor that went into a dry hole, so the surviving company must pay for the economic loss of its competitor's failure. In 1941, for example, about 40 per cent of all American corporate enterprises did not make a profit; they barely covered their replacement costs or lost money.

The dry hole, the competitive failure, are wastes that any individual enterprise may avoid but a society of enterprises cannot. They even perform a necessary function: that of keeping the economy's bowels open. They are nevertheless economic losses, and society must demand correlative gains from its successful enterprises over and above what the successful enterprise needs to provide for its own risks. If they are not provided for, the economy as a whole will shrink.

If all enterprises could be successful—that is, could cover their private risks successfully—there would of course be no need for this additional social premium. But even the Russian planned economy has not been able to make all its enterprises successful. On the contrary, the profit margins in Russian industry—three to five times as great as those of American industry—indicate that planning actually increases the amount of social risk these industries must cover. This is probably because uncertainty is a larger problem in a planned than in an unplanned economy. For the essence of planning is to accept unduly long odds in the bet on timing: the planner bets he will roll not one seven but an unbroken series of sevens. Everything comes to depend on the correct or lucky forecasting of when a new product or process will be successful. Many new developments must reach the stage of success at the same time, or the whole plan collapses.

Thus it is not by eliminating competition that the social waste of failure can be avoided. Competition is merely one rather efficient way by which the elements of risk in any changing industrial economy can be explored. These risk factors, not competition at such, cause the social losses of which the successful enterprise must bear a share.

THE SOCIAL BURDEN

Finally, the enterprise must bear—again out of its current production —a share of all those social services that do not pertain to the economic process: schools, churches, hospitals, armies and navies, foundations, zoos, the custodial overhead of the Grand Canyon, what not. It does not concern us here whether these social services are supplied by government or by the enterprise itself, or to what extent they contribute indirectly to productive capacity, or how much of them we can afford. However evaluated, they are a non-economic burden on production, and their cost must therefore come out of a surplus of current production over the enterprise's own replacement cost and risks.

To sum up, the current production of the enterprise must cover:

1: The current costs of doing business,
2: The future costs of staying in business, which are replacement, risk proper, uncertainty, and obsolescence,
3: A share of the future losses of unsuccessful enterprises, and
4: A share of society's non-economic burden.

Only if the enterprise can cover all these costs out of current production will it preserve its own and its society's resources intact. But if the economy is to expand and improve, still more is required.

CHANGE AND PRODUCTIVITY

All societies change; but changes in pre-industrial economies were mostly the result of outside forces. The dramatic changes of history—war, conquest, exploration—caused great dislocation in the use of existing resources. Thus the discovery of America, by shifting the centers of trade from the Mediterranean to the Atlantic, made England and the Netherlands wealthier at the expense of Venice, Genoa, and Augsburg. Dislocations of the same sort followed the Crusades, the great gold discoveries in California, Alaska, etc., the collectivization of Russian agriculture, the total conversion of the English economy after Dunkerque; men and resources were moved into new employment, for good or bad. When economic expansion resulted from these huge dislocations, it was usually an unintended byproduct. The change was physical or political in origin, and did not come out of the economic system itself.

Quite otherwise is the change to which the industrial economy is subject. Now change is self-generated, built in. We must always be either expanding or contracting; increasing our economic resources or using them up. Expansion therefore is the very purpose of the industrial economy, and its imperative need. Lest it contract, society demands of its tool, the industrial enterprise, that it increase its productivity. This is the second basic law of the enterprise: the *law of increasing productivity*.

EXPANSION OLD STYLE

Adam Smith, and even more so the classical economists who followed him, knew of only one way to increase economic production. That was the employment of existing resources for the activity they were best fitted for. How to bring about the most economical application of the existing resources was the great problem to which the whole classical tradition from Adam Smith to John Stuart Mill addressed itself. But the resources themselves were considered God-given and unchangeable. Only on this assumption of changelessness can the classical doctrines be understood, above all the free-trade doctrine and that of an automatic, self-adjusting gold standard.

Marx, unlike the classical economists, understood that expansion is not only desirable but necessary to the new industrial economy that was coming into being in his lifetime. But he saw only one possibility of expansion: expansion into new territory. Out of this grew the Marxist theory of "imperialism" as developed by Hobson and Lenin, according to which capitalism in order to expand must enslave. Out of it grew also Henry George's theory of new land as the source of all enrichment and Franz Oppenheimer's theory of conquest as the dynamic principle in history. But even Marx and the Marxists did not believe that expansion was possible for long; indeed they based their prediction of the inevitable collapse of capitalism on their conviction that expansion, while necessary to the capitalist system, was inherently impossible except at somebody's expense.

Fuller and better use of existing resources is still one of the major ways to greater wealth, as is the exploitation of virgin resources. But what is basically new about the industrial system is its power to expand at nobody's expense. The application of technology results in an actual transformation of old and fully utilized resources into bigger and more productive resources.

This expansion is called increased productivity. The way to increase productivity—the only way—is through an improvement in the art by which the same resources employed in the same activity are made capable of producing more. Hence the economy can produce more of the same goods, or it can, without any cut in existing production and without dislocation, shift resources to produce something new.

The industrial system has made this expansion a normal process. We have grown so familiar with it that we underestimate its miraculous nature. Among an infinity of examples, take rayon. The basic chemical processes of this industry were all in use by the middle twenties. Yet with no new chemistry of any significance the output per worker in the rayon industry has multiplied in the past twenty years through innumerable small, anonymous, on-the-site improvements, the total effect of which has been revolutionary. Moreover, any good production man undoubtedly could have predicted twenty years ago that something like this would happen, without being able to specify what the particular improvements were going to be.

ARE PROFITS RESPONSIBLE?

This habit of increased productivity is the chief characteristic of the industrial system. In traditional economic terms, how is it obtained? The traditional answer is, by the reinvesting of profits; and the many examples of this process cited before the Flanders Committee show how ingrained is this notion in practical corporate accounting. Yet in theory it is a misleading answer. An increase in productivity does not really come out of profits, which are payments to capital, for the increase does not require new capital at all. In fact it releases capital; its agent is not the capitalist but the innovator. (The marriage between the constitutionally timid capitalist and the innovator was very recent, and a shotgun marriage at that.) When capital is directly released by increased productivity in the form of repayment or bigger dividends, then profits are the vehicle by which this transfer is made. But if the released capital takes the form of higher wages or lower prices—which may well be the more normal case under competitive conditions—it does not even show up as a profit.

Yet clearly there is a continuing social profit from increased productivity. In this sense *profitability* is the better, more inclusive word. Profit, as understood by accountants, is a crude and inaccurate prototype of the gauge we need to measure profitability. Crude and inaccurate as it is, it is the only approximation that corporate management has.

PROFITS VS. PROFITABILITY

The meaning of profitability may be clarified if we compare it further with profits. The average corporate profit account both understates and overstates profitability; it is based on a false time sense; and there are aspects of productivity that are still beyond its reach.

Profits understate profitability because they fail to include such social dividends as higher wages, lower prices, and contributions to the social burden (the latter are symbolized rather than measured by taxes). Profits overstate profitability because they have to cover risks that are really future costs of staying in business. Except replacement, all these costs are made to appear as profit, which they are not.

Moreover, accounting on an annual or quarterly basis is but a picayune enlargement of the instant or day that was the time unit of Ricardo's trading economy. Industrial production neither begins nor ends with the production of a given unit. The farmer's natural unit is the cycle of four seasons. The cattleman's is the two or three year reproduction cycle of the herd. What is the natural time unit of industry: the depreciation period of the machine? Or the business cycle? Or even longer? Whatever it may be, the calendar year has long since ceased to make sense as the unit of industrial measurement.

Also the rate of productivity increase, and indeed the measures of risk, are realms of wild surmise to most corporate accountants. The art has not yet yielded the figures needed for determining the optimum rate of change; we have only hunches. Without wishing here to prejudge problems in the nature of capital formation, I will own to a hunch that none of the great industrial economies today operates on so high a rate of profit as Soviet Russia.

PROFITABILITY IS A FUNCTION

The search for the optimum rate of change will of course raise all manner of social and moral questions: how, and by whom, should future risks be covered? How, and to whom, should increased productivity be distributed? The questions of justice involved here, though real, would be much easier to solve if it were no longer necessary to justify or vindicate the enterprise's need for profitability. That should be accepted on functional grounds.

The function of profitability *has nothing to do with the profit motive*. Whether this motive still exists in our society, and what good it does if it does exist, are beside the point. If archangels ran our enterprises, profitability would be the first law of their actions. It is also the dominant consideration of the commissars who run Russia's industries. Profitability has nothing to do with any individual's motives. It is founded in the objective necessities and purposes of industrial production. Nor has profitability anything to do with the legal or poltical environs. It works the same way whether a labor government disapproves of profits or a capitalist government smiles on them. Changes in the legal or political system, however they may affect the individual's life or livelihood, will not affect the structure or behavior of the industrial enterprise.

Profitability is the whole rationale and purpose of the modern industrial enterprise. It includes the first law of the enterprise—the covering of all costs; and the second law—the law of increased productivity. Profitability is also what society demands, or what it should demand, of the enterprise; for the coverage of future costs and the release of capital for expansion through increased productivity are as important to society as they are to the enterprise.

When this concept is more widely understood, many of the most heated arguments over the role of profits in the U.S. economy will be found to be sterile, if not pointless. The only trouble with profits is that they measure profitability too crudely. Profitability is the lodestar of economic performance, by which the enterprise, in order to serve itself *and* society, must necessarily set its course.

---

32. CORPORATE MANAGEMENT AND ECONOMIC DEVELOPMENT*

THE GREAT size of many corporations requires that they be owned by thousands of stockholders, since no single person or small group is likely to have sufficient resources to establish a large enterprise. However only a few persons—the management—can control the operations of a corporation. The stockholders as such have no power other than to elect the managers and for many stockholders such a power is never, or can never be, exercised. This results in what has been called the separation of ownership from control. Some of the effects of such a separation are described in this selection.

WHAT EFFECT did the separation of ownership from control have on economic development? In theory, the division of managerial responsibility and the greater degree of specialization made business enterprise more rational and improved the efficiency of the business process. Experts made the decisions in each field of business enter-

* E. A. J. Johnson and Herman E. Krooss, *The Origins and Development of the American Economy*. Copyright, 1936, by the Macmillan Co. Copyright, 1947, 1953, by Prentice-Hall, Inc., New York, pp. 204-207. Reprinted by permission of the publisher.

E. A. J. Johnson (1900——) formerly taught at Harvard, George Washington, Cornell, and New York Universities and the University of California. Editor of the *Journal of Economic History,* 1940-43. Adviser to the United States government and to the government of Korea. Author of *An Economic History of Modern England; The Predecessors of Adam Smith* and other works in economic history. Herman Krooss (1912——) is Professor of Economics at the Graduate School of Business Administration, New York University. Formerly Educational Supervisor of the Penn Mutual Life Insurance Company. Co-author of *Financial History of the United States.* Author of *American Economic Development.*

prise. Research became more scientific and innovation more a matter of routine than of vision. But the new system also had great disadvantages so that the separation of ownership from control did not have a wholly beneficial effect on economic progress. It bred bureaucracy, for the splitting down of complicated decisions, the creation of staff and line organizations, and the departmentalization of management meant routine and systematized administration, which is the essence of bureaucracy. Although bureaucracy might be the most efficient system for handling day-to-day routine administration, it stultified initiative and made business management a dull routine rather than a stimulating adventure; it emphasized stability and security and deemphasized risk, thereby removing the effectiveness of the old business incentives. In many respects, the problems of managing big business were the same as the problems of managing big government. Many members of the business managerial group adopted the same psychology and the same working plan held by the typical civil service employee. The preservation of the job became the paramount goal. The ideal was to become an anonymous cog in an enormous machine. Initiative was repressed, because "going out on a limb" might imperil the security of the jobholder. Alfred P. Sloan, Jr., who was a large stockholder in General Motors in addition to being its president, recognized the nature of the problem when he said, "We seem to suffer from the inertia resulting from our great size." Admittedly, the stultifying effects of bureaucracy were most prominent in the lower echelons of management, but even among top executives there was a tendency to avoid risk and to seek stability. This was especially true in industries dominated by bankers.[1]

Most of the members of the new managerial class had relatively little share in the ownership of the businesses for which they made decisions. Consequently, profits, which had formerly offered by far the greatest business incentive, lost some of their effectiveness in stirring entrepreneurs to ever greater heights.[2] In like manner, financial considerations no longer served as well to discourage mistakes, because management, having little ownership in the business, did not have to pay for its mistakes with its own money. Substitute incentives, such as bonus plans, pensions, stock options, and management funds, were tried but proved to be imperfect solutions. In some companies, General Motors, for example, competition between management groups was en-

[1] In 1927 a General Motors director said, "Bankers regard research as most dangerous and a thing that makes banking hazardous, due to the rapid changes it brings about in industry."

[2] Sloan said in 1938, "Making money ceased to interest me years ago. It's the job that counts."

couraged and definite attempts were made to formulate ways of increasing the prestige of management. It was becoming clear that where ownership was lacking money rewards were not sufficient to call forth the most productive effort. The problem of spurring management to achieve the optimum economic development involved, to a greater extent than ever before, prestige, security, morale, and social recognition.

The separation of ownership from control tended to weaken the businessman's position in American society. He began to lose his traditional supremacy; society was no longer impressed by him but began to take him for granted. As the process became more routine, success in making business decisions seemed to be accomplished without a struggle. It appeared so easy that it came to be accepted as part of ordinary day-to-day existence. Professor Schumpeter recognized this as imperilling the whole structure of capitalist society when he wrote, "Success no longer carries that connotation of individual achievement which would raise not only the man but also his group into a durable position of social leadership. . . . Since capitalist enterprise, by its very achievements, tends to automatize progress, we conclude that it tends to make itself superfluous—to break to pieces under the pressure of its own success."

The separation of ownership and control also emphasized the divergent interests of the different players in the business game and served thereby to create antagonisms. Conflict among stockholders, financiers, laborers, and the different members of the managerial hierarchy became sharply defined. Financiers, attracted by profits from security sales or security speculation, often engaged in freebooting at the expense of the business itself. Thus, Drew, Gould, and Fisk milked their railroad empires in the latter part of the 19th century, and Insull, Krueger, and Hopson were guilty of financial practices which hurt business in the 1920's. Stockholders were interested in dividends and very often thought that managment wasted money on meaningless doodads or by rewarding itself over-generously. But management was more concerned with its own security and with the stability and continuity of the business enterprise than in paying large dividends. More and more, businesses retained earnings in order to enable management to stabilize dividends and to gain independence from financiers in raising capital for expansion. By 1950, corporations were financing about half their total investments from retained earnings and depreciation accruals. At the same time, they were retaining about 60 per cent of their earnings after taxes, paying only 40 per cent in cash dividends to stockholders.

Who then was the entrepreneur in the modern corporate business and what had happened to the doctrine that to the owner belongs the profits? Certainly the stockholder was no longer the entrepreneur, if he had ever been. Equally certain, the owners of business were no longer reaping the profits. New elements had been introducd into the economic system; much of the entrepreneurial function had been taken over by professional management, and, in the phrase of James Burnham, a "managerial revolution" had taken place. Here and there, boards of directors and finance-capitalists still retained some control over the larger goals, but management made the bulk of all business decisions. Since top management was primarily interested in stability and continuity, in striking a balance between the various groups—stockholders, consumers, labor, and the government—that had an interest in the business, this transformation of the entrepreneurial function added rigidities to the business system and made it less resilient and flexible.

Even the members of the managerial class itself had divergent interests which created hostility and open antagonism. Some were exclusively interested in production. Their goal was plant expansion, machinery replacement, advanced techniques, and cost reduction. They were the engineers, the technicians, the scientists, and the production bosses, with little or no concern for finance and no sympathy with the aims of the financial men. On the other hand, the financial managers—those who were interested in selling, distribution, public relations, and pure finance—were not much concerned with production, and often prevented the production men from accomplishing their goals of expansion. In the average corporation, the financial manager receives greater money rewards than the production man. But, more important, the financial manager's very existence is dependent upon the private enterprise, profit system, whereas the production men would have status in any society. Thus, the advertising man, the salesman, those whose function it is to stimulate demand, have the greatest stake in capitalism and are its stoutest defenders. Before the separation of ownership from control, every businessman had a stake in capitalism, for every businessman combined in himself an interest in both production and finance.

VII

Money, Banking, and Price Levels

33. A DIALOGUE ON MONEY *

MONEY has achieved such widespread acceptability in our modern world that few of us pause to consider the significance of the promises connected with it or the basis for its issue. Indeed, we might find ourselves in the same dilemma as the economist in this dialogue imagined by Professor Robertson if we were asked to explain the logic of our monetary system.

THE BRITISH monetary system, as it has emerged from the furnace of the last eight years, is on the face of it a somewhat eccentric contraption. Between some enquiring Socrates from another planet and an economist instructed to explain its nature some such dialogue as the following might well take place:—
SOCRATES: I see that your chief piece of money carries a legend affirming that it is a promise to pay the bearer the sum of one pound. What is this thing, a pound, of which payment is thus promised?
ECONOMIST: A pound is the British unit of account.
SOCRATES: So there is, I suppose, some concrete object which embodies more firmly that abstract unit of account than does this paper promise?
ECONOMIST: There is no such object, O Socrates.
SOCRATES: Indeed? Then what your Bank promises is to give me.

* Dennis H. Robertson, *Essays in Monetary Theory* (London, Staples Press Limited, 1939), pp. 158-59. Reprinted by permission of the author and the publisher.

The author (1890——) is Professor of Political Economy at Trinity College, Cambridge University. Author of many articles and books, particularly in the field of money and banking. Among his books are *Banking Policy and the Price Level* and *Essays in Monetary Theory*.

another promise stamped with a different number in case I should regard the number stamped on this promise as in some way ill-omened?

ECONOMIST: It would seem, indeed, to be promising something of that kind.

SOCRATES: So that in order to be in a position to fulfil its promises all the Bank has to do is to keep a store of such promises stamped with all sorts of different numbers?

ECONOMIST: By no means, Socrates—that would make its balance-sheet a subject for mockery, and in the eyes of our people there resides in a balance-sheet a certain awe and holiness. The Bank has to keep a store of Government securities and a store of gold.

SOCRATES: What are Government securities?

ECONOMIST: Promises by the Government to pay certain sums of money at certain dates.

SOCRATES: What are sums of money? Do you mean Bank of England notes?

ECONOMIST: I suppose I do.

SOCRATES: So these promises to pay promises are thought to be in some way solider and more sacred than the promises themselves?

ECONOMIST: They are so thought, as it appears.

SOCRATES: I see. Now tell me about the gold. It has to be of a certain weight, I suppose?

ECONOMIST: Not of a certain weight, but of a certain value in terms of the promises.

SOCRATES: So that the less each of its promises is worth, the more promises the Bank can lawfully make?

ECONOMIST: It seems, indeed, to amount to something of that kind.

SOCRATES: Do you find that your monetary system works well?

ECONOMIST: Pretty well, thank you, Socrates, on the whole.

SOCRATES: That would be, I suppose, not because of the rather strange rules of which you have told me, but because it is administered by men of ability and wisdom?

ECONOMIST: It would seem that that must be the reason, rather than the rules themselves, O Socrates.

34. THE ISLAND OF STONE MONEY *

THROUGHOUT history various objects have been used as money. In the following article Mr. Furness tells the story of the inhabitants of the Island of Yap, who successfully operated a monetary system based upon stones. Although the use of beads (wampum) by the American Indian is generally familiar, consideration of the advantages and disadvantages of such a seemingly preposterous money substance as stone will clarify one's thinking about the nature of money. The reader should ask himself how this stone standard differs from the gold standard and from the modified gold standard used in the United States today.

IN A land where food and drink and ready-made clothes grow on trees and may be had for the gathering, it is not easy to see how a man can run very deeply in debt for his living expenses,—for which, indeed, there need be no barter, and if no barter, there is no need for any medium of exchange. In fine, as far as mere existence is concerned in Yap, there is no use for money. But nature's ready-made clothes, though useful, are not ornamental, and the soul of man, especially of woman, from the Equator to the Poles, demands personal adornment. And like all adornments, polished shells, tortoise-shell, variegated beads, etc., demand labour in the making. Here then the simple-hearted natives of Yap, who never heard of Adam Smith nor of Ricardo, or even if they should hear of them would care no more for them than for an English song from the phonograph, have solved the ultimate problem of Political Economy, and found that labour is the true medium of exchange and the true standard of value. But this medium must be tangible and enduring, and as their island yields no metal, they have had recourse to stone; stone, on which labour in fetching and fashioning has been expended, and as truly a representation of labour as the mined and minted coins of civilization.

This medium of exchange they call *fei,* and it consists of large, solid, thick, stone wheels, ranging in diameter from a foot to twelve feet, having in the centre a hole varying in size with the diameter of the stone,

* William H. Furness III, *The Island of Stone Money* (J. B. Lippincott Company, 1910), pp. 92-100. Reprinted by permission of the Land Title Bank and Trust Company, Trustee for Lillian Landers MacLaughlin u/w William Henry Furness, dec'd.

The author (1866-1920) was a physician and anthropologist. One time secretary and Curator of the Free Museum of Science and Arts, University of Pennsylvania. Author of *The Home Life of Borneo Head Hunters, Its Festival and Folklore.*

wherein a pole may be inserted sufficiently large and strong to bear the weight and facilitate transportation. These stone "coins," if I may so call them, are not made on the Island of Yap, but were originally quarried and shaped in Babelthuap, one of The Pelao Islands, four hundred miles to the southward, and brought to Yap by some venturesome native navigators, in canoes and on rafts, over the ocean by no means as pacific as its name implies; and, with the stones safely landed, these navigators turned speculators, and, with arguments as persuasive as those of the most glib book-agent, induced their countrymen to believe that these "novelties" were the most desirable things to have about the house. Of course, the larger the stone the greater its worth, but it is not size alone that is prized; the limestone, of which the *fei* is composed, to be of the highest value, must be fine and white and of close grain. It is by no means any large stone, however skillfully fashioned, from The Pelaos that will be accepted as a *fei;* it is essential that a *fei* be made of this particular variety and quality of limestone.

After having been stored in houses, out of sun, wind and rain, the *fei* present a white, opaque appearance, somewhat like quartz, but not so translucent nor of so fine a grain; when by luck it happens that a man's wealth outgrows the capacity of his house, his money is then stored outside, and, thus, exposed to tropical weather, its colour changes to a dirty gray, somewhat like sandstone, and the surface becomes rough and covered with moss and lichen. As far as purchasing power goes, this does not, however, detract from its value; this "unearned increment" can be readily scraped off and the quality of the stone and its diameter, on which depends its value, be no whit diminished. I saw several æsthetic possessors of stone money polishing their wealth and cheerfully chipping away at their riches, thereby plainly evincing that they did not deem the acquisition of moss desirable for rolling stones.

Fei are cut as nearly circular as primitive resources permit, and through their centre a hole is cut whereof the diameter is, roughly speaking, about one sixth of the total diameter; this hole is, as I have said, for the insertion of a pole sufficiently strong to bear the weight of the wealth upon the shoulders of men when passed as currency. The smaller, more portable "coins," used for the purchase of fish from the *failu,* or of pigs from the wealthy chiefs, slope from the center in one or two step-like gradation; wherefore, if at the centre they are six or eight inches thick, they are but an inch and a half, or two inches thick at the periphery. Their diameter, and, therefore, their value, is measured in spans, which in Yap means the stretch of the index finger and thumb.

In front of a *failu* there are always many *fei,* which are thus displayed as evidence of the industry and wealth of the inmates; they are acquired by the hard work of members either on fishing expeditions or by their labour in building houses for the villagers.

Another noteworthy feature of this stone currency, which is also an equally noteworthy tribute to Yap honesty, is that it is not necessary for its owner to reduce it to possession. After concluding a bargain which involves the price of a *fei* too large to be conveniently moved, its new owner is quite content to accept the bare acknowledgement of ownership and without so much as a mark to indicate the exchange, the coin remains undisturbed on the former owner's premises.

My faithful old friend, Fatumak, assured me that there was in a village near-by a family whose wealth was unquestioned,—acknowledged by every one, and yet no one, not even the family itself, had ever laid eye or hand on this wealth; it consisted of an enormous *fei,* whereof the size is known only by tradition; for the past two or three generations it had been, and at that very time it was lying at the bottom of the sea! Many years ago an ancestor of this family, on an expedition after *fei,* secured this remarkably large and exceedingly valuable stone, which was placed on a raft to be towed homeward. A violent storm arose and the party, to save their lives, were obliged to cut the raft adrift, and the stone sank out of sight. When they reached home, they all testified that the *fei* was of magnificent proportions and of extraordinary quality, and that it was lost through no fault of the owner. Thereupon it was universally conceded in their simple faith that the mere accident of its loss overboard was too trifling to mention, and that a few hundred feet of water off shore ought not to affect its marketable value, since it was all chipped out in proper form. The purchasing power of that stone remains, therefore, as valid as if it were leaning visibly against the side of the owner's house, and represents wealth as potentially as the hoarded inactive gold of a miser of the middle ages, or as our silver dollars stacked in the Treasury at Washington, which we never see nor touch, but trade with on the strength of a printed certificate that they are there.

There is one undeniable advantage in this form of weighty wealth among people whose houses are as fragile as those in Yap:—when it takes four strong men to steal the price of a pig, burglary cannot but prove a somewhat disheartening occupation. As may be supposed, thefts of *fei* are almost unknown.

There are no wheeled vehicles in Yap and, consequently, no cart roads; but there have always been clearly defined paths communicating with the different settlements. When the German Government assumed the ownership of The Caroline Islands, after the purchase of them from Spain in 1898, many of these paths or highways were in bad condition, and the chiefs of the several districts were told that they must have them repaired and put in good order. The roughly dressed blocks of coral were, however, quite good enough for the bare feet of the natives; and many were the repetitions of the command, which still remained unheeded.

At last it was decided to impose a fine for disobedience on the chiefs of the districts. In what shape was the fine to be levied? It was of no avail to demand silver or gold from the chiefs,—they had none,—and to force them to pay in their own currency would have required, in the first place, half the population of the island to transport the fines; in the second place, their largest government building could not hold them; and finally, *fei,* six feet in diameter, not having been "made in Germany," were hardly available as a circulating medium in the Fatherland. At last, by a happy thought, the fine was exacted by sending a man to every *failu* and *pabai* throughout the disobedient districts, where he simply marked a certain number of the most valuable *fei* with a cross in black paint to show that the stones were claimed by the government. This instantly worked like a charm; the people, thus dolefully impoverished, turned to and repaired the highways to such good effect from one end of the island to the other, that they are now like park drives. Then the government dispatched its agents and erased the crosses. Presto! the fine was paid, the happy *failus* resumed possession of their capital stock, and rolled in wealth.

---

35. THE PAPER MONEY OF KUBLA KHAN *

"IN XANADU did Kubla Khan a stately pleasure dome decree. . . ." After reading the next article one may be tempted to add "And he created his own money to pay for it!" This may or may not be true, but, as Marco Polo relates, the "Great Khan" did issue fiat paper money. The reader is asked to compare this practice with a procedure sometimes followed by modern governments—the sale of bonds to commercial banks which create money to pay for them.

NOW THAT I have told you in detail of the splendour of this City of the Emperor's, I shall proceed to tell you of the Mint which he hath in the same city, in the which he hath his money coined and struck, as I shall

* *The Book of Ser Marco Polo,* translated by Col. Sir Henry Yule (3rd edition, Charles Scribner's Sons, 1926), pp. 423-26. Reprinted by permission of the publisher.

relate to you. And in doing so I shall make manifest to you how it is that the Great Lord may well be able to accomplish even much more than I have told you, or am going to tell you, in this Book. For, tell it how I might, you never would be satisfied that I was keeping within truth and reason!

The Emperor's Mint then is in this same City of Cambaluc, and the way it is wrought is such that you might say he hath the Secret of Alchemy in perfection, and you would be right! For he makes his money after this fashion.

He makes them take of the bark of a certain tree, in fact of the Mulberry Tree, the leaves of which are the food of the silkworms,—these trees being so numerous that whole districts are full of them. What they take is a certain fine white bast or skin which lies between the wood of the tree and thick outer bark, and this they make into something resembling sheets of paper, but black. When these sheets have been prepared they are cut up into pieces of different sizes. The smallest of these sizes is worth a half tornesel; the next, a little larger, one tornesel; one, a little larger still, is worth half a silver groat of Venice; another a whole groat; others yet two groats, five groats, and ten groats. There is also a kind worth one bezant of gold, and others of three bezants, and so up to ten. All these pieces of paper are issued with as much solemnity and authority as if they were of pure gold or silver; and on every piece a variety of officials, whose duty it is, have to write their names, and to put on their seals. And when all is prepared duly, the chief officer deputed by the Kaan smears the Seal entrusted to him with vermilion, and impresses it on the paper, so that the form of the Seal remains printed upon it in red; the Money is then authentic. Any one forging it would be punished with death. And the Kaan causes every year to be made such a vast quantity of this money, which costs him nothing, that it must equal in amount all the treasure in the world.

With these pieces of paper, made as I have described, he causes all payments on his own account to be made; and he makes them to pass current universally over all his kingdoms and provinces and territories, and whithersoever his power and sovereignty extends. And nobody, however important he may think himself, dares to refuse them on pain of death. And indeed everybody takes them readily, for wheresoever a person may go throughout the Great Kaan's dominions he shall find these pieces of paper current, and shall be able to transact all sales and purchases of goods by means of them just as well as if they were coins of pure gold. And all the while they are so light that ten bezants' worth does not weigh one golden bezant.

Furthermore all merchants arriving from India or other countries, and bringing with them gold or silver or gems and pearls, are prohibited from selling to any one but the Emperor. He has twelve experts chosen for this business, men of shrewdness and experience in such affairs; these appraise the articles, and the Emperor then pays a liberal price for them in those pieces of paper. The merchants accept his price readily, for in the first place they would not get so good an one from anybody else, and secondly they are paid without any delay. And with this paper-money they can buy what they like anywhere over the Empire, whilst it is also vastly lighter to carry about on their journeys. And it is a truth that the merchants will several times in the year bring wares to the amount of 400,000 bezants, and the Grand Sire pays for all in that paper. So he buys such a quantity of those precious things every year that his treasure is endless, whilst all the time the money he pays away costs him nothing at all. Moreover, several times in the year proclamation is made through the city that any one who may have gold or silver or gems or pearls, by taking them to the Mint shall get a handsome price for them. And the owners are glad to do this, because they would find no other purchaser give so large a price. Thus the quantity they bring in is marvellous, though those who do not choose to do so may let it alone. Still, in this way, nearly all the valuables in the country come into the Kaan's possession.

When any of those pieces of paper are spoilt—not that they are so very flimsy neither—the owner carries them to the Mint, and by paying three per cent on the value he gets new pieces in exchange. And if any Baron, or any one else soever, hath need of gold or silver or gems or pearls, in order to make plate, or girdles, or the like, he goes to the Mint and buys as much as he list, paying in this paper-money.[1]

[1] The issue of paper-money in China is at least as old as the beginning of the 9th century. In 1160 the system had gone to such excess that government paper equivalent in nominal value to 43,600,000 ounces of silver had been issued in six years, and there were local notes besides; so that the Empire was flooded with rapidly depreciating paper.

The *Kin* or "Golden" Dynasty of Northern Invaders who immediately preceeded the Mongols took to paper, in spite of their title, as kindly as the native sovereigns. Their notes had a course of seven years, after which new notes were issued to the holders, with a deduction of 15 per cent.

The Mongols commenced their issues of paper-money in 1236, long before they had transferred the seat of their government to China. Kublai made such an issue in the first year of his reign (1260), and continued to issue notes copiously till the end. In 1287 he put out a complete new currency, one note of which was to exchange against *five* of the previous series of equal nominal value! In both issues, the paper-money was, in official valuation, only equivalent to half its nominal value in silver; a circumstance not very easy to understand. The paper-money was called *Chao.*

Now you have heard the ways and means whereby the Great Kaan may have, and in fact *has,* more treasure than all the Kings in the World; and you know all about it and the reason why.

---

36. THE EDICT OF DIOCLETIAN *

A Study of Price Fixing in the Roman Empire

WE ARE inclined to think of price regulations as a modern device for economic control; however, the following study reveals that this is not the case. Professor Michell reviews the history of monetary inflation during the reign of the Roman Emperor, Diocletian, and tells of the price regulations that he instituted in the year 301 A.D. The record of the failure of these regulations to halt rising prices may give pause to those who think this device particularly appropriate to the solution of the inflationary problem in the United States.

IN 301 A.D. the Emperor Diocletian, with whom were associated his three co-rulers, promulgated an edict which fixed for the whole Roman Empire maximum prices for commodities, freight rates, and wages. According to the evidence available, and it is certain that the whole edict has not been recovered, price "ceilings" for over 900 commodities, 130 different grades of labour, and a considerable number of freight rates, were fixed and severe punishment promised to all "black market" operators who dared to buy or sell above the maximum. So elaborate a scheme of price control was not tried again until 1,600 years had passed. The reasons that led to this drastic interference in the economic life of the Empire and the success it attained, or rather did not attain, in regulating prices, provide a study for the historian which is well worth while.

THE CHAOS OF THE THIRD CENTURY

In order to understand the circumstances that led to the issuing of this edict, it is necessary to envisage the appalling state of affairs which marked the third century of the Christian era. Utter anarchy engulfed

* Humphrey Michell. Reprinted from *Canadian Journal of Economics and Political Science,* February, 1947, pp. 1-12, by permission of the author, the editors of the *Journal,* and the University of Toronto Press.

The author (1883——) is Professor Emeritus of Economics at Bishop's University.

the Roman world; emperors and pretenders to the imperial throne struggled for the great prizes of power. Armies marched and remarched over every province, plundering the wretched inhabitants. In 193 the Empire was put up for sale by auction by the Praetorians, the imperial guards, and bought by Didius Julianus. It is interesting to note that he enjoyed his bargain for exactly sixty-six days. Such cynical disregard for the glory of the imperial purple was too much even for those days and he was murdered. As each claimant reached the goal of his ambition, the first thing he had to do was to pay the soldiery that backed him. The imperial treasury was looted and empty, and the enormous sums necessary to satisfy the army could only be met by piling tax on tax, by confiscating the wealth of opponents and, worst of all, by debasing a currency that already was fast approaching the point when it was next to worthless. In 260, there came the last and most shocking degradation when the Emperor Valerian, who was trying to defend the eastern frontier, was captured by the Persians and held for six years in captivity until his death. The Empire was clearly breaking up in misery and confusion, bankruptcy and anarchy.

But the complete dissolution of the Empire was still postponed. The amazing thing was that it rallied and the barbarians were driven back. Italy and Gaul were saved and the Persians were repulsed in the east. By the time of Aurelian (270-5) the Empire was on the mend; his successor Probus (276-82) decisively beat off the last of the invaders, and Diocletian (284-305) reigned, with his three co-regents, over an Empire that was, in comparison with the anarchy of the last century, at peace. But it was the peace of exhaustion and, as Tenney Frank has remarked, it is doubtful if the Empire was worth saving under such conditions. Such was the almost incredible history of what was, probably, the most unhappy and intolerable century in which mankind has suffered for the ambitions of head-strong men.

DEBASEMENT OF THE CURRENCY

The story of anarchy in the Roman Empire is reflected by the evidence we have of bankruptcy of the imperial exchequer. If an emperor could not raise money by heavier taxation, or by confiscating the wealth of his rivals, the only way left to him was to debase the currency, in precisely the same way as modern governments increase the note issues of their central banks. Numismatic evidence gives us a very clear picture of the progressive decline of the purity of the silver *denarius,* the "penny" of the New Testament. The *denarius* of Augustus was, for all practical purposes, pure silver. Some alloy was necessary to harden it and preserve it against excessive loss by abrasion or clipping. Nero (54 A.D.)

struck a *denarius* of 94 per cent pure silver, and with unimportant variations this standard was maintained until the time of Hadrian (117), whose *denarius* was 87 per cent pure. There was obviously a certain amount of debasement; but it was not serious and the coins were accepted everywhere at their face value. With Antoninus Pius (138) really serious depreciation began, which ended in the complete degeneration of the currency, as Table 1 very clearly shows.

TABLE 1

Silver Content of Roman Coin of Denomination

Issuing Authority	*Per Cent Silver*
Nero 54 A.D.	94
Vitellius 68 A.D.	81
Domitian 81 A.D.	92
Trajan 98 A.D.	93
Hadrian 117 A.D.	87
Antoninus Pius 138 A.D.	75
Marcus Aurelius 161 A.D.	68
Septimius Severus 193 A.D.	50
Elagabalus 218 A.D.	43
Alexander Severus 222 A.D.	35
Gordian 238 A.D.	28
Philip 244 A.D.	0.5
Claudius Victorinus 268 A.D.	0.02

Gold coins *(aurei)* practically disappeared from circulation, and what did remain were so reduced by clipping that they passed only by weight. Down to the time of their complete demoralization, the debased silver coins had passed current, simply because they represented the only currency available. As these became more and more debased, they were issued with a silver or tin wash to make them look respectable. But so poor and thin was this coating that it soon wore off and the sham "silver" coins were revealed for what they really were. With the monetary system in complete confusion, trade, except on a barter basis, was seriously hampered. Enormous fortunes were made by farseeing and utterly unscrupulous speculators and the sight, so familiar to the world since then, of profiteers enjoying their gains amid ruin and bankruptcy was common, until these same speculators attracted too much attention and an emperor confiscated their fortunes. The middle class —the *bourgeoisie*—was almost obliterated and the proletariate was quickly sinking to the level of serfdom. Intellectually the world had fallen into an apathy from which nothing could rouse it. Men lost heart; they were afflicted with an overpowering boredom, a *taedium vitae,* in which nothing was worth while.

The reasons for this economic and spiritual collapse are not far to seek. Basically it can be summed up in a few words—the task of ruling the world had been too great for Rome. It was physically impossible to concentrate so much administrative power into one centre. During the time of the Republic, the Senate had tried to carry out this impossible task and failed. The Empire inaugurated by Augustus had been more successful; but the efficiency of the imperial administration, the upkeep of the armies, and the payments for the doles which supported the Roman proletariate had been paid for at a ruinous price in taxation. How often in the Bible do we hear of the exactions of the Roman tax-gatherers, the "publicans and sinners."

THE ERA OF DIOCLETIAN

To the Emperor Diocletian, fell the task of reconstruction, and he went about it with energy and wisdom. His "reforms," if we may call them that, may be summarized as follows: (1) To overcome the paralysis of administration through over-centralization, he divided the task of ruling into four, associating with himself three "associate emperors." (2) He reorganized the civil service, increasing its efficiency, but, unfortunately, also enhancing its cost. (3) Since the taxes could not accurately be measured in terms of money that was so violently depreciated as to be next to worthless, he instituted a system of payment of taxes in kind, *"annona"* as they were called. This system was a good one only in so far as it was the only possible one. But it led to the last degradation of the free peasantry; since obviously, if taxes were to be paid in natural products, such as wheat or other grains, their production must be guaranteed and agricultural workers must be on hand to till the soil. In other words, the peasantry must be bound to the soil *(ascripti glebae),* they became serfs, "villeins," and for them the transition to the feudal system was natural and inevitable. (4) He reformed the monetary system of the Empire. (5) He attempted to set maximum prices for commodities, freight rates, and services, as will be seen hereafter.

DIOCLETIAN'S REFORM OF THE CURRENCY

As is unavoidable in any study of monetary systems of the ancient world, some of the details of the new system introduced in 293-6 are by no means perfectly clear, and have given rise to considerable controversy among numismatists. It does seem certain, however, that Diocletian put the imperial mint to work turning out coins of gold, silver, and bronze, which, at least for the first two categories, were a return to the best standards of the early Empire. In gold, a coin called the *aureus* was issued at the rate of sixty to the pound weight of 12 ounces, and in silver an *argenteus* of which ninety-six went to the pound, a return to the silver *denarius* of Nero. So much is certain; it is over the bronze coins that the experts fall out. The best conclusion seems to be that Diocletian minted three bronze pieces of 150, 60, and 20 grains Troy weight respectively. Without going into the hopelessly involved and obscure problems connected with the issue of these coins, it may be said that Diocletian demonetized the coin known as the *valentinianus,* which was tariffed at 25,000 to the pound of gold, and substituted the *follis,* or what was officially called the "common penny" or *denarius communis,* at 50,000 to the gold pound. In other words, copper was revalued in terms of gold at one-half of its former entirely fictitious worth.

That we are on safe ground in this conclusion is found, amusingly enough, in a private letter from an official named Dionysius to an underling named Apion saying that he has "inside" information that the currency is about to be recast and that the *"nummus"* is to be reduced by half, i.e., tariffed at 50,000 instead of 25,000 to the gold pound. He bids Apion buy any commodity he can lay his hands on and at any price to hold for a rise. The letter ends with a warning to Apion not to give the writer away or try to do Dionysius out of his cut of the profits, a thoroughly characteristic communication from one rogue to another.

The whole episode of the monetary reform of Diocletian bristles with difficulties. Tenney Frank is surprised that he had enough silver at his command to coin the new *argentei,* and surmizes that he had brought a good deal in booty back from his campaigns on the eastern frontiers, the balance being made up by plundering temples of their sacred vessels, and private individuals of their plate. That is quite possible, although there is no evidence to substantiate it; but what is apparent is that there was not enough silver, and less gold, to support a price structure founded on the precious metals. The bronze coins, the *nummi* that Dionysius was talking about, were tariffed too high in relation to the new gold standard that the emperor sought to introduce. The pound weight of gold was fixed as being worth 50,000 bronze *denarii.* In the open market it was worth a good deal more, and no one was going to sell gold at the mint rate when a handsome profit could be made by dealing in the open or "black" market. The *denarius* was not worth what it was officially tariffed at in gold, and the whole structure of the newly reformed monetary system was in danger of breaking down in a confusion as bad as any that had gone before. Diocletian had done his best to give the Empire an honest currency in gold and silver, which would have been successful if the stock of precious metals at the disposal of the imperial mints had been sufficient to support it. But that was exactly what it was not, and we may be sure that "Gresham's Law" was hard at work. Bad money—the grossly inflated bronze *denarii*—was driving the good, the *aureus* and *argenteus,* out of circulation.

Diocletian and his co-regents were faced with a deadly dilemma, either to inflate or deflate and one was as disastrous as the other. It was true that the Empire had been saved from complete collapse; it was at least a going concern, albeit hardly and painfully. But to keep it going was a costly business. To maintain a disciplined army, without which the frontiers could not be held, was a never-ending drain upon the exchequer, for without regular and sufficient pay it would become mutinous and the old anarchy would break out again. An efficient civil service was almost as costly and we know that Diocletian had greatly increased the number of officials, which made for efficiency and also for greater expense. The administration of the Empire had been turned into a vast bureaucracy over which presided four imperial courts, maintained with oriental luxury and ostentation, which may have been highly impressive but cost enormously. To deflate was, therefore, impossible; to do so would bring down the whole elaborate fabric of civil and military government. To inflate would be equally disastrous in the long run. It was inflation that had brought the Empire to the verge of complete collapse. The reform of the currency had been aimed at checking the evil, and it was becoming painfully evident that it could not succeed in its task. There was only one chance to maintain economic equilibrium. It was a poor chance and not likely to succeed, but at least it was worth trying. That was to maintain a stationary price level, or as near stationary as could be hoped for, by decreeing maximum prices, wages, and freight rates, and enforcing the decree with the utmost rigour.

THE EDICT ON MAXIMUM PRICES

This remarkable document, promulgated in 301 A.D., fixed "ceilings" or maximum prices on most, if not all, commodities and freight rates, and maximum wages for all workers. Even in the incomplete form in which it is at present extant, its comprehensive nature is abundantly evident. In the various categories into which the document may be divided, price maxima are set for the commodities listed in Table 2. Although we may be certain that the list is incomplete in its present form, it is to be observed that the omissions here are even more remarkable than the number of commodities included. For instance, where are the metals, iron, copper, lead, tin, bronze? There are no prices for clay products. Gold and silver are included for a special purpose, as will be seen later. Some of the schedules of prices seem curiously over-elaborate. Vegetables, herbs, and meats are in great variety, while fish, which might reasonably be expected in even greater detail, have only five quotations, seafish first and second quality, fresh water ditto, and salted fish.

TABLE 2

Schedules of Prices and Wages Covered by Edict

Prices	
Foods	222
Hides and leather	87
Timber and wood products	94
Textiles and clothing	385
Wicker and grass products	32
Cosmetics, ointments, incense	53
Precious metals	17
Miscellaneous	31
Wages	
General, skilled, and unskilled	76
Silk workers and embroiderers	13
Wool weavers	6
Fullers	26

The schedules for wages are highly detailed, and worthy of more intensive analysis than can be given here. In general the standard wage for unskilled labour is 25 *denarii* per diem; for skilled 50, with maintenance, with considerably higher rates for the most skilled classes. For instance, a wall painter receives 75 *denarii* and a figure painter 150. Why a shipwright working on a sea-going vessel should receive 60, and one on a river-going ship only 50 is hard to say. The extremes in piece rates are sometimes extraordinary and amusing. Thus, for an advocate in opening a case the rate is 250 *denarii;* for pleading a case, 1,000, while a clothes-guard receives 2 *denarii* per bather. The rates for teachers are interesting. An elementary instructor may charge 50 *denarii* per pupil monthly; a teacher of arithmetic or shorthand 75; a teacher of Greek or Latin literature and geometry 200; and a teacher of rhetoric or public speaking 250. The most highly paid workers are those in the precious metals in which a craftsman in gold receives 5,000 per pound weight. This must refer to skilled smelters, refiners, and assayers, while gold cutters receive 3,000 *denarii* per pound. A gold spinner receives 2,500 per ounce and for unornamented gold work 2,000 plus per ounce.

The most important item in the whole edict is that which values a pound of gold at 50,000 *denarii*. This item is the key to the whole revaluation of the currency that had been brought into effect some five years earlier. The bronze unit of denomination, the so-called *valentinianus,* had been grossly overvalued at 25,000 to the pound of gold: the new coin, the *follis,* was tariffed at exactly double that amount. The "black market" price for gold must have been considerably more than 25,000 *valentiniani* per pound, and it is permissable to suppose that the new *follis* was put at the free market rate.

FREIGHT RATES

Fragments of this famous edict have been discovered in a good many places, the latest and a very important one in Italy, a discovery which disproves the idea previously held that the edict applied only to the eastern provinces. This provides a remarkable schedule of maximum freight rates for commodities in inter-Empire trade. Thus, from the port of Alexandria to Rome and nine other places a tariff of charges is laid down for grain per *castrensis modius.* For instance, it cost from Alexandria 16 *denarii* to ship one to Rome; 8 to Ephesus, and so on. There are fourteen rates to other points from "Oriens" and "Asia." The latter refers to the Roman province bordering on the Aegean. The term "Oriens" is puzzling and no certain explanation of it can be given. It will be noticed that the rate from "Asia" to Rome is 16 *denarii* per *castrensis modius;* from "Oriens" it is 18. From Africa, i.e. the Roman province bordering on the Mediterranean, there are thirteen rates varying from 18 *denarii* to Salona to 4 "to the Gauls." The schedules are obviously incomplete, many more rates from various ports must have been originally tabulated. It is also to be observed that "fiscal" rates are much lower than the ordinary commercial charges, which meant that goods carried on account of the imperial treasury *(fiscus)* were tariffed at prices which can hardly have paid the unfortunate shipowner who was forced to carry for the government. There is some indication that grain transported on government account went at half rates.

As denoting the importance of Nicomedia (the modern Ismid at the head of a gulf opening out of the Sea of Marmara south of Constantinople), which Diocletian had designated capital of the Roman province of Bithynia, some thirty freight rates are listed. Its commercial importance lay in the fact that it stood at the confluence of some of the busiest caravan routes from further Asia, and until Constantine made Byzantium the capital of the Eastern Empire, Nicomedia was one of the most important centres of trade. Unfortunately, this fragment of the edict is badly mutilated and only scattered quotations can be deciphered. For instance, the rate from Nicomedia to Rome was 18 *denarii* per *castrensis modius,* to Ephesus, 6, to "Phoenicia," 12. The whole schedule of freight rates, imperfect as it is, awaits careful analysis. It obviously casts considerable light upon the commerce of the later Roman Empire.

REASONS FOR THE EDICT

A careful study of the preamble to the edict will reveal two things. First, it was primarily an effort to fix a universal figure for the new *denarius* that had been introduced at the "reform" of the coinage. For that reason it was not an elaborate price list of all sorts of articles in daily use in terms of a well-established and universally accepted currency, but rather a tariff whereby the new unit of denomination was fixed in terms of goods. In short, the edict on prices cannot be understood unless it be closely related to the new coinage. The two enactments stand or fall together, a fact of which Diocletian and his advisers were very well aware. Was the new coin, the *follis,* really worth half of the old *antoninianius?* Was it tariffed too high or too low in terms of gold? Five years' experience had been enough to demonstrate that the chances of making money in arbitrage dealings were very numerous. The edict waxes indignant over the unconscionable gains made in this fashion. "For who is so insensitive and so devoid of human feeling that he cannot know, or rather has not perceived, that in the commerce carried on in the markets or involved in the daily life of cities, immoderate prices are so widespread that the uncurbed passion for gain is lessened neither by abundant supplies nor by fruitful years, so that without a doubt men who are busied in these affairs constantly plan actually to control the very winds and weather." This is a picturesque way of saying that trade had fallen very largely into the hands of profiteers who through combines and cartels, controlled the markets. Almost identical words had been used 700 years before in Athens, when the city had prosecuted the grain merchants and Lysias declaimed on the wickedness of those who sought to turn public misfortunes to their own gain. All through history, and today as never before, the profiteer has been hated, and when his depredations became too flagrant, prosecuted and punished. Those who fly in the face of nature and seek to control the weather itself so that even in times of abundance prices are kept up are the money changers who, by "rigging the market" and driving the exchanges up or down as is most advantageous to themselves, can make profits whether the harvests be rich or scanty. If arbitrage operations could be stopped, or at the very least considerably hampered, the new coinage and the latest tariffing of bronze in terms of gold could be allowed a chance to make itself decisively felt, and the wild inflation and monetary confusion of the past century be checked.

And secondly, an inspection of the items of the edict will reveal that a majority of the maximum prices ordered refer to articles that enter largely into military stores. Indeed, the words of the preamble make it very clear that it is directed against profiteers who sell to the army so that "sometimes in a single purchase a soldier is deprived of his bonus and salary and that the contribution of the whole world to support the armies falls to the abominable profit of thieves, so that our soldiers seem with their own hands to offer the hopes of their services and their completed labours to the profiteers." The edict is not primarily a price list for army victuallers nor a tariff for quartermaster's stores; but since the army was the single greatest buyer of commodities, if the prices at which these must be sold can be, if not fixed, at least in certain measure controlled, the effect upon the general price level would be highly salutary.

In confirmation of this view of the purpose of the edict, a passage in the *Chronographia* of Joannes Malalas is apposite. Speaking of Diocletian he says, "He also established warehouses for the storage of grain and provided everyone with measures both for grain and other forms of merchandise so that no retailer should be cheated by the soldiery." Joannes Malalas (491-578) was a sixth-century historian or compiler of chronologies in Constantinople and his authority is not beyond criticism. In this case there seems no reason to doubt his accuracy. If the army was to be protected against the profiteer, so must the people in general be protected against the army. It was entirely to the advantage of the four rulers of the Empire that the ruin of the countryside at the hand of an army be avoided. If "ceilings" were to be imposed on purchases for the army, the sellers must be protected against seizure and/or confiscation at impossibly low prices. It is true that no mention is made of minimum prices in the edict, but on the contrary much is made of the blessings of low prices, yet as the chronographer says, it must soon have been realized that "ceilings" demand "floors." The references to warehouses for the storage of grains and other commodities is interesting and important. We know that in Rome and other large cities government storehouses and granaries were maintained largely in order to control supplies for the "dole" to needy citizens. It is not impossible that we see here the inauguration of a system of supply depots for the army, of which we have no previous knowledge. The point, however, is incapable of exact proof.

FAILURE OF THE EDICT

As Tenney Frank very truly remarks, "The principle of a planned economy within a single unified state was in itself not necessarily wrong, for imperial trade in the Empire was practically all domestic, importing and exporting could be forbidden or confined to barter and payment could be made in a coinage that was regulated throughout the trading world. It had not to find its level through foreign exchange." This is broadly true, granting the most vigorous and relentless enforcement, as has been demonstrated during the Second World War.

Tenny Frank puts the failure down to the fact that the edict was too simple and too rigid, and that no differences were allowed wholesale and retail prices, and seasonal variations. This is also true, but it may be remarked that our information is very incomplete on these points. It might well be that within the price structure so set up a good deal of leeway was possible, and that administrative officers, using the edict as a term of reference, were empowered to administer it in fairly elastic fashion.

It is curious to realize that the only other extant reference to the edict comes from the writings of an early Christian father, Lactantius, who, in his book, *Concerning the Deaths of Persecutors,* dwells with considerable, and excusable, satisfaction on the unhappy end of the Roman emperors who persecuted the Christians. Among other things he says of Diocletian, whom he calls "the author of ill and deviser of misery": "When by various extortions he had made all things exceedingly dear, he attempted by an ordinance to limit their prices. Then much blood was shed for the veriest trifles: men were afraid to expose anything for sale and the scarcity became more excessive and grievous than ever until in the end the ordinance having proved disastrous to multitudes was from mere necessity annulled." The evidential value of so violently prejudiced an observer is naturally not high; but it is significant to realize that he does grasp that it was through the "reform" of the coinage five years previously that the alarming rise of prices had been caused. Lactantius is, of course, grossly exaggerating after the manner of all propagandists, but even though we heavily discount what he says, yet it is evident that a strenuous attempt at enforcement was made and that this failed.

Actually this is the only extant reference to the breakdown of the experiment in price regulation, but that it did fail we may be quite certain for other evidence is available which admits of little doubt on the subject. Diocletian had given to the Empire an honest gold and silver currency, an action which, so far as it went, was all to the good. But he had not provided it with an "honest" bronze currency; the same silvered coins were being struck and the so-called *denarius* or *follis* simply was not worth the rate at which the emperor sought to tariff it, namely 50,000 to the pound of gold. There is reason to suppose, although admittedly the evidence is not perfectly clear, that within two years of the issuing of the edict the impossibility of maintaining that rate had been recognized and the official rate raised to 60,000. That prices rose very rapidly thereafter can be safely inferred from the fact that after 305 the weight of the 20 *denarii* piece of silvered bronze begins steadily to diminish at the mint. In a word, the same disastrous process was at work again.

The emperors could, with perfect justice, point to the splendid gold and silver coins they issued, but there were not enough of them and the trade of the Empire was done on silver-washed bronze which was constantly deteriorating in value and driving out any gold or silver coins that did creep into circulation. Indeed there is evidence that the imperial mint gave up the hopeless job of striking silver altogether, for the instant they appeared they were swallowed up. All commentators are agreed that the purchasing power of the *denarius* constantly depreciated. Unfortunately, however, the widest divergence of opinion arises when the extent of this depreciation is considered. If we follow Mattingly the course is probably as follows. Within four years of the promulgation of the edict the price of gold had risen from 50,000 to 120,000 *denarii* per pound. Subsequently the advance in price, while not so violent was still steady, rising to 168,000 some time before 324. In that year Constantine seems to have been successful in stabilizing the price at 172,800, and this figure was probably accepted, more or less, throughout the west. It seems certain that this did not endure for long, and as the security of the Western Empire steadily deteriorated, so did the worth of the *denarius,* until it reached the fictitious figure of 473,000 late in the fourth century and in the middle of the fifth it stood at 504,000. These are impossible figures and simply mean that any attempt at preserving a market, let alone a mint ratio, between the bronze denarius and the pound of gold was lost. An even more interesting parallel might be drawn from the efforts of the Greek government to stabilize the drachma which had become valueless. In December, 1944, it issued new drachmas tariffed at a certain rate *vis-à-vis* the English gold pound, and sold gold sovereigns to the public at that rate. As in the case of Diocletian's attempt to stabilize the bronze *nummus* in terms of gold, the stock of gold sovereigns proved inadequate and the new drachma fell violently.

CONCLUSIONS

The whole episode of the attempt to impose "ceilings" upon commodity and wage levels through the edict of Diocletian is of great interest and deserves more attention from economic historians than it has received. The course of events that led up to it and its failure to achieve its object are quite clear. Diocletian and his advisers thought, or perhaps we had better say hoped, they had given to the world an "honest" currency of gold and silver coins. But the stock of precious metals was not sufficient to make the standard effective; the great mass of bronze in circulation was too overwhelming and what gold and silver currency there was passed out of circulation as soon as it came from the mint.

The mines of the precious metals known to the Romans had been exhausted and no more could be found. The Christian bishop of Carthage, the redoubtable Cyprian, writing about 250 A.D. says, "The diminished quantities of gold and silver suggest the early exhaustion of the metals, and the impoverished veins are straitened and decreased day by day." Strenuous efforts were made to increase production but in vain, neither persuasion nor threats could induce more to appear when the mines had been worked out. Davies, in his *Roman Mines in Europe,* which is a most careful compilation of all extant evidence, comes to the same conclusion as to the exhaustion of the supply of precious metals, and suggests that the Eastern Empire with its capital in Constantinople was able to survive the eclipse of the west because it was still able to produce at least enough gold and silver to keep its currency on a sound footing. This is perhaps a somewhat too extreme view to take and is open to several severe limitations. It might very plausibly be argued that the shrinkage in trade caused by the downfall of the Empire in the west made the stock of gold and silver in the east adequate to support the price level, or at least make the decline a slow and long drawn out affair. Probably Mr. Davies is right, coupled with this consideration.

The Western Roman Empire declined and fell because it was bankrupt. The task of ruling the world was too great and too expensive. The business of government, the upkeep of the armies, and the holding of the frontiers cost too much: there simply was not enough gold and silver in existence to pay for the crushingly expensive bureaucratic and military organization of the imperial government. But if there was too little gold and silver, there was too much copper, which, in ancient days, was the substitute for our modern paper currency. Copper coins could very easily be manufactured; numismatists testify that the coins of the fourth century often bear signs of hasty and careless minting; they were thrust out into circulation in many cases without having been properly trimmed or made tolerably respectable. This hasty manipulation of the mints was just as effective as our modern printing presses, with their flood of worthless, or nearly worthless, paper money.

The fantastic rise in prices that accompanied this inflation at last sank under its own weight; it toppled over and collapsed. It has often been said that the "dark ages" were dark because they were an era of low prices which prevented manufacture and commerce being carried on profitably. While this is not the whole explanation, it does at least point to one major factor in the eclipse of ancient civilization—the destruction of capital and the inability of medieval finance to provide a new supply. It was not until the coming of the treasures of Mexico and Peru to Europe in the sixteenth century that money in sufficient quantity was available and made possible the next great advance in the evolution of the capitalistic system.

---

37. 100% MONEY *

PROFESSOR FISHER maintained that a number of economic problems related to money and banking could be solved, in part at least, by requiring commercial banks to hold cash equal in amount to the total of their demand deposits. His proposal, familiarly referred to as the One Hundred Per Cent Reserve Plan, is summarized below.

SUMMARY IN ADVANCE

IN THE United States, as in a few other countries, most of our bills are paid by check—not by money passing from hand to hand.

* Irving Fisher, *100% Money* (3rd edition, New Haven, City Printing Company, 1945), pp. 3-20. Reprinted by permission of the executor of the author.

The author (1867-1947) was a mathematician and economist; Professor of Economics at Yale University. Began career as a mathematician. Wrote his doctoral thesis on the mathematics of the theory of value and prices, and became one of the foremost mathematical economists in the world. Particularly well known for his time-preference theory of the rate of interest, for his work with price indexes and the Quantity Theory of Money, and for his various plans for the stabilization of the economy. Author of *The Nature of Capital and Interest, Rate of Interest,* and *The Money Illusion.*

When a person draws a check, he draws it against what he calls "the money I have in the bank" as shown by his deposit balance on the stub of his check book. The sum of all such balances, on all such stubs in the whole country, i.e. all checking deposits, or what we ordinarily think of as the "money" lying on deposit in banks and *subject to check,* constitutes the chief circulating medium of the United States. This I propose to call "check-book money" as distinct from actual cash or "pocket-book money." Pocket-book money is the more basic of the two. It is visible and tangible; check-book money is not. Its claim to be money and to pass as if it were real money is derived from the belief that it "represents" real money and can be converted into real money on demand by "cashing" a check.

But the chief practical difference between check-book money and pocket-book money is that the latter is bearer money, good in anybody's hands, whereas check-book money requires the special permission of the payee in order to pass.

In 1926, a representative year before the great depression, the total check-book money of the people of the United States, according to one estimate, was 22 billion dollars, whereas, outside of the banks and the United States Treasury, the pocket-book money—that is, the actual physical bearer money in the people's pockets and in the tills of merchants—amounted, all told, to less than 4 billion dollars. Both together made the total circulating medium of the country, in the hands of the public, 26 billion dollars, 4 billions circulating by hand and 22 by check.

Many people imagine that check-book money is really money and really in the bank. Of course, this is far from true.

What, then, is this mysterious check-book money which we mistakenly call our "money in the bank"? It is simply the bank's *promise to furnish* money to its depositors when asked. Behind the 22 billions of checking deposits in 1926, the banks held only some 3 billions in actual money. The remaining 19 billions were assets other than money—assets such as the promissory notes of borrowers and assets such as Government bonds and corporation bonds.

In ordinary times, as for instance in 1926, the 3 billions of money were enough to enable the banks to furnish any depositor all the money or "cash" he asked for. But if *all* the depositors had demanded cash at one and the same time, the banks, though they could have gotten together a certain amount of cash by selling their other assets, could not have gotten enough; for there was not enough cash in the entire country to make up the 22 billions. And if all the depositors had demanded *gold* at the same time, there would not have been enough gold in the whole world.

Between 1926 and 1929, the total circulating medium increased slightly —from about 26 to about 27 billions, 23 billions being check-book money and 4 billions, pocket-book money.

On the other hand, between 1929 and 1933, check-book money shrank to 15 billions, which, with 5 billions of actual money in pockets and tills, made, in all, 20 billions of circulating medium, instead of 27, as in 1929. The increase from 26 to 27 billions was inflation; and the decrease from 27 to 20 billions was deflation.

The boom and depression since 1926 are largely epitomized by these three figures (in billions of dollars)—26, 27, 20—for the three years 1926, 1929, 1933.

These changes in the quantity of money were somewhat aggravated by like changes in velocity. In 1932 and 1933, for instance, not only was the circulating medium small, but its circulation was slow—even to the extent of widespread hoarding.

If we assume that the quantities of circulating medium for 1929 and 1933 were respectively 27 and 20 billions and that its turnover for those years was respectively 30 and 20, the total circulation would be, for 1929, 27 x 30 = over 800 billion dollars and, for 1933, 20 x 20 = 400 billion dollars.

The changes in quantity were chiefly in the deposits. The three figures for the check-book money were, as stated, 22, 23, 15; those for the pocket-book money were 4, 4, 5. An essential part of this depression has been the shrinkage from the 23 to the 15 billions in check-book money, that is, the wiping out of 8 billions of dollars of the nation's chief circulating medium which we all need as a common highway for business.

The shrinkage of 8 billions in the nation's check-book money reflects the increase of 1 billion (i.e. from 4 to 5) in pocket-book money. The public withdrew this billion of cash from the banks and the banks, to provide it, had to destroy the 8 billions of credit.

This loss, or destruction, of 8 billions of check-book money has been realized by few and seldom mentioned. There would have been big newspaper headlines if 8 thousand miles out of every 23 thousand miles of railway had been destroyed. Yet such a disaster would have been a small one compared with the destruction of 8 billions out of 23 billions of our main monetary highway. That destruction of 8 billion dollars of what the public counted on as their money was the chief sinister fact in the depression from which followed the two chief tragedies, unemployment and bankruptcies.

The public was forced to sacrifice 8 billion dollars of 23 billions of the main circulating medium which would not have been sacrificed had the 100% system been in use. And, in that case, there would have been no great depression.

This destruction of check-book money was not something natural and inevitable; it was due to a faulty system.

Under our present system, the banks create and destroy check-book money by granting, or calling, loans. When a bank grants me a $1,000 loan, and so adds $1,000 to my checking deposit, that $1,000 of "money I have in the bank" is new. It was freshly manufactured by the bank out of my loan and written by pen and ink on the stub of my check book and on the books of the bank.

As already noted, except for these pen and ink records, this "money" has no real physical existence. When later I repay the bank that $1,000, I take it out of my checking deposit, and that much circulating medium is destroyed on the stub of my check book and on the books of the bank. That is, it disappears altogether.

Thus our national circulating medium is now at the mercy of loan transactions of banks; and our thousands of checking banks are, in effect, so many irresponsible private mints.

What makes the trouble is the fact that the bank lends not money but merely a promise to furnish money on demand—money it does not possess. The banks can build upon their meager cash reserves an inverted pyramid of such "credits," that is, check-book money, the volume of which can be inflated and deflated.

It is obvious that such a top-heavy system is dangerous—dangerous to depositors, dangerous to the banks and above all dangerous to the millions of "innocent bystanders," the general public. In particular, when deflation results, the public is deprived of part of its essential circulating medium through which goods change hands.

There is little practical difference between permitting banks to issue these book credits which perform monetary service, and permitting them to issue paper currency as they did during the "wild cat bank note" period. It is essentially the same unsound practice.

Deposits are the modern equivalent of bank notes. But deposits may be created and destroyed invisibly, whereas bank notes have to be printed and cremated. If eight billion bank notes had been cremated between 1929 and 1933, the fact could scarcely have been overlooked.

As the system of checking accounts, or check-book money, based chiefly on loans, spreads from the few countries now using it to the whole world, all its dangers will grow greater. As a consequence, future booms and depressions threaten to be worse than those of the past, unless the system is changed.

The dangers and other defects of the present system will be discussed at length in later chapters. But only a few sentences are needed to outline the proposed remedy, which is this:

THE PROPOSAL

Let the Government, through an especially created "Currency Commission," *turn into cash* enough of the assets of every commercial bank to increase the cash reserve of each bank up to 100% of its checking deposits. In other words, let the Government, through the Currency Commission, issue this money, and, with it, buy some of the bonds, notes, or other assets of the banks or lend it to the banks on those assets as security.[1] Then all check-book money would have actual money—pocket-book money—behind it.

This new money (Commission Currency, or United States notes), would merely give an all-cash backing for the checking deposits and would, of itself, neither increase nor decrease the total circulating medium of the country. A bank which previously had $100,000,000 of deposits subject to check with only $10,000,000 of cash behind them (along with $90,000,000 in securities) would send these $90,000,000 of securities to the Currency Commission in return for $90,000,000 more cash, thus bringing its total cash reserve up to $100,000,000, or 100% of the deposits.

After this substitution of actual money for securities had been completed, the bank would be required to maintain *permanently* a cash reserve of 100% against its demand deposits. In other words, the demand deposits would literally be deposits, consisting of cash held in trust for the depositor.

Thus, the new money would, in effect, be *tied up* by the 100% reserve requirement.

The checking deposit department of the bank would become a mere storage warehouse for bearer money belonging to its depositors and would be given a separate corporate existence as a Check Bank. There would then be no practical distinction between the checking deposits and the reserve. The "money I have in the bank," as recorded on the stub of my check-book, would literally *be* money and literally be *in the bank* (or near at hand.) The bank's deposits could rise to $125,000,000 only if its cash also rose to $125,000,000, i.e., by depositors depositing $25,000,000 more cash, that is, taking that much out of their pockets or tills and putting it into the bank. And if deposits shrank it would

[1] In practice, this could be mostly "credit" on the books of the Commission, as very little tangible money would be called for—less even than at present, so long as the Currency Commission stood ready to supply it on request.

mean that depositors withdrew some of their stored-up money, that is, taking it out of the bank and putting it into their pockets or tills. In neither case would there be any change in the total.

So far as this change to the 100% system would deprive the bank of earning assets and require it to substitute an increased amount of non-earning cash, the bank would be reimbursed through a service charge made to its depositors—or otherwise.

ADVANTAGES

The resulting advantages to the public would include the following:

1. There would be practically no more runs on commercial banks—because 100% of the depositors' money would always be in the bank (or available) awaiting their orders. In practice, less money would be withdrawn than now; we all know of the frightened depositor who shouted to the bank teller, "If you haven't got my money, I want it; if you have, I don't."

2. There would be far fewer bank failures—because the important creditors of a commercial bank who would be most likely to make it fail are its depositors, and these depositors would be 100% provided for.

3. The interest-bearing Government debt would be substantially reduced—because a great part of the outstanding bonds of the Government would be taken over from the banks by the Currency Commission (representing the Government).

4. Our Monetary System would be simplified—because there would be no longer any essential difference between pocket-book money and check-book money. All of our circulating medium, one hundred per cent of it, would be actual money.

5. Banking would be simplified—at present, there is a confusion of ownership. When money is deposited in a checking account, the depositor still thinks of that money as his, though legally it is the bank's. The depositor owns no money in the bank; he is merely a creditor of the bank as a private corporation. Most of the "mystery" of banking would disappear as soon as a bank was no longer allowed to lend out money deposited by its customers, while, at the same time, these depositors were using that money as *their* money by drawing checks against it. "Mr. Dooley," the Will Rogers of his day, brought out the absurdity of this double use of money on demand deposit when he called a banker "a man who takes care of your money by lending it out to his friends."

In the future there would be a sharp distinction between *checking* deposits and *savings* deposits. Money put into a checking account would belong to the depositor, like any other *safety* deposit and would bear no interest. Money put into a savings account would have the same status as it has now. It would belong unequivocally to the bank. In exchange for this money the bank would give the right to repayment with interest, but *no checking privilege.* The savings depositor has simply bought *an investment* like an interest-bearing bond, and this investment would not require 100% cash behind it, any more than any other investment such as a bond or share of stock.

The reserve requirements for savings deposits need not necessarily be affected by the new system for checking deposits (although a strengthening of these requirements is desirable).

6. Great inflations and deflations would be eliminated—because banks would be deprived of their present power virtually to mint check-book money and to destroy it; that is, making loans would not inflate our circulating medium and calling loans would not deflate it. The volume of the checking deposits would not be affected any more than when any other sort of loans increased or decreased. These deposits would be part of the total actual money of the nation, and this total could not be affected by being lent from one person to another.

Even if depositors should withdraw all deposits at once, or should pay all their loans at once, or should default on all of them at once, the nation's volume of money would not be affected thereby. It would merely be redistributed. Its total would be controlled by its sole issuer —the Currency Commission (which could also be given power to deal with hoarding and velocity, if desired).

7. Booms and depressions would be greatly mitigated—because these are largely due to inflation and deflation.

8. Banker-management of industry would almost cease—because only in depressions can industries in general fall into the hands of bankers.

Of these eight advantages, the first two would apply chiefly to America, the land of bank runs and bank failures. The other six would apply to all countries having check-deposit banking. Advantages "6" and "7" are by far the most important, i.e. the cessation of inflation and deflation of our circulating medium and so the mitigation of booms and depressions in general and the elimination of *great* booms and depressions in particular.

OBJECTIONS

Naturally, a new idea, or one which seems new, like this of a 100% system of money and banking, must and should run the gauntlet of criticism.

The questions which seem most likely to be asked by those who will have doubts about the 100% system are:

1. Would not the transition to the 100% system—the buying up of the assets with new money—immediately increase the circulating medium of the country and increase it greatly?

Not by a single dollar. It would merely make check-book money and pocket-book money completely interconvertible; change existing circulating deposits of imaginary money into circulating deposits of real money.

After the transition (and after the prescribed degree of reflation had been reached), the Currency Commission could increase the quantity of money by buying bonds, and could decrease it by selling, being restricted in each case by the obligation to maintain the prescribed price level or value of the dollar with reasonable accuracy.

But it is worth noting that the maintenance of 100% reserve and the maintenance of a stable price level are distinct; either could, conceivably, exist without the other.

2. Would there be any valuable assets "behind" the new money?

The day after the adoption of the 100% system there would be behind the new money transferable by check the very same assets—mostly government bonds—which had been behind the check-book money the day before, although these bonds would now be in the possession of the Currency Commission.

The idea is traditional that all money and deposits must have a "backing" in securities to serve as a safeguard against reckless inflation. Under the present system (which, for contrast, we are to call the "10% system"), whenever the depositor fears that his deposit cannot be paid in actual pocket-book money, the bank can (theoretically) sell the securities for money and use the money to pay the panicky depositor. Very well; under the 100% system there would be precisely the same backing in securities and the same possibility of selling the securities; but *in addition* there would be the credit of the United States Government. Finally, there would be no panicky depositor, fearful lest he could not convert his deposits into cash.

3. Would not the gold standard be lost?

No more than it is lost already! And no less. The position of gold could be exactly what it is now, its price to be fixed by the Government and its use to be confined chiefly to settling international balances.

Furthermore, a return to the kind of gold standard we had prior to 1933 could, if desired, be just as easily accomplished under the 100% system as now; in fact, under the 100% system, there would be a much better chance that the old-style gold standard, if restored, would operate as it was intended.

4. How would the banks get any money to lend?

Just as they usually do now, namely: (1) from their own money (their capital); (2) from the money received from customers and put into savings accounts (not subject to check); and (3) from the money repaid on maturing loans.

In the long run, there would probably be much more money lent; for there would be more savings created and so available for lending. But such an expansion of loans—a normal expansion generated by savings—would not necessarily involve any increase of money in circulation.

The only new limitation on bank loans would be a wholesome one; namely, that no money could be lent unless there was money to lend; that is, the banks could no longer *over*lend by manufacturing money out of thin air so as to cause inflation and a boom.

Besides the above three sources of loan funds (bank capital, savings, and repayments), it would be possible for the Currency Commission to create new money and pass it on to the banks by buying more bonds. But this additional money would be limited by the fundamental requirement of preventing a rise of prices above the prescribed level, as measured by a suitable index number.

5. Would not the bankers be injured?

On the contrary, (a) they would share in the general benefits to the country resulting from a sounder monetary system and a returned prosperity; in particular they would receive larger savings deposits; (b) they would be reimbursed (by service charges or otherwise) for any loss of profits through tying up large reserves; (c) they would be almost entirely freed from risk of future bank runs and failures.

The bankers will not soon forget what they suffered from their mob race for liquidity in 1931-33—each for himself and the devil take the hindmost. Such a mob movement would be impossible under the 100% system; for a 100% liquidity would be assured at all times and for each bank separately and independently of other banks.

6. Would the plan be a nationalization of money and banking?

Of money, yes; of banking, no.

IN CONCLUSION

The 100% proposal is the opposite of radical. What it asks, in principle, is a return from the present extraordinary and ruinous system of lending the same money 8 or 10 times over, to the conservative safety-deposit system of the old goldsmiths, before they began lending out improperly what was entrusted to them for safekeeping. It was this abuse of trust which, after being accepted as standard practice, evolved into modern deposit banking. From the standpoint of public policy it is still an abuse, no longer an abuse of trust but an abuse of the loan and deposit functions.

England effected a reform and a partial return to the goldsmiths' system when, nearly a century ago, the Bank Act was passed, requiring a 100% reserve for all Bank of England notes issued beyond a certain minimum (as well as for the notes of all other note-issuing banks then existing).

Professor Frank D. Graham of Princeton, in a statement favoring the 100% money plan, says of President Adams that he "denounced the issuance of private bank notes as a fraud upon the public. He was supported in this view by all conservative opinion of his time."

Finally, why continue virtually to farm out to the banks for nothing a prerogative of Government? That prerogative is defined as follows in the Constitution of the United States (Article 1, Section 8): "The Congress shall have power . . . to coin money (and) regulate the value thereof." Virtually, if not literally, every checking bank coins money; and these banks, as a whole, regulate, control, or influence the value of all money.

Apologists for the present monetary system cannot justly claim that, under the mob rule of thousands of little private mints, the system has worked well. If it had worked well, we would not recently have lost 8 billions out of 23 billions of our check-book money.

If our bankers wish to retain the strictly banking function—loaning—which they can perform better than the Government, they should be ready to give back the strictly monetary function which they cannot perform as well as the government. If they will see this and, for once, say "yes" instead of "no" to what may seem to them a new proposal, there will probably be no other important opposition.

---

38. THE MONEY MARKET *

THE MONEY markets are markets in which money is exchanged for debt. Like other markets, they have a significant bearing on the al-

* Harold V. Roelse, *Money Market Essays* (Federal Reserve Bank of New York, 1952). Reprinted by permission of the author and the publisher.

The author (1894——) is Vice President of the Federal Reserve Bank of New York.

location of resources. Beyond this, they are intimately connected with the banking system and with forces that are crucial in the determination of the level of economic activity. As such, they serve as important avenues of Federal Reserve policy implementation. The student is well advised to be familiar with their operation.

THE FINANCIAL pages of the newspapers, economists' professional publications, and other periodicals make frequent reference to "the money market," but the term is rarely defined. Probably the reason is that the money market is, in fact, a rather nebulous affair, consisting of interrelationships and transactions among varying participants, rather than a definite group of individuals like the members of the New York Stock Exchange or the Chicago Board of Trade; it has no specific location, as does an organized security or commodity market; and its principal activities have changed gradually but markedly over the years. In earlier periods, references to the money market were frequently so narrowly limited as to mean chiefly the market in which security trading and speculation was financed—the market for "call" and "time" loans to security brokers and dealers, or "street loans" as they used to be called. At other times, the term has been used so broadly as to include long-term borrowing and lending operations in the form of security floatations.

For the purposes of this discussion, "the money market" may be defined as the central national market in New York City where temporary surplus funds of various types of organizations (including secondary reserves of the banks) go to find income-producing employment without sacrifice of liquidity, and where short-term needs for funds are satisfied, usually at interest rates that are advantageous to the borrower. It is a place where final adjustments between the supply of funds and the demand for funds are made for the country as a whole, after much regional clearing has been effected. In general, it is an impersonal market involving the usual lender-customer relationships only to a limited extent. The open-market borrower frequently has certain sources from which he expects to obtain part of the funds he needs fairly regularly, but he usually feels no obligation to go to any particular lender or group of lenders for his financing any longer than he considers that to be in his interest, and he gets his money from whatever source he can on the most favorable terms. Similarly, the lender in the money market ordinarily assumes no responsibility for financing the borrower any longer than suits his convenience.

SOURCES OF FUNDS

By far the most important source of money market funds, usually, is commercial banks. For many years considerable amounts of the secondary reserves (and even primary reserves) of the commercial banking system have tended to concentrate in New York City through the correspondent banking system, the amounts varying with the fluctuations in public demands for currency and credit and the flow of funds throughout the country. This condition was especially true before the establishment of the Federal Reserve System when the large New York City banks provided a kind of limited central banking system.

At that time, some of the funds of out-of-town banks were loaned or invested for them in "street loans," short-term business paper, or securities, but considerable amounts were simply deposited with the New York City banks and those banks employed them in the money market if suitable outlets were available. In addition to facilitating deposits and withdrawals of funds by correspondent banks, the New York City banks could to some extent (within the limits of their own reserve positions) increase the total volume of bank reserves by making loans to their correspondents. But their own reserve requirements were high and they seldom had very large amounts of excess reserves, so that their ability to supply additional funds to correspondent banks was rather narrowly limited. Consequently, when demands for funds from other parts of the country were heavy, they tended to cause stringencies in the New York money market, which occasionally reached the point of becoming money panics. It was this kind of situation that led to the creation of the Federal Reserve System.

It was expected that the establishment of the twelve regional Reserve Banks would end the concentration of bank reserve funds in New York and the dependence of the commercial banking system on the liquidity of the New York money market after a transitional period. To a considerable extent it did. But the practice of sending secondary reserves to New York (also primary reserves in the case of many nonmember banks) continued and still prevails on a large scale. And, of course, the New York City banks lend or invest in the money market not only the funds of their correspondents, but also considerable amounts of their own funds. Some of their most temporary lending is to other banks, in the form of sales of "Federal funds," which will be discussed later.

The second major source of supply of funds for the New York money market has been temporary surplus funds of business concerns. Many national corporations maintain accounts with the New York City banks in which they deposit funds for meeting interest and dividend payments, taxes, and other general expenses, and also such additional funds as are not needed at other points around the country for the conduct of their business. When these funds accumulate in amounts in excess of needs for current working balances, and appear likely to remain idle at least for some foreseeable period ahead, it has been the common practice of corporations to employ them in short-term loans or investments if suitable outlets are available and offer sufficient return to make it worth while. Furthermore, business concerns frequently invest the proceeds of long-term security issues temporarily, pending their use for capital expenditures.

A smaller source of money market funds is investing institutions, such as insurance companies. These institutions normally employ most of their funds in longer-term investments, but sometimes enter the money market for substantial amounts of short-term securities, pending disbursements on their investment commitments or the development of more attractive long-term investment opportunities.

Another, distinctly minor and quite irregular, source of funds is State and local governments and their subsidiary organizations, as well as some agencies of the National Government. For example, if a State government sells a bond issue for purposes which will involve disbursements over an extended period, such as a veterans' bonus or a construction program, or accumulates funds to pay off a bond issue, it may wish to invest some of the proceeds temporarily in the money market.

For many years, especially since the first World War, during the period in which New York City has gained in importance as an international financial center, it has been the custom of many foreign central banks to keep some of their reserves in New York in the form of earmarked gold or dollar assets of various kinds. To a considerable extent dollar assets are kept on deposit in the Reserve Banks, but frequently the foreign central banks like to obtain some income on dollar funds they do not need to draw upon immediately. The Federal Reserve Bank of New York began more than 25 years ago to buy bankers' acceptances for foreign central banks in the market, and added its guarantee of payment (for a fee), in behalf of all Federal Reserve Banks. But in recent years, the supply of bankers' acceptances has been insufficient to supply all such demands and several foreign central banks have requested the investment of some of their dollar funds in Treasury bills and other short-term Government securities.

New York agencies of foreign commercial banks also supply fairly sizable amounts of funds to the money market through loans to security dealers and short-term investments.

Finally, the Federal Reserve Banks serve as a residual source of supply of funds for the New York money market, but further discussion of that matter will be left until later.

SOURCES OF DEMAND FOR FUNDS

Reference was made previously to the predominance of brokers' loans ("street loans") as a source of demand for funds in the money market in earlier years. For many years security brokers and dealers have borrowed on either a demand or a time basis to finance their customers' trading on margin, and to carry their own holdings of securities, to the extent that their "portfolios" have been in excess of their capital funds. Usually the greater part of their borrowing has been on a "call loan" basis—that is, it has been repayable on demand in clearing house funds, so that the lender could get his money back on one day's notice. These "street loans" were for many years considered the safest and most liquid available use for temporary surplus funds of banks and others. The only disadvantage—and frequently it proved to be an advantage—was that the yield was unpredictable, depending upon the relationship between the total supply of funds and total demand for funds in the money market, and the consequent fluctuations in interest rates. The amount of such loans has fallen far below the volume of earlier years—to a range of about 200 to 800 million dollars since 1945, as compared with several billion dollars in the late '20's. In recent years borrowings on a demand basis by Government security dealers have been substantial (frequently 500 million to 1 billion dollars or more), but they have by no means taken the place of the "street loans" of earlier years.

At least until the '20's the next most important outlet for money market funds was open market commercial paper—that is, short-term notes of well-known business concerns with strong credit ratings (for example, some of the big milling companies and mail order houses), which are purchased by commercial paper dealers and resold by them, chiefly to banks. Such paper has long been attractive to banks all over the country (especially the "country" banks) as a means of employing their secondary reserves. This is still an active market, but not as important as in earlier years.

Another type of business paper which was developed in the United States after the Federal Reserve System was established, and with its encouragement and support, is bankers' acceptances or "bankers bills" (which were commonly referred to simply as "bills" until a new type of bill—the Treasury bill—was created about 20 years ago). These bankers' acceptances, which are used mainly in the financing of exports, imports, and storage of staple commodities, soon attained the rating of top-quality business paper, as in the form in which they are sold in the open market they represent two-name paper—that is, the bankers' acceptance is not only the obligation of the concern by which it is drawn, but it is also the unconditional obligation of the "accepting" bank. In some instances it may also carry the endorsement of the dealer by whom it is sold. Use of bankers' acceptances has diminished considerably in the past 20 years because of low rates on direct loans, but has shown some revival recently.

A minor and sporadic source of demand for money market funds is short-term borrowing by State and local governments. The commonest form is tax anticipation notes, which are frequently issued by local governments to provide them with funds, pending the receipt of large periodic tax payments. A considerable part of such borrowing is done in local communities, but a fair amount is done in the New York money market.

A far more important type of government borrowing in the money market developed from the adoption by the United States Treasury in 1929 of the practice of selling securities in the form of discount bills, generally maturing in 91 days, through competitive bidding.[1] This represented an adaptation of British practices to the financial system of the United States. These Treasury bills are, of course, offered throughout the country, but a large proportion has been absorbed in the New York money market, and most of the trading subsequent to issuance is done in the New York money market. Even earlier—as far back as the first World War—short-term Treasury obligations in the form of certificates of indebtedness had been a fairly important money market instrument. The certificates were sold at a fixed price, and for a number of years were commonly of one-year maturity, whereas the Treasury bill provided weekly issues and redemptions of securities with shorter maturities (most commonly three months), and at prices and yields to be fixed in the market. For several years, Treasury bills replaced certificates of indebtedness entirely, but the use of certificates was resumed during the second World War, and the volume of both types rose to unprecedented levels. Certificates were rapidly replaced by short-term Treasury notes during 1950, and disappeared entirely at the beginning of 1951, but their use was resumed after a few months.

In addition, obligations of Government-sponsored organizations, such as Federal Intermediate Credit Bank debentures, are minor sources of demand for funds in the money market.

A final source of demand for short-term funds in the money market is the banks themselves, chiefly the large city banks. The reference here is to interbank borrowings of immediately available reserve funds

[1] These Treasury bills carry no interest coupons but are sold at prices slightly below par, the difference between the purchase price and the par value at maturity providing the income, or yield, on the investment.

or "Federal funds." These dealings involve the transfer of reserve balances on the books of the Federal Reserve Bank, from the reserve account of the lending bank to the reserve account of the borrowing bank, generally through an exchange of checks, one drawn by the lending bank on the Federal Reserve Bank payable immediately, and the other by the borrowing bank on itself payable through the clearing house the next business day (i.e., "clearing house funds"). In other words, they represent day-to-day loans between banks. Most of the transactions are between New York City banks, although not infrequently large banks in other cities are also involved—probably more often as lenders than as borrowers—in which case borrowings and repayments of reserve funds are effected by telegraphic transfers.

ORGANIZATION OF THE MONEY MARKET

Several different types of organizations are involved in the mechanism of the money market:

1. The large New York City banks, sometimes referred to as the "money market banks" or the "Wall Street" banks (although most of them are not located on Wall Street);
2. Dealers in securities, especially Government security dealers;
3. Commercial paper dealers;
4. Bankers' acceptance or "bill" dealers;
5. Money brokers, whose function it is to know who in the money market is in need of quickly available funds, and who has money to lend (although much less is heard now of this function than in earlier times);
6. Federal Reserve Banks.

There is no clean-cut separation of functions among all these various types of organizations. For example, the dealer in bankers' acceptances is likely to be a dealer in Government securities, and at times may also serve as a money broker. The Government security dealer may be a dealer in other securities as well; he may act as a broker as well as a buyer and seller on his own account; he is almost always a borrower. The role of the commercial bank in the money market is predominantly that of a lender of funds, either on its own account or on behalf of its correspondent banks or other customers; but the commercial bank is also a buyer and seller of short-term Government securities and frequently of other types of open market paper; and, as was noted previously, the large city banks are often day-to-day borrowers of reserve funds. A few of the large New York City and Chicago banks serve as dealers in Government securities, in which case they are sometimes referred to as "dealer-banks."

While all the different organizations have important functions to perform in facilitating the smooth operation of the money market, easily the most important and essential (with the possible exception of the Federal Reserve Banks) are the New York City banks. Most money market transactions are cleared through their books, and all inflows or outflows of funds between New York City and other parts of the country (except for Federal Reserve or Treasury account) go through their reserve accounts on the books of the Federal Reserve Bank of New York.

The Federal Reserve Banks were referred to earlier as residual suppliers of funds to the money market. Federal Reserve credit may be considered a balancing factor in the market—supplying funds when they are needed and absorbing them when there is a surplus. There has never been any question but that the Reserve System should supply, through the money market or directly to the banks (at a price), whatever amount of funds is needed to enable member banks to maintain their reserves at the required levels. But the Reserve System has never willingly accepted the obligation to supply passively, at a fixed level of rates and at the option of the market, all the funds that might be in demand (except perhaps in periods of national emergency when major national objectives, such as the winning of a war, could not be permitted to be impeded by a lack of adequate financial support), since that would conflict with its responsibility for maintaining, as far as it is able, the monetary conditions necessary for economic stability.

FACTORS AFFECTING MONEY MARKET CONDITIONS AND OPEN MARKET INTEREST RATES

Conditions in the money market and changes in the levels of open market interest rates reflect, of course, the interaction of changes in the supply of and demand for funds. While the aggregate demands from Federal, State, and local governments and from business organizations in the open market fluctuate considerably over fairly long periods, the day-to-day and week-to-week changes in money market conditions are usually determined much more largely by changes in the supply of funds. As was mentioned earlier, the commercial banks are by far the most important single source of funds in the market, and that supply is determined chiefly by the banks' reserve position, especially that of the large New York City banks.

The reserve position of the commercial banking system as a whole reflects the various factors that are shown in the weekly statements published by the Board of Governors of the Federal Reserve System, such as gold inflows or outflows and changes in the deposits of foreign central banks in the Federal Reserve Banks, changes in public demands for currency, net receipts or disbursements by the Treasury reflected in changes in its balances with the Federal Reserve Banks, fluctuations in the volume of Federal Reserve "float," and changes in the reserve requirements of the banks. It is through the last named factor that business and public demands for credit in the form of direct borrowings from the banks have their indirect effect upon money market conditions. As bank loans expand or contract, the volume of deposit liabilities and the reserve requirements of the commercial banks change correspondingly. Changes in the banks' reserve requirements as a result of action taken by the Board of Governors of the Federal Reserve System to increase or decrease the percentages of reserves which member banks are required to maintain are, of course, also an occasional influence of some consequence upon the money market. Changes in Federal Reserve credit, which are also included in the weekly statement—especially Federal Reserve credit in the form of discounts and advances to member banks and holdings of United States Government securities—constitute the balancing factor, and the readiness and the rates at which such credit is supplied to the banking system are a major factor in determining money market conditions.

Not all the changes reflected in the weekly statement have an immediate impact upon the money market, but their influence usually is not long delayed. For example, a demand for currency in the Dallas Federal Reserve District may be met initially by drawing upon the excess reserves of banks in that area, but if it attains considerable volume it is likely to result in withdrawals of balances from city correspondents or sales of short-term Government securities in the New York money market. Similarly, an increased demand for credit in the San Francisco District, and a resulting rise in the reserve requirements of banks in that area, may be met for a while by drawing upon excess reserves or borrowing from the Federal Reserve Bank of San Francisco, but if continued it is likely sooner or later to have some reflection in the money market.

The most important immediate determinant of day-to-day money market conditions is the reserve position of the New York City banks, through which practically all transfers of funds in and out of the money market are made. The reserve position of the New York City banks is, of course, affected by the local impact of all the factors mentioned above which affect the reserve position of commercial banks generally, but in addition there are day-to-day movements of funds between New York City and other parts of the country which frequently amount to 100 million dollars or more. Consequently, even though banks in other areas may be experiencing an increase in their excess reserves, if the New York City banks are short of reserves, firm money market conditions are likely to prevail at least temporarily. Similarly, when New York City banks have substantial amounts of excess reserves, money market conditions are likely to be easy, and the most sensitive open market interest rates are likely to decline temporarily, even though banks in other areas may be losing reserve funds through Government tax collections, public demands for currency, or other factors. Through deposits or withdrawals of correspondent bank balances and business transfers of funds, however, such disparities between the reserve positions of the New York City banks and of banks in other areas are likely to be equalized quite rapidly. Thus by putting funds into the money market or taking funds out of the market, the Reserve System can exert an immediate influence on money market conditions and, fairly quickly, an influence on credit conditions, throughout the country, even though the initial effect is reflected only in the reserve position of the New York City banks.

The essence of effective regulation of credit and the money supply is to retain control over the amount and cost of reserve funds supplied to the commercial banks, and the manner in which they are supplied. Reserve funds can be made available to the banking system on the initiative of the Federal Reserve System through the purchase of Government securities in the market, or by forcing the banks to come to the Reserve Banks and borrow the reserve funds they require. Offerings of securities to the Reserve System can be greatly influenced by the willingness or unwillingness of the System to take the securities at current market prices, and the extent to which the banks are ready and willing to borrow can be influenced by the Reserve Bank discount rate. In general, it is the policy of the Reserve System to limit the availability of reserve funds to the banks in periods of inflation, and to make reserve funds easily available in periods of business recession and deflation.

CHANGES IN THE MONEY MARKET OVER THE YEARS

Aside from major changes in supply and demand conditions which have been reflected in broad movements in the general levels of interest rates, the money market has been subject to gradual but important changes in its functioning and principal activities over the years. The creation of the Federal Reserve System itself was probably the most important single development affecting the functioning of the money market. It lessened the dependence of the commercial banks of the country on the New York City banks (or, more broadly, on the New York money market) by providing twelve regional institutions to hold the reserves of banks that became members and to provide facilities for supplying banks in their respective areas with additional reserve funds and with currency to meet the demands of their customers. As was noted earlier, however, it did not break down correspondent bank relations, nor end the use by commercial banks of the facilities of the New York money market for employment of their surplus funds and secondary reserves.

Other major changes (some of which have been more gradual, so that their significance was not at first so readily recognized) include:

1. The great change in supply and demand relationships in the money market, which grew out of the depression of the '30's and the great inflow of gold that followed, and the resulting major lowering of the general levels of interest rates;

2. The virtual disappearance, as an important factor in the money market, of call loans to security brokers and dealers;

3. The shrinkage in business borrowing through the open market in the form of sales of commercial paper and bankers' acceptances, because of the diminished advantages of such forms of borrowing, compared with direct borrowing from the banks;

4. The great increase in the volume of short-term Government securities available for trading in the money markets;

5. The growth of the market for "Federal funds" (rates on which have now taken the place of the call loan rate as the most sensitive and the most widely fluctuating interest rate in the money market).

The extent of some of these changes may be illustrated by a few figures comparing the present volume of loans and short-term securities available for trading in the money market with the amounts available 25 years ago.

(Approximate amount in millions of dollars)

	1925	*1950*
Brokers loans*	2,400–3,500e	500– 800
Commercial paper	600– 800	250– 350
Bankers' acceptances	600– 800	200– 400
U. S. Treasury bills, certificates of indebtedness, and short-term notes†	2,500–3,000	42,000–46,000

* Borrowings in New York City by members of the New York Stock Exchange; 1925 figures estimated on basis of related data; 1950 figures represent borrowings on collateral other than Government securities.

† Certificates and notes only in 1925; Treasury bills initiated in 1929; notes maturing within two years are included in both 1925 and 1950.

e Estimated.

It is evident from these figures that the importance of business borrowing (including the securities business) as a source of demand for funds in the money market has greatly diminished, both absolutely and even more relatively. Short-term Government securities have become by far the most important type of money market instrument.

The present predominance of Government securities (and the growth in the public debt which it reflects) has important implications for the freedom of the money market, since it involves, of course, greatly increased interest and influence of the Government in money market conditions. One reflection of this influence is the very narrow range of fluctuation in most interest rates during recent years; day-to-day changes in rates now are usually not even in eighths of one per cent—on short-term Government securities they are in "basis points" or 1/100th of 1 per cent. (The one exception is the rate on "Federal funds" which has fluctuated between rates as low as 1/16 of one per cent and rates only slightly below the Federal Reserve discount rate.)

Nevertheless, the tremendous growth in public debt and the dominant position of Government securities in the over-all debt structure of the country and in the investments of its financial institutions have induced much greater sensitivity to small changes in interest rates, and especially to changes in the *direction* of rates. There is reason to believe, therefore, that the Federal Reserve System may in the foreseeable future be able to carry out its credit policies effectively within the limits of considerably narrower fluctuations in interest rates than was the case some years ago. In fact, it does not seem likely that, even if the System had a completely free hand to influence the money market as it deemed most appropriate, without having to consider the effect of its actions on the market for Government securities, this country will again in the near future witness anything like the rate fluctuations of earlier days, when the rate for call loans to security brokers fluctuated by 1 or 2 per cent (and sometimes much more) from day to day.

---

39. THE KEY TO EISENHOWER'S ECONOMICS—SOUND MONEY*

THE CONCEPT of "sound money" is no longer the exclusive property of those who champion the gold standard. Sound money is an objective of those who would pursue a dynamic monetary policy within

* Reprinted by special permission of *Business Week*—March 28, 1953 issue.

the framework of our managed monetary system. The article below explains the *modus operandi* of this system.

WHEN candidate Dwight D. Eisenhower stumped the country last fall, one of the first planks he nailed into his platform was "sound money."

In whistle stop talks, he used a bit of business with a piece of lumber to make his point—breaking off pre-sawed sections of it and throwing them away to illustrate the shrinking purchasing power of the dollar. In formal speeches, he hammered away at the same point, without the lumber but with all the statistics of a 10-year inflation to toss at his audience.

At first the reporters who rode the campaign train thought it was the usual election-year malarky. "The sound dollar," one of them remarked, "is all sound and no dollar."

But as the campaign went on, the sound dollar became more and more an Eisenhower trademark. By election day, the reporters—and apparently the voters—were convinced that he meant it.

Since the election, everything that Eisenhower has done suggests that he does mean it. His Cabinet and sub-Cabinet appointments, his State of the Union message to Congress, some of the first acts of his Administration, all point the same way.

Resonant Note

Now, it is true that no administration on record has ever in so many words endorsed anything but a sound dollar. The phrase has a nice ring to it, even when the dollar hasn't. But when Eisenhower talks about sound money, he has a fairly definite idea in mind. To him and to such men as George M. Humphrey, Secretary of the Treasury, and W. Randolph Burgess, Humphrey's special deputy, it implies at least two things:

1. A dollar that will purchase approximately the same amount of goods from one year to the next.
2. Use of the government's power to make credit hard to get as one of the main ways of keeping the purchasing power from changing.

Thus, for the first time in 20 years, the U.S. has an administration with no soft spot in its heart for easy money. In the long run, this may turn out to be one of the biggest and most important differences between the Eisenhower Administration and the Democratic regime that preceded it.

Managed Money

The sound dollar that Eisenhower is talking about isn't the sound dollar of McKinley. To the Republican stalwarts who turned out to whip William Jennings Bryan, sound money meant just one thing: money that was freely redeemable in gold. There's no question now of going back to a system that lets gold circulate freely. In the 50 years since Bryan's impassioned plea for free silver, both gold and silver have fallen out of favor as the base for a monetary system. The swings are too wide in a gold standard country, the expansions and contractions too erratic. Congress will go through the ritual of counting the gold in Fort Knox, but once it is finished it will lock up the vaults and keep them locked just as the Democrats did.

What Eisenhower means by a sound dollar is a dollar redeemable not in gold but in more or less the same quantity of goods whenever the holder decides to spend it. In other words, he is thinking of a managed system of money and credit. The main difference between him and the Democrats is that he intends to use all of the government's powers over money and credit to keep money management from becoming a one-way street to inflation.

LESSONS FROM HISTORY

This concentration on monetary control has set the economists to blowing the dust out of the old books, updating and revising a body of theory that has been on the shelf for the better part of 20 years.

The theory of monetary control is one of the neatest and intellectually most satisfying branches of economics. The practice over the past 100 years has been one disappointment after another. Again and again, something has happened to spoil the Swiss-watch precision that the theory says is possible.

Miscalculations

Take 1937, for instance, the one time when the Roosevelt Administration tried its hand at tightening up credit. Early in 1937, government economists started worrying about the way commodity prices were climbing. The federal budget had been running a deficit since 1931, and a lot of economists, appalled by the $20-billion increase in government debt, were predicting a howling inflation.

And so the Administration decided to put a damper on prices. The Federal Reserve Board tightened up on credit, and Roosevelt made a speech. What everybody forgot was that the federal budget in 1937 was starting to run a surplus rather than a deficit. And what everybody underestimated was the skittishness of business after seven years of depression. The Administration wanted to put the brakes on gently. It succeeded in demolishing the infant boom completely and starting the 1937 recession. There is room for argument as to whether or not the

Reserve Board was guilty of bad timing in its restrictive policy. But justly or unjustly, the board got much of the blame.

A lot of economists got burned in the 1937 fiasco. Many have been afraid of monetary controls ever since. Manipulation of money and credit, they concluded, is too heavy-handed and too uncertain. This line of thinking is one reason why the Truman Administration never warmed to the idea of using forceful monetary controls to check the postwar inflation.

Sadder But Wiser

But Eisenhower's experts are convinced that they have learned enough from the discouraging history of monetary controls to handle the ax without cutting their feet off. They are willing to bet their political shirts that they can use the money mechanism to stabilize the dollar—without starting a serious recession in the process.

To see just what they hope to do and why they think they can do it, you have to take a look at the U.S. money and credit system. To a large extent, the success or failure of the first Republican administration in 20 years is going to be determined by what goes on at the desks back of the paying and receiving windows of the country's banks.

MONETARY POLICY

Just a little less than 100 years ago, the governors of the Bank of England made a bad mistake in what a later generation has come to call public relations. Smarting under criticism of the policies they followed during the financial panic of 1857, they declared that fundamentally the Bank of England was no different from any other bank. Its policies, they argued, should be exactly the same policies that an ordinary banker would follow.

Walter Bagehot, the brilliant editor of the London Economist, took their argument and beat their brains out with it. In a series of articles, he demonstrated, once and for all, that a central bank is basically different from all ordinary banks. It sits at the end of a long lever that extends through the whole credit system. Its policies, with all the leverage of the system behind them, determine whether the man who comes into an ordinary bank for a loan gets a frosty look or a hearty handshake and one of the vice-president's cigars.

Since 1873, when Bagehot's articles were consolidated and polished up in his book, Lombard Street, it has been obvious that the central bank can control the credit policies of the ordinary banks. And so, to the extent that the availability of credit sets the level of prices, monetary control, through the central bank, has been indirect price control.

Policymakers

In the U.S., the function of the central bank is handled by the 12 Federal Reserve Banks and the seven-man Board of Governors that lays down general policy for them.

The ordinary businessman never goes inside a Federal Reserve Bank, unless he is invited for lunch and a guided tour—a public relations program that would have scandalized the stiff-necked governors who so offended Bagehot. Week in and week out, the businessman deals with an ordinary commercial bank—making deposits, writing checks, and, when he needs money, negotiating a loan.

The commercial banks, collectively, are the machine that generates most of the country's money supply. And much of the creation of money arises out of the relation between the businessman and his bank.

CREATING MONEY

This is the place where the argument starts in any discussion of banking. There are still a lot of bankers who will swear up and down that they never created a dime in their working lives. And they will drag out their books to prove that the amount of money they can loan is limited to what comes in at the receiving window in the form of deposits or repayment of old loans.

But the fact is that the commercial banks create money. And you can see the process of creation at work if you follow through a series of transactions with a bank.

To start with, take a look at the U.S. money supply and ask what it consists of.

Altogether, the money supply now adds up to about $145-billion. About $30-billion of it consists of currency—paper money issued by the federal government and coins stamped by the federal mints. The other $115-billion is in the form of demand deposits on the books of the country's commercial banks.

Familiar Faces

Fundamentally, there is not much difference between these two kinds of money. A $5-bill is a piece of paper a little less than 3 in. wide and a little over 6 in. long, with a picture of Abraham Lincoln in the middle and the signature of the Secretary of the Treasury in the lower right-hand corner. A $5-check drawn on a commercial bank is a piece of paper of approximately the same size, with a picture of the bank's whiskery founder in the middle and the signature of some depositor in the lower right-hand corner.

When you get right down to it, the only difference between the two is the fact that Abraham Lincoln and the Secretary of the Treasury are somewhat better known than the particular bank and depositor whose names are on the check. And that, when you get down to it, is the only difference between currency and deposit money. Currency is accepted somewhat more freely than checks simply because it involves less danger of fraud, but the only reason that anybody accepts either checks or currency is the fact that he expects other people to accept them.

Thus, if banks can create deposits, they can create money. So the next question is: How do the banks create deposits?

Chain of Reactions

To answer this one, ask yourself what happens when a bank gets a new deposit. The chances are that the depositor comes up to the receiving window and hands the teller a check drawn on another bank. Bank No. 1 credits the depositor's account with the amount of the check, say $1,000, and takes over the check drawn on Bank No. 2.

At this point, the Federal Reserve Bank comes into the picture. Bank No. 1 doesn't send the check directly to Bank No. 2. Instead, it turns the check over to the Federal Reserve Bank for its district. Both Bank No. 1 and Bank No. 2 have accounts with the Federal, and so to collect the check all the Federal has to do is transfer $1,000 from one account to the other. It then forwards the check to Bank No. 2, which charges it against the drawer's account, and the deal is complete. If the two banks are in different districts, two Federal Reserve Banks are involved, but the principle is the same.

So far, no new money has been created. But something has happened that is important to both banks. Bank No. 1 has gained $1,000 in deposits; Bank No. 2 has lost $1,000 in deposits. More than that, the account that Bank No. 1 has at the Federal is now $1,000 larger; the account of Bank No. 2 is $1,000 smaller.

Keystone

These accounts that the commercial banks keep with the Federal Reserve Banks are the keystone of the banking structure. For under the law they are the legal reserves of the banks.

The law specifies that each bank must hold reserves equal to a specified fraction of its deposits. (The percentages now are 24% for New York and Chicago banks; 20% for banks in other large cities; and 14% for "country" banks.) These reserves must be kept in the form of deposits with the Federal Reserve Banks. Currency doesn't count for this purpose. A bank could have a vault full of $100-bills and still be deficient in reserves if its account with the Federal was too low.

When the Federal Reserve Bank, in the course of collecting the check, transferred $1,000 from the account of Bank No. 2 to the account of Bank No. 1, it changed the reserve position of both banks.

Shifting Reserves

What that does to the money supply will depend on a lot of things, including the policies of the individual banks and the policies that the Federal Reserve Banks are following at the time.

Suppose the Federal Reserve is taking a neutral line—neither tightening nor loosening credit. Suppose Bank No. 1 is a hustling eager beaver trying to expand its business; and suppose Bank No. 2 is a stodgy outfit that hasn't been carrying all the deposits that the size of its reserve account would permit.

Bank No. 2 now has $1,000 less in reserves, but that doesn't particularly bother it, because it already had more reserves than the law required.

But Bank No. 1 now has $1,000 more in reserves, and it intends to make the most of that happy circumstance. It also has $1,000 more in deposits, but—assuming that it is subject to a 20% reserve requirement—that has increased required reserves by only $200. And so it has $800 excess reserves. That $800 will cover the legal reserve requirements on another $4,000 of deposits.

The next time a likely looking borrower comes in, Bank No. 1 will have the red carpet out for him. It has money to lend.

Two Schools

Now, this is where the dispute starts between the bankers and the economists. The president of Bank No. 1 will argue that he has only $800 to lend—because as soon as the borrower gets his loan he will draw out the $800, and Bank No. 1 will have no more excess reserves.

But the fact is that Bank No. 1 won't slap $800 in currency in the man's hand and encourage him to take it away. It will either give him a check drawn on itself or open an account for him and give him an $800 balance in it.

The borrower will then start checking against the account. The checks will go to the other banks, but if the banks are hustlers like Bank No. 1, they will start making loans against their expanded reserves. By the time the process is complete, the $800 in reserves will be backing a full $4,000 of new deposits.

A little work with a scratch-pad will show just how it happens.

On the first round, Bank. No. 1 got $1,000 in excess reserves from Bank No. 2, and increased its deposits $1,000; this rise in deposits was offset by a reduction of $1,000 in Bank No. 2's deposits.

On the second round, Bank No. 1 expanded its deposits by another $800 and when the borrower drew that out, the $800 of excess reserves went to Bank No. 3.

On the third round, Bank No. 3, with an $800 increase in deposits and a $160 increase in required reserves, found itself with $640 excess reserves. It expanded deposits by another $640; when the borrower drew that out, the $640 in excess reserves went to Bank No. 4.

And so on, until deposits have expanded to the point where there are no more excess reserves—or at least none held by banks with an aggressive lending policy.

Added Up . . .

This kind of scratch-pad computation shows how the commercial banks create money. It also shows the crucial role that the member accounts at the Federal Reserve Banks play in the whole monetary system. Anything that affects those accounts affects the money supply of the whole country.

In the case of Bank No. 1 and Bank No. 2, it was a shift of reserves —from a passive bank to an aggressive bank—that created new money. But ordinarily shifts in reserves are less important than variations in the total volume of the reserve accounts. Whenever these reserve accounts are increasing, the potential lending power of the banking system is expanding. When the reserve accounts are shrinking, the lending power of the member banks is shrinking.

CONTROLLING DEPOSITS

The enormous power that the Federal Reserve Banks have over the banking system comes primarily from the fact that there are several things that the Reserve Banks can do to increase or decrease the total volume of deposits that the members have with them. Thus, the Reserve Banks can deliberately open the way for an expansion of the money supply or force a contraction of it.

Suppose, for a moment, that the Reserve Banks decide that credit is getting too tight and that the reserve balances of the member banks should be fattened up so that the member banks can make more loans. There are two main ways in which the Federals can increase reserve deposits:

(1) By making loans to the member banks, accepting some of their assets (notes or other securities) as collateral. In banker's jargon, this is called "rediscounting."

(2) By going into the open market and buying securities, paying for

them by checks drawn on the Federal Reserve Banks. Theoretically, the Federals could buy any sort of securities in these open market operations. In practice, they stick almost entirely to government obligations of one sort or another.

Rediscounting

The immediate effect of either rediscounting or open market purchasing is to increase the total of member bank deposits with the Federals.

Say that the Federal Reserve Bank of San Francisco rediscounts a $1,000 note for the First National Bank of Drygulch. It takes over the note and gives the bank of Drygulch credit for an additional $1,000 in its reserve account. The Drygulch bank is subject to a 14% reserve requirement, so this extra $1,000 in reserves will support some $7,000 in additional deposits.

Or say that the Federal Reserve Bank of New York buys a $1,000 government bond in the open market. It gives the seller a check for $1,000 drawn on itself. The seller deposits this check in the First National Bank of Wall Street, which promptly presents it to the Federal. The Federal then adds $1,000 to the Bank of Wall Street's reserve account. The Wall Street bank is subject to a 24% reserve, and so the extra $1,000 in reserves will support something over $4,000 in new deposits (including, of course, the $1,000 in new deposits that were created when the seller of the bond deposited his check in the First National of Wall Street).

Open Market Purchase

So far as the arithmetic goes, there isn't much difference between rediscounting and open market purchasing, assuming that the same bank is involved in either case. But from the commercial banker's point of view, there is all the difference in the world.

An open market purchase by the Federal gives the member banks the additional reserves with no strings attached. Rediscounting forces the member banks to go into debt to the Federals to get the additional reserves. And bankers hate to be in hock to the Fed. For one thing, it costs them money, because the Federals charge interest—the rediscount rate—on the loans. More than that, bankers feel that it looks bad to be in debt for any length of time.

Consequently, bankers won't rediscount, except when they have to. They regard rediscounting as a device to get them over seasonal peaks in the demand for credit. They won't undertake a permanent expansion of their deposits (via new loans) if they have to rediscount to get the reserves. And when they do rediscount, they scratch frantically to get the money to pay off the loans from the Federal as fast as possible.

For Example

You can see how all this works if you take a look at a typical rediscounting operation—say the one between the First National Bank of Drygulch and the Federal Reserve Bank of San Francisco.

Last November, Joe Jones, proprietor of Jones Hardware Emporium, borrowed $1,000 from the Drygulch bank to help carry the inventory he had laid in for the Christmas season. He gave the bank a 90-day note, and the bank charged him 6% interest.

Two weeks later, Henry Pennyfeather, proprietor of Pennyfeather's Dry Goods & Draperies, came in to borrow $7,000, also with the Christmas season in mind. Consulting his books, the banker found that he was already loaned up. If he gave Pennyfeather a deposit of $7,000, the bank's reserve account would show a deficiency of nearly $1,000.

But Pennyfeather was a good customer, and he had a legitimate need for the money. And so the bank gave him a 60-day loan. Then—to get the necessary reserves—it took Jones' note for $1,000 to the Federal Reserve Bank and borrowed the $1,000, pledging the note as collateral. The Reserve Bank charged the Drygulch bank 1¾% of interest—the rediscount rate at the time.

This took care of things for the time being, but the fact that it was in hock to the Federal made the Drygulch bank uncomfortable. Toward the end of the year, when Pennyfeather came around to say it would be nice if that note could run another 30 days, the banker gave him a hard look and said no dice. Pennyfeather went back to his store and staged a special cut-price sale—a good example of the deflationary effect of tight money. He paid up on the nose; the bank promptly paid off its loan from the Federal; and the rediscount was wiped out in time for the bank to make up a year-end statement that gave no hint of the fact that two weeks before it had been borrowing from the Fed.

FRB'S DUAL CONTROL

It is the reluctance of the member banks to stay in debt that gives the Federal Reserve Banks their power to check a credit expansion—or even to force a credit contraction. The rediscounting procedure is there to take care of individual hardship cases and to ease temporary squeezes on credit, but the commercial banks won't use it to engineer a permanent expansion of their credit structure.

If they should ever try to, the Federals have ample power to stop them. For one thing, the Federals can raise the rediscount rate, thereby putting a heavier penalty on borrowing. And theoretically at least, they can refuse to lend to the members. Actually, the Reserve Banks feel that as the lender of last resort they can never give a member bank an outright turndown, but they can make the borrowing process tough enough to be discouraging if they think the member is taking advantage of them.

Active and Passive

In rediscounting, the initiative lies with the member banks. The rediscount policy that the Federals adopt makes itself felt only as the members find it necessary to borrow.

But in open market operations, the initiative lies with the Federals. This makes open market policy the most powerful single tool that the money managers have.

When the Federal Reserve System was first set up in 1914, each Reserve Bank did its own buying and selling in the open market. Often the purchases of one would be offset by the sales of another, and there was no real open market policy. In fact, in the early days the managers of the Reserve System realized only dimly that their open market buying and selling made a difference in the credit situation.

Under present law, open market operations are handled by a 12-man committee, consisting of the seven members of the Federal Reserve Board and the presidents of five of the Federal Reserve Banks. This committee buys and sells "for System account," that is, for all 12 Federal Reserve Banks collectively. And it is always acutely aware of just what each move that it makes is doing to credit in general.

When it buys securities, the Open Market Committee is increasing the reserve balances of the member banks (page 363), broadening the base of the country's money supply. When it sells securities, it is whittling away the member balances, putting a squeeze on money supply.

Example

Suppose, for instance, that the Open Market Committee sells a $1,000 government bond out of its portfolio. The buyer, whoever he may be, pays for it with a check drawn on his own bank. When this check is presented, the bank debits the buyer's account, and the Federal Reserve Bank debits the bank's account with it.

If the member bank is fully loaned up (that is, if it has no excess reserves), it now finds itself in an uncomfortable spot. It has lost $1,000 in reserves, and those reserves were backing up not just the $1,000 in deposits that the buyer has now drawn out but another $4,000 in other deposits as well (assuming a 20% reserve). In short, the bank now has $4,000 more deposits than its reserves permit.

What to Do

In a spot like this, a bank can do various things. For example, it may sell an asset of its own. This would buck the problem over to some other bank, but for the banking system as a whole it wouldn't solve the question of where the $800 in reserves to back that $4,000 of deposits is going to come from.

In the end, one of two things has to happen: (1) Some bank or group of banks has to cut deposits by $4,000, which means retiring loans; or (2) some bank or group of banks has to borrow $800 from the Federal through rediscounting, thereby bringing back into existence the $800 of reserves necessary to support the $4,000 in deposits.

The chances are that the banks will rediscount temporarily. But they will immediately start trying to get out of hock. That means they will tighten up on their lending policies; as old loans are repaid the banks will not try to replace them with new ones. As soon as possible, they will get deposits down by $4,000 and clean off the debt to the Federal.

Neat Theory

By using a combination of rediscount policy and open market policy, the money managers can tighten or relax credit to suit the business situation—at least, they can in theory.

Suppose business is booming and prices are getting out of hand. Then is the time to use a tight monetary policy to head off inflation. The first step is for the Reserve Banks to raise the rediscount rate and indicate to the member banks that they think credit expansion has gone far enough. If that doesn't work, the Open Market Committee can start selling securities. That will cut member bank reserves and force them to start rediscounting. Sooner or later, the pressure will get intense enough to make the member banks contract their loans and deposits. This contraction in the money supply will put a damper on prices and take some of the zip out of business generally.

Or suppose that business is slow and prices wobbly. Then credit should be relaxed so that businessmen will be encouraged to expand. In a situation like this, the Federals lower their rediscount rates and the Open Market Committee starts buying securities. The commercial banks find that they have excess reserves and are therefore ready to make loans freely. The new loans swell the money supply; business picks up; prices get firmer.

So the theory goes, anyhow. And it's a beautiful theory—logical enough to suit Aristotle himself. Neat, tidy, and clean-cut, as becomes a theory about a neat and tidy subject such as banking.

THE PATTERN DOESN'T FIT

The trouble is that things have never worked out according to the books.

Always, something has happened to ball up the smooth working that the theory says is possible. Some loophole has developed, or something unexpected has turned up. Take a quick look at the history of monetary policy in the past 25 years:

In 1928 and 1929, the Federal Reserve Board was worried about the amount of credit that was going into the stock market. It tightened up on credit as much as it thought it safely could. But there were problems. The farmers were in serious trouble and needed easy credit. England, then as now, was having trouble keeping the pound stable; high interest rates in this country would have started gold moving across the Atlantic and put the British in a hole.

And so the money managers never dared make credit so tight that the lure of Wall Street couldn't siphon any more of it off. The boom in the stock market, fed by credit, ran its course and collapsed, starting the Great Depression.

In 1932 and 1933, the Reserve Banks faced another kind of problem. Bank failures were rising, and depositors all over the country began to lose their heads. At first, they drew out their deposits, demanding currency to take home and hide in the mattress. Then, as the panic spread, they began to doubt the currency. They turned it in and demanded gold.

Impact on Banks

All this played hob with the banking system. An increase in the demand for currency has the same effect on bank reserves as an open market sale of securities by the Reserve Banks. In many respects, it is the same kind of transaction. The depositor draws out his account and demands cash; the bank gets the cash from the Federal Reserve Bank, which issues it (most hand-to-hand currency in this country consists of Federal Reserve notes). The Reserve Bank debits the member bank's account by the amount of the currency withdrawn.

Thus, the flight into currency was trouble enough for the banks. And the flight into gold was disaster.

Empty Cupboard

Under the law as it stood then, the Federal Reserve Banks had to keep a reserve of 40% in gold against all currency that they issued and a reserve of 35% in gold against all deposits that they held. And so, as the gold reserve ebbed away, the power of the Reserve Banks to help out the commercial banks ebbed with it.

When a money panic starts, it is like an explosion. It goes all the way. On Mar. 4, 1933, when Franklin D. Roosevelt was inaugurated, the banking system was paralyzed. Every bank in the country was closed.

No Solution

Under the New Deal, the banking system was overhauled; the gold standard was abandoned; the power of the Reserve Banks was greatly increased. Belatedly, the power of the stock market to outbid business for credit was checked by giving the Federal Reserve Board authority to prescribe margin requirements for loans on securities. By that time, of course, the stock market wasn't outbidding anybody.

But still things didn't work out according to the theory. In an effort to loosen up credit, the Reserve Banks embarked on a program of easy money. Excess reserves shot up, but the banks didn't take advantage of this opportunity to expand their loans and deposits. Nobody wanted to borrow—or at least nobody who looked like a good risk to the bankers.

Gradually, it became evident that in a real depression you can give the banks all the reserves you like and still the money supply won't expand. Disgustedly, the money managers concluded that trying to promote recovery through credit control was like "pushing on a piece of string."

Meanwhile, gold was flowing into the U. S. on practically every ship that docked in New York. The $35-an-oz. buying price that Roosevelt established after devaluation looked good to the rest of the world.

The gold had to be sold to the Treasury, and the selling process added to the already bloated excess reserves of the member banks. The Treasury took the gold and put it in the vault, giving the importer a check drawn on a Federal Reserve Bank, and giving the Federal Reserve Bank a gold certificate to keep in its vault. As soon as the importer deposited his check in a commercial bank, it became part of the banking system's reserve balance.

Drug on the Market

In 1937, when a few faint signs of inflation began to crop up, the

Federal Reserve Board got nervous about the $2.5-billion of excess reserves that the banks were sitting on. Theoretically, those reserves could have supported an expansion that would have almost doubled the money supply.

At that time, the Reserve Banks had only about $2.5-billion of government securities in their portfolios. To have sold the whole amount would have disrupted the market. And so the Reserve Board decided to try another trick. It got permission from Congress to increase reserve requirements and thereby blot up the excess reserves.

It looked like a good idea, but when the new requirements took effect the banks didn't respond as they were supposed to. Apparently they had become accustomed to working with a wide margin of excess reserves and had no intention of going back to the old system of rediscounting and lending to the limit. They hastily sold assets and tightened up on their own credit. Rightly or wrongly, the Reserve Board got a large part of the blame for starting the 1937 recession.

It was a considerably chastened group of money managers, therefore, who came up to the beginning of 1942, the first year of World War II and the start of a new period in monetary policy.

The experience of the past 10 years had left them deeply discouraged about their ability to promote a business recovery with monetary methods once a depression was started. And the 1937 crackup had shaken their faith in their ability to check an upward movement without bringing every thing down in a heap.

Both of these attitudes were to have an important influence on the policies that were adopted during the war and postwar inflation.

DEBT MANAGEMENT

The year 1942 marks a turning point in monetary policy, because ever since then the Federal Reserve Board has been forced to take a new factor into account in all its calculations: the government debt.

The U. S. has had a public debt ever since the days of Alexander Hamilton, who thought it was a good thing because it gave people a stake in the success of the new government. But never in history has the federal debt played so big a role in the economic life of the country as it does today.

At the end of 1941, the federal debt stood at $64.3-billion—and that looked like a staggering figure in those days. At the end of 1945, it was up to $278-billion. In succeeding years, the Treasury managed to get it down to $252-billion, but Korea started it up again. At the end of 1952, it was back to $267-billion.

A debt of that size is something that money managers have never been forced to deal with before. It presents them with an endless series of problems and complications.

Snags

Government securities are not money, but they are something very like money—especially if they are short-term obligations. A 91-day Treasury bill with a face value of $1,000 has many of the qualities of a $1,000 Federal Reserve note. The man, or the bank, who owns the Treasury bill is apt to act very much as though he had $1,000 in cash.

The problem is complicated by two policies that the Treasury followed in its wartime financing:

1. It took the easy course of selling a very large part of the new debt to the commercial banks instead of doing everything it could to get individuals and nonbanking investors to buy.
2. It kept a large part of the new debt it short-term issues—which for many years have carried a low rate of interest in comparison with long-term bonds, but which have to be refunded again and again.

The two policies were closely related. Both were byproducts of the Treasury's determination to do its wartime borrowing at the lowest possible rates. These low rates meant that the Treasury had to lean heavily on the commercial banks—who were willing lenders because as long as they had the reserves they could pay for the securities simply by expanding their deposits.

Deposit Inflation

At the end of 1941, the commercial banks held $22-billion of U. S. securities. At the end of 1945, they were sitting on the tremendous total of $91-billion.

This expansion of about $70-billion in their holdings of governments just about matched the expansion of their demand deposits—from $44-billion in 1941 to $106-billion in 1945. And the correspondence is no accident. The banks paid for the securities by drawing checks on themselves, that is, by creating deposits.

Obviously, these new deposits had to have reserves behind them. To create these reserves, the Federal Reserve Banks bought a total of $22-billion in government securities. This gave the banks elbow room to take all the securities the Treasury would sell them and to expand credit in other directions, too.

But the Fed's program of open market purchasing did more than just provide the banks with reserves. It kept the price of governments from wobbling under the impact of the enormous new issues the Treasury was putting out.

In World War I, the government had to pay a higher interest rate on each successive issue of Liberty Bonds. In World War II, there was none of that nonsense. In 1942, the Treasury set up the "pattern" of interest rates it proposed to pay on its wartime financing. From a banking standpoint, it was a starvation-low pattern—ranging from ⅜% on 91-day bills to 2½% on the longest marketable bonds. (E-bonds, sold to individuals and redeemable on demand, paid 2.9%, but were not marketable.)

The Federal Reserve Banks passed the word through the money market that they would take any securities that couldn't find buyers at par. That put an absolute floor under the market. Throughout the war, the Treasury never paid more than its pattern.

Spur to Inflation

During the war period, this policy of pegging the price of government securities made a lot of sense. After 1946 it was a dangerous mistake. It forced the Federal Reserve System to collaborate in the postwar inflation instead of using its power to check the upward rush of prices.

The end of the war and the start of the postwar inflation should have been the cue for the Reserve System to put on the monetary brakes. It was a time to sell securities, soak up excess reserves, sweat down deposit totals, let interest rates go up to discourage borrowing.

Supports Continued

But Secretary of the Treasury Fred M. Vinson and his successor, John Snyder, insisted on continuing the support program, not only in 1946 but all through the postwar period. In part, they argued:

1. That if government bonds were allowed to drop below par in the open market, it would start a financial panic.
2. That any rise in interest rates would run up the cost of carrying the government debt and unbalance the federal budget.
3. That a restrictive policy by the Reserve System wouldn't check the rise in prices anyhow, because "a fractional increase in interest rates won't stop inflation."
4. That a low structure of interest rates is healthy for the economy in general because it promotes investment and expansion of plant.

The Reserve Board argued that the rise in interest rates would be a by-product of a restrictive policy, not the main weapon. It pointed out that inflation was running up the federal budget faster than any possible increase in interest costs could run up the cost of carrying the debt. It cited the records to show that government bonds had often sold below par in the past, without starting any panics.

The Treasury wouldn't listen. And the Treasury had a clincher for its argument. The heavy concentration of government debt in short-term securities meant that the Treasury was constantly in the market with refunding operations. If one of these refundings had flopped, there might very well have been a financial panic. And the Federal Reserve Board would have taken the blame for it—just as it took the blame for the 1937 recession.

And so the Reserve Board squirmed and wiggled, but it kept on supporting the market.

BOOM VS. INFLATION

In a sense, the postwar boom vindicated the Treasury's argument for easy money. A really tough monetary policy in 1946 and 1947 might have proved a serious drag on all business. For the banks were not the only investors in government securities. Corporations and life insurance companies, among others, also held huge blocs of them. And the liquidation of these securities financed a large part of the postwar expansion. Corporations used the money to build new plant and equipment. Life insurance companies used it to extend mortgages on new homes or new plants. If the corporations and the institutional investors had been locked into their governments too early, the boom might never have got started.

But the postwar experience also vindicates the arguments of the Federal—because it brought inflation as well as boom. And there was little that the money managers could do to check the inflation.

Upset

The support program they were following in the government market turned the whole theory of monetary control inside out; it gave the initiative in open market operations to the commercial banks instead of the Reserve Banks. Any time a member bank needed reserves, it could just sell one of the government securities that it held. There was no way for the Reserve Banks to put a real squeeze on the money supply, because the first hint of a squeeze would have brought a rush of offerings on the government security market.

Fast Footwork

The Open Market Committee did some fast footwork during this period to keep the support program from wrecking the country's money system entirely. If the market forced it to buy one kind of government security to keep the price from breaking par, it tried to sell another kind out of its portfolio. In that way, it kept bank reserves from getting out of hand entirely.

The Treasury also discovered that debt management could make one contribution to stability. Between 1945 and 1949, it was able to retire about $25-billion of the government debt—first by drawing down the enormous cash balance it had built up at the end of the war and later by using the budget surplus. The issues that the Treasury picked to retire were ones that were held mainly by commercial banks and Reserve Banks. This had the effect of shrinking the assets and deposits of the banking system by the amount of the debt that was retired.

Still, the basic policy from 1946 to 1950 was easy money by any standard. The Reserve Banks never had a chance to use their traditional weapons to hold down the inflation.

The Showdown

It was the Korean war that brought the final showdown between the Treasury and the Federal Reserve Board. Faced with the prospects of new federal deficits, Secretary Snyder put the Reserve Board on notice that he expected the support program to go on indefiinitely. The Reserve Board finally balked.

New Policy

The result was the famous "full accord" between the Treasury and the Reserve Board, negotiated with all the trappings of an international peace treaty in March, 1951 (BW—Mar.10'51,p.132). The substance of the full accord was that over a period of time, the Reserve Board would wind up the support program and leave the government market standing on its own feet.

The full accord marked the beginning of a gently restrictive credit policy—the first in 20 years. Bit by bit the Open Market Committee dropped the pegs in the government market. Governments broke par, and there was no panic.

With governments selling below par, the member banks suddenly began to think twice about selling them just to fatten up reserves. They had bought at par or a premium; to sell at the market price would mean taking a loss. Most banks—and other investors as well—decided to sit tight and keep their governments until maturity.

Light Hand

The Reserve Banks could have put on a real squeeze by selling governments out of their portfolios, but they didn't want to get that rough.

They simply refused to do any more buying. The rapid expansion of bank loans was soaking up excess reserves, and the time was obviously near when the banks would come up against the ceiling.

By the end of 1952, the Federal Reserve was at last back in its traditional role as the manager of the country's money supply. The government market was standing on its own feet—with the long bonds selling something like five points under par. Excess reserves were down to practically nothing. The banks were rediscounting again—a sign that money was tightening up. Rediscounts were close to $2-billion in December, and when the Reserve Banks boosted the rediscount rate from 1¾% to 2% shortly after the turn of the year, the banking system knew that the free-wheeling days of easy money were finished.

By the end of 1952, the great postwar inflation was also finished, at least for the time being. Production was still booming; consumers were still living high on the hog. But prices had leveled off or turned down.

The Federal Reserve Board is careful not to take credit for bringing the inflation under control. The past 20 years have taught it to be wary of claiming anything. But Chairman William McChesney Martin, Jr., likes to tell a story about a prize fighter who was being systematically beaten to a pulp. To get him back into the ring at the start of each new round, his seconds kept telling him that his opponent wasn't touching him—couldn't lay a glove on him. Finally the fighter turned on them angrily. "This next round," he snarled, "watch that referee. Somebody in that ring is beating the hell out of me."

WHAT'S IN THE CARDS?

The record that the Reserve Board has made in the two years since the full accord with the Treasury is one of the main reasons why the Eisenhower Administration thinks it can use monetary controls to head off the threat of any future inflation. Unless and until there is a defiinite break in the business boom, you can expect the Reserve Board to go ahead with a mildly restrictive program.

You can also expect the Treasury to start a systematic program of tidying up the government debt, putting it into a shape that will make it easier to handle and less of a threat to monetary stability.

A Free Hand

What Secretary Humphrey and Burgess, his special deputy, want to do is "push out" the maturities on the debt. By that they mean refunding the heavy load of short-term issues into longer-term securities. If they succeed, the time will come when the Treasury no longer has to handle over $100-billion of refunding operations a year, as it does today. Instead, it will be able to stay out of the market for months at a stretch, giving the Reserve Board a free hand to do what it thinks best with the money supply.

By and large, funding the debt will have a deflationary effect on the U. S. credit system:

To get investors to take the new long-term issues, the Treasury will have to pay a higher schedule of interest rates. The market is now talking about a 3% coupon on long-term bonds—as against the old peg of 2½%.

Funding will tend to take securities away from the banking system and put them in the hands of institutions and private investors. In the process, it will tend to squeeze down bank assets and deposits.

Juggling the Debt

To see how this will work, make one last calculation on your scratchpad:

Suppose the Treasury sells a $1,000 30-year bond to a life insurance company and uses the money to retire a $1,000 1-year certificate that has been held by a commercial bank. The life insurance company pays the Treaury by giving it a $1,000 check drawn on a bank. The Treasury, in effect, pays off the bank by giving it that check and taking back the certificate. The result is that both the assets and the deposits of the bank go down $1,000.

With deposits off by $1,000, the bank now has $200 in excess reserves—which means that it can put out $1,000 in new credit if it wants to. But if the Federal Reserve is following a restrictive policy, it may not want to, or it may not be able to find borrowers. If the bank has been rediscounting, it will almost certainly use the money to get out of hock instead of expanding again.

It will take time for the Treasury to work out all the variations of deflationary and inflationary effects that can be obtained by switching the debt around among the various classes of holders. The whole problem of debt management on the present scale is so new that nobody knows all the possible tricks of the trade.

More Leverage

The combination of Treasury policy in debt management and Federal Reserve policy in money management will give the Eisenhower Administration more leverage on the money supply than anyone has ever had before. Fundamentally, it is an understanding of this leverage that makes Eisenhower's money men so confident that they can head off any further inflation by using indirect rather than direct controls.

The new Administration isn't forgetting the unhappy record of money management in the depression. If business turns down, nobody will expect easy money alone to pull it out of trouble. There is no reason to think that pushing on the piece of string would work any better in the 1950's than it did in the 1930's. And so if Eisenhower's sound dollar begins to get uncomfortably sound, the money managers will be the first to yell for help.

VIII

International Economics

---

40. PETITION OF THE CANDLEMAKERS *

Petition From the Manufacturers of Candles, Wax-Lights, Lamps, Chandeliers, Reflectors, Snuffers, Extinguishers; and From the Producers of Tallow, Oil, Resin, Alcohol, and Generally of Everything Used for Lights

THE ISSUE as to whether free trade or protection of domestic industries is the better policy for a nation to follow has been debated for the past one hundred and fifty years. The issue remains alive today in very much the same form as in the early nineteenth century, when Frederic Bastiat hurled his criticisms at the protectionists of his day. In the following selection Bastiat satirizes the type of argument normally presented to the Chamber of Deputies of his native France by those seeking protection from foreign competitors. Compare this selection with "Crisis in the American Bike Industry," which follows it. In what respects do the two "petitions" differ?

To the Honorable Members of the Chamber of Deputies:

GENTLEMEN, you are in the right way: you reject abstract theories; abundance, cheapness, concerns you little. You are entirely occupied with the interest of the producer, whom you are anxious to free from

* Frederic Bastiat, *Sophisms of the Protectionists* (New York, American Free Trade League, 1870), pp. 73-80.

The author (1801-1850) was a French economist and member of the Constitutional and Legislative Assemblies during the Revolution of 1848. A staunch believer in free trade. His major works were *Economic Harmonies, Essays on Political Economy,* and *Economic Sophisms.*

foreign competition. In a word, you wish to secure the *national market* to *national labor.*

We come now to offer you an admirable opportunity for the application of your—what shall we say? your theory? no, nothing is more deceiving than theory;—your doctrine? your system? your principle? But you do not like doctrines; you hold systems in horror; and, as for principles, you declare that there are no such things in political economy. We will say then, your practice; your practice without theory, and without principle.

We are subjected to the intolerable competition of a foreign rival, who enjoys, it would seem, such superior facilities for the production of light, that he is enabled to *inundate* our *national market* at so exceedingly reduced a price, that, the moment he makes his appearance, he draws off all custom from us; and thus an important branch of French industry, with all its innumerable ramifications, is suddenly reduced to a state of complete stagnation. This rival, who is no other than the sun, carries on so bitter a war against us, that we have every reason to believe that he has been excited to this course by our perfidious neighbor England. (Good diplomacy this, for the present time!) In this belief we are confirmed by the fact that in all his transactions with this proud island, he is much more moderate and careful than with us.

Our petition is, that it would please your honorable body to pass a law whereby shall be directed the shutting up of windows, dormers, sky-lights, shutters, curtains, vasistas, *oeil-de-boeufs,* in a word, all openings, holes, chinks and fissures through which the light of the sun is used to penetrate into our dwellings, to the prejudice of the profitable manufactures which we flatter ourselves we have been enabled to bestow upon the country; which country cannot, therefore, without ingratitude, leave us now to struggle unprotected through so unequal a contest.

We pray your honorable body not to mistake our petition for a satire, nor to repulse us without at least hearing the reasons which we have to advance in its favor.

And first, if, by shutting out as much as possible all access to natural light, you thus create the necessity for artificial light, is there in France an industrial pursuit which will not, through some connection with this important object, be benefitted by it?

If more tallow be consumed, there will arise a necessity for an increase of cattle and sheep. Thus artificial meadows must be in greater demand; and meat, wool, leather, and above all, manure, this basis of agriculture riches, must become more abundant.

If more oil be consumed, it will cause an increase in the cultivation of the olive-tree. This plant, luxuriant and exhausting to the soil, will come in good time to profit by the increased fertility which the raising of cattle will have communicated to our fields.

Our heaths will become covered with resinous trees. Numerous swarms of bees will gather upon our mountains the perfumed treasures, which are now cast upon the winds, useless as the blossoms from which they emanate. There is, in short, no branch of agriculture which would not be greatly developed by the granting of our petition.

Navigation would equally profit. Thousands of vessels would soon be employed in the whale fisheries, and thence would arise a navy capable of sustaining the honor of France, and of responding to the patriotic sentiments of the undersigned petitioners, candle merchants, *etc.*

But what words can express the magnificence which *Paris* will then exhibit! Cast an eye upon the future and behold the gildings, the bronzes, the magnificent crystal chandeliers, lamps, reflectors, and candelabras, which will glitter in the spacious stores, compared with which the splendor of the present day will appear trifling and insignificant.

There is none, not even the poor manufacturer of resin in the midst of his pine forests, nor the miserable miner in his dark dwelling, but who would enjoy an increase of salary and of comforts.

Gentlemen, if you will be pleased to reflect, you cannot fail to be convinced that there is perhaps not one Frenchman, from the opulent stockholder of Anzin down to the poorest vender of matches, who is not interested in the success of our petition.

We foresee your objections, gentlemen; but there is not one that you can oppose to us which you will not be obliged to gather from the works of the partisans of free trade. We dare challenge you to pronounce one word against our petition, which is not equally opposed to your own practice and the principle which guides your policy.

Do you tell us, that if we gain by this protection, France will not gain, because the consumer must pay the price of it?

We answer you:

You have no longer any right to cite the interest of the consumer. For whenever this has been found to compete with that of the producer, you have invariably sacrificed the first. You have done this to *encourage labor,* to *increase the demand for labor.* The same reason should now induce you to act in the same manner.

You have yourselves already answered the objection. When you were told: The consumer is interested in the free introduction of iron, coal, corn, wheat, cloths, etc., your answer was: Yes, but the producer is interested in their exclusion. Thus, also, if the consumer is interested in the admission of light, we, the producers, pray for its interdiction.

You have also said, the producer and the consumer are one. If the manufacturer gains by protection, he will cause the agriculturist to gain also; if agriculture prospers, it opens a market for manufactured goods. Thus we, if you confer upon us the monopoly of furnishing light during the day, will as a first consequence buy large quantities of tallow, coals, oil, resin, wax, alcohol, silver, iron, bronze, crystal, for the supply of our business; and then we and our numerous contractors having become rich, our consumption will be great, and will become a means of contributing to the comfort and competency of the workers in every branch of national labor.

Will you say that the light of the sun is a gratuitous gift, and that to repulse gratuitous gifts, is to repulse riches under pretense of encouraging the means of obtaining them?

Take care—you carry the death-blow to your own policy. Remember that hitherto you have always repulsed foreign produce, *because* it was an approach to a gratuitous gift, and *the more in proportion* as this approach was more close. You have, in obeying the wishes of other monopolists, acted only from a *half-motive;* to grant our petition there is a much *fuller inducement.* To repulse us, precisely for the reason that our case is a more complete one than any which have preceded it, would be to lay down the following equation: $+ \times + = -$; in other words, it would be to accumulate absurdity upon absurdity.

Labor and Nature concur in different proportions, according to country and climate, in every article of production. The portion of Nature is always gratuitous; that of labor alone regulates the price.

If a Lisbon orange can be sold at half the price of a Parisian one, it is because a natural and gratuitous heat does for the one, what the other only obtains from an artificial and consequently expensive one.

When, therefore, we purchase a Portuguese orange, we may say that we obtain it half gratuitously and half by the right of labor; in other words, at *half price* compared to those of Paris.

Now it is precisely on account of this demi-gratuity (excuse the word) that you argue in favor of exclusion. How, you say, could national labor sustain the competition of foreign labor, when the first has everything to do, and the last is rid of half the trouble, the sun taking the rest of the business upon himself? If then the *demi-gratuity* can determine you to check competition, on what principle can the *entire gratuity* be alleged as a reason for admitting it? You are no logicians if, refusing the demi-gratuity as hurtful to human labor, you do not *a fortiori,* and with double zeal, reject the full gratuity.

Again, when any article, as coal, iron, cheese, or cloth, comes to us from foreign countries with less labor than if we produced it ourselves, the difference in price is a *gratuitous gift* conferred upon us; and the gift is more or less considerable, according as the difference is greater or less. It is the quarter, the half, or the three-quarters of the value of the produce, in proportion as the foreign merchant requires the three-quarters, the half, or the quarter of the price. It is as complete as possible when the producer offers, as the sun does with light, the whole in free gift. The question is, and we put it formally, whether you wish for France the benefit of gratuitous consumption, or the supposed advantages of laborious production. Choose, but be consistent. And does it not argue the greatest inconsistency to check as you do the importation of coal, iron, cheese, and goods of foreign manufacture, merely because and even in proportion as their price approaches *zero,* while at the same time you freely admit, and without limitation, the light of the sun, whose price is during the whole day at *zero?*

---

41. CRISIS IN THE AMERICAN BIKE INDUSTRY *

FOR AN introductory statement to this selection, see the headnote for Selection 40 on page 377.

THE RISING tide of foreign bikes coming into this country has been directly responsible for the serious crisis that now exists in the American bicycle industry.

This problem has beset the industry at the very peak of its contributions to American life. The tremendous increase in imports, resulting in a great loss of employment, production and sales, threatens the very survival of the industry.

As a result of repeated reductions in the tariff rate, the American bike industry, by the end of 1953, had lost one-quarter of its entire market to foreign competition. This happened in the unbelievably short period of four years.

Currently, in 1954, the industry's losses are substantially higher, and show every evidence of continuing. All the resourcefulness and know-

* John Auerbach, "Bike Crisis—An American Industry's Fight for Survival," published in 1954 by the American Bicycle Industry Tariff Committee.

The author (1911——) is Executive Manager of the Bicycle Manufacturers Association and the Bicycle Institute of America. Prior to that, he acted as Executive Manager of the New York State Restaurant Owners Association. A graduate of New York University in Aeronautical Engineering. Author of many booklets and pamphlets, he has contributed various articles to leading magazines.

how at our command, covering 77 years' experience, cannot help us solve the problem.

For this is a problem that has resulted not from any failures on the part of the bike industry, but from government acts over which we have no control—acts that have ignored the realities of the situation as it has affected our plants.

The continuance of the bike industry as a healthy and profitable part of our economy rests solely on our ability to obtain the help of the Federal government. It is within their power alone to put an immediate halt to the unrestricted influx of foreign two-wheelers.

LOW TARIFF STRUCTURE PLAYS HAVOC

The extremely low tariff structure and the low wages paid bicycle workers abroad is at the heart of the problem. These factors have given foreign bikes an unbeatable price edge. The unfair competitive advantage imported bikes now have threatens the productive output of our industry—and the jobs of thousands of workers who derive their income from the manufacture and sale of bicycles.

American producers, dealers and workers have no argument with imports entering this country. In fact, the industry sympathizes with the government's program to stabilize the economies of friendly nations. But we believe such programs should not be permitted to place an unnatural and unfair burden on the American bicycle industry.

If sacrifices are required for the sake of encouraging international trade, we believe they should be assessed proportionately against the entire economy. We simply desire to remain a vigorous and useful part of the nation's economy.

Whether we do or not depends entirely on the willingness of the government to grant us the right to compete equally with foreign-made bikes in the home market.

LOW WAGES IMPERIL U. S. WORKERS

The domestic industry has not been able to compete successfully against the low wages paid abroad. American workers, among the highest paid in the metal fabricating trades, receive more than four times the wages paid foreign bike workers.

American bike producers, who have traditionally operated on a low margin of profit, do not desire nor could they expect American workers to perform their highly skilled tasks for the 15 to 45 cents an hour which bicycle workers in foreign countries receive. American bike workers receive in excess of $1.90 an hour for producing bicycles and parts in this country, plus many additional benefits.

What it boils down to is that *imports entering this country are making rapid progress at the expense of the standard of living of American bike workers*—and only the government has the power to halt this trend that threatens to swallow up the domestic bike industry.

DOMESTIC SALES DECLINE RAPIDLY

The statistics shown give you an accurate picture of how the increased rate of imports in recent years has resulted in a disastrous loss of sales and output in the home market. You will note that imports have made their greatest strides in the past four years.

Foreign Bike Sales in U.S. Market

	Foreign Units Sold in U.S. Market	*Per Cent of Foreign Sales to U.S. Market*
1931-1939 (—Average)	11,500	1.3
1940	11,329	.9
1941	6,041	.3
1946	46,469	2.7
1947	19,758	.7
1948	16,874	.6
1949	15,757	1.1
1950	66,289	3.4
1951	176,263	9.0
1952	245,163	11.8
1953	593,659	22.8
1954 (6 months)	291,314	40.0

A study of the figures above shows that in 1953 alone more bicycles were imported into the United States than the cumulative total for the 20-year period of 1931 to 1951. In 1953 the sale of imports skyrocketed to 23 percent of the total market here.

Frequently in 1954 more bicycles were imported in one day than came into this country in a former full year period in the past! Until 1949 imports seldom exceeded a mean average of 1.3 percent in comparison to domestic sales. Today, imports often run at nearly 50 times that figure.

Already in a single month early in 1954 imports have exceeded domestic sales—the first such experience in the industry's 77-years of existence.

LOSSES IN THE MILLIONS AS PRODUCTION LAGS

It is no wonder, therefore, that domestic sales in the first part of 1954 were by far the worst ever recorded in the modern history of the American bicycle industry.

There followed, naturally, crushing financial losses to the bicycle industry. The normal productive output of many plants was suspended. Tax contributions to the government were seriously curtailed.

This situation was accompanied by the worst siege of unemployment the bike industry has ever encountered under normal business conditions. Thousands of bike workers were made jobless during the first half of the year—causing hardship not only to their families but to scores of communities dependent upon bike income for the economic well-being of the entire community.

Imports of bicycles and parts cost American labor five million man-hours of work in 1953, resulting in losses of millions of dollars in take-home pay. This figure will approach 10 million man-hours in 1954—and the future is even more discouraging as long as the rate of imports continues upward.

Along with other wage-earners in this country, bicycle workers, whose purchasing power is vital to the nation's prosperity, pay taxes to the government. The rise in unemployment sharply reduced their tax contributions and buying power.

AMERICAN PRODUCERS SATISFY ALL BIKE NEEDS

The producers of foreign bicycles have not brought anything new or of superior quality into the American market. The two-wheelers received from Great Britain, France, Germany, Japan and others are the same type lightweight and balloon-tire models which have been available here for many years.

The lightweight, also known as the Continental or English-type bike, provides an efficient ride for adult use. But it is costly to maintain and is possessed of equipment that is unsafe in the hands of many youngsters who do not have the ability or experience to operate it properly. In most parts of the world, this type of wheel is principally used as a means of transportation by adult riders.

The standard or balloon-tire bike has been traditionally popular among younger riders in this country because of its low upkeep, easy maintenance, dependable coaster brake, sturdy construction, stability and ability to take much abuse without serious damage to any important parts. This bicycle was designed to meet the special needs of active hard-playing American youngsters.

LOW TARIFF AIDS SALE OF FOREIGN LIGHTWEIGHTS

Imported lightweights did not fill a vacuum or create a new market for bicycles in this country.

Long before the importers flooded our market with their merchandise, American lightweights were available in this country. In fact, they could be bought in retail stores as far back as 1936.

Although the bike-riding public then, as now, showed a preference for the standard-type two-wheeler, the record shows that until recently, American producers outsold foreign manufacturers on the very type of lightweights being imported in large quantities today.

In the record-breaking year of 1948, 2,761,437 American bikes were sold in this country. Despite a heavy demand for anything on wheels, it is worth noting that only 16,874 foreign lightweight bikes were sold. Several thousand less foreign lightweights were sold in 1949—indicating no great demand for these bikes at that time, even though our peacetime production had not yet caught up with the accumulated war-time demand.

Suddenly, however, import sales jumped to 66,289 in 1950—and since then have not stopped their upward trend. Why did this change occur? For no other reason than that duty rates on imported bikes were cut drastically to as low as 7½ percent in 1948, followed by the British devaluation of their currency in 1949, resulting in the equivalent of another 30% duty cut.

As a result, the prices of foreign bikes dropped sharply. It was these prices, beyond our control, that broke down sales resistance in many quarters.

EFFICIENCY ALONE CANNOT HELP US

The present crisis in the bike industry has not resulted from any inefficiency or failure in production and merchandising techniques. Despite the disadvantage of cheaply-produced imports, the industry has applied its full resources to meeting the challenge of unfair competition.

The industry has employed all kinds of emergency measures and stop-gaps. It has consulted some of America's outstanding industrial experts and designers. Despite our efforts, the odds against us have proved too great. We find ourselves seriously handicapped in trying to bridge the gap which finds foreign workers receiving one-quarter to one-eighth the wages American workers earn.

American bike workers are well-trained and highly skilled. American management has been equally competent in the maintenance of first-rate plants, and the employment of the latest methods of production.

The industry's superior merchandising achievements have been nationally acclaimed by the American Trade Association Executives, Public Relations News, Tide Magazine, the National Safety Council and many leading newspapers and publications. Their citations under-

or other benefits which enable them to maintain a high productive capacity in their native lands.
score the enterprise which our industry has exercised during its time of crisis.

Actually, only because of the industry's remarkable degree of productive and technical efficiency has it been possible to operate at all in the present declining market.

NEW PRODUCTS NO CURE-ALL

It has been suggested that perhaps the bike industry's salvation lies in changing over to new products. As ludicrous as this proposal may seem, we are compelled to alternately suggest that if this is feasible and easy to accomplish, why haven't foreign producers been asked to do the same—and thereby avoid disrupting this market!

In all fairness, we must state that we not only question the logic of being asked to make new products, but we resent being asked to default the market we have cultivated for 77 years.

Aside from the impracticalities and unfairness of seeking such a solution, the industry has been on the alert to the possibilities of adding new products for many years. It is not a simple matter. The skills involved in bike production are not easily transferred to other modes of production.

In changing over to new competitive products, the industry's labor force would be compelled to learn new techniques and skills to assure their continued employment. Many workers would face the loss of seniority rights which would entail labor union problems of a highly complicated nature.

Finally, when all is said and done, the bike industry would have no guarantee that its new products would not run the full risk of a second foreign attack!

FOREIGN INDUSTRIES ENJOY PROTECTION

We are limited considerably by the absence of any substantial export market for our merchandise, such as the British and other nations enjoy in this country and other parts of the world.

The American industry is getting the worst of it coming and going. U. S. bike exports fell from 105,000 in 1948 to a mere 9,300 in 1953. Barriers have been set up against our exports. Other countries have imposed high protective tariffs and varied restrictions, but violently oppose such measures when proposed here to protect our industry.

Moreover, British and other leading foreign producers are well-protected by their governments. They are aided by government subsidies

Lastly, they are protected at home by high tariffs. Our State Department has said, for example: "That of all the bikes in use in Great Britain, 100% may be said to be British made." We don't blame the British for erecting barriers to preserve their own market. In contrast, however, the American bike tariff is by far the lowest among all the major nations of the world. Thus our industry is exposed to continuous import assault.

Here we see an unusual paradox. The domestic bike industry is completely dependent on the home market. It has no foreign outlets for its products. On the other hand, protected foreign industries have their own home market and the markets of the world for the sale of their bicycles!

IMPORTERS USURP OUR CULTIVATED MARKET

It took the American bicycle industry more than half a century to cultivate the present market. By contrast, the importers have achieved their stronghold in the disproportionate period of four years, without making any contributions to the development of the current interest in bicycling.

They have opportunistically succeeded in exploiting the very market that the business ingenuity and farsightedness of American producers, distributors and dealers were able to create.

The importers have no deep roots in our industry. Yet they have been faring handsomely at the expense of long-established businesses and are managing to destroy well-established policies, patterns, and harmonies.

The importers are invincible in pricing their bikes. *They are able to sell standard and lightweight models for less than the manufacturing cost of American producers.* Such a price advantage will doom American bike workers and management—unless immediate tariff relief is forthcoming.

UNFAIR COMPETITION VIGOROUSLY OPPOSED

What has made it possible for foreign producers to seize an unequal share of the bicycle market? What is it that American labor and management so sorely resent?

It is nothing more than the fact that foreign producers enjoy the exceptional advantages of low wages, high volume and low tariffs. *It is not the superiority of their merchandise that gives them an edge—but the price factor which has enabled them to gobble up a substantial part of the U. S. market.*

American bike producers are not fearful of competition—either domestic or foreign. In fact, the industry welcomes *fair* competition and readily accepts the challenge of applying its maximum ingenuity, productive skill and merchandising know-how in the day-to-day struggle for recognition and sales.

We believe, however, that such competition should thrive in an economic atmosphere which affords equality to all competitors alike. Regardless of how well intentioned our government may be in attempting to stimulate international trade, we see no plausible reason for giving foreign competition advantages in our market, which can only lead to bankrupting our plants and forcing thousands of American workers into unemployment.

WHAT THE INDUSTRY IS SEEKING

Today's duty rates on bicycles are 7½ to 15 percent, the lowest in the industry's entire history. The overwhelming majority of imported bikes come into this country at the lower 7½ percent duty.

The restoration of duty rates to levels that previously existed would only serve as a minor roadblock. For example, even if the government were to impose the 1930 tariff rate of 30 percent, foreign wheels could still manage to undercut American products, as is currently the case with bicycle parts and accessories.

Accordingly, we are seeking a reasonable limitation on imports through the establishment of flexible quota limitations based on a fair relationship of imports to domestic sales.

We have asked the government to undertake an immediate survey to determine the extent of the industry's distress. We believe that such an approach will lead to tariff relief.

BIKE INDUSTRY UNITED AGAINST IMPORTS

Despite the fact that American wholesale and retail buyers are making money selling foreign wheels in this country, most of them have expressed support for the industry's position. They are fearful of becoming permanently dependent on foreign sources of supply thousands of miles away. They realize that overnight they might find themselves a captured market, subject to deprivations utterly beyond their control.

In fact, all elements of the industry—manufacturer, jobber, wholesaler, retailer and worker—are united in a determined effort to put an end to the present inequitable competition which the industry finds itself powerless to combat on an effective basis.

INDUSTRY'S POSITION WINS SUPPORT

The bike industry is determined to obtain help before it is too late. It has mobilized all of its resources and forces to protect its future. It believes that the public strongly favors its continuance on a healthy and sound basis—able to compete freely, fairly and equally with foreign merchandise sold in the American market.

The position of the industry has won support in many State Legislatures. The Massachusetts and New York legislatures have passed resolutions opposing the unrestricted influx of bicycle imports. City and municipal governing bodies, ranging from Chicago to Little Falls, N. Y., and numerous other communities, have protested the hardship imports have created for our industry.

Labor unions, representing bicycles workers in many plants and workers in plants supplying materials to the industry, have expressed powerful support for the industry's plea for action. Numerous resolutions have been passed by these unions strongly condemning unfair tariff rates and the unnecessary unemployment it has caused for workers in the industry.

HOW YOU CAN HELP OUR INDUSTRY

The bicycle industry has applied to the United States Tariff Commission for the establishment of reasonable quota limitations—as the only means of solving the pressing problem of unfair competition from imports.

It is within the power of the Tariff Commission to rule favorably on our application, which is now before them for consideration, and then recommend to the President of the United States the adoption of changes that will preserve our industry.

We hope that you have been convinced of the justness of our cause. If so, we urge you to support our application for tariff relief by writing to the President and the state and federal legislators who represent your district.

There are many ways in which you can help the bike industry in this hour of crisis. We urge you to contact your civic, community and business groups—your city and municipal government—your labor union—and urgently request that they pass resolutions supporting the bicycle industry in its fight to survive.

42. THE DOLLAR CRISIS IN NEW ENGLAND *

An Economic Fable for Our Times

WHAT HAPPENS when interregional trade also becomes international trade through the separation of one country into two? Mr. Galbraith describes the dollar shortage and other problems that arise out of the imposition of trade barriers between two countries by inventing the fiction of the secession of New England from the rest of the United States, and the establishment of that region as a sovereign nation. The reader will find that this fable has what all good fables must have—a moral.

AN UNEXPECTED consequence of the secession of the six New England states was the severe financial crisis experienced by the new commonwealth. It was all the more surprising, for New Englanders had a well-established reputation for caution and prescience in financial matters. The bankers in Boston, the financial capital of the new state, had always handled their own and other people's money with commendable prudence and rectitude and the New England banks, alone, had been unembarrassed by the severe banking crisis some fifteen years earlier. New England had suffered little disorganization and even less physical damage from the second world war, and some caution is called for in comparing the position of New England with that of the European states of the period.

Prior to partition, however, economic conditions in New England had been a cause for some apprehension. A contemporary authority had observed that, although wages in New England were lower than in most other parts of the United States, production per man was frequently even lower. Some branches of the manufacturing industry, on which the area was singularly dependent, were in a precarious position. Partly as a result, New England had been buying more food, raw materials, and other goods from the rest of the country than it had been selling in return. This deficit had been made up by payments received for such services as insurance and private education and from earnings on investments in other parts of the then U.S.

In spite of the uncertain state of its balance of payments, the New England area never experienced an actual dollar shortage in the pre-partition years. Apparently, as manufacturing enterprises found themselves unable to compete with newer and more modern plants in other

* John Kenneth Galbraith. Reprinted from the April, 1948, issue of *Fortune* Magazine by special permission of the Editors; Copyright 1948, Time, Inc.

For a brief biographical sketch of the author, see Selection 10 on page 114.

parts of the country (a condition that had characterized the New England textile industry for many years), they simply closed down. The younger and more energetic workers then migrated to other parts of the country. There were no immigration barriers to stop this movement and, by the middle of the twentieth century, travel facilities, though often primitive, were no barrier to the hardy. As a result of this migration, the population of New England had increased less rapidly than that of other sections. In 1880 it had about 8 per cent of the population of the U.S. as a whole and by 1940 only about 6.4 per cent.

In retrospect, it would appear that it was the closing down of inefficient enterprises and the migration of workers that prevented New England from having balance-of-payment problems while it was still part of the U.S. The plants that remained in operation were, inevitably, those with the lowest costs and best management and hence the ones that were best able to maintain or expand their exports to other parts of the U.S. At the same time the closing of inefficient plants and the emigration of workers reduced, relatively speaking, the volume of raw materials, food, and consumers' goods that had to be imported into New England. This crude process had kept New England's imports automatically in balance with her income from exports, services, and investments.

No nation ever came into existence under circumstances more auspicious than those attending the inauguration of the New England Union on that Arbor Day that has since become a sacred memory of all New Englanders. Except for some southern politicians who were inclined to draw parallels with 1860 and mutter about discrimination, the right of the people of New England to govern themselves in their own way was conceded. Mild communal disturbances in Boston and Bridgeport were quickly suppressed. A Maine senator who had been expected to oppose partition declared that it was "the will of the people" and devoted himself to organizing the commercial air services of the new country. The facilities of the federal government, including post offices, dams, internal-revenue offices, and the headquarters of the regional soil-conservation service were turned over to the infant republic. The mayor of Boston became the first ambassador to Washington.

Unhappily, financial difficulties followed almost at once. While the principal incentives to the creation of NEU were social and cultural, the founding fathers were aware of the unsatisfactory state of their industries. They took steps to provide modest tariff protection for those in most serious trouble and launched a carefully designed program of industrial rehabilitation. The predecessor state governments, while they could accord minor tax concessions and other subsidies to industrial enterprises, had been generally unable to raise capital on behalf of private industry. The borrowing power of these primitive governments was usually exhausted in providing needed public works and improvements. For reviving and recapitalizing depressed industries, local officials had been forced to rely mostly on oratory and incantation, which, though greatly used, had never been completely effective.

The men who forgathered at the new capital at Increase, Massachusetts, were under no such handicaps. They had at their disposal the credit resources of a sovereign power. In Wall Street the first bond issues of NEU encountered the then prevailing suspicion of foreign loans but patriotic New Englanders subscribed generously and what remained was readily absorbed by the new central bank. Plans were drawn to recapitalize the cotton-textile, shipping, shoe, and farm wood-lot industries, and to modernize the New Haven Railroad. With an adequate supply of public capital to supplement the efforts of private enterprise, chances for success seemed promising.

Partition, unfortunately, made the new commonwealth subject to the tariff of the U.S. Although it received most-favored-nation treatment and quickly negotiated a reciprocal-trade treaty as well as a treaty of friendship, commerce, and navigation with the U.S., products of the NEU entered the latter country at a considerable handicap. New York farmers, after drawing attention to the substandard labor and sanitary conditions in Vermont, were able also to have fresh dairy products from that state excluded from the New York market.

There were other minor sources of irritation in the trade between the two countries. New England, for example, had long been a manufacturer of inexpensive watches, and these cheap timepieces flooded the U.S. market, endangering, it was believed, the watch industry of the latter country. Fortunately, a previous arrangement between the U.S. and Switzerland provided a formula for resolving this problem, and NEU watch manufacturers undertook, voluntarily, to limit their exports to the U.S. Tobacco was also a source of difficulty, for the U.S. Government was then engaged in supporting the price of this product for its own farmers. It was necessary to keep Connecticut tobacco producers from taking advantage of a market that, in the contemporary phrase, was being maintained "at the expense of the American taxpayer." It would be unfortunate, however, were the trade problems of the two countries exaggerated unduly. At this particular period the U.S. was actively engaged in promoting world trade. Its policy, which had been enunciated with great force and clarity, was a source of much encouragement to the manufacturers and exporters of the NEU.

Had it not been that times were good and the labor requirements of the new industrial-rehabilitation program substantial, unemployment in

NEU might have been serious. Inevitably there was dislocation in industries that had been accustomed to market their products in the U.S. At the same time the extraordinarily strict immigration quotas established by the U.S. for the NEU effectively prevented workers from the latter area from seeking employment in the U.S. As it happened, most of the actual suffering was confined to the part of NEU adjacent to New York City. The people of that area had long found employment in New York and many of them had rather specialized talents coupled with an attitude toward manual labor that made it difficult to absorb them into the NEU economy.

The difficulties the new country encountered in selling its products, together with the restraints on emigration, coincided with its growing need for steel, nonferrous metals, and other raw materials and certain types of machinery for its industrial-rehabilitation program. As a result there was a heavy demand from NEU for U.S. dollars to buy U.S. goods and a considerably more limited demand from the U.S. for NEU dollars to buy New England products. The NEU dollar, for that reason, went to a sharp discount in New York. Fearing a further fall, holders of NEU dollars, bank deposits, and other liquid assets endeavored to convert their money into U.S. dollars and this capital flight added to the instability of the new currency.

The government of the New England Union, although opposed in principle to the step, was forced to institute exchange control to halt the flight of capital. All U.S. dollars earned from exports were turned in to the central bank and these were doled out only for approved imports. In addition U.S. dollar assets in NEU were registered and their transfer out of the country was prohibited. It was the latter regulation, incidentally, that led to the disgraceful "Greenwich incident." This was the result, apparently, of an NEU frontier inspector having been told, inadvisedly, to be on the lookout for a middle-aged Boston spinster who was suspected of having concealed several hundred thousand dollars worth of Telephone bonds in her corset.

The government of NEU also curtailed imports of citrus fruits, automobiles, films, alcoholic beverages, and other non-essentials, and it launched a "Buy New England" program that was a model of its kind. The tourist trade was encouraged and unnecessary travel in the U.S. was prohibited.

These steps were not taken without some sacrifice in the standard of living or, indeed, without some criticism from within NEU. At no time, however, did this criticism seriously jeopardize the future of the young country since most of it was directed at the regulations and the manner of their administration—at what a speaker in a much quoted address to a meeting of the New England Council spoke of as "the cancerous red tape and the capricious job holders who are the sole architects of our agony."

The firm measures taken by the government of NEU, criticism notwithstanding, served to arrest the deterioration in the exchange position. It was not possible, however, to eliminate the deficit in the balance of payments entirely. Eventually the assistance of Washington had to be solicited and, after some hesitation, Washington made a series of advances to the young republic. This help proved temporary, for Washington itself was in difficulty after California left the union and Texas reasserted its independence. The Canadians, who provided aid for a time, were always inclined to make their assistance conditional on closer economic cooperation between the secession states.

---

43. THE UNITED STATES IN THE WORLD ECONOMY *

IN 1954 the Commission on Foreign Economic Policy, better known as the Randall Commission, presented its report to President Eisenhower and the Congress. The Commission also released a series of staff papers dealing with various aspects of international trade. Four short excerpts from the staff papers are reproduced here. Selection 43 emphasizes, first, the necessity for a high and rising level of income in the United States as a means of helping foreign nations sell goods here. Next, the balance of payments, or rather the unbalance of payments, between the United States and the rest of the world is examined. Selection 44 stresses the importance of foreign trade to American farmers as producers, consumers, and citizens and then describes the conflict between domestic programs for support of the farmer and the aims of our foreign economic policy.

THE UNITED STATES is by far the richest and economically the most powerful nation in the world and by reason of that position exercises a dominant role and influence in the world economy. Our domestic and foreign economic policies have a far-reaching impact on the economic and trading positions and policies of the rest of the world. Through appropriate policies, therefore, we can help to shape significantly the kind of world economy in which we want to live. If, however, we pursue inappropriate policies, our actions will adversely affect economic and trading conditions in the rest of the world, to the detriment of ourselves and of our over-all foreign policy objectives.

* *Staff Papers;* presented to the Commission on Foreign Economic Policy, February 1954 (Government Printing Office, 1954), pp. 1-14.

Although the United States has only about 5 percent of the world's population, we produce well over 40 percent of the world's total output of goods and services. In terms of certain major products, e. g., steel, automobiles, and crude petroleum, we produce well over 50 percent of the world's supply of these particular products.

The United States also generates perhaps as much as two-thirds or more of the world's flow of savings. This has made it possible for us to be the world's greatest exporter of capital and creditor nation.

Another indication of the tremendous weight that we exert in the world economy is provided by the fact that we are now both the world's largest exporter and importer. *In 1952 our exports amounted to over 20 percent of total world exports and our imports to about 15 percent of total world imports.* (With regard to world imports of raw materials alone, our share in the total is much larger.) We are the largest single supplier to, and the largest single market for, a very large number of individual foreign countries. Some countries, in fact, including Canada, the Philippines, and many Latin American nations, sell us more than 50 percent of their total exports and buy more than 50 percent of their total imports from us.

A high level of United States imports of goods and services is of great importance to the rest of the world (and to us) for two reasons. For one thing, United States imports play an important part in affecting the level of domestic economic activity in many foreign countries, especially raw-materials-producing countries which are heavily dependent on exports. Second, and of more importance, United States imports constitute the main source to foreign countries of earning the dollars which are needed to finance the purchase of essential goods and services from the United States. Many of the goods and services in question cannot be obtained elsewhere, or, if so, only at higher prices, in inadequate quantities, or of inferior quality.

The magnitude of our imports of goods and services is closely related to the level of our national income. When our income rises, both the volume and the value of our imports tend to rise. Conversely, when our income falls, the volume and value of our imports fall. Our imports of raw materials are especially sensitive to changes in our national income. Changes in our national income, in fact, tend to cause even greater changes, percentage-wise, in the aggregate value of our imports. The modest downward readjustment in United States business conditions in 1949, for example, caused a drop of as much as 10 percent in the aggregate value of our merchandise imports between the second half of 1948 and the second half of 1949, with far-reaching repercussions on the rest of the world. It forced other nations, because of the drop in their dollar earnings and the relative inadequacy of gold and dollar reserves at their disposal, to tighten their import controls against United States goods and services, and also helped to precipitate the widespread devaluation of foreign currencies against the dollar that occurred in September of that year.

Foreign countries, therefore, obviously fear a downturn, however modest, in United States business activity. For such a downturn, by causing a decline in our imports, would tend directly to depress the income of export industries abroad and through this impact exert a deflationary influence on foreign economies as a whole. Of more importance, it would tend to deprive foreign countries of dollars needed to finance imports of goods and services from the United States and other dollar countries. Even in cases where individual foreign countries do not themselves export heavily to the United States, the same adverse consequences would tend to ensue because of the close economic interdependence of all foreign countries. Another reason why foreign countries fear a United States recession is that there is a tendency for the outflow of private investment capital from the United States to foreign countries to decline in times of receding business activity in this country, further depriving the rest of the world of needed dollars. It might also be noted that the *fear of a United States recession, because of the effect that it would have on the flow of dollars, is one of the important factors inhibiting foreign countries from moving in the direction of liberalizing their trade and payments restrictions against imports of American goods and services.*

A United States recession would tend to force foreign countries to tighten their restrictions against American imports, if it were of such severity as to cause a significant depletion of their limited gold and dollar reserves. Such action would not only run counter to our objective of obtaining a relaxation of foreign restrictions against American goods but also would tend to deprive foreign countries of goods needed to sustain the strength of their economies and to support their rearmament programs. The resultant weakening of foreign economies could also have serious political and social consequences by weakening the ties of these countries to the democratic way of life and their willingness to resist Communist intrigue and subversion, and by strengthening the Communist propaganda line.

Foreign countries also fear, though to a lesser degree, sharp *speculative* upswings in United States economic activity of the sort that followed upon the outbreak of the Korean war. Such upswings, as the experience of 1950-51 amply indicated, can have a seriously disturbing impact on foreign economies through the artificial bidding up of the prices of primary products on world markets to a level which cannot be sustained.

It follows from all this that *essential requirements for world economic stability and growth, for a better balance in the payments positions of foreign countries vis-a-vis the United States, and for a continuing liberalization of the trade and payments restrictions of foreign countries on dollar expenditures, are a high and rising level of national income in the United States and the avoidance of sharp downturns or sharp speculative upturns in United States business activity.*

Although, as noted before, a high volume of trade with the United States is of strategic importance to the economic well-being of foreign countries as a whole, our trade with the rest of the world has admittedly a much more limited significance from the viewpoint of our own economic activity. This stems from the fact that *at present our merchandise exports constitute only about 5 percent of our national income* (and about 7 to 9 percent of our total production of movable goods), *while our merchandise imports constitute only about 4 percent of our national income.* Movements in our exports or export surplus rarely, if ever, have a decisive influence on the level of our economic activity.

But it would be a serious error to assume that a high level of foreign trade is of little or no importance to us. Apart from the fact that a reduction in our imports and exports could have serious effects abroad which would endanger our security objectives, there is also the consideration that imports and exports play a role in our economic life far more important than is suggested by the low ratio of our exports and imports to our national income. In the case of our exports, many individual sectors of our economy depend heavily on foreign markets. For two leading field crops, cotton and wheat, for example, annual exports during the past few years have averaged more than one-third of the total domestic production; and approximately one-quarter of our total tobacco output was exported during the same period. A sharp decline in these and in other agricultural exports could have seriously disturbing effects on our farm population and on predominantly rural areas, especially the South. In the field of manufactured goods, moreover, exports in many individual industries comprise much more than 10 percent of total domestic production; in some, e. g., textile machinery, sewing machines, and tractors, over 20 percent of the total output is exported. The *indirect* effects of a fall in our exports also should be considered. A decline in exports would result in a reduction in the incomes of exporting groups which would react on the rest of the economy and, in addition, would affect those industries, e. g., transportation, that derive a large part of their incomes from servicing the export industries.

The low ratio of our imports to national income likewise gives a misleading picture of the importance of imports in our economy. Indeed, our dependence on many critical raw materials and on certain foodstuffs is great. An exceedingly high proportion of our total absorption of such materials as tin, copper, lead, manganese, nickel,and chromite, for example, is supplied by imports. With the growing demands of our economy for these strategic materials and the growing pressure on our available resources, our dependence will tend to rise. In the case of foodstuffs, we depend heavily on foreign sources for coffee, sugar, tea, cocoa, spices, and other products which provide us with a more varied pattern of consumption. Our imports of these and of manufactured goods, moreover, provide us with goods that can be acquired more cheaply from abroad than from domestic sources, even when similar goods are produced at home. Furthermore, our imports of certain raw materials, foodstuffs, and especially manufactured goods, are impeded by tariffs and other restrictions and would rise significantly if these barriers were relaxed. To be sure, if our imports were suddenly cut off or sharply reduced, we could develop substitutes for some and do without others, but only at the expense of higher costs and of substantial dislocations to ourselves.

The main theme of this paper has been to demonstrate the importance of a high, relatively stable, and growing level of United States business activity as a means of maintaining a large and steadily growing flow of dollars to foreign countries by means of imports of goods and services and exports of private capital in order to enable them to finance their needs for goods and services in this country from their own dollar earnings. The tremendous role of the United States in the world economy as a supplier of goods and services gives strategic importance to the flow of dollars to the rest of the world. Although our economic intercourse with other nations is of less direct economic importance to us than it is to them, our interests in maintaining a high level of imports and exports are no less great than theirs. This is so, not only because a high level of foreign trade is of great importance to many of our individual industries as a source of their supplies or as a market for their production and because it raises our standard of living, but more especially because it helps to strengthen the economies of our allies and thus their ability and willingness to remain on our side and to contribute to the common cause of the free world.

THE WORLD DOLLAR PROBLEM: 1946-53

The dollar problem has been the central international economic problem of the postwar period. Foreign countries as a group have wanted to buy in the United States a volume of goods and services larger than they have been able to finance from their sales of goods and services to this country and from other "normal" dollar receipts. Although nearly all foreign countries have tightly restricted their expenditures in the United States by means of exchange and direct trade controls, they have nevertheless had huge deficits in their payments with this country throughout the postwar period.

According to the particular statistical procedure adopted here, the "world's dollar deficit" in the period 1946-53 as a whole, which was accounted for largely by Western Europe, aggregated approximately $32 billion.[1] The *annual* deficit reached a peak of almost $10 billion in 1947, but by 1953 it had become a slight surplus. Over the period as a whole, the aggregate deficit was financed by United States Government economic aid and loans. Foreign countries as a group transferred over $6 billion of their gold and dollar reserves to the United States in 1946-49 to help finance their deficits in those years; but they subsequently gained back from us an approximately equal amount of reserves in view of the fact that since 1949 our economic aid and loans have exceeded the "world's dollar deficit" with us by that amount.

The following table summarizes the picture *for the period 1946-53 as a whole:*

BALANCE-OF-PAYMENTS ITEMS	*Billions of dollars*
1. United States net surplus on account of goods and services (excluding goods and services exported under military aid)	35.2
2. Net exports of private United States capital	6.8
3. Net imports of foreign long-term capital and miscellaneous items	3.7
4. World's dollar deficit (1−2+3)	32.1
FINANCED BY:	
5. U. S. Government *economic* aid and loans	32.5
6. Net transfers of gold and dollar reserves *to* foreign countries	0.4
7. Total financing (5−6)	32.1

Now it is clear that *had we not extended aid of this magnitude, the*

[1] In the computation of this figure, United States exports of goods and services financed by *military* grants have been excluded in order to give a more accurate picture of the size of the world's "commercial" payments deficit with us. If military-aid items were included, the world's payments deficit with us in 1946-53 would have been larger by almost $10 billion.

dollar deficits of the rest of the world could not have existed on the scale that they did, since foreign countries would have been forced to take measures (further import restrictions, severe deflationary policies, or exchange adjustments) to reduce drastically their dollar expenditures to the point where these expenditures could have been financed out of current dollar earnings and drafts on available gold and dollar reserves. *But had foreign countries been forced to restrict their purchases of United States goods and services to such a degree, economic and political chaos would have ensued abroad.* The aid which the United States Government gave was thus designed to make it possible for the rest of the free world, on the basis of the additional resources which our aid placed at their disposal, to maintain politically tolerable levels of consumption; to carry out programs of reconstruction and development needed to raise their over-all levels of production and gradually to reduce their dependence on United States aid; and, after June 1950, to speed up their rearmament programs in the interests of the common defense of the free world.

The point to emphasize, therefore, is that had we given less aid, the "dollar gap" would have been smaller; had we given more aid, it might have been larger. In short, the "dollar gap" is a measure of the difference between the amount of dollar goods and services that the United States, in order to achieve certain foreign policy objectives, has deemed it necessary for foreign countries to purchase, and the amount that they have been able to finance out of their own resources. The fact that foreign countries have maintained tight payments and trade restrictions during the postwar period against purchases in the United States, moreover, is an indication of the fact that there is also a *suppressed* or *latent* "dollar gap," i. e., that foreign countries have wanted to buy even more goods and services from us but could not do so because of insufficient means to pay for them.

Causes of the World Dollar Problem

As compared with before 1939, the postwar dollar-payments deficit of foreign countries as a whole has reflected a vastly enlarged demand for dollars to finance purchases in the United States. During this period the supply of dollars made available to them through United States purchases of goods and services abroad and through exports of private American capital has also risen sharply. In fact, in 1951 and 1952 the supply of dollars, thus defined, was about five times as large as the 1936-38 average; and, even after adjustment for the rise in prices in the United States, the supply of dollars was still twice as large as it was in 1936-38. The postwar dollar shortage has thus been wholly a matter of an *increased demand for dollars,* the reasons for which are outlined below.

Although the dollar-shortage problem has been essentially a world-wide phenomenon, it is misleading to generalize in global terms. *The core of the dollar problem has been centered in Western Europe;*[2] and the dollar problem of that area is of a complex sort that should be distinguished from the dollar problems of most other areas and countries.[3] The postwar dollar difficulties of Western Europe have fundamentally reflected the weakening of that area's position in the world economy, especially relative to the United States, as a result of the severe dislocations and losses caused by two world wars, and of structural changes in the pattern of world production and trade.

Western Europe's dollar-payments problem must first be examined against the background of the deterioration of its payments position vis-a-vis the world as a whole. During World War II Western Europe had to liquidate a substantial part of its overseas investments, the earnings from which had previously covered much of its traditional merchandise trade deficits. It also assumed large overseas debts during the war and in the early postwar years which had to be serviced. Its opportunities for earning overseas income from shipping and from other services (e. g., insurance and international banking) were also impaired by the war. Moreover, prices of Western European imports, consisting mainly of foodstuffs and raw materials, have been considerably higher, relative to the prices of its exports (mainly manufactured goods), than before the war. This adverse shift in Western Europe's "terms of trade" has meant that that area has had to export a correspondingly larger *volume* of exports to purchase a given *volume* of imports and has added to the over-all deterioration in its balance of payments. Another burden on Western Europe's postward balance of payments has been the heavier overseas expenditures on military account that it has had to

[2] Including the United Kingdom.

[3] The dollar-payments difficulties of most underdeveloped countries, for example, have mainly reflected the accelerated urge that they have had since the war to develop and diversify their economies and their attempt to do so at a rate faster than their available resources have permitted. This has led them to rely heavily on an expansion of bank credit as a means of financing their development programs, with marked inflationary results. These inflations have greatly enlarged the demand for imports from all sources (especially from the United States), and have absorbed resources for domestic production that would otherwise have been available for producing goods for export. As a result, many underdeveloped countries have had persisting difficulties in balancing their payments with the United States. A number of other foreign countries, even when in approximate balance or surplus in their over-all external payments, have also suffered from a dollar problem as a result of their inability to convert their surpluses in one direction (because of the inconvertibility of the currencies concerned) into gold or dollars needed to finance their traditional deficits with the United States.

carry out as compared with before the war, especially because of the French campaign in Indochina.

All this meant that Western Europe after the war was faced with the problem of having greatly to enlarge its merchandise exports to the rest of the world if it were to be able to finance even its prewar volume of imports. But the wartime dislocation and damage to its productive facilities, coupled with the heavy postwar demand on its available resources to meet the requirements of domestic consumption, reconstruction, and, later, rearmament, as well as the disruption to long-established overseas trade ties, made this task virtually impossible in the early postwar years. The strong inflationary pressures that prevailed in Western Europe, moreover, accentuated this task by drawing exportable supplies into the inflated home market and by increasing the demand for imports.

Western Europe's *over-all* balance-of-payments problem, the causes of which have been described above, has taken the form primarily of a *dollar* payments problem, largely because of structural changes in the pattern of world production and trade.

1. Compared with before the war Western Europe has had increased difficulties in obtaining from nondollar countries its requirements of basic foodstuffs and raw materials, notably bread grain, coarse grain, and vegetable oils and fats, in view of a shrinkage of such supplies available from these countries. Its dependence upon the United States (and certain other countries in the Western Hemisphere where payment has had to be made in dollars) has correspondingly increased. The inability of Western Europe to obtain needed supplies from nondollar areas has reflected: the political division of Europe and the greater demands of Eastern European countries for domestic goods, formerly exported, because of their large-scale industrialization programs; the relative shift in underdeveloped countries in general from agricultural to industrial production in keeping with their development programs; and, in many underdeveloped countries, inflation and increased population which have further tended to cause a larger domestic absorption of primary products that would otherwise be available for export. Western Europe has also had to turn, to a relatively greater degree than before the war, to the dollar area in order to satisfy its needs for heavy equipment, machinery, and manufactured goods which could not be obtained in adequate degree at home or in other foreign countries.

2. Western Europe has found it increasingly difficult, as compared with before the war, to earn dollars from its trade with primary-materials-producing countries outside the dollar area. Before the war it used to cover a large part of its dollar deficit with the dollars which it earned in this way. But after the war, despite the great increase in the supply of

dollars resulting from expanded United States imports of goods and services, the great bulk of those dollars accrued to countries in the Western Hemisphere where Western Europe's competitive position had always been weakest. The bulk of these dollars in turn has flowed back directly to the United States, not only because of the close trade ties of these countries with the United States, but more especially because the import demands of these countries have tended to focus more heavily on capital goods, raw materials, and foodstuffs of a sort which the United States has been best equipped to supply, and less heavily on manufactured consumer goods in which Western Europe has traditionally been strongest and most competitive.

Although the volume of Western Europe's aggregate exports has expanded very considerably since the war (in fact, by 1951 there had been an expansion of over 40 percent as compared with 1938), the bulk of the increase has gone to countries and areas where dollars could not on balance be earned (notably, to the sterling area and European dependent territories), rather than to third countries from which dollars could have been earned and to the dollar area itself. The diversion of so large a part of Europe's exports to the countries in its affiliated overseas currency areas has reflected the greater ease and profitability to exporters of selling in these countries, and the ability of the latter to run large trade deficits with Western Europe in view of their large accumulated holdings of sterling and the large volume of financial resources currently placed at their disposal by the metropolitan countries (notably, Britain and France) through capital movements and military expenditures.

3. Before the war, part of Western Europe's dollar deficit had been covered by sales to the United States of gold acquired from current gold output in the overseas countries associated with it, notably South Africa, Australia, and African territories. Between 1938 and 1951, however, the dollar value of gold production in these particular countries declined by approximately one-fifth and more than one-half of the reduced supply found its way into private hoards. Moreover, whereas the prices of United States export goods have more than doubled, the United States price of gold has remained fixed at $35 per fine ounce, thereby cutting in half both the dollar purchasing power of current gold production coming into official hands, as well as of existing monetary gold reserves. All this has greatly accentuated Western Europe's dollar-payment difficulties.

Very considerable progress has been made since 1945 towards world economic recovery and towards solving the world's dollar problem and the problem of imbalance in international payments in general. Aided in very large part by grants and loans of the United States Government, production abroad has risen markedly, inflationary pressures have abated, and the magnitude of the dollar problem has substantially been reduced. Foreign countries have also been able to rebuild their gold and dollar reserves from the low point reached in mid-1949; and to some degree they have been able to relax their trade and exchange controls against each other and against the United States.

1. World industrial production, excluding the United States and the Union of Soviet Socialist Republics, was in mid-1953 twice as high as in 1946 and about 50 percent above the 1938 level. Industrial production in Western Europe is nearly twice as high as it was in 1946. Agricultural production in Western Europe has not expanded as much, but it is almost 20 percent above prewar and much more above the immediate postwar level. The postwar process of physical reconstruction of productive facilities has been largely completed. Inventories have been rebuilt and "pipelines" have been refilled. The abnormal shortages of goods and of critical key materials which featured the early postwar years, as well as the abnormal demands on resources in general, are no longer in evidence, especially in Western Europe. Some progress has also been made in raising production levels in underdeveloped countries, thanks to the unusually large volume of imports which they have been able to finance in the postwar period; but the over-all internal economic situation in many of these countries is still unsatisfactory.

2. Inflationary trends throughout the world, which had so accentuated the dollar shortage in the early postwar years, and which were given a renewed impetus by the post-Korean boom, now have very substantially abated. This has reflected not only the greater availability of goods and the easing of the abnormal postwar and post-Korean demands but also since mid-1950 the resort by many countries, especially European ones, to "disinflationary" monetary and fiscal policies. As a result, European and other nondollar goods are now more competitive with dollar goods, a situation which was partly aided by the widespread currency devaluations of September 1949. Direct price controls have been increasingly abandoned in many foreign countries; there has been greater reliance on the price mechanism, and internal economies have become more flexible.

3. In large part because of the above mentioned developments, assisted as they were by foreign aid from the United States Government, there has been a remarkable drop in the "world's dollar deficit," as defined in an earlier section, during the postwar period as a whole. That deficit, which rose from $6.8 billion in 1946 to a peak of $9.7 billion in 1947, had declined to only $0.3 billion by 1950. Under the impact of post-Korean developments, it rose rather sharply in the last half of 1951 and

the first half of 1952, but it virtually has disappeared since the middle of 1952. This has been true with regard not only to the rest of the world as a whole but also to Western Europe. During 1953, in fact, the rest of the world has actually had a slight "payment surplus" with the United States.

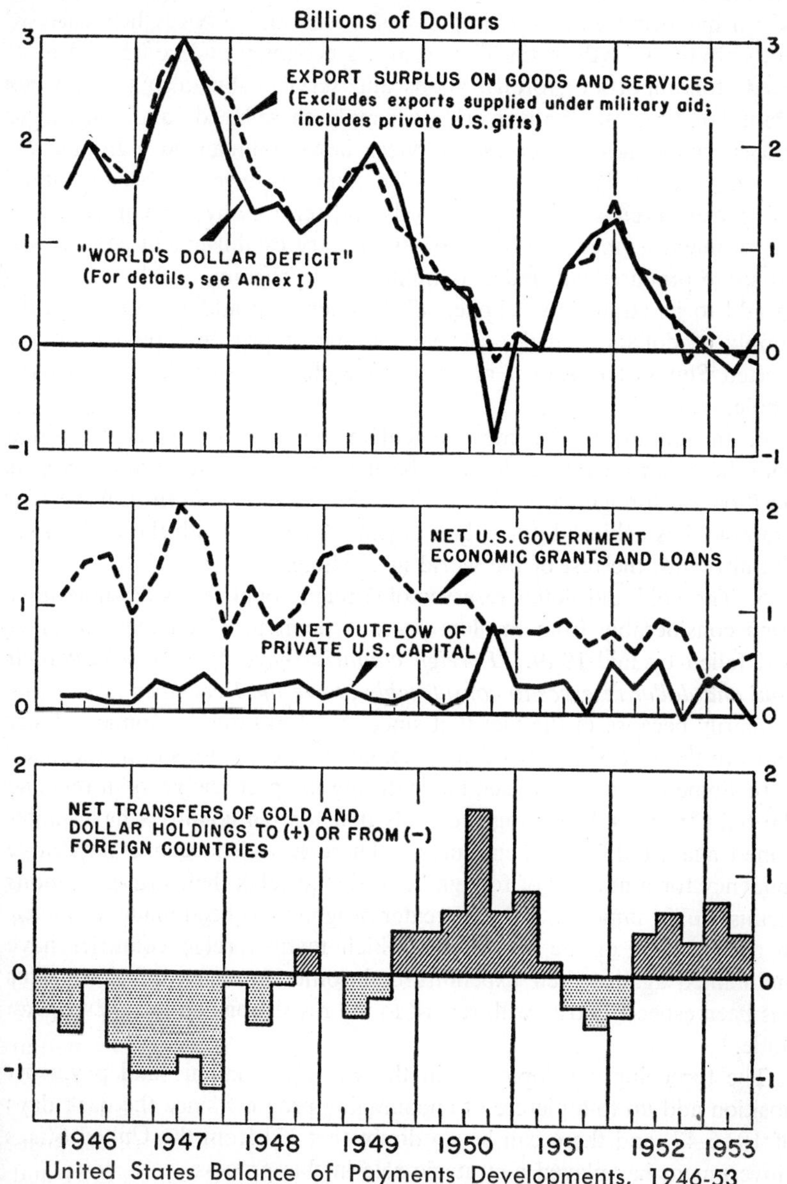

United States Balance of Payments Developments, 1946-53

This remarkable improvement in the world's payments balance with the United States between 1946 and 1953 has resulted entirely from increased United States imports of goods and services and not from a decline in our total "commercial" exports of goods and services; indeed, the latter rose somewhat between the two years. The great expansion which has occurred in our imports of goods and services has reflected not only the growth in the United States economy and consequently its needs for imports of foreign goods and services, but also the growing ability of the rest of the world to supply these needs and the higher prices which these goods and services have commanded. In the last few years the dollar earnings of foreign countries have also been enlarged by special purchases of foreign goods and services by the United States Government to meet the needs of its military establishment abroad and off-shore procurement under its military aid program, and by purchases to add to its strategic stockpile. The other item adding to the world's supply of dollars, namely, the net outflow of private capital from the United States, has shown no significant change over the period as a whole.

4. In addition to the improvement in the world's payments position with the dollar area, there has also been an improvement in the payments position of foreign countries with each other. Western Europe, for example, has achieved not only a payments balance with the dollar area but also with the rest of the world as a whole.

5. The gold and dollar reserves of foreign countries as a whole have risen considerably from the low postwar point to which these reserves had fallen by mid-1949. *Foreign countries have by now rebuilt their gold and dollar reserves to considerably above the December 1945 level,* primarily because of the fact that since mid-1949 our economic aid and loans to the rest of the world have exceeded the "world's dollar deficit."

6. Some progress has been made during the past few years in relaxing the tight trade and exchange controls that foreign countries have maintained against dollar expenditures. There has also been a noticeable tendency for a number of foreign countries to relax their *discriminations* against dollar imports. Much greater progress has been made, however, in a relaxation of the restrictions which many foreign countries have maintained against their expenditures in other foreign countries. This has been especially true with regard to the restrictions on intra-European trade.

The foregoing developments in the world's economic and payments position add up to a picture of encouraging progress since the dark days of 1946-47, and there can be no doubt that aid from the United States Government has played a strategic role in this process.

The fact remains, however, that there is still a concealed world dollar

The fact remains, however, that there is still a concealed world dollar problem of considerable magnitude. For one thing, the present statistical balance in the payments of foreign nations with the United States has been made possible only by continuing severe trade and payments controls of a discriminatory sort against imports of United States goods and services by foreign countries. If those controls were removed—and it has been one of the objectives of United States foreign economic policy that they should be removed—a "dollar gap" of substantial size undoubtedly would reappear. Secondly, the present statistical balance is based in part upon large-scale United States military expenditures abroad of a magnitude that cannot be expected to remain for long at their present high levels.

Part of the recent improvement in the dollar positions of foreign countries reflects continuing large-scale economic grants and loans by the United States Government which are not likely to continue indefinitely at their present levels. Moreover, the volume of foreign gold and dollar reserves is still believed inadequate to enable foreign countries safely to remove all discriminatory restrictions against United States goods and to restore the convertibility of their currencies. For these and other reasons the present payments situation, despite the progress made, calls for no complacency.

44. FOREIGN TRADE AND AGRICULTURE*

FOR AN introductory statement to this selection, see the headnote for Selection 43 on page 394.

AGRICULTURE has the same kind of interest in foreign trade as does every other group. As *producers,* farmers are interested in the development of broader markets for their products; as *consumers,* they desire to have available a wide variety of goods and services at reasonable prices.

To provide in abundance the many things that add up to an "American standard of living," it has long been recognized that we must specialize in our productive activities. Specialization, however, is of no purpose unless combined with its Siamese twin, trade.

The advantages to be gained from each person doing the job he knows best—farmer, merchant, mechanic, lawyer, doctor, etc.—are obvious. Generally apparent also are the advantages of specialization by region. Many commodities can be produced outside their usual areas only at great cost and a very considerable list not at all. Well known agricultural, mining, and industrial areas have emerged as a

* *Staff Papers;* presented to the Commission on Foreign Economic Policy, February, 1954 (Government Printing Office, 1954), pp. 148-53; 157-61.

result of the regional differences in soil, climate, location, and other factors. But there is little object in specializing—by occupation or region—unless there is an exchange of the results of such specialization. International trade merely permits the widespread realization of the benefits of specialization. These benefits accrue to agriculture as to other sectors of the economy.

Farmers' interest in trade, however, is not limited to agricultural commodities alone. A step-up in exports of nonagricultural products in which the United States enjoys production advantages allows expansion in these lines and thereby enlarges the domestic market for farm products. Furthermore, the availability of imported materials helps to hold down farm production costs by broadening sources of supply and providing items which otherwise would be available only at high cost or not at all.

Probably even more important than their interest as producers and consumers, however, is farmers' *interest as citizens* in the development of amicable relations between nations and economic progress throughout the world. Expansion of international trade is an extremely important ingredient in the recipe for economic progress for most nations. The wide range of natural resources found within the borders of the United States is an extremely rare occurrence. Few countries stand in so favorable a position.

The narrower a nation's economic base—the more specialized its resources—the greater is its dependence on international trade for improvement of living standards. Measures which restrict the ability of such nations to sell the limited types of goods produced with their specialized resources necessarily shrink their ability to purchase from other countries. It is understandable, therefore, that they may view such restrictions with grave concern. Insofar as the goodwill and co-operation of these nations are important to the future welfare of the United States, it is in the best interest of all our citizens that the channels of trade be so ordered that they aid, rather than hinder, economic progress.

Volume and Value of Agricultural Exports

United States agricultural exports have declined sharply from the record $4 billion reached in 1951-52. Nevertheless, they continue to play an important role in the markets for a number of farm commodities. In view of the high level of production and the rapid accumulation of stocks of several of our principal commodities, the decline has aroused widespread concern.

Totaling $2.8 billion in fiscal 1952-53, agricultural exports were off 30 percent from the previous year and were well below the $3.5 billion average of 1947-48 through 1951-52. Contributing to the sharp decline were the reduction in United States foreign economic aid, which at its peak in 1948-49 provided funds to pay for about two-thirds of our agricultural exports,[1] recovery of agricultural production in Western Europe, drawing down of inventories in importing countries as the supply situation eased, continued stringency in the supply of dollars available to some countries, and decline in prices below the level at which commodities were supported in the United States.

The value of agricultural exports since 1945 has been equal to about one-eighth of our cash farm income; the volume has accounted for the commodities produced on over 40 million acres, about one-tenth, of our cropland. Both measures are appreciably larger than in the pre-war years 1935-39 when, following the persistent decline of the twenties and the first half of the thirties, exports accounted for less than one-tenth of cash farm income and for the product of only 22 million acres of cropland (see Figure 1).

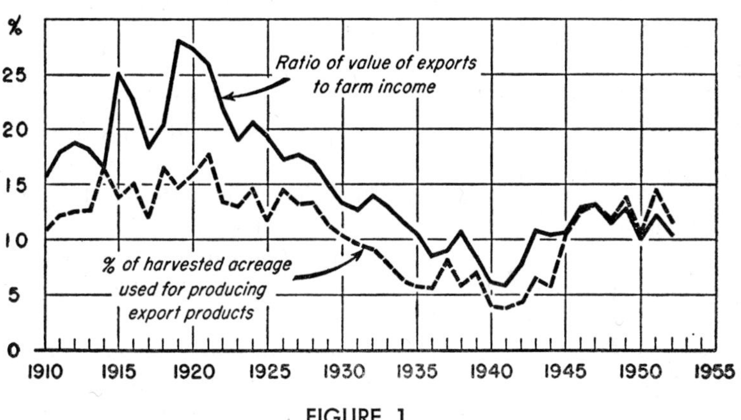

FIGURE 1

United States Agricultural Exports: Harvested Acreage and Relation of Value of Exports to Farm Income

The over-all value and quantity of agricultural exports, although useful measures, fail to indicate the high degree of dependence of a number of commodities on export outlets. In 1952, for example, we exported over one-half of our rice crop, two-fifths of our wheat crop, and one-fourth of our cotton and tobacco crops. Exports were important also for soybeans, barley, lard, tallow, raisins, prunes, grain sorghums, and a number of other commodities.

Wheat and cotton, each grown on about one-fifth of the nation's farms,

[1] Such funds accounted for about one-seventh of our agricultural exports in 1952-53.

account for about three-fourths of the acreage from which agricultural commodities are exported. It does not follow, however, that the farmer interest in exports is confined only to the producers of these crops. Although agricultural resources are sufficiently specialized to result in regional specialization in certain kinds of production, these specialized areas blend into one another and very substantial acreages can be readily shifted from one product to another. A severe cutback in cotton acreage, for example, would release land which could be shifted in some areas to peanuts; in other areas, to soybeans; and in many areas to feed crops, pasture, and livestock. Land that is well adapted to corn usually can be used effectively for other feed crops or soybeans, and much wheat land can be used for grazing or for the production of feed grains and livestock. Thus dairy, hog, and beef producers may well be concerned with developments affecting markets for wheat and cotton. A substantial shrinkage of outlets for any one of the widely grown crops affects not only that crop but many other commodities as well. The effects of shifts in markets for specialty crops, grown on much smaller acreage, would be similar but the impacts on other crops and areas would be less widespread.

The physical volume of agricultural exports since the end of World War II, although far above the average for the 1930's, has been about the same as in most of the years between 1900 and 1930. Reflecting the inflation of prices, however, the value of exports has been much higher than in most of the earlier years (see Figure 2).

Despite the large fluctuations in value of agricultural exports and the lesser fluctuations in volume, there has been a decided downward trend

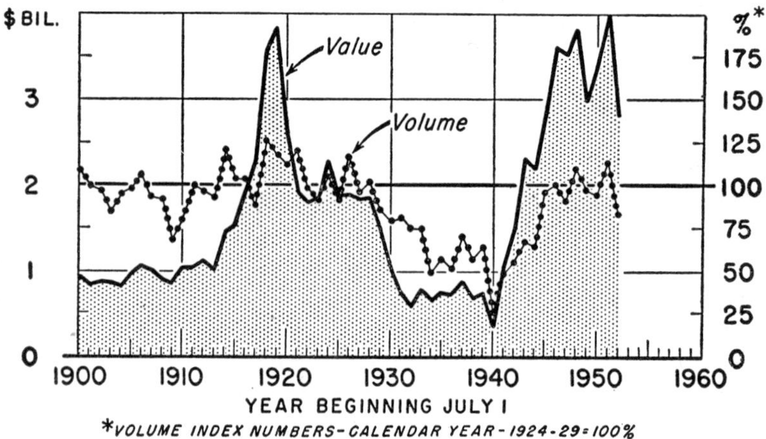

FIGURE 2

Value and Volume of United States Agricultural Exports

in their proportion of total United States exports. Prior to 1890 farm products accounted for about four-fifths of our total exports. By 1910 they had dropped to one-half and in 1930 they accounted for about one-third. They declined further in relative importance during the thirties, but in postwar years through 1951-52 they ranged between about one-fourth and one-third of the total (see Figure 3). The broad decline in relative importance has been due primarily to industrial development and the expanding domestic market for farm products. However, measures

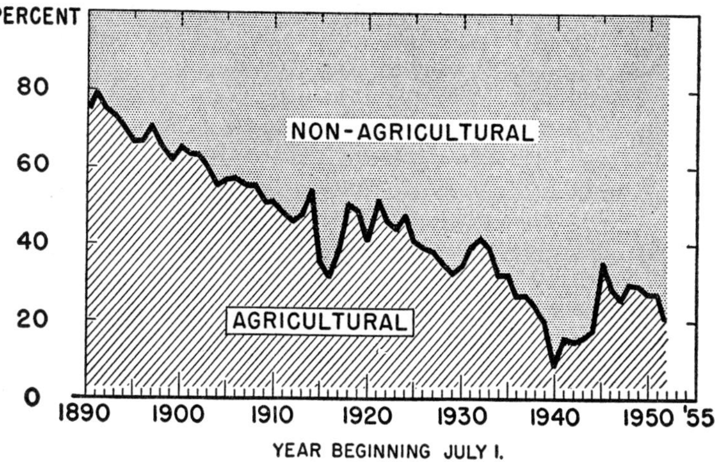

FIGURE 3
United States Agricultural Exports

which (a) have restricted United States imports, thereby limiting the ability of other nations to earn dollars, and (b) have raised domestic prices of farm products above the world level have also played a role in this trend. Although exports of agricultural commodities have accounted for a declining proportion of our total exports, foreign markets nevertheless continue to provide important outlets for United States farm products.

Agricultural Imports

Agricultural imports have increased as the United States economy has grown, but the rise has been at a nominal rate. The physical volume in 1940, for example, was only 8 percent above the 1924-29 average, and the 1950-52 volume showed a gain of only 12 percent over the pre-depression years.

As with exports, the share of agricultural products in the total import picture has been a declining one, especially since 1940. Here again, the major reason is the rise in relative importance of non-agricultural goods and services as our economic progress has permitted a rise in living standards.

The growth in imports of agricultural commodities not produced in this country has been somewhat greater than for those which supplement supplies of domestically produced items. These complementary or "noncompetitive" imports—coffee, rubber, cocoa, carpet wool, bananas, pepper, tea, and the like—constitute about two-thirds of total agricultural imports. These commodities are of interest primarily for their contribution to the variety of goods available for consumption. In the so-called "competitive" or "supplementary" group the leading items are wool, sugar, and hides and skins, which together account for nearly one-half of the group total.

The tendency to focus attention primarily on the export side of trade probably gives a misplaced emphasis. It reflects the fact that individually our interest as producers commonly overshadows our interest as consumers. Basically, however, the reason for exporting is to be able to import—to be able to buy that which we need but which we produce in inadequate volume or not at all. Agriculture, therefore, has an interest in all programs that affect our imports and thereby influence the ability of nations to earn dollars, since the size of the potential export market for farm products is rather rigidly circumscribed by this factor.

CONFLICTS BETWEEN DOMESTIC AGRICULTURAL PROGRAMS AND OUR INTERNATIONAL AIMS AND OBJECTIVES

A primary goal of domestic agricultural policy is that of improving economic opportunity for farm people by raising farm income and increasing price and income stability. This goal need not conflict with the objectives of our international economic policies.

Greater freedom of trade can contribute to a higher level of living for farmers as well as other groups in the United States by achieving a more effective use of the resources of the "free world." This is consistent with the goal of domestic farm policy.

An expanded volume of international trade may contribute also to greater price and income stability for agriculture. With broad markets and supply areas, the effects of supply changes in any one area are frequently offset by opposite changes in other areas.

Similarly, although possibly to a lesser degree, demand changes may tend to balance out as markets encompass larger areas. It must be recognized, however, that when large changes in demand have occurred they usually have extended over much of the world and have caused wide swings in prices of agricultural commodities and in farm income. Instability originating from this source, other than that associated with wars, probably can be attacked most effectively by measures designed to maintain high levels of employment and income generally.

The United States has provided price supports on various farm products and other aids to agriculture in the past two decades. During the 1930's these programs were intended to raise farm prices and incomes from their depression lows. Farm exports during the depression were at a relatively low level. The outbreak of World War II soon strengthened both domestic and foreign demand. Price supports were not needed to raise market prices during the war period, but were used to provide incentives for farmers to engage in all-out production without fear of a sudden market collapse. Price supports, which previously had been at lower levels, were raised to 90 percent of parity (a ratio between the indexes of prices received and prices paid by farmers) on a wide range of farm products in 1942. Farmers responded magnificently to the call for more output, with the result that not only was the domestic demand met effectively but sizable amounts were available for export to our allies. During the war and much of the postwar period, price supports were largely inoperative because other forces held prices above support levels. The lend-lease program played an important role in moving wheat and other farm products overseas during the war; foreign aid programs since the war did likewise; and the upsurge of demand after the Korean outbreak had a similar effect.

As agriculture in Western Europe has recovered and United States foreign aid has centered more on mutual defense, exports have slackened. However, price supports have been continued at 90 percent of parity on "basic" crops (wheat, cotton, corn, rice, peanuts, and tobacco) and on some other commodities. These have encouraged farmers to maintain production at or near record levels. *The price-support system has become a price-fixing system.* In consequence, the Commodity Credit Corporation owns or has under loan large stocks of such products as wheat, cotton, corn, wool, butter, cheese, dried milk, and certain vegetable oils. Additions to these stocks are continuing, and the end of accumulation is not in sight. The Congress has extended present supports through 1954, after which variable supports will come into operation unless current rates are extended again. The 90 percent support rates, originally provided for two years following the end of hostilities in World War II, have been extended on several occasions since 1945.

Conflicts between agricultural programs and our international aims lie not with the objectives but with the means used to attain them.

They arise in no small degree from the widespread acceptance of parity prices as goals of agricultural programs and from rigid supports at 90 percent of parity, regardless of quantities produced.

Once a specific set of prices has been established as a goal, *domestic programs come into sharp conflict with international aims whenever world prices fall below those in domestic markets.* In this situation, our products tend to be priced out of world markets and any excess of supply above domestic requirements is *accumulated as surplus stocks.*

Such withdrawal from world markets invites *other areas to expand output* to fill the void. This was evident in the 1930's, for example, on cotton.

Domestic production meanwhile may need to be controlled in order to provide some limit to the cost of the price-support program.

Imports are attracted by the high domestic prices. If allowed to enter they tend to increase domestic stocks, thereby adding to the difficulties and/or cost of making the support program effective. Objection arises also to allowing imports to share in the supported market. This leads to demands for *added restrictions on imports.*

Congress foresaw this result and provided authority for the imposition of such measures when imports threaten to interfere with farm programs, under Section 22, Agricultural Adjustment Act of 1933.[2]

Because some Members of Congress apparently thought Section 22 was not used by the Administration with full force, Section 104 of the Defense Production Act was added to make embargoes, quotas, and other restrictions mandatory under specified circumstances for the period this act was in force. Expiration of the latter legislation in mid-1953 has led to renewed reliance on Section 22, as further revised and strengthened.[3]

As domestic surpluses accumulate, *interest in expanding exports to* dispose of them grows.

[2] This section was adopted initially on August 24, 1935 and provides, in part, that "whenever . . . any article or articles are being or practically certain to be imported into the United States under such conditions and in such quantities as to render or tend to render ineffective or materially interfere with any program or operation . . . undertaken by the Department of Agriculture . . . with respect to any agricultural commodity or product thereof, or to reduce substantially the amount of any product processed in the United States from any agricultural commodity . . . with respect to which any such program or operation is being undertaken . . ." and . . . "the President finds the existence of such facts, he shall by proclamation impose such fees not in excess of 50 per centum ad valorem or such quantitative limitations on any article . . . as he finds and declares . . . to be necessary. . . ." As amended in the Trade Agreements Extension Act of 1951, Section 22 also provides that "no trade agreement or other international agreement heretofore or hereafter entered into by the United States shall be applied in a manner inconsistent with the requirements of this section."

[3] The Trade Agreements Extension Act of 1953 added the following to subsection (b) of Section 22: "In any case where the Secretary of Agriculture de-

This brings resort to subsidies to make export sales below domestic prices. Such a program of dumping often is viewed with disfavor by producers in receiving countries and may *lead to retaliatory action.* The United States itself has employed countervailing duties in some instances of this sort (authorized in Section 201 of the Anti-Dumping Act, 1921, and Section 303 of the Tariff Act of 1930). Nor is the adverse reaction to dumping limited to countries receiving the surpluses. Other exporting countries may feel that such action encroaches unfairly on their markets. This can engender ill will and result in a proliferation of retaliatory action in respect to other goods and markets.

Thus, domestic programs which result in attempts to insulate them against imports, bring into use practices which the United States has been urging other nations to abandon in the interest of an expanding multilateral trade of mutual benefit to all participants.

This brings the conflict into the clear. To make our European aid program effective in strengthening the economies of overseas countries and to enable them to acquire the dollar exchange they need for buying commodities from us, we have urged them to increase their productivity, to integrate their production more effectively, to adapt themselves to exporting, and to remove some of their trade barriers to imports.

The position of the United States as the leader of the free world focuses the spotlight on this conflict between our domestic agricultural programs and our international objectives, particularly overseas. It is not yet apparent that Americans generally appreciate its extent or seriousness. There is an evident tendency to view our domestic programs as paramount and to underrate the tremendous stake which our Nation has in effective international cooperation to maintain the peace and to build a successful mutual security program to protect the free world.

45. WHAT FOREIGN TRADE MEANS TO INDIANA*

MANY textbooks and teachers of economics preach free trade as a desirable goal from both the economic and the political point of

termines and reports to the President with regard to any article or articles that a condition exists requiring emergency treatment, the President may take immediate action under this section without awaiting the recommendations of the Tariff Commission, such action to continue in effect pending the report and recommendations of the Tariff Commission and action thereon by the President."

* Carroll Kilpatrick, "Unexpected Evidence on Foreign Trade," *Harper's Magazine,* February, 1954, pp. 61-64. Reprinted by permission of the author.

The author (1913——) is an editorial writer for *The Washington Post and Times-Herald.* Former Nieman Fellow at Harvard. Author of *Roosevelt and Daniels—A Friendship in Politics.*

view. However, there are other groups that are equally strongly committed to the maintenance of protection. In the United States these latter groups have often been well organized and have maintained strong lobbies in Congress. Partly as a result of such pressures many Senators and Representatives have lent their support to tariff programs probably with little or no knowledge of the over-all effect of such programs on the economy. The following selection presents the results of a study made by one Congressman who decided to ascertain for himself the effects of a high tariff program on the residents of his particular district.

A FEW months ago a freshman Republican Congressman from Indiana decided to try to find out what, if any, effect foreign trade has on his District. From the day he arrived in Washington for the opening of the 83rd Congress, D. Bailey Merrill of Evansville had been buffeted by pleas of free traders on one hand and high-tariff advocates on the other. Lobbyists representing every point of view had begun knocking on his door almost before he could take his oath of office.

After some weeks of this, and after listening to the impassioned debate on extension of the Reciprocal Trade Agreements Act, Merrill appealed to the Library of Congress. Two staff men from the Library's Legislative Reference Service—Howard S. Piquet and Howard T. Lamar—were assigned to his project.

As a result, we now have a detailed case study showing exactly what foreign trade means in one fairly typical Midwestern constituency. It is the *only* comprehensive study of its kind and it will be invaluable when the great national debate on trade policy erupts again after the Randall Commission makes its recommendations for a new foreign economic policy.

The seventeen-man Randall Commission has been wrestling with trade and currency issues since last fall and has already held debates throughout the country. But these have been mostly between people speaking either purely theoretically or on the basis of only their own personal business experience. The Merrill study is something else.

The Eighth Indiana, the subject of the study, is an eleven-county district of 393,000 people in the southernmost part of the state. It has 225,000 city dwellers and a rural population of 168,000. Like almost any other area in the country, it has among these people determined free traders and stubborn protectionists. A leading furniture manufacturer in the district, for example, recently argued for a high tariff wall against all countries except those "that are founded on a true and absolute democracy." Another furniture maker from the same area, arguing for low tariffs, replied that trade with all nations should be on an equal basis. "When one nation is out of balance in relation to the others," he said, "the people suffer."

Both Indiana's Senators—Republicans Homer E. Capehart and William E. Jenner—are conservative protectionists of the old school. But Congressman Merrill's study shows clearly that if they were successful in erecting a high tariff wall around the United States, there would be immediate unemployment on the farms and in the factories of the Eighth District of Indiana. In fact, a severe depression could easily follow.

THE FARMER'S STAKE

Take agriculture first. Almost one-fifth of the District's population lives on farms, and 12 per cent of the labor force works on them. The farmers produce corn, soybeans, tobacco, and other field crops that were worth $15,169,000 in 1949, the last year for which detailed statistics are available. Livestock production the same year brought them $31,420,000.

"Most of the major agricultural commodities produced in the Eighth District are important export commodities," the Library of Congress report said. "Such products as corn, small grains (including wheat, oats, barley, and rye), soybeans, tobacco, milk and cream, eggs, and hogs not only account for the major portion of the District's agricultural production, but are among the most important agricultural commodities exported by the United States."

The District's wheat crop in 1949 brought $2,780,000—and 33.5 per cent of all United States wheat produced in 1949 was exported. Soybean production brought District farmers $3,013,000 in 1949—and 25.1 per cent of the nation's soybean production was sold overseas. Eighth District farmers produced $954,000 worth of tobacco in 1949—about 25.1 per cent of the United States tobacco production was exported. The corn crop in the District was worth $5,272,000—and 3.5 per cent of the nation's corn was exported. (Actually, a much larger percentage of the corn found its way abroad in the form of meat products, for most corn is fed to livestock.)

It is not possible to give exact figures on dairy exports because of inadequate statistics. While most of the District's dairy products were undoubtedly sold locally, in 1949-51 more than half the dried whole milk produced in this country was exported, as were 13.5 per cent of the condensed milk, 7.1 per cent of the evaporated milk, and 6.3 per cent of the cheese. So it is clear that District dairymen too have a stake in foreign trade. So do the hog producers, who took in $10,680,000 in 1949. Their precise stake is also uncertain because of inadequate statistics, but one per cent of the pork and 22 per cent of the lard produced by American farmers are sold abroad. Egg production brought Eighth District farmers $3,526,000 in 1949—and 2.7 per cent of domestic egg production was exported.

The effect of foreign trade on District minerals is not so clear as it is on agriculture. About 3,300 men in the District (2 per cent of the labor force) are employed in the production of minerals; two-thirds of them in coal mining. They have been producing 5.5 million tons of bituminous annually at a time when 10 per cent of America's soft coal has been exported.

Petroleum production brings about $15,000,000 annually to the District. Coal and oil producers elsewhere in the country have complained bitterly that they are subject to severe competition from imports of crude and fuel oil. The Library of Congress study found, however, that the Eighth District is not materially affected either by exports or imports of coal and oil, and it concluded that on balance producers seem to share to a greater extent in coal exports than in the competitive impact of fuel oil.

JOBS FOR FACTORY WORKERS

Manufacturing is the most important economic activity in the Eighth District. The value of manufactures in 1947, when the last Census of Manufactures was taken, was about $250,000,000. The following table shows the 1950 breakdown of employment:

Industry	*Number of Employees*
Machinery	15,896
Furniture and lumber	8,955
Foods and related products	5,277
Motor vehicles	2,073
Chemicals	2,473
Fabricated metals	2,179
Apparel and related products	2,105
TOTAL	39,959

Evansville, the largest city in the District, is the world's largest refrigeration center. The significant fact for this industry is that 13 per cent of all refrigerators produced in the United States in 1952 were exported. Servel, Inc., of Evansville, which employs more than 10,000 refrigerator workers, reported that every type of refrigeration equipment it manufactures is exported.

Furniture and lumber producers export some of their products, but of the four District companies that expressed concern over imports, three were in this field. (The fourth, a small cement manufacturer, said he had had trouble from import competition before World War II but none since.) Three lumber and furniture men said that competition is not serious now, but they were worried about the future. One of them, a manufacturer of single-ply face veneers, said imports "will eventually become serious." Another, a manufacturer of fancy veneer, said he faced the possibility of competition from imported mahogany veneers; and the third, a plywood manufacturer, said imports of thin plywood, while not directly competitive with his product, had forced some other thin plywood manufacturers "to go after our customers for relief."

In the food products field, the Mead Johnson Company, which employs, 1,100 workers to make baby-formula products, vitamins, and nutritious foods, reported that at least 10 per cent of its sales are for export.

The 3,073 auto workers, chiefly in assembly plants of Chrysler, Briggs Manufacturing Company, and the Hercules Body Corporation, know that about 5 per cent of American passenger cars are exported. Also in this group are farm-machinery manufacturers, 12 per cent of whose output is exported. The Bucyrus-Erie Company of Evansville, manufacturers of road-building and heavy construction equipment, reported that between 40 and 50 per cent of its production is for export.

In chemicals, the Colgate-Palmolive-Peet Company plant in Clarksville reported that they counted little on exports, but depended heavily on the import of such items as coconut oil, palm oil, olive oil, talcum, and crude glycerine.

A leading wholesale druggist in the District explained that though he does not import directly, he sells imported merchandise. "We feel quite strongly," he added, "on the free trade side of the question."

"Among the products manufactured in the District," the researchers concluded, "there are no conspicuous instances where imports are injurious to domestic producers." Or, if there are, the Library team was unable to find them.

On the contrary, it found "other manufacturers in the District who, while not producing directly for export markets, are vitally affected by exports. For example, the expansion of the refrigeration industry has influenced the growth of a number of metal-working industries in Evansville, including metal stamping and fabricating plants, furnishing parts and fittings for refrigerator cabinets, along with a variety of other metal parts and supplies for other kinds of manufacturing and assembly plants. . . .

"Such establishments as railway companies, motor transport concerns, warehouses, banks, and insurance companies all profit from foreign trade. Several hundred in nonmanufacturing enterprises are directly dependent upon foreign trade for their livelihood. These include railroad engineers, brakemen, switchmen, and mechanics, truck drivers, office workers, and warehouse employees."

FACTS VS. PREJUDICE

Expansion of foreign trade would inevitably mean "increased development and economic growth for the Eighth District," the Library of Congress researchers concluded. By the same token, contraction of foreign trade would mean the reverse. It would not only injure those industries that depend upon exports, it would fail to give substantial aid to the few producers who want protection—for some of these are high-cost manufacturers who suffer as much from more efficient domestic industries in related fields as they do from foreign competition.

Moreover, more workers in the Eighth District are employed in the manufacture of refrigeration products alone than in all the industries that might benefit from tariff protection together.[1] If there were layoffs in the refrigerator, automobile, and construction-machinery industries, and lower farm prices, as a result of the loss of export markets, the consumption of coal, oil, and gas would be cut.

Perhaps the most significant thing about the Eighth District study is its substantial refutation of the popular argument that only the mammoth corporations of the country benefit from foreign trade. Clearly, most of the industries in the Eighth District that are dependent upon exports for their margin of profit are small companies.

The consumer's interest was not considered in the study, but he is the one who should benefit most from competitive international trade. Neither was the security interest of the United States. But the expansion of the market for American industry means a consequent increase in the economic and military strength of the nation. The interests of our allies were not considered, but the development of the widest possible area of economic freedom clearly would strengthen the nations on whom we must rely in any future conflict.

Another study somewhat similar to this one but on a less intensive

[1] There are 13,000 refrigerator workers and 12,000 workers in the coal mines, the oil fields, and the furniture and lumber industries.

scale was completed a short time ago in the Eighteenth District of Pennsylvania. The Pennsylvania study, conducted by the United States Council of the International Chamber of Commerce, was an attempt to find out whether Representative Richard M. Simpson (R), the Eighteenth District Congressman, actually was representing the best interests of his constituents in his crusade for protectionism. It found that he was not; that if he had his way, he would do his District more harm than good.

Many detailed studies like these are needed to fortify Senators and Representatives against the special pleas of producers who want protection without regard to the effect on the community as a whole. During the recent Congressional recess Representative Merrill continued his study, interviewing scores of persons and double-checking the experts' findings. Now he is convinced that "mutually profitable world commerce is essential for world peace" and for the welfare of the Eighth District. Unlike many of his fellow Congressmen, he is able to speak on the basis of knowledge rather than from prejudice or what might have been true half a century ago.

---

46. TARIFF CUTS: WHO GETS HURT? *

MUCH LIKE the proverbial blind men describing an elephant each had touched from a different vantage point, economic observors have made many different explanations to describe the effects of tariff cuts upon our economy. Our author below supplies evidence which indicates that the effects may be many and varied depending upon where and when the tariff cuts are made.

IN A World War II cartoon, Bill Mauldin's unkempt Willie remarks that his foxhole is the most important spot in the world—because he is in it. Many businessmen, under fire from foreign competition and urged by free traders to crawl out of their tariff-protected shelters, feel somewhat the same way. They are puzzled or angered by the bland assertion that, in the long run, they too would benefit from freer world trade. From where they sit, a good solid tariff barrier looks far more important, and often it is. What free traders too frequently fail to realize is that protectionists are usually motivated, not by chauvinism or cussedness, but by genuine fear of injury.

* Reprinted from the April, 1954 issue of *Fortune* Magazine by special permission of the Editors; copyright, Time, Inc.

The fact is, tariff reductions *would* injure a certain number of American businesses and employees. Indeed, tariff cuts are worth striving for only on the assumption that there *are* some products other countries can make better and more cheaply than we can. The question that has not had enough attention is how many U.S. firms and workers would be hurt—and how much. The general, or national, pros and cons of the tariff have been well hashed over. What is needed now is more concentration on the specific cases and arguments.

The protectionists no less than the free traders are prone to indulge in generalities. The protectionists warn that any substantial increase in imports would paralyze the U.S. economy or jeopardize the national defense. Actually only one quantitative study of the probable impact of free trade has been made. In *Aid, Trade, and the Tariff,* Dr. Howard Piquet of the Library of Congress computed that suspension of all U.S. import duties would have increased imports in 1951 by a maximum of $1.8 billion, or 17 per cent of the import volume that year—an amount equivalent to less than 1 per cent of the U.S. gross national product. Using Piquet's figures, the Randall Commission staff estimated that a 50 per cent cut in present tariff rates might displace 100,000 U.S. workers all together. More than twice that number are laid off *every month* in the U.S., even in periods of rising employment, and most of them quickly find other work.

But the Piquet-Randall estimates do not purport to be more than informed guesses. To get any clear idea of how a more liberal trade policy might affect protected industries, individual companies must be studied, for the degree of tariff protection and vulnerability varies widely from industry to industry. Here, therefore, is a close look at three individual corporations—an appraisal of how each is being affected by imports now and an estimate of how each might be affected by the reduction or elimination of existing duties.

One of the three probably would be hurt but not irreparably; another might conceivably be put out of business by suspension of duties; and the third would be affected hardly at all. All three corporations, however, have led their respective industries in their fights for stiffer trade barriers and they share a conviction that any lowering of tariffs would seriously weaken the U.S. economy. The three: Bausch & Lomb Optical Co., of Rochester, New York, the only fully integrated U.S. optical manufacturer (1953 sales: $51 million); Homer Laughlin China Co., of Newell, West Virginia, the world's largest manufacturer of earthenware (1953 sales: $11 million); and Monsanto Chemical Co., of St.

Louis, the sixth-largest U.S. chemical manufacturer (1953 sales: $341 million).

I. BAUSCH & LOMB: ESSENTIAL

The $43-million Bausch & Lomb Optical Co. is a prime example of a firm that can legitimately claim it should be protected, but has more difficulty proving it needs to be. B. & L. is beyond question a vital defense producer. It is not only one of the Defense Department's major suppliers of range finders, fire-control instruments, aerial photography and mapping devices, airplane observation domes, binoculars, and laboratory equipment, but is also a major supplier of optical glass and lenses for other optical manufacturers. Since B. & L. is the only fully integrated U.S. optical manufacturer, it is the only domestic firm able to make a number of war-critical specialty prisms, lenses, and instruments.

At present B. & L.'s products are protected by duties averaging 40 per cent. Despite this seemingly substantial barrier, B. & L. has had to contend with rising imports of German, Italian, and Japanese microscopes and binoculars in recent years. The company insists that any substantial reduction in present tariff rates would almost certainly open the market to a number of other foreign optical and ophthalmic instruments and lenses that now come in only in small quantities. And, the argument goes, the elimination of any one of B. & L.'s interrelated product lines would very likely cripple the entire company. *Ergo:* any reduction of duties on optical equipment would be detrimental to the national security of the U.S.

That foreign competition in binoculars and microscopes has cut into B. & L.'s sales is a matter of record. Japanese prism binoculars, usually advertised as "B. & L. type," sell in the U.S. for about a quarter of the B. & L. price—$40 vs. $155. In 1953, 135,000 of these Japanese "imitations" were sold here. Largely as a result of rising imports, Bausch & Lomb's unit sales of binoculars have been halved since 1947, when some 12,000 pairs were sold, and even B. & L.'s dollar share of the domestic market has been cut from three-fourths to less than a fifth.

B. & L.'s microscope sales have been hard hit too. Imports of laboratory-type microscopes from Germany, Italy, and Japan rose from less than 1,000 in 1948 to over 5,700 in 1953. In that same period B. & L.'s unit sales dropped by 60 per cent. B. & L. will not divulge dollar sales figures for individual products but it seems probable that B. & L. sales of laboratory microscopes during the same period slipped from over $4 million a year to less than $2 million. Foreign competition has hurt Bausch & Lomb not only in the domestic market but in the profitable and expanding Latin-American market as well. There optical instruments of foreign manufacture undersell B. & L. products by 25 to 40 per cent.

Differences in labor costs, of course, are primarily responsible for the wide price differentials. According to B. & L.'s Vice President L. B. McKinley, wages absorb 55 to 60 cents of each B. & L. sales dollar. German and Italian wages average only one-quarter as high as Bausch & Lomb's and Japanese wages only one-ninth as high.

The wage disadvantage cannot be offset by improved productive processes, McKinley claims, since the limited demand for each product makes it uneconomical to use mass-production methods. As a result, the revival of German, Italian, and Japanese competition has almost completely wiped out Bausch & Lomb's export sales, and B. & L.'s Executive Vice President Carl Hallauer thinks the U.S. should prevail on Latin-American countries to allocate their imports and thus assure U.S. firms a quota in these markets.

So far as imports of binoculars and microscopes into the U. S. are concerned, the company professes that if they are permitted to continue at current levels B. & L. may eventually be forced to abandon the manufacturer of all optical instruments. For microscopes and binoculars have traditionally been B. & L.'s bread-and-butter items. The substantial markup on these products has helped pay the overhead on less profitable prestige and specialty items. A progressive decline in microscope and binocular sales, moreover, would scatter much of B. & L.'s skilled labor force, which may be needed for defense expansion.

The Other Lens

If an industry as essential as the optical industry were really in danger, certainly some means would have to be found to ensure its survival. But despite the sharp drop in sales of binoculars and laboratory microscopes, Bausch & Lomb's total sales and profits have actually improved since 1948, the year imports began to grow troublesome. B. & L. sales were one-third higher last year than in 1948. Employment was up more than 25 per cent (not counting overtime), and the company's net earnings were up 80 per cent. In fact B. & L.'s 1953 sales of $51 million and net of $1,500,000 were the second-best peacetime figures in B. & L.'s hundred-year existence; they were exceeded only in 1952, when sales topped $52 million and net was almost $1,700,000.

To be sure, defense business has accounted for a good part of the company's recent sales growth. Government deliveries rose from an estimated $2 million in 1948 to nearly $10 million in 1952. But this business has already started to decline; defense sales dropped to about $8 million last year. In any event defense orders have not been solely responsible for B. & L.'s recent prosperity.

Bausch & Lomb has most successfully met the threat of foreign competition by developing new products and improving old ones. Its binocular division, for example, is now marketing a new non-fogging telescopic rifle sight, and a 60-mm. telescope half the size of earlier models that sells for less than half the former price. Bausch & Lomb also makes lenses for CinemaScope and for the Polaroid Land camera. The basic skills used in making these products are essentially the same as those required for binocular assembly; thus war skills are preserved intact.

Despite the sharp drop in sales of laboratory microscopes, moreover, B. & L. actually sold more microscopes last year than in 1948. This was due primarily to a big increase in sales of industrial microscopes and partly to rising sales of inexpensive "student microscopes" to high schools and colleges.

Also favorable to B. & L. is the fact that optics is a genuine growth industry; new equipment and new applications are turning up all the time. There is the echelle spectrograph, for example, which permits rapid identification of any elements present in a material in proportions as minute as one part in a million. B. & L. expects this instrument to make the analytic techniques now used in the U. S. chemical industry obsolete.

In the U. S. market, finally, Bausch & Lomb enjoys one general advantage over foreign competitors. Industrial customers usually prefer to buy from U. S. firms, even though their prices are higher, because domestic firms can more readily supply technical advice and services.

Galileo's Influence

If tariff rates on optical goods were lowered, B. & L. would undoubtedly have to contend with foreign competition in a number of lines besides microscopes and binoculars. Within limits, such competition might be healthy, at least from the standpoint of consumers—and taxpayers. The fact that an Italian firm, Officine Galileo, won some government microscope contracts, for example, persuaded Bausch & Lomb and American Optical to reduce their government bids by 10 to 20 per cent (they had been basing them on retail prices).

What if B. & L. had absolute protection from foreign competition? Because of the industry's defense role, Britain has banned practically all imports of optical equipment since the end of World War I. The result: Britian has lagged seriously behind the U. S. and Germany in optical development.

As a vital and unique U. S. resource, B. & L. can legitimately demand protection against any foreign competition that is really threatening its survival. But there is some evidence that such foreign competition as B. & L. has so far faced has had the effect of stimulating and strengthening the company. Should that situation change, open subsidy, rather than the concealed subsidy of the tariff, is the way to preserve this company and its unique productive facilities.

II. HOMER LAUGHLIN CHINA: FRAGILE

Unlike Bausch & Lomb, the Homer Laughlin China Co., of Newell, West Virginia, would unquestionably be hard hit by any substantial tariff reduction. Were duties removed entirely, the company might even be wiped out. Although protected by a 75 per cent duty, Homer Laughlin is already feeling the effect of the recovery of the Japanese dinnerware industry. Since 1948, imports of Japanese china have increased from \$2 million to \$5 million. In the same period Homer Laughlin's sales have declined almost one-third—from an estimated \$16 million to \$11 million. A family-owned corporation, Homer Laughlin publishes no sales or profit figures, but industry sources estimate that its net profits in the past five years have dropped from approximately \$500,000 to \$100,000. Employment has dropped from 3,000 to 2,200.

All this has happened, according to H. L.'s Secretary-Treasurer Joseph M. Wells, because Japanese fine china is being sold here at prices not far above Homer Laughlin's prices for ordinary earthenware. In one New York department store, for example, five-piece place settings of Japanese china sell for as little as \$3.99, as compared with \$2.90 for one of Homer Laughlin's higher-priced earthenware patterns.

The biggest cost factor in pottery making, of course, is labor. In Homer Laughlin's case it accounts for about two-thirds of total production costs. Since Japanese pottery wages are only about one-tenth as high as Homer Laughlin's, the company finds the differential hard to overcome. It has tried to offset this, says Mr. Wells, by installing laborsaving machinery, but so far has been able to narrow the yawning wage gap by only a little.

To date, only Homer Laughlin's department-store sales have been seriously affected by imports from Japan. These sales have fallen two-thirds since 1948. Thus far, however, Japanese dinnerware has hardly penetrated Homer Laughlin's most important markets: the variety chains, mail-order houses, and premium distributors. Sales to such outlets have declined less than 15 per cent. These stores can get two to three weeks' delivery from Homer Laughlin, thus minimizing their inventory risk. (Homer Laughlin, in turn, minimizes its risk by keeping the bulk of its inventory in the form of undecorated whiteware.) By contrast, there is an average three-month delivery period for Japanese dinnerware, which is usually sold in complete settings for eight or twelve places. Low-income consumers prefer to buy open-stock china like H. L.'s because new pieces can be added, broken pieces replaced.

The Japanese, however, are beginning to ship open stock themselves, and H. L. fears that any further reduction in Japanese prices will offset its current advantages. The W. T. Grant variety chain, in fact, now carries an open-stock Japanese bone-china pattern selling in Homer Laughlin's price category (sixteen-piece starter set for $8.95). According to Dr. Howard Piquet's estimates, the elimination of duties might increase chinaware imports from all sources by as much as 300 per cent, i.e., $35 million, vs. a total domestic chinaware volume of approximately $80 million in 1953. Right now, however, H. L. is more worried about the Randall Commission's recommenation that all duties be cut back to a maximum of 50 per cent within three years. Wells doubts that even the existing 75 per cent rate is high enough to preserve the domestic industry. The only hope, as he sees it, is for the U. S. to impose a rigid quota on chinaware imports, based on the 1948 level of imports.

"We Tried Advertising"

It may well be asked whether a firm or industry that cannot survive with a 75 per cent tariff subsidy should be accorded still more protection. To be sure, if foreign competition were allowed fuller play, Homer Laughlin's 2,200 employees might conceivably lose their jobs, at least temporarily. But certainly no considerations of national security or of stability for the economy as a whole apply here. There is nothing that demands perpetuation of a domestic pottery industry.

Actually, the entire industry would probably not fare as badly as Homer Laughlin. For foreign competition is only one of Homer Laughlin's troubles. The company sat out the postwar revolution in U. S. dinnerware tastes; slowness in adopting new styles, new materials, and new merchandising techniques, along with reluctance to diversify, made H. L. far more vulnerable to foreign incursions than the more alert domestic producers.

Smartly styled and colorfully decorated earthenware created by firms like Gladding, McBean, Stangl, Red Wing, and Steubenville has blurred the once-sharp demarcation between "fine" china (invariably bone or porcelain) and "everyday" earthenware. Extensive advertising has helped create a new "mass-class market" for high-styled earthenware at prices two to three times as high as Homer Laughlin's—while Homer Laughlin sales have dropped about one-third since 1948, sales of Gladding, McBean's Franciscan Ware have grown 40 per cent.

Lately Homer Laughlin has been improving its designs and it now offers as attractive a line as any mass producer. But the firm is reluctant to spend money for advertising or promotion. "We tried national advertising in the 1920's," Mr. Wells recalls, "and it didn't work." Last year, on sales of $11 million, H. L. spent $23,000 for advertising; it plans no increase this year. Gladding, McBean, by contrast, spent $740,000 in 1953 and is spending $850,000 this year on national advertising.

Distress Area?

Not all workers in the territory Homer Laughlin draws on are waiting to be displaced. According to union estimates the average age of the 8,000 pottery workers in the West Virginia—eastern Ohio district is over fifty. Young people dislike the three-to-five-year apprenticeships in the potteries; they can earn $1.57½ an hour to start in the nearby Midland plant of Crucible Steel as compared to $1.37½ at H. L. Mr. Wells complains that he can no longer rehire his entire work force after a layoff: each time some drift into the steel mills or wander elsewhere in search of steadier jobs.

Even so, if Homer Laughlin and its local competitors were suddenly to shut down, considerable social dislocation would result in this essentially one-industry area. Potters who have spent thirty years in one craft would have difficulty acquiring new skills and jobs. The transition could be facilitated, of course, by action at the state and community level to attract new and diversified industries. Still, if the pottery industry's towering protective wall were razed or even substantially lowered, some federal aid would probably be needed to tide the area through a difficult adjustment.

As *Fortune,* among others, has often suggested, there are three requisites in any workable program for elimination (or drastic reduction) of U. S. tariffs: (1) The reductions must be gradual. (2) Production that is really essential to U. S. defense *and* really helpless before foreign competition should get its protection in the form of direct subsidy rather than tariffs. (3) The labor and capital that went into tariff-protected businesses like Homer Laughlin should be eligible for some kind of short-term federal help in making the transition to more productive employment.

III. MONSANTO CHEMICAL: MORBID

No U. S. corporation has attacked free trade so vigorously as the Monsanto Chemical Co., the nation's sixth-largest chemical producer. Monsanto feels so strongly about tariffs that it resigned from the National Association of Manufacturers last October in protest against a relatively mild N.A.M. statement in favor of more liberal trade policies. The statement was finally killed; meanwhile Monsanto had written the N.A.M.: "We believe your present stand on free trade is detrimental to the chemical industry, and we cannot in honesty align ourselves with an organization whose beliefs and active promotion are, in this instance, contrary to our own."

What Monsanto is primarily worried about is rising imports of organic chemicals, i.e., those based on carbon. Imports of organic chemicals from West Germany alone climbed from virtually nothing in 1947 to more than 10 million pounds in 1953. Total organic-chemical imports, meanwhile, have increased fourfold—from 24,500,000 pounds in 1947 to 125 million pounds last year.

The Wage Gap

The danger, according to Vice President Francis J. Curtis, Monsanto's spokesman on the tariff controversy, lies in the trend rather than the amounts presently imported. These are admittedly trifling compared to U. S. output (nearly 30 billion pounds in 1953) or even to U. S. exports (650 million pounds). But chemical tariffs were cut an average 50 per cent under the GATT agreements negotiated at Torquay, England, in 1951, and since the German chemical industry is just getting back on its prewar feet, Monsanto fears the ultimate result of the GATT agreements will be a tremendous resurgence of German chemical exports.

Like Bausch & Lomb and Homer Laughlin, what Monsanto worries about most is its ability to compete with low foreign wages. The average West German chemical worker gets less than one-fifth of the $2.03 an hour the average Monsanto worker is paid. Moreover, according to the chemical industry's statement before the Randall Commission, "few organic chemicals lend themselves to the 'continuous process' of manufacture." Most must be made by the old-fashioned "batch method," requiring a large input of skilled labor. Already, Curtis points out, some German-made chemicals like phthalic anhydride are being sold here at prices below Monsanto's despite import duties of 20 to 40 per cent.

High U. S. wage costs are pyramided all through the chemical-refining process, according to Curtis. Research is more costly, too. German Ph.D.'s, for example, get $2,500 to $3,000 a year (and work six or seven days a week), while Monsanto's starting salaries range from $6,500 to $8,500. U. S. construction costs are higher. "This is an industry of pipes," says Monsanto President Charles Allen Thomas, and the biggest cost in pipes is the labor of pipefitters and plumbers.

Curtis also charges that the old I. G. Farben cartel has been revived and is subsidizing exports below cost in an effort to destroy the U. S. chemical industry. Even limited quantities of imports can do serious damage, he argues, because chemicals are so interrelated that efficient use of all byproducts is essential to profitable operation. Following this reasoning, Monsanto not only opposes cutting the tariff rates on any chemical but urges protectionist changes in the Tariff Act's escape clause and peril-point provision. These changes would permit the Tariff Commission to act when only a single product, or firm, or segment of the industry is hurt or even threatened with injury from imports.

Looking Backward

Monsanto's fears of German competition seem to be largely retrospective. For the first fifteen years of its history—until World War I—Monsanto had to fight the powerful German chemical trusts for a share of the U. S. market. Probably neither Monsanto nor the U. S. chemical industry could have grown to their present strength without the aid of tariffs and occasional embargoes in the period between the two world wars.

But the once-feeble U. S. chemical industry has long since outgrown its swaddling clothes. It has, in fact, been growing twice as fast as the rest of U. S. industry. Today it dwarfs the chemical industry of Germany and every other country in the world. U. S. exports of organic chemicals last year were five times as large as imports (650 million pounds vs. 125 million). Monsanto alone exported about $17 million of chemicals in 1952 (as compared with total West German exports to the U. S. of $6,400,000), not counting the sales of Monsanto subsidiaries in England, France, Canada, Australia, Latin America, Japan, and elsewhere. Imports amounted to less than one-half of 1 per cent of the volume of U. S. chemical production; in no single category did imports exceed 5 per cent of domestic production.

Most chemical imports, moreover, have entered the U. S. in response to temporary shortages in domestic production. Even in the absence of tariffs, foreign firms could not increase their output limitlessly or invade the U. S. Market in force. Raw-material prices are generally higher in Germany than in the U. S., and interest rates are two to three times as high.

Low German wages, moreover, are substantially offset by the U. S. industry's very high investment per worker. In the U. S. industry this averages $20,000; in Monsanto's case this high investment means that the company's labor bill is less than 30 per cent of total production costs and absorbs little more than 20 per cent of revenues. Mass-production techniques apparently are used in a larger proportion of Monsanto's operations than the industry's tariff spokesman usually intimates.

Actually, almost all petroleum-based chemicals (these comprise three-fifths of Monsanto's output) and many coal-tar chemicals are made in continuous or near-continuous processes. Though Monsanto claims imports are injuring its phthalic anhydride sales, for example, the company turns out 30 million pounds a year—10 per cent of the U. S. supply—in a completely automatic factory not much bigger than a large basement playroom. Monsanto produces half the U. S. asprin supply in a semi-automatic continuous process. At another Monsanto plant eight men per shift turn out half the U. S. supply of the gasoline additive TCP.

Germany, actually, has lagged behind the U. S. in chemical technology since the mid-Thirties—particularly in the field of plastics research. The German chemical industry is still largely coal-tar based, and progress in petrochemicals has been comparatively slow: German science faculties lost some 60 per cent of their members between 1933 and 1950 by death, emigration, or exile.

Worrying For The Record

Under normal circumstances it is difficult to see why German firms should be able to undersell American manufacturers except in a few dyes, pharmaceuticals, and other "fine" chemicals made in small batches and requiring large amounts of highly skilled labor. Even these specialized markets are no push-over for the Germans. As John Powers Jr., of Chas. Pfizer & Co., recently observed in a discussion of foreign-trade problems, "I do not see how any of us who survive the rigors of American competition can permit ourselves to be fearful concerning foreign competition."

In fact, in trade discussions most chemical firms show considerably more confidence in their ability to meet foreign competition than they do when arguing against lower tariffs. A poll conducted by *Chemical Week,* for example, shows that more than half the companies think their own exports abroad would increase sharply if they were not blocked by high foreign tariffs. One out of four firms thinks it could sell its own products more cheaply in the U. S. if it were not for the high import duties on basic and intermediate chemicals like phthalic anhydride and coal-tar products.

And then there is the fabulous American market. Domestic chemical sales have been growing 10 per cent a year, on the average, ever since 1925. The domestic demand for Monsanto's most important products —plastics, detergents, and synthetic rubber—is expected to increase five to ten times by 1975, according to the 1951 Paley Commission report. A market of these dimensions could not only support but might even require an increased volume of imports.

At present Monsanto and the other domestic chemical producers enjoy a type of tariff treatment accorded to no other major U. S. industry; chemical tariff rates are applied to the U. S., not the foreign, price. Even for chemicals not produced in this country, customs appraisers must compute what the "U. S. value," i.e., wholesale price, would be if the chemicals *were* made here.

Undiscriminating and wholesale tariff cuts, to be sure, might be dangerous to an industry as vital as chemicals. But the chemical industry has cut most of its prices 50 per cent or more since 1920, while the general U. S. price level has more than doubled. It has introduced new products in such profusion that half its sales each year are in products that did not exist ten years earlier. Those few strategic chemical lines in which the U. S. is a hopelessly high-cost producer, e.g., certain low-volume dyestuffs and drugs—should continue to receive some tariff protection—as long as any U. S. production continues to receive tariff protection—or direct subsidies. But for the rest, increased imports would serve to shake the industry loose from pricing practices that have no sanction other than tradition, and stimulate further cost reduction and product innovation.

IX

Collectivism and Planning

---

47. THE PARABLE OF THE WATER TANK*

SOCIALISTS have indicted capitalism on a number of counts, one of which is the recurrence of economic fluctuations. The basic cause of business cycles, according to some Socialist writers, is the inequality in the distribution of income, which prevents workers from buying back what they produce. Edward Bellamy expressed these views in the following parable.

THERE was a certain very dry land, the people whereof were in sore need of water. And they did nothing but to seek after water from morning until night, and many perished because they could not find it.

Howbeit, there were certain men in that land who were more crafty and diligent than the rest, and these had gathered stores of water where others could find none, and the name of these men was called capitalists. And it came to pass that the people of the land came unto the capitalists and prayed them that they would give them of the water they had gathered that they might drink, for their need was sore. But the capitalists answered them and said:

"Go to, ye silly people! Why should we give you of the water which we have gathered, for then we should become even as ye are, and perish with you? But behold what we will do unto you. Be ye our servants and ye shall have water."

* From *Equality* by Edward Bellamy. Copyright, 1897, D. Appleton & Company. Reprinted by permission of the publishers, Appleton-Century-Crofts, Inc. The author (1850-1898) was a journalist. Author of *Looking Backward*.

And the people said, "Only give us to drink and we will be your servants, we and our children." And it was so.

Now, the capitalists were men of understanding, and wise in their generation. They ordered the people who were their servants in bands with captains and officers, and some they put at the springs to dip, and others did they make to carry the water, and others did they cause to seek for new springs. And all the water was brought together in one place, and there did the capitalists make a great tank for to hold it, and the tank was called the Market, for it was here that the people, even the servants of the capitalists, came to get water. And the capitalists said unto the people:

"For every bucket of water that ye bring to us, that we may pour it into the tank, which is the Market, behold! we will give you a penny, but for every bucket that we shall draw forth to give unto you that ye may drink of it, ye and your wives and your children, ye shall give to us two pennies, and the difference shall be our profit, seeing that if it were not for this profit we would not do this thing for you, but ye should all perish."

And it was good in the people's eyes, for they were dull of understanding, and they diligently brought water into the tank for many days, and for every bucket which they did bring the capitalists gave them every man a penny, but for every bucket that the capitalists drew forth from the tank to give again unto the people, behold! the people rendered to the capitalists two pennies.

And after many days the water tank, which was the Market, overflowed at the top, seeing that for every bucket the people poured in they received only so much as would buy again half of a bucket. And because of the excess that was left of every bucket, did the tank overflow, for the people were many but the capitalists were few, and could drink no more than others. Therefore did the tank overflow.

And when the capitalists saw that the water overflowed, they said to the people:

"See ye not the tank, which is the Market, doth overflow? Sit ye down, therefore, and be patient, for ye shall bring us no more water till the tank be empty."

But when the people no more received the pennies of the capitalists for the water they brought, they could buy no more water from the capitalists, having naught wherewith to buy. And when the capitalists saw that they had no more profit because no man bought water of them, they were troubled. And they sent forth men in the highways, and byways, and the hedges, crying, "If any thirst let him come to the tank and buy water of us, for it doth overflow." For they said among themselves, "Behold, the times are dull; we must advertise."

But the people answered, saying: "How can we buy unless ye hire us, for how else shall we have wherewithal to buy? Hire ye us, therefore, as before, and we will gladly buy water, for we thirst, and ye will have no need to advertise." But the capitalists said to the people: "Shall we hire you to bring water when the tank, which is the Market, doth already overflow? Buy ye, therefore, first water, and when the tank is empty, through your buying, will we hire you again." And so it was because the capitalists hired them no more to bring water that the people could not buy the water they had brought already, and because the people could not buy the water they had brought already, the capitalists no more hired them to bring water. And the saying went abroad, "It is a crisis."

And the thirst of the people was great, for it was not now as it had been in the days of their fathers, when the land was open before them, for everyone to seek water for himself, seeing that the capitalists had taken all the springs, and the wells, and the water wheels, and the vessels and the buckets, so that no man might come by water save from the tank, which was the Market. And the people murmured against the capitalists and said: "Behold, the tank runneth over, and we die of thirst. Give us, therefore, of the water, that we perish not."

But the capitalists answered: "Not so. The water is ours. Ye shall not drink thereof unless ye buy it of us with pennies." And they confirmed it with an oath, saying, after their manner, "Business is business."

But the capitalists were disquieted that the people bought no more water, whereby they had no more any profits, and they spake one to another, saying: "It seemeth that our profits have stopped our profits, and by reason of the profits we have made, we can make no more profits. How is it that our profits are become unprofitable to us, and our gains do make us poor? Let us therefore send for the soothsayers, that they may interpret this thing unto us," and they sent for them.

Now, the soothsayers were men learned in dark sayings, who joined themselves to the capitalists by reason of the water of the capitalists, that they might have thereof and live, they and their children. And they spake for the capitalists unto the people, and did their embassies for them, seeing that the capitalists were not a folk quick of understanding neither ready of speech.

And the capitalists demanded of the soothsayers that they should interpret this thing unto them, wherefore it was that the people bought no more water of them, although the tank was full. And certain of the soothsayers answered and said, "It is by reason of overproduction," and some said, "It is glut"; but the signification of the two words is the same. And others said "Nay, but this thing is by reason of the spots on the sun." And yet others answered, saying, "It is neither by reason of glut, nor yet of spots on the sun that this evil hath come to pass, but because of lack of confidence."

And while the soothsayers contended among themselves, according to their manner, the men of profit did slumber and sleep, and when they awoke they said to the soothsayers: "It is enough. Ye have spoken comfortably unto us. Now go ye forth and speak comfortably likewise unto this people, so that they be at rest and leave us also in peace."

But the soothsayers, even the men of the dismal science—for so they were named of some—were loath to go forth to the people lest they should be stoned, for the people loved them not. And they said to the capitalists:

"Masters, it is a mystery of our craft that if men be full and thirst not but be at rest, then shall they find comfort in our speech even as ye. Yet if they thirst and be empty, find they no comfort therein but rather mock us, for it seemeth that unless a man be full, our wisdom appeareth unto him but emptiness." But the capitalists said: "Go ye forth. Are ye not our men to do our embassies?"

And the soothsayers went forth to the people and expounded to them the mystery of overproduction, and how it was that they must needs perish of thirst because there was overmuch water, and how there could not be enough because there was too much. And likewise spoke they unto the people concerning the sun spots, and also wherefore it was that these things had come upon them by reason of lack of confidence. And it was even as the soothsayers had said, for to the people their wisdom seemed emptiness. And the people reviled them, saying: "Go up, ye bald-heads! Will ye mock us? Doth plenty breed famine? Doth nothing come out of much?" And they took up stones to stone them.

And when the capitalists saw that the people still murmured and would not give ear to the soothsayers, and because also they feared lest they should come upon the tank and take of the water by force, they brought forth to them certain holy men (but they were false priests), who spake unto the people that they should be quiet and trouble not the capitalists because they thirsted. And these holy men, who were false priests, testified to the people that this affliction was sent to them of God for the healing of their souls, and if they should bear it in patience and lust not after the water, neither trouble the capitalists, it would come to pass that after they had given up the ghost they would come to a country where there should be no capitalists but an abundance of water. Howbeit, there were certain true prophets of God also, and these had compassion on the people and would not prophesy for the capitalists, but rather spake constantly against them.

Now, when the capitalists saw that the people still murmured and would not be still, neither for the words of the soothsayers nor of the false priests, they came forth themselves unto them and put the ends of their fingers in the water that overflowed in the tank and wet the tips thereof, and they scattered the drops from the tips of their fingers abroad upon the people who thronged the tank, and the name of the drops of water was charity, and they were exceeding bitter.

And when the capitalists saw yet again that neither for the words of the soothsayers, nor of the holy men who were false priests, nor yet for the drops that were called charity, would the people be still, but raged the more, and crowded upon the tank as if they would take it by force, then took they counsel together and sent men privily forth among the people. And these men sought out the mightiest among the people and all who had skill in war, and took them apart and spake craftily with them, saying:

"Come, now, why cast ye not your lot in with the capitalists? If ye will be their men and serve them against the people, that they break not in upon the tank, then shall ye have abundance of water, that ye perish not, ye and your children."

And the mighty men and they who were skilled in war harkened unto this speech and suffered themselves to be persuaded, for their thirst constrained them, and they went within unto the capitalists and became their men, and staves and swords were put in their hands and they became a defense unto the capitalists and smote the people when they thronged upon the tank.

And after many days the water was low in the tank, for the capitalists did make fountains and fish ponds of the water thereof, and did bathe therein, they and their wives and their children, and did waste the water for their pleasure.

And when the capitalists saw that the tank was empty, they said, "The crisis is ended"; and they sent forth and hired the people that they should bring water to fill it again. And for the water that the people brought to the tank they received for every bucket a penny, but for the water which the capitalists drew forth from the tank to give again to the people they received two pennies, that they might have their profit. And after a time did the tank again overflow even as before.

And now, when many times the people had filled that tank until it overflowed and had thirsted till the water therein had been wasted by the capitalists, it came to pass that there arose in the land certain men who were called agitators, for that they did stir up the people. And they spake to the people, saying that they should associate, and then would they have no need to be servants of the capitalists and should thirst no more for water. And in the eyes of the capitalists were the agitators pestilent fellows, and they would fain have crucified them, but durst not for fear of the people.

And the words of the agitators which they spake to the people were on this wise:

"Ye foolish people, how long will ye be deceived by a lie and believe to your hurt that which is not? For behold all these things that have been said unto you by the capitalists and by the soothsayers are cunningly devised fables. And likewise the holy men, who say that it is the will of God that ye should always be poor and miserable and athirst, behold! they do blaspheme God and are liars, whom he will bitterly judge though he forgive all others. How cometh it that ye may not come by the water in the tank? Is it not because ye have no money? And why have ye no money? Is it not because ye receive but one penny for every bucket that ye bring to the tank, which is the Market, but must render two pennies for every bucket ye take out, so that the capitalists may have their profit? See ye not how by this means the tank must overflow, being filled by that ye lack and made to abound out of your emptiness? See ye not also that the harder ye toil and the more diligently ye seek and bring the water, the worse and not the better it shall be for you by reason of the profit, and that forever?"

After this manner spake the agitators for many days unto the people, and none heeded them, but it was so that after a time the people harkened. And they answered and said unto the agitators:

"Ye say truth. It is because of the capitalists and of their profits that we want, seeing that by reason of them and their profits we may by no means come by the fruit of our labor, so that our labor is in vain, and the more we toil to fill the tank the sooner doth it overflow, and we may receive nothing because there is too much, according to the words of the soothsayers. But behold, the capitalists are hard men and their tender mercies are cruel. Tell us if ye know any way whereby we may deliver ourselves out of our bondage unto them. But if you know of no certain way of deliverance we beseech you to hold your peace and let us alone, that we may forget our misery."

And the agitators answered and said, "We know a way."

And the people said: "Deceive us not, for this thing hath been from the beginning, and none hath found a way of deliverance until now, though many have sought it carefully with tears. But if ye know a way, speak unto us quickly."

Then the agitators spake unto the people of the way. And they said:

"Behold, what need have ye at all of these capitalists, that ye should yield them profits upon your labor? What great thing do they wherefore ye render them this tribute? Lo! it is only because they do order you in bands and lead you out and in and set your tasks and afterward give you a little of the water yourselves have brought and not they. Now, behold the way out of this bondage! Do ye for yourselves that which is done by the capitalists—namely, the ordering of your labor, and the marshaling of your bands, and the dividing of your tasks. So shall ye have no need at all of the capitalists and no more yield to them any profit, but all the fruit of your labor shall ye share as brethren, every one having the same; and so shall the tank never overflow until every man is full, and would not wag the tongue for more, and afterward shall ye with the overflow make pleasant fountains and fish ponds to delight yourselves withal even as did the capitalists; but these shall be for the delight of all."

And the people answered, "How shall we go about to do this thing, for it seemeth good to us?"

And the agitators answered: "Choose ye discreet men to go in and out before you and to marshal your bands and order your labor, and these men shall be as the capitalists were, but, behold, they shall not be your masters as the capitalists are, but your brethren and officers who do your will, and they shall not take any profits, but every man his share like the others, that there may be no more masters and servants among you, but brethren only. And from time to time, as ye see fit, ye shall choose other discreet men in place of the first to order the labor."

And the people harkened, and the thing was very good to them. Likewise seemed it not a hard thing. And with one voice they cried out, "So let it be as ye have said, for we will do it!"

And the capitalists heard the noise of the shouting and what the people said, and the soothsayers heard it also, and likewise the false priests and the mighty men of war, who were a defense unto the capitalists; and when they heard they trembled exceedingly, so that their knees smote together, and they said one to another, "It is the end of us!"

Howbeit, there were certain true priests of the living God who would not prophesy for the capitalists, but had compassion on the people; and when they heard the shouting of the people and what they said, they rejoiced with exceeding great joy, and gave thanks to God because of the deliverance.

And the people went and did all the things that were told them of the agitators to do. And it came to pass as the agitators had said, even according to all their words. And there was no more any thirst in that land, neither any that was ahungered, nor naked, nor cold, nor in any manner of want; and every man said unto his fellow, "My brother," and every woman said unto her companion, "My sister," for so were they with one another as brethren and sisters which do dwell together in unity. And the blessing of God rested upon that land forever.

---

48. THE COMMUNIST MANIFESTO *

THE DICTIONARY defines manifesto as a public declaration of intention and motives by a sovereign or political group. The *Communist Manifesto* is more than that. It is a short but bitter history of class struggle and a prophecy of revolution. It is an indictment of the property owners *(bourgeoisie)* and a prediction of the downfall of the capitalist system. It opens with the ominous words, applicable today as never before, "A specter is haunting Europe—the specter of Communism" and closes with a call to arms—". . . their ends can be attained only by the forcible overthrow of all existing social conditions . . . Working men of all countries, unite!" Compare this document with an earlier manifesto, also provoked by economic and political injustice, which gave rise to a bloody but effective overthrow of an existing order—a manifesto adopted in Philadelphia, July 4, 1776.

A SPECTER is haunting Europe—the specter of Communism. All the powers of old Europe have entered into a holy alliance to exorcise this specter: Pope and Tsar, Metternich and Guizot, French Radicals and German police-spies.

Where is the party in opposition that has not been decried as communistic by its opponents in power? Where is the Opposition that has not hurled back the branding reproach of Communism, against the

* Karl Marx and Friedrich Engels, *The Manifesto of the Communist Party,* 1848.

Karl Marx (1818-1883) was a German political philosopher; regarded as the founder of modern socialism. Editor of various radical newspapers and a revolutionary leader in Continental Europe. After being driven from Germany, France, and Belgium he sought refuge in England in 1849 and spent most of the rest of his life in study and in the writing of his masterpiece, *Capital.* Author of *The Poverty of Philosophy, Toward a Critique of Political Economy,* and *The Communist Manifesto* (with Engels). Friedrich Engels (1820-1895) was a writer and revolutionary leader. Played an important part in both the First and Second International. Engels was a life-long friend of Marx, and after the death of Marx, edited the second and third volumes of *Capital.*

more advanced opposition parties, as well as against its reactionary adversaries?

Two things result from this fact:

I. Communism is already acknowledged by all European powers to be itself a power.

II. It is high time that Communists should openly, in the face of the whole world, publish their views, their aims, their tendencies, and meet this nursery tale of the specter of Communism with a manifesto of the party itself.

I: BOURGEOIS AND PROLETARIANS

The history of all hitherto existing society is the history of class struggles.

Freemen and slave, patrician and plebeian, lord and serf, guild-master and journeyman, in a word, oppressor and oppressed, stood in constant opposition to one another, carried on an uninterrupted, now hidden, now open fight, a fight that each time ended, either in a revolutionary reconstitution of society at large, or in the common ruin of the contending classes.

In the earlier epochs of history, we find almost everywhere a complicated arrangement of society into various orders, a manifold gradation of social rank. In ancient Rome we have patricians, knights, plebeians, slaves; in the Middle Ages, feudal lords, vassals, guild-masters, journeymen, apprentices, serfs; in almost all of these classes, again, subordinate gradations.

The modern bourgeois society that has sprouted from the ruins of feudal society has not done away with class antagonisms. It has but established new classes, new conditions of oppression, new forms of struggle in place of the old ones.

Our epoch, the epoch of the bourgeoisie, possesses, however, this distinctive feature: it has simplified the class antagonisms. Society as a whole is more and more splitting up into two great hostile camps, into two great classes directly facing each other—bourgeoisie and proletariat.

. . . . .

The bourgeoisie, during its rule of scarce one hundred years, has created more massive and more colossal productive forces than have all preceding generations together. Subjection of nature's forces to man, machinery, application of chemistry to industry and agriculture, steam navigation, railways, electric telegraphs, clearing of whole continents for cultivation, canalization of rivers, whole populations conjured out of the ground—what earlier century had even a presentiment that such productive forces slumbered in the lap of social labor?

We see then: the means of production and of exchange, on whose foundation the bourgeoisie built itself up, were generated in feudal society. At a certain stage in the development of these means of production and of exchange, the conditions under which feudal society produced and exchanged, the feudal organization of agriculture and manufacturing industry, in one word, the feudal relations of property became no longer compatible with the already developed productive forces; they became so many fetters. They had to be burst asunder; they were burst asunder.

Into their place stepped free competition, accompanied by a social and political constitution adapted to it, and by the economical and political sway of the bourgeois class.

A similar movement is going on before our own eyes. Modern bourgeois society with its relation of production, of exchange and of property, a society that has conjured up such gigantic means of production and of exchange, is like the sorcerer who is no longer able to control the powers of the nether world whom he has called up by his spells. For many a decade past the history of industry and commerce is but the history of the revolt of modern productive forces against modern conditions of production, against the property relations that are the conditions for the existence of the bourgeoisie and of its rule. It is enough to mention the commercial crises that by their periodical return put the existence of the entire bourgeois society on its trial, each time more threateningly. In these crises a great part not only of the existing products, but also of the previously created productive forces, are periodically destroyed. In these crises there breaks out an epidemic that, in all earlier epochs, would have seemed an absurdity—the epidemic of over-production. Society suddenly finds itself put back into a state of monetary barbarism; it appears as if a famine, a universal war of devastation, had cut off the supply of every means of subsistence; industry and commerce seem to be destroyed. And why? Because there is too much civilization, too much means of subsistence, too much industry, too much commerce. The productive forces at the disposal of society no longer tend to further the development of the conditions of bourgeois property; on the contrary, they have become too powerful for these conditions, by which they are fettered, and so soon as they overcome these fetters, they bring disorder into the whole of bourgeois society, endanger the existence of bourgeois property. The conditions of bourgeois society are too narrow to comprise the wealth created by them. And how does the bourgeoisie get over these crises? On the one hand by enforced destruction of a mass of productive forces; on the other, by the conquest of new markets, and by the more thorough exploitation of the old ones. That is to say, by paving the way for more extensive and more destructive crises, and by diminishing the means whereby crises are prevented.

The weapons with which the bourgeoisie felled feudalism to the ground are now turned against the bourgeoisie itself.

But not only has the bourgeoisie forged the weapons that bring death to itself; it has also called into existence the men who are to wield those weapons—the modern working class—the proletarians.

In proportion as the bourgeoisie, i.e., capital, is developed, in the same proportion is the proletariat, the modern working class, developed —a class of laborers, who live only so long as they find work, and who find work only so long as their labor increases capital. These laborers, who must sell themselves piecemeal, are a commodity, like every other article of commerce, and are consequently exposed to all the vicissitudes of competition, to all the fluctuations of the market.

Owing to the extensive use of machinery and to division of labor, the work of the proletarians has lost all individual character, and, consequently, all charm for the workman. He becomes an appendage of the machine, and it is only the most simple, most monotonous, and most easily acquired knack, that is required of him. Hence, the cost of production of a workman is restricted, almost entirely, to the means of subsistence that he requires for his maintenance, and for the propagation of his race. But the price of a commodity, and therefore, also of labor, is equal to its cost of production. In proportion, therefore, as the repulsiveness of the work increases, the wage decreases. Nay, more, in proportion as the use of machinery and division of labor increases, in the same proportion the burden of toil also increases, whether by prolongation of the working hours, by increase of the work exacted in a given time, or by increased speed of the machinery, etc.

Modern industry has converted the little workshop of the patriarchal master into the great factory of the industrial capitalist. Masses of laborers, crowded into the factory, are organized like soldiers. As privates of the industrial army they are placed under the command of a perfect hierarchy of officers and sergeants. Not only are they slaves of the bourgeois class, and of the bourgeois state; they are daily and hourly enslaved by the machine, by the overlooker, and, above all, by the individual bourgeois manufacturer himself. The more openly this despotism proclaims gain to be its end and aim, the more petty, the more hateful and the more embittering it is.

The less the skill and exertion of strength implied in manual labor, in other words, the more modern industry becomes developed, the more is the labor of men superseded by that of women. Differences of age and sex have no longer any distinctive social validity for the working class. All are instruments of labor, more or less expensive to use, according to their age and sex.

No sooner is the exploitation of the laborer by the manufacturer so far at an end that he receives his wages in cash than he is set upon by the other portions of the bourgeoisie, the landlord, the shopkeeper, the pawnbroker, etc.

The lower strata of the middle class—the small tradespeople, shopkeepers, and retired tradesmen generally, the handicraftsmen and peasants—all these sink gradually into the proletariat, partly because their diminutive capital does not suffice for the scale on which modern industry is carried on, and is swamped in the competition with the large capitalists, partly because their specialized skill is rendered worthless by new methods of production. Thus the proletariat is recruited from all classes of the population.

. . . . .

Hitherto, every form of society has been based, as we have already seen, on the antagonism of oppressing and oppressed classes. But in order to oppress a class, certain conditions must be assured to it under which it can, at least, continue its slavish existence. The serf, in the period of serfdom, raised himself to membership in the commune, just as the petty bourgeois, under the yoke of feudal absolutism, managed to develop into a bourgeois. The modern laborer, on the contrary, instead of rising with the progress of industry, sinks deeper and deeper below the conditions of existence of his own class. He becomes a pauper, and pauperism develops more rapidly than population and wealth. And here it becomes evident that the bourgeoisie is unfit any longer to be the ruling class in society and to impose its conditions of existence upon society as an overriding law. It is unfit to rule because it is incompetent to asure an existence to its slave within his slavery, because it cannot help letting him sink into such a state, that it has to feed him, instead of being fed by him. Society can no longer live under this bourgeoisie; in other words, its existence is no longer compatible with society.

The essential condition for the existence and for the sway of the bourgeois class is the formation and augmentation of capital; the condition for capital is wage labor. Wage labor rests exclusively on competition between the laborers. The advance of industry, whose involuntary promoter is the bourgeoisie, replaces the isolation of the laborers, due to competition, by their revolutionary combination, due to association. The development of modern industry, therefore, cuts from under its feet the very foundation on which the bourgeoisie produces and appropriates products. What the bourgeoisie therefore produces, above all, are its own grave-diggers. Its fall and the victory of the proletariat are equally inevitable.

II: PROLETARIANS AND COMMUNISTS

In what relation do the Communists stand to the proletarians as a whole?

The Communists do not form a separate party opposed to other working class parties.

They have no interests separate and apart from those of the proletariat as a whole.

They do not set up any sectarian principles of their own, by which to shape and mold the proletarian movement.

The Communists are distinguished from other working-class parties by this only: 1. In the national struggles of the proletarians of the different countries, they point out and bring to the front the common interests of the entire proletariat, independently of all nationality. 2. In the various stages of development which the struggle of the working class against the bourgeoisie has to pass through, they always and everywhere represent the interests of the movement as a whole.

The Communists, therefore, are on the one hand, practically, the most advanced and resolute section of the working-class parties of every country, that section which pushes forward all others; on the other hand, theoretically, they have over the great mass of the proletariat the advantage of clearly understanding the line of march, the conditions, and the ultimate general results of the proletarian movement.

The immediate aim of the Communists is the same as that of all the other proletarian parties: formation of the proletariat into a class, overthrow of the bourgeois supremacy, conquest of political power by the proletariat.

The theoretical conclusions of the Communists are in no way based on ideas or principles that have been invented, or discovered, by this or that would-be universal reformer.

They merely express, in general terms, actual relations springing from an existing class struggle, from a historical movement going on under our very eyes. The abolition of existing property relations is not at all a distinctive feature of Communism.

All property relations in the past have continually been subject to historical change consequent upon the change in historical conditions.

The French Revolution, for example, abolished feudal property in favor of bourgeois property.

The distinguishing feature of Communism is not the abolition ot property generally but the abolition of bourgeois property. But modern bourgeois private property is the final and most complete expression of the system of producing and appropriating products that is based on class antagonisms, on the exploitation of the many by the few.

In this sense, the theory of the Communists may be summed up in the single sentence: Abolition of private property.

. . . . .

We have seen above that the first step in the revolution by the working class is to raise the proletariat to the position of ruling class, to win the battle of democracy.

The proletariat will use its political supremacy to wrest, by degrees, all capital from the bourgeoisie, to centralize all instruments of production in the hands of the state, i.e., of the proletariat organized as the ruling class; and to increase the total of productive forces as rapidly as possible.

Of course, in the beginning, this cannot be affected except by means of despotic inroads on the rights of property, and on the conditions of bourgeois production; by means of measures, therefore, which appear economically insufficient and untenable, but which, in the course of the movement, outstrip themselves, necessitate further inroads upon the old social order, and are unavoidable as a means of entirely revolutionizing the mode of production.

These measures will, of course, be different in different countries.

Nevertheless, in the most advanced countries, the following will be pretty generally applicable:

1. Abolition of property in land and application of all rents of land to public purposes.
2. A heavy progressive or graduated income tax.
3. Abolition of all right of inheritance.
4. Confiscation of the property of all emigrants and rebels.
5. Centralization of credit in the hands of the state, by means of a national bank with state capital and an exclusive monopoly.
6. Centralization of the means of communication and transport in the hands of the state.
7. Extension of factories and instruments of production owned by the state; the bringing into cultivation of waste lands, and the improvement of the soil generally in accordance with a common plan.

8. Equal obligation of all to work. Establishment of industrial armies, especially for agriculture.

9. Combination of agriculture with manufacturing industries; gradual abolition of the distinction between town and country, by a more equable distribution of the population over the country.

10. Free education for all children in public schools. Abolition of children's factory labor in its present form. Combination of education with industrial production, etc.

When, in the course of development, class distinctions have disappeared, and all production has been concentrated in the hands of a vast association of the whole nation, the public power will lose its political character. Political power, properly so called, is merely the organized power of one class for oppressing another. If the proletariat during its contest with the bourgeoisie is compelled, by the force of circumstances, to organize itself as a class; if, by means of a revolution, it makes itself the ruling class, and, as such, sweeps away by force the old conditions of production, then it will, along with these conditions, have swept away the conditions for the existence of class antagonisms and of classes generally, and will thereby have abolished its own supremacy as a class.

In place of the old bourgeois society, with its classes and class antagonisms, we shall have an association in which the free development of each is the condition for the free development of all.

Position of the Communist in Relation to Various Existing Opposition Parties

In short, the Communists everywhere support every revolutionary movement against the existing social and political order of things.

In all these movements they bring to the front, as the leading question in each, the property question, no matter what its degree of development at the time.

Finally, they labor everywhere for the union and agreement of the democratic parties of all countries.

The Communists disdain to conceal their views and aims. They openly declare that their ends can be attained only by the forcible overthrow of all existing social conditions. Let the ruling classes tremble at a Communist revolution. The proletarians have nothing to lose but their chains. They have a world to win.

Working men of all countries, unite!

49. VISIT TO A MODEL COLLECTIVE *

GREAT strides have been made in recent decades in the industrialization of the U.S.S.R. Nevertheless, the majority of the population is still engaged in agriculture. Roughly one tenth of the agricultural products in the Soviet Union come from the State Farms; the rest from the Collectives. Mr. Daniel here describes the operation of a Collective Farm, a State Farm, and a Machine Tractor Station whose equipment is used to service both types of farms.

"One of Russia's 'showplace' collective farms is Pamyat Ilyicha, near Moscow. It is not a typical farm—in fact, it is exceptional, having won the Order of Lenin—but its methods of operation are typical in that they show how collectives throughout Russia produce goods, met quotas and pay the men and women who work them."

ON THE Yaroslav highway about seventeen miles north of Moscow stands a wooden building with a façade of startling blue. Beside the building is a full-length statue of Nikolai Lenin (Vladimir Ilyich Ulianov), arm outstretched in an oratorical pose familiar all over the Soviet Union. Anyone who has ever traveled through rural America would recognize the building as a country store, with an apartment, a small meeting hall and an office on the second floor. In fact, the store is publicly owned, and the office is the headquarters of the Pamyat Ilyicha ("In Memory of Ilyich") collective farm founded twenty-four years ago on the anniversary of Lenin's death.

For twenty-two of those years, Osip Ruzin, a former bookkeeper whose parents were peasants in that vicinity, has been chairman of the collective. A man of 61 with a shaven head, horn-rimmed spectacles, and a typical Russian blouse under his blue serge suit, Ruzin receives visitors in his office, and, slapping his hand against the abacus that sits on his desk, rapidly rattles off facts and figures. They are the facts and figures of life and work on a Soviet collective, a Socialist institution that has been described, discussed and argued about for three decades. And now it is being subjected to severe new tests of practicality and productivity by the demand of the high authorities for greater farm output.

* Clifton Daniel, *The New York Times Magazine,* November 14, 1954, pp. 19ff. Reprinted by permission of *The New York Times* and the author.

The author (1912——) is a newspaper correspondent with extensive foreign experience. Mr. Daniel worked with the Associated Press and with *The New York Times* in the United States and Europe, also serving as war correspondent for the U. S. Army. After World War II he worked in the Middle East, and in 1954 became Moscow correspondent for the *Times.*

The chairman of Pamyat Ilyicha has the facts of collective agriculture at his fingertips, and with his fingers he deftly flicks the beads of the abacus as he recites the statistics. The staccato clacking of the beads puts an exclamation mark after every figure.

Size of the farm—700 hectares (1,730 acres). Clack! One hundred planted in vegetables. Clack! One-hundred-twenty in potatoes. Clack! And so on for fruit, fodder, turnips and beets, corn, cabbage, pasture and private gardens.

Population of the farm—about 1,000. Clack! Able-bodied adult workers—230 women (Clack!) and 140 men. Clack! The predominance of women, he explains, is due in part to losses of men in the war (Ruzin himself was a major in the supply services) and to the fact that some men who live on the farm work in near-by factories.

Specialized personnel—seventy, including five agronomists, two of them with university degrees; three animal husbandry experts; one veterinarian; six bookkeepers, fifteen drivers, one plumber and fitter, and, of course, the chairman himself.

Livestock—225 cattle, including 140 milk cows; 250 pigs, including fifty breeding sows; 2,500 chickens; 100 horses; 100 beehives.

Equipment—ten trucks; two small cars; repair shops; a new cow barn; seven greenhouses, including three big new ones; ten thousand new forcing frames; a potting shed; a steam generating plant for the greenhouses and forcing frames; and so on.

Social services—a kindergarten; a crêche for fifty children; a clinic with five doctors, who also serve the village; a school, with compulsory attendance for seven years; a club with dramatic circles and other recreational groups; a movie theatre; an orchestra; and a library with 10,000 books.

"We have educated our own intellectual specialists," Ruzin says.

Then he comes to methods of payment for the sale of produce and for sharing the proceeds among the members of the collective. One begins to understand why Ruzin needs the abacus, why there are six bookkeepers in the collective, why cartoons in Krokodil, the Soviet humor magazine, are always ridiculing farmers who are so busy shuffling papers that they have no time to dig potatoes.

The produce of the farm, Ruzin explains, is marketed in three ways. There are, first, compulsory deliveries to the Government; second, additional voluntary sales to the Government; and, finally, free sales on the open market. This year, Pamyat Ilyicha sold approximately half of its output to the Government and half on the open market.

For compulsory deliveries, which have been drastically reduced since last year's agricultural decrees by the Soviet Council of Ministers and the Central Committee of the Communist party, there are fixed prices. For further voluntary sales to the Government, the farm now receives, instead of fixed prices, 75 per cent of the retail prices of the produce in state stores. These prices are generally, but not always, higher than the farm gets from compulsory sales. The highest rates of all come from sales in the open market, where the law of supply and demand and not official decrees govern the price level.

Just to take one staple product, in early September Pamyat Ilyicha was receiving 30 kopeks per kilogram (2.2 pounds) for compulsory deliveries of potatoes. The retail price in state stores was 50 kopeks, 75 per cent of which would be 37.50 kopeks. And the retail price in the open market was two rubles—that is, 200 kopeks.

When it comes to telling how the members of the collective are rewarded for their labor, Ruzin's abacus chatters louder and faster.

Workers at Pamyat Ilyicha, Ruzin says, have an average of 500 working day units a year. A working day unit is not a measure of time, but of output. For example, the working day unit for a dairymaid, a member of one of the cattle barn brigades, is fifty liters (13 gallons) of milk a day, the milk to have an average butter fat content of 3.8 per cent. If her section of the herd produces 100 liters a day, she gets credit for two working day units. A tractor driver who plows four hectares (10 acres) gets credit for three working days. And so on.

Every worker is required to fulfill a minimum of 150 working day units a year. If he (or she) does less, it is assumed that the worker is devoting too much time to his own personal garden plot, and he must pay double the annual tax of 300 rubles. For each working day unit, a worker at Pamyat Ilyicha received this year: 8.8 pounds of potatoes, 8.8 of vegetables, a pound of fruit, a pound of fodder and eight rubles in cash.

Taking a representative list of farm products and their prices in state stores, one can calculate roughly that the cash value of a working day unit is 20 or more rubles, or 10,000 rubles a year for the average worker at Pamyat Ilyicha. (For foreign exchange purposes the ruble is valued by the Soviet Government at four to the dollar, but that rate does not necessarily reflect the relative domestic purchasing power of the two currencies.)

In addition to their shares from the collective, the workers each have, under the rules of that particular farm, a private plot of 300 square meters or three-quarters of an acre to use as the individual wishes. On that plot the worker has his own home, and may keep one milk cow, two calves, one sow, ten sheep, ten beehives and as much poultry as he likes. He may grow any crop he wishes or has room for.

The crops and the livestock on the individual plots are for personal use and may be either consumed or sold on the free market. The worker may also sell any surplus from his daily earnings of produce.

In addition, collective farmers may receive bonuses if, in the Soviet phrase, they "overfulfill their plan." Each farm and each brigade on the farm has a plan for the year—that is, a production quota. At the end of the year there is a general meeting of the collective to assess the farm's record.

If the plan has been overfulfilled—and therefore more money earned—25 per cent of the extra earnings goes to the chairman and other executives and specialists. Brigades that have exceeded their quotas get the next bite. The rest is distributed among the rank and file in the form of increased pay.

Aside from bonuses, the chairman receives a salary of 500 rubles a month and gets credit for 100 working days a month. Ruzin says he owns a radio, a television set and a new Pobeda sedan, for which he paid 16,500 rubles last year.

The collective pays income tax at the rate of 8 per cent on its net earnings. Individual members pay the homestead tax and, if they earn enough to be in a tax bracket, the usual income tax. The collective pays 2 per cent of its income from state sales into the farm's mutual aid fund for pensions, disability benefits and relief. The individual also pays 2 per cent of his share from the collective. For each child who is cared for in the crêche while its parents are working there is a charge of 4 per cent of one parent's income from the collective. The fee is calculated on the higher income of the two.

Now and then, as he runs through these complex figures, Ruzin changes pace to expound on the accomplishments of collective agriculture. He is not only a statistician, but a propagandist, an evangelist for the system in general, his farm in particular and especially for the aims and objects of the new Soviet agricultural drive.

Twenty-five years ago, he declaims dramatically, there were no buildings on the site of Pamyat Ilyicha except the homesteads of the peasants, including his own parents' home, and two country inns. Pamyat Ilyicha, he says, had twenty-seven founding members. In a glass case on his office wall is a book as broad as an atlas in which the deed to the farm is preserved. An imposing document adorned with flourishes of calligraphy, it conveys the land of Pamyat Ilyicha to its members in perpetuity.

Above Ruzin's head is another glass case, a tiny one, enclosing the medal and ribbon of the Order of Lenin, awarded to Pamyat Ilyicha for being represented three successive pre-war years in the great agricultural exhibition down the highway toward Moscow. Pamyat Ilyicha, whose products are in the fair again this year, is obviously an exceptional Soviet farm.

Ruzin leaves his desk, takes a pointer and goes to a multicolored map of the farm affixed to the opposite wall. Here, new greenhouses. There, new orchards. In that section, new forcing frames for vegetables. Over there, a new cow barn. Almost every operation on the farm is now mechanized, he says. The hundred horses? They are used in the long Russian winter when tractors and cars are snowbound. They are also lent to the workers to take their personal produce to market.

The task of Pamyat Ilyicha under the new farm program is to double its production. In one year, Ruzin says, it has already achieved a 25 per cent increase. Its plan, he explains, calls for the creation of a group of agricultural "factories"—"a vegetable factory," "a milk factory," and so on. And in the fields, waving and pointing, the chairman shows where each new "factory" will be centered.

Across the fields and not far away is another type of farm, a state farm called Lesniye Polyany ("Forest Glades"), which breeds dairy cattle and horses, grows early vegetables and experiments with improving fodders. Its grounds are well kept and its central administrative building, yellow and white in the Russian style, is neat and clean.

In the assembly hall are rows of chairs with fresh linen covers, and around the walls photographs of the Soviet leaders. In one long narrow frame are the pictures of several farm employes who have been decorated as Heroes of Socialist Labor. One of them is Fyodor Ivanovitch Trizno, the present director of the farm, whose two immediate predecessors became deputy ministers in the Soviet Government.

State farms generally are engaged in one specialized type of production that the state wishes to promote. Lesniye Polyany's specialty is breeding Kholmogor cattle, a type that resemble the Holstein-Frisian, and raising the yield and quality of their milk. The average yield in its herd of 400 cows is 5,500 liters (1,453 gallons) a year, Trizno says. The milk is sold to state agencies, and the farm supplies breeding cattle to other state farms, collectives and institutions.

Lesniye Polyany also produces its own fodder and breeds both race horses and draft animals. In its stables is a famous Soviet racer, Godach, who once ran the 1,600 meters in 2 minutes 6 seconds, and is now retired to stud.

Unlike Pamyat Ilyicha, the state farm does not share out its produce. It operates on a state budget, like an agricultural experiment station in the United States, and its 300 workers receive cash wages. They live in two-family houses or in state-owned apartments with communal dining halls and five to six square yards of floor space per person.

Sixty per cent of the workers are women and the average wage for a dairymaid, Trizno says, is 625 to 650 rubles a month. Workers who exceed their production norms get more pay and the best workers earn from 1,000 to 1,500 rubles a month. The director's salary is 2,400 rubles a month, and last year he received an extra 12,000 from the bonuses earned by Lesniye Poyany in "socialist competition" with other farms.

Ivan Markov, a 38-year-old tractor driver who lives in one of the two-family houses and has a broad smile for visitors, says he and his wife have a combined income of 1,500 to 2,000 rubles a month. Her earnings as a farm worker are actually larger than his.

As she is away at work, he is minding their month-and-a-half-old son, their third child. The child sleeps in his arms as he conducts his visitors through his three rooms and the kitchen that the Markovs share with another family. One of the Markovs' rooms is a glassed-in porch. The second is a sitting room with rough though clean embroidered cotton covers on tables and chairs. The third room is the bedroom. The kitchen has a wood stove built into the chimney in a way unfamiliar in the West and a one-ring electric hotplate that stands on a ledge covered with tough brown paper. Water is brought in from outside.

When Markov is asked about a refrigerator, he reports that they are building an underground storehouse for ice that will be cut from the ponds and will last all summer long. As for an automobile—well, he would rather have a television set, and is saving his money.

Back along the highway to Moscow is still another agricultural institution invented in Russia, a machine-tractor station (MTS) whose bright red brick buildings and walls and plots of flowers resemble the premises of a prosperous factory.

Machine-tractor stations provide mechanized plowing, cultivating, harvesting and construction services to state and collective farms, and this one, the Matishchin MTS, serves five farms. It has six tractor "brigades" and employs a total of about 100 persons, including "brigadiers" (brigade leaders), tractor drivers, combine operators and agricultural and animal husbandry experts who assist the farms. It has sixty tractors of various sizes, four grain combines, one hay combine and four potato combines.

The farms served by the MTS have a total area of 4,631 hectares (11,443 acres), of which 2,714 are plowed land. For tending these lands the station receives payment in kind—for example, one ton of potatoes for each hectare. The farm collects seventeen to eighteen tons, says the director, Nicholau Dimitry Akulinin. Construction work, such as the new greenhouses at Pamyat Ilyicha, is paid for in money.

However, the MTS does not pocket the cash or sell the produce it collects. That goes to the state and the MTS operates on Government appropriations, like the state farm. Machine-tractor stations in grain regions pay their own way, Akulinin says, but this one, being in a vegetable region where the crops require more attention, does not meet expenses.

As elsewhere, workers at MTS are paid on a piece-work basis, which is complicated by a differential between the summer, when the tractors are busy, and the winter, when they are idle. The workers are paid in cash and in kind, receiving the same amount of produce as other workers on the collectives where they live.

The total value of the station, Akulinin says, is 2,500,000 rubles. The latest addition to its equipment is a large repair shop with machine tools, overhead cranes and a trolley line across its wood-block floor. It is one of eighty such shops erected in the Moscow region this year.

---

50. SOVIET LABOR LAW *

WHAT are the functions and powers of a labor union in a communist state? To what extent are economic decisions vested in the manager of a communist enterprise? What incentives are given to a communist worker or manager? These questions, as they relate to the Russian brand of communism, are taken up in the following article. One should compare the arrangements discussed with those of a free enterprise, capitalist economy.

"Soviet Russia does not know of any 'free' contract of employment, nor of any legal relations usually connected with the concept of the employment contract. . . . In Soviet Russia labor duty is the basis of labor relations."

THUS did a contemporary Soviet authority on labor law characterize the situation in 1920. He was not referring to forced labor, so widely used in Soviet Russia, especially after 1930, but to the Soviet equivalent of "free" labor, the subject of the present article.

* Vladimir Gsovski, "Elements of Soviet Labor Law, Part I," *Monthly Labor Review* (Government Printing Office, 1954), pp. 15-26.

The author (1891——) is Chief of the Foreign Law Section of the Law Library of the Library of Congress. Author of *Soviet Civil Law: Private Rights and Their Background Under the Soviet Regime.*

Generally speaking the concept put forward in the quotation is largely held today by the Soviet State; it governs to a great extent the functions of the trade-unions and reflects the attitude of the Communist Party. Over the years it resulted in separate labor laws which are punitive rather than protective.

True, in 1920, private enterprise had been effectively barred under the policy known as Militant Communism. This was superseded in 1922 by the so-called New Economic Policy (N. E. P.), under which private enterprise, within certain limits, was readmitted and freedom of the employment contract was accorded some recognition. But this policy came to an end about 1929 with the inauguration of the first Five Year Plan, which, according to Stalin, had been framed and executed to eliminate capitalist elements and to create an economic basis for a socialist society. Since then private enterprise has been banned.

THE NATURE OF SOVIET ENTERPRISE

When private enterprise finally disappeared in Russia the great majority of persons engaged in industry and commerce—from top executives to manual laborers—became employees of a single owner—the government.[1] In that sense there is no contrast between capital and labor in the Soviet Union. The Soviet Government claims that there is a "unity between the interests of the toilers of the Soviet Union and those of the Soviet Socialist State," as an official textbook on labor law stated in 1946. However, such unity can hardly be demonstrated in reality. Soviet industrial organization shows that the fixed relationship between labor and State management took the place of the free relationships between labor and capital in capitalist countries.

Government-owned industry and commerce now operate on a different basis from that of the first years of the Soviet regime (1918–21). At that time, private enterprise and profit-making were outlawed without offering a substitute for satisfaction of personal ambition or an opportunity for extra earning.

In contrast, the policy adopted after the drive began for total socialization was popularly called "whips and cookies." On the one hand, concessions are made to the ever emerging personal ambition; but on the other, criminal law is put into operation in an effort to check the inefficiency of the entire economic system.

Government agencies engaged in business operate on a "commercial" basis (*Khoziaistvenny raschet*) and enjoy a degree of formal independence and enter into contracts with each other and with private persons.

[1] Members of the so-called productive cooperatives are in fact paid for their work and not according to their shares.

Although they are government agencies they are supposed to act with the competitive vigor of a private enterprise (the principle of "socialist competition"). This "independence" should not be overrated. As a Soviet text puts it: "The commercial basis is merely a special method of management of the national economy." Planned assignments of higher bureaus set definite limits to their independence, to say nothing of continuous supervisory control by various government agencies and political control by the secret police and Communist Party.

Nevertheless, the management of a Soviet quasi corporation is as interested in obtaining the lowest unit labor cost as its capitalist prototype. A single executive is appointed by the head of the bureau under whose authority the enterprise (called "trust" in industry and *torg* in commerce) operates. He hires and fires, allocates wages, imposes penalties, and grants bonuses. Bonuses are paid from a special director's fund based on a percentage of the profits or savings. His own bonus also depends upon the efficiency of the enterprise. In case the output falls below standard quantity or quality, he is liable to imprisonment up to 8 years.

THE SOVIET WAGE PRACTICE

Private profit-making is barred and the earnings of the bulk of the population are practically limited to wages and salaries. But the governmental scale of compensation for work, whether in money or comfort, aims to offer a substitute for profit-making to stimulate efficiency. A system of wages and salaries is designed to allow wide latitude for differentials in wage, salary, and bonus payments. To this end, the principles of piecework and bonuses for efficiency, without any guaranteed minimum wage, constitute the basis of compensation for work in government industry, in collective farming, and in cooperatives.

Regardless of whether the employee is paid by time or by piece, he must attain a standard of output established by the management. If he fails to do so through his fault he is paid according to the quality and quantity of his output.[2] Progressive scales of piecework and bonuses for extra efficiency are issued by the government for individual industries and industry groups.

Numerous honorary titles—"Hero of Labor" and others—and medals

[2] Soviet Labor Code, Sec. 57 as amended in 1934. "If an employee at a governmental, public, or cooperative enterprise, institution, or business fails through his own fault to attain the standard of output prescribed for him, he shall be paid according to the quantity and quality of his output but shall not be guaranteed any minimum wage. In other enterprises and businesses (private enterprises including those under a concession) such an employee shall be paid not less than two-thirds of his scheduled rate."

carry with them distinct material benefit, such as tax exemption, right to extra housing space, etc. There are also "personal salaries" and "personal pensions" awarded without reference to any scale, and Stalin prizes amounting to as much as 300,000 rubles in a lump sum.

All this affords professional, managerial, and skilled labor remuneration in money and comfort greatly exceeding that given to the ordinary laborer. For example, a scale of salaries and wages for electrical power plants, established in 1942 and still in force as late as 1946, ranged from 115 to 175 rubles monthly for janitorial services to 1,000 to 1,300 rubles for a director.

In 1934, Stalin frankly declared the underlying philosophy of his policy as follows: "Equalization in the sphere of demands and personal life is reactionary, petty bourgeois nonsense, worthy of a primitive ascetic sect and not of a socialist society organized in a Marxian way."

However, material benefits thus promised evidently proved to be insufficient stimuli for good work.

Heavy responsibility is imposed upon both workers and management. Inefficiency involves not only loss of material benefits and possible loss of job, but prosecution in court as well. Workers are subject to penalties imposed by managers for "loafing on the job" and to court action for absenteeism and unauthorized quitting of the job. From 10 to 25 years in a forced labor camp, with or without confiscation of property, can be imposed for "misappropriation, embezzlement, or any kind of theft" of the property of the principal employers, the government, or public bodies. Prior to 1946, the death penalty could be invoked. In case of damage to or loss of property of the employer—tools, raw materials, fuel, even work clothes—if due to employee negligence can result in deductions from wages, in some instances in an amount 10 times the value of the property.

MANAGERIAL PRESSURES

A series of laws penalize inefficient management for such things as poor quality or small volume of output, failure to penalize workers for absenteeism and other violations of labor discipline.

A potent incentive to the efficiency of the individual establishment is the principle that earnings depend in part upon the efficiency of the whole enterprise (principle of "check by ruble"). Business success brings definite individual profit; business failure incurs heavy punishment for those holding administrative posts. Although the total amount of regular wages to be paid in an individual enterprise is established by central government bureaus ("wages fund"), bonuses are dependent upon the profits or savings of an individual enterprise.

THE ROLE OF TRADE-UNIONS

Under such an arrangment there is no less reason for the rise of labor conflicts than under capitalism. But under the Soviet system labor is deprived of the main effective devices by which it may protect itself in a labor dispute in the capitalist world. Neither the constitution nor any law or decree mentions the right to strike and the strike is tacitly outlawed.

In general, all the channels through which labor can pursue its objectives in the capitalist world—legislation, courts, administrative agencies, the press, and trade-unions—are in Soviet Russia agencies of the principal employer of industrial labor—the State.

For a time when private enterprise was tolerated under N. E. P. (1922–28) the Soviet leaders visualized the protection of the interests of labor in this conflict through trade-unions. But the unions were regarded as an arm of government and of the Communist Party rather than as an independent force. Still they were to be an arm specialized in protection of labor. As the drive for socialization progressed, this special protective quality of the unions was pushed to the background. Instead, the notion of the identity of interests of the workers and the Soviet State was put forward, and the primary function of Soviet labor unions is to serve the interests of the State.

THE PROMISE OF 1922

The eleventh congress of the Communist Party in 1922, when the N. E. P. was inaugurated, recognized that if government enterprise operates on a commercial basis "inevitably certain conflicts of interests on the issue of labor conditions in the enterprises are created between the working masses and the directors, managers of the government enterprises, or the government bureaus to which the enterprises are subordinated." Consequently the resolution "imposed upon the trade-unions the duty to protect the interests of the working people."

Thus, the Labor Code of 1922, then enacted, relegated to the collective agreements between management and trade-unions the settlement of all the basic working conditions, including wage rates, standard of output, shop rules, etc.

Nevertheless, even then, both before and after this period, the trade-unions were not considered as a force independent from the Communist Party or the Soviet Government. The ninth congress of the Party (1920) had stated that "the tasks of trade-unions lie primarily in the province of economic organization and education. The trade-unions must perform these tasks not in the capacity of an independent, separately organized force but in the capacity of one of the principal branches of the government machinery guided by the Communist Party." The tenth congress went further and in 1921 passed the resolution, drafted by Lenin, and stressing the role of the trade-unions in Soviet Russia as a "school of communism." The fifteenth congress in 1925 stressed that "trade-unions were created and built up by our [Communist] Party."

"The most important task of the trade-unions," says the official textbook on Civil Law of 1944, "is the political education of the toiling masses, their mobilization for building up socialism, and the defense of their economic interests and cultural needs . . ."

"Formally," says the official textbook on Administrative Law of 1940, "the trade-unions are not a party organization but, in fact, they are carrying out the directives of the Party. All leading organs of the trade-unions consist primarily of Communists who execute the Party line in the entire work of the trade-unions."

THE REALITY AFTER 30 YEARS

Thus the trade-unions were transformed from a labor protecting arm into an arm for execution of government policy, and achievement of production goals. According to Soviet jurists, "the socialist industrialization of the country required that labor law . . . serve the successful struggle for productivity of labor and strengthening of labor discipline."

Such transformation of the trade-unions into a government arm, enforcing official economic policy, began soon after the onset of the first Five Year Plan. Accordingly, the sixteenth congress of the Communist Party directed in 1930 that the trade-unions, striving in collective agreements for improvement of the standard of living of the workers, must take into account the financial status of the enterprise with which the agreement was made and the interests of the national economy. In making the agreement, the resolution insisted, each party must undertake definite obligations in carrying out the financial and production plan of the enterprise. The unions in particular were obligated to guarantee, on behalf of the workers, the productivity of labor contemplated by the plan.

The central agency of all the Soviet trade-unions—their Central council—was granted the status of a government department in 1933. It officially took the place of the People's Commissariat for Labor, which was then abolished, and the Council was also charged with administration of social insurance. But then the Central Council of Trade-Unions lost the character of a representative body of trade-unions even in terms of the Soviet "democracy." Under law this Council must be elected by the Congress of Trade-Unions which is designated as "the supreme authority of the trade-unions of the Soviet Union." Nevertheless, since the Ninth Congress in 1932 no such Congresses were convoked for 17 years, during which the whole Soviet social order and the position of labor were radically changed.

When the Tenth Congress convened in 1949, no explanation was asked or offered for the delay. The Congress adopted a new statute which reaffirmed the total control of the Communist Party over the trade-unions:

> The Soviet trade-unions conduct their entire work under the direction of the Communist Party—the organizing and directing force of the Soviet Society. The trade-unions of the U.S.S.R. rally the working masses behind the Party of Lenin-Stalin.

Among numerous tasks assigned by the new statute to the trade-unions the generalized political objectives are described in the first place at great length. For example, the trade-unions "strive to enhance in every way the socialist order in society and State, the moral-political unity of the Soviet people, the brotherly cooperation and friendship between the peoples of the Soviet Union; they actively participate in the election of the agencies of governmental power; they organize workers and clerical employees for the struggle for the steady development of the national economy."

In contrast, "the duty to protect the interests of the working people" which had been emphasized by the Party Congress in 1922 is not expressly stated. It may have been considered unnecessary because the statute assumes that "in the conditions of the Soviet socialist order the State protects the rights of the working people." But in any event the labor-protection tasks of the unions are couched in cautious language.

At the very end of the above quoted passage it is mentioned that the unions "look after *(zabotiatsia)* the further rise of the material well being and the full satisfaction of the cultural needs of the toilers." At another place the unions' monopoly to represent the workers is stated with a hardly accidental lack of specificity: [unions should] act on behalf of workers and clerical employees before the governmental and social bodies in matters concerning labor, culture, and workers' everyday life."

Collective bargaining, provided for in the Labor Code of 1922, was discontinued in 1933. As the official Soviet text on labor law explained in 1946: *"The collective agreements as a special form of legal regulation of labor relations of manual and clerical employees has outlived itself.* Detailed regulation of all sides of these relations by mandatory acts of governmental power does not leave any room for any contractual agreement concerning one labor condition or another."

In plain English, this means that the Soviet leaders chose to abandon the last vestige of contract in relations between labor, even as represented by party-controlled trade-unions on the one hand and State management on the other, for the sake of outright government regimentation. Capitalist free collective bargaining was frankly declared unfit in the socialist surroundings of the Soviet Union.

However, in 1947 a campaign for making new collective agreements was suddenly ordered after a lapse of 14 years.

AGREEMENTS WITHOUT BARGAINING

Collective agreements were declared the most important measure "to achieve and exceed the production plan, to secure further growth of the productivity of labor, improvement of the organization of labor, and the increase of responsibility of management and trade organizations for the material condition of living of the employees and cultural services rendered to them." Nevertheless, the new policy is far from introducing free collective bargaining. Certain matters are definitely excluded from any negotiation and agreement and are reserved for government regulation.

The new rules positively require that "the rates of wages, of piecework, progressive piecework, and bonuses as approved by the government must be indicated" in the agreement. It is expressly forbidden to include any rates not approved by the government. In other words, wage rates are excluded from bargaining, but if included in the agreement are no more than applications of the governmental schedule to the establishment for which the collective agreement is drawn. This is true, to a large measure, of other points covered, particularly standards of output. The official act and the jurisprudential writings insist that the primary purpose of such agreements is to translate the abstract terms of the general plan for economic development into specific assignments and obligations within each particular establishment. They appear to be merely a form in which the orders of the government are made more precise.

A Soviet writer of authority comments:

> It is understood that the present day collective agreements could not but be different by content from collective agreements which were made at the time when the rates of wages and some other conditions of labor were not established by the law and government decrees.

The purpose of the present day collective agreement is to make concrete the duties of the management, shop committees, workers, technical, engineering, and clerical personnel toward the fulfillment of the production plans and production over and above the plan as well as to raise the responsibility of business agencies and trade-unions for improvement of material living conditions of workers and cultural services rendered to them.

As before, the new regulations are based on the assumption that "the interests of the workers are the same as the interests of production in a socialist state" and that the collective agreements are designed to be the "juridical form of expression of this unity." Accordingly, a model agreement is drafted by each ministry upon consultation with the central offices of the appropriate trade-unions. Then the model agreement is sent as a fait accompli to the establishments concerned.

While such collective agreements are not the result of collective bargaining, it may be observed that when the Soviet Government faced the task of postwar rehabilitation of its economy, it preferred to give decreed labor conditions the appearance of an agreement.

THE DOCTRINE OF NORMATIVE ACTS

Negotiation and mutual agreement are in fact proscribed in the Soviet Union in many important respects. Government regulation of wages and other basic conditions of labor took their place. However, it does not mean that labor is thus protected by law as we understand it. True, a Code of Labor Laws still exists on the statute books of the republics of the Soviet Union. But it was enacted in 1922 when private enterprise was within some limits tolerated and the government was not the sole employer in industry and commerce. At that time the code sought to regulate labor relations on the basis of free contract and to protect labor by methods resembling advanced democratic labor legislation.

However, these provisions of the code were either repealed or for the most part became inoperative being superseded, without a formal repeal, by various laws and decrees.

Under the totalitarian concept of government power, the accepted relationships of the administrative and legislative branches of the government do not apply. Although the terms "constitution," "legislative act," and "administrative decree" are used in Soviet law, the authority attached to each of these sources of law in the Soviet Union is different from that associated with these terms in the democratic countries. A constitutional provision may be set aside by an administrative decree and the newly enacted rule is incorporated into the constitution only at a later date. For example, the 7-hour working day was provided for in the 1936 constitution (section 119).

However, on June 26,1940, the Presidium of the Supreme Soviet, an executive body in terms of the constitution, decreed the 8-hour normal working day. This edict became operative immediately. It was ratified by the Supreme Soviet in August 1940, but without following the procedure prescribed for constitutional amendment. Not until 7 years later was section 119 constitutionally amended.

The Soviet jurists are fully aware of such practices. In discussing the sources of Soviet labor law in the treatises on this subject, they seek to blur the distinction between the authority of a constitutional provision, a legislative enactment, and an administrative decree or directive. In a recent (1949) standard treatise, designed for use in university law schools, a doctrine of "normative acts" (rule making) as the source of Soviet labor law is promulgated. Normative acts are in general terms defined as "acts by which the will of the ruling class is 'elevated to law.'" This not too clear definition is fortunately followed by an enumeration of the specific acts issued by Soviet authorities which, according to the author, fall under the definition. These are "laws" enacted by the Supreme Soviet (Soviet equivalent to legislature), "edicts" by its presidium (a body of 47 members constituting the Soviet collective President), "normative resolutions" (i.e., rule-making resolutions) of the Council of Ministers (cabinet), joint resolutions of the Council of Ministers and the Central Committee of the Communist Party, regulations issued by individual ministers and by the Central Council of the Trade-Unions.

In other words, any decree or order by any of the central governmental authorities is law. No matter what it is called and by what body it is issued, it prevails until the action of another authority supersedes it.

The survey of recent trends in the Soviet legislation thus far made suggests the conclusion that the disappearance of private enterprise from the Soviet economy has not been followed by the increase of rights of labor in labor law. If compared with the time when private enterprise was tolerated, the legal status of labor has worsened. Another striking feature of the Soviet regulations on labor are the numerous penal provisions.

51. A PROBLEM FOR PLANNERS *

ONE CRITICAL shortcoming of the capitalist system is the tendency toward magnified fluctuations of activity in the construction and certain other industries. This deficiency has led to various proposals and actual programs for public works and other forms of government support for these industries. Socialist planners are sometimes inclined to deride a system subject to such recurrent and acute disorders. However, the planned economy may find itself afflicted with the same malady and undergoing the same therapy, suggests Professor Wright as he raises a penetrating theoretical question for planners.

THE BUSINESS CYCLE—"PLANNED" CASE

DURING the earlier part of this study we set out to find the "ideal" size of the investment goods industries, relative to consumption, and it was suggested that a planning board able to enforce the "right" relationship could avoid jerks in production to go a long way toward solving the problem of social stability. However the argument . . . led to the conclusion that there was no *a priori* long run ideal relationship, but merely a series of fluctuating and rather indefinite short run limits. Furthermore we have found that there is no adequate spontaneous mechanism by which short run consumption can adjust itself in an unplanned market economy. But now the question arises: "Can the planners do any better?"

The problem confronting us may be approached from two sides. The planners may (a) try to induce a series of changes in consumption, or (b) endeavor to "smooth out" capital demand. Policy (b), in turn, is capable of yet further subdivision. Investment may conceivably be planned in advance so as to produce a smooth aggregate, or else a program of "filling in" or compensatory finance may be adopted designed merely to keep fluctuation within bounds.

The writer does not feel very optimistic concerning the chances of "planning" rapid shifts in consumption. One must remember that short run stability requires not high saving, or low saving, but *variable* saving. The Russian government has shown what can be done toward compelling a high average proportion of saving in an impoverished so-

* From David McCord Wright: *The Economics of Disturbance,* pp. 70-76, copyright 1946 by David McCord Wright and used with the permission of The Macmillan Company and the author.

The author (1909——) is Professor of Economics at the University of Virginia and the author of *The Creation of Purchasing Power, The Economics of Disturbance, Democracy and Progress,* and *Money, Trade, and Economic Growth.*

ciety. Contrariwise, in the alleged "economy of abundance" of the West, it is certainly arguable that socialism by making life more secure, reducing the motive to accumulate, etc., etc., would obtain a higher *average* propensity to consume. But as far as the cycle is concerned it is frequently not the average but the marginal propensity which is of first importance. Planning may change the average volume of saving but can it change the rate of change? Again, when rapid changes in consumption levels are needed, may the government simply proclaim, "Everyone will now spend money this month" and later announce, "Everyone will now start saving"? Should the government try to do so, could the planners be sure of estimating the results correctly in a free society?

Since most comprehensively planned economies which we have known so far have been very poor in consumer's goods, any slight extra margin allowed the consumer has been speedily taken up. But it remains to be seen whether in a wealthy free socialism you can both lead the consumer to water and make him drink.[1] The more likely choice of a planned economy, it would seem, will be to endeavor to smooth out, or fill in, investment goods demand.

In this connection we are confronted by the choice between planning nearly the whole field of investment *ex ante* to produce a smooth flow—as apparently advocated by Lord Beveridge for example, and the much more modest concept of planning which seeks merely to organize social desires in slump so as to prevent violent fluctuation. In much of the radical literature of today the latter policy is viewed as an unworthy compromise. A deal of ridicule is heaped upon "public works" or "deficit finance," as a crutch which barely enables us to hobble despite the mistakes of the capitalist market. But is this attitude justified?

. . . Men usually assume that the "over" expansion of the durable goods industries is the result of lack of forethought. Thus Lord Beveridge has suggested that the instability of the construction trades is due to "many headed control of industry."[2] M. Ilin, in *New Russia's Primer,* gives a dramatic exposition of how the capitalist order period-

[1] We are not here discussing the problem of the secular choice between goods and leisure, but of short run fluctuation in consumption levels complementary to fluctuations in investment demand. Of course the workers in the investment industry might be allowed to loaf and draw their salaries during slack times but this would scarcely be good for the morale of the remainder of the economy.

[2] Lord Beveridge, *Full Employment in a Free Society* (London, G. Allen & Unwin, 1945), p. 308. Lord Beveridge in the passage referred to assumes that the "supply of houses does not follow the demand closely." The writer submits that Lord Beveridge in this statement may be confusing need with effective monetary demand.

ically "overbuilds" itself because of "lack of plan." Mr. Kalecki puts the blame upon a decisions lag. Mr. J. A. Hobson blames it on over-building due to too much "saving," and so on. Whatever the reasoning the problem is viewed as the outgrowth of the present economic order.

Now it cannot be denied that "planlessness," mistakes, cumulative over-estimate of profits, etc., can cause depression. But is this the whole story? What is frequently forgotten is the possibility of cyclical waste, distortion and/or unemployment in a comprehensively planned state *abstracting from the problem of error in forecasting.*

To sift the matter thoroughly let us assume that the planners wish to follow not a compensatory policy, but one of anticipatory smoothing out. To further this aim they are willing to license and plan the growth of all industry. Their endeavor will be first to select, or ascertain, the average proportion of saving in their economy, and then so to direct the flow of new investment as to ensure a perfectly smooth flow of demand—and yet give the consumer what he wants. Can the job be done? The answer depends upon the social values to be followed and the circumstances under which the task is undertaken.

The preceding chapter [omitted] intimated that the problem of stabilizing the business cycle in a society that has already experienced several booms is quite different from that of preventing the development of the cycle in a society still in full employment equilibrium. This point may turn out to be of great importance to socialist states. For the odds are enormously in favor of the prediction that socialist governments, or other type governments advocating the comprehensive planning of society will take office in periods of unemployment, or slack production. Either the planners take over a backward country or else one whose industrial structure has experienced the cycle. In any case there will be slack and in any case they will be faced with the problem of deciding on the optimum rate of expansion.

In order to bring out clearly the essential difficulty let us suppose a very strong case. Suppose the United States governed by a politically omnipotent, and economically omniscient, planning board possessed of every moral virtue. Assume that there is initially no failure of consumption to keep pace with the actual output of consumer's goods,[3] no monopolies or pressure groups, no price rigidities, no inflation, and to give a perfectly clear field no problem of foreign investment or foreign trade. But suppose further that such an economy be confronted with the problem we now face after the war; a large, newly released labor force, considerable deferred demand, a large potential rise in the output of consumer's and capital goods. This case closely resembles, save in degree, the situation in the beginning of an ordinary boom. Does not the way seem open for peaceful and rapid expansion? Unfortunately one further question remains: How *fast* shall consumer's demand be satisfied?

THE SINGLE INDUSTRY

We may best begin our study of the equilibrium rate of expansion by concentrating upon a single commodity—say housing. Let us suppose that the only houses in existence are palm leaf huts which fall to pieces after a single night and which must be rewoven each day by primitive savages who use only their bare hands in the process. If this were the case there would be no problem of stabilizing the housing "industry" nor of selecting an optimum rate of expansion. The optimum rate would simply be to build as many houses as were needed each day as fast as possible—having due regard to the conflicting uses to which labor can be put. It follows that if our primitive tribe be assumed stationary in numbers, skill, age distribution, tastes, and resources, there would be a perfectly definite daily optimum rate of house production at which the industry would be permanently stabilized.

But now let us suppose that while the tribe still desires a certain number of houses relative to other satisfactions, say 100, that these houses are durable—lasting say ten years. We may also say that house construction is placed under the control of a planning board desiring to stabilize the "industry." Yet we further suppose that the board starts from scratch—that is to say that initially there is not a house in existence.[4] At what rate will the board permit expansion? Putting the matter so baldly of course exaggerates the problem but it is well to get essentials clear and qualifications will soon be added.

A very brief calculation will show that if the board places perfectly smooth housing demand above all other virtues it cannot allow the construction of more than ten houses per period. For each house lasts ten years. If all were built at once there would be no further housing demand whatever for ten years. The industry would be highly unstable. On the other hand, if we build at the rate of ten a year there will be a perfectly smooth demand for an indefinite period. Replacement will take over when expansion leaves off. We may conclude that, considering a single industry alone, the rate of expansion con-

[3] I.e., if total output and income drop, consumption may be supposed to drop with it, but while income is rising consumption will be supposed to keep pace with actual consumer's goods output.

[4] The problem would not be greatly different, if there were some houses already built, but the Board were deciding how rapidly it should make a large addition to the total stock.

sistent with stability is a rate *no faster than the equilibrium replacement rate in full employment equilibrium.*

For example, if in full employment equilibrium, the total relative demand for commodity A would be 500 units lasting 15 years the equilibrium rate of expansion would be 33⅓ units per period. If 400 units for 20 years it would be 20 per period. The calculation may be adjusted to fit not merely given amounts but also given amounts plus given rates of expansion in a dynamic equilibrium. In any event the reason why non-durable industries are more stable than durable ones is immediately apparent. In the non-durable industry the equilibrium replacement rate *equals* the total equilibrium flow. There cannot be either replacement "waves" or a "drop" to replacement requirements. But with durable goods all sorts of distortions and "gluts" are possible.

All this, one may say, is very well. We have "found" the "equilibrium" rate of expansion. But let us look a moment at the other side of the picture. Suppose that there are enough men and resources "free" to build not ten but one hundred houses a year and that the demand for the equilibrium figure of one hundred houses is intensely felt. In that case there arises a fundamental conflict between speed in the satisfaction of consumer's wants on the one hand, and stability on the other. For if the equilibrium rate is equal to the replacement rate, so also *the time taken to attain full equilibrium satisfaction is equal to the length of life of the individual equipment unit.*

The so-called equilibruim rate of expansion will have the following paradoxical results. If we consider the single housing industry alone, a rate of ten a year will leave "permanently" unemployed[5] men and resources sufficient to build ninety houses, and it will keep consumers in the streets for ten years waiting for shelter. The price of stability becomes "permanent" unemployment and an unnecessary ten-year delay in satisfying the consumer. Yet this conclusion has nothing to do either with planning or not planning. Given slack in the productive system, intensely felt desire for certain durable goods, and a wish to give the consumer what he wants when he wants it, and Lord Beveridge himself with the aid of all H. M. Army, Navy and Marines could not stabilize the construction industry.[6]

[5] The word "permanently" is put in quotes because, if the housing industry were stabilized, as indicated, the surplus portion could, in fact, be diverted to some other employment—were sufficient demand forthcoming.

Professor Haberler has shown that similar difficulties can occur regarding rapid accumulation of an inventory of "single use" goods.

[6] We are at this point excluding public works. I think this legitimate in the

52. THE SOVIET SYSTEM OF PLANNING *

THE ECONOMY of the U.S.S.R. is often cited as an important example of a planned economy. A more distinctive characteristic of this economy is that it is administered or operated by the state. State operation, however, requires careful planning. The process by which the Soviet Union plans its economic activities is described in this selection.

THE GENERAL PROBLEM OF PLANNING

IT IS both true and misleading to describe the Soviet system as a planned economy. It is true because for twenty-five years the Russian economic plan has been crucial for the determination of how and to what end the Russian economy should be operated. It is misleading, because it is not planning, nor even control of the economy, that sets the Russian system off from others. There are elements of planning in every contemporary economy, and every contemporary economy is in some measure controlled. The fascist economies are both planned and tightly controlled; there are indeed many similarities between the fascist and the soviet systems. There are, nevertheless, differences, and the differentia† of the Russian system consists in the *operation by the state* of almost all industry and a substantial part of agriculture and commerce. The description of the Russian economy as planned is true, but its description as administered is distinctive: In the Russian economy the state is entrusted with the ownership and operation of substantially all enterprise.

This, however, makes planning all the more essential, so that while planning may not be a differentia of the Soviet system it is a most important element in it. An introductory word about the nature and implications of economic planning, accordingly, seems called for.

---

initial exposition, for Lord Beveridge seems to imply that "single headed" control of the housing industry could stabilize it—without public works. In view of the model just given I doubt this very much.

* George P. Adams, Jr., *Competitive Economic Systems* (New York: Crowell, 1955), pp. 318-321, 325-337.

The author (1909——) is Professor of Economics and Chairman of the Department of Economics at Cornell University. Formerly Economist, Department of State, and Assistant to the Director, Army Specialized Training Program at Cornell.

† "The *differentia* is that part of the essence of anything—or, as we may say, of any species—which distinguishes it from other species in the same genus . . ." H. W. B. Joseph, *An Introduction to Logic,* 2d. edition, Oxford, 1916; p. 74.

In the Western World, at least, the appeal of planning has probably been greatest during periods of depression. These are just the times when resources, set against the opportunities for their employment, appear most abundant; in other words when the costs of error appear least, because any waste in the use of resources appears positively desirable. When manpower is employed in "boondoggling" and when other resources are under-utilized, the most urgent economic and social need appears to be the taking up of slack, and if the market does not promise to do so other means must be planned. Under those circumstances, the host of statisticians and accountants required to prepare the details of the plan and to keep track of its progress are easily regarded less as manpower diverted from physical production than as labor for which employment has been found.

Although the popular *appeal* of planning is high when resources appear abundant, that appeal nevertheless rests, not upon abundance, but upon scarcity—in this case, the scarcity of employment. Planning appears to be the offspring of necessity. The *need* to plan emerges when physical resources themselves come into acute shortage.

It thus may appear reasonable to plan the employment of resources for which spontaneous employment is apparently not to be had, but it is imperative to plan when resources are in such short supply that their utilization cannot be left unplanned. Wartime provides a conspicuous illustration, because war, economically, is simply a condition in which everything but problems become scarce. During the Second World War even the individualistic United States was driven to ration, to allocate, to hunt for substitutes, to control prices—in short, to plan.

To this powerful incentive to planning must be added its aesthetic appeal to those seeking a kind of visible order in economic activity which, to them, the market is incapable of imposing, and its moral appeal to those seeking a distribution of income which, again, the market does not appear to provide.

In consequence, the running controversy over planning which is still in process has, at least in its popular manifestations, taken the form of assertion and counter-assertion regarding its necessity or desirability with little attention given to its *difficulty*. That difficulty is not insurmountable, but it is great and warrants a quick glance at its elements. The concept of an economic plan has become so popular that its content no longer arouses wonder; yet it should.

Disregarding temporarily the important problem of what to plan for, let us assume that a planner knows precisely what economic structure he wishes to bring to birth, what the composition of gross output should be, what total volume of production so composed he wishes to see attained, and how rapidly he desires—or hopes—to achieve those ends. It is true that the determination of those ends is in itself a prodigious problem, but we have provisionally put it aside.

The planner, if he is to be at all effective, must know in considerable detail the resources, equipment, tools, and materials at his disposal; otherwise, his plan is no more than a daydream. He must know how to make use of what he has; otherwise, his plan may produce something as unsatisfactory as the proverbial bride's cookies. Moreover, if planning is technically to justify itself, the planner must provide for improvement in the effectiveness and economy with which his resources are used. The conscientious planner, indeed, must frequently be haunted by the tension between the security of staying with proved procedures at the risk of failing to keep abreast, and the lure of experimentation which carries the risk of failure. Having no competitor, moreover, he has available no market standard by which he can determine at least whether he is as efficient as he should be; but that, perhaps, is not invariably taken as a disadvantage.

Like a navigator, the planner must keep his bearings. If he gets off course, he must realize it before he gets hopelessly lost. That means three things: (1) he must have at his disposal a constant flow of information on how his plan is progressing, on the points at which it may be ahead of schedule, and on the channels in which it may be lagging; (2) he must be capable of grasping, classifying, and absorbing this information without becoming hopelessly entangled in streams of paper festooning themselves about his desk faster than he can clear them away; and (3) his reaction time must be quicker than the onset of surplus or shortage in order that he may make adjustments in both his plan and its operations as they become necessary and before they become unmanageable.

If we now relinquish our initial assumption and add to these problems that of determining what to plan for—that is, the degree of emphasis to be placed upon national economic power as against individual material welfare, or standardization compared with variation in the goods produced, and so on—we can see that the effective planner must combine qualities verging upon both omniscience and omnicompetence. But even that is not all. In contrast to *laissez-faire* systems in which responsibility is diffused, in which the compromise between following proved rules of thumb and venturing upon alluring but hazardous innovation is reached according to the boldness or conservatism of separate entrepreneurial personalities and the opportunities they believe to confront them, in *planned and administered systems* all responsibility is ultimately borne by the planner. The failure of an individual entrepreneur is indeed a tragedy for him and those dependent upon him, but society generally can absorb the shock of his failure. The wrong decision made by a national planner, however, may have repercussions extending far beyond a single enterprise and may even entail a political as well as an economic penalty. The unsuccessful private entrepreneur is seldom suspected of having committed deliberate sabotage against himself, but the unsuccessful state planner, particularly in a suspicion-ridden society like the Russian, may find himself indicted for guilt as well as for incompetence.

. . . . .

THE PROCESS OF PLANNING

Character of the Plans

. . . Russian planning did not really come into existence until the Soviets hit upon the device they call control figures, or constantly revised estimates of available resources and practicable output, . . . After this point had been reached economic planning proceeded in five-year jumps.

It is important at this point to grasp precisely what these plans are. They are, *first,* political decisions as to how resources should be allocated, and *second,* economic decisions about how to make that allocation effective. The planners must decide upon what they are to concentrate: the development of heavy industry, for example, or the manufacture of consumers' goods; the provision of armaments or of agricultural equipment; or the production of goods for domestic consumption or for export. Planners must determine the location of new industries, right down to the decisions where particular new plants should be established and what each plant in the economy should produce.

These decisions determine the *direction* of economic activity. The *rate* of activity is determined by the resources at hand and the means for processing, transporting, and distributing them, all of which must be known to the planners, and in detail. Moreover, these two essential factors are mutually dependent: political decisions determine the way resources shall be used, but the availability of resources (and in the broadest sense) determines which political decisions are practicable.

So far, the Russians have found the basic political decisions, what to do, easier than the economic, how to do it. From the very beginning they have sought to industrialize, to develop heavy industry, and they have been willing to depress the standard of living in order to do this. In consequence, approximately one quarter of the national income has been applied to economic development from the very beginning.

The Collection of Information

The starting point of each plan, therefore, is the collection of essential information as to resources. An estimate is made of the working population, excluding children, old folk, invalids, students, governmental employees, soldiers, and the like, for labor constitutes the basic resource. Questionnaires are then sent to every productive enterprise in the economy, covering its operations in the recent past, its current activities and its expectations for the immediate future. These statements must include figures concerning the numbers of workers of different grades and categories, the amounts and kinds of materials and components which have been or will be required, and the corresponding demands upon financial and transportation services. At the same time, retailing and marketing institutions of all kinds must report on the number of customers they have been supplying and expect to supply, with what kinds of goods and services and in what amounts, and they must state which of these they expect to procure from domestic sources and which must be imported from abroad. The state itself must estimate, largely on the basis of past records, what demands and output can be expected from individual peasants and nomads. Finally, similar information is sought from transportation, communication, and even cultural institutions. To secure all this, *Gosplan* maintains a corps of inspectors who are sent into the field to give assistance and to prod laggards.

Analysis of Information

Analysis of all this material enables *Gosplan* to derive, for each line of production, figures showing the quantities of labor, fuel, materials, and so on, that are needed to achieve a given output program. The next step is to examine these figures to see whether resources are, in fact, available to meet this complex of output programs, both nationally and regionally. The whole calculation is complicated still further by the Russian desire, not only for national self-sufficiency *vis-à-vis* the outside world, but also for a measure of regional self-sufficiency in order to ease the strain upon the transportation system.

Correlation of Information

In the meantime, the economic ministries, under guidance from the Party, have been reaching decisions as to the direction and rate of further development and expansion, and these decisions from above have to be correlated with the estimates of future activity which have come up from below. *Gosplan* eventually emerges with a master plan for the allocation of all resources, and this is then passed down the line finally to reach every individual plant and enterprise for comment, for suggestions and for criticism, and in the end for a breakdown into detailed, subordinate plans. When these have at last been returned, *Gosplan* is in a position to prepare the final, definitive plan for the approval of the Government. The Plan is thus an estimate, made in advance, of what ought to be achieved; but not every element in the complicated series of balances which comprise the plan is susceptible of control, so that constant revision of the estimates is necessary. The weather, for example, to say nothing of the carelessness or even interference of man, may prevent the delivery of the agricultural quota imposed upon some collective farm. As time passes, therefore, the annual and quarterly plans take on the character of revisions of the basic Five-Year Plan. In the end, it is the quarterly plans which are the really operative ones.

As far as physical resources are concerned, the plan is no more than a procedure for shuffling things about and a technique for keeping track of the results. However, human resources are required as well as physical, and this introduces two complications. Human beings are not quite so easy to manipulate, and they demand remuneration. With the exception of individuals who can be assigned specific tasks, like members of the party or the unhappy victims of the forced labor system, the allocation of labor is on the whole determined in the long run by adjusting training opportunities open to young workers, and in the short run by campaigns to recruit labor for plants and industries in need of it and by setting differential wage rates in accordance with the "social value" of any kind of labor in scarce supply. The continual complaints about the high rate of labor turnover attest the resort to these devices in addition to the forced labor imposed upon those who incur the disfavor of the authorities.

The Effects of Planning on Prices

In contrast to free economies in which private expenditure is permitted to determine the direction of production, in Russia consumers' sovereignty neither exists nor is it wanted. In Russia, accordingly, planners have the additional problem of preventing the price system from significantly influencing the allocation of resources; priorities take the place of prices. It it true that, even in Russia, excessive demand may be followed by higher prices, as happened between 1928–1935 and again during the Second World War. This happens because the Government permits it; it might just as easily impose rationing and hold prices as constant as it is able to. People obviously cannot purchase *more* than the total output of consumers' goods, and the volume of that output is determined by what resources are left over after the needs of heavy industry have been met. At the same time, however, Russians are unlikely to buy *less* than the total output of consumers' goods, for Russian living standards are still low and there is less incentive for personal saving (which reduces consumption) than elsewhere. Subsidies for children, the provision of free education, and the comprehensive social-security system shift to the state those financial responsibilities which in many other countries are borne by individuals out of their personal savings. Russian consumers, accordingly, are left free to spend their incomes on the goods and services permitted them under the plan; they are not free to change either the volume or the composition of what they are permitted to buy.

The Effects of Planning on Savings

The volume of saving on a national scale, therefore, is largely determined by the planners, from above, rather than from below by the aggregate decisions of independent individuals; and its determination consists, quite simply, in deciding by how much the income distributed to consumers shall fall short of the national income. If prices are not to change, and they sometimes do, this decision must be consistent with the decision determining the allocation of resources between the heavy and consumers' goods industries. If the government fails to hold aggregate consumers' incomes to an amount which will clear the market at current prices, national saving still can be brought about by curtailing consumption either through inflation, or through rationing, or through a combination of both.

Thus savings, in the large, represent deferred or unsatisfied individual consumption. They may appear in some forms familiar to us, such as deposits in savings banks or purchases of state bonds. They may also, however, appear in less familiar guise: as planned or realized profits accruing to particular enterprises.

The Effects of Planning on Profits

Profits are planned by adding to the price of output a permitted margin over average, planned costs of production, allowing for regional and other peculiarities. Such planned profits represent savings rather than industrial success (to which *we* attribute profits), because they are calculated not by any standard of efficiency to which an enterprise presumably should be held, but by the prices deemed necessary to adjust aggregate demand to planned supply. The function of planned profits, therefore, is to reduce consumption. Sometimes, to be sure, planned profits may be negative; the firm is expected to incur a loss. The planning of loss, in this sense, occurs when the price a firm would have to charge in order to make a profit is too high to be consistent with the plan under which the firm, and its customers, operate. The firm is then subsidized.

Sometimes, also, the profits actually realized by a firm fail to correspond with the profits planned for it. In such cases the planned savings (corresponding to the planned profits of industry) are either greater or less than the realized savings (corresponding to realized profit). Discrepancies between planned and realized savings (or profits) are not necessarily undesirable; they may even be useful. If an excess of realized over planned profits in one firm, for example, is greater than in another firm, there is some reason to believe that the first firm is more efficient than the second. That information is useful to have. Or, if an excess of realized over planned profits rises as time goes on, the conclusion might be drawn that efficiency was increasing. That, too, is useful knowledge. Both those kinds of knowledge are matters of concern to planning officials.

TYPES OF PLANS

The Production Plan

The core of the plan, then, is the program for capital construction which determines the relationships between different branches of industry which are to prevail within the planning period. From these are derived, by the method of balancing resources against needs, the entire system of output programs for all the products of the economic system.

Planning of this sort may sound easy in principle, but has turned out to be highly complicated in detail. In both preparation and implementation, a wealth of statistical information must be at hand, and it must be accurate, pertinent, and up-to-date. That has not been easy to insure. It is reported, in fact, that the Russians have had greater difficulty in checking the progress of their plans than in preparing the plans themselves. The statistical procedure involved in both preparation and checking consists in striking certain significant balances. The method was worked out simultaneously with the development of the control figures to which, indeed, they are necessary.

Initially, balances were struck separately for important groups of commodities—grains, metals, and so forth—as a necessary but still imperfect device for ascertaining whether the various sectors of the economy were developing in proper alignment with each other. As facility increased, these balances came to be more purposefully compared with one another so that, when the 1928–1929 control figures were drawn up the balances themselves constituted the core of the plan for the ensuing year. This was possible because, with the balances brought into a system and properly coordinated, impending bottlenecks were immediately revealed, the kinds and volume of production needed to fulfill the assignments set forth in the plan became immediately evident, and, in result, the responsibilities assigned particular industries together with the capital expansion to be planned for each, and the composition and volume of imports and exports, could be more or less precisely determined. With this information at hand, *Gosplan* is in a position to coordinate separate balances into an integrated system, and this done, it can then very easily determine whether the program submitted to it by its subsidiary agencies and departments are mutually consistent and compatible with the approved plan.

All this, complicated as it is, constitutes only a production plan. Provision has still to be made for pricing the various products and for determining the incomes of the various workers engaged in these processes. Specifically, the production plan serves as a basis for formulating a credit, or financial, plan, a cash plan, and a system of prices. To these we must now turn.

The Financial Plan

The credit, or financial, plan is designed not only to facilitate the execution of the production plan, but also to enable its fulfillment to be watched and to insure against the improper use of resources.

Let us recall how both current operations and programs of capital development in both industry and agriculture are financed by a series of specialized banking institutions. At the center is the State Bank of the U.S.S.R. *(Gosbank),* which operates as a central bank and as a source of short-term credit. The provision of long-term credit is the responsibility, according to the sector concerned, of the *Prombank* for industrial development, the *Selkhozbank* for agricultural expansion, the *Tsekombank* for municipal construction, and the *Vsekobank* for financing cooperative societies. There is also a savings bank which can be used as a source of short-term loans, but which usually invests its deposits in Soviet Government bonds.

Under a centrally planned economy, financial considerations tend to be subordinated to economic. Central banking consists primarily in facilitating the execution of the economic plan, and credit is extended to particular enterprises *not* according to their financial prospects, but only in amounts and for purposes consistent with the plan. Thus, the central bank and the central offices of the other banks exercise very little initiative, but they still exercise more than their various branches throughout the country. These are autonomous only for accounting purposes; they are expected to cover their expenses out of the interest and commissions they are permitted to charge, but in other respects these branches do little more than to keep accounts, make payments, and check applications for loans for compatibility with the plan.

Procedure. The process of financial planning starts with the submission to the appropriate bank of applications for credit. These come from enterprises, farms, in fact from all the great variety of institutions which are preparing their programs for the impending planning period. Those applications are compared with the corresponding production plans and, when approved, are passed downward through the planning hierarchy until each operating unit knows its exact assignment and the financial resources to be made available for its fulfillment. At the beginning of each accounting period, therefore, every enterprise in the economy is provided with an amount of working capital theoretically just sufficient to enable it to carry out its expected minimum program. This fund is supposed to be divided into separate accounts for such things as fuel, wages, raw materials, and so forth; but beyond this, the firm has general control over its capital.

If, in the course of its activity, the enterprise finds it needs additional capital, it may apply to the appropriate bank, but any such application is subject to minute scrutiny. Banks grant credit only when they are satisfied that the loan is for purposes already approved under the plan, and they may recall loans which have been put to uses they consider improper.

Control by the Ruble. Banks, moreover, must investigate the causes of any losses which appear, and they must examine invoices to assure themselves that price regulations are being observed. In addition to all this, the power of the banks extends still further to affect suppliers of raw materials and component parts. They may extend "transit credit" to finance the purchase of materials, but they may also, if they choose, withhold payment until the finished product has been sold.

Planned loans, as the name indicates, are granted for approved purposes for which a firm's working capital is inadequate, and are automatically self-liquidating as finished products are sold and the proceeds credited to the firm's account. By watching the rate at which these credits are liquidated, the banks are able to keep track of the progress of the production plan and to spot delays, hitches, and bottlenecks, with respect both to day-by-day operations and to each major accounting period.

Unplanned loans are also made to tide an enterprise over an emergency, such as the tying up of inventories as a result of congestion in the transportation system. These loans are made for very short periods, and, being indicative of difficulties, they occasion some sensitiveness. Unplanned loans may also have to be made when the plan is revised; a firm having to adapt its activity to the revision of the plan may need supplemental credit.

This system of financial control, or "control of the ruble" as it is sometimes called, serves as an effective checkrein upon the proclivity of industrial managers to hedge against potential trouble by accumulating and hoarding unnecessarily large inventories. It operates in three ways: (1) By rationing capital and controlling credit the authorities can keep inventories under firm control. (2) By making each enterprise an individual accounting unit and by planning its costs and prices so that the "normally" efficient firm will just pay its way, the income statements of other firms will either reveal inefficiency, or, in the case of exceptionally efficient firms, will enable the accumulation of a surplus which can be partly used for reinvestment within the firm, partly paid into the State Budget, and partly used as "socialized" wages—organized cultural or recreational activities—for the firm's employees. (3) By pooling the other portions of these surpluses, the government can keep capital development itself under control.

Planned and Unplanned Profits. It is important to distinguish between the "planned" and "unplanned" profits of a Soviet enterprise. The former is the sum for which the plan provides and which ought to emerge if prices, costs, and volume actually do correspond to their planned quantities. Part of this planned profit, when realized, goes directly into the State Budget through taxation, part of it is paid into the fund held by the Prombank for financing capital development generally, and part is retained by the enterprise to be used for improving the working and living conditions of the labor force. "Unplanned" profit comprises whatever may be earned in excess of the planned figure; up to half of this is retained by the enterprise, and may be used at the discretion of the management. Bonuses and premiums are frequently paid from this sum to the laborers and staff members of the fortunate enterprise.

Taxation. About three quarters of the country's capital expenditure is normally financed through the budget, supplemented by the reserves of the Prombank. The government's income is largely derived from taxes, the most important being the "turnover tax" which bears most heavily upon the output of the consumers' goods industries. This tax is similar to a sales tax, except that, formally, it is levied upon the industry rather than upon the consumer; but it is passed on in the form of higher prices just the same. It is extraordinarily high by Western standards, ranging from thirty per cent to almost one hundred per cent *ad valorem.* The tax is concentrated upon retail prices for two reasons: (1) it is useful to have that method of adjusting prices paid by consumers to the amount of purchasing power possessed by consumers, and (2), it is pointless to levy such a tax upon goods purchased by industry, for to do that would mean, simply, that the government was taxing itself. This is so because, since the state is the only consumer of such products, the only effect of such a tax would be to increase the amount of capital necessary to carry out the objectives of the Plan. Government funds are supplemented by the private savings deposited in the savings banks or invested in Soviet bonds, and by the collective savings accumulated by the methods already described. Through the budgets of the various banking institutions, financial resources are concentrated in the hands of the state. This results in their being used to foster the harmonious and even development of the national economy. Reddaway makes the observation that this system gives to capital, as a factor of production, the full mobility taken for granted by Western economic theorists, sometimes without empirical warrant.

The financial plan consists, as we would expect, in a program of planned receipts and expenditures. These, balanced against each other, indicate the necessity for expanding or contracting the currency, and thus lead directly to the formulation of the cash plan.

The Cash Plan

In the Soviet Union, just as in other countries, the amount of currency that will be needed in any given period of time is a function (1) of the aggregate disbursements to be made, and (2) of the average time period elapsing between disbursement and the return of the cash to the issuing authority. The first of these, aggregate disbursements based upon the estimated number of transactions, is easily determined in the Soviet

Union, at least as far as advance planning is concerned. For industry, the cash plan depends simply upon the total planned wages and salaries bill; for agriculture, it depends upon the planned payments to members of collective farms for compulsory deliveries of agricultural produce to the State, plus the estimated amount of currency needed for sales of agricultural produce on the free market. Revision of the production and financial plans bring corresponding adjustments in the cash plan.

The second factor significant for the cash plan, the velocity, or rapidity of turnover, of the currency is calculated regionally as well as nationally, and is based upon the return of currency to the state in the form of taxes, savings, or expenditures in the state stores. From these calculations each regional bank determines whether its holdings of cash seem to be adequate to meet expected withdrawals, whether it can retire part of its holdings, or whether it must draw upon the central bank for additional amounts.

More than this, the cash plan plays its part in facilitating the regional and local distribution of supplies. Each financial institution analyzes anticipated conditions in its territory for the purpose of determining the total value of the consumers' goods that will be needed in the coming planning period, and thereby is aided in its determination of the total amount of credit to be granted the various retail establishments.

Under the Soviet system it is, in principle, not too difficult to plan the whole currency issue within fairly precise limits. The production plan fixes the output and the distribution of commodities, and the financial plan determines disbursements. Prices in the very substantial, socialized sector of the economy are planned, and so are incomes. Hoarding is no problem since most personal incomes are too low to provide much surplus, and savings pass through the channels previously described right back to the state. With most incomes disbursed by the state and the greater part of most incomes returning to the state, there is not much of anything left that is beyond the reach of state control.

THE PRICING SYSTEM UNDER PLANNING

The smooth operation of this system of inter-related plans for production and finance clearly depends on the consistency of those plans with the plans concerning prices and costs. Prices are cumulatively built up by adding a planned profit to the planned costs (including provision for depreciation, overhead, and so on) of each enterprise. That profit is usually calculated at rates varying according to the importance accorded the product; it is figured as a percentage upon turnover, and the aggregated total of all costs plus profit becomes the planned price at which the finished product will be credited to the producer when final delivery is made.

We have observed that unplanned, or efficiency, profits may also arise; in fact, they are encouraged as a sort of socialized incentive to economy and efficiency. Since, however, these unplanned profits arise through success in reducing costs below their planned level, they do not constitute an ingredient of price in the way that planned profits do.

As wc also have seen, efficiency can be tested by fixing planned prices on the basis of planned costs at each stage of the operations, and by then examining income statements to see how *realized* costs and prices correspond to their planned levels. Here, however, one difficulty arises which has plagued other governments than the Russian in their experiments with price control. When many plants of varying sizes and different degrees of efficiency all produce the same article, the costs of production in the several plants will not necessarily be the same, and this complicates the determination of a single price for their collective output. The Russians have occasionally made allowance for this by permitting different prices to prevail in different regions, but more generally the Trusts have been utilized as economic shock absorbers to equalize these differences.

The Trusts, be it remembered, are organizations of all plants producing the same product. These institutions serve as agents for assessing the planned cost of each enterprise, for comparing those costs, and for determining the average cost of production of the product for the economy as a whole. Being an average, that cost is higher than the actual cost of the efficient plants, and less than the average cost of the inefficient; consequently, the Trust concerned must re-allocate planned costs and planned profits among its constituent members. This the Trust does by purchasing, at different prices (based upon the particular costs of each enterprise), the entire output of the product. That product is then re-sold at a single price determined by the Price Fixing Commission. If the Trusts have normal skill in negotiating with their constituent plants the particular price to be paid each, on the basis of its own cost, the emergent single price for the product as a whole will bring about equality between the Trust's total receipts and its total expenses, including the cost of the Trust's own operations and its own profits. A Trust which is more than normally efficient, in this sense, will reap an unplanned profit, which is treated exactly as unplanned profits arising elsewhere; and, contrariwise, a less than normally efficient trust will incur unplanned losses.

The sale price of any commodity is, therefore, essentially an accounting price at which transactions among various state enterprises take place.

Since, until the final consumer is reached, the finished output of one industry is the raw material of the next, the price-forming process is cumulative until the final emergence of the market prices at which consumers' goods are bought. At this final stage, the accounting price, which includes the costs and planned profits of manufacturers, of wholesale and retail distributors, and of transportation agencies, is transformed into market price by adding certain supplementary charges designed to equalize the demand and supply of particular goods. The first of these charges is the turnover tax, already mentioned. The second is a high supplemental tax paid by establishments which, for one reason or another, sell at higher prices than prevail elsewhere although the cost of their supplies is the same. Throughout the entire Soviet system, the basic pricing principle is the simple one that the normally efficient enterprise should just pay its way.

---

53. PLANNING AND THE RULE OF LAW *

MANY opponents of planning have argued that it leads to a centralization of economic and political power and eventually to a loss of political freedom. Once we begin planning, the argument runs, we are on the road to totalitarianism. Professor Hansen gives a succinct answer to these allegations in the following selection.

THERE are those who allege, led by Professors Mises and Hayek, that conscious planning is not compatible with personal freedom. They would rely upon the automatic forces alone. Only such institutions as are basic to the necessary automatic processes are acceptable to them. All other planning is regarded as "bad planning." That, at least, is the logic of the case, and it is in fact the position of Mises. Hayek, a little less rigid and doctrinaire in his thinking than Mises, is forced to abandon logical consistency in the face of the hard realities of the modern world. Thus, he admits, somewhat reluctantly, the necessity of social security and some other measures involving a minimum of social planning.

* By permission from *Economic Policy and Full Employment,* pp. 27-28, by Alvin Hansen. Copyright, 1947. McGraw-Hill Book Company, Inc.

The author (1887——) is Professor of Political Economy at Harvard University. Known in particular for his work in the fields of business cycles and fiscal policy, and for his discussion of secular stagnation Author of *Business Cycle Theory, Full Recovery or Stagnation, Fiscal Policy and Business Cycles,* and *Monetary Theory* and *Fiscal Policy.*

THE RULE OF LAW

Hayek fears a world that requires human management. He has a great deal to say about the "rule of law." Yet he confuses automatism in social life with the rule of law. He forgets that the very concept of the rule of law was developed in England just at the time when there was a vast amount of governmental control of economic life. It was precisely because this was the case that the rule-of-law concept was developed. The rule of law does not mean that human management is replaced by automatic forces. It means that the conscious management of social life is conducted under established canons that preclude *arbitrary* action. The rule of law substitutes rational principles of management for the arbitrary acts of arbitrary men.

The widespread acceptance of social and economic planning by all modern governments is evidence that the hard experience of recent decades have driven home the lesson that the functioning of modern economic life cannot be left to automatic forces. But it does not mean that we thereby deliver ourselves up to the arbitrary management of irresponsible men. That is not now, and never has been, the method of political democracy. The plans we are devising, both domestic and international, are not ships let loose on an uncharted sea with instructions to the captains to steer as they see fit. Rational and democratic planning involves the development of rules of law that preclude arbitrary action by those who are chosen to administer the plans. This could be illustrated in any one of the plans, domestic or international, that I have reviewed. For example, while the International Monetary Fund does not mean that we have abandoned the moorings of the old international gold standard, it will not leave us in international monetary matters adrift upon a sea of arbitrary decisions by the Governing Board of the Fund. New moorings to take the place of the old gold standard are established. Rules of law are set up which constitute a framework within which decisions are made.

In the decades that lie ahead, a major task of economic and social statesmanship must be undertaken precisely in this field. We must evolve rules of law under which the social planning of the future can be made a rational and democratic method of managing our social order. Only thus can we achieve the high goals of progress, stability, and full employment combined with the undying human values of personal and individual liberty. Without exception, all the great democracies are today embarked upon programs of social planning. In our own Anglo-Saxon tradition, the concept of social control *under law,* not control by irresponsible and arbitrary men, reaches far back into history.

It antedates the age of modern capitalism. It reaches back into the early beginnings of local government. And it was never wholly lost sight of even in the heyday of *laissez-faire*. We have a rich heritage of legal and political tradition which gives us high confidence and faith that we can achieve the great social and economic goals we seek without losing our personal freedoms.

CORRELATION TABLES
AND
INDEX

CORRELATION OF THIS BOOK WITH INTRODUCTORY TEXTS

Bach
Economics: An Introduction to Analysis & Policy
Prentice-Hall, 1954

Ch. No.	*Related Selections*
1	—
2	1, 4, 6, 23
3–4	—
5	3, 17
6	36
7	33–35, 37
8	—
9	14–16, 18
10	3, 4, 6
11	17–19, 21, 47, 51, 52
12	22, 32
13	12–16
14	10, 11, 30
15	1, 2
16–17	—
18	7–9, 23–26
19	7–9, 12, 13
20	23–26
21	3
22	30
23	27–30
24	—
25	31
26	22–26, 32
27	5, 10, 11, 49
28	30
29–30	—
31	20, 21, 37–39
32	18, 20, 21, 51, 52
33	30
34	—
35	6, 43–45
36	—
37	40–42, 46
38	43–45
39	47–53

Burns, Neal, and Watson
Modern Economics,
2nd ed.
Harcourt, Brace, 1953

Ch. No.	*Related Selections*
1	2, 6, 12
2	3, 4
3	1, 2, 4, 6
4	32
5	17
6	33–35
7	14–16, 18
8	17, 19–21, 47, 51, 52
9	—
10	12–16
11–15	—
16	7–9
17	—
18	5, 10, 11, 49
19	—
20	4, 28–30
21	—
22	38
23	31
24	3
25	—
26	32
27	—
28	22–26
29	4, 28, 30
30	27, 29, 50
31–32	—
33	18, 20, 21
34	—
35	38, 39
36	20, 21, 36–39
37–38	43–45
39	6, 40–42, 46
40	47, 48, 51–53
41	49–53
42	—
43	3

Bye and Hewitt
The Economic Process
Appleton-C-C, 1952

Ch. No.	*Related Selections*
1	—
2	1–4
3	1, 2
4	3, 4, 17
5	1, 2
6	3, 4, 6
7	32
8	22
9	19, 32
10	9, 22–26, 32
11	—
12	12–16
13	—
14	33–36
15	37–39
16	36–39
17	17, 18
18	18, 20, 21
19	17–21, 47, 51, 52
20	12–16
21	—
22	7–9
23	—
24	10–13
25	5, 9–11, 30, 49
26	3
27	4, 28–30
28	38, 39
29	—
30	31
31	3
32	30, 31
33–34	43–45
35	6, 40–46
36	27–30, 50
37	27–29
38	30, 50
39–41	—
42	18, 20, 21, 51
43	47
44–45	47–53

Dodd and Hasek *Economics: Principles and Applications,* 2nd ed. South-Western, 1952		Gemmell and Balsley *Principles of Economics,* 2nd ed. Heath, 1953		Gemmill *Current Introductory Economics* Harper, 1955	
Ch. No.	*Related Selections*	*Ch. No.*	*Related Selections*	*Ch. No.*	*Related Selections*
1	—	1–2	—	1	4, 6, 12
2	3	3	31, 52	2	—
3	12–16	4	3, 4, 6	3	1, 2
4	2, 6, 17	5	—	4	1, 27
5	1, 2, 27	6	17	5	3
6	—	7	17–19, 47	6	22, 26, 32
7	32	8	20, 21	7	—
8	22–26	9	—	8	33–35
9–11	—	10	1, 2	9	37
12	7–9	11	32	10	37–39
13	5, 10, 11, 30	12	—	11	17
14	3	13	22–26, 32	12	14, 15, 18
15	4	14	9, 23–26	13	20, 21, 36, 37
16	38	15	—	14	17–21, 47, 51
17	—	16	12–16	15	18, 20, 21
18	31	17	—	16	—
19	3, 47	18	7, 8	17	3
20	33–35	19	33–35	18–20	—
21	37	20	—	21	22–25
22	38, 39	21	37–39	22	7–9
23	36, 37	22	20, 21, 36, 37	23	—
24	43–45	23	40–46	24	40–46
25	18	24	43, 44	25	42–45
26	—	25	3	26–27	—
27	18, 20, 21	26	29–31	28	28–30
28	28, 29, 50	27	38	29	4
29	27	28	—	30	38
30	27, 30	29	27–29	31	31
31	17–21, 39, 47	30	30, 50	32	12–16
32	14–16, 18, 20, 21, 39	31–32	5, 10, 11, 44, 49	33	47–53
33	—	33	4, 6		
34	5, 10, 11, 49	34	47–53		
35	18				
36	6, 40–46				
37	47-53				
38	—				
39	3, 4, 6, 53				

Harriss *The American Economy* Irwin, 1953	
Ch. No.	*Related Selections*
1	—
2	1, 2
3	—
4	2, 4, 6
5	4
6	3, 17
7	—
8	32
9	19, 26
10	22–26
11	29
12	27–30
13	33–35
14	37–39
15	37
16	36
17	14–16, 18, 20, 21
18	17, 19–21, 47, 51, 52
19	12–16
20	11, 30
21–22	—
23	7–9
24	8, 9, 22–24
25	9, 23–26
26–27	—
28	3, 4
29	28–30, 50
30	—
31	38
32	31
33	3
34	—
35	12, 13
36–37	43–45
38	6, 43–45
39	40–46
40–42	—
43	20, 21
44	4, 30, 36
45	5, 10, 11, 51
46	3, 4, 6
47	53

Ise *Economics,* rev. ed. Harper, 1950	
Ch. No.	*Related Selections*
1	—
2	6
3–4	4
5	1
6	2
7–8	32
9	22–26
10	—
11	12
12–14	—
15	23–26
16	22–26
17	23–25
18	7–9
19	—
20	11, 30
21	12–16
22	33–35
23	—
24	37–39
25	36, 37
26	17–21, 37
27	14–16, 18, 20, 21, 39
28	43–45
29	40–42, 44–46
30	4, 29
31	—
32	27–30, 50
33	38, 39
34	—
35	5, 10, 11, 44, 49
36	31
37–38	—
39	3, 4
40	3, 4, 6
41	47, 48, 51–53
42	48–50
43	—
44	3, 47, 48
45	26, 32
46	—
47	3

Kiekhofer *Economic Principles, Probs. & Policies,* 4th ed. Appleton-C-C, 1951	
Ch. No.	*Related Selections*
1	—
2	1, 2, 4, 6
3	5
4	1–3, 32
5	22–26, 32
6	29, 30, 50
7	27, 28
8	17
9	33–35
10	37–39
11	43–45
12	40–42, 46
13	—
14	19, 38
15–19	—
20	7, 8
21	9–11, 30
22	4, 28–30
23	38
24	—
25	31
26	36
27	17, 19–21, 47, 51, 52
28	12–16
29	13, 18
30–31	—
32	4
33	18
34–35	—
36	20, 21
37	—
38	45, 46
39	—
40	9, 22–26
41	—
42	47–53

Nordin and Salera *Elementary Economics,* 2nd ed. Prentice-Hall, 1954		Peach *Principles of Economics* Irwin, 1955		Peterson *Economics,* rev. ed. Holt, 1954	
Ch. No.	*Related Selections*	*Ch. No.*	*Related Selections*	*Ch. No.*	*Related Selections*
1–2	—	1	3	1	—
3	3, 4, 6, 14–17	2–3	4	2	3
4	1, 2	4	6	3	1, 2
5	17	5	1, 2	4	17
6	12, 13	6–7	17	5	1, 53
7	22–26, 32	8	14–16, 18	6	4, 6
8–9	—	9	17, 19, 47,	7	2
10–11	7–9		51–53	8	1, 22–25
12	22–26	10	18, 20, 21	9	26, 32
13	31	11	3, 4	10	33–35
14	5, 10, 11, 44,	12	33–35	11	37–39
	49	13	37	12	30, 36
15	28, 29	14	20, 21, 37–39	13	43–45
16	27, 30	15	36	14	14–16, 18
17	28, 29	16	26, 32	15	17, 19, 47, 51,
18–19	—	17	—		52
20	31	18	22–25	16	18, 20, 21, 30
21	33–36	19	9, 23–25	17–18	—
22	37, 39	20–24	—	19	12–16
23	37–39	25	18, 20, 21, 39	20	—
24–25	—	26	12, 13, 16	21	7–9
26	18	27–28	—	22	8, 9, 22–26
27	17, 19, 47	29	7–9	23	5, 9–11, 49
28	20, 21	30	4	24	3
29	37	31	31	25–26	—
30	18, 20, 21	32	—	27	27–30, 50
31	5, 10, 11, 44,	33	3	28	—
	49	34	4	29	31, 38
32	—	35	30, 50	30	—
33	40–42, 44–46	36	27–29	31	20, 21
34	43	37	43–45	32	40–46
35	6	38	40–42, 46	33	47–53
36	48–50	39	42–45		
37	47, 51–53	40	43–45		
		41–42	—		
		43	5, 10, 11		
		44	3, 51		
		45	53		
		46	47–49		

Reese *Our American Economy* Houghton Mifflin, 1953		Samuelson *Economics: An Introductory Analysis,* rev. ed. McGraw-Hill, 1955	
Ch. No.	*Related Selections*	*Ch. No.*	*Related Selections*
1	3, 4, 6, 17	1	—
2	1–4, 6	2	1–4, 6
3	3, 6	3	1, 2, 34, 35
4	4	4	3
5	—	5	22–26, 32
6	47	6	18, 20, 21
7	32	7	—
8	22–26, 32	8	27–30, 50
9	12, 15, 16, 31	9	3, 12–16
10–11	12–16	10	17
12	—	11	14–16
13	31	12	18, 20, 21
14	11	13	33–36
15	7–9	14	37
16	18	15	38, 39
17	5, 10, 11, 18, 20, 21	16	37–39
18	27–30, 50	17	19–21, 47, 51, 52
19	33–35	18	4, 16, 18, 20, 21, 51, 52
20	36–39	19	12–16
21	17	20	10, 11, 30
22	3, 4	21	5, 10, 11, 47, 50
23	14–16	22	19
24	17, 19, 47	23	12–16
25	16, 18	24	—
26	18, 20, 21	25	7–9, 22–26, 32
27	40–42, 45, 46	26–27	—
28	43, 44	28	27–30
29	47–53	29	—
		30	31, 32
		31	43–45
		32	42
		33	40–42, 46
		34	6, 43–45
		35	—
		36	6
		37	47–53

Index